A Reluctant Traveler in Russia
Modigliani: Prince of Montparnasse
Time Stopped at 6:30

COMMISSAR

COMMISSAR

The Life and Death of
Lavrenty Pavlovich Beria

THADDEUS WITTLIN

THE MACMILLAN COMPANY · NEW YORK, NEW YORK

COLLIER-MACMILLAN LIMITED · LONDON

The Macmillan Company
866 Third Avenue, New York, N.Y. 10022
Collier-Macmillan Canada Ltd., Toronto, Ontario

Library of Congress Catalog Card Number: 74-189683

First Printing

Printed in the United States of America

"Beria . . . who gained such a position in the Party and in the State, so as to become the First Deputy Chairman of the Council of Ministers of the Soviet Union and a member of the Central Committee Political Bureau . . . had climbed up the Government ladder over an untold number of corpses."

NIKITA S. KHRUSHCHEV

(From the Secret Speech delivered at a Closed Session of the 20th Congress of the Communist Party of the Soviet Union on February 25, 1956.)

ACKNOWLEDGMENTS

For helping me with this book, on which I worked for over six years, I should like to express my gratitude to Madeline T. Hawes, Simon Kobiashvili, Wesley Pedersen, Andrew Pomian, and Adam Schmidt.

I should like, as well, to pay tribute to the late Lieutenant General Wladislav Anders, C.B. Commander in Chief of the Polish Forces in the USSR, who in several talks and letters furnished me with many details about his personal conversations with Stalin at the Kremlin and with Beria in Lubyanka Prison.

THADDEUS WITTLIN

September, 1972
Washington, D.C.

Contents

Contents

PART TWO: MOSCOW

Contents

LIST OF APPENDICES

PROLOGUE

The Man Who
Was Killed Three Times

LAVRENTY PAVLOVICH BERIA, Chief of Security of the Soviet Union during Stalin's regime, master of many bloody purges and the hatchetman who destroyed thousands of people, the highest members of the Communist Party included, led such an obscure life that he was called "the man without a history." No less mysterious was his death. Besides the official announcement published by the Soviet government in the State-run newspapers, there exist three different versions of the end of Beria, and every one of them is almost equally proved.

They are as follows:

Version No. 1

Sitting in his huge black limousine behind bulletproof windows and drawn curtains, Lavrenty Pavlovich Beria nervously looked at his wristwatch. As the First Deputy Chairman of the USSR Council of Ministers and Minister of Internal Affairs of the Soviet Union, he should have been in the Bolshoi Theatre at least a half hour ago. As number two man in the Government and the First Deputy of Premier Malenkov, he should appear at the theatre just after his superior, beside whom he would sit in the first official box. That day, however, Beria, also the Minister of State Security of the USSR, was kept in his office by some exceptionally important duties. Since the morning he had been studying reports from East Berlin about

xix

the riots that had erupted ten days before. He also had to check the files on the incident of a shooting at the car of Premier Malenkov. On the night of May 31, 1953, two military guards fired at the Prime Minister's automobile as Malenkov was leaving the Kremlin through the main Spassky Gate. The Premier was unhurt, but one of the bullets wounded his chauffeur. The guards reported that the driver did not answer the password demanded from officials' limousines and did not stop to produce his documents. To shoot was their duty according to regulations. However, their behavior could still be interpreted as an organized plot to assassinate Premier Malenkov, since the guards were from the Security Police subordinate to Beria who, in case of Malenkov's death, would take his position. To disperse any suspicions, Beria immediately ordered the guards arrested.

These two important cases, which Beria had to close as soon as possible, kept him busy for several hours. Evening had fallen when Beria locked the dossiers in the fireproof safe in his office at Lubyanka Prison. There was not much time before the show at the Bolshoi Opera would start. But since the Lubyanka Prison was not far from the theatre, Beria could make it in no more than ten minutes.

The evening was clear and warm. From afar, the golden domes of St. Basil's Cathedral shone against the background of the darkening sky. In the beams of spotlights the powerful silhouette of the medieval citadel of the Kremlin grew to gigantic size. On the spires of several tall towers, big red stars lighted from the inside gleamed like torches. They were made of real rubies taken from churches all over the country. Red Square, spread out at the foot of this ancient castle like an enormous courtyard, was overcrowded. It was June and the oncoming night was pleasant. It was Saturday and tomorrow no one had to go to work in a factory, in an office, or at school, but could fully relax after six days of an exhausting week.

In front of Lenin's Mausoleum, where recently the coffin with the body of Stalin who had died less than four months before had also been placed, there was a changing of the guard of honor. There were firm commands, snappy salutes, port arms, clicking of heels, and springy departure of the platoon, with the new sentries left at their posts.

Near Red Square, where Sverdlov Square is located, is the Bolshoi Theatre. That night the theatre was richly illuminated. At the entrances stood several militiamen in their new navy-blue uniforms. There were also reporters from *Pravda*[1] and *Izvestia*[2] newspapers, taking notes. At a distance from the theatre, many militiamen kept order in the streets. Some military trucks were parked in an alley and a few tanks moved slowly by. It was almost the same as in the days after Stalin died.

That night at the Bolshoi Theatre there was the gala performance of the new opera *The Decembrists*, by Yuri Sharpoin, and all the Government leaders, the highest personalities of the Communist Party, as well as the diplomatic corps, were to attend the premiere.

At the main door the ushers in black livery and white gloves were checking the personal invitations. They did their job courteously and efficiently, being watched by the plainclothesmen standing not far from them.

A spacious old-fashioned Rolls-Royce with a British banner arrived in front of the theatre. The chauffeur opened the door of the car and helped a middle-aged lady step out. The woman, in a crimson evening gown with pearls around her neck, was followed by the British ambassador: a gray-haired, lanky gentleman wearing a dinner jacket with a white carnation.

They entered the opera house. The passersby behind the line of militiamen glanced at the couple, but nobody stopped to look closely at them. No crowd of bystanders was allowed. Such gatherings were banned in the Soviet Union in those times. The gapers would be dispersed at once and anyone who looked suspicious to the shrewd security men might be arrested. It was much safer to pass by as if noticing nothing.

Soon after, a Cadillac with the American flag approached the theatre. The United States, known as the most capitalistic country in the world, a notorious warmonger and imperialist, was damned by the official authorities equally with England, the corrupted and perverted decadent. In other words, it was also dangerous to stop on the street to watch the Americans. It was much better to look in the opposite direction and go your way. The militiamen let the cars with C.D.—Corps Diplomatique—tags pass by one after another. The representatives of other countries—France, Italy, and Den-

[1] *Truth.*
[2] *News.*

mark, as well as those of the friendly Peoples' Republics of China, Hungary, Czechoslovakia and Poland—arrived with increasing frequency as it drew closer to eight o'clock, the hour when the show was to start. The Government and the Party leaders evidently were already in the theatre. At a secretly specified time, they had entered the building by the back door. In front of the theatre some last cars stopped and from each of these there hurried diplomats with their companions: the Swedish, Japanese, Dutch, or some of the new African republics.

The auditorium of the Bolshoi Opera Theatre was illuminated by thousands of lamps. The main floor and all the balconies were filled to capacity. In the general buzz of the excited public one could hear the musicians in the orchestra pit tuning their instruments. The performance would begin at any moment.

When Beria's big black limousine left the prison yard and drove toward Sverdlov Square, it met exceptionally heavy traffic, and the street became more jammed as his car approached the theatre. The chauffeur had to blow the horn again and again to pass other cars and buses. At the point where the huge automobile had to cross the street, it found some tanks blocking the way. The driver approached the nearest one and, presenting his credentials, asked the officer to move aside. While the commander was busy checking the chauffeur's identity card, the other tanks moved as if their crews recognized the official Packard and intended to open a path wide enough for the automobile to go through. Now, if the driver went fast, his boss would be on time.

The boxes of the Bolshoi Theatre reserved for the members of the Cabinet were not yet fully occupied. But if anyone in the audience noticed the absence of Lavrenty Beria, he was not yet late, as there were still a few minutes until curtain time.

At exactly eight o'clock the lights in the auditorium began to dim slowly, at first those on the walls, then the many upper ones, and at last the cluster of small lamps in the magnificent chandelier in the center of the ceiling. The big white sun of the spotlight was thrown on the scarlet curtain. The conductor, in formal evening attire, entered the orchestra pit. He was a tall man in his sixties, with an artistic mop of gray hair and big, bushy gray eyebrows above intelligent eyes. Greeted by a storm of applause, he bowed, then turned to the musicians and lifted his baton.

At that very moment, the black limousine with First Deputy

Premier Lavrenty Pavlovich Beria was still moving between two tanks, which protected it like two big battleships guarding a small vessel to give her a safe escort. However, they did not tow him to the theatre. They were going much further, to the outskirts of Moscow, where the heavily guarded Lefortovo Prison was located. That same night Beria was executed in the cellar of that jail.

The next morning, on the sunny Sunday of June 28, 1953, the Muscovites, in no hurry for their daily work, could leisurely read in *Pravda* or *Izvestia*, the reviews of the gala performance of the new opera, *The Decembrists*, by Yuri Shaporin. The opera was based on an historical event of the Russian revolutionists in 1825 in St. Petersburg. They also could scrutinize the list of Party leaders present at that performance. The names of the Cabinet members were mentioned, with the title of every one of them. They were all there, except for one man—the First Deputy Premier, who was also Minister of Internal Affairs and Minister of State Security—Lavrenty Pavlovich Beria.[3]

In such official announcements published in State-run newspapers, the omission of the name of a man regarded as next in line to Premier Malenkov, was too significant to be taken by the Soviet people as an oversight by a typesetter. It was beyond any doubt that on the previous evening, Saturday, June 27, 1953, Beria had just vanished. It was also certain that the tanks had not found themselves in Moscow by accident, but that the event in the streets of the city was prepared with the same care as the opera on the stage of the Bolshoi Theatre.

Such was the first version of the epilogue of Lavrenty Beria and of the end of his life. *The New York Times* of June 29, 1953, published the news from Moscow, repeating from the Soviet press of the day before that this Soviet leader had not appeared in the theatre according to the attendance roster. Later, after reliable dispatches by the press of Paris, London, and Washington on July 11, 1953, the world learned that the day before all newspapers of the Soviet Union had revealed that Beria had been arrested as a traitor and accused of being "the enemy of the people."

Version No. 2

A warm summertime dusk embraced the city. From behind the bulletproof windows and drawn curtains of Beria's long black

---

[3] Appendix 1.

Packard, the passengers occasionally glimpsed the life of the city: men wearing caps, women with scarfs on their heads or, more seldom, wearing hats. There were overcrowded streetcars, buses and trolleys, soldiers strolling in twos or threes, some peasants from the country not far away. At a subway station a big crowd, its members pushing each other, poured through the gate that led to the underground level. The people looked like ants rushing into a funnel of sand. In front of a movie theatre a long line, mostly young people, stretched for a block. The limousine passed Sverdlov Square with the State Academic Bolshoi Theatre; then the immense Red Square with the Lenin and Stalin Mausoleum and with the impressive walls of the Kremlin and St. Basil's Cathedral. From there, the car took the Kremlevskaya Embankment along the Moskva River and soon turned to the right, into a small, beautiful, tree-lined street, Tolstoy Street. There, at number 30-A, stood a white, medium-sized classical building of Empire style. Its many high windows shone with lights from huge crystal chandeliers. From the balcony on the second floor hung a long white and red flag. Above the widely opened main entrance was the national emblem, a shield with a white eagle against a red background. This was the Embassy of the Polish People's Republic.

The limousine stopped at the gate. Lavrenty Pavlovich Beria and his two companions, his best friends and closest Party comrades, got out of their automobile and entered the building. They felt obliged to come here, for it would seem rude to ignore the invitation to a reception given by the Polish ambassador, in honor of the friendship between the People's Poland and the Soviet Union.

The Ambassador, his wife, and the First Secretary of the Embassy awaited their honored guests at the top of the staircase and greeted them with due respect and demonstrative Slavic cordiality. Among the visitors Beria was the highest, but not the only, Soviet dignitary. Besides him, there was Molotov, third in rank after Malenkov and Beria. This was the triumvirate that took the power and became rulers at the Kremlin, succeeding the late Stalin. There was also Marshal Bulganin, an old versatile Bolshevik who, with his little goatee, looked like a goodhearted philosopher, and Marshal Voroshilov, Chairman of the Presidium of the USSR Supreme Soviet. The latter came to this reception in his gala uniform with dozens of decorations on both sides of his chest. There was also the First Deputy Minister of Defense, Marshal Zhukov, the great defender of Moscow against the Nazis, the hero who led his troops into Berlin, and Marshal Govorov, famed in the defense of Leningrad.

There were already on hand some representatives of several peoples' republics as well as of other friendly countries. The general mood was happy, gay and carefree. A servant carried a tray with glasses of Polish vodka, known as the best in the world. "Probably the only thing the Poles can do well," one of the Soviet dignitaries remarked, lowering his voice and raising his glass.

In the company of their hosts, Beria and his friends accepted the goblets. Three British officers who looked like schoolboys were trying to empty their glasses in one gulp, Russian style. Another round of vodka with some superb hors d'oeuvres—a paradise in your mouth. It was impossible to decline accepting one more drink and still another.

The butlers opened a door to display the banquet room with a big table arranged in a horseshoe shape and set for dinner. Beria offered his arm to the ambassador's wife and led her in. This formality was also a pleasure for him because the lady was pretty, had charming dimples, a peachlike complexion, and wore French perfume.

The dinner started. A wonderful tasting soup, meats melting on your palate, and white wine. Everyone had to admit the Polish cuisine was terrific. Again wines, champagne, and fruits on ice. Talking Russian with a strong Polish accent, the ambassador delivered a speech praising the Treaty of Friendship and Mutual Support between Poland and the USSR. Bravo! Bravo! Molotov answered the toast with his characteristic personal charm and eloquence, and with the wit of a professional diplomat. His listeners were all smiles, pretending they were delighted. From time to time a woman's laughter resounded. It rang like a silver bell, but only at the appropriate moments, so as not to disturb the speaker. Finally, spontaneous applause rewarded the oration. Everybody seemed to be delighted, even those foreign representatives in attendance who did not understand a single word of Russian. The Polish hosts were the happiest and most enchanted of all. But Beria hated the Poles with his whole heart. Those conceited, supposed noblemen, lords, sirs, and esquires full of pride! Those stupid daydreamers and Don Quixotes, eager to die for honor, dignity and other nonsensical slogans of the sort. Long ago, Beria hated the late Feliks Dzerzhinsky in spite of the fact that the Pole, called by Lenin "True Knight of the Proletariat," was one of the great Bolsheviks and had become Beria's model in executing thousands of people. It was none other than this popularly named "Iron Feliks" who was the founder of the *Cheka*—the Secret Police, the Communist terror apparatus, and the Soviet Security System.

After more toasts of champagne the rich dinner was over. The guests rose and moved to the adjoining room where a band was playing Russian melodies, Gypsy romances and Polish folk songs. Again, Beria offered his arm to the ambassador's wife, attractive, brunette, intelligent and witty.

The orchestra played a waltz, and a few couples danced. The butlers were serving Mocha coffee, liqueurs, and cognac. You could sit with a glass in hand, sipping a good drink, and pretend to listen to the flattering words of the ambassador.

It was late when Bulganin and Voroshilov approached Beria to suggest that it was time to leave. Beria had brought them here in his huge limousine and now they expected to get a lift home. Escorted to the front door by the hosts, the three Soviet dignitaries left the building. The night, lighted by the white moon, was beautiful. The weather was calm and refreshing. It was especially pleasant after so many drinks that had gone to one's head more strongly than one had expected. Soon, Beria's automobile approached the entrance. The limousine was followed by two similar official cars for the other Soviet representatives who had attended the party: Generals Ivan Konev, Rodion Malinovsky and a few others. Beria entered his limousine in the company of Bulganin and Voroshilov, who had come here with him after he had picked them up at their offices. It was good to have these two comrades on both sides. Just after Beria's car started, the two other automobiles with Soviet celebrities left the Polish Embassy.

The motorcade proceeded through the sleeping city. When it entered the capital's center and passed St. Basil's Cathedral, the Kremlin, and Red Square, Beria's chauffeur, instead of turning left on Gorky Street to Marshal Bulganin's home, turned the car to the right, to Dzerzhinsky Square with the huge statue of the "Knight of the Proletariat." In this vicinity was located the big, gray building of Lubyanka Prison, where Beria had his office in which he liked to work until very late at night. Often, after a party or dinner, his driver took him back there, since Beria customarily continued work that had been interrupted. But this time, in spite of having had more drinks than he intended, Beria was almost positive he had told his chauffeur to go first to Marshal Bulganin's home, and then to Marshal Voroshilov's. The car turned to the right again at "Children's World," the big toy store, moving toward Lubyanka. But that night Beria did not want to work there. It could only be his driver's mistake, bringing him to the office because he was accustomed to his boss' routine. Or maybe it was a joke prepared by Beria's companions, who were tipsy like himself, and now were going to make fun of him as the official who was always so busy and dutiful. Perhaps they had told the driver to come here. It was obviously a joke since, in the glare of the searchlights that flooded the prison walls as they approached, it was easy to see the two other cars with more friends, who had trailed his limousine all the way here. They had certainly all come to laugh at him together. Lubyanka's gate opened, letting in the familiar automobiles of the chief and his companions. The chauffeur stopped in the center of the courtyard. Half amused, Beria asked him what the joke was. To answer his superior, the driver turned around and pulled down the turned-up collar of his black leather overcoat. Beria looked at his face and realized that this time he was not being driven by his regular subordinate who also was his bodyguard, but by a high-ranking officer only slightly known to him. The prank was really very well staged indeed.

Taking Beria's arm, Marshal Voroshilov started to get out, and Bulganin also firmly took Lavrenty by the hand. The other generals had already left their automobiles and were waiting for them. But as yet nobody laughed. Held securely under the arms by his two friends, and followed by the other officers, Beria walked toward the building's back door, which he used every day or night on his way to his office. On the threshold stood the prison's commander with two officers. They escorted the party to the courtroom of the prison where sessions of a panel of *Troyka*—three judges who pronounced sentences in a short court-martial trial—were usually held. This time, the panel of judges consisted not of a *Troyka*: the staff had been enlarged to an eight-man tribunal headed by Marshal Ivan S. Konev, Chief Inspector of the Red Army and Hero of the Soviet Union. Beria was tried for treason. He was accused of (a) trying to seize "total power in Russia, (b) being a foreign spy, and (c) attempting to bring capitalism to Russia." There was no counsel; the defendant was allowed to say a last word in his own behalf. The judges did not repair to the conference room to discuss the sentence. They exchanged a few remarks among themselves and in a few seconds they reached a unanimous decision. The sentenced announced by the President of the eight-judge tribunal of Marshals and Generals read:

To declare Laventry Pavlovich Beria guilty of all the crimes he was charged with, and to sentence him to deprivation of all his posts, civil rights, property and possessed titles, awards and decorations, namely: the Honorary Title of Hero of the Socialist Work, granted to him by the Presidium of the Supreme Council of the USSR; the Honorary Title of Marshal of the Soviet Union; five orders of Lenin; an Order First Class of Suvorov; two Orders of the Red Banner, and seven Medals of the Soviet Union; and to sentence him to capital punishment: the death penalty. The verdict is definitive, there is no appeal of any sort.

The execution by a firing squad was to be performed immediately.

A captain, a sergeant, and two soldiers of the guard took the condemned man from the courtroom to a cellar some floors below. In this place hundreds of captives had been destroyed by order of the Chief Minister of State's Security: Beria himself.

Such was the second version of Lavrenty Beria's epilogue and the end of his life, according to a reliable dispatch by the Associated Press published in the newspapers of West Berlin, London and New York on February 18, 1954.

Version No. 3

It was almost four o'clock in the afternoon on June 26, 1953. In the main conference room at the Kremlin the Party's Presidium was about to meet. Premier Malenkov, his First Deputy Beria, and Molotov, who were Stalin's successors and the triumvirate that had taken power after his death less than four months before, were expected to show up at any moment and begin a discussion of several important problems. They would appear momentarily. In the reception room the other members of the Cabinet were already gathered. Soon after their arrival other important and famous personages came: Nikita S. Khrushchev, Marshals Kliment Voroshilov and Nikolay Bulganin, the heavy-set, dark Lazar Kaganovich and lanky Anastas Mikoyan. All were close comrades and good friends, and several of them were Old Guard Bolsheviks and founders of the Party. Besides them, the highest commanders of the Red Army were also present, called here to serve because of their experience and judgment in the military matters that were supposed to be on the agenda. In this group an atmosphere of sincere brotherhood prevailed, as is usually the case in a circle of comrades-in-arms who, together, had shed their blood for their country—and victoriously ended the Second World War. Among these generals, richly decorated with medals and orders, one could recognize the stout silhouette of the Marshal of the Soviet Union, Georgy Zhukov, who saved Moscow as a Commander of the Defense of the Nation's Capital against the Germans; Marshal Ivan Konev, Hero of the Soviet Union and Chief Inspector of the Soviet Army, General Moskalenko, Deputy Defense Minister, and Marshal Malinovsky, the hero of Stalingrad. The officers, standing aside, kept their own company and did not mix with the civilian ministers with whom they had just exchanged greetings, handshakes and sincerely polite smiles.

Outside the thick walls of the Kremlin castle the weather was sultry and sticky. The city sizzled. The green overcrowded street-cars and trolley-buses were as hot as huge pots on a stove. On the several street corners the round kiosks with soda water and lemonade were besieged not only by schoolchildren and soldiers as they ordinarily were, but by people from all walks of life. It was hard to believe that such tropical heat could occur in Moscow, where the winter is proverbially frosty. The huge onion domes of St. Basil's Cathedral, glittering blindingly, remained suspended above Red Square like big fiery suns that would suddenly drop from the sky. The old bricks of the ancient walls around the medieval Kremlin Citadel seemed to be still hot, as if taken straight out of the furnace. Fortunately, in the ancient Kremlin the air was nice and cool, protecting the men from the scorching heat.

When the Cabinet gathered in full force, with all members present, it moved to the conference room to begin the meeting. At the head of the long table covered with red cloth sat Premier Malenkov, a serious, fat, heavy man with the round face of a eunuch and chubby cheeks that looked as if they were never touched by a razor. He was wearing a black *roobashka*, a tunic with a small collar buttoned at the side of his neck under his left ear. Next to Malenkov, at his left, sat Molotov, the famous Minister of Foreign Affairs and now one of Malenkov's deputies. Molotov, a statesman with the appearance of a university professor, wearing glasses and a small mustache, was clad in a well-tailored suit, a white shirt with a starched, snowy collar and a faultlessly knotted tie. On Malenkov's right sat his First Deputy Premier, Lavrenty Pavlovich Beria. After Premier Malenkov he was the number two man, and the powerful Minister of Internal Affairs. This stocky, bald, rather fat man in a dark flannel suit, with an old-fashioned pince-nez on a prominent nose and a bulging, worn briefcase full of papers on his lap, looked more like a banker or businessman from some capitalistic foreign country than the Minister of State Security of the Soviet Union. Next to him sat Nikita Khrushchev, a friendly Ukrainian. In his gray suit of coarse fabric he resembled a middle-aged peasant in his Sunday best attending some relative's wedding party. After these four celebrities, which one of whom it was still impossible to predict would take the late Stalin's place and grasp his dictatorial power, there were Marshal Bulganin, Minister of Defense; Marshal Voroshilov, Deputy Chairman of the Council of Ministers; Lazar Kaganovich, the oldest member of the Bolshevik Party; the always enigmatically smiling Anastas Mikoyan, and five other members of the Administration.

The conference was opened by the Chairman, Premier Malenkov. Unheedful of the fact that after Stalin's death he had won the Premier's post thanks mostly to the support given him by Beria for the sake of the fatherland, Malenkov moved on to two important problems. The first involved the recent revelations about the "Jewish Doctors' Plot." These arrests, which six months ago had scandalized the whole world as being proof of an extremely strong anti-Semitism deeply rooted in Russia, demolished the Soviet Union's reputation as a country where everybody enjoys equal rights. But now, although in half a year's time the world had forgotten the case, Beria had recently brought it back into the daylight, declaring that the defendants were innocent. Comrade Beria decided to free all the imprisoned, as victims of a fabricated affair where confessions had been forced from them by torture during a period when Beria was not active as Minister of State Security. Why did Beria make such a revealing announcement in the Soviet press of April 4?[4]

By his statement Comrade Beria denounced publicly the activity of the former Ministry of State Security, describing its methods as

---

[4] Appendices 2 and 3.

unlawful. Didn't he know that for the masses no Soviet authority is ever wrong? Certainly he knew it. He knew it very well. So why did he belittle the prestige of the Soviet Administration in the eyes of the people and sabotage that important Agency? Did Beria behave as a Soviet-minded person should? Of course he did not. So, the only answer was that he did it to discredit the reputation of Soviet justice and of the Communist jurisprudence.

The next, and even graver case, concerned recent events in East Berlin. Just ten days before this meeting, on June 17, 1953, riots had broken out in East Berlin, and had lasted several days before they could be suppressed. Such a fact must encumber Beria, as the Minister of Security, with guilt. Certainly, riots can happen anytime and anywhere. But if they grow to such a size as they had in East Berlin, where the inner forces were not strong enough to overpower the rebels and restore peace and order, and where it became necessary to send Red Army tanks and armored units for pacification action, it meant that the revolt had been prepared on a large scale and that Beria should have been informed in advance. Otherwise, he proved to be a very poor guardian of the State's security. By such indolence Beria brought shame on the whole Soviet Union and discredited it before the world, because he let it be revealed that famine prevailed in East Germany, driving its people to despair. Advantage of this fact was immediately seized by anti-Soviet propaganda in America, where President Eisenhower made a display of declaring fifteen million dollars in aid for the supposedly starving Germans. By this political maneuver the United States presented the Soviet Union with a real dilemma: If East Germany accepted the American offer, she would admit that without the support given her by the capitalistic, decadent West it was impossible to solve her problem of hunger. If, on the other hand, East Germany rejected American help, how could she justify her decision against the background of the desperate step taken by the people? All these troubles were caused by nothing other than the inadequacy of Beria, the Minister of Internal Affairs and State Security. However, Malenkov continued, it is highly doubtful that this was really only a case of inadequacy. Such an experienced and shrewd politician and statesman as Lavrenty Pavlovich Beria, who for fifteen years had been the most powerful person in the Soviet Union next to the late great Comrade Stalin, could hardly be described as being inadequate. It is widely known that during the

rebellion in East Berlin the Chief of the East German Police
Forces, Inspector Zaisser, was Beria's man and that after the revolt,
not only was he never arrested or even removed from his post, but
was still kept there by Beria. It should be obvious to everyone that
an event such as the revolution in East Berlin, which shocked the
whole world and was featured on the front pages of every newspaper in every country of the globe, had been very well foreseen—
if not staged—by the man who for years had been an expert at
preparing convincing trials, often directed against the most eminent Bolsheviks and outstanding members of the Communist Party.
All of this proved, Malenkov said in a low, calm voice, that Beria
did not serve his country well. On the contrary, he consciously
acted against the good of his fatherland and in the interests of the
enemies of the Soviet Union, especially by furthering the aims of
the United States of America, with which he doubtless had connections. Beria acted as a subversive agent for American dollars.
Strictly speaking, Lavrenty Beria was a traitor who should be accused of being an enemy of the people of the Soviet Union and be
put on trial as a foreign agent charged with treason.

"You are not a true Communist, Lavrenty Pavlovich"—remarked
Nikita Khrushchev with a broad smile during a short pause in
Malenkov's speech—"and you never even joined a Party organiza-
tion."[5]

In answer, Beria opened his briefcase and put his hand inside, as
if to produce documents that could prove his innocence. However,
instead of papers, he took out a big black revolver. But Khrushchev
was swifter. With the elbow of his heavy left arm he pressed Beria's
hand to the table, while with his other hand he directed the barrel
toward the ceiling. At the same moment, Malenkov stepped on a
button under the table. The door opened wide, and a group of high-
ranking Red Army officers appeared, led by General Moskalenko
with a tommygun in his hand. One more step forward, another to
make sure that nobody would get hurt but the marked man, and
Moskalenko triggered the gun, firing a volley of bullets aimed at
the bald, round head with the pince-nez and the stocky chest of the
Chief of the Soviet Secret Police.

This is the third version of Lavrenty Pavlovich Beria's epilogue.
The news of such an end to his life, according to the most reliable

---

[5] News dispatches, *The Washington Post*, November 17, 1961.

sources, was announced in the international press of November 16, 1961.

These are the three epilogues of Lavrenty Pavlovich Beria. His death was one of the most mysterious on the Russian political scene, especially since there are even more versions; a number of public figures wished to credit themselves with adding an extra bullet to the corpse of the Chief of the Soviet Secret Police. Among these was Nikita Khrushchev. The American writer, John Fisher, revealed that during a conversation between Khrushchev and a Western diplomat, the latter asked him: "You know, one thing I never understood was how you managed to get rid of Lavrenty Beria. With his absolute control of the Secret Police, I should have thought he would be invulnerable."

"He should have been," Khrushchev replied, "but he made one silly mistake. Beria came into a conference room one day without his bodyguard. I shot him."[6]

In May 1956, Khrushchev said to a visiting French senator: "Beria had refused to follow the instructions of the Presidium and was striving to build up his own power. After a four-hour session of the Presidium in the Kremlin, Beria admitted his plot. He left the room with the others, and in an adjoining circular hall, Anastas Mikoyan fired a bullet from behind and killed him."[7]

However, in his tape-recorded reminiscences which were later translated into English and published in the United States, *Khrushchev Remembers*, Khrushchev once again changed his recollections of Beria's death. In these memoirs Khrushchev declared that at the session of the Presidium of the Central Committee at the Kremlin in June 1953, Beria was not shot but was only arrested by Marshal Zhukov and General Moskalenko. Then, in December Beria was tried, sentenced and executed according to the official announcement of the Soviet press.

On the other hand, according to Boris I. Nicolaevsky, formerly of the Marx-Engels Institute in Moscow, Beria's killer was Anastas Mikoyan. In *The Crimes of the Stalin Era*, published by *The New*

---

[6] John Fisher, "Easy Chair—Some Guesses About the Next Kremlin Conspiracy." *Harper's Magazine*, March, 1969. Vol. 238, No. 1426.

[7] *Facts On Communism*, Volume II. *The Soviet Union, From Lenin to Khrushchev.* Committee on Un-American Activities. House of Representatives, Eighty-Sixth Congress, Second Session. U. S. Government Printing Office. Washington, 1961.

Leader, Nicolaevsky commented: "One newspaper report has Khrushchev telling the recent French Socialist delegation that Beria was killed during a session of the Party Presidium by Deputy Premier Anastas Mikoyan."[8]

There is also an official declaration, carried in the government newspapers *Pravda* and *Izvestia* of December 24, 1953, that Beria was put on trial, sentenced to death for treason, and executed.

But the *Great Universal Encyclopedia*, published by the Polish Communist government in Warsaw in 1962, stated in a biographical note about Beria that he died in July 1953. By this announcement it was revealed that Beria had been liquidated long before the official Soviet newspapers *Pravda* and *Izvestia* declared that his trial had occurred in December 1953.

These were the many deaths of Lavrenty Beria.

But what was his life, his background and his career, during which Beria climbed from a peasant boy in a small Caucasian village in Georgia, to a paramount post as the most powerful man in Russia and became a master of life and death to the millions of people in the whole Communist Imperium?

---

[8] Boris I. Nikolaevsky, "The Crimes of the Stalin Era." *The New Leader*, New York, 1962.

PART ONE

THE CAUCASUS

1

Kingdom of the Golden Fleece

ABKHAZIA IS A SUNNY LAND of Georgia—a land of fragrant acacias and shiny leaves of tea with its delicate flowers. It is a country where the light wind tenderly swings the plumes of the tall palm trees, which grant a blessed shadow. Here are ripening golden oranges and bright tangerines, yellow lemons, purple pomegranates and pink apples of paradise. Here is the country of red peppers, green olives and heavy bunches of grapes for the sweet Caucasian wine. On the eastern coast, washed by the waters of the Black Sea, there are two towns: Sukhum in the North and Batum in the South. Their harbors smell of grease and coal tar from the freighters that are swaying at anchor. Between these two ports there are fishermen's villages lining the length of the extended shore like small shells threaded on a brown string forming the semicircle of a huge necklace.

At night, when the white moon is sailing through the navy-blue sky, it sheds its light on these tiny hamlets, which are quiet, as if spellbound. In the cool moonlight, mute huts stand with roofs covered with wooden shingles, each with its little garden, wide barn, low pigsty, and narrow chicken coop. Nearby, on high poles, big black fishermen's nets are drying, spread out like huge cobwebs. Farther on, boats pulled out of the water are sleeping. They lie about like big-bellied fish thrown upon the sand by angry waves.

All around, silence prevails. Not a single dog is barking. Only the

3

sea murmurs rhythmically, splashing white foam on the dark shore. The windows in the chalk-white huts are dead, like black, empty eyesockets. Sometimes the windowpanes reflect, like dark mirrors, the pale moon or the gray sea waves, or the swinging meshes of the nets, or a long arm of a shadow well. They all look alike, as do the boats, the oars, the fish, the seagulls. Farther from the Black Sea, deep in the mainland, there are hamlets where peasants grow olives, grapes, tobacco and corn, and tend orchards of apple, peach, pear and plum trees.

Such were the hamlets of Abkhazia, villages inhabited by Mingrelians, an ancient tribe of over 400,000 souls belonging to the Georgian group of Caucasian peoples, supposedly already known in Greek mythology, and certainly already settled during the Crusades.

One of dozens of such villages was called Merkheuli, a few miles inland and not far from the town of Sukhum. In summer the nights there are warm and clear, bathed in moonlight. But in early springtime, in March, when the moon hides behind the clouds, it is so pitch-dark that you cannot see your hand in front of you. The wind is chilly, dashes you with a cold drizzle and leaves you wet to the bone.

On the night of March 29, 1899, the hamlet of Merkheuli was asleep as usual. However, in the windows of one white dwelling there was a light, the swaying flame of a kerosene lamp. This house, larger than any of the abodes in the village, did not belong to any of the peasants in particular, but was the property of the whole community. It was popularly called *samrevlo* and was founded and supported by the church. *Samrevlo* in Georgian means maternity home run by the parish, or *mrevli*. Expectant mothers come here a few days before giving birth. The Georgians, who took many customs from Eastern nations, believe that during that time a woman is impure and should be isolated.

On this particular night, a woman was there who had been admitted to the maternity house less than a week before. Above her bed an icon hung in a corner. A small taper placed in a red glass threw flickers of light on the picture of the black Madonna and Child, painted against a gold background. In the adjoining kitchen, there was a big clay stove where a fire was crackling. On top of the stove stood a big black kettle full of boiling water.

Two older women, neighbors and good friends of the pregnant

one, were at her side. They were sitting on the edge of the bed. They held the woman's hand and prayed aloud so the pains would stop and the baby would come soon, nice and healthy. With a wet rag, they wiped the sweat from the woman's forehead and from her almost blue face. They prayed and waited. That was all human beings could do. The rest was in God's hands and in those of Holy Mary . . . and in the hands of the good spirits who live near every person. Her time might come in an hour, or two, or five, or before dawn. Who knows? So let's pray.

Suddenly, the woman in labor yelled as if stabbed with a knife straight through her chest. But that was good. Shortly everything would be over. The two women, themselves each the mother of several children, knew what to do when a woman was giving birth. They were quick and experienced. Soon the young mother calmed down and was breathing with less difficulty. While one of her friends took care of the young mother, the other busied herself with the small new arrival. In a tin bowl of water, she washed the little creature who looked like a skinned rabbit. Everything was fine. In a few minutes' time, the younger of the two midwives left the *samrevlo*. In spite of the pitch-dark, moonless, windy and drizzly night she had no difficulty in finding the hut where the new mother lived with her husband and with Datiko, her son from a previous marriage. The woman knocked at the low window, once, and a second time, louder. A man got up, opened the door of his hut and stopped on the threshold. "How is she?"

"She's all right. You have a son, Pavel Beria, a nice, healthy boy whom your wife, Tekle, wants to name Lavrenty."

"Well, let him be Lavrenty."

When the geography teacher started lecturing, all the boys in the class listened to him attentively. On that particular day, the teacher told them a kind of fairy tale or story from Greek mythology. But evidently he was driving home a certain point. He told them of how once upon a time, long ago in very ancient times, there was in Thessaly a king, Aeson by name, a good and righteous monarch. Alas, he had a brother, Pelias, a treacherous and unscrupulous character who, with a gang of subordinates, wove a plot against the king. One night, they entered the castle and after disarming the guards, they captured Aeson and deprived him of his throne. Later, in order to prevent the dynasty from continuing,

Pelias decided to kill Aeson's infant son, Jason, because when he grew up, he could claim the right to the throne. However, the baby's mother, warned by a faithful servant, escaped from the town with her child and took him to the cave of the good Centaur, Chiron. She asked him to take care of the boy, and left her son in his care. From that time on until he was twenty, Jason was brought up and tutored by the wise Centaur. Then he bade his mentor good-bye and went away to learn about the wide world and to see it with his own eyes. Soon after, he started a long voyage, seeking the Golden Fleece of a ram that had lived in the kingdom of Colchis on the eastern shore of the Black Sea and, after a long life, had been sacrificed to Jupiter.

The speaker was well aware of the interest he evoked in his young audience. Not one of the students played tic-tac-toe or a game of buttons, as they did during other teachers' lessons. Now they were all ears, listening intently, while he told them that the mythological kingdom of Colchis was their own native land; that the very town of Sukhum where they attended school and the Sukhum harbor that they all knew well—were located in Colchis' lowlands.

The old teacher in his worn, dark suit knew well how to capture the youths' imaginations. Continuing the story, he told them about the expedition led by Jason who, with fifty of his men built a huge boat he called *Argo*, meaning "Swift." Then the crew, called Argonauts, started their voyage. After navigating the Black Sea, so familiar to everybody in Sukhum, they at last arrived in Colchis. There, in the Caucasian mountains so dear to the heart of each of his listeners, stood the magnificent castle of King Aetas, who kept the Golden Fleece. The Colchian king promised Jason the Golden Fleece if the young adventurer would overpower and tame two fire-belching bulls, use them to plow a field and sow there the poisonous teeth of a slain dragon. As soon as Jason accomplished this task, there sprang from the earth a horde of warriors who attacked the young hero. But Jason was a smart fellow. He threw a large rock at them and the dragon's breed immediately started a fight against one another and mercilessly slew each other until the very last one lay dead.

Later on, before the end of the story of the Argonauts roaming over the Caucasus, many other adventures occurred, colorful, cruel and horrible. It was really an exciting tale full of gruesome conspiracies, intrigues, treason, blood, murders, escapes and chases. Yes, Caucasus, the boys' fatherland, was indeed the fabulous setting of such heroic tales. Another thing that had happened nowhere else but in the mountains of their native Caucasus was the Titan Prometheus' deed. He stole fire from heaven for men's sake and was chained to a rock where vultures tore out his liver. Of course, every student in the class knew these mountains.

The clatter of the hand-bell shaken by the mustachioed school janitor announced the end of this hour. Later, after other lessons —Russian grammar, or arithmetic, or history, or religion—the school day came to its end and at last the boys could leave and go home. They noisily collected their textbooks, papers and pencils and ran to the door, jostling one another. Once outside, they hurried through the streets to their homes and then to the seaside for bathing and swimming. The town was covered by a glow from the golden rays of the sun. From the onion-domed church one could hear the ding-dong of bells striking two o'clock in the afternoon. At the stands of the street market a row of fat peasant women were selling silvery fish, quarters of red watermelon cut in such a way that they looked like half-moons in the green halo of their peel. There were also yellow peanuts in shells and black sunflower seeds, a full measure of which—a small glass—you could buy for half a kopeck, pour into your pocket and, while walking, bite and eat them, spitting out the hulls far in front of you.

After leaving the dilapidated building of the high school at Podgornaya Street, the boys passed the market house and the street vendors' stands with their goods outside. From there one only had to turn a corner to be on a sandy road where could be seen the ships anchored far from the harbor. When walking past the line of town houses on your right, you had on your left the vast beach covered with gravel. The white waves of the sea repeatedly invaded the coast with a murmur and then silently withdrew, leaving big brown spots. Here you could take off your clothes and bathe and swim to your heart's content until you got hungry as a devil and hastened home for dinner.

But Lavrenty Beria did not like to join his colleagues and go swimming with them in a group. He did not care for friends either, except for a few: Semyon Danilov and Nestor Lakoba. Generally, however, Lavrenty was a lone wolf. During the recesses between lessons when walking alone in the school yard or in the hall, Lavrenty was always ready to fight and often provoked a scuffle. Being less than medium-sized he suffered a complex common to short boys. When looking for a brawl Lavrenty wanted to prove that he was not inferior to any of the tall fellows. Beria was broad-shouldered, thick-necked and almost athletically strong, with stubby hands. When he fought he did not behave like schoolboys usually do, just expending energy. Lavrenty tried to do some special harm to his adversary either by hitting him in an eye, or making his nose bleed, or by throwing him against the sharp edge of a class desk to injure his back. No wonder his classmates avoided him. However, Beria was not violent by nature, but rather grim and unapproachable. Knowing that he was unpopular he was possessed by a feeling of being rejected by society as an unpleasant, short and ugly being. It set him against people, most of whom he considered his potential foes. In revenge, Lavrenty wanted to show them that he was not a mere nobody who could be ignored, but was an individual who must be respected and should be feared.

Besides, such pleasures as bathing, swimming and playing on the beach were for boys from well-to-do families, not for those who had to work. Lavrenty had to work, and so he envied and hated the rich. From school he had to go straight home. His house was in the center of the town, on Dvorskaya Street, which was the principal avenue. It was one of the most prominent buildings, having a store with two big shop windows and a wide entrance door in the middle. Overhead hung a signboard with the name SVIMONI IERKOMOSHVILI printed in golden letters against a blue background surrounded by hand-painted lengths of colorful fabrics, spools of thread, ribbons, a pair of scissors and many buttons of all sizes and shapes. On the second floor was the apartment of the owner of this enterprise, a rich merchant, the proprietor of the biggest dry-goods store in Sukhum. He was a businessman who brought various materials—silk, cotton, wool, velvet and so on— from Kutais, the faraway large town in Georgia, or even by ship from Odessa.

To be able to study in Sukhum, Lavrenty had to live there. His mother, whose most beloved child he was, found him this place with the good man Ierkomoshvili, whom she had met once and who was kind enough to do her this favor. In the rear of the shop Lavrenty had a small room where he slept and could prepare his homework. He ate his meals upstairs in the kitchen, which he entered by the servants' staircase. He paid for his room and board by working in the shop, and the tuition was paid by his father. Lavrenty swept and cleaned the store before it was opened, tidied it up in the evening, washed the windows and prepared tea for his boss and the two salesmen, who also sent him out to buy the daily newspaper or cigarettes. He hated them for making him their messenger. Lavrenty also delivered parcels to customers. This duty could be a pleasant one since the boy could take walks through the town, and made some money in tips. But he liked best of all to be left alone in his dark, tiny room behind the shop, and not to be disturbed by anyone.

Lavrenty's only amusement was to go from time to time to the main square to watch an old bearded beggar who sat at the wall of the church, a cup for alms in front of him, and whispered monotonous pleas. That crippled man pretended to be blind, too. But he was not. Lavrenty noticed that the beggar's tired eyes were expressionless only when people passed him indifferently. Yet, when an individual who listened to his plea dropped him a coin and then went his way, the beggar lifted his bowed head and looked after him with a spark of hatred in his eyes, while his lips whispered curses.

This scene always fascinated Lavrenty, who had been waiting for just that moment. He grasped the beggar's feeling. The boy understood that those hundreds of pedestrians who showed no pity for the beggar did not count. He did not exist for them, while for him they were just faceless silhouettes. But the person who stopped and gave him alms became his personal foe because he was rich and had so much money he could spend it without getting anything in return, while the beggar was poor and miserable. The rich man and his donation humiliated the poor beggar, so he envied and hated him. Beria knew the popular ancient saying: "I have no idea why he hates me so much. I never did anything good for him." And Lavrenty agreed entirely with the wisdom of this old adage.

Once a week, on Sundays, Lavrenty had to leave his hiding place and go on foot to his native village, Merkheuli. His shoes, bound together by their laces, hung on his shoulder, while he walked fast to get home in time to attend high mass with his family. He had to start his trip quite early, even before sunrise, because on holidays you never knew when you would find a country wagon with a friendly peasant who, going in the same direction, would be

willing to give you a lift. In the late afternoon, Lavrenty started
back. At that time, his father usually drove him in their wagon, to
which their old mare was hitched. During summer vacation from
school Lavrenty had one week free from work in the shop. But,
since he was in his village during that time he had to get up at
daybreak and go to work with his father and half-brother Datiko. It
seemed to Lavrenty that such a way of life would last until he
finished his education in the sixth-grade school. One could not expect any changes or surprises.

Once, however, he was told to go home on a weekday. Lavrenty,
who was twelve years old then, was called by his employer to
his office, a small booth behind the counter. The old man told
him with a very solemn face that one hour or so ago Lavrenty's
younger brother Irakly had come with the sad news that their father had died. The little boy had been sent to the kitchen to have
some food and rest after his long, tiring walk from the village, and
to wait for his brother. The sympathetic merchant gave Lavrenty
some money so the boys could take a coach and be home as soon as
possible. The droshkies were at the railway station.

As the two brothers approached Merkheuli, Lavrenty was proud
to see a crowd in front of their hut. It was as if the whole village
had gathered there. There were not only women and children, but
also men, who evidently had left their work in the fields earlier
than usual in order to come. When the boys arrived, the crowd
before the hut parted in silence to let them pass.

Inside, Pavel Beria was lying on his bed under the pictures of the
saints and the icon, which hung there as always, only now, many
candles and tapers were burning in front of them, although it was
still daylight. Pavel was clad in his work clothes. He had died
working in the field, and the neighbors brought the corpse to his
hut. His eyes were closed. On the middle of his forehead a holy
picture of Jesus Christ had been placed, held tightly by a band of
coarse cloth. In his hands the dead man held the big crucifix which
had been taken from the wall. He seemed to be pressing it to his
chest. The mirror hanging above the crude commode was now covered with a rug. Little Tamara, Lavrenty's younger sister, stood at
the bedside waving a bunch of leaves to shoo away flies that tried
to get into the dead man's nostrils, ears, under his closed eyelids
and between his lips. On the bench against the opposite wall their
mother was sitting, lamenting loudly. On both sides were two old

women, her friends and neighbors. They were holding her by the arms to protect her from herself should she try to scratch her face with her fingernails, or pull her hair out, or break a finger while wringing her hands because of the great grief which she was demonstrating before all the spectators. These two old women helped the widow, in accordance with tradition, but their stony faces did not reveal any sorrow, pity or sympathy.

To Lavrenty the whole scene looked like a very stupid hoax. The event was not of the kind where such feelings should be expressed. Death is a part of everybody's life and it comes to everyone sooner or later. So what? Why pity someone because of something common to all? Datiko did not cry, neither did Tamara. Datiko just stood there and looked at his father, while Irakly was happy and excited after the recent ride in a real droshky. Nor did Lavrenty regret his father's death. He considered this man an old goat ready for his grave. Once he disciplined Lavrenty with a spanking, and from that time on Lavrenty wished him the worst. So now it serves that old man well. Some women, widows themselves and the poorest creatures in the vicinity, cried from the bottoms of their hearts. They were professional mourners who, after the funeral, would be paid for their job.

The dwelling was full of kneeling people, like church on a Sunday. They prayed, often crossing themselves with the broad signs of the holy cross. But truly this event in the hamlet was nothing but a novelty, a change in the routine life, and a relief from boredom. The crowd in front of the hut grew bigger and bigger, as more folks returned from work in the fields. Everybody was eager to look inside and see what was happening. Those who had been there for a long time explained Pavel's accident to the newcomers. They gladly repeated their story hundreds of times, since this made them centers of interest.

That night and the following day candles burned constantly in the room where the body of Pavel Beria was lying. The women came from time to time, knelt down and prayed. The next morning the village carpenter stopped his horse-drawn country wagon in front of the hut and brought in a coffin which he had made of coarse planks. The mother and her children approached the corpse and kissed the little holy picture on the dead man's forehead. They also kissed his lips and his hands, which were pressing the cross to his chest. They each did it, one by one, except Lavrenty who only pretended because he had never liked that old man, who always seemed a stranger to him. Then, with the help of one of the neighbors, the carpenter removed the body from the bed, placed it in the coffin, covered it with the lid, carried the coffin out of the house, put it on the cart and drove to the parish house.

The open casket, surrounded with flowers and flickering candles, had to remain in the church for three days and three nights, in accordance with the religious custom. After the required time elapsed, the coffin was taken from the church and put on a funeral wagon driven by a black horse; then the procession started on its way to the cemetery. A choir boy marched first, wearing a surplice and carrying a tall crucifix. He was followed by the Orthodox priest, who preceded the black van, while behind it walked the family of the deceased and the mourners. They were singing a church hymn. For Lavrenty the whole procession was funny nonsense.

At the cemetery they put the coffin beside the grave, which had already been dug. They opened the coffin once more, and the priest prayed for the peace of Pavel Beria's soul. The widow, the orphans, and some friends of the dead man approached to kiss him goodbye. Finally, the gravediggers nailed the lid on the coffin and lowered it into the grave on long, homespun webbed belts. There was a moment of general whispering of the short prayer *Eternal Rest*, repeated three times. Then someone opened a bottle of sweet, red Caucasian wine, filled a glass and poured the contents into the grave. This would guard against the earth's becoming too heavy for the deceased. It was an ancient tradition, a pure absurdity, in Lavrenty's opinion. Afterwards, the gravediggers started shoveling the sand into the pit with their wide spades. At first they threw the yellow sand, then the black dirt until a small mound rose. Then their job was done. The family adorned the grave with a wooden cross, a wreath and some flowers, and the funeral was over.

After the ceremony the widow invited the mourners to a repast in her home. She had already prepared a tremendous reception. According to tradition, there was a huge country cake baked with hot meat inside, a chicken, dumplings with white cheese, red and white Caucasian wine, vodka and homemade beer. Also, there were various fruits and a lot of sweet goodies, pastries, balbalo, rahat-loukoum and halvah. Beria's widow wanted to treat her guests with all this food and drink. Besides the friends and neighbors who showed so much sympathy and heartfelt affection for her, and such respect for her late husband's memory, she also invited the priest and his wife. A reception for such an eminent couple had to be appropriately lavish.

It was late in the evening when the party was over. The Orthodox priest, pleased and drunk, left the hut with the help of his spouse and took his seat in the coach. Then the other guests took leave. This time, as always after a funeral in the village, the mourners went home tipsy and in a good mood, enjoying the fact that they were still alive and their stomachs were full of excellent food and drink. Now they left the hut of Beria's widow who—who knows—possibly had spent all her savings for the funeral and the lavish wake. From now on, she would be expected to work for her living and that of the youngsters. Surely, they speculated, the lives of these orphaned children and their mother would soon undergo a change. Obviously, now the widow and her four offspring would have a hard time. When Tekle lost her first husband, Kvaratskhalia, she was still young, not bad-looking, and had only one child—her boy Datiko. So she was able to find another man—Pavel Beria—to marry her. But from now on, she could count only on herself. She was not young and pretty any more. She was the mother of four brats, and she was poor. Who would care for such a woman? She certainly would be able to manage as long as she remained strong and healthy. But would she be able to let her Lavrenty stay in school, or would the boy have to abandon his studies and look for a job to help his poor mother? Anyhow, who cared? Everyone had his own troubles and tomorrow was another day for work. But this was the only thought and feeling that bothered Lavrenty: would he be allowed to go back to town and to his studies?

Standing in the center behind a long table covered with a heavy green cloth, the schoolmaster was delivering a speech. He wore a black frock-coat and looked quite official. However, the knot of his tie slid down a bit from under the stiff collar, revealing a shiny copper stud by which the collar was pinned to his white shirt. On both sides of the headmaster sat all the teachers of the school. Opposite them, at a distance from the table, stood the students. Some of them had brought their parents, for whom chairs had been reserved.

It was mid-June. The crowded room was very hot, although the windows were wide open. From time to time the headmaster reached for water and drank from a thick glass filled from a nearby decanter. He was obviously tired, but the long annual oration which he delivered at the ends of the terms and on graduation day was his responsibility, adding a special note to his prestige. At last the speech was over. The listeners rewarded the orator with resounding applause. The headmaster sat down, wiped the sweat from his face with a handkerchief, and exchanged a few words with the two professors sitting on either side.

Now followed the ceremony of distribution of diplomas to those who were graduated from the Municipal Public High School for Boys at Sukhum in the year 1915. The professor of the Russian language began calling out the names of the students. When each of them approached the table, the schoolmaster handed him a document written in calligraphical characters on a big sheet of paper, and honored him by shaking hands. Since the boys were summoned in alphabetical order, soon the name—Beria, Lavrenty Pavlovich—was called.

Lavrenty took a few steps forward. He was a middle-sized but stoutly built sixteen-year-old boy, with a round head and crew-cut black hair. His face was pale in spite of its dark complexion, and his mouth, with a heavy, thick, sensual lower lip, was tightly closed. Balanced on his wide and prominent nose, wire-rimmed glasses covered his gray-green-blue almost transparent eyes, which had an unpleasant gibing, penetrating, and cool watery look. He wiped his perennially perspiring palms on his trousers and accepted his diploma from the schoolmaster, bowed, and returned to the ranks of his classmates.

When all the students had received their diplomas, the social part of the ceremony began. Professors, alumni and the boys' parents joined in informal conversation while sipping cold lemonade, or hot tea from a samovar. They also sampled some cookies baked every year for this celebration by the janitor's wife, on the schoolmaster's order. In the large room there was a general murmur of gay voices, typical for such a pleasant party. However, everybody was eager to leave the place as soon as possible. At first the younger students left, those who still had some years ahead of them before graduation. Then, the alumni who had come by themselves took leave, while those accompanied by their parents had to stay longer. It would be considered impolite to depart before the others, and besides, the parents were glad to talk to the teachers.

Tekle Beria was genuinely proud of her Lavrenty and happy because she could take part in the ceremony. This was the greatest day in her life. For the occasion she wore her best dress. On her head she had knotted a shiny kerchief of pure black silk with red and white roses, which she customarily wore only on Sundays to church. With pious respect she looked at her son's diploma and even read it. She knew her three R's, although a simple peasant woman of her origin wasn't usually so educated. Both her late husbands had been illiterate. But Tekle had been born in the environs of the village of Merkheuli, in a community called Uria Sopeli. This hamlet was inhabited by Jews and their derivative, the Karaim tribe; and both of those peoples like to educate their children. So Lavrenty's Karaim mother could read and write and was able to scrutinize her own son's graduation paper.

The party slowly dispersed. It was late in the afternoon when the widow Beria and her son left the dark, one-story school building and headed uptown in the direction of Dvorskaya Street, where well-to-do residents lived. Now Lavrenty began to dread the approaching unavoidable annoyance, the moment of thanking his benefactor for making his education possible. You have to be thankful, and there is no feeling more unpleasant than gratitude. It is common knowledge that nobody likes his benefactor, and the old, fascinating, supposedly blind beggar, whom Lavrenty remembered well, was no exception.

Alumnus Lavrenty Beria was no different from the rest of humans in the matter of expressing thanks, and he disliked doing it. He did not even know how to put his gratitude into words. It was not because he was shy, but because people annoyed him by disturbing his personal thoughts and intentions—some of them perhaps unspecified as yet—in his own inner world. Perhaps this was the reason he did not want and need people. People bothered him.

This time he had to go to his benefactor and give thanks for everything the man had done for him. After his father's death, Lavrenty's mother had to find work in town. She took the job of cook at Mr. and Mrs. Ierkomoshvili's home. Luckily her daughter Tamara was already old enough to take care of the household and look after Irakly. The money the widow Beria earned covered just the bare necessities. When Datiko, her oldest son, together with some other youths from the village, was drafted into the army, she had lost his help around the house and the income from his work. Moreover, because of the great war where, on faraway front lines

Tsar Nicholas was fighting Germany's tsar, everything became
much more expensive. Even the price of salt rose half a kopeck. It
was hard to make a living. Fortunately, once, when talking to her
mistress, Tekle Beria mentioned that it was a big problem for her to
pay for her Lavrenty's schooling. The good lady promised to discuss the matter with her husband. Next day, the merchant let his
cook know that the burden would be taken from her shoulders,
because from that moment on he would pay for her boy's education.

So it was, and now they had to thank Mr. and Mrs. Ierkomoshvili
for their good hearts and generosity.

Mother and son entered the apartment by the rear door. In the
kitchen, Tekle took off her Sunday silk kerchief, replacing it with a
regular white *babushka*. She also changed her clothes and shoes,
and tied a big white apron around her hips. Then she went to the
living room to ask her masters whether she could come in with her
boy. Yes, this was the best time. She came back and, in the company of her son, entered the drawing room.

Lavrenty stopped at the threshold and did not approach the
honorable couple sitting on a sofa, as was appropriate for dignified
and rich people. He looked around and noticed many beautiful
pieces of furniture, a Bokhara carpet, white fragile china, many
expensive leather-bound books displayed behind the glass of a tall
bookcase, several pictures in golden frames hanging on the walls,
and heavy embroidered draperies at the windows. All of a sudden
Lavrenty experienced a feeling of hatred against those two old
people for possessing all these goods while he had nothing more
than a small dim room behind their store. He despised that couple
for whom he and his mother had to work, and to whom he now had
to express his gratitude. Since Tekle had told them previously that
her son wished to thank his benefactors, she saved Lavrenty the
necessity of chokingly blurting out the difficult words. Now, the
mother encouraged him to produce for the masters his diploma,
which he carried rolled in a tube for fear it would be crushed. The
merchant read the certificate and nodded approval, although the
marks were just average. Then he asked the boy about his plans
for the future. Was their cook's son looking for a job? Yes, indeed.
But what kind of work, since his education was more than basic?
To take any indifferent job available would mean a waste of energy
and of the money spent on his studies. If he was thinking about a
better job, then what kind of post? As an assistant claims inspector?

In an office of the Georgia Railways? At the Post Office? In the Internal Revenue Bureau, or in a bank?

Lavrenty listened without a single word in reply. What could he say? It was lucky his mother was bold enough to let the Ierkomoshvilis know that her son would like to get a higher education. He dreamed about becoming a technician, an engineer or a builder. He would be happy to go to an appropriate college. There was, however, no institute of the kind at Sukhum, while the schools in Tiflis, the Georgian capital, were not the right ones for a potential engineer. The only suitable school was located in Baku, in Azerbaijan, on the Caspian Sea. True enough, it was quite far—over 425 miles away—on the opposite side of the vast Caucasus, but the schooling there would not be very expensive, and the living was cheap. Besides other assets, educated natives were always wanted and could find good and well-paid jobs in the many huge refining plants owned by foreign companies. The tuition should not amount to a very large sum, and Lavrenty could work to pay for his upkeep. The merchant listened attentively, as if doing mental calculations, and then he agreed. All right, let the youth go there. Mr. Ierkomoshvili was prepared to pay for his further studies.

Lavrenty thanked his benefactors once again. He approached and kissed the hands of Mr. and Mrs. Ierkomoshvili. His mother did likewise, crying for joy and barely able to find words to express her gratitude. She was at a loss to invoke God's blessings for her good masters who cared for her orphaned boy "Lara" as much as if he were their own son.

On the slopes of the land the Transcaucasian train moved through a rolling terrain, going up and down like a tremendous snake creeping along. The journey was going to be long. The engine stopped at every station not only for the passengers' sake, but also to replenish the supply of water and coal, or to take on goods. The locomotive puffed, blew and whistled every time the train climbed upward, or when it meandered on the serpentine curves of the trail winding through the mountains. There were also endless halts at crossings to let pass the long columns of red-painted cattle wagons, full of troops going to the front. On the platforms were cannons and carts loaded with ammunition.

Sixteen-year-old Lavrenty was sitting in the cheapest third-class car, going from Sukhum to Baku. He put under his bench his green wooden box with his Sunday suit, a change of underwear, a few copybooks, pencils, a pen, an eraser and some provisions given him by his mother. He also had some dry tea leaves in a paper bag. At every railway station boiling water was distributed free of charge, so the passengers could prepare their own tea, which they sipped from their tin cups through a lump of sugar held between their teeth. The boy kept his personal documents, as well as the money his mother had given him for the trip, in a linen pouch she had sewn for him especially for this journey. People of his origin, when going on a journey, usually had such a little sack for their valuable possessions. This primitive kind of wallet was hung around one's neck on a long string, and the traveler kept it hidden on his chest under his *roobashka*.

The trip from Sukhum in Georgia in Baku in Azerbaijan should normally take no more than two days and a night. But now, in wartime, when military trains had priority and right-of-way everywhere, it would last much longer. During the nights, stretched on the hard wooden benches before falling asleep, the passengers turned on their bellies to protect their wallets from anyone who might try to steal them. They also kept their boots on, afraid to take them off lest they awaken the next morning to find their footwear gone.

All these secrets Lavrenty had learned before this trip, his first by train. So he had to be careful. Now, sitting next to the window, he watched everything with great interest although without any special excitement or enthusiasm. He was glad to see all these new things, but he looked at them with a feeling of cold indifferent calculation, as if he already had seen them before and knew them well, and now was only checking to make sure they were what they should be and that they were in their proper places.

Finally, after more than three days and two nights of travel, the rails of the tracks on both sides of the train multiplied suddenly and branched out into more lanes. There also appeared more railway signals and semaphores. There were lines of tank cars. There were more and more of these black tanks, showing huge white letters painted in the unfamiliar Latin alphabet, new to a stranger who knew only the Russian ones and his native Georgian characters. Lavrenty understood that these tank cars belonged to foreign companies which exploited crude oil from the bottom of the Caspian Sea, refined it in their plants and shipped it away to the wide world to make a lot of money. Now, as the train approached the station, the smell of petroleum gradually grew stronger. The locomotive increased its speed and quickly passed some dark warehouses and depots, tall elevators, high platforms for loading goods, huge piles of coal and gravel, old railway cars deprived of their wheels and blackened, roofless skeletons of burned-out houses destroyed by fire. Here were the dwellings of the poor—dirty yards with clotheslines stretched across them, heavy with washed linen, skirts, and trousers and underwear. . . . Then huge houses built of red brick. Sometimes, on a windowsill, there was a flowerpot with a crimson geranium, or a cat, or a cage with a canary, or a little child, or an old toothless woman, the ugly poverty for which Lavrenty never had any compassion, and which he hated and despised with all his heart. Tank cars of the impressive companies, again, rows and rows of them, the suffocating smell of kerosene, semaphores with their gigantic arms stretched out, a miserable railway guard gazing thoughtlessly at the train, his little red banner in his hand, and, at last, the gray, short station building. Baku.

Lavrenty donned his cap, took from his linen wallet the tiny brown cardboard rectangle of his ticket to produce at the exit and, carrying his wooden trunk, left the train. For a new life—to be rich and powerful. Like the men from the foreign oil refineries.

2

Toward a Better World

IN THE HUGE AND MURKY CLASSROOM where the dust-covered windows overlooked a narrow gray courtyard, one could hear only the creaking of chalk against the big blackboard. Under the quick fingers of the professor, the white figures appeared on the black slate and grew into long, obedient columns. Upon these logical mathematical formulae depend a lot of important events; especially for one who is going to construct bridges, or railway tracks, or steel frameworks under the roofs of the foundries. Lavrenty was carefully copying everything that was put down. He was an assiduous student who did not want to be disturbed during the lessons. His professors could easily note this, because Beria, being a nearsighted boy who had to wear glasses, was placed in the front row of desks.

As long as the professor was busy writing, the students sitting in the back of the room occupied themselves with many activities that were out of place. They played cards or smoked cigarettes. Some of them secretly read the banned newspaper, *Pravda*, which had been established by Lenin three years earlier and was printed by the Bolshevik Party in Petrograd. Or they were perusing the local illegal paper, *Bakinsky Rabochy*.[1] You could easily keep such papers in your textbook and, when you finished reading them, you just closed the book and passed it to one of your pals without evoking

---

[1] *The Baku Worker.*

any suspicion on the part of the teacher. Only the eight students sitting two to a desk in the first row of four desks could not share in the privileges of card-playing or reading subversive papers.

In the Baku Mechanical-Construction Technical School, called Technicum for short, which Lavrenty Beria attended, the students ran an organized discussion circle. Officially, for the headmaster and for the authorities, the club was described as a self-educating literary association. However, at meetings held in the classroom after schooltime, the boys discussed politics.

The meetings usually were presided over by a certain student named Vsevolod Merkulov with the ardent assistance of two other most enthusiastic and active members of that club: a short, dark Azerbaijani with an Oriental name, Mir Djaffar Bagirov, or by Evgeny Dumbadze, a Georgian like Beria. If Dumbadze and Bagirov had not lured him into that group Lavrenty would probably never have joined. He preferred to be left alone to make some money by tutoring a few boys from an elementary school, children of well-to-do families. During the gatherings there were also talks about literature and poetry, since the organizers' idea was to attract as many students as possible from other institutions of learning. The movement needed young members of the intelligentsia from the poor and laboring class rather than from the aristocracy. For this purpose, and in order to attract the brighter students, the discussions touched on all kinds of subjects of interest. Such a broad program was also advisable as an alibi in case of a sudden, unexpected visit by a professor. So there were always at hand a few copies of recent issues of the local literary and drama magazine, *Molla Nasreddin*.[2] In this periodical one could find nice, harmless, clean-cut short stories and poetry approved by the school authorities. In their library they had volumes of verses by Shirvani, Sabir and Samed Vurgun, the famous Azerbaijani poets. However, no matter what subject was discussed—a novel by Tolstoy or Dostoevsky, a play by Ostrovsky or Chekhov, poetry by Lermontov or Pushkin— sooner or later Merkulov switched the conversation to the living conditions of Russian peasants and workers and to the necessity of fighting for the social, economic and political changes which would lead to a new order and a better world.

This movement was so popular in the Technicum that it was

---

[2] *Mullah Nasreddin.*

almost impossible for Beria to stay out of it if he did not want to remain a stranger among those clever and active colleagues who, in the future, might become dignitaries, or at least influential men. Of course, they would succeed if they were lucky enough not to be arrested, imprisoned and whisked off to Siberia. In that case, it would be advisable not to know them. Since Beria did not officially belong to the group, it wouldn't be difficult for him to deny any connection with any of them. At the moment, Merkulov was a good friend of Lavrenty, whom he supplied with illegal literature. It was usually delivered to him during the recess between lessons, and Lavrenty was able to read the newspapers the same day he got them, and to return them immediately. The reading was done in the rest room, but not in the regular school lavatory where the provost could enter at any moment and catch the conspirator. It took place in the primitive "johnny" in the corner of the courtyard, where one could lock himself inside by means of a hook and then read undisturbed. If some official should order the occupant to open the door, he always had time enough to throw the papers into the latrine. Lavrenty occasionally accepted these banned pamphlets, only so his friends would not be dissatisfied or suspect that he, Beria, was not one of them, at least spiritually. But he was not a member of this circle and preferred not to be involved. It was much wiser to stay a little outside, to look, observe and wait. The end of the Great World War was undoubtedly far away; in the meantime, it would be better to study at the Technicum and earn a degree.

Not being a brilliant student, Beria had to work very hard for promotion. But Merkulov and the others knew he was a fellow who could keep secrets, and that meant a lot. Backed by such a reputation, Lavrenty did not risk much. He only had to be careful when receiving and returning the illegal literature. This was a trifle that he could manage very easily, while knowledge gained from such reading could be useful. In wartime like the present, you should watch, listen, keep your ear close to the ground and your nose straight, sniffing in the direction *kooda vyeter dooyet*—"from which the wind is blowing," as the old Russian saying goes. You had to think soberly and watch how events were going to develop.

Besides legal books which everyone could borrow from the school library, the leaders of the circle lent you some banned literature. Merkulov, who became Lavrenty's closest friend, brought him a few booklets: *What Is to Be Done?*, *Burning Questions of Our*

Movement, and *Letter to a Comrade,* written by Vladimir Lenin, who was living in exile. Merkulov also lent Beria some brochures written in Lavrenty's native language and printed in the Georgian alphabet. The authors were two eminent political writers of the movement in Georgia: Avel Yenukidze, an Old Guard Bolshevik who organized underground Communist printing offices and Suren Spandaryan, who although an Armenian, was born and educated in Tiflis and became the best friend of Lenin and Stalin.

Lavrenty realized well enough that such clandestine literature would bring repression not only from the school authorities but even from the Tsarist Secret Police, *Okhrana.* It did not pay to look for trouble. You could be ousted from school once and for all and be branded with a so-called "pitfall ticket." This meant that on your personal documents, which had to be produced when applying for acceptance to a school, they would put a stamp warning everybody that you were a black sheep, and therefore should not be admitted to any educational institution in the country. So why take such a risk, for the sake of whom or of what? It was much wiser to study diligently as long as your mother's employer—that oldster Ierkomoshvili—paid the tuition regularly, and as long as mother sent you some of her saved money and food parcels. There was no need to look for a headache. If it were really true that new and different times were approaching, and the day of a revolution's outbreak was nearer than one could predict—as Merkulov and Dumbadze deeply believed—then the one who lived long enough would witness it. There was always time to adjust to new circumstances and to the heralded new times.

Lavrenty read the borrowed brochures very carefully. It was always better to know what was brewing and to be acquainted with the questions, than to remain an ignoramus. Then, in a short time, he returned the books to his friend. He did so not because Merkulov asked him to give them back as soon as possible, since other students were also eager to read them, but because keeping them at home was not safe. In wartime it was wiser to be doubly cautious and alert. You could never tell whether or not the landlord who rented you a room in his basement flat, although an illiterate tailor himself, had a friend or relative working for the *Okhrana.* Such watchdogs are nosy by duty and by vocation and can easily rummage through your belongings when you are in school. And then you are finished. This is no exaggeration. The Baku police had recently increased their vigilance, and the Municipal Bailov Prison was one of the most dreadful jails in the whole Russian Empire.

In spite of all these obstacles and warnings, Lavrenty took risks and read the brochures he had been lent. He did it not without interest. The ideas expressed there were new to him; they were inspiring and it was useful to know them well, for . . . who could predict? Some day they might turn into reality, and one should not be caught unaware by the sudden changes and the new order. It is always good to be ready and able eventually to take part in these changes. To join this group of students, however, and to attend their meetings regularly—that was another matter. It was more advisable to stay away and offer as an excuse the necessity of cramming for examinations or tutoring some kids. But why should it be only an excuse? This was the truth. Beria liked to get home as early as possible, straight from school, and to study. If you come to your flat when there still is daylight and sit down to your textbooks, you save the kerosene in your lamp or the candles you had to buy with your own money. There were also some pupils Lavrenty was coaching in their homes at certain hours. He had not much time to spare.

It was hard to go straight home, however, and study for the next day after any of the supposedly literary gatherings, where students argued over social and political problems. It was soothing to take a solitary stroll and think over what one had heard during a lecture on *The Communist Manifesto*, or *Capital* by Karl Marx. It was also safer to say good night to your colleagues immediately after the meeting was over and walk home alone like any other innocent passerby, instead of rushing out of the building with the group, like a bunch of conspirators. The Security Police were aware of the fact that some undesirable movements existed among the students, and it was easy to get into trouble. If the youths were stopped by the Security Police and searched, the *Okhrana* men could find some banned literature on them. On the other hand, to possess such power as an *Okhrana* official could be an exciting experience. He had the right, at any time he chose, to stop anyone he wanted to. He could search the suspect's pockets or check all corners of his chosen victim's flat. He was then able to arrest people if he wished; this could be a magnificent job, which impressed Beria immensely. But, right now, Lavrenty preferred to wander around the town alone, unnoticed, and mingle with the tremendous, variegated and colorful crowd. In the stony canyons of the streets, above which white mosques displayed huge blue domes, and the big gilded onions of the Orthodox churches shone in the sun he could see the most diverse kinds of people. Short, broad-shouldered Tatars of dark-yellow complexion, pockmarked and slant-eyed, in their black garb of sheepskin and fur caps with earmuffs. Lezghins in their long, black tunics and black breeches stuffed into black boots, daggers in their belts. Bow-legged Talyshes wrapped in rugs and wearing shoes made of linden bark. Some rode mules, donkeys or camels. Persians in their small skullcaps adorned with tiny beads. Azerbaijanis in long, white robes and turbans. Tall, dark-haired Tadzhiks. Jews with their patriarchal beards. Cossacks yelling to one another in a strange language unlike any other tongue. Fat Armenians with kind but insincere smiles. Cherkesses in red caps. Kirghizes in their big, round fur hats and with whips in their hands even when they were not astride their small horses. Turkmen, Uzbeks, Kurds in their cowherds' garb with hoods. Mongolians smelling of sweat, tar and garlic. Many of them were driving herds of goats or sheep, which were trotting on the sidewalks. Mohammedan women in black or white robes, their faces covered by veils. Merchants, vendors, craftsmen, artisans, thieves, whores and beggars. A tremendous human whirlwind. Hot, noisy, loud and fetid.

Here Beria observed how different this was from sunny, quiet Sukhum where life flowed slowly, lazily and pleasantly. Here, in Baku's crowd a single human being was a nullity—like a drop in the Caspian Sea from which the huge companies extract the crude oil to be refined for Western European foreigners. Beria could hate from the depth of his heart this filthy and noisy mob of never- or badly-washed, perspiring creatures. "If mankind had but one head, I would cut it off with the greatest joy," as Beria had read somewhere. Who said it? Wasn't it Nero, the Roman Emperor who ordered Rome to be burned? If Rome was as overcrowded and as foul-smelling as Baku, then Nero was right when he ordered his men to set the city afire.

Only here, in the multinational town of Baku where he found himself, Lavrenty realized suddenly that an individual did not mean anything. You could fall on the sidewalk and die, and nobody would care. A silly horse might be frightened by the corpse and jump aside; that would be all. But a philosophical donkey, a quiet mule or a stoical camel would step over you indifferently, if he didn't drop some manure onto your dead face. A teen-age thief would empty your pockets and take off your boots if you had any. At night, someone else would take your belt and trousers, and later a few homeless starving dogs would worry your dead body with their teeth. They would do so for many nights until the flesh decayed because of the heat and started stinking, or until a street cleaner put the corpse on his cart to throw it into the sea. If someone wants to remain an individual and to swim above that human hogwash, he must become a personality. He should obtain a degree, at least from the Institute where Lavrenty was studying, the Mechanical-Construction Technical School. But this would be only the first step in his career, if he still did not want to bow his head low before any foreman, or supervisor, or manager, or deputy director or any other kind of boss, and not be afraid that at any moment he would get sacked. So he should obtain the best education, a diploma from a Polytechnic University. Beria did not want to become just a technician master builder, who is only a little more than a mere carpenter who erects barracks, halls, warehouses and one-story huts. Lavrenty desired to be a real architect; to create huge factories with tall smokestacks, powerful petroleum refineries, railway terminals, bridges and harbors. Then he would be equal to those rich directors, those English and Swedish aristocrats who lived in their white villas high above sweating, stinking Baku; those men who managed the great Western businesses, the companies that leased the oil fields on the bottom of the sea, who produced kerosene and shipped it away in tanks by rail and by sea. Lavrenty hated these people with his whole heart because they were rich and had everything, while he had to struggle for his existence, although he didn't feel that he was inferior to them. Yes, all that really matters is power. Power over people; over the mass of millions and millions of brainless, two-legged creatures whom one can govern and hold in one's fist while despising them. The power that means mastership, ruling, riches, good food, servants, luxury and women. It was enough to look at the ancient castles surrounded by turreted walls rising above Baku and its present shabby suburbs, where hundreds of low, dilapidated clay and mud huts were lined up in endless rows. In the self-taught left-oriented circle of young demagogues in Baku, the leaders claimed that new times were coming; that a different world would emerge out of the present war, which was lasting so long; that there would be other, different governments, a new order; and that the rich would rule no more.

It sounded very promising. But it gave Lavrenty a lot to think about. Who would reign if the rich were swept from the surface of the earth? The speakers claimed the ruling would be done by the people. But who were these people? Was it this stinking human spittle, that compost on which the rich grow and bloom? Those illiterate Tatars, Cossacks, Lezghins, Mongolians, Kirghizes, who drive their herds and who eat and sleep with their animals? These Armenians who, sitting on the dirty sidewalks, offer you watermelons and corn for a few kopecks, who feed on horsemeat or raw sparrows? These Mohammedans who pray five times a day, their stupid faces turned to the East? These cobblers who made sandals and repair boots in front of their workshops, which look more like caves and dog-holes than like human dwellings? These hawkers who sell stinking fish, or the barefoot water carriers who distribute drinking water from two buckets hanging on a stick carried across their shoulders? What do these people know about ruling? What can they do? They would get cheated by any Greek, Persian or Jew.

Merkulov and Dumbadze, or sometimes other smart boys, like Goglidze and Kobulov, replied that these men should be educated, first of all. All right. But who would supply them with knowledge if the rich were exterminated? Perhaps the leaders who, before starting the revolution, wiped out the rich? Nonsense! As soon as the leaders started ruling over the poor, they would stop thinking about education for the masses, being aware of the fact that clever masses would no longer accept the role of obedient slaves. What did the Great Revolution in France give to the French people? It gave them the empire of Napoleon and the monarchy with the Bonaparte dynasty. In other words, it was another oppression, bringing with it new wars and a new and worse misery. This problem was not so simple. No siree!

When thinking about the main slogan, which said that all working people should unite, and that peasants and workers should go arm in arm, Beria wondered how this could be possible? A peasant stays in his village far from towns and is busy farming for himself, while a worker is in town in a factory toiling for someone else—for the government, or the plant's owner—and is himself far from villages. A worker does not care about the stupid peasant and a peas-

ant does not care about the damn worker. They do not have anything in common. A worker cannot tell wheat from rye, while a
peasant is afraid of machines. They even speak different languages,
so they do not understand each other. And why should they? You
could do a lot for them, so they would lead a better life, or at least
an existence fit for human beings. All right. However, why should
you work for them? Why sacrifice your precious time, privacy and
energy for others? There could be only one logical reason for doing
it: to grasp the power and to govern them. That would be the only
sensible aim to this job: the power; to become a master of these
masses, to be the individual whom the brainless mob would obey
and fear because of your strength. If a man of such power should
be, for instance, an engineer or an architect, he could use people as
a tool to build canals, bridges, dams—even whole towns. It could
be as it had been in long-past ages in Egypt, Greece or Rome, when
the pharaohs, kings and emperors had used the masses to build
mines, irrigation systems, palaces and garden cities.

During his lonely strolls, after wading through a driveway full of
muddy bumps and drowned in odorous smells, Lavrenty plunged
into the dimness of a narrow alley. Far ahead the stony shores
could be seen, and beyond shone the Caspian Sea. From here, turning to the right, he found a shortcut, a path leading to the freight
port. That spacious, blue-pointed frame building of the terminal
was a kind of gigantic barge, almost a Noah's Ark. It was moored to
the short, thick poles of the wharf. However, it swung under your
feet when you entered it by a wide, slanting gangplank, as if you
were boarding a boat.

Inside, there was a counter of rough wood reinforced with iron
bands for luggage and freight, and a big scale for trunks, boxes and
barrels. There was a ticket office with a barred window and a
storage room for luggage. There also was a buffet where one could
buy cigarettes, tobacco, beer, lemonade or soda water from a huge
siphon. There were also cheap candies, hard-boiled eggs, salted
corncakes, sunflower seeds and peanuts, combs and safety pins,
postage stamps and newspapers. The floor, made of raw planks, was
covered with litter. The room stank of kerosene, herrings and seaweed.

On the dirty walls covered with obscenities written in pencil,
chalk or charcoal, were pasted enormous sheets of complicated
timetables that nobody understood, and Government announce-

ments that nobody respected, and a big warning: DO NOT SPIT
ON THE FLOOR, that nobody paid any attention to. Under them,
on crude benches around the waiting room, sat folks with suitcases
tied with pieces of string, or with small wooden trunks or with
wicker ones. Some women held babies in their arms and suckled
them at their breasts. Men smoked, spat, and read newspapers. On
the front pages of their dailies were big headlines:
   GREAT RUSSIAN VICTORY OVER THE AUSTRO-
      HUNGARIAN ARMY!
   MAGNIFICENT OFFENSIVE OF GENERAL BRUSILOV
      DEVELOPS ON THE WHOLE FRONT!
   GALICIA TAKEN!
   THE RUSSIAN ARMY FIGHTS BRAVELY FOR TSAR AND
      FATHERLAND!
   TURKISH TROOPS DEFEATED BY OUR HEROIC MEN!
   FIFTEEN MILLION RUSSIAN SOLDIERS ADVANCE!
   MOTHER RUSSIA IS THE GREATEST POWER IN THE
      WORLD!
This was not an exaggeration, but the truth. And at such a time,
a handful of students like Dumbadze, Merkulov or Goglidze and a
few other teen-agers, gathering after school, proclaimed the over-
throwing of the powerful Tsar and the introducing of a new regime, a people's government. Were they fools? Or, perhaps, men of
the future? Who could tell? But in the meantime, in the boathouse,
with a daily newspaper in his hands, far from his friends and
schoolmates, Lavrenty could sit next to a man also busy with his
newspaper, and exchange a few words with him about the present
situation.

Because Beria, who by tutoring a few students, barely could earn
pocket money, made some extra rubles as an informer for the Azerbaijan *Okhrana*.

3

For the Country

AT THAT TIME, many unexpected history-making events occurred. Only in December of the previous year—less than three months earlier—Rasputin had been murdered. The assassination initiated a chain reaction of incidents. The newspaper *Pravda* revealed a lot about Grigory Rasputin, an illiterate peasant, a criminal, a dubious monk who gained power over the Tsar and the Tsarina and made their palace his home. There he used to stage drinking and sex orgies with the ladies of the Court, whom he forced to join him in his perverted pleasures. He exacted obedience from the Tsarina, who had to kneel in front of him and kiss his tar-smelling boots. This obscure character used to give orders to the Tsar, telling him which members of the Cabinet and which generals should be dismissed, and whom the Tsar should appoint to fill vacant positions. At last, after a decade of his rule, that villain was swept out of existence, killed by Prince Felix Yusupov, the leader of the plot. Beria read all those articles with great excitement. Rasputin, who arranged bacchanals with dozens of ladies, made a slave-girl of Tsarina and gave orders to Tsar, impressed Lavrenty tremendously.

From the day after Rasputin's assassination several important incidents occurred one after another. Shortly after Rasputin's death on December 17, 1916, beginning in January of the next year, the workers of several Petrograd factories organized mass meetings demanding an increase in their low wages. Soon, every few days strikes were proclaimed in one plant after another. The city was in permanent fear of riots, as if a hidden bomb had been planted, ready to explode at any moment.

On the Tsar's orders more and more troops poured into Petrograd. The press presented this phenomenon in its daily news commentaries as the arrival on leave of some regiments recalled from the Northern Front for a well-deserved rest in reward for their heroic and heavy fighting. However, the people of the capital were aware that these troops had been sent to Petrograd for the purpose of pacification and as support for the police in case the strikes grew to the size of riots. In addition to such reinforcement of the ranks of the regular foot and mounted police, there were brought to Petrograd a regiment of gendarmes, a squadron of regular cavalry and a regiment of the Ural Cossacks. A shipment of machine guns sent from England for the Russian Army on the front was directed to the capital for use in the event of a rebellion.

The tension of the city grew from hour to hour. Every day it was more difficult to obtain bread in Petrograd. Endless lines of women in front of bakeries waited for long, exhausting hours. The price of bread rose immensely.

The bakeries in Petrograd delivered their products mostly to the troops stationed in town. The civilians were starving. Throughout the night bakeries and groceries that usually sold bread were besieged by crowds of hungry people who waited for the opening of the premises. But many shops kept their front doors permanently closed, while selling bread on the black market at steep prices. Finally, the crowd of angry and determined women broke into some of the stores and looted the entire stock. A platoon of mounted police dispersed them with rifle butts, sabers and knouts.

But these repressions could not solve the problem. In the whole of great Petrograd there was not one broad street where, after mass meetings at their factories, crowds of hungry workers were not marching in parades of protest to the tunes of revolutionary songs. The Duma, the Russian Parliament, was helpless. Its suggestion that the factories and plants producing goods for the Government's needs should supply the workers with food was only an empty paper resolution that nobody intended to respect.

The starving masses filled the streets. Armed with sticks and their tools, the jobless workers were determined to fight the police, the symbol of oppression. At the outlets of some avenues, from which the squadrons of Cossacks on their horses could raid unexpectedly, the people erected barricades. Overturned streetcars, horse cabs and two-wheeled pushcarts, bars, heavy benches brought from squares and parks, and streetcar rails from the roadways were stacked to the height of the second floors of buildings. General Sergius Khabalov, Commander in Chief of the pacification plan, was ready to set his soldiers on the mob at any moment. He was a man with an iron hand, not only for the rebels but for his own troops, too. Knowing the commander's ruthlessness, the townsfolk did not expect any mercy for themselves. However, neither a power nor a fear existed that could prevent the determined people from going to extremes.

Nevsky Prospect, the capital's main avenue, was filled day and night with crowds carrying red banners and singing revolutionary songs. The detachments of mounted gendarmes and Cossacks stationed nearby were alerted to charge the crowd if the demonstrations should turn into riots.

On February 25, 1917, when the workers organized a mass meeting at Tsar Alexander the Third's statue, a squadron of mounted gendarmes, led by their captain, attacked the gathering with drawn swords. A platoon of Cossacks was grouped on the opposite outlet of the street. One of them grabbed his rifle from his back, leveled it at the crowd and pulled the trigger. This first shot was aimed at the captain of the gendarmes, who fell from his saddle to the cobblestoned roadway. The event provoked a general outbreak of shooting. People ran in all directions, hiding in doorways, pushing one another and stamping on anyone who fell to the ground. There was a panic under the fire of the Cossacks, who were shooting the officers of the gendarmes. They did not do this in order to protect the civilians, or to unify themselves with the striking workers. They were not concerned for them at all. Shooting them—such poor helpless creatures—was no fun either. They got much more pleasure from killing gendarmes, their own oppressors, the hated officers in their shiny uniforms with golden epaulets; those men who until now had been masters of their life and death. Now was a good opportunity to let yourself go, firing to your heart's content. Especially since no penalty was threatened, and also since you were tipsy after a few gulps of vodka, which your commander had previously ordered to be poured lavishly into your field bottle, so you would be more eager to quiet this crowd of jobless beggars.

The mounted police units, in self-defense, fired a volley into the Cossacks. The people who now were running away from the Cossacks—their supposed defenders—hurried in the opposite direction, but were halted by their own barricades. They fell over ramparts of dirt bristling with stones, barbed wire, glass from crushed bottles, iron bars, pieces of bricks and broken pots and pans. Those who fell on that bulwark were trampled under the feet of the ones who ran over them.

During the night of February 26, 1917, the city was in a frenzy. In the suburbs, several fires broke out. Downtown, the mob looted shops and demolished squares and parks. The next morning the revolt was still growing. The rebels were joined by a battalion from a guards regiment. The mutinous soldiers were shooting their own officers. The detachment of cavalry which, on demand of General Khabalov, was called away from the front, had not arrived yet. Hospitals in the city were full to the brim. The wounded and sick did not get proper care, because many physicians as well as professional nurses were out of town, mobilized and sent to the field hospitals. Now the municipal and private hospitals were invaded by the mob, who stole pillows, bed linen and furniture. The sick were thrown out of their beds, which were taken by the looters. Anarchy prevailed. The Prime Minister, Prince Nicholas Golitsyn, resigned his post, and as a result, the whole Cabinet was dismissed.

At the time of these events, the Tsar was at the Supreme Headquarters at Mogilev, near the front. The President of the suspended Duma, Michael Rodzyanko, sent the Tsar a telegram informing him that the capital was in a state of chaos. In Petrograd platoons of soldiers filled the streets, but they did not have any commanders, since they had previously shot their officers. They did not represent the army any more; they were just part of the mob, only in military uniform. They wore no emblems on their caps, no belts on their topcoats, no insignia of rank on their epaulets. When drunk, they gladly sold their rifles to civilians for a bottle of vodka. They did not need that weapon now. If you wished to kill someone, you could do it with your bayonet, and you could open a door of the shop you intended to loot with a few kicks of your military boots.

On the night of February 27th, the Petrograd was overpowered by rebels. The yelling soldiers, the pockets of their long overcoats filled with bottles of liquor and with loot from shops and private apartments, felt themselves masters of the situation. Along with these marauders, the throng of civilians was in a frenzy of joy because of its victory. In two state jails, Litovsky Zamok and Peredvarilka, the prisoners broke open the gates and ran free into the town. Several thousands of criminals sentenced for theft, robbery, arson, rape and murder joined the crowd. Wearing their prisoners' black-and-gray striped uniforms, round caps and wooden sandals, they seemed to be dressed for a carnival. Suddenly, the grim atmosphere became gay. It is commonly known that criminals are vivacious chaps, especially when sniffing the fresh smell of freedom. In the darkness of the night the Peredvarilka Prison glared like a huge torch, set afire by the departing convicts. The buildings of the Municipal Court and the Secret Police, *Okhrana*, as well as some police precincts and gendarmes' barracks, were aflame. Many civilians sang *La Marseillaise* to Russian lyrics, and the *Red Banner*, or a new revolutionary ditty, *Get Up and Arise, Working People* or chanted slogans: "Long Live the Proletariat!," "Death to the Capitalists!" and "Down with the Intelligentsia!"

The riots spread over Petrograd. In some other cities the rebels arrested local officials and formed their own administration. In Kronstadt, on Kotlin Island in the Finnish Gulf not far from Petrograd, at the base where the main force of the Russian Navy was stationed for the capital's defense, the sailors murdered their commanders and their supreme chief, Admiral Wiren, whom they literally tore to pieces alive.

But the final victory was still far away. In the suburbs of Petrograd, the police force dug trenches, erected barricades and fought desperately, pouring a hail of bullets from their machine guns. Before sunrise, the belated infantry regiment entered the city. It began a regular military operation in defense of the police, gendarmes and army. Every civilian caught with firearms and every drunk and irresponsible soldier in the mob was arrested and, if he resisted, was executed on the spot. Soon the crowd melted and dispersed, not wanting to show resistance or to engage in an organized battle. The next morning several armored cars patrolled the devastated streets of the capital. Some regiments, faithful to the Tsar, had been pulled from the front lines and arrived in the city. In a few hours' time the railway stations, the telegraph and telephones were back in the loyalists' hands. The Petrograd garrison was estimated at over 150,000 troops. That very morning a new Cabinet was established and took power. Red Cross ambulances staffed with male nurses picked up the corpses from the streets and brought order back to the hospitals. Engineer units dismantled the barricades and cleared the city of the carcasses of dead horses as well as the smoldering ruins of the burned-down buildings. In the suburbs several military field kitchens distributed free food to the poor: a bowl of pea soup, a quarter-loaf of dark bread and a cup of sweetened tea.

High-ranking officers with their subordinates firmly backed the Duma, which took office with a roster of new personnel.

The inhabitants of many other cities and towns expressed their solidarity with the Tsar, so the war against the main enemy—the Germans—could be continued. More trains with troops, equipment and ammunition directed to the front were leaving regularly for their destinations.

Two days later, the Duma announced that the Tsar would be asked to abdicate. The regency would be given to the Tsar's brother, the Grand Duke Michael Alexandrovich, who would then declare Russia a constitutional monarchy. In the meantime, however, power was taken by the Provisional Government led by a new Prime Minister, Prince Georgy E. Lvov.

As soon as this government was constituted, it issued a manifesto which declared an amnesty for all political crimes, including terrorist activity. Alexander Kerensky, a Socialist, who was the new Minister of Justice, telegraphed all district attorneys in the whole country ordering them to free from jails all political trespassers, and to transmit to them greetings from the new democratic administration.

Along with this amnesty, it was announced that soldiers who had taken part in riots would not be punished. Under such circumstances, it was no wonder the new regime became very popular. From the farthest parts of the country there flowed to the capital messages of assurance of support, words of appreciation, greetings for the statesmen actually in office, and tributes calling the government "The Morning Star of Liberty."

The Grand Duke Michael Alexandrovich, the Tsar's only brother, who was asked to accept the crown, answered the Provisional Government that he would ascend the throne only if it were offered to him by a Constituent Assembly. When this news spread, general joy poured over the whole of Russia. Even the revolutionary deportees, confined by order to live in Siberia, could return from

exile. Among the Bolsheviks who were freed were Grigory Ordzhonikidze, Stepan Shaumyan and Joseph Stalin.

The Tsar abdicated. The new Russia was born.

The city of Baku did not remain indifferent to these historical
events taking place in Petrograd. Long before Kerensky's Manifesto
had been announced, a group of oil workers broke into the Bailov
jail and liberated the political prisoners. It was not very hard to
discern that the leaders of the adherents to the new movement
were going to come to power. In times like these, Beria realized he
should not stand aside unless he wanted to be an outsider to the
end of his life. He had to act, and act wisely; in other words, his
activity should not involve risking his neck. Lavrenty intended to
leave this pleasure to others who did not mind experiencing imprisonment, interrogations and beatings. Such brave fools usually pave
the way to success for others who follow them. If any of these
pioneers like Ordzhonikidze or Stalin eventually became a leader
he was the exception, not the rule. And even with good luck Stalin
and the others had to pay a high price for their popularity. There
were arrests and inquisitions to be survived, and life in distant
locations in Siberia where they had been deported—that, for certain, was no pleasure. It was much more clever to be on good terms
with both sides at the same time, with the *Okhrana* as well as with
the conspirators. Lavrenty Beria, the informer and revolutionist,
could serve both sides faithfully, without doing much harm to
either of them.

On his birthday, March 29, 1917, Lavrenty received a gift parcel
and a letter from his mother. She wrote that his younger sister
Tamara and his youngest brother Irakly were attending schools,
and that Datiko was still in the army. Lavrenty's mother was happy
about her dear Lara's progress in his studies. Now, being eighteen,
he would soon become an educated man.

It was true that, if one was eighteen years old, he was a grown-
up person. However, he still had his whole life ahead of him. And
his life should be managed with sense. Undoubtedly, those who
distributed the daily paper *Pravda* in Petrograd, organized general
strikes and created the February Revolution, would in one way
or another, become important personalities. But if one should like
to join them years from now, he might be asked where he was
when they were struggling and suffering. What would his answer
be then?

The underground newspaper, *Bakinsky Rabochy*, was now distributed almost openly. So was the *Izvestia of the Baku Soviet*, a new daily established in Baku after the February Revolution. Its editor-in-chief was Anastas Mikoyan, a devoted Bolshevik and a member of the Party since 1915. Now Lavrenty had to decide: if he intended to become a political personality, he had to make up his mind. There was no time to waste.

The February Revolution had failed and was attacked by *Pravda*, as well as by the Baku underground papers. All these dailies described it as a "bourgeois" movement, which gave nothing to the proletariat. At the head of the Provisional Government stood Prince Georgy Lvov, an aristocrat. All the Cabinet members also belonged to the upper class. In the whole government there was not a single worker or peasant.

Yet the Russian troops were still fighting on several fronts. They even attained some success. General Alexey Brusilov, who a year earlier had began a great offensive, pushing the Germans back from Galicia and Bukovina, by his bold operations the previous August had caused Rumania to declare war on the side of Russia.

On April 16, 1917, in Petrograd, a crowd of several thousands welcomed Lenin's arrival in the capital from his voluntary exile in Switzerland. His return awakened hope in the hearts of all Bolsheviks. But just ten days before his homecoming, the United States of America entered the war, supporting Russia. With that help the war could soon be over, and Beria calculated that a capitalistic country such as America would do her best to choke any activity of the Bolshevik State. Obviously, America would never let Russia become a Bolshevik regime. Under these circumstances Beria came to the conclusion that it would be good to become one of those who was fighting arm in arm with the Americans. The more so if one were to join the Russian Army as a volunteer, since students of educational institutes were exempt from the draft.

The risk of being sent to the front did not seem to Lavrenty to be too great. The Americans should finish the war soon, and the international slaughter would be over before you were sent to the battlefield. In case you should find yourself at the front while the war was still on, it is true there would be some danger, but if you knew how to use your brain, you would be able to avoid any unpleasantness. A soldier with some education was not usually sent to the trenches, but to the headquarters as a clerk. Thus, the whole business was not so dangerous. Although there were some personnel changes in the Provisional Government, Prince Georgy Lvov was still Prime Minister, while the former Minister of Justice, Alexander Kerensky, who became Minister of War, Army and Navy, decided to fight with the Western Allies until a final victory was won over Germany. If, after the war, Kerensky's Cabinet remained in power, volunteers of his army would be in an especially favorable position as the opponents of the Bolsheviks, and they would be honored for being brave patriots who had fought for the country.

In June, 1917, Beria passed his examinations at the Technicum and was promoted to the next semester. Graduation from the school was now a matter of one final year. He could easily receive his diploma at any time. At present, there were more important things to do if Lavrenty was considering his future on a broader range.

After one of their clandestine meetings Beria asked Merkulov whether it wouldn't be advisable for the Bolshevik Party to have more of its men in the ranks of the Tsarist Army, someone dependable, who could spread Communist propaganda among the soldiers at the front. If so, he, Lavrenty, would be glad to sacrifice his studies in behalf of the Party's cause. Merkulov was enthusiastic about the suggestion. Beria impresed him and even somehow put him to shame. Merkulov, who was hungry for knowledge and who first of all wished to get his diploma, never had thought of becoming a voluntary dropout. He promised Beria that he would mention his idea to some older and more experienced comrades, especially to Mikoyan.

Soon Merkulov brought the good news: Mikoyan would like to see Beria. Thanks to the notion of joining the Tsarist Army, Lavrenty had the opportunity to be introduced to Mikoyan who, although only four years older than he, was already an established figure among the Bolsheviks.

On the same day, Lavrenty wrote his mother a long letter. He hastened to tell her about the good results of his examinations as well as his decision about volunteering to fight the enemy, which was the principal duty of a citizen loyal to the present government.

After dropping the letter into the blue mailbox hanging on the wall of the post office, Lavrenty went to the army recruiting bureau. The sergeant on duty was neither impressed nor overjoyed that a student wished to join the army. If someone wanted to stick out his stupid neck, that was his business.

Soon the new volunteer stood before a military medical commission. Its opinion was positive. The young man was healthy and strong. His nearsightedness was a trifle. To overcome this shortcoming he wore glasses, and anyhow, when firing his rifle he would close his left eye. This reduced the problem by fifty percent. Lavrenty Pavlovich Beria was enlisted as category *A* and got a red draft card: Good for active service.

4

The Mysterious Telegram

THE RED CATTLE CARS of a long train carrying troops were moving smoothly and without haste. They were passing golden fields of grain and the green pastures of Azerbaijan. From time to time the engine whistled once or twice. It did so at crossroads, when approaching the small hut of a railroad guard or when the machinist pulled the string for his own personal reason: to break the prevailing silence, to dispel the boredom of a quiet ride or just for a change. The bystanders who watched the moving train, whose cars had their doors wide open, could see the heads of horses inside, dark loaves of bread stacked like a high wall of black bricks and boxes of ammunition. The soldiers, standing framed in the doors, were looking at the sunny countryside or singing military ditties. A few of them usually sat on the edge of their cars, their legs in high boots hanging outside between the front and rear wheels of the wagon, swinging to the rhythm of the train. They rode as if going to some harmless maneuvers, not to a real bloody battlefield. They did not even care to what destination they were heading, since they were going according to someone else's will, not their own, and had to go where they were ordered.

In the whole tremendous string of cars there was perhaps only one person who knew where he was going. He was eighteen-year-old Private Lavrenty Pavlovich Beria. Since a volunteer had a choice of the branch of service Beria, as a student of the Technicum, asked for the Hydro-Engineering Unit. This had been suggested by Mikoyan during their talk. Lavrenty was aware that the general direction of the train was toward Rumania, a country that had entered the war on Russia's side almost a year before. He also knew he was being sent where he wanted to go. Enlisted in the Hydro-Engineering Regiment, he understood that such troops were primarily sent to Rumania where, as in Azerbaijan, there were many large oil fields. Before his departure from Baku the Party, through Mikoyan, gave him special instructions as to his duties. They did so more in order to check his activities as a beginner and to see if in the future he could be considered eligible for other tasks, than to entrust him with any important mission. While in other regiments of the Russian Army morale was very low, on the Rumanian-Black Sea front the spirit of the troops was still unbroken. The soldiers were obedient and determined to fight until the final victory. Supplied with this information, the Party wished to have there someone young, sensible, properly indoctrinated, and at the rank of a simple private. Such an individual, working wisely, could drop an appropriate word among the soldiers or make some remarks that would undermine the boys' confidence in their superiors or in the Government in Petrograd. The reasoning that Beria got from Mikoyan to use among his comrades in arms was: "Why should we rot in the trenches and die in battle fighting for a cause nobody knows about, while a new democratic administration has been recently organized in our country, and a new life is just beginning for the people? Why should we sacrifice our young lives for a cause that does not exist?"

But would it pay Beria to undertake such activity? If one managed to make for himself the reputation of a thoughtful, promising young fellow, he really should be wise. As long as the Provisional Government was legal, there was no reason to be a black sheep. Especially if one was a volunteer, he had to pretend to be an ardent patriot and a hero, even while being subversive.

The train rolled across Lavrenty's native Georgia, full of familiar vineyards, pink magnolias, delicate yellow mimosas and sweet-smelling white jasmine. There was a long halt at the huge station of Tiflis, Georgia's capital. The troop train remained there for almost half a day. Then, there was one more long stop before the trip, which was to last many days, was continued through the Caucasian mountains. Finally, the train arrived in Batum. Thousands of soldiers poured out of the train, which had stopped on a side track close to the harbor. They led their horses out of the murky wagons into the sunny daylight. In twos or threes, the men carried machine guns or trucks full of ammunition or hand grenades, or erected gangplanks leading to the flatcars and pushed the cannons down, to which horses were then hitched. At last, the platoons were formed into ranks, and marched to the pier to be loaded onto the ship. They left the cattle cars behind, with some walls broken by the kicking horses, the floors covered with trampled, carroty straw still wet from horses' and human's urine and excrement, littered with beer and lemonade bottles, empty cans of fish preserves, pieces of newspapers, and torn rugs.

After three days' journey the ship docked in Odessa, which was the rear base for the Rumanian-Black Sea front. From there, after disembarkment, there was again a journey by another train to Yassy where, on the northern wing of the Rumanian Front, the Russian Fourth Army was occupying fortified positions. The troops had to be prepared for a great offensive. Of course, nobody knew the exact moment when Zero hour would strike, but everyone was aware that it would come soon, perhaps tomorrow at sunrise. Fortunately, here, as at any headquarters, there was always a vacancy for a clerk, a telephone operator or a telegraphist, especially for someone whose education extended further than the three R's, and who was technical-minded. Soon, volunteer Private Lavrenty Pavlovich Beria had been detailed to such duties. It was almost the end of June 1917 when he took his new job.

On July 1, 1917, the Commander's Staff, with Generals Alexey Brusilov and Anton Denikin from the Supreme Headquarters in Molodetchno, gave the order to initiate Kerensky's Great Offensive. At dawn, protected by artillery fire, huge masses of Russian soldiers surged forward with a horrifying cry: "Kill!" The murderous fight halted the march of the German troops, who had been advancing for two days. Yelling "For the Country!," "On to the Enemy!," "Beat the Germans!" thousands of infantry and cavalrymen charged the front. With the initial blow, the Russians broke the German defenses. They literally wrecked the first lines of the Landwehr and took a large portion of the front along a considerable length. In their assault, they jumped into the enemy's trenches to fight with bayonets, rifle butts, knives, fists, and teeth, dealing blows the peasant way, with blind passion. The Germans could not resist

such an onslaught. Their army, under General Erich von Ludendorff, Commander in Chief of the Supreme Staff of the German
Forces of the East, had to retreat. Soon the Russians took the second line of the front defended by the Landwehr. Equally murderous battles, resulting also in victory for the Russians, were fought
on the Southwestern Front, where the Russians cracked six German
divisions of infantry and artillery freshly transferred from the
Western Front.

The strong Rumanian Eastern Front, personally managed by the
Commander in Chief, General Brusilov, from his headquarters in
Kamenets-Podolsky, was a subject of particular interest for the
Party and could provide a good training ground for the undermin-
ing activity of a young follower of the Bolsheviks.

The German Staff was aware of the important role of subversive
action developed by Communist agents and saboteurs in the Russian Forces and recognized it as a great support. Many of these
conspirators worked along the lines of Lenin's directions, according
to his principle: "The worse matters get, the better," and were
doing everything possible to break the soldiers' fighting spirit and
their morale. Lenin realized that the Bolsheviks could take power
into their hands only with the fall of democratic Russia and her
present rulers and administrators. Therefore, he decided to support
the Germans in their war against the Russian Empire. For this
purpose every act of sabotage was welcome to him.

The Party, in response, had to deal a blow which would undermine the confidence of the whole Russian population in the Government.

During the night of July 6th-7th, an official report had been
cabled to Petrograd, supposedly from the southwestern headquarters. The next day it was printed in every daily paper all over
Russia. The telegram stated that at ten o'clock in the morning the
607th Regiment left the trenches without orders and withdrew
from the line. The other regiments stationed nearby did the same
and soon after the Germans took the abandoned Russian positions.
This communiqué was entirely false. It was even very poorly concocted. But it was wartime, when nerves were strained to the utmost, and the news shook the whole nation.

It was never clearly explained who edited the text of this treacherous telegram and who personally dispatched it to the capital, to
break the hearts and morale of millions of Russian people. There

exist many versions of the event, but no definite proof. However, in the *Great Soviet Encyclopedia* of 1952 where, some years later, Commissar Lavrenty Pavlovich Beria's biography was to take almost two pages, the historians described Beria's service in the Russian forces as a period of "immensely diversive activity in the Army on the Rumanian Front."

5

Back to School

AFTER SIX DAYS OF FIGHTING, several new German divisions launched a counteroffensive, halting the Russians.

Lenin decided to use the new situation for his own purposes. On July 16, 1917, in order to cause commotion in the capital, he inspired some new riots there. The next day about twenty thousand sailors from Kronstadt, aroused to revolution by Bolshevik agents, arrived in Petrograd from their Baltic fortress. Straight from the harbor on the Neva River, shouting, "All power to the Soviets!," they marched to the former palace of the Tsar's protégée, ballerina Kshessinska, where Lenin now stayed. Soon after the sailors gathered there, Lenin appeared on the balcony. When the cheers in his honor calmed down, he delivered a fierce speech against the Provisional Government. He ended his harangue by calling the sailors to defend the Revolution and to remain devoted Bolsheviks. With the slogan "Down with the Provisional Government!" the crowd ran into town.

The liquor stores, which had not been locked in time by their owners and closed with iron shutters, were immediately broken into and looted, and the vodka was consumed on the spot. The drunken sailors were joined by the mob, by hooligans, and by some soldiers, mostly marauders and deserters. Shortly they were supported by thousands of striking workers from several plants.

Chanting, "Hang the Cabinet members on the lamp posts!," the

45

mob marched to the Tauride Palace, the Cabinet's headquarters. On the Nevsky Prospect several military trucks appeared, full of men and women yelling threats against the members of the Cabinet. Some better-dressed passersby were stopped by the crowd, who called them by the most-hated word "bourgeois," and beat them severely. This was also a good opportunity to rob these people of their wallets and watches. A rebellious soldier shot at a streetcar. The vehicle stopped, and frightened passengers ran in panic to the nearest doorways of the apartment houses to hide. The mob overturned the car to block traffic.

That day, the whole city had been thrown into chaos. Lenin realized he had unleashed a power which he, himself, would not be able to control. During the night and the next day the riots grew almost to a civil war. The mob looted shops, the drunken soldiers shot at the windows of private apartments in the residential section. Some individuals recognized as being bank or factory directors had been hanged.

Yet the Reds were still not masters of the situation. In the residential section of the capital as well as on some main streets and boulevards, troops loyal to the Government installed their machine guns and started firing at the mutineers. Rebels, hidden in doorways and in the buildings, shot back from windows, balconies and roofs. But the workers did not know how to use their weapons properly, and the rioting sailors and soldiers were mostly too drunk to be good snipers. Soon the revolutionaries had to retreat. Regular troops were taking over street after street and one section of the city after another. Before midnight of the third night, order was restored in Petrograd.

The result of the two days of fighting, with several hundred people killed and more than twice as many wounded, was the whole nation's disenchantment with the Bolsheviks. The Communists' popularity declined even among many workers whose comrades had senselessly lost their lives for no apparent reason, since the Provisional Government ruled along Socialist and Democratic lines.

In order to show the nation the subversive role of the Bolsheviks, the Government unveiled in the press the main parts of some confidential documents that until then had been kept secret. In the newspapers of July 19, 1917, there was shown proof that Lenin was an enemy agent on the German payroll. The statement revealed the names of two German staff officers, Schiditski and Luebers, who for a long time had been in contact with Lenin. The Russian officials also mentioned the names of some banks in Germany, Sweden and Russia[1] where the Germans had deposited over two million rubles in gold at Lenin's disposal, to be used for his subversive activity.

Lenin, afraid that at any moment he might be accused of being a German spy and arrested, decided to leave the country as soon as possible. In the shabby suburban flat of a railroad worker and a devoted Party member, Sergo Alliluyev, Lenin shaved his characteristic beard and mustache, dyed his red hair a darker shade and donned a railroad man's uniform. At night on July 24th, along with his best friend and comrade, Grigory Zinoviev, Lenin left the town on foot. Far beyond the suburbs both escapees jumped onto a flatcar of a train going to the Finnish border.

After the first few days of successes, the great Kerensky's offensive collapsed. The German armies under Generals Paul von Hindenburg and Erich von Ludendorff were reinforced, and several new divisions of German artillery were thrown into the battle. The German army even used a newly-invented diabolical weapon— poison gas. The Germans launched a fierce and desperate attack, penetrating deeply into the Russian lines. From that time on, the Great Russian Retreat began. On the Rumanian and southwestern fronts, Russian armies were almost entirely smashed. Shortly, Hindenburg's army, which had already occupied Galicia and Bukovina, took the city of Riga in a violent attack on the northern front, while in the meantime, the combined forces of Germans, Austrians and Bulgarians entered Rumania, taking half of her territory.

The disastrous situation on the battlefields caused an increase of antiwar feeling all over Russia. From September 1917 on, strikes broke out in Petrograd almost every day. Bread mutiny occurred again, Communist agents and saboteurs directed by Leon Trotsky fomented defeatism and confusion by every means possible. In the middle of the night, there were sudden fusillades in the streets, or shouts, or explosions or fires broke out. Next morning, passersby

---

[1] "Diskonto Gesellschaft" in Berlin, Nya Bank in Stockholm and the Siberian Bank in Petrograd.

were horrified at the sight of a dead man, killed at night and still lying on the sidewalk.

In October, when the situation seemed ripe for the outbreak of a revolution, Lenin returned to Russia from Finland, and came back to Petrograd to reorganize his rebellious forces. His emissaries worked successfully among the soldiers in the Petrograd garrisons. This time Lenin realized that the uprising could succeed if it got the backing of the army.

On November 7, 1917, the Great Revolution burst out. Under the slogans "Peace and Bread for the Masses!" and "Death to Capitalists and Bourgeois!" the mutinous soldiers and the mob ran into the town, armed with rifles, bayonets and knives, killing everyone who appeared to be middle class, an official, a professional man, or a clerk. The next day the Winter Palace was taken, and Kerensky's Provisional Government was overthrown. A newly organized administration, "The Soviet of People's Commissars," took its place. At the head of the new Cabinet were Lenin as Chairman, Trotsky as Commissar of Foreign Affairs, Stalin as Commissar for Nationalities, and nine others. Under the new regime all private enterprises, banks, factories and estates were closed and confiscated by the State, while the owners of these institutions were either arrested or shot to death on the spot. Justice was in the hands of Special Tribunals of Soldiers, Workers and Peasants who tried cases of defendants accused of treason, sabotage against the Revolution, different political opinion, or belonging to the upper classes of society. The sentences—usually death—were executed in twenty-four hours. There was no appeal from these courts. Slogans such as "Down with the Intelligentsia!" and even "Down with the Literate Ones!" were among the most popular. The administration installed special offices for censorship of the press and all printed and published material, and the duties of policemen killed in mass executions were taken over by the new Red Militia. The *Cheka*—The Extraordinary Commission for Combatting Counterrevolution and Sabotage—was led by Lenin's best friend, comrade Feliks Dzerzhinsky, who once declared, "We have no need for justice now. Now we need a battle to the death." His squads carried out arrests and executions of the White Army officers, their wives and children, aristocrats and well-to-do people. The cellars in the basements of the *Cheka*, in the former Police Headquarters not far from the Tsar's Winter Palace, were full of these victims. Every night, some of these people were taken from their cells to the courtyard where they were shot to death by machine guns. It was none other than Lenin himself who proclaimed, "We cannot be victorious without using the most cruel terror" and "If we cannot shoot a man who sabotages, a member of the White Guard, then what kind of revolution is this?"

In a month the armistice pact between Russia and Germany was signed. It was a separatist peace treaty without any agreement with the four Allies—the United States, Great Britain, France and Italy. The historic signing of the armistice with the Germans, concluded by the Soviet delegation led by Adolf Ioffe, Lev Kamenev and Leon Trotsky, took place at Brest-Litovsk in December 1917.

In the meantime Lavrenty Pavlovich Beria could leave Kerensky's army and return to his Technical School to continue his interrupted studies. He had only one semester left before obtaining his degree, and Baku had not been disturbed by the revolution. Lavrenty truly wished to get his diploma, the more so since Petrograd and Moscow were too far from Azerbaijan for the slogan, "Down with the Intelligentsia!" to reach Baku.

As a former volunteer who had joined the army to fight for the fatherland, Beria had priorities everywhere. He reentered the Technicum without any obstacles and devoted all his time to his studies, remote from any political activity.

It was advisable to stay away from any subversive movement and to appear to be just an indifferent student because in Azerbaijan, as everywhere in the Caucasus, the Bolshevik idea was not accepted at all. On the contrary, Communism had a bad reputation in Baku, the capital of Azerbaijan, as well as in Tiflis, the capital of Georgia, and in Erevan, the Armenian capital. In these three Caucasian countries, Mensheviks still ruled; a Bolshevik orientation and membership in the Party did not help at all. Beria's native Georgia, especially, always yearned to throw off the yoke of Russia's hegemony and to win her independence. The new times seemed to serve this purpose. Thanks to the Soviet Declaration of the Rights of Nationalities proclaimed on November 15, 1917, and stating the right of every nationality to self-decision, Georgia, Azerbaijan and Armenia aimed to obtain their autonomies. In Tiflis, the Menshevik government was represented mainly by the Georgian liberal intelligentsia. President Nikolay Chkheidze and Prime Minister Chkhenkeli were very popular in their country; both were well-known personalities in the Georgian political field, and the Cabinet was on good terms with the regional centers of the local Boards of Workers', Peasants' and Soldiers' Delegates under the guidance of Noah Jordania, a leader of the Georgian Menshevik Party.

In Tiflis—called in the Georgian language, Tbilisi—after the autonomy the ruling Menshevik Government was supported by the whole nation. In such a situation, for someone who sooner or later would like to make a career in the Georgian democratic Menshevik administration, it was wise to be in touch with these circles. With such assets as being the son of a poor Georgian peasant from the village of Merkheuli and of a simple maidservant from Sukhum, and of being, however, an educated young man with an engineer's diploma, and a veteran who voluntarily fought the Germans, Beria understood he could go far in the future free Georgia. In other words, he shouldn't remain aloof to their political movement and tendencies, but should involve himself in the trend of their politics.

Lavrenty went to the editorial office of the newspaper *Izvestia of the Baku Soviet* and asked to see Mikoyan, the Editor-in-Chief. Soon in Mikoyan's small room with a huge, old-fashioned desk covered with papers, Beria talked in private with the always-smiling Armenian. Lavrenty asked the influential Bolshevik whether it would be useful to the Party to have a reliable man, and a Georgian, in the Mensheviks' camp. If so, he, Beria, would be glad to undertake this dangerous and responsible mission. Mikoyan promised to put Lavrenty in touch with two eminent members of the Party, Stepan Shaumyan and Ordzhonikidze who, after the Revolution, had been directed to Baku by Lenin.

Grigory Ordzhonikidze, generally beloved by his comrades and nicknamed "Dear Sergo," himself a Georgian thirteen years older than Beria, expressed paternal feelings toward Lavrenty when his young compatriot was introduced to him by Mikoyan. "Dear Sergo" was one of the Party's top bosses in Baku. One of the best friends of Stalin, with whom he shared a room while in exile in Siberia, and also a good friend of Lenin, Trotsky and Zinoviev, Ordzhonikidze was among those who prepared the July revolt in Petrograd and later, the victorious October Revolution. Here in Baku this Old Guard Bolshevik of high merit was a great authority. Knowing the terrain well—because years before he had organized strikes of the oil refinery workers—he came here again to prepare the ground for a revolution which, in its final result, would bring subdued Azerbaijan under the power of the central Soviet Government.

During their talk, Beria explained his plan. Because his and Ordzhonikidze's common country, Georgia, was ruled by Mensheviks who intended to make use of the benefits of Lenin's magnificent Soviet Constitution to aim for an autonomy and to detach Georgia from Red Russia, Beria suggested that perhaps it would be profitable for the Communists to have their own man in the Georgian Menshevik Party. Such a watchdog, being himself a Georgian, could keep an eye on them, and report everything to "Dear Sergo," to comrade Stalin, and to the genius Lenin. Thanks to such an arrangement the Bolshevik Party would know everything that was cooking in the Mensheviks' headquarters and in time would be able to foil the enemy's plots. If such a man could be useful to the common cause, he, Beria would be happy to accept this task and as soon as possible would infiltrate the Mensheviks' innermost circles.

Ordzhonikidze was delighted. Now Beria had a free hand to join the Mensheviks at once in Baku and to go to his native Tiflis. If the Mensheviks kept power and survived the pressures, he would remain with them. If, however, they were overthrown by the Reds, he would emerge a faithful Communist who had helped his older comrades from Baku, Petrograd and Moscow overpower the hated capitalistic liberals. Moreover, the post was not as dangerous as it seemed. In case the legal Menshevik Government in Tiflis found out he was double-crossing them, the only thing they could do would be to put him in prison for a few years. In Georgia, capital punishment for political transgressors had been abolished some time before, and the sentences were very light. So if the worst came, after being released from jail or liberated from it by Bolsheviks, Beria would play a martyr who had suffered for Communism. It was not too bad.

6

Watch and Wait

HAVING THE COMMUNIST PARTY'S APPROVAL to enter the Mensheviks' camp in the role of a Trojan Horse, Beria could stay outside any Bolshevik activity in Baku. He even was told to avoid giving any knowledge of his clandestine work to his school circle, in order to be beyond suspicion. In the meantime, the year 1918 was, for Azerbaijan, and especially for Baku, full of disturbances and violence.

After the October Revolution Azerbaijan, taking advantage of Lenin's Declaration, which granted to every nation the right of self-determination, announced itself an independent country. The same was done by two other Caucasian countries, Armenia and Georgia. In the latter, the government was still in the hands of the liberal Mensheviks, supported by the Social-Federalists. In Armenia the administration was secured by the Nationalistic Christian Party of Dashnaks. In Azerbaijan, where the Mensheviks had their own big organization, the new Cabinet included them, the nationalists and the Moslem Party Mussavatists—"Equality"—representing the great majority of that country.[1]

However, in Baku, where the population represented a mixture of various nationalities, some Russian Communist workers employed in the refineries started organizing riots and demonstrations

---

[1] Appendix 4.

under the leadership of Mikoyan. Soon, in spite of the fact that Azerbaijan was ruled by the Mussavatists, an Azerbaijan Board was created in the capital city of Baku; the so-called Soviet of Workers' Delegates of Baku. On November 31, 1917, they declared the power of Boards; in other words, of the Soviets. On April 25, 1918, disregarding the separatistic tendencies of the whole Azerbaijani nation, the new Russian regime in Moscow created for Baku a Council of People's Commissars, which called itself Baku Komuna.

In this committee, which became a government for Baku only, there was an administration of twenty-six Soviet Commissars. This body was led by a triumvirate composed of Lenin's closest friend, Stepan Shaumyan, Prokofi Dzhaparidze—alias "Alyosha"—and M. Azizbekov. Dzhaparidze, powerful "Dear Sergo" Ordzhonikidze's best friend, was a Georgian, while Shaumyan, although of Armenian extraction, was born and educated in Tiflis.

Iosif Dzhugashvili—Joseph Stalin—Commissar of Nationalities in Moscow, knew very well that his Georgian compatriots would be the best henchmen for strangling any independent tendency in their common motherland, Georgia, should she try to make any use of the benefits granted by the Soviet Declaration, which was very liberal in theory but not at all in practice. With the full support of Stalin, who had pronounced Baku to be "the fortress of Soviet power in Transcaucasia," the new Baku Komuna immediately introduced economic and political reforms and tried to impose Bolshevik rule and the dictatorship of the proletariat throughout Azerbaijan. Besides these twenty-six Baku Commissars heading various agencies, there were also a few others who were directed by Lenin and Stalin through Anastas Mikoyan, and were supported by Soviet troops under Ordzhonikidze's command. However, the legal National Azerbaijani Government consisted of counterrevolutionary-oriented Mussavatists, Mensheviks and Socialists, determined to fight openly for its independence and to throw its forces against the Bolshevik troops.

For a sensible young man like Lavrenty Beria the most advisable course of action was to stand aside and watch and wait to see who would emerge the final victor.

In the hot Caucasian July of 1918, fierce and bitter fights burst out in the sloping, narrow streets of Baku. The Soviet units there were too small in comparison to the National Azerbaijani Forces. Support for the tiny Bolshevik units struggling in the ancient alleys and mews came from an organization calling itself the Socialist League of Working Youth. These battalions fought arm in arm with the Bolsheviks as only young idealists can.

In the first ranks of those youths were several students of the Technicum, members of the clandestine club. They fought with Merkulov, Goglidze, Dekanozov and Kobulov as their leaders. Beria failed to join them, as did Mir Diaffar Bagirov, whom he had befriended not long before. Lavrenty had become a close colleague of Mir Diaffar since the day he had accidentally spotted Bagirov in a shabby suburban tearoom sitting next to the same man from *Okhrana* with whom Beria sometimes had secret meetings at the boathouse.

In these impressive battles, full of heroism the brave boys, deeply devoted Communists and members of that school circle, proved the most faithful ally of the Bolsheviks. They joined the Red Army troops and lent support to the Soviet Administration with an admirable spirit of self-sacrifice. But Beria did not participate in that movement at all. Although nineteen years old at the time, Lavrenty was already an experienced soldier, and as a veteran of the regular Russian Army, he undoubtedly could have performed military service with much greater skill than many of his younger fighting friends. The more so as there were in the ranks of the Socialist League of Working Youth many fifteen-year-old boys who had no knowledge about operating a machine gun, or even how to use a rifle properly.

The Azerbaijani Army enjoyed a strong advantage over the Bolsheviks and their followers. By the end of July the battle was over and the Bolshevik rule in Baku ceased to exist. In the meantime, however, the Azerbaijani Government, realizing that even a victory would be only temporary, decided to establish its power with some support by Great Britain. Soon envoys were sent from Baku to Teheran on a secret mission to the headquarters of the British military forces stationed in Persia. During the conference in Teheran the Azerbaijani delegates suggested that the British troops in Persia could intervene and establish the peace. Great Britain, being directly interested in cutting off oil wells from Soviet Russia, as well as in securing the terrains with oil refineries for her own use, accepted the proposition of support and promised to send a military expedition. Soon British regiments under the command of General L. C. Dunsterville entered Baku and occupied the city. Now rule in Baku was provided by a provisional government which called itself "The Centrocaspian (Transcaspian) Dictatorship." This Cabinet, however, relayed its power to the Mussavatists. The Soviet authorities in Moscow tried to evacuate their troops, but the Azerbaijan Government stopped them and interned them in camps for prisoners of war, and the twenty-six Commissars of the Baku Komuna were imprisoned.

The Azerbaijan Government severely punished all members of the Socialist League of Working Youth. Leaders and older boys who belonged to the organization were arrested and jailed, while youngsters under seventeen were expelled from their schools with red stamps on their personal documents. This identification was a warning to all it might concern, that the bearer was too dangerous to society to be admitted to any educational institution. Fortunately, Goglidze, Merkulov and a few other leaders, thanks to false papers, avoided repressions.

Undisturbed by his comrades and not bothered by the local security, Beria could continue his studies in peace.

The British occupation of Baku did not last long. General Dunsterville's troops had to leave the city less than six weeks after they had entered it. They had been forced to retreat in face of the danger of being exterminated down to the very last man by an approaching huge army of fanatical and determined Turkish soldiers. The next day, the Turks captured Baku without firing a single shot.

A few hours before the town was taken by the Turks, Anastas Mikoyan succeeded in convincing the British to release the twenty-six Commissars of the Baku Komuna and to let them out of the country aboard a steamship. Mikoyan joined them to be evacuated himself. Beria, being a member of the Menshevik Party, had no reason to fear persecution, and stayed in Baku. The Commissars left Baku on that boat not knowing that the captain and crew were anti-Bolsheviks.

After two days' voyage on the Caspian Sea, the ship docked in Krasnovodsk in Turkestan. This place, however, offered no asylum. The local government was Socialist, and all the passengers were immediately arrested. On September 20, 1918, the twenty-six Commissars were tried by a court-martial and sentenced to death. At night, they were driven to the sandy shores of the Caspian Sea and executed there. Only one member of the group—Anastas

Mikoyan—escaped the death sentence. In prison he worked in the kitchen as a cook's helper and eluded the attention of the firing squad's leader.

In November 1918, just after the First World War ended and Turkey no longer represented any power, the British again took Baku. The Bolshevik movement and the *Komsomol* activities went underground once more. *Komsomol*—the Young Communist League—was a new organization which replaced the decimated Socialist League of Working Youth. In such circumstances it was nearly impossible to establish with any degree of certainty who took part in secret and clandestine activities, and because it was difficult to find out whether or not a person was a key figure in these activities, Beria remained unmolested. He was not persecuted and was not even suspected by the Security Police, especially since he was listed in their files as belonging to the official Menshevik Party. He also was left alone by his own comrades as their man serving in the enemy camp.

In December 1918, in accordance with the new Declaration, the Commissar of Nationalities, Joseph Stalin, and the entire Soviet Cabinet approved the autonomous tendencies of the three Caucasian countries—Azerbaijan, Armenia and Georgia—and accepted their national governments. The consent was given in the belief that the British would evacuate their troops from these countries as soon as they become independent. This Machiavellian stratagem proved to work perfectly. Indeed, soon after the fall of Turkey, the British troops were withdrawn from the Caucasus. Azerbaijan rose from the dead again as an independent state with its national government. Now the Soviet Administration grasped the most appropriate moment to attack Azerbaijan. The Baku Bolshevik Party and the local *Komsomol* were ordered by Moscow to prepare an uprising. They were assured of full support by the Central Committee of Workers and Peasants of the Bolshevik Party. In February 1919, to arrange the proper maneuvering of the oncoming events in Baku, Old Guard Bolshevik Armenian, Anastas Mikoyan, was sent there once again. He had been released from Krasnovodsk prison in Turkestan not long before and had gone to Moscow. Mikoyan undertook the leadership of the plot being organized. In April 1919, Ordzhonikidze arrived in Baku as a delegate of the Central Committee of the Russian Communist Party and as Stalin's representative. The popular Sergey Kirov, an ardent Communist partisan and participant in the 1905 revolution, also came as an emissary and assumed leadership of the people's uprising that had been prepared.

Beria immediately renewed his personal relations with Mikoyan, as well as with Ordzhonikidze. However, he did not perform any special services as an adherent, preferring to continue his education. In 1919 Lavrenty quickly terminated his studies in the Mechanical-Construction Technical School and received a diploma of an engineer-builder.

7

Down with the Bourgeois!

WITH HIS DEGREE from the Technicum, Beria could choose one of several career possibilities. Closest to his heart's desire was to obtain a higher education and become a real architect. To receive such a diploma, he should study at a polytechnic university in Petrograd, Moscow or Odessa. These dreams, however, were only plans for a profession without any emotional involvement, and they did not fulfill Beria's ambitions. Lavrenty experienced a strong feeling of envy when, perusing the Communist Party newspaper *Pravda* he read articles signed "Koba," the pen name of Joseph Stalin, his Georgian countryman, born Iosif Dzhugashvili in the village of Gori, near Tiflis; or when he watched "Dear Sergo" Grigory Ordzhonikidze, from a village near the town of Kutais and also a Georgian like himself, and now a leader who delivered speeches to thousands of workers and was recognized as an authority everywhere he appeared; or when he observed the constantly smiling, mild-mannered Anastas Mikoyan, an Armenian, but born in a village called Sanain, near Tiflis. At the same time, Lavrenty consoled himself by reasoning that, if every one of these three dignitaries had achieved so much, then these honors, positions and power were available to him, too. Beria hailed from the same country as they, he was young, even younger than they were, and, being a poor peasant's son, he came from the same very low class they did. On the other hand, he had the highly technical education so much needed for building the foundations of a new state and for the new times, so different from the past. He had many assets and held wonderful cards. All Beria needed was to play these cards wisely, in order to win the game. It was true that the top boss, with his almighty power, was Lenin. But after an attempt on his life almost a year before—in a factory in Moscow, on August 30, 1918, when he was shot by Dora Kaplan—Lenin had never entirely recovered from his wounds, and it was doubtful if he would live much longer. In view of such prospects, it would be advisable to become acquainted with the boss' successor, who would be one of the three: Trotsky, Kamenev or Stalin. Beria calculated that Trotsky, who had virtually provoked the Great October Revolution and led the Red troops to victory, had little chance because his real name was Lev Davidovich Bronstein. In other words, he was a Jew, so the masses would not accept him for long. The same was true of Kamenev-Rosenfeld. These two men could not be leaders, and even if they did attain such a position, it would be easy for Stalin to sweep them away. To Lavrenty it seemed indubitable that the only person apt to succeed Lenin was Stalin. This meant that it would be good to meet Stalin, called by his friends "Comrade Koba," or "Soso," and become his close disciple and worshiper. For this purpose Beria could obtain help from his influential friends Ordzhonikidze or Mikoyan. And last—but not least—a third, perhaps the most important of this trio, Sergey Kostrikov, known by his pseudonym "Kirov." Since these three men came to Baku to grab power for the Soviet regime, they intended to take not only Azerbaijan as a first bite but also to swallow the whole Caucasus. Beria's planned return to his native country would be worthwhile only if he came triumphantly as an architect who would erect beautiful modern buildings in Georgia's capital, or as a high political executive, a governor or a proconsul—a master of life and death, a man at whose name everybody would shake with fear. For these reasons, in times like the present, Lavrenty should not stay in Baku with his diploma hidden in his trunk, but should make contact with eminent people and wait for the right moment.

Beria was introduced to Kirov by Mikoyan a month after Kirov arrived in Baku, in April 1919. It was in May, just after Lavrenty's graduation. Kirov, a Russian peasant's son, good-looking with a big blond mop of hair, blue eyes, and an air of sincerity about him, was devoted body and soul to the Great Cause of the Party. A magnificent speaker, always full of enthusiasm, he was sure to be greeted by a hurricane of applause as soon as he mounted the platform to start a meeting. From the first words of his address, "Comrades! Brothers! Eagles! Falcons!" to the very last ones, "Long Live the Great Revolution!," he captivated the hearts and minds of the audience who listened to him with bated breath. He delivered his orations in a beautiful, melodic, purely Russian pronunciation, unlike Stalin, Ordzhonikidze, Mikoyan, or Mir Djaffar Bagirov, whose speaking voices were harsh, unpleasant and marred by Georgian or Armenian accents. This even applied to Beria, in spite of the fact that he did his best to master the Russian language, being aware that the masses disliked a foreign accent, and that it would be useful to speak a Russian as unflawed as possible.

Kirov received Beria favorably in his Baku office. He regarded Beria as a young comrade and a friend of Mikoyan. The latter recommended Lavrenty warmly, as an exceptionally promising member of the Bolshevik ranks, a young fellow who, if used properly, could fulfill any important job. Kirov trusted Mikoyan and promised to keep Lavrenty in mind and entrust him with a position of responsibility as soon as the Bolsheviks came to power in Azerbaijan.

This event happened soon. In May 1919 a conference of the Transcaucasian Bolshevik Organizations took place in Baku under the leadership of Ordzhonikidze and Mikoyan. During this time, Kirov directed the activities of the Bolshevik underground's work in Baku. Because in that city, as well as in the rest of Azerbaijan, the Bolsheviks represented only a small minority, the Soviet regime decided to take the country by force.

Before the end of 1919, the British troops departed, leaving Baku under the rule of the democratic Mussavatist administration as the only legal government of Azerbaijan. The Allies believed their withdrawal could be accomplished safely, as the Soviet Declaration on the Rights of Nationalities assured every country's independence. However, before Azerbaijan could take advantage of this privilege, and while it was unprotected by any Allied troops, the Soviets decided this was the best opportunity to arrange a *coup d'état*. At sunrise on April 20, 1920, the Soviet Eleventh Army under the leadership of Kirov and his aîde-de-camp, *Komandarm* Gekher entered Baku and overpowered the city without a shot. The members of the Azerbaijan National Republic's Government were arrested and taken to Bailov Prison, where they were executed in the courtyard the same day.

As a reward for the victory of the Red Forces, the soldiers were allowed to have a good time in the town for the next twenty-four hours. The one condition was that the object of their fun should be exclusively the bourgeoisie. Soon, the windows and doors of the houses of the rich were smashed, and convents were robbed and demolished. A spectacle was made of nuns forced to dance naked before being raped and then shot to death. There were also numerous lootings of well-to-do homes and rapings of young women from prominent families.

In the course of the night many houses in Baku were set afire. The blazes lighted the shores of the Caspian Sea, while the buildings burned down to their foundations because nobody extinguished the fires. In the smoldering ruins lay the charred bodies of the inhabitants, killed with bayonets or knives. The corpses lay among clothing and linen that the looting soldiers had failed to take, or that they lost when they left in a hurry.

The next day, at six o'clock in the morning, the soldiers had to be in their barracks or they would be considered guilty of deserting the garrison. At this time, in accordance with the orders of the recently created Special Department of Secret Political and Intelligence Services of the Red Army, units of the promptly organized Baku Security Commission, *Cheka*, appeared on the streets. The very first day, all officers of the former National Azerbaijan Army were arrested and jailed, their families thrown out of their homes into the streets, and their apartments requisitioned for Soviet officials. Government employees were also arrested; not only those in the higher positions, but even the small fry—supervisors of the post office and of harbor facilities, and the station masters. At night, trucks stopped in front of many houses and occupants were brutally taken out of their beds. Whole families were loaded onto trucks and carted away to jail. In a few days' time, the Bailov Prison became so overcrowded that the inmates had no place to lie on the floor, or even to sit. They had to stand tightly packed together—men, women and children, aged and the sick—jamming the cells as well as the halls, baths, laundry room, kitchen, storage rooms and the prison hospital. All these places were converted into temporary cells, which had to be emptied soon to receive new batches of the arrested.

From the early morning of the next day, two small steamboats started to ply between the Baku wharf not far from the Bailov Prison, and nearby Nargen Island. In the following twenty-four hours, hundreds of prisoners were transferred by these ships to a compound on the island, circled all around by a barbed wire fence. In this camp people did not get any food—not even bread—or drinking water to quench their thirst in the hot and salty air of the Caucasian May-time. There was no doubt that in a few days' time an epidemic of dysentery, typhoid fever or cholera would erupt there. But this danger was never permitted to materialize. The captives were brought to that island not to stay in isolation, but to meet a quick death. The executions started soon after the arrival of the first shipments, and were performed without any trials or sentencing. People were killed en masse by machine guns that shot volley after volley into targets consisting of 100 or 200 people arranged in a row on the embankment above a long trench. The dead fell into the trench, into which some soldiers immediately poured quicklime thick enough to cover the bodies, but leaving room for the next layer of corpses that would fall into the trench soon after the next transport arrived. There were from three to four such transports daily.

These horrors lasted six days and were eventually known in the history of Baku's revolution as the infamous "Week of Suppression of the Bourgeoisie."[1]

The entire operation was personally directed by "Dear Sergo" Ordzhonikidze who especially passionately exterminated not only the rich, but particularly the intelligentsia against whom he—a rude village barber by profession—felt a particular, almost psychopathic, hatred. When the massacre was over, proud of his achievement, Ordzhonikidze sent a detailed report to Lenin in Moscow. An important part in this action was played by the Baku *Komsomol* and some of its leaders—Dumbadze, Bagirov and Dekanozov—with the assistance of their friend, Lavrenty Beria.

On May 5th and May 6th, 1920, the first All-Baku Bolshevik Party Conference was called, with Kirov, Ordzhonikidze and Mikoyan as principal speakers. This trio, with help from Beria who, acting as a planted cog in the Menshevik and Mussavatist Party machinery, supplied them with the proscription lists, was responsi-

---

[1] Appendix 5.

ble for the mass murder on Nargen Island. The papers, prepared by Lavrenty, contained the names and addresses of people described by Beria as the enemies of the Soviet regime. In the course of the Convention, the Communist Party of Azerbaijan was created. The definitive downfall of Azerbaijan's National Government and the country's autonomy was announced, as well as the extermination of all opponents of the Soviet authority. A resolution was also accepted to send to Moscow a telegram expressing Azerbaijan's plea to be incorporated into the Soviet Government for a common struggle against the world's international imperialism. On that day, the Azerbaijan Socialist Soviet Republic was proclaimed.

Lavrenty Beria showed his three powerful sponsors that he could assuredly be their most valuable follower.

8

A Visit to Sunny Georgia

THE FIRST STEP in conquering Transcaucasia for the Soviets had
been taken. Now, in order to overpower the entire Caucasus, there
remained two more countries to subject: Georgia and Armenia.
Turning first to Georgia, the Soviet Government had a very complicated problem to solve. If the Bolsheviks formed a tiny minority in
Azerbaijan and even in the Baku area, and Soviet Russia had to
take that country by dint of force, then the Bolsheviks would have
to face a more difficult task in conquering Georgia. There, the
Marxist idea was completely unpopular and the Communist Party
had no significance at all. The Georgians were aware that now,
having established the new regime in neighboring Azerbaijan, the
Red Eleventh Army would attack their own fatherland. However,
they were determined to defend it. Soon, after the Russians crossed
the Azerbaijan-Georgia border and struck at the Georgian guards,
the war broke out.

While the Georgian Army was locked in combat in the border-
land, a subversive group of Georgian Communists tried to seize the
National Cadets' Academy building on Plekhanov Street in Tiflis.
The idea behind this attack was that if the cadets, representing the
most patriotic young element of the Georgian National Army and
the best-trained, promising fresh cadre of officers, were overpowered, the morale of the whole Georgian Army would be broken.
Then it would not be too hard to take the entire country.

During the night a detachment of fifty men under Sergo Makharadze's command overran the cadets' quarters. Makharadze, Ordzhonikidze's friend, was an experienced partisan and an old hand at similar tasks.

But this time, in Tiflis, his plan failed. The young cadets fought back against their assailants and killed almost all of them by shooting at them from the school's windows and later attacking them with their sabers in the courtyard and in the streets.

Soon, events took an entirely different course, and Soviet Russia had to shift her troops in the opposite direction, to the west. Just before the end of the First World War, Poland gained independence by disarming the German forces occupying her territory. Now, after Russia's attack on Azerbaijan in April 1920, the Poles realized the danger threatening them from the Soviets who, in spite of assuring every country of the right to self-determination, were ready to swallow one foreign country after another. The Polish government did not intend to wait idly, but decided to take the initiative into its own hands. The proposed treaty delineating future Polish eastern boundaries, suggested by the Soviet Administration in March 1920, proved unacceptable. It would undermine Poland's existence as a sovereign state and sounded more like a provocation than a sincere offer. The only possible answer to the Russian proposal was military action. On April 26 the Polish Army, under Marshal Joseph Pilsudski, attacked the Soviet Forces and invaded Russia. The impact of the attack was so powerful that the Reds were unable to counter the blow and retreated. Following the fleeing armies closely, the Poles pushed the Russians back to the east, besieging the city of Kiev.

Faced with such a blow, the Soviet Administration dared not fight two enemies, Georgia and Poland, at once. The plan of waging a similar war against Georgia accompanied by such bloodshed as in the case of Azerbaijan—although demanded by two Georgians, Stalin and Ordzhonikidze—had to be postponed. The advancing Polish Army was more dangerous than war for the conquest of the Caucasus.

Lenin sent Ordzhonikidze a telegram ordering him to desist from further invasion of the Caucasus and to withdraw all forces from Georgia's territory back to her boundaries.

The next day, Russia proposed a pact to the Georgian Government based on friendly noninterference and mutual tolerance.

On May 7, 1920, the Polish Army took Kiev. The next day the Soviet authorities signed a peace treaty with the independent Menshevik Georgian Government in Tiflis. Thanks to this agreement, Georgia avoided bloody battles against Russian Forces and gained full Soviet recognition of her regime. Notwithstanding the pact, however, Russia did not abandon her plans of incorporating Georgia. But from now on, the action of the Reds went underground. Men were needed for such subversive activity. They must be known to the Party as cunning and reliable. Moreover, they must be Georgians. Later, the Russians had to be able to claim that the movement had been purely Georgian, and that the new order was brought on by the natives themselves.

While Kirov had already been appointed by Lenin as the Soviet representative in Georgia and was living in Tiflis, Mikoyan and Ordzhonikidze in Baku were developing plans for the new action according to Stalin's directions. When considering candidates for the assignment of subversive agent in Georgia they came to the conclusion that the best-suited person for the job was Beria. He proved to be so shrewd in preparing the proscription lists for the mass executions on Nargen Island that the Red rulers of Baku decided to send him to Georgia. He was to join the local Communist cell and pave the way for the future revolution against the legal National Government.

Boarding a train to his native land and furnished with instructions by *Komandarm* Gekher, now Chief of the Special Department of the Eleventh Red Army, Beria was returning home as a promising, successful young fellow. He was coming as an educated man with a diploma from the Mechanical-Construction Technical School in Baku and a volunteer veteran who had fought the Germans. He was now a young scholar and a patriot who obviously was not involved in any political activity. He had never been bothered either by officials of the Tsarist *Okhrana*, which was fighting the underground movement so popular then among the young, or by the Red Army, the Soviet militia, or the Bolshevik Security as an individual who supported anti-revolutionary forces. Quite the contrary. He was an immaculately pure, clean-cut young man with a fine future as an architect wide open to him. His mother, sister and brothers, as well as all his friends, neighbors and acquaintances, could be proud of their "Lara." He left his country as a poor sixteen-year-old village boy and now, in less than five years, he was returning as a mature young man, an engineer-builder.

When the train stopped at the station of his native Sukhum, called now in Georgian Sukhumi,[1] and Beria left his compartment, he realized that nothing had changed here. There was the same cashier who, busy in his ticket office, paid no attention to his arrival. The same news vendor was at the kiosk, a disabled man with a wooden leg. The sleepy oldster was sitting on a low stool near his stand and dozed as usual.

Carrying his suitcase, Beria crossed the station building and found himself in the street, where stood a droshky drawn by a brown horse. As he rode along the sunny, sandy road, Lavrenty looked around, observing the familiar landscape. The dust from under the cab's wheels rose high behind and spread away. The Black Sea glittered with a silvery hue and exuded the well-known smell of seaweed, mussels and fish, a fragrance so different from the Caspian Sea's fumes of crude oil. Soon the seashore disappeared from view, as the road turned inland.

The huts of his native village of Merkheuli stood unchanged from the days before his departure. Small, covered with roofs of black wooden shingles, they were poor but clean and nice. On lines stretching high above the backyards, the washed dark clothes were drying. In the little fenced gardens stood tall, golden sunflowers, reaching far above the multicolored flowers which are probably found nowhere in the world except in Abkhazia. They were glittering and smelling as sweetly as five years ago and surely as hundreds of years before, even as in the times of Jason, who arrived here on his ship *Argo* while sailing in pursuit of the Golden Fleece. Everything here was exactly as it was during Lavrenty's boyhood.

At home also, nothing had changed. Stepping out of the garden, Lavrenty crossed the threshold of the low door and entered the kitchen. Beria could see the same pots standing on the stove. On the right, the same small room he shared with his brothers was still as he left it. On the other side of the stove, there was a bigger room containing his parents' large double bed with a high pile of pillows and above them in the corner, a hanging icon with a taper burning in a red glass cup. Next to the bed, there was a table with a kerosene lamp on it, and two stools. Everything the same. Even the same cobweb on the window, and probably the same fly caught in its net.

---

[1] Sukhumi: The Georgian name for Sukhum after Georgia proclaimed her independence.

However, only someone who did not know Beria would suppose that all these rustic and nostalgic scenes made him sentimental and softened his heart. Such feelings were entirely alien to him. Beria despised the stillness of his poor, simple and provincial birthplace where nothing ever happened. He firmly believed that someday he would be ruling that country.

There also were no changes in his family's life. Tamara, a little taller but still as fat as ever, was busy with the household, because mother came home from her work in town only once a week. Their half-brother, Datiko, after being discharged from the army, returned home, got married, and was now living a few houses away. The youngest brother, Irakly, worked at Sukhumi in the shop of the good merchant Ierkomoshvili, at whose home mother was still employed as a cook.

Lavrenty already knew these details from his mother's letters. Some less important news, for instance, about this or that neighbor's death, or marriage, or having a baby, or being killed in the war, was insignificant. Just a normal occurrence in life.

Soon Beria began his new activities. First of all, he had to pay a visit to his benefactors, Mr. Svimoni Ierkomoshvili, and his wife, Maro, to thank them for their help in the past and to show them the diploma of an engineer-builder from the Technicum in Baku, as well as his honorable discharge from the army. The visit was a necessary step for starting his mission in Georgia. Beria still needed the friendship and sponsorship of this rich merchant, who was an outstanding figure in Sukhumi. He also had to go there to greet his old mother and that little brat Irakly. After exchanging a few kisses with his mother Lavrenty asked her if he could see the master of the house. Soon he was invited to the living room.

The atmosphere of the meeting was warm and cordial; tea was served, and preserved fruits and pastries. It was a great joy to Lavrenty's old mother, full of pride and happiness, to listen when her dear son "Lara" talked about his studies, examinations, and wartime adventures on the faraway front. Beria also did not neglect to express his deep disgust when describing the horrible days of riots in Baku, the dreadful occupation of Azerbaijan by the brutal Eleventh Red Army, and the bloody liquidation of the Baku nationalists. He professed that, as a loyal Georgian, his heart was fully on the side of the Mensheviks, whose party ruled his native country. He voiced deep conviction that this truly democratic government consisted of representatives of liberal and even radical, well-to-do intelligentsia, moved by patriotic feelings and strong ambitions for independence and liberty.

Ierkomoshvili, one of the wealthiest businessmen in Sukhumi, a well-read and enlightened man and an ardent Georgian patriot, was also an active member of the Menshevik party. He was glad that his protégé, Lavrenty, shared his beliefs. This promising young man did not have to try to convince him that his opinions were right. The merchant realized that, were Lavrenty not telling the truth, he wouldn't have been able to get his diploma in Baku, or at least he would have been in trouble with the *Okhrana*. Ierkomoshvili also believed Beria's explanation that he avoided the massacre committed by the Special Department of the Bolshevik Security thanks only to the help of one of his friends; namely, Dumbadze, who hid him on the outskirts of the town. Otherwise Beria, who belonged to the Mensheviks, would have been executed. Dumbadze, a schoolmate in the Technicum and countryman of Beria, took part in the occupation of Baku by the Eleventh Red Army which he had joined before and, as Lavrenty now revealed, was active in the group which arrested and jailed the political trespassers. At last, Beria was happy to have returned to his native Georgia which he, along with all good sons of the fatherland, wished to see free, independent and ruled by her own people. Soon, he would renew old friendships with his pals from the high school, see again the dear familiar places in his homeland, and then he would go to Tiflis, where he had never been before, to look for a suitable job.

The visit with the Ierkomoshvilis ended on a warmhearted note. When bidding good-bye to their young guest—the "wonderful Lara"—his hosts wished him good luck and much success. Beria once more thanked his benefactors for their past generosity and their help in making his dreams of becoming an educated person come true. He also thanked them for providing employment to his mother and younger brother. Then he left the home of the merchant, whom he hated, calling him a stupid bourgeois. Beria could not stand his benefactor. He saw him as a narrow-minded, stubborn, dirty Menshevik and a capitalist living comfortably in his luxurious three-story house with plush-covered sofas and mahogany furniture. He also hated that couple as two parasites who did no work, while being served by an exploited maid, Beria's poor, weary mother.

After that obligatory diplomatic visit, Lavrenty dropped in at his high-school on Podgornaya Street to greet his old headmaster and his teachers, to check on how many of them still were there, to get acquainted with the new ones, and to see whether they brought up the youngsters in the poisonous spirit of the national, patriotic, anti-Communist and independent Georgia. It was also useful to learn whether the members of the teachers' board were active in the Menshevik Party, and to memorize their names. Then he would say hello to his friends and former schoolmates, Semyon Danilov and Nestor Lakoba. Each of them was a devoted worshiper of the genius, Lenin, and Nestor was also proud of his friendship with Stalin.

Lavrenty went to see Lakoba. Nestor looked somewhat pale. He, like Danilov, had lost weight because both had spent a few months behind bars, jailed for their subversive activity. Just a few days earlier they had been released from prison, thanks to the amnesty based on the recent pact between the Georgian Government and the Soviets, signed on May 7, 1920.

Lavrenty brought them greetings from their protectors in Baku, Ordzhonikidze and Mikoyan, and conveyed words of encouragement from these men for their action. He also delivered to them some papers signed by these two outstanding comrades, so his friends could be sure he was not a provocateur, but a genuine liaison man. They told him that the Party planned to establish in Tiflis a new newspaper, *Communisti*, in the Georgian language and that Lavrenty could make a personal contact with the editors when he went to that city.

Soon after that Beria left for Tiflis. There was nothing suspicious about a young, ambitious Georgian with an engineer-builder's diploma going to search for a suitable job in that city. In a few days' time, however, he returned to Sukhumi, bringing to the circle of his former schoolmates some orders from the Communist headquarters in Tiflis, led there by Kirov.

Six weeks after Beria's return from Azerbaijan, in mid-July 1920, he was arrested and imprisoned in Kutaisi,[2] a town not far from Sukhumi, on charges of being a Soviet spy. He was caught there in possession of some confidential notes with instructions for a foreign intelligence man. Beria faced several years in jail for carrying on subversive activity against Menshevik Democratic Georgia on or-

---

[2] Kutaisi: The Georgian name for Kutais after Georgia proclaimed her independence.

ders of the Caucasian Bureau of the Central Committee of the Russian Communist Party.

But his stay behind Kutaisi prison bars did not last even a month. His release came only a few days after Lakoba informed Kirov of Lavrenty's arrest. Kirov, the Plenipotentiary Representative to Tiflis of the Soviets from Moscow, officially asked the Georgian Administration in his letter of July 9, 1920, to release Beria and to immediately send him back to Azerbaijan. Thanks to his powerful protector, Lavrenty was shortly deported under guard to the Georgian-Azerbaijani border.

In August, Beria was at liberty and again walked freely the familiar streets of Baku.

9

Guest of Honor

BERIA COULD NOW PERFORM the role of martyr and hero. He realized that at last he had become a personality known to the whole Georgian Democratic Government as a man protected by the Soviet authorities, as well as someone popular in the circle of the rulers of Red Azerbaijan. During his briefing with Mikoyan and Ordzhonikidze in the office of the Executive Committee Beria reported that in the Kutaisi prison he went on a hunger strike because he was not permitted to have any visitors. Only thanks to this action, he said, had he been able to send a message to Comrade Kirov.

Such methods as refusing food were frequently used in jails all over the world, so in Beria's case it would be hard to check whether his story was true or false. When speaking of his mission in Tiflis to the editors of *Communisti*, and to Sergo Makharadze, who had led the unsuccessful attack on the Georgian National Cadet Academy, and who had recently been released from prison, thanks to the amnesty, Beria reported that Makharadze could not be successful without a detachment of supporting troops to be sent to him from Baku by the Special Department of the Eleventh Red Army. The chief of that unit, *Komandarm* Gekher, a short, bow-legged Latvian, an unscrupulous brute, soon became Lavrenty's friend. The power Gekher represented fascinated Beria. When he first saw Gekher, during the "Week of Suppression of the Bourgeoisie," the officer had a pistol in his hand and was personally shooting to death some of the arrested officers of the disarmed National Azerbaijani Army. The interrogation of these prisoners by the *Komandarm* during the mock trials excited Beria more than he could ever have imagined. Such power was spellbinding.

Since his return to Baku, Beria was in the habit of spending evenings and nights with the *Komandarm*, drinking in his company and listening to stories of his great achievements during the October Revolution in Russia. Soon Lavrenty realized that, while Gekher got drunk very quickly he, Beria, could drink a lot and still stay sober. But this did not mean he should waste too much time in the company of this narrow-minded soldier. All Beria needed was the powerful *Komandarm*'s friendship.

In September 1920, a new college opened in Baku—a Polytechnical University. Now Beria did not have to go to a big city in Russia to study architecture, as he still wished to do. He could enroll in the Polytechnic right here, in the town, where he was among influential friends, and where he himself was, to some extent, a personality. Beria realized that in spite of his achievements he was still considered small-fry. He knew he should not rely exclusively on his friends who, one day, could be called off to another assignment, transferred to another job, or promoted, and who would then forget him. In the event of any such occurrences it would be advisable to have a real and steady profession as an architect.

Lavrenty studied hard for two months, taking time out only to attend his Party's meetings, according to regulations.

During one such gathering, held on November 2, 1920, in the House of the Central Committee of the Azerbaijan Communist Party, Ordzhonikidze announced that he had received a telegram from Comrade Stalin in Moscow advising that in three days' time he would come to Baku. This would obviously be a triumphant return for the leader to the town where in the past Stalin had engaged in conspiratorial work, and where he served his terms in Bailov Prison.

His official visit must be celebrated according to the status of the hero who, together with the genius Lenin, ignited the Great October Revolution. The program and schedule of the festivities during Stalin's stay in Baku would be prepared by a special committee which was to be organized right away at the meeting. The gathering elected a board comprised of three of the most outstanding personalities—Ordzhonikidze, Mikoyan and Kirov, who was coming from Tiflis for this occasion. The first was to preside. Having been elected chairman, the popular "Dear Sergo" invited on to the board *Komandarm* Gekher and—as an assistant—Lavrenty Pavlovich Beria. Lavrenty was now known as that young and promising Communist who had suffered in the prison in Georgia and who previously had been so helpful in the overpowering of Azerbaijan by the Bolsheviks.

This new distinction, expressed personally by Ordzhonikidze, made Beria proud and happy. At last he had the great opportunity to be introduced to Stalin. However, his pride did not stem from admiration for his famous countryman Stalin. Beria was not impressed by him at all. Such feelings as admiration or devotion were alien to his cold and calculating nature. In his opinion the great Comrade Stalin was a vulgar, pockmark-faced Georgian peasant, Iosif Dzhugashvili, a chauvinistic bastard from the filthy outskirts of the Gori community in the Tiflis area, the son of a drunkard cobbler, and a dropout from a deacons' seminary, a frustrated candidate for Orthodox priesthood, an activist more lucky than clever, a conspirator rude, ruthless and unscrupulous enough to be on top. To boot, he owed his position to Lenin, whose close aide he was. Being an educated young man, Beria despised rather than adored Stalin. But an acquaintanceship with Comrade Stalin represented the first step to a big-time political career and to power. And only that really counted. In these times, when wielding power was equivalent to being a butcher, the names of Lenin, Stalin or Trotsky stood for authority.

The newly created committee spent the three days in a feverish mood. From the very morning of November 5, 1920, the railway station had been surrounded by a cordon of Red Army troops and militiamen. The station building was full of delegates—all Party members—of workers from oil refineries and factories. When at last the long-awaited train rolled up to the platform, Ordzhonikidze, Kirov and Mikoyan climbed into the first Pullman car. There, they searched the corridor looking for their comrade and leader. Soon, they met their eminent guest, with whom they rode to the House of the Executive Committee. They came in a shabby-looking military truck, escorted by a similar car carrying security men. The motorcade's route was not announced to the people beforehand, so it passed unnoticed.

On this memorable day of November 6, 1920, there was a meeting of the Baku Soviet called for ten o'clock in the morning at the House of the Central Committee of the Azerbaijan Communist Party and the Council of Commissars of the Azerbaijan Soviet Socialist Republic. Entrance was granted only to persons having a special pass issued the previous day by the Security Department of the Eleventh Red Army. This document had to be presented at the door, where it was carefully checked by militiamen. At a quarter to ten the big room was packed. The podium was decorated with long banners displaying, on a red background, a white hammer and sickle, and slogans: "Death to the Bourgeois!" and "Death to the Capitalists!" Now the panel entered, composed of four dignitaries: Stalin, Ordzhonikidze, Kirov and Mikoyan. The audience sprang to their feet and gave them a standing ovation. The Powerful Four took their seats behind a table covered with red cloth. After a long period of applause "Dear Sergo" Ordzhonikidze stood up. With a friendly gesture of outstretched arms and a broad, warm smile, he announced, "Attention, comrades. Comrade Stalin is going to speak."

Stalin rose and began his oration. In the crowded room his coarse, harsh voice with its hard Georgian accent sounded like woodchopping in a quiet, desolate forest. His speech was neither sentimental nor nostalgic. In the very town, where some years before he had carried on his underground activity, in the very same city of Baku, where he had twice been arrested and put behind bars, Stalin did not reminisce, or refer by even one word to his past. The subject of his lecture was: "Three Years of the Proletarian Revolution." It was a dry account of struggles, achievements and victories; a sober statement supported by facts and dates. At each mention of Marx's, Engels' or Lenin's name, Stalin stopped and applauded. He was immediately joined in applause, first by members of the panel, and then by all present.

In the center of the first row in the auditorium sat Beria, his eyes glued with an expression of worship to the speaker's face. He applauded the moment he noticed that Stalin intended to clap again.

The next two days were spent in meetings during which Stalin and his three top rulers of the new regime in Azerbaijan discussed plans for overpowering Georgia and Armenia. Then, on November 9, 1920, one day before his departure, Stalin delivered another program-delineating speech at a meeting of the Central Committee of the Azerbaijan Communist Party. This time Beria again sat in the front row and enthusiastically applauded every time the speaker stopped for a dramatic pause.

10

Nomination

THE POLISH-SOVIET WAR was rolling on with varying luck. After many bitter battles the Poles, who occupied Kiev and even crossed the Dnieper River, had to abandon their positions and withdraw. The masses of Cossack cavalry under *Komandarm* Semyon Budyonny and the infantry under *Komandarm* Mikhail Tukhachevsky pressed the Polish troops almost to the river Vistula and threatened Warsaw.

When Lenin became convinced that Poland's fall was only a matter of a few days, he decided to change his previous peaceful policy toward Georgia and execute Stalin's and Ordzhonikidze's plans for conquering the Caucasus. Before breaking the Soviet-Georgia treaty of May 7, 1920, by which the Soviet Government guaranteed the independence of this country, the proposed action had to be well planned in advance. It had to start from neighboring Azerbaijan, and primarily from its capital, Baku.

The Azerbaijan Communist Executive Party in Baku was appointed to a new task. All Party members were to be on the alert.

After a meeting with Trotsky and Alexey Rykov—the former, People's Commissar of Foreign Affairs and the latter, Commissar of the Interior—Lenin announced that the time had come to deal Georgia a blow. On February 9, 1921, Lenin personally allowed Stalin to decide on the Zero hour for the attack.

Eight days later, at six o'clock in the morning, the Eleventh Red

Army launched an unprovoked attack on Georgia from Azerbaijan, stepping over the border of this peace-loving, but noble and by no means humble, country. The proud Georgians did not intend to give up their fatherland and bow before the enemy. In a gallant fight, their cavalry stopped the foe on the first day of the war, while their machine guns, hidden on the slopes of the high, imposing Caucasian mountains, forced the enemy to retreat. However, the outcome of the war, or rather of the desperate defense waged by that brave nation, could be predicted from the very beginning. The hordes of tens of thousands of drunken Red Army soldiers, swarming in successive waves, burned down whole villages, hanging their entire populations—innocent peasants, men, women and children.

Even after the Russian troops occupied their capital, Tiflis, the Georgians did not put down their arms, but withdrew to Batumi[1] in search of reinforcements. Then, however, neighboring Turkey decided to take advantage of the Soviet-Georgian war and moved to take Batumi. When the first Turkish regiments arrived at the outskirts of Batumi, an important port on the Black Sea, the Soviet Army halted its advance. Lenin did not want any involvement in a new war against Turkey, which could be long and hazardous. He preferred to leave to Turkish hands the dirty job of decimating the Georgian National Army, which the Red troops had started to sweep out. The Georgian forces found themselves trapped in fire from two sides. They were able to force the Turks to retreat, but could not withstand the pressure from the Russians.

Thus, the Georgian people faced the danger of total extermination. Under such circumstances, their democratic government realized it would be madness, if not outright suicide, to carry on a hopeless war, let the civilians be massacred and villages, towns and cities turned into ashes. After several weeks of such warfare, the Georgians had to ask Moscow for an armistice. They were forced to agree to unconditional surrender, leaving the country at the mercy of a ruthless conqueror.

When the hostilities ended, the Special Department of the Soviet Security arrived in Georgia just after the military occupation had been settled.

The victories in Georgia, and soon after in Armenia and on the Polish front, required huge supplies of food and equipment for the

---

[1] Batumi: The Georgian name for Batum after Georgia proclaimed her independence.

Red Army. The inhuman exploitation of the peasants and workers inside Russia created unbearable living conditions. On the Polish Front the Red Army, defeated August 14, 1920, on the outskirts of Warsaw, had to retreat from Poland. Russia was completely exhausted. The *Cheka's* terror destroyed the majority of professionals, intelligentsia and specialists, who were arrested and exterminated according to Dzerzhinsky's orders. Many factories, their machines smashed by rioting workers during the 1917 Revolution, were still closed. Famine and misery prevailed. At last the sailors of Kronstadt, previously the most ardent believers in Communist ideas, decided to protest again in favor of their brethren, the workers and peasants. In the course of a great gathering, called on February 28, 1921, they elected representatives to be sent to Petrograd to discuss the problem with Grigory Zinoviev, the Region Party leader and one of the best friends of their beloved Great Comrade Lenin, whom they had admired and enthusiastically applauded before the October Revolution.

On March 1, 1921, the 30-man delegation was received by Zinoviev in his office at Smolny Palace in Petrograd. He promised them to wire a telegram to Moscow. The reply came immediately: Lenin decided that the Kronstadt resolution was just a counterrevolutionary act, and by his, Lenin's, personal order, the delegates should be imprisoned and treated as simple traitors. The order was fulfilled instantly. The sailors were arrested and executed the next morning.

The Soviet country is the land of the proletariat. Therefore, if somebody protests, it means he is protesting against the proletariat, against his own fatherland. In that case, he is not a patriot, but a parasite spitting into the common well of drinking water. There is no place for such men in the people's country. There is also no place there for strikes, demonstrations or any other kind of mutiny directed against the Administration which, representing the proletariat, is devoting every minute to the citizens' good. Such treacherous elements must be eliminated from the healthy community and destroyed to their very roots, for they do not deserve to live.

When the Kronstadt sailors got the news of their delegation's execution, they proclaimed an uprising. The same seamen who supported Lenin with all their hearts and deep devotion in his struggle during the February and October Revolutions in 1917 now declared a rebellion against the Administration.[2] But Lenin's govern-

---

[2] Appendix 6.

ment was not as generous as the democratic socialist Kerensky, who announced an amnesty for all soldiers and sailors who had fought against him. Now Lenin acted quickly and mercilessly by leaving the problem to Trotsky as the chief organizer and leader of the Red Army and now Commissar for War. Trotsky entrusted to Mikhail Nikolayevich Tukhachevsky the touchy and responsible task of dealing with the sailors. The choice was very cunning. *Komandarm* Tukhachevsky, who during the Polish war exhibited bravery and experience, previously had been a Tsarist officer and had joined the Bolsheviks in 1918. As a former White Russian commander, he undoubtedly hated the Kronstadt sailors for murdering his colleagues, some of whom had been his best friends. He would have no scruples about extinguishing the mutiny.

Before embarking on this action, Tukhachevsky pointed out that his only problem was the question of the troops he was to use. At a conference with Trotsky he mentioned that the Red Army soldiers, instead of fighting the rioters, might join them and together with them turn against the Government. To prevent rebellion, Trotsky ordered the Petrograd garrison disarmed. He also promised to supply Tukhachevsky with armed battalions of 60,000 men who would be told they were going to attack Kronstadt because it was a base of Whiteguard revolt against Communism and had organized a petty-bourgeois counterrevolutionary plot. They would be given adequate bread rations, better food and enough vodka to make them angry with the parasites. Besides, there would be units of Communist military cadets. Also, Dzerzhinsky promised to lend some of his own troops of *Cheka* men.

On March 5, 1921, Trotsky issued a proclamation warning the mutinous sailors in Kronstadt that, unless they surrendered, they would be shot, as he described in his own words, one by one "like ducks on a lake."

But the seamen did not think of giving up their bastion. On March 7, Tukhachevsky's forces, supported with heavy artillery, approached Kronstadt. Although the attackers outnumbered the 15,000 sailors more than four to one, the latter greeted the invaders with a hail of bullets. The war of Lenin's and Trotsky's Red Army, led by Mikhail Tukhachevsky against the navy men, whose delegates were asking for bread and justice for the peasants and workers, lasted ten days. The Red units had to take one bunker after another in bloody battles. "They fought like wild beasts," wrote

Tukhachevsky when, on March 17, 1921, he reported to Lenin in Moscow that Kronstadt had been taken. On the ground around the bunkers and in the fortress lay thousands of mariners killed "one by one." Those who were taken prisoner were later executed down to the last man by *Cheka* firing squads. In accordance with Trotsky's statement, in the name of the Communist Government, they were shot "like ducks on a lake."

Such was the end of Lenin's most devoted worshipers, the Kronstadt falcons, the comrades-in-arms of the crew of the famous battleship *Aurora*, the enthusiastic seamen the Party once had called "the Pride and Glory of the Revolution," and the best sons of the workers and peasants.

Near the end of March 1921, when Georgia had been defeated, the sailors' mutiny in Kronstadt toppled and drowned in blood, and the peace treaty with Poland signed, the final pacification of the Georgian and Armenian nations and the crushing of any sign of opposition and of anti-Bolshevik feeling had to be carried out according to the pattern for such action as applied previously to Baku. For this task the farsighted Ordzhonikidze had already chosen his faithful and promising young comrade—Lavrenty Beria.

During the entire academic year, since September 1920, Beria had studied assiduously at the Polytechnic University, preparing for the summer examinations. Only from time to time did he see Ordzhonikidze or Mikoyan, and then just so he would not lose contact with these important comrades. Suddenly, in April 1921, he was called to the House of the Executive Committee. Ordzhonikidze wished to see him. He was needed.

11

The Right Man

WHEN BERIA ARRIVED at the Executive Committee building, he was
told by the male secretary that Comrade Ordzhonikidze was busy
and Lavrenty Pavlovich should wait. This was the first time such a
formal approach had been used with him. Since he was never late
for a meeting, he always was able to go right in to see any of the
authorities. This time he had to wait in the hall until he was called.
At last, the door of Ordzhonikidze's office opened and Dumbadze
came out. His face expressed determination, discipline and obedience to the necessity of accepting orders, even against his own
wishes. He looked at Lavrenty and passed by him. He might have
been instructed not to talk to anybody he would meet in these
headquarters, or perhaps he just wasn't in a mood for conversation.

Soon afterwards "Dear Sergo" Ordzhonikidze appeared at the
threshold and, stretching out both arms in a friendly gesture, invited Beria into his office. They sat at his beautiful, richly inlaid
desk, confiscated from the home of one of the capitalists evicted
during the bloody purge. Talking in his native Georgian, "Dear
Sergo" revealed that despite the victory of the Communist idea and
of the Red Administration in Azerbaijan, opposition in Baku still
existed and the anti-Bolshevik movement was quite active. The
anti-Soviet parties—the Mensheviks, the Dashnaks and the Mussavatists—had gone deep underground. These subversive organizations must be smashed by all means. The Special Unit of the Elev-

enth Army, the Security Department under *Komandarm* Gekher, worked quite well, but this was not enough. This great burden had to be taken over by those who already had some experience in watchfulness and investigation, by shrewd and cunning men, particularly those who were not just soldiers or militiamen, but clever young people devoted to the Party. This task was to be their main job, a full-time one and their only interest and pursuit. Ordzhonikidze knew that Beria presently was studying architecture, but the country's security was more important than anything else. Comrade Lenin, the Genius, once said that "a good Communist is at the same time a good *Chekist*,"[1] which means that every Bolshevik should be a Security Police Officer, a spy and undercover man. Under these circumstances, Beria had to embrace immediately the new duties the Party was entrusting to him. This meant that he would have to discontinue attending school; but he should be proud that the Party chose him for a special task. The same thing had happened to Dumbadze, who dreamed about becoming a high-ranking officer in the Red Army. However, in these great times of creating a new Communist power, good architects and even brilliant regular army officers were not as essential as good and skilled *Chekists*. What use would good professionals be if the Soviet fatherland should be undermined by enemies? As a devoted Bolshevik in Baku, Dumbadze was also being rewarded with the same kind of honorable responsibilities. He understood that the Party's interests were above all else, and he would quit his studies. The *Cheka* in Moscow was a model office. It was led by the experienced hands of the closest personal friend of Lenin, Comrade Dzerzhinsky, who acquitted himself perfectly in his duties. But the Party still needed new cadres of bright men, especially Georgians. Sooner or later, Georgia would be incorporated into the Soviet Union and there would be a great demand for well-prepared, outside-trained Communists, young men ready to assume new posts of responsibility at once. These officials would become high executives as soon as the new regime was introduced in the country. Ordzhonikidze was aware of the fact that during the memorable days of the "Week of Suppression of the Bourgeoisie" Beria showed quite a talent. Now, "Dear Sergo" was eager to become Lavrenty's personal guide in the latter's work at the Baku *Cheka*: the smashing of the underground

---

[1] V. I. Lenin, in a speech delivered at the Ninth Party Congress on April 3, 1920.

movement in that city. This would be Beria's training prior to his future appointment in Georgia. There was no time to waste. The next day Lavrenty would start his new job in the Bailov Prison's office. Ordzhonikidze shook hands with his young comrade and wished him good luck.

The dream about becoming an architect vanished forever. But a new dream was beginning to come true: to be a master of life and death over thousands of people here in Baku and later, in his native Georgia. This was even more exciting than building houses, erecting dams and drilling tunnels. From now on all Beria had to do would be perform skilfully and efficiently in his new occupation, be loyal, useful and—if possible—irreplaceable to the Party.

The next morning, at eight o'clock sharp, Beria appeared at Bailov Prison. His office was ready and waiting for him. It was a narrow room, its walls covered with brown wallpaper. However, the moire pattern was ruined by big dark spots of moisture, while the dull gray ceiling had not been repainted for years and was peeling like a leprous skin. On the floor was a worn green carpet. On a low, crude desk covered with a green cloth similar to the one on the floor, stood an electric lamp, a telephone and writing accessories. There were two chairs and a filing cabinet. A big round clock on the wall, a picture of Lenin and a coat rack in the corner completed the furnishings. On Beria's right, when he was seated at the desk, was a narrow window, with thick bars partly covered by brown drapes. It overlooked the courtyard.

The personal supervision and guidance of Ordzhonikidze meant, as Beria learned the very first morning from his telephone conversation with him, that Lavrenty had practically a free hand. "Dear Sergo" delegated full responsibility to his protégé. Beria could phone Ordzhonikidze any time he needed special advice, and that was all there was to it. Such power suited Lavrenty's ambitions well. He realized that the task he was entrusted with—the crushing of the underground movement—was only his admission examination. If he passed it, the door to a great career would open. This was a big stake, and he had to win it. His job must be carried out systematically and without haste.

To begin, Beria acquainted himself with the list of prisoners. In Bailov Prison, this statistical material showed the names in alphabetical order, with the number of the cell in which each inmate was jailed. Checking the list, Beria found the names of several men he personally knew and had denounced. Now it would be interesting to see some of these people and interrogate them. It would be his first meeting with the inmates in his new capacity and his first interrogation as a *Chekist*.

Beria pressed the button of a round metal bell on his desk. The jailer who appeared was ordered to bring Marat Bossadzhogly from his cell. The guard left but promptly returned, reporting there was no man of this name in the cell specified. Beria phoned the prison commander and asked him to come to his office for a conference. As a *Chekist* with the rank of Deputy Chief of the Secret Operation Section, Beria was superior to a mere head warden of a jail. Lavrenty learned from the latter that there could be several explanations for the absence of the inmate Marat Bossadzhogly from his cell. (1) He could have been shot during the "Week of Suppression of the Bourgeoisie," when there were mass executions of several transports of people without any checking of names. (2) The man could have died in prison, as happened there almost every day and every night. He could have been taken to the mortuary and later buried in a common, nameless grave. (3) The man could have given a false name to the officer. Perhaps he had been taken from his home at night straight from bed and loaded on a truck with a crowd of other arrested people, leaving his papers at home. Now, when called, he does not answer to the name Bossadzhogly. (4) He could have been transferred to a different cell which, by mistake, was not shown in the ledger.

Not satisfied with these explanations, Beria asked if the four circumstances discussed really exhausted all possibilities, and whether the commander was sure there was no fifth reason; namely, that the prisoner could have escaped. Hearing that such an event was almost impossible, Beria retorted that the word "almost" had no place in a Soviet prison and should be erased from existence once and for all. After the conference Beria decided his first task would be to organize the whole prison system properly. Such an undertaking would show "Dear Sergo" that Lavrenty was extremely efficient and assuredly the right man for the job.

It was not hard for Beria to gratify his ambition. As a former student at the Technicum he had learned enough about the group of schoolmates who carried out illegal activities for the Bolsheviks. From his own experience, Lavrenty took two guiding rules. First of all, if the professors who had been against such activity were still alive and enjoying freedom, they belonged to the opposition. They must be arrested, and under interrogation would surely reveal a lot about the anti-Bolshevik movement. Beria listed their names on an arrest warrant to seize these men and bring them to his office for questioning. Second, in the educational institutions—in high schools and colleges—there probably were associations and groups of students who now were disseminating political propaganda against the present administration under various pretexts such as literary clubs, sports teams, or drama circles.

Beria sent a memorandum to the headmasters, deans and presidents of all educational institutions in Baku demanding exact lists of all students and details of their whereabouts. He also reminded the authorities that no student organizations were allowed, except the one under the special patronage of the State, which was led and controlled by professionally trained and officially appointed instructors. This was the Young Communist League, *Komsomol.*

Having obtained the lists of students, Beria marked the names of those who were children, or close relatives of people known to him previously as prominent Mussavatists, Mensheviks or Dashnaks. To be so singled out was equivalent to bearing the name of somebody already imprisoned or liquidated as an opponent. Beria knew very well that these youths, slightly over fourteen years old, could mean trouble to the State's security. Even twelve-year-old children could be used as couriers, messengers or as helpers in hiding emissaries coming to town. These brats had to be mercilessly punished. Beria marked the names of all students over twelve who sounded familiar or suspicious to him. Soon, every day one or two students, the older ones at first, were summoned from their classes to the dean's or headmaster's office. There, two plainclothesmen arrested them. The teachers reassured their schoolmates by telling them that their colleagues had been called home.

After several sessions of student interrogations personally carried out by Beria, the procedure started to bore him. If a boy tearfully mentioned some names or affirmed everything he was accused of, he had to sign his deposition and was sent back to his cell to be released in a few days, or rather, nights. But if he did not know anything, or stubbornly refused to answer questions, he was ordered to stretch out his arms and was beaten on the hands with a reed stick. If this did not help, Beria used to slap the victim's face. At first he did it like an exacting village teacher punishing a naughty pupil, or a craftsman cross with his clumsy apprentice for ruining his material, or like a brutish sergeant ordering about his recruits. But the more unyielding the boy being questioned was, the harder he would be hit, and with increasing frequency. The interrogator slapped the youth's left cheek with his right hand and his right cheek with his left hand. At first Beria did it as the simplest method of getting the needed information. Then he discovered it gave him a peculiar pleasure. Being an intelligent person, he soon found that the enjoyment he felt came not from the action of beating, or from seeing the victim bleeding and crying with pain. In other words, Beria was not a sadist. The pleasure generally had its roots in his consciousness of the tortured one's helplessness, and in his certainty that none of the victims would dare attack the interrogator, even in desperation. The realization of the prisoner's helplessness when he entered Beria's office was for Lavrenty more pleasant than the beating itself.

The schoolgirls, when interrogated, were not hit on their outstretched hands. Nor did they have to be especially stubborn to get beaten. But they had to endure some suffering to scare them into telling everything they knew. They were ordered to take off their shoes and lie on the floor with their face to the rug, to lift their skirts, and to pull down their underwear. Then Beria put one foot on the victim's neck and started horsewhipping the girl. The poor child was allowed to weep, but was warned beforehand that should she try to cry aloud, the punishment would never be stopped.[2]

Spanking the girls excited Beria sexually, and not only because they lay half-naked in front of him. Of course, a partly undressed girl was exciting to a man twenty-one years old, as Lavrenty was at that time. But this was not the main reason Beria's senses were affected, for after the first few strokes of the horsewhip the victim's body turned purple, started bleeding, and finally, when the system was unable to bear the pain any longer, the call of nature had to be answered. This sight was not pleasant, and the odor was disgusting. The true reason for the pleasure was the girl's youth. The more helpless and innocent the young girl was, the more exciting and desirable she became, and the greater the pleasure.

In spite of being mature, strong, healthy and animally volup-

---

[2] From the report of a female prisoner the author met in the Vorkuta hard labor camp in ASSR Komi Republic, where he was detained during 1941-1942.

tuous, Beria had led a spartan life and until then his sexual experiences had been limited. He knew that, with his head round as a watermelon, his wide, short nose, thick lips, rotten teeth, permanently perspiring stubby hands, and thinning hair, he was ugly. He had developed a complex about being ugly. He remembered from his school days how the girls laughed at him and giggled among themselves every time he attempted to accost them in a tea shop or in a public garden. In dance halls, they usually refused to dance with him. Aware that he was an ugly man, Beria despised women and wanted to take revenge and punish them. At the same time, he tried to look, if not handsome, then at least interesting, and he hated and envied any good-looking fellow he happened to see. His ambition to become a great personality and a dignitary wielding enormous power also had its source in his complex about his ugliness. Beria felt that, thanks to his position, he would impress people with his power, at least as much as he would if he were handsome. Rejected by girls he met socially, Beria had to limit his sexual life to relations with streetwalkers. As he was usually short of money, however, he could not spend much on them. The pretty young prostitutes were too expensive for Lavrenty, and he had to satisfy himself with old, cheap whores he loathed. Later, when he became *Komandarm* Gekher's friend, he participated in drinking orgies the man arranged in his one-room flat in the garrison's barracks. There, Lavrenty had to accept and be content with the wenches his friend brought in at his own expense, the middle-aged females of a vulgar type, with big bosoms and fat buttocks. The parties in their company were quite different from intimacy with a young, innocent girl. Now when Beria became a *Chekist*, he got a chance to take his revenge; he could punish young lasses for all the others in the past who had rejected him, or never showed up for dates as they promised and made fun of him.

In his work of smashing enemies, Beria had a trump card up his sleeve with which he could impress his powerful friends, Ordzhonikizde and Mikoyan, and Gekher. Before the "Week of Suppression of the Bourgeoisie," when Beria had produced proscription lists with names he was able to gather as a planted cog in the Menshevik Party's machinery, he did not reveal the names of several outstanding conspirators who were well hidden. He kept them secret at that time for two reasons: first, because in case of the failure of the revolution in Baku, these people might emerge on top, and could then help him; and second, because at the right time, Beria could sell his information about them as valuable goods. Now the right time had come. But Lavrenty realized he should not rush. Quite the contrary. Such a move should appear to be the grand finale after the difficult and exacting work of a long search. During the first two months of his *Chekist* activity, Beria started to sign the first arrest warrants for these people. This would really be a mighty blow to any opposition, if it still existed. The men caught this way should have been known to the Communist Party as its enemies, but until now they were still free, protected by fake papers and living at different addresses than before. Beria, who knew them personally, invented a special method. Since he always dressed in civilian clothes, and since his post was an obscure one, he was not afraid of being recognized as a *Chekist*. He used to take a stroll, wandering through the streets with two of his aides following him. They were Riza-Zade, a native of Baku and former executioner on Nargen Island, and Orbeliani, an Armenian agent and a spy. When Beria spotted one of his chosen victims in the crowd of pedestrians, or noticed the person working in a shop or in an office, he greeted him with a cordial smile and a kind "good day." The next day the person was shadowed by one of Beria's companions to his hidden lodgings. Later, during the night, he was arrested.

During one such walk Beria noticed a dubious character in a tattered jacket and trousers and a worn cap low on his forehead. He was sneaking through a narrow alley, avoiding observation. Beria ordered his ferrets to follow that man and bring him to the jail at once. He was the same man Lavrenty used to meet at the boat-house and he also was an acquaintance of Mir Djaffar Bagirov. Both Lavrenty and Bagirov were paid by him for their information. The same night of his detention the man was executed in the prison cellar. From now on Lavrenty could sleep peacefully. By ordering that character shot he got rid of a witness to his work for the *Okhrana*.

Lavrenty evidently did not take into consideration that his name, as well as the name of his friend Bagirov, was still on the pay list in the archives of the Tsarist Secret Police, and that not all those documents were burned or destroyed during the Revolution.

Beria remembered well the names of the well-to-do parents of the pupils he used to tutor in the past. They should be punished for humiliating him by paying him a few lousy rubles and for exploiting him.

Several weeks later, the success of that fruitful and efficiently performed task, accomplished by Beria, thanks to his shrewd preservation of these people until this moment, was fully rewarded by Ordzhonikidze. The good "Dear Sergo" soon promoted Lavrenty, appointing him Chief of the Secret Operation Department of the Deputy Chairman of the Azerbaijan *Cheka*.

12

A Banquet in Tiflis

IT WAS A HOT, sunny, dry summer in the Caucasus in 1921. Three
months had passed since the war between Georgia and Communist
Russia had ended, but the new regime established by the conquerors could exist only because of the Red Eleventh Army, which still
occupied the defeated country. The Committee of the Communist
Party in the Caucasus consisted of a handful of Old Bolsheviks:
Budu Mdivani, who after the Soviet invasion became Chairman of
the Council of People's Commissars in Georgia; Mamia Orakhelashvili, Chairman of the Georgian Revolutionary Committee; Philip
Makharadze; Alexey Svanidze, brother-in-law of Stalin's first wife,
Ekaterina; Sergo Alliluyev, father-in-law of Stalin's second wife
Nadezhda; Nestor Lakoba and a few others. This committee was
too small to be able to create the Party. A tiny group of workers, lured to Marxism by the promise of better jobs, could not pretend to the name of "the masses." Svanidze, in a letter to Stalin,
asked "Soso" to make a personal visit, to appear in front of his
countrymen to encourage them all and lift the general spirits.

At the end of June, Stalin arrived in Tiflis. His comrades were
sure that Iosif Vissaryonovich Dzhugashvili—Joseph Stalin's real
name—born the son of a poor Georgian cobbler, risen from a village boy to such power and authority, would impress the nation.

A few days after his homecoming, Stalin entered the main hall of
the Railway Workshop in Tiflis, where a great meeting had been

announced for ten o'clock in the morning. Over three thousand workers were gathered there, waiting for the speaker. Together with Svanidze, Alliluyev, Mdivani and Makharadze, Stalin mounted the podium, which was decorated with red banners. He was greeted more with cold curiosity than with admiration. To this crowd Stalin was simply a member of the Soviet Politburo[1] and one of the Bolshevik Commissars, but by no means a hero. Only sporadic and relatively light applause was heard when Makharadze introduced the guest of honor, Iosif Vissaryonovich Dzhugashvili Stalin, a great son of the country.

"Comrades! Brothers!" Stalin began in Russian.

"Why don't you talk Georgian?" someone shouted from the audience. "Have you forgotten your mother language? Shame on you!"

"I haven't forgotten my mother language," Stalin replied, "but I am using the language of the Great October Revolution."

A roar of laughter answered this declaration. The prepared speech could not be delivered.[2] The workers started asking questions. Why were they "liberated" from their independence and their freedom? Why were all meetings banned except those called by officials? Why was the press censored? Why are the Georgian grain, fruit and other products shipped away to Russia? Why is the Russian Army still occupying the country?

Stalin gave a short, sober reply to each and every question. His harsh voice was quiet and monotonous as always, but it was evident the speaker could hardly contain his impatience. The questions could have been asked *ad infinitum*. At last, Makharadze announced that Comrade Stalin would answer only three more questions, then the meeting would be over. After the gathering, the workers returned to their machines and tools. They were disappointed and depressed, realizing they had nothing in common with the new regime, which was instituted to repress them and to harm their interests.

Stalin and his associates decided to sit back and wait for at least a week or so. The people would have a chance to cool off and forget the unsuccessful meeting before the next one was arranged.

On the 6th of July 1921, the Central Committee of the Georgian

---

[1] Politburo: contraction of the Political Bureau of the Central Committee of the Communist Party.

[2] This incident was told to the author by someone from that audience, a man who later emigrated to the United States.

Communist Party in Tiflis called another meeting for the following day at eleven o'clock in the morning. This time, the duty of chairman was entrusted to the good-looking Nestor Lakoba, who had a more lofty mind and more pleasant appearance than the bald and bearded Philip Makharadze. With a friendly, disarming smile, Lakoba announced that Comrade Stalin would deliver a most interesting speech on which he had been working for several days; that was why the dear comrades should not interrupt the speaker. Amidst a deep silence, Stalin rose and with a deadpan expression on his dark, pockmarked face delivered, or rather, recited his speech titled *The Instant Tasks of the Communists in Georgia and the Transcaucasia.* In his lecture Stalin pointed out that the narrow-minded local patriotism of the three small Caucasian countries, Georgia, Azerbaijan and Armenia, was an obsolete phenomenon, dangerous to the attainment of the great common goal of international Communism. He emphasized that any nationalist uprising should be smashed and uprooted by all available means.

The speaker went on for almost an hour. When he finished, the factory hooter whistled, announcing twelve o'clock noon, lunch time. Everyone made for the exit to grab his sandwich box and a bottle of tea or coffee brought from home. Of course, nobody cared to ask questions. The meeting had been staged and timed wisely.

In the afternoon, the Central Committee prepared a farewell banquet for Stalin. In the Committee's headquarters, located in the former National Theatre building, a lavish dinner had been arranged. According to ancient Georgian traditions and old-time customs, the long table was covered with a white, handmade tablecloth embroidered in red, blue and yellow folkloristic designs. The room was decorated with bunches of fresh flowers in vases on the table, the windowsills and the floor. On the table in front of every guest stood a specially carved, large buffalo horn, or *khanty*, used by the Georgians as a drinking cup. These unique goblets are big enough to contain three or four bottles of wine each. At the head of the table was a tall armchair for the guest of honor, who was also to be toastmaster, or *Tamada*, in Georgian. To the right of Stalin-*Tamada* sat "Dear Sergo" Ordzhonikidze, who had come from Baku especially for the occasion of "Soso's" visit to Georgia. Next sat other veterans of the "Old Georgian Communists." The dinner had been arranged in the best Caucasian manner. The food and drinks were prepared following the rules of Georgian cuisine which—as everyone knew—was the best. There was *pilav*: rice with lamb and raisins; *mcvadi*: a Georgian shish kebob; *satsivi*: turkey with chestnuts; and red and white wines from the famous Kakheti vineyards. The guests were served by the three youngest members of their group. According to custom, nobody dared say anything before the *Tamada* started. But Stalin was in a bad mood, unwilling to talk. He realized he had not gained any popularity in the capital of his own country, but was treated as a visible symbol of a hostile occupant. The general atmosphere of the banquet was heavy with gloom. The young attendant standing behind the *Tamada's* chair was ready at any sign to put more food on his plate and to refill the horn with wine. When the dinner was drawing to its end, *Tamada* finally lifted his cup and said: "There are still many weeds in Georgian soil. We shall plow it anew. We have to liquidate any of the opposition, every one of our enemies to the very last. We shall exterminate and burn them out with a red-hot iron." Then he drank, emptying his horn. There was neither an answer nor applause. The most devoted members of the Party understood that these words presaged a bloody massacre of thousands of the best Georgians. In deep silence, they gulped down their wine. Now one of the oldest veteran Communists was expected to answer the toast. All the guests' eyes were directed on Mdivani; but he sat motionless, deadly pale.

Suddenly, the young attendant who stood behind the *Tamada* reached over to a small table nearby, lifted a spare horn full of wine and shouted in a fiery and enthusiastic manner: "We shall uproot and destroy the weeds, and we will plow Georgia throughout!" Then he drank the wine, emptying the horn to the last drop. Such behavior from a servant was against all regulations. But the dark, pockmarked face of the *Tamada* was all smiles.

The next day, Stalin was going back to Moscow. Just before his departure he left some orders for "Dear Sergo" Ordzhonikidze. Among them was the nomination of a chief for the *Cheka* in Georgia. The promotion went to the young attendant attached to the *Tamada* at the banquet the previous evening. The name of the daredevil eager to live, work and die for Stalin only was Lavrenty Pavlovich Beria.

13

Homecoming

ON THE TRAIN TO BAKU, Ordzhonikidze told Beria the good news and congratulated him on his success. "Dear Sergo" told his young comrade that he was truly happy about the promotion. Ordzhonikidze knew that Lavrenty was the right man for this tough post. However, Sergo still needed this efficient comrade who was so helpful in Azerbaijan. Since Stalin did not specify Beria's immediate transfer to Georgia, and since the Red Eleventh Army was still occupying the country and insuring security there, Ordzhonikidze decided that for the time being Lavrenty Pavlovich would remain in Baku to complete his job. Beria, who had to obey the wishes of his superior, expressed his great joy at not leaving his friend "Dear Sergo" so soon. He returned to his office in Bailov Prison to continue his work with the same eagerness as before so the Party would be pleased, despite the fact that this would prolong his stay in Baku. In truth, Ordzhonikidze, knowing Beria to be an over-ambitious man, was not particularly pleased by Stalin's choice.

In this feeling Ordzhonikidze was supported by one of his best associates, Kartvelishvili, an Old Georgian Bolshevik who did not trust Beria, regarding him as a sly careerist. To disperse Kartvelishvili's apprehensions, "Dear Sergo" assigned a certain Snegov as Beria's deputy. Snegov, a Communist Party functionary and Kartvelishvili's man, was told to watch Lavrenty closely.

Fortunately, some trails of the Dashnak and Mussavatist organizations traced by Beria in Baku led to Georgia. Through several reports of his agents—Riza-Zade and Orbeliaui, Kazasse, a Tatar from Crimea, and Tryandofilov, a Greek from the Caucasus—Beria learned that many prominent Mensheviks had fled from Baku too, and were living in Tiflis and other cities in Georgia and Armenia.

This information provided him with a good opportunity for frequent visits to his homeland in the line of duty. In Sukhumi, Beria had several informal meetings with Lakoba. The latter, after the Soviet invasion or, as it was officially called, "the liberation by the Workers' and Peasants' Red Army," became Chairman of the Central Executive Committee of the Soviets in Abkhazia. Although much younger than Stalin, Nestor Lakoba was one of his friends.

Lavrenty did not have to assure Nestor of his friendship and gratitude. On every occasion Beria emphasized that he felt very thankful to Lakoba and that he would always remember how helpful Nestor was when he, Lavrenty, had been imprisoned in Kutaisi. At that time it was Lakoba who alerted Kirov, asking him to intercede on Beria's behalf. This had happened just in time, before the trial, so Beria had been immediately deported without a sentence. Now it was quite understandable that, should Beria be transferred to Tiflis as soon as possible to become Chief of the Georgian *Cheka*, as was Stalin's wish, Lakoba would have in Lavrenty a great sponsor and protector. Nestor promised his support by sending word to Stalin.

According to his duties as Chief of the Secret Operations Department and as Deputy Chairman of the Azerbaijan *Cheka* hunting down Mensheviks and Mussavatists, Beria went from Sukhumi to Tiflis. There he had some personal talks with Philip Makharadze. The Old Caucasian Bolshevik assured Lavrenty he would remind "Soso" to bring Beria to Georgia. Lavrenty received the same promise from two other friends of Stalin. One was Philip's brother, Sergo Makharadze, who in 1920 tried unsuccessfully to overpower the Georgian Military Academy, and the other was Budu Mdivani. The last, but not the least important, promise of recommendation came from Mamia Orakhelashvili, also a good friend of Lenin and Stalin, and a member of the Council of the People's Commissars.

All these veteran Bolsheviks had no doubts whatsoever that Lavrenty Pavlovich was a promising young Communist with a wonderful future, that he fully deserved their friendship, and that it was therefore good for the Party to lend him a hand. Assured of their support for his transfer, Beria returned to Azerbaijan to work, as usual, for "Dear Sergo."

On March 10, 1922, a Congress of the Communist Representatives of Azerbaijan, Georgia and Armenia was called in Baku. On March 12 they declared the organization of the Transcaucasian Federation of these three Socialist-Soviet Republics. This convention was held under the constant surveillance of Ordzhonikidze and Beria.

Lavrenty's friends did keep their promises and sent letters to Stalin. Soon after receiving these pleas Stalin wrote to Sergo urging him to send Beria from Azerbaijan to Georgia at once. This time, Ordzhonikidze could not resist. He summoned Lavrenty to his office and informed him of the order. Beria was sorry to leave his post in Baku and "Dear Sergo," but there was nothing he could do. Stalin knew better than Lavrenty what was useful for the Party. Ordzhonikidze wished all the best to his young friend. After all, they were not to entirely sever their contact, since "Dear Sergo" was Chief for the whole of Transcaucasia. The two comrades shook hands and kissed three times, according to the traditional Georgian custom: first on the left cheek, then on the right, and again on the left. There were tears of emotion in their eyes.

Beria immediately handed over to his successor his duties as Chief of the Security Department and Deputy Chairman of the Azerbaijan *Cheka*. However, he took with him some of the top secret and most important files when he left Baku for Georgia.

Two days after his arrival in Tiflis in November 1922, Beria paid courtesy visits to the powerful Old Caucasian Bolsheviks: Alexey Svanidze, Sergo Alliluyev, Philip and Sergo Makharadze, Budu Mdivani and Mamia Orakhelashvili, thanking them for their help and assuring them of his cordiality and gratitude.

The next day, Lavrenty Pavlovich Beria went to his newly assigned office to take his post as Chief of the Secret Operative Division.

The headquarters of the Georgian *Cheka* in Tiflis were located near the State Prison on Olginskaya Street, on the outskirts of the city. When Beria appeared there for the first time, at eight o'clock in the morning, he was greeted by the authorities already awaiting his arrival: Commandant Dombrovsky, *Komandarms* Kvantalyani and Shulman, two of Shulman's deputies, Antishkin and Nagapetov, and a functionary known by his pseudonym, "Mikhail Moodry,"[1] an interrogator and executioner. Except Kvantalyani, all of them were Russians—not Georgians—sent there from Moscow after long service in the Russian *Cheka* under Dzerzhinsky. Dombrovsky was a high-ranking experienced *Chekist* and Shulman had been transferred to the capital of Georgia to be the head of the Investigation Department; the three others were his aides. In this small Caucasian country they not only represented the power, but were also men trusted by Dzerzhinsky, Stalin and Lenin. Therefore, they must be respected. Beria greeted them in a rather official manner, as became a newcomer. At the beginning, before one got firmly planted on one's feet, it was better to act like a modest, well-mannered officer than to try to impress already-established functionaries with having been sponsored by Stalin. It was wiser not to behave like a prima donna, a protégé of the Opera's director.

Before being shown through the building, Beria was eager to learn about the staff in the various offices of his new assignment. He was to become the boss of the Special Agency covering espionage and counterespionage, intelligence operations, arrests, and interrogations. Also, having been appointed Chief of the Secret Operative Division, Lavrenty Pavlovich had particular authority. This Department carried out the death sentences passed not by the court in public trials, but by the *Troyka*—three *Cheka* high functionaries, including Beria as the chairman.

Just after the new boss sat down in his office and started perusing local regulations prepared for Georgia in Moscow, there was a knock at his door. Beria answered. The door opened, and a man entered the room. He was young, around the new Chief's age, very cordial, all smiles and open-heartedness. He wore on his uniform the badge of a distinguished member of the Fighters for the Liberation of Azerbaijan. He only held the rank of Lieutenant but was visibly proud and happy about it. Now he rushed in to greet his classmate, a comrade he had politically and ideologically educated and helped to climb to the top of his career.

But Lavrenty could barely recall him. He did remember him from the Technicum in Baku and even from some clandestine meetings of the underground students' organization. But he was not at all cordial and did not show any sign of brotherly enthusiasm. He was glad to learn that Dumbadze had been promoted to the rank of

---

[1] "Michael the Clever."

Lieutenant and now was working in *Cheka* under Nagapetov's orders. Lavrenty recalled that the last time he had seen Evgeny was at the office of comrade Ordzhonikidze in Baku, but he did not know that soon afterwards Dumbadze had been transferred to their native Georgia and assigned to Tiflis. Perhaps Beria had heard this piece of news, but if he had, it didn't interest him. After the Revolution Evgeny joined the ranks of the Red Army which later took Baku, while Lavrenty cautiously had not participated in that action. But the fact that Dumbadze still was a small fry made it apparent that he never would be a high executive. For that he was too enthusiastic and too idealistic. He was just a mere rung on the ladder that others climb to get to the top. He was a born loser, a country sucker, and didn't count at all. A new Chief should not get too chummy with such a small cog. After exchanging a few words about the new post and work, and having thanked Evgeny for his congratulations, Lavrenty said he was sorry, but he had to go back to his work. He was too busy to waste his time, which belonged to the Party and its lofty aims, on unimportant personal talk. Perhaps some other time.

Later that same day Beria, accompanied by Commandant Dombrovsky and his two aides, visited every office in the Division. His subordinates expected a general meeting, with a speech by their new boss exhorting them to work untiringly for Bolshevism. But Beria did not plan anything of the kind. He knew the procedure was routine with every boss and he did not want to copy exactly what others did. In the afternoon he asked Antishkin, the man responsible for the imprisonment of political criminals, to advise him about the regulations of the local jail: How many people to a cell, the food and accommodations they were getting, the hours of rest at night, the roll calls, how often the inmates were taken for a stroll in the courtyard, and even how many times a day the prisoners were allowed to go to the lavatory. Beria intended to introduce some changes like those he had already established in the Bailov Prison in Baku, and which had proved to be right.

Soon the new Chief ordered plank beds removed from all cells as well as buckets with water, washing bowls, and pitchers with drinking water; these objects were to be sent to the neighboring city hospitals. The only utensil left in each cell was a so-called *parasha*—a big iron container that served as a urinal. The prisoners were taken to the washrooms only twice daily, in the morning and in the evening. Also, the morning and evening cup of tea they received should be sufficient to satisfy their thirst. The strolls in the courtyard were reduced to one, for fifteen minutes, every three months.[2] Taking away the beds made more space in each cell, so there was room for more people who had been arrested. The inmates were also denied the luxury of mattresses, pillows and blankets, which were donated to the hospitals. "The Soviet prison is neither a health resort nor a boarding house."[3] This was the saying created by Beria and it became a popular proverb for many years to come. The new Chief also ordered the rearrangement of some cellars where potatoes and coal were kept for the needs of the prison. These supplies could be kept in the prison yard in the open air, while the small, windowless basements now emptied could serve as transit cells for newly arrested men and women awaiting interrogation. After spending several days and nights in darkness, in solitary confinement without food and water, and usually stripped of their clothes, barefoot and in their underwear only, the persecuted were morally broken and their resistance was lowered. During the investigations they were unable to concentrate and to think carefully before answering the questions, and generally told the truth, or accepted everything suggested to them, which was helpful to the inquisitor.

In less than four weeks Lavrenty was again back in Baku. He went there because of a great event. On December 13, 1922, a Congress of the Representatives of Azerbaijan, Georgia and Armenia was held. As a result of their two-day debates, the delegates of those three countries, which previously, on March 12, constituted themselves the Transcaucasian Federation of the Socialist Soviet Republics, now decided to become one Transcaucasian Socialist Federated Soviet Republic. This resolution was accepted under pressure from Stalin, Kirov and Dzerzhinsky in Moscow, with the support of Ordzhonikidze and Beria, present at the convention.

In the spring of 1923, a few months after Beria took his post in Tiflis, the Circassian tribe in the Abkhazian area started an upris-

---

[2] This regulation the author experienced personally when he was imprisoned in the USSR during the rule of L. P. Beria.

[3] The author heard this many times in the USSR jail.

ing. An appeal had been directed to them, urging them to deliver voluntarily a certain number of horses for the Red cavalry. An added warning threatened to seize the animals by force if they did not obey the order. Since a Circassian cannot imagine life to be possible if deprived of his horse, the riots were unavoidable. The rebellion was rather small and insignificant, and soon was smothered by the local Abkhazian Red militia. It was, however, alarming enough to cause Beria to decide to go to Sukhumi and investigate the incident on the spot.

In a few days' time he arrived in Sukhumi, where he was met by Lakoba and other dignitaries. Beria soon immersed himself in office paper work, studying reports and files on the riots. But he did not sign any arrest warrants. The next morning he went to the village of Merkheuli to visit his family. His mother no longer worked at the Ierkomoshvilis. Such jobs as domestic servant had been abolished under the new regime. The old woman glanced with pride at her son clad in a uniform and wearing some decorations on his chest. Moreover, he was a high-ranking officer and came in a chauffeur-driven automobile. The whole village gathered around her house to gaze at the car, and everybody was happy to shake hands with this dignitary who had left their area as a poor boy. His older half-brother Datiko interrupted his work in the field and came at once to kiss "Lara" in front of all neighbors. While serving in the army he had seen automobiles, but for the younger generation in the village they were a miraculous novelty. Datiko's four children whose uncle this great personage was, became the envy of all the children. Lavrenty's younger brother Irakly worked on their small farm, while Tamara helped her mother with the household chores. She was eager to tell Lavrenty she was engaged. Her fiancé, a certain Nicholas Kvichidze, was only a simple, almost illiterate, poor boy, a mere street vendor who sold soda water, lemonade, *khlebney kvas*,[4] peanuts and sunflower seeds from a pushcart. But he was a handsome man and Tamara was madly in love with him. She was happy to learn from Lavrenty that in present times the poor, simple and uneducated folks were the rulers on behalf of the masses, and there was nothing to be ashamed of because she had chosen Nicholas, whom Lavrenty would like to meet.

A big dinner had been prepared to honor the important guest. All

---

[4] A bubbling beverage made of fermented dark bread.

the eminent personalities from the neighborhood were invited, such as the hamlet's chief and some elders, who toasted the visiting celebrity. It was late when Lavrenty left his native village; his mother bid her beloved "Lara" good-bye, and with tears of joy made a sign of the cross in the air, as the car started on its way back.

14

"Dear, Good Boy Lara"

THAT NIGHT BERIA CONTINUED his interrupted work in the Sukhumi prison. He learned a lot from the huge volume of reports. The leaders of the rebelling Circassian tribe had been either killed in the short battle or imprisoned. Several other arrests had also been made. There was no reason for imprisoning more of these simple Caucasian peasants and shepherds who just couldn't control their tempers and acted on the spur of the moment. The uprising, as such, was of no importance at all. But to the authorities it seemed most significant from the psychological point of view. It proved that an active spirit of liberty and a strong will to fight for independence was still alive among the people. This idea had to be eradicated and destroyed by all means—burned out with a red-hot iron, as Stalin had said. But if this were to be done successfully, it had to be done slowly and methodically, and in such a way that the leaders and organizers would not become suspicious. They had to be caught like flies in a cobweb. A spider never hurries when spinning his net. Therefore, the initiators of the uprising should be left alone, secure in the feeling that the authorities were satisfied with their easy victory over the small Abkhazian tribe. However, there should be some interrogations and the extraction of a few names of the men known as enemies of the regime. Such people had to be investigated and jailed at once.

Beria knew too many eminent Sukhumi citizens to find it difficult to select one for this purpose. But his first personal inquest, carried out in the city where he was remembered as the delivery boy of a dry goods store, had to be his great revenge and triumph. There was nothing pleasurable in grilling somebody unimportant and indifferent, but there was much satisfaction in questioning a person one knew well; to torture someone to whom you should be grateful. Beria remembered the old beggar in the square, about whom he later liked to tell his friends. He shared the feeling of that man who, loudly thanking his benefactor, wished him in his thoughts a sudden death and Hell.

In the middle of the night a military truck stopped on Dvorskaya Street in front of the dry goods store that had belonged to Svimoni Ierkomoshvili before the Red regime had confiscated and nationalized all shops. The aged gentleman had been awakened and told he had to come to the militia station, just to attend to some trifling formality. The officer on duty assured the merchant's wife that her husband would be released soon. It would be such an unimportant bureaucratic formality that he was advised not to take any additional clothing, a blanket or food.

Two days passed, and Ierkomoshvili still wasn't back home. His wife, learning that "her boy Lara" was in charge of the *Cheka*, went to his office to talk to him. But she was told that Commandant Beria was very busy and couldn't see anyone. The miserable woman rushed to the village of Merkheuli and asked her former maidservant for help. Both of them went to town, crying, and again asked to see Lavrenty Pavlovich. This time he let them come to his office. Beria advised them to be calm and assured them he didn't know anything at all about citizen Ierkomoshvili's arrest. If the man really had been arrested, he surely was as innocent of any evil as his wife claimed, and would be released immediately. Beria promised to take the case into his own hands and, of course, to do his best. He also asked his mother not to come to his office in the future, and not to interfere with his duties, which he always kept separate from family affairs. Such behavior on her part was quite inappropriate.

On the third day the old merchant was called for interrogation. When he entered the office, he was happy to see his protégé. He had no doubt that he could not find a more helpful friend to lend him a hand and end his misfortune.

Beria asked Ierkomoshvili to take a seat and offered him a cigarette. It tasted wonderful. Then Lavrenty Pavlovich asked the prisoner if he knew why he had been jailed, and explained there were many accusations against him. It was said that the merchant had exploited working people. Among these had been two salesmen in his store and a delivery boy who had to live in a small room at the rear of the shop and be on hand any time he was called. The capitalist was also accused of exploiting two maidservants working for him for very poor pay. These crimes proved clearly enough that the arrested man was a parasite, taking advantage of poor helpless people. But this was not all. Ierkomoshvili was a political personality, an eminent citizen of Menshevik leanings. Wasn't it so? Yes, Ierkomoshvili admitted it; anyhow, it was known he belonged to this party, the one that included the majority of Georgia's population. He did not hide his membership. Good thing he didn't. But what did he know about the recent uprising? Nothing at all. This did not seem probable. Beria insisted, but the merchant really wasn't involved with the mutiny of that small tribe and could not supply his interrogator with any details. All right, then, perhaps a longer stay in the jail would refresh his memory. Beria pressed the bell and ordered the guard to return the prisoner to his cell.

A few days passed and Ierkomoshvili had not been called for another questioning session. Neither had he been released. It seemed he was forgotten in his solitary cell in the basement by authorities too busy with many other cases more important to the administration to remember a single prisoner. His pleas to be seen again by the Commandant were left unanswered.

After waiting in vain for the return of her husband, Mrs. Ierkomoshvili decided to see dear Lavrenty again and beg for his help. It seemed unbelievable to her that "Lara," that young man she liked so much and had given his education as if he were her own son, could deny her his support if he were able to do anything at all. Especially as he was now a person of great power. She went to the State Prison and asked Beria's male secretary whether she could see Lavrenty Pavlovich. Beria received her at once. He assured her everything was going well, but there were still some formal matters to be attended to. She asked whether she could see her husband, and Beria gladly granted her request. Instantly he pressed the bell button on his desk and asked the guard who appeared to bring in the arrested Ierkomoshvili. Soon the prisoner was ushered into Beria's office. Seeing his wife, he was sure she had come to take him home, thanks to that "good boy, Lara." The old man, exhausted, emaciated, unshaved and in tattered clothes, looked like a sick wretch. His torn trousers had been deprived of suspenders, buttons and belt, his shoes were without laces. Eyes full of tears but smiling happily, he ran to his wife and embraced her. Sobbing, she kissed him. After a long while, uninterrupted by the "kindhearted Lara," Beria asked the man to sit down and calm himself until his case could be closed. Mrs. Ierkomoshvili returned to her chair, while her husband was shown a stool behind which the guard took his post. After glancing once more through the files, Beria recalled the old times of his childhood and his work in the dry goods store. He reminded them how he had to be the first one to get up before dawn to sweep the floors and clean windows; how he had to be always at hand, ready at every call of his master to hop to the corner tobacco kiosk for cigarettes, or to fetch the newspaper; how he had to make and serve tea innumerable times each day and run around the town with deliveries, whether or not he had to study and prepare his homework for the next school day. Yes, true enough, his tuition at the Technicum in Baku had been paid by the merchant, but the sum was not very large and the rich store owner only did it to show he had enough money to humiliate a poor boy unable to pay for his own education. Now the new, wonderful Communist regime, which had come to power thanks to the genius of Lenin and Stalin, was providing everyone with free schooling. Therefore, there was no need now for acts dictated by pride, such as in the case of this particular rich capitalist, who had exploited a poor boy and two salesmen working for him six days a week. Beria also reminded his former employer that he once fired one of his salesmen, a married man and father of two children. It is true that the man stole some money from the cash box. But it was for the first time and, if reprimanded, he would have promised never to do it again. But no! The unscrupulous merchant sacked the worker on the spot. Yes, Lavrenty Pavlovich agreed with the prisoner's remark that if the merchant had called the police and had the dishonest man arrested, it would have been worse for the culprit. But Beria did not believe in the sincerity of Ierkomoshvili's claim that he did not send the salesman to jail because the man had to provide for his wife and little children. The rich capitalist probably wanted to avoid a scandal, should the townspeople learn he employed thieves in his shop, because this would have harmed his business. That was the true reason for his actions. Then, the merchant used to have housemaids; one of them was Beria's mother. The boy saw with his own eyes that his mother had to kiss not only the hands of her mistress, but those of her master as well. Once the poor woman almost knelt before Ierkomoshvili, embracing his legs. Beria could not find valid the explanation of the arrested man that their maid-servant had never been forced to kiss her employers' hands—that this was simply a generally accepted custom and ancient tradition of the country. But by doing this, the woman wanted to show her gratitude and thank the good master for the generosity he lavished on her son "Lara." Beria retorted that by all means his mother should have been advised against behaving like a slave girl.

He, Lavrenty Pavlovich, also had to kiss his boss' hand. Of course, he wasn't forced to do it, but if he had resisted, he would have been called an arrogant youth and would be denied everything. His and his mother's employers were bourgeois, full of pride and capitalist prejudice, who enjoyed belittling and humiliating the poor peasants and workers whose existence depended on them, a couple of exploiters. Fortunately, the times of suppression were over once and for all.

Walking to and fro before his desk, Beria stopped briefly in front of the Ierkomoshvilis. The watery gray-blue eyes behind his pince-nez shone coldly and did not express any anger. In a calm and quiet voice, Lavrenty Pavlovich told them how wildly he hated them. But this was the past, done with and over; personal affairs wouldn't be discussed any more. There were now different, more important problems, dealing with the welfare and safety of the whole Bolshevik country, like the recent uprising in Abkhazia. Was the prisoner one of its organizers? No? All right, then. But maybe he knew the names of persons who were? Didn't he, really? Or perhaps he did not want to reveal them? No, he truly didn't know them. Well, that would be seen. Beria stopped in front of Mrs. Ierkomoshvili and, as a good boy should, "her Lara" slapped her face with his right hand. The woman almost fell from her chair, but another blow, this time from the left, kept her in balance. The merchant tried to rise to his feet in defense of his wife, but the guard standing behind his stool put his heavy hands on the old man's shoulders. Would the prisoner now reveal the names of the Communist regime's enemies? He didn't know any. All right! Beria hit the woman straight in the face, this time with his fist. Once, then twice.

Blood was trickling from her left ear and from her nose, her teeth had cut open her lips and a thin stream of blood started flowing down her chin. Ierkomoshvili begged the tormentor to stop. He was going to confess. It was he, himself, who instigated the uprising, using the simple, illiterate Circassians as a Mensheviks' tool in the fight against the new administration. Beria was back at his desk and recorded the deposition. Having put it in writing, he read it aloud and asked the prisoner whether everything had been stated correctly, whether the merchant accepted it as being exact and whether he would sign it voluntarily. The old man was willing to sign the document. The investigation was over. Commandant Beria allowed the couple to bid good-bye to each other and to kiss; then the woman was told to go home. When she left, Beria arranged and tidied the file with the confession and locked it in a drawer. Then he ordered the guard to take the prisoner back to his cell. He accompanied them. In the basement, Beria entered the cell with Ierkomoshvili, telling the guard to stay outside. He quickly took his pistol out of his pocket, put it to the old man's forehead and pulled the trigger. Then he left the cell. This was the first time Beria had killed a man. But Dumbadze, who saw him just after that execution, in later years said Beria managed his first shooting calmly and without any excitement—as if it were for him a trifle, an act as easy as lighting a cigarette.

It was early in the afternoon when Mrs. Maro Ierkomoshvili returned home. During the night she suffered a heart attack and died before the doctor arrived. Before that, however, she had been visited by several neighbors to whom she related what had happened to her that morning. Soon the execution of the merchant Svimoni Ierkomoshvili in the prison was revealed.

Later, one of the acquaintances of that unhappy couple escaped from Georgia and found shelter in Paris. From him, the author of this book learned the details related here.

15

Insurrection

JANUARY 22, 1924. The whole population of the Soviet Union, from Moscow and Petrograd to the most remote village in the Caucasus was deeply absorbed in grief and official mourning. On the previous day the great Vladimir Ilyich Ulyanov Lenin had died, but the sad news was not divulged until the following morning. The funeral was scheduled for January 27, at the Kremlin, and the general mourning was to cover a whole week. On that memorable day, at four o'clock in the afternoon, the coffin with Lenin's body had been carried to the crypt on the shoulders of Old Guard Bolsheviks, best friends and comrades of the deceased: Stalin, Molotov, Bukharin, Dzerzhinsky, Kamenev, Rudzutak, Tomsky and Zinoviev. Then Stalin delivered a speech vowing before the entire Soviet nation to pick up the flag that had fallen from the hands of Lenin, the Genius of the October Revolution, and to continue the dead Leader's task as became a faithful son of the Bolshevik Party.

Among other dignitaries, Yekukidze, Mikoyan, Ordzhonikidze and Kirov also attended the funeral. From Georgia, Lakoba, Orakhelashvili and Mdivani rushed to Moscow. Beria chose not to leave his post and was absent from the funeral. He had to keep an eye on Trotsky, who had come to the Caucasus two weeks earlier because of ill health and was now convalescing there. Beria realized that because Stalin was now coming to power, he, Lavrenty Pavlovich, was on the road to a real career. Therefore, it was much more useful to stay in Tiflis and trail Trotsky—who sooner or later would have to be eliminated—than become one more mourner attending the elaborate obsequies taking place in Moscow. The day after Trotsky left Moscow for the sunny Caucasus, being forced to follow the instructions of doctors who examined him at the Kremlin, Stalin attacked him in his speech at the Party Conference, pointing out his many mistakes and errors in judgment. That is why Beria calculated it was wiser to remain in Georgia as Trotsky's shadow.

In his eulogy over Lenin's coffin, Stalin promised the nation to continue Lenin's political line. It was obvious, however, that his words were only politic. People close to the Kremlin knew very well that there existed basic differences of opinion between the two men, that frictions had occurred, and that Lenin did not wholly approve of many of Stalin's decisions and actions, particularly his cruel, bloody invasion of Georgia. They represented two entirely different personalities as to creed, national origin, temperament, and background. All of these factors could play a part in the shaping of coming events and policy. Everyone who knew Stalin's mentality could be sure his discipline would be harsher than that of his predecessor. Thus, it was not difficult to predict that there would be protests, demonstrations and riots, and that as a consequence the Secret Operative Division would be more alert and efficient than ever before. Then, it could be expected that before a new Cabinet of People's Commissars was created and the new administration established in full power, uprisings would occur in some of the conquered countries, such as Azerbaijan, Armenia and Georgia. To prevent these outbreaks in Transcaucasia was the job of the Chief of the Georgian *Cheka*, Lavrenty Pavlovich Beria.

Beria—and not only Beria—remembered the unfriendly reception the Georgian railway workers gave to Stalin at the mass meeting in July 1921. Later on, several arrests had been made and there was no doubt about the hostile spirit prevailing among these workers. In the Tiflis railway plants Beria had a few informers who reported signs of dissatisfaction, and repeated to him critical comments and the names of the dissenters. Expressions of disappointment also occurred in other places and communities of Georgia. From his agents and investigators Beria received reports about a strong opposition movement in the longshoremen's communities in the harbor of Batumi. They also reported that in Kutaisi and Sukhumi there still existed organizations of the intelligentsia, Mensheviks, and officers of the former Georgian National Army, and that this independence movement was very active. The most dangerous center of unrest seemed to be Chiaturi, a big coal basin and manganese mine, where thousands of workers were employed.

Supplied with the names of several leaders of the opposition, Beria could have arrested them, thus preventing the uprising and bloodshed. This, however, would run counter to his plans. The job had to be done quietly, unemotionally, and inconspicuously. Rather, there should be fostered a great national anti-Communist movement, which then would be choked and smothered by Beria. He would thus become a Soviet hero and the savior of the Russian domination of Stalin's fatherland, Georgia, Transcaucasia, and the whole Caucasus.

On the other hand, the uprising should not be too well prepared, too popular, or too widespread. It would then become too hard to subdue. In view of this, some arrests must be made. But only single imprisonments, occurring sporadically.

Acting according to this premise, Beria decided to detain a few potential leaders still at liberty, intellectuals presumably opponents of the regime. These arrests had to be arranged in such a way as not to alarm the population. They had to occur at long intervals in order not to evoke any notion that the Security Police was suspicious. And detentions must not look like a mass hunt. The GPU— State Political Administration—previously called *Cheka,* must work with precision. During an eight-month period there were only a few arrests. The victims were eminent citizens such as Banya Tchikishvili, former Mayor of Tiflis, and Noah Khomeriki, a member of the Constituent Assembly that had prepared and declared a new democratic constitution for independent Georgia before her invasion by Red troops.

The uprising was organized by the National Underground Committee under Valiko Dzugheli, a General of the former Georgian National Army. The rebels consisted mainly of officers of the former National Army, alumni of the Military Academy in Tiflis, men who later hid themselves in the port of Batumi, in the caves of the Caucasian mountains, or worked in coal and manganese mines in the Chiaturi region disguised as simple miners. Weapons for the use of these fighters were mostly obtained by smuggling transports of arms from Turkey en route to Batumi and Sukhumi ports. Or they came from the weapons of the Georgian National troops that were not surrendered to the enemy, but hidden in cellars or basements, or else buried in the earth in the forests. The date for the insurrection's outbreak all over Georgia had been announced: August 25th, 1924, at six o'clock in the morning. The Chiaturi region in western Georgia would be under General Dzugheli's command, while Colonel Cholokashvili was to take command of the Kartalina area, in eastern Georgia.

Two days before the date of the outbreak, however, General Dzugheli was arrested. The Liberation Army of the western region found itself without a commander, left with Dzugheli's aide-de-camp, a young and inexperienced lieutenant, as its leader. It was feared that the imprisoned general, subjected to torture, might disclose important secrets to the enemy, and the uprising would be annihilated even before it took place. In view of this, Colonel Cholokashvili decided to strike first, one day before the agreed date. He expected the fight would be joined soon by the National Forces of the western region. The launching of a great revolution throughout the whole country was not too advantageous, but it seemed to be the only plan possible in view of the tragic capture of General Dzugheli.

On August 24, 1924, before sunrise, Colonel Cholokashvili's forces attacked the barracks of the local Red units and set them afire. Soon, fights erupted in the other districts: Kartalina and Katecchia. In a suburb of Tiflis the Soviet troops, attacked by the patriots, fled from their quarters and left the town. The partisans barricaded themselves and shot mortars, machine guns and light cannons; single snipers were firing from the tops of the trees.

A few hours later, one of the coal mines at Chiaturi had been blown up with dynamite. This was the signal for the general outbreak of the insurrection to the Liberation Forces in western Georgia. Hundreds of miners and workers armed themselves not only with machine guns, rifles and bayonets, but also with lances and sabers used by the national cavalry, long Georgian daggers, or simply heavy pitchforks.

The Soviet troops were unable to resist the first furious impact. Several fires were set in Sukhumi, Kutaisi, Batumi and in other towns. The volunteers were joined by fishermen, peasants and even schoolboys fighting with weapons taken from fallen enemies or comrades-in-arms.

Despite its start, which was not in accordance with the plan, the insurrection became too widespread to be easily smothered by the Soviet invaders. During the first week of hostilities, the patriots seemed to be victorious. But their equipment and supplies soon became inadequate. On the tenth day, the Red Army began to regain its predominance. More and more fighters, wounded, hungry, short of bread, drinking water and munitions, were taken prisoner, while the survivors of the surrounded platoons and scattered soldiers retreated to Batumi, to board ships that would take them to Turkey. In less than three weeks the uprising was over. The prison camps were full of captives, almost all of them wounded.

These men, however, not being officers and soldiers of a foreign enemy army, were not regular prisoners of war. They were simply rebels to be treated and punished as mere hooligans and destructive elements. If, in this case, Beria, as Head of the Secret Operative Division, wanted to show mercy, it would be interpreted as proof of generosity, but at the same time, of carelessness and weakness. Lavrenty decided to show his Boss Stalin that, to the Chief of the Georgian GPU Beria, these hoodlums were enemies of the Communist idea, the Soviet country and the regime; they were an abscess on the nation's healthy body, and they should, therefore, be radically and completely eliminated. Following Stalin's own idea Beria, the victorious Commander of the Security Police and the savior of the Communist rule in the Great Stalin's homeland, decided "to uproot the weeds of subversion and burn them out with a red-hot iron."

The next day, the Georgian Communist Party daily, *Zarya Vostoka*,[1] published in Russian, printed on its front page an official announcement advising that, as a result of the rebels' crushing defeat, the only legal Soviet Forces had taken over the mutineers' headquarters and captured three leaders of the riots: Valiko Dzugheli, General of the former Georgian National Army; Banya Tchikishvili, former Mayor of Tiflis and Noah Khomeriki, a member of the National Constituent Assembly. These three leaders of the hooliganish and irresponsible attack against the Soviet regime were tried and sentenced to death by a summary court-martial. They had been executed by firing squad the previous morning at five o'clock in the courtyard of Metekhy Castle.

---

[1] *Dawn of the East.*

This bulletin, however, told only part of the truth; namely, that the men had been killed. To be exact, these three Georgian patriots, arrested in separate times before the uprising, were never tried by any court martial, but had been murdered in their cells on Beria's personal order. The killing took place during the first day of the uprising, when the victims were in solitary confinement.

The extermination of the rebels took several months. The men were usually killed during the night, as a rule in batches of from 50 to 120. As the prison camp was quickly dissolved, the captives were transferred to the State Prison on Olginskaya Street or to the jail in Metekhy Castle and locked up in cells already so overcrowded that the guards, when slamming the doors, had to push on them, forcing them closed with their knees.

At night, the time when Beria liked best to work in his office, prisoners were called out individually from their dungeons. They were taken to Beria who personally questioned them, asking politely their names, ages, marital status, education, employment, home address and other particulars. After every person had signed an appropriate report, they were escorted by armed guards to the prison courtyard.

There they had to form lines for a roll call and wait until the whole batch was ready for transport. The action took several hours. The prisoners were told to sit on the ground, six abreast. The order did not have in view the inmates' comfort, but rather security reasons. It is much easier to run away from a standing position than when crouching on the ground. The prisoners were warned that any attempt to get up would result in the immediate shooting down of the culprit. When the whole batch had been assembled, there still were hours of waiting ahead; nobody knew for what. The guards, their rifles at the ready, circled the sitting men. Then the entrance gate opened, letting in a military truck—one, if there were about 50 inmates gathered in the courtyard; two or three, if there were more. Under the supervision of *Komandarms* Shulman and Kvantalyani and their deputies, Antishkin, Nagapetov and Moodry, the guards made each row of six men rise, one after the other. They tore from each prisoner's clothing—shirt or jacket—a strip of fabric and bound his wrists securely behind his back. Now the inmates were instructed to step onto the open platform of the truck and sit down with their backs against the driver's cab. When the first row of prisoners filled the width of the car, they were ordered to open their thighs so the next line of men could sit between their legs. When the truck had been fully loaded in this way, the tailboard was lifted and secured with hooks. It was then impossible for anyone to get up and try to escape. This new method of transportation had been introduced by Beria, who was able to concoct this crafty system thanks to his engineering studies.

Every such car then had an escort of four guards armed with rifles with fixed bayonets. They sat on top of the tailboard that barred the truck's exit, and pointed their rifles at the prisoners.[2] Following a small Ford with Kvantalyani and the Deputy *Komandar* in the Georgian *Cheka*, Antishkin, the trucks left the prison courtyard and rolled along the long narrow Olginskaya Street on their way to a place called Vake, on the outskirts of Tiflis. It was an empty plain, far from the town, a place where the clay soil was hard and unfit for farming. The truck stopped there, but the prisoners were not unloaded. Again they had to wait, sometimes for hours. At last an elegant shiny automobile appeared and halted at some distance. Now the captive patriots, hurried by the soldiers, were told to get off the truck. Those who did not obey orders quickly enough were speeded up by blows from rifle butts and kicks. After the last one had left the truck, the men were arranged in columns, six abreast, and led a few hundred yards farther, where trenches had been dug. Here they were halted, facing the trench, while the two officers emerged from the Ford. Now the prisoners were ordered to stand in one line. The officers, Kvantalyani and Antishkin, approached. Soon the execution started.

Even if there were mass killings of 120 persons, machine guns were never used. The whole procedure had to be carried out as silently as possible, so the townsfolk couldn't hear.

The execution over, the guards brought buckets of quicklime and shovels from the truck driver's cab. They poured the slaked lime over the dead bodies in the trenches and covered the ditch with dirt. If they noticed that someone was still alive among the cadavers, they finished him with a blow of a shovel or with a rifle butt. They dispatched their job efficiently and accurately, as well-trained GPU functionaries should, under the vigilant eyes of their superiors. When everything was finished, the commander of the

---

[2] A similar ride was experienced by the author when, among other prisoners, he was transferred from one Soviet jail to another, with one difference: his hands were not tied.

execution, Kvantalyani, approached the elegant automobile and, with a snappy salute reported that the orders had been carried out.

The authorities who watched the proceedings through field glasses and acknowledged the report, were two members of the Central Committee of the Georgian Communist Party: Mikhail Kakhiani and Ivan Maskhulia, and their superior, the Chief of the Georgian GPU Lavrenty Pavlovich Beria.[3]

By drowning the provoked uprising in bloodshed, Lavrenty had gained his goal. In appreciation of his outstanding service for the Soviet Union by crushing the rebellion in Georgia and cleaning that country of the parasitic element of nationalists, Stalin decorated Lavrenty Pavlovich Beria with the Order of the Red Banner.

---

[3] Evgeny V. Dumbadze, *Na Sluzhbe Cheka i Kominterna* (*In the Service of the Cheka and the Comintern*) (Paris: Mishen, 1930).

16

The New Era

EVERY NIGHT one or more trucks took the victims to the outskirts of Tiflis, to be shot on the edge of trenches—graves prepared for them —and buried under the personal surveillance of the Georgian GPU's Chief, Beria. Lavrenty Pavlovich could liquidate these men more quickly by skipping interrogations and using machine guns. Such a streamlined system was employed by "Dear Sergo" Ordzhonikidze during the "Week of Suppressing the Bourgeoisie" in Baku. But Beria, a methodical-minded student—as a future good architect should be—was in no hurry; he had plenty of time. He interrogated every one of his victims several times, for many hours at each session. Thus he collected a tremendous amount of material for his files and was able to order additional arrests. Simple peasants, the small fry who joined the uprising as riflemen, were treated by the Chief of Security as faceless beings, mere numbers. He asked the men routine questions and made them sign their confessions. Then he dealt every one of them a blow with his fist, straight into the teeth.

When, at the end of an inquest Beria hit such a prisoner in the face, he did it without passion or anger. He acted coldly, with premeditation, to prove to himself that his hand was sure and strong. He used it as training in case he should sometime need to use his fist to extort a confession from a more important victim, or to deal with someone deserving such correction. For the intelligentsia and the officers of the crushed Underground Army, Beria used a different sort of exercise. When interrogating such a person, he started the procedure in a pleasant manner, asking questions politely, sitting quietly behind his desk. Then, the Chief of the Georgian GPU—a civilized high-ranking officer and a college graduate—suddenly climbed onto the desk top and jumped straight down on the seated defendant, knocking him and his chair to the floor. Beria was a stocky, heavy man weighing almost 175 pounds, and when he landed on a man's chest he usually broke one or more of the prisoner's ribs. Standing on the fallen prisoner's body, Lavrenty continued his interrogation in a calm, indifferent voice. It was a very good exercise for a twenty-five-year-old man who liked to check up on his physical fitness. Often a tortured man, not being a milksop, called his tormentor the dirtiest of names. If this occurred, before moving off the fallen man Beria kicked him under the chin so hard the victim's teeth rattled. Then he proceeded with the interrogation, still in a detached, indifferent tone of voice. Afterwards, the inquisitor called a guard and ordered the inmate to be taken to his cell. A few nights later the man, his files completed, was called out of his cell and, together with a batch of prisoners, was driven in a truck through Olginskaya Street to the Vake suburb, where he was shot to death under Beria's supervision.

The liquidation of the former fighting patriots ended in the spring of 1925. In time, there were arrests of people whose names had been learned in the course of the interrogations, but the mass executions at dawn in the town's outskirts were discontinued. Some sporadic killings of the inmates occurred in the ancient Metekhy Castle dungeons. Such sentences were performed by men of a special branch, the Agential Department, whose boss was Beria's subordinate, Mikhail Moodry. The person condemned by Beria was taken to the prison's basement, formerly a coal or potato storage place. Besides the guard, the prisoner was accompanied by Moodry, also nicknamed "Helper of Death," or by one of his aides. Seldom was he left to Beria's personal disposal. In such cases Lavrenty used to come a little later, when the inmate already had been locked up in the basement. The windowless cellar had a heavy wooden door strengthened by iron parts and fitted with a small peephole. It was about 3 feet long, 6 feet wide and less than 6 feet high. There was no plank floor, only a clay one; the ceiling was black, the walls covered with mold from dampness persisting from time immemorial. On the walls were fresh white spots of quicklime, splashed there to cover the remnants of blown-out brains of prisoners who had been ordered to stand against the wall before getting a bullet from a Nagan revolver in their foreheads or in the back of their heads.[1]

Arrests in Tiflis and in other Georgian towns occurred every night, and the victims were people from all walks of life. Prominent Mensheviks, rich merchants, aristocrats, professors or lawyers disappeared suddenly from sight. So did some workers; a machinist or a miner from the Chiaturi coal and manganese mines simply did not show up on his regular shift. The co-workers and pals of the missing man did not inquire what had happened to him; they were afraid to ask such questions and could predict the answer, anyhow.

One night, the families of the three so-called leaders of the uprising were taken from their homes. Among them were the wife of the former Mayor of Tiflis, Banya Tchikishvili; the wife and ailing old mother of a member of the Constituent Assembly, Noah Khomeriki; the wife and four little children of the Chief of the former National Army, General Valiko Dzugheli. These women and children were arrested and deported to an unknown destination.

The Vake area became not only a place of mass murders, but also an invisible graveyard for people killed individually in the Metekhy Castle cellars and brought for burial to the outskirts. However, this state of affairs could not go on indefinitely. Beria, who once had ambitions to become an architect, now decided to erect a new district and a residential section in this Tiflis suburb. This idea initiated Beria's five-year plan for Georgia. From that time on, after exhumations performed at night, hundreds of bricklayers and stonemasons busied themselves building tenement houses. Many of the projects, supervised personally by Beria, were ready in a couple of months and tenants moved in during the summer. There were rows of three-story whitewashed houses divided into one-bedroom flats, with running water and electric installations; the rent was very low. The new road leading to the town was broad and soon had buildings on both sides, thus becoming a model street called Stalin Avenue. This new addition to the city was quite different from the ancient Caucasian town with its narrow alleys, bumpy

---

[1] Evgeny V. Dumbadze, *Na Sluzhbe Cheka i Kominterna* (*In the Service of the Cheka and the Comintern* (Paris: Mishen, 1930).

roadways, dirty squares and dilapidated houses. Lavrenty the architect decided to change completely the look of the old capital of his and Stalin's homeland and to remodel it into a modern city.

In August of that year Beria's younger sister, Tamara, was to be married to her beloved fiancé, Nicholas Kvichidze. Beria went to his native village of Merkheuli to attend the wedding. His old mother firmly insisted that the marriage be blessed by the Orthodox priest in church; she refused even to hear of a Godless civil ceremony in the People's Hall, a practice that had been recently introduced. In her opinion, such a civil marriage would be wholly meaningless; Tamara would live in sin, the mistress of a man. To placate his mother, her "dearest Lara" joined the religious wedding and, together with his family and friends, went to the church service. He even left a lavish donation on the silver tray, as a good Georgian boy should.

Lavrenty brought the newlyweds many valuable gifts, mostly jewelry—surely robbed from his rich victims, as some of the villagers whispered. He also had a lovely gift for his mother, something she always dreamed about: a gold necklace with a gold cross set with large rubies. Of course, Beria was sorry about the bad luck experienced by the Ierkomoshvili couple. He assured his worried mother he had done everything possible to free the poor man, but he, Lavrenty, was not so powerful as one might suppose and did not have influence enough to save his old benefactor. Lavrenty also promised a good job to his new brother-in-law. The latter's lack of education was not an insurmountable obstacle, so the illiterate soda water street vendor, Nicholas, need not worry. He was told to come to Sukhumi and talk to Commissar Lakoba, who would nominate him Chief of the Water Supply Workers' Union. "Good Lara" did not forget to help his two brothers, either. They were told to see Commissar Lakoba the next day at his Sukhumi office. He would make Datiko the Deputy Manager of the Oil Syndicate in Sukhumi, while the younger one, Irakly, would also get a good job in the Abkhazia region.

The wedding feast was lavish, with plenty of food, wine, music and dancing. Lavrenty danced with his sister, who wore a beautiful national wedding dress adorned with colorful ribbons. He also whirled in a dance with several of the beautiful village girls, and with his good old mother.

A few days later, Chief of the Secret Operative Division, Lavrenty Pavlovich Beria, was back in his main office, in the ancient castle of Metekhy, now the Georgian GPU prison. From this fortress, perched atop a high hill overlooking the town, he watched over the security of the Soviet power in the once-free Caucasus.

In Tiflis Beria found another problem awaiting solution. Evidently many of the newly nominated Bolshevik dignitaries were enjoying to the full their recently obtained power, but were misusing it or did not understand it. There were already grounds to prove that Georgia's People's Commissar of Agriculture, Alexey Gegechkori, was by no means a model Party member whose behavior should be admired. Dumbadze was on duty when the authorities were called to the luxurious Orient Hotel in Tiflis. There they had to bodily overpower Commissar Gegechkori, who had taken a whole floor of the hotel and was throwing a party for his friends and deputies. Some of the girls working in his Department were ordered to come. The party turned into a drunken orgy, the girls were stripped of their clothes and had to submit to the attentions of several of the men present. A few young boys also were provided for the revelers who were homosexuals. When this enjoyable celebration was at its climax, Commissar Gegechkori, completely drunk, drew his military Nagan revolver and started shooting at random.

Beria could order Commissar Gegechkori's arrest, but he did not act rashly. Lavrenty preferred to work with a cool mind. After examining the reports, Beria called Dumbadze to his office and questioned him. The report showed beyond any doubt that People's Commissar Gegechkori was a drunkard and was responsible for the murderous brawl in the Orient Hotel where one of the girls was shot to death. Dumbadze was an eyewitness to the horrible ending of the orgy and was eager to proceed with the inquest in the Georgian Agriculture Department and to take an action against its Commissar. Beria, however, halted any further investigation. The case was serious and could dangerously undermine the prestige of the Communist Party in the Caucasus. The Chief of the Georgian Secret Police told his subordinate to sign his testimony, which would be used at the appropriate moment, and assumed responsibility for the matter himself. Dirty linen should be washed at home, not in public. The conversation was over, Dumbadze was dismissed and could go back to his routine, everyday duties. Gegechkori's case could wait. Lavrenty decided to save the life of the Commissar not because he liked him so much, but because Alexey "Sasha" Gege-chkori was a very close friend of Avel Yenukidze, Budu Mdivani, Philip Makharadze and Sergo Ordzhonikidze. Thus his hushed-up case could be useful at some later time to use as leverage on them, if they were at the top. Or, it could be exposed and used against them, if the right time came to topple them over.

17

Two Kidnapings

ON THE ROOFS of Metekhy Castle and the State Prison on Olgin-skaya Street the red flags were lowered to half mast for one week.

Only July 22, 1926, the front pages of the dailies published in Tiflis brought sad news to the people. One of the best Bolsheviks, one of the unshakable fighters who had helped the Genius Lenin and the Great Comrade Stalin to win the October Revolution and later to strengthen the Soviet power, had passed away. Two days before it was announced, Feliks Dzerzhinsky, the creator of the *Cheka*, later the GPU, subsequently renamed the OGPU—Unified State Political Administration—died in Moscow while at his post of duty. He died of a heart attack while attending an important meeting at the Kremlin. He was just 48 years old.

Before the news appeared in the local papers, Beria called the editors to his office for a briefing and ordered them to write long biographical articles about the Soviet hero, one of the genial Lenin's and Stalin's closest friends. Quotations from Dzerzhinsky's writings and speeches were to be inserted, and the deceased's martyrdom in exile in Siberia, as well as in the Tsarist prisons before the Revolution, were to be emphasized. Beria was aware that Dzerzhinsky, known by the Georgians for his memorable visit to their country in 1921, was hated by the whole Caucasian nation, so his merits as an Old Bolshevik should be built up.

From his personal informers, however, Beria learned that Dzerzhinsky died of an apoplectic stroke while attending a Politburo meeting at the Kremlin. The stroke had been the result of a discussion with Stalin, whom the Chief of the OGPU tried to oppose in some unimportant matter. Stalin became angry and cursed him, shouting in an outburst of rage. Dzerzhinsky became so frightened he fainted and died before a doctor could be summoned. Beria despised that Polish nobleman for being mortally scared by a few dirty words used against him. The man who had proved to be such a coward had written in one of his papers: "I am in the front line and I want to be merciless, to tear the enemy to pieces as a watchdog would do."

And now that butcher of the Kronstadt sailors and of many thousands of civilians was so shocked by Stalin's bad-tempered outburst that he died on the spot. What a "True Knight of the Proletariat" —as he was generally called. A dirty craven, a typical product of the decadent aristocracy.

Beria condemned Dzerzhinsky with all his might.

The day after the official announcement of Dzerzhinsky's death, Lavrenty sent to the Politburo in Moscow a telegram with words of deepest grief and sympathy. Realizing that someone would be needed to fill the vacant post of OGPU Chief and that the new candidate would be nominated very soon, he expected to be chosen. He had been made by Stalin Chief of their native Georgia's *Cheka*, in Transcaucasia. He had influential friends, Lakoba, Orakhelashvili, Mdivani and Makharadze, and he was a protégé of Kirov, Ordzhonikidze and Mikoyan. Finally—a most important detail—for several months in 1925, he, Beria, had been Trotsky's shadow, sending weekly reports to Stalin of the man's activity at every hour during the day and night.

However, after three days the vacant post had been permanently entrusted to Vyacheslav Rudolfovich Menzhinsky, the acting Chief of the OGPU who, as Feliks Dzerzhinsky's deputy, assumed his responsibilities immediately following his death. That such a nomination should be signed by Stalin was unbelievable, but true. Menzhinsky was a Pole and an aristocrat, like his deceased boss. It was hard to understand how Stalin could have nominated him; but still, he had; the reality had to be accepted. Lavrenty knew well that if he wanted to achieve his supreme goal, he had to keep his mouth shut, do the job at hand and wait for the right moment.

Beria was busy with many activities besides his regular duties of supervising the work of the Secret Operation Division. It was Lavrenty's job to indoctrinate the Georgian population with Communist ideas. The editors of the newspapers published in the country —*Pravda Gruzzi*[1] and *Zarya Vostoka* were printed in Russian, while *Communisti*, a Georgian language paper, and several other dailies and periodicals—not only had to send their galley proofs to the censor's office for approval, but had to appear at weekly meetings in the Security Office, where they were told what they were to write about in their lead articles. According to Beria's Five-Year Plan of reconstruction and indoctrination in the schools, teachers were instructed to apply pressure to the pupils, persuading them to join the *Pioneers*, the Soviet children's organization, while the university students were urged to enter the ranks of the *Komsomol*. Special agents and agitators were sent to small towns and villages to organize public meetings at which they delivered speeches praising Stalin and the Soviet regime. In order to bring up the new generation in the spirit of Communism, Lavrenty took care to establish schools in every town and in the rural communities consisting of a few villages each. It was an innovation for Georgia that schooling was obligatory under penalty to the schoolchildren's parents. The teachers, however, had to stress the ideological and political significance of the Soviet rule. In Sukhumi, Beria ordered the dilapidated one-story high school, where he had obtained his basic education, torn down and replaced by a modern three-storied structure with large, well-lighted classrooms. Podgornaya Street, where the school was located, was renamed Beria Street. In Tiflis, which was progressively becoming a clean and modern city, two universities were established, primarily for members of the Young Communist League and for children of Party members. Several new schools were also opened in Batumi and Kutaisi, while Sukhumi was granted a Technicum. Throughout Georgia education was free of charge. The teachers were compelled to belong to the Party, and their lectures had to be composed primarily of political propaganda. Every lesson was supposed to start with a reading from the works of Marx, Engels, Lenin or Stalin. Quotations from the works of these four Communist geniuses served as material for lectures, lessons and home assignments. Sukhumi, Batumi and other towns were cleaned up; their mayors were made responsible for smooth-

---

[1] *Georgia's Truth.*

ing the roadways and paving new sidewalks. The façades of the houses were ordered repainted. In the Colchis area, in the Mingrele Valley near Batumi, drains had been laid in the many hundreds of acres of swamps. This damp region in the Poti Delta, infested with swarms of mosquitoes, had been spreading malaria and yellow fever epidemics throughout this part of western Georgia every year.

Slowly, people were forgetting the ruthless bloodshed that followed the thwarted national uprising. The Georgians, whose towns had been improved and who received free education, hospitalization and medical attention would even be ready to praise Beria, if there were not still secret arrests every night. However, the OGPU's armored cars and platoons were still patrolling the towns and townships in the vicinity of mine basins. Every time, five to ten people from the intelligentsia, as well as peasants and workers, were arrested. Nobody knew under which code the arrests were decided and the people dragged from their homes. It was not known whether these arrests were carried out in order to frighten the citizens into submission, whether the victims were chosen because of their social origins, activities or something in their past. They could also have resulted from informants' tips, or simple gossip. Anyway, the terror still lasted and nobody could be sure of sleeping peacefully through the night.

Beria was in reality the master of life and death of the whole population of Georgia.

On October 23, 1926, Trotsky was expelled from the Politburo and, a year later, from the Party. In January 1928 he was banished from European Russia and sent to Asia, where he was compelled to live in Alma-Ata, the capital of the Asiatic Kazakh Soviet Republic. While there, despite constant surveillance by local and Russian agents of the OGPU, he busied himself writing a defense against accusations of being hostile to the Soviet regime and a traitor, as Stalin once had called him at a Party Conference. Among the plainclothesmen watching him were two planted by Beria, who wanted firsthand reports of the activities of the former People's Commissar of Foreign Affairs and of War, and the once Commander-in-Chief of the Red Army, whom Beria himself had spied on previously in Tiflis. It was evident that sooner or later Stalin would want to crush Trotsky, although now the latter had too many thousands of followers and was still too popular to be destroyed. Nonetheless, it was good to be able to perform this service for Stalin.

In the meantime, however, Beria faced a problem of his own which he had to solve. A delegate representative of the OGPU, arrived in Tiflis from Moscow. Supposedly, his was an official courtesy visit. But Beria soon learned that it was a kind of inspection and that the delegate was a plenipotentiary and protégé of Menzhinsky. This unwelcome guest was eventually to replace Beria, whose fate had not yet been decided. There was no time to lose. Lavrenty Pavlovich immediately left for Moscow. The very next day after his arrival in the capital Beria talked to Stalin and the delegate was recalled from Tiflis. Along with this man Beria managed to arrange a call back to Moscow Headquarters for *Komandarms* Dombrovsky, Shulman and their deputies, Antshiskin and Nagapetov. Those functionaries Lavrenty decided to replace with his old pals from Baku, Goglidze, Merkulov, Dekanozov and Kobulov.

During his stay in Moscow, Lavrenty, as Chief of the Georgian OGPU, was given a new special assignment. He was told to see Mikhail Trilisser, Chief of the OGPU's Foreign Administration. There Beria learned that a certain Miasnikov, an agent of the Armenian OGPU, who had been working in Erivan in the Armenian Financial Administration, had escaped to Persia. The latest news about him was that, after crossing the border in the town of Julfa, Miasnikov went to Tabriz, where the local authorities stopped him as an illegal immigrant and put him into prison. If, however, he insisted on being a political refugee and asked for asylum, he could not be extradited. The Central Committee ordered that the escapee be brought back to Moscow alive, and the Tiflis OGPU was charged with the task. While carrying out the assignment, Beria was instructed to keep in touch with the Chief of the OGPU's Oriental Section, who would meet the Chief of the Georgian OGPU in his hotel room in a few hours' time. In the afternoon, Lavrenty awaited his visitor in his suite at the Hotel Select, which was maintained by the OGPU for eminent functionaries. Exactly at the appointed time the chief of the Oriental Section of OGPU appeared. He was Georges Agabekov.[2]

Agabekov, given his present position after his return from a secret commission in Persia, informed Beria that both of them had to go immediately to Georgia, to prepare the plan for Miasnikov's

---

[2] Georges Agabekov, *OGPU: The Russian Secret Terror* (New York: Brentano's, 1931).

kidnaping. He repeated what Trilisser had stressed before, that the captive had to be brought back alive. The next morning, Beria and Agabekov left Moscow for Tiflis. During the three days' trip Agabekov tried to abandon small talk and turn the conversation to more important matters. He mentioned the many problems the Party had had to face recently, because this time the "Rightists" were starting a campaign against the Central Committee. But Beria smelled a provocation and preferred to play the part of simpleminded policeman, unaware of the great inner politics and entirely absorbed by the fulfilling of his local duties.

It was late evening when their train reached Tiflis, but there was no time for rest. They had to act fast. In a few hours' time, they organized the first meeting on the matter of Miasnikov's abduction. At the conference, Beria and Agabekov were joined by Kaul, Head of the Secret Operative Section of the OGPU in Georgia, and a certain Tite Lordkipanidze, one of Beria's subordinates.

Kaul advised the gathering that Miasnikov was in the Tabriz prison under special guard. The Persian authorities realized who he was, and they were aware of the possibility of an assassination attempt. The informant who related the details to Kaul was a specially trained man sent to Persia to abduct Miasnikov. But he had found the job impossible. The four-man committee would have to invent some subterfuge.

Lordkipanidze suggested attacking the prison, kidnaping Miasnikov and recrossing the border with the victim in a car. To avoid the possibility of the Persian frontier guards stopping the car, Lordkipanidze proposed to order the Red Army Frontier Troops to engage in some shooting and tie down the Persians in a border incident. Beria would eventually accept this plot, but at first he advocated instead bribing the Tabriz chief of police, a man who had previously accepted money from the Tiflis *Cheka*. Agabekov was not quite sure the scheme would work this time and announced that someone should go to Tabriz and examine the situation on the spot. He offered to go to Persia personally and explore the possibility of bribing the police officer in exchange for having the prisoner delivered to the border. All he needed was a passport enabling him to enter Persia. Beria did not accept the plan wholeheartedly. He realized it was quite possible that after getting to Persia with enough cash to bribe the Tabriz police chief, Agabekov would keep the money for himself and remain abroad. It was four o'clock in the morning, and the men gathered still had not arrived at any conclusion when they received a long distance call. It came from the Moscow OGPU Headquarters. The authorities had decided to desist from abducting Miasnikov. The plan for the kidnaping had to be postponed. That time Lavrenty lost an opportunity to display his skill as a kidnaper.

It was revealed later that Miasnikov succeeded in bribing the Tabriz authorities, and was allowed to depart for Paris.

Agabekov returned immediately to his duties in Moscow, while Beria, Chief of the Georgian OGPU, with power over the whole of Transcaucasia, a few months later received a different, very delicate and responsible task. This time the target was Leon Trotsky.

Although living in exile in faraway Alma-Ata under the watchful eye of the local OGPU, which sent weekly reports to Moscow, Trotsky managed to mail many letters to his followers, opposing Stalin's rule.

At the beginning of 1929, a rumor spread in Moscow to the effect that Trotsky was seriously ill, and that the Central Committee barred him from receiving any medical treatment. Trotsky's place of exile, a primitive town in Kazakhstan, was said to have been chosen by Stalin because of its lack of good doctors and efficient medical facilities. Trotsky, a man in poor health, wasn't supposed to survive long under such conditions.

In the meantime, the OGPU reports mentioned Trotsky's increasing popularity and the constant flow of sympathizers visiting him in ever greater numbers. Even several of the men sent as spies from Moscow to Alma-Ata became Trotsky's followers instead of spying on him.

The Politburo could not ignore Trotsky any longer; it had to act. As a result of secret talks with the Turkish representative in Moscow, the Kremlin got from the government in Istanbul every assurance that Trotsky and his family would be granted asylum in Turkey if they were expelled from the Soviet Union.

On January 18, 1929, Stalin asked the Politburo to have Trotsky deported to Turkey. With the exception of Nikolay Bukharin, who opposed the plan, everybody accepted it. The transfer had to be arranged with special precautions. Since Trotsky had many followers who would gladly fight in his defense, and since several armed OGPU agents had joined the ranks of his supporters, it would be easy to trigger a revolt that could spread beyond the small town of Alma-Ata and have dangerous repercussions even in Moscow.

These fears were not groundless. When the OGPU agents appeared at Trotsky's place to escort him, they met with a certain resistance.

They came under the supervision of Pavel Petrovich Bulanov, a secretary of Menzhinsky's deputy, Yagoda. Bulanov was a confidant of Stalin, who had personally commissioned him to escort Trotsky abroad.

The finishing touch was supplied by Beria. At night, a group of Bulanov's men surrounded the little house hidden in an apple and cherry orchard, overpowered Trotsky and took him and his family to Georgia by force. There, accompanied by Beria, they were taken to the port of Batumi and, under armed guard, put on board a steamer to Istanbul.

18

Family, Friends and Subordinates

THE SMALL HUT on the outskirts of the village of Gori where Iosif
Vissarionovich Dzhugashvili—Joseph Stalin—was born on December 21, 1879, had been turned into a shrine: the Stalin House and
Museum. Originally it was a poor, dilapidated abode, the former
home of Stalin's parents. Here also, Stalin's father Vissarion Ivanovich Dzhugashvili, a cobbler by trade, had his workshop where he
repaired boots and sandals, drank, and beat his wife Ekaterina.
Here also he died, when Iosif was eleven. He died in a drunken
brawl, stabbed with a knife. When, however, Beria decided to
transform this small hovel into a shrine to Stalin, it soon became
unrecognizable. Using his skill as an architect, Beria erected over it
a lavishly designed building, forming a marble canopy over the old
shack. Inside, every detail had been preserved, not as an exhibit,
but as a relic piously kept there with the greatest devotion and
most tender care.

Stalin's mother, after being persuaded by her son to move to
Tiflis, lived there in a luxurious house chosen for her by Beria from
many confiscated private estates. It was a magnificent old palace
surrounded by a huge garden. Beria himself had a splendid apartment in the same city and an equally beautiful summer house, or
dacha, in the capital's suburbs, less than a half hour's drive from
Stalin's mother's residence. Both the apartment and the *dacha* had
previously belonged to two Georgian democrats who were exe-

cuted by Beria and whose entire possessions had been confiscated —officially, for the State—and turned over for the use of Beria as Chief of the Georgian OGPU.

Beria's mother did not want to abandon her hut in the village of Merkheuli. She opposed all suggestions offered by her "dear boy Lara" about leaving sunny Abkhazia for big, faraway Tiflis, Lavrenty tried many times to talk his mother into living near him and Stalin's mother, but he never convinced her. She did not change her mind to her last day. In the summer of 1929, Tamara wired Lavrenty that their mother was quite ill. When he arrived at her home, Tekle Beria was already dead. After the funeral, there were some domestic problems for the powerful Lavrenty to solve. His brother-in-law Nicholas Kvichidze, former street vendor, later Chief of the Water Supply Workers' Union, although only half-literate, proved smart enough to embezzle, with the help of his two deputies, large sums of public money. Tamara implored her omnipotent brother to help her. Fortunately, Lara was a very understanding man toward his relatives. It required Beria to stay a few days in Sukhumi. But thanks to his intervention, the trial did not result in great harm for his in-law. The two deputies got jail sentences of seven and ten years respectively; Kvichidze was acquitted. Soon afterwards he was nominated Director of Gagri, a health resort near Sochi, the famous seaside locality where Stalin, Mikoyan, Kirov, Ordzhonikidze, Beria and other great dignitaries had their *dachas*. These villas had previously belonged to Georgian magnates and aristocrats who had either fled abroad in time, or had been arrested and executed by the *Cheka*. Two of these summer houses were especially luxurious, beautiful estates with enormous parks, classical statues, fountains and tennis courts. One, called *Zubalovo*, was owned by Stalin, while the other, *Maindorf*, had been taken by Mikoyan. Both names, Zubalov and Maindorf, were well known to Stalin and Mikoyan. They were the names of oil magnates who operated refineries in Batum and Baku. They also had similar villas near Moscow and in Baku, where they had permanently lived. Their refineries had been targets of strikes arranged by Stalin, Mikoyan and their agents. On the first day of Azerbaijan's Soviet occupation, Mikoyan ordered these two rich men and their families arrested and executed that same night. Their houses in Baku had been taken by Ordzhonikidze, Kirov and Mikoyan.

Lavrenty also looked after his stepbrother Datiko, promoting him to the rank of Chief of the Oil Syndicate in Sukhumi, while his youngest brother, Irakly, became Director of a health resort trade organization called *Kurort-Torg*.

During his stay in Abkhazia Beria lived on his luxurious special train, in which he had traveled to Sukhumi. It was switched onto a siding some distance from the station building. The train consisted of three Pullman cars: a sleeper, a saloon car equipped with a bar and a restaurant wagon. The evening before Beria planned to depart for Tiflis he was approached near the station by a young girl about sixteen years of age. She was of medium height with black eyes and a creamy white complexion. The girl had come from her native Mingrelian village neighboring Lavrenty's Merkheuli to ask Beria to intercede for her brother, who had been arrested. She was positive that one word from the powerful Chief of the Secret Police would be sufficient to release her brother from his unjust imprisonment.

Beria noticed the beauty of the girl. To get more details about her brother he invited her into his train—but not to the saloon or the restaurant. In his bedroom compartment Lavrenty told the girl to undress. When, frightened, she started to leave the car, Beria locked the door. Then he slapped her face, twisted her arms behind her back, pushed her onto the bed and pressed her down heavily with his body. The fragile girl was overpowered and raped. A few minutes after everything was over, Beria let her go free. Now he could call a guard and order him to take that little waif to a jail. Or, he could just kick her out onto the railroad track. But looking at her beautiful tear-streaked face, Beria knew that in less than half an hour he would desire her again. He locked her up in the compartment and went to the restaurant car for supper and some vodka.

Beria kept the girl the whole night. The next morning he told his orderly to bring breakfast for two. Later, before leaving for his duties, Lavrenty locked up his victim again. Beria was not only spellbound by the freshness and charm of that girl, he realized she was the type who appealed completely to his senses. She was young and innocent, but looked mature. She was delicate, but by no means thin. She had small breasts, big eyes that cast demure glances and a full, ripe mouth. Lavrenty saw that it would be stupid of him to throw such a creature away right now.

Beria spent a few more days in Sukhumi in order to supervise the progress of the Five-Year Plan of 1928-1933 for the improvement of the country roads and highways, construction of new dwellings, hospitals and schools. During this entire time he kept his little prisoner locked up in the train.

The settling of the family affairs of his sister and brothers made Beria aware of the fact that he, too, should arrange his own personal life. All his superiors and friends—Stalin, Ordzhonikidze, Mikoyan, Kirov—were married. The sole bachelor was Yenukidze, but he was a handsome seducer, a skirt-chaser, and since the Party enforced severe moral rules, this weakness could sooner or later be turned against him. Lavrenty, who liked girls in their early teens, which was not a secret, would be safer if he married, even for appearance's sake, than if he stayed single.

Beria was a man of quick decision. He came to the conclusion that he should be married too. It would strengthen his position. The night Lavrenty Pavlovich left Sukhumi for Tiflis, he took his captive with him. That was the way the little Nina became his wife.

Beria arrived in Tiflis with his new bride. On the day the Chief of the Georgian OGPU returned to his office in the dreary ancient Metekhy Castle, there were two surprising pieces of news awaiting him. The first was that Georges Agabekov, Chief of the Oriental Section, the man who had been designated to bring the defector Miasnikov back to the Soviet Union, had himself defected. He went to Turkey on an assignment and, after a short stay there, left for France. According to the latest reports, Agabekov had already reached Paris and had met there with Miasnikov, who supplied him with money. The other news concerned Evgeny Dumbadze.

Disenchanted with the regime and the mass executions in his native Georgia, Dumbadze had left the Soviet Union, escaping abroad.

19

The New Assignment

DESPITE ALL THE PURGES and mass executions in Georgia, Azerbaijan and Armenia; despite individual arrests following denunciations by OGPU agents and informers planted in every factory, every Army and Militia detachment, every club or sports association; despite controversial discussions in meetings organized by professional provocateurs, the opposition to Stalin and the Soviet regime still existed in these three countries of Transcaucasia. The love of independence and freedom still was alive in the hearts of Caucasian people, mountaineers and fishermen, folks of the plains and horsemen. It was impossible to suppress them even by bloodshed. On the contrary, the more they were persecuted, the more they were obstinate and resistant to Bolshevik ideas.

Being a Georgian himself, Stalin was well aware of the general feeling of revolt and the vigorous trend to freedom. He realized his dictatorial power over the Soviet Union would never be complete as long as opposition against him persisted in the Caucasus. In addition to the constant aversion to Communism and the great inclination toward the liberal national democratic movements of Mensheviks, Dashnaks and Mussavatists, there still existed a tremendous antagonism against Russia, remembered from the times of Tsarist rule. This phenomenon meant that Stalin would encounter in Transcaucasia more difficulties in establishing his power than in other parts of the vast Soviet Union. In order to complete the difficult and complicated task of overwhelming and subjugating these stubborn peoples, some radical steps had to be taken.

In November, 1931, by decision of the Central Committee of the Communist Party at the Kremlin, Beria was elevated to the post of First Secretary of the Georgian Communist Party. From now on Beria became, on Georgia's soil, the counterpart of Stalin, who was First Secretary of the Communist Party of the entire Soviet Union. Now Lavrenty Pavlovich was no longer only a high officer of the Secret Police and Security, but a statesman with a wide range of political responsibilities.

Beria received this nomination after some friction with Kartvelishvili, who, as the protégé of "Dear Sergo" Ordzhonikidze, was Chairman of the Georgian Council of People's Commissars and expected to get the post that was given to Lavrenty Pavlovich. But Kartvelishvili was an Old Bolshevik, so he was not in good favor with Stalin, who made him Beria's deputy.

Lavrenty went to Moscow to thank personally his superior for this promotion. He was received by the Dictator at an informal reception in Stalin's villa at Zubalovo. When speaking about some bureaucratic formalities Beria still had to fulfill, he mentioned that in an inquiry form he was going to state on the line for "Party membership" his answer, "From 1920." Comrade Stalin advised him to put down "From 1917" because it would look better in view of Beria's present responsible job.

During that conversation Lavrenty also suggested the recall from Georgia to Moscow of his new deputy Kartvelishvili, a useless character, and his plea was granted.

Beria understood exactly what his promotion meant. He was being given unwritten directions to start a new purge even in the ranks of the Georgian Party's members, or at least to correct basic errors and misinterpretations of the guiding idea of which the leaders of the Transcaucasian Federation were guilty. Stalin's opinion of these characters was that they were more nationalistic deviationists than true Bolsheviks.

In reality several of the Old Guard Communists of the same age, or even older than Stalin, were ardent worshipers of the Marxist-Engels-Leninist idea. At the same time, however, they were Georgian or Armenian or Azerbaijan patriots, who wished their countries to be only loosely associated with the Soviet Union as a Transcaucasian Federative Republic, not forcibly incorporated into, and swallowed by, Russia. Stalin, although a Georgian, as they were, wanted to rule over the Soviet Union, forming one country consisting of a number of obedient satellites and by no means free autonomous republics. Besides, the old Georgian, Armenian and Azerbaijani Bolsheviks who had been active in the early underground work with Stalin well knew his own part in that movement and were aware of the size of his contribution to this uncommon achievement. Such knowledge could be most unfavorable for the leader of the USSR.

Budu Mdivani, Mamia Orakhelashvili, Nestor Lakoba and many others were real Georgian patriots, being at the same time Communists and fierce fighters for its idea. Beria understood what he should keep in mind. One of the most devoted Georgian Communists, Philip Makharadze, much older than Stalin and one of Communism's pioneers, wrote his memoirs, *Twenty-Five Years of Struggle for Socialism*, soon after Georgia had been conquered by the Red Army. In this book, published in Tiflis in 1923, and revealing many facts of sabotage and terrorism, Stalin was not shown as the principal hero. The former chief of the Georgian *Cheka*, Kote Tsintsadze, committed the same fault of carelessness when he published his diary in one of the Tiflis magazines in 1924. Such men, who stressed their own part in the movement for the Great Cause while dismissing Stalin's attainments as less important, could sooner or later become unwanted witnesses.

By entrusting Beria with such enormous power, Stalin knew well what he was doing. Beria was only 32 and Stalin, 20 years his senior, needed just such a young man, desirous of making a political career, who would not hesitate to liquidate the old cadres of Stalin's contemporaries. The old pioneers who remembered quite well the beginning of the twentieth century and took an active part in changing the course of history, were in evidence not only in the Kremlin and the Party's top echelons, but even belonged to Stalin's family and were residents, or at least frequent guests, at Stalin's villa, Zubalovo. They had been ardent fighters for Communism a long time before the Revolution's outbreak and during its course. Alexey Svanidze, an Old Georgian Marxist and a close friend of "Soso" Stalin, was a brother of the latter's first wife. She was Ekaterina Svanidze, who died in 1907, three years after their marriage, leaving a son, Yakov. Alexey Svanidze lived in Georgia but visited Stalin at the Kremlin very often. So did two sisters of Stalin's late first wife, Maria and Alexandra Svanidze. Sergo Alliluyev and his wife Olga, parents of Stalin's second wife, Nadezhda Alliluyeva, lived near the Stalins. So did Stalin's two brothers-in-law, Fyodor and Pavel Alliluyev, outstanding revolutionaries, as well as their sister, Anna, who was married to a Pole, Stanislav Redens, a ruthless *Chekist* and a close friend of Dzerzhinsky and his deputy.

For all these people, including his son Yakov, Stalin felt a great antipathy, either because they reminded him of his first wife, the only person he had really loved; or because, being Old Guard Bolsheviks, they remembered that the part he played, including his activity before the Revolution, did not amount to too much and did not entitle him to the position of greatest hero of the Soviet Empire. Moreover, many of these Marxists were Jews. For instance, First Secretary of the Moscow Party Committee Lazar Kaganovich, the Trade-Union leader Solomon Abramovich Lozovsky, Commissar of Foreign Affairs Maxim Litvinov and Dzerzhinsky's deputy, Iosif Unshlicht. Or else they were married to Jewesses, as Bukharin, whose wife was Kozya Gurvich; Molotov, with his Jewish wife, Paulina; Alexander Svanidze, the brother of Stalin's first wife. This man, three years younger than Stalin and one of the first pioneering Georgian Communists, with the Party pseudonym "Comrade Alyosha" when in the underground, married a Jewish girl, Miriam. Her origin was sufficient to cause Stalin to hate both of them. Stalin could not stand Jews. His feelings against the Jewish people were more like a blind animal hate, stronger than just an anti-Semitic prejudice. This was also part of the reason for Stalin's antipathy to Leon Trotsky, whose real name was Lev Bronstein; to Kamenev-Rosenfeld, who was expelled from the Politburo; Zinoviev-Apfelbaum, who had been ousted from the Party; and to Adolf Abramovich Ioffe, who was forced to commit suicide. Stalin needed someone young, ambitious, and cold-blooded. He needed a man who would be glad to further his own career over the dead bodies of any of these unwanted people; a man who, being himself a Georgian, could present Stalin as one of the genial leaders of the Communist movement and the initiator of the Great October Revolution, starting from his native Caucasus. To bring this task to completion, Beria was the right man, when equipped with the powers of First Secretary of the Georgian Communist Party.

Lavrenty Pavlovich was a systematical engineer, a shrewd policeman and an industrious government official, and he played his

cards carefully and cautiously. His spies and agents were shadow-
ing every eminent member of the Party in Transcaucasia. Soon
every one of the Old Georgian Bolsheviks had his own special dossier in Beria's filing cabinet devoted to top secret documents. In the
course of many months of investigations Beria collected some very
incriminating charges, data and materials pertaining to many of the
most respectable Communists of the Caucasus, such as Budu Mdivani, Mamia Orakhelashvili, Philip Makharadze, Avel Yenukidze,
who was attached to the Kremlin, and even "Dear Sergo" Ordzhonikidze. These Old Revolutionaries, whose friendship Lavrenty
Pavlovich had always mentioned with pride and gratitude, had
helped him to rise to power, and could serve him now to climb
higher over their dead bodies. Of course, they were still too powerful to be eliminated at once, but they could be pushed out one by
one, and would be liquidated sooner or later. Political expediency
was not Beria's only reason. He shared with Stalin one feature. To
them, condemning enemies was a normal and sensible activity, and
annihilating unknown people was simply the consequence of introducing certain rules and orders. But to Beria and Stalin the real
personal pleasure consisted of destroying their own colleagues and
friends, people who had helped them, trusted them, and liked or
even loved them, and who expected their good feelings to be recip-
rocated. As Stalin said once with a disarming smile, "To choose the
victim, to prepare the blow with care, to sate an implacable vengeance, and then to go to bed . . . There is nothing sweeter in the
world!"[1] It was the refined joy of a higher sensitivity.

By studying the biographies of prominent Georgian Marxists
Beria learned that Yenukidze, Makharadze and Orakhelashvili had
joined the ranks of revolutionaries long before Stalin did and their
record of achievements in the first decade of the twentieth century
was much more impressive than that of Comrade Stalin. He also
read their memoirs, published in 1923 and 1924, when Lenin was
still alive, as well as their historical works about the Transcaucasian Bolshevik movement. In these papers, Stalin's role received so
little mention that such a treatment would never satisfy the Great
Dictator. Makharadze, Chairman of the Presidium of the Supreme
Council in Georgia, was known as the mentor of a whole generation

---

[1] Boris Souvarine, *Stalin* (New York: Alliance Book Corporation, Longmans, Green
& Co., 1939).

of Georgian Bolsheviks. A personality no less important was Orak-helashvili, Chairman of the Georgian Central Committee in 1922, and Yenukidze, the organizer of the underground printing offices for illegal newspapers and leaflets distributed in Baku and Tiflis. During the October Revolution, Yenukidze fought in the streets of Petrograd. Later, for many years, he had been the Secretary of the All-Russian Central Executive Committee of the Soviets. This also applied to Alipi Tsintsadze, known as "Kote," who published his memoirs in 1924. All these men were close friends of Stalin. Tsintsadze who, before the Revolution was a guerrilla leader in the Caucasus, was one of Stalin's closest friends. In their writings these men mentioned in passing Stalin's role in the common activity but also stressed that Comrade Stalin was by no means the only one to fight. So did other Old Bolsheviks. Now, Beria realized he had to begin a long-range work, either to make all these writers change their memoirs, or to silence them forever. However, his main goal was the liquidation of men opposed to the disbanding of the Trans-caucasian Socialist Federated Soviet Republic and the incorporation of Georgia, Azerbaijan and Armenia into the USSR. Beria, a plotter who directly or indirectly caused the death of several outstanding persons, some very well guarded and inaccessible, did not have to be a shrewd psychologist to discover that Stalin, always gloomy and alien to everyone, had an obsessive fear of being assassinated by his best friends or even close relatives. Because of this fear, it would never be hard to convince Stalin that an attempt on his life was being prepared somewhere. Exploiting this mania of Stalin's in an appropriate way would make it possible to liquidate almost everybody. In his new job Beria proceeded slowly but cunningly.

The first person among the Georgian Old Communist dignitaries to become his victim was the People's Commissar of Georgia's Agriculture, Alexey Gegechkori, the same "Sasha" who had arranged the famous orgy in the Orient Hotel in Tiflis. That time Lavrenty Pavlovich had spared his life, but now there was no reason to let him live longer. Beria had kept in his office the proof of Gegechkori's embezzlement of a large sum of government money. The Commissar was summoned to the OGPU's headquarters on Olginskaya Street. After a brief interrogation Beria advised him to kill himself. It would be the easier and quieter way and everybody could be happy. "Sasha" Gegechkori returned home and contemplated the difficult choice facing him: to be tried publicly the next day and then to be dragged to a cellar where, with his hands bound behind his back, he would receive a bullet in his head; or, to die by his own hand. He chose to commit suicide. He drank a whole bottle of vodka and then shot himself.

The next in line was Kote Tsintsadze. Beria had a personal reason for eliminating him. Tsintsadze whom once Stalin had introduced to Lenin with the words, "This is Kote, the former Georgian terrorist expropriator," knew too many secrets. But Tsintsadze had once been the closest associate of the legendary Communist hero, Kamo, who was worshiped as the greatest of daredevils and was beloved throughout the Caucasus. Therefore, Tsintsadze could not be liquidated now with a single stroke. A long, detailed and convincing report to Stalin had to be prepared, making insinuations against Tsintsadze, recalling his bad temper, which had once resulted in a quarrel with the Great Comrade. There were also Tsintsadze's writings, published years before, which were not too favorable concerning Stalin's activity. Soon, Tsintsadze was invited to the Kremlin to receive, as he was told, a new assignment. From Moscow, however, he was whisked to Siberia and died in exile.

In 1932 Stalin promoted Beria from the post of First Secretary of the Georgian Communist Party to that of First Secretary of the Transcaucasian Territorial Committee of the Communist Party. By this new nomination Beria became dictator of the entire Transcaucasia.

20

Writer and Biographer

IN THE POST of First Secretary of the Transcaucasian Territorial Committee of the Communist Party, Lavrenty Beria was Stalin's long arm in the Caucasus. He realized that if he were to have a chance of becoming Stalin's Deputy for the entire Soviet Union in the future, he would have to erase all autonomous notions and patriotic feelings from the Caucasians, to level the Transcaucasian Federation, and to exterminate all leaders who were not bound blindly to Stalin. In short, Beria had to introduce an unwritten slogan that whoever was not entirely for Stalin, was against the Soviet Union. Lavrenty Pavlovich also decided that a new History of the Revolution should be created and, consequently, a new History of the Bolshevik Party. In it should be no mention of men who did not deserve to be considered builders of the Soviet Union—men like Trotsky or Ioffe. Also, the deceased Lenin's role should not be shown as much more important than that of Stalin, who was alive. Therefore, the new version of Stalin's biography should be altered from the previous ones, building up the Dictator's personality from the very beginning. Stalin would be the only one glorified, and his part in founding a new country would be made to look at least as important as that of Lenin.

The clock of history had to be turned back so it could start running again according to the will and aims of the watchmaker, Lavrenty Pavlovich Beria. From now on, Iosif Vissarionovich

Dzhugashvili, the "Dear Soso," "Koba" and the "Great Comrade Joseph Stalin" must be elevated to the dimension of a genius, shown to be the greatest hero and a mythical god who stepped down from Olympus to the land of Caucasus, from which he began his long and nearly solitary walk to his throne at the Kremlin. But if God created man in His image, so Stalin made Beria to his likeness.

On November 9, 1932, Beria had to drop everything and hurry to Moscow. He went to take part in the funeral of Nadezhda Allilu-yeva, Stalin's wife, who died at the age of thirty. The cause of this untimely death was officially given as acute appendicitis. But only ignoramuses or people who wished to avoid trouble would accept this explanation. The Muscovites who on November 7, 1932, watched the gigantic parade in honor of the Revolution's fifteenth anniversary could see Nadezhda Sergeyevna Alliluyeva in the Red Square, standing among the wives of the other dignitaries. She seemed in perfect health, not like a person suffering from any physical ailment. The next day, on November 8, a crowd of hundreds of Soviet personalities watched her at even closer range at a concert at the Kremlin, given in celebration of the anniversary. She looked sound and in perfect health. The next night, however, she was dead. It seemed impossible to believe that in modern times, in the 1930s, when an appendix removal was considered by medical science as a minor operation, Stalin's wife, living in the Kremlin, could not have skilful and quick aid from the best doctors available.

Beria had no reason to be sorry for her. He had seen too many women killed, so one more or less didn't matter, even if she was a Dictator's wife. What's the difference? Just another female. Moreover, Lavrenty was aware of the fact that Nadezhda despised him. Whenever Beria visited Stalin and his family—at their Kremlin home or at their country house at Zubalovo, or when he entertained them in Georgia when they came with their daughter Svetlana to spend summer vacation in the Sochi health resort in the Caucasus —Nadezhda Alliluyeva Stalin never hid her hatred of him. Now she was dead. Whether she had died of acute appendicitis or had killed herself, Beria had one potential foe less.

As to the widowered Stalin, why should Lavrenty shed tears over him? Beria was neither his brother nor friend. Besides, Stalin at any moment could turn his back on him and deprive Beria of his power and honors.

In Moscow, however, Lavrenty expressed his deepest grief to the bereaved Leader before returning to his office in Georgia to continue his aim of changing the past, a work that would be most pleasing to the Big Boss.

By removing from the Central Committee of the Party such eminent Communists and devoted Lenin supporters as Kamenev and Zinoviev, who were excluded as early as 1927; by forcing Adolf Ioffe to commit suicide the same year; and by whisking Trotsky beyond the boundaries of the Soviet Republic two years later, Stalin showed clearly that he intended to get rid of all the Old Bolsheviks. It was evident that, after Lenin's death, he decided to eradicate systematically and ruthlessly all of the Communists who had any credit in the success of the October Revolution and who, by the parts they themselves played in this momentous movement, outshone the glory of the new Caesar Imperator, Joseph Stalin.

Beria realized that a new biographer could not lose time. The sooner he wrote the new epic of Stalin's immortal deeds, based on concocted documents supposedly captured from the Tsarist Secret Police, the sooner would the schoolchildren start learning about him and the older generation accept it as truth. Certainly such a new history would in many places contradict the one already published; there would also be discrepancies in many articles, memoirs and autobiographies of some of the pioneers and veteran fighters. The fate of such authors would be the worst. They would be obliged to admit that their memories were poor and had failed them. Consequently, they would be forced to confess their errors and introduce corrections into their published works. This would be the first step toward their downfall. They would be swept aside and the previous editions of their writings confiscated and destroyed. The more new and imaginary facts of Stalin's heroism mentioned, and the more names of old heroes included as authors who, for their own aggrandizement, had hidden the magnificent activity of the Great Comrade Stalin, the better it would be. The new history of the Communist Party of the Bolsheviks, and the corrections of the other authors would provide nails for their coffins, while Beria would gain favor in the Dictator's eyes. Of course, such a delicate task had to be carried out slowly and cunningly. One imprudent false step, one little error, and the whole work so laboriously prepared could be turned against its creator and destroy him. This had to be a long-range plan. The names of the future victims had to be chosen very carefully, because at the moment these men were still in power.

Since the first steps of Stalin's revolutionary activity took place in Tiflis and Baku, Georgia and Azerbaijan had to be chosen as the places where the underground Bolshevik movement started. Thus, the history of the Soviet Union should have its roots in the history of the subversive work in the Caucasus. Stalin would be shown as the one and only hero, the initiator of every magnificent idea, while the other members of the revolutionary circles had to be presented as supporting actors, just small cogs in the tremendous machinery of the organization, obediently and blindly executing the Chief's orders. Anyone who had previously revealed facts praising himself or someone else was a liar and must be made to confess his effrontery and receive his rightful punishment.

Operating with such motives, Lavrenty Pavlovich began planning to write a book: *Stalin's Early Writings and Activities: On the History of the Bolshevik Organizations in Transcaucasia.*

Somewhat earlier, Stalin had publicly pointed out severe distortions in the writings of Yemelyan Yaroslavsky, official historian and member of the Party, whose works showed, in the Dictator's opinion, several basic mistakes. This was the first sign indicating that the time had come to publish a new history of the Communist Party.

Approaching his work as an educated man should, Beria first collected all the necessary material. In his office he gathered all memoirs, autobiographies and reminiscences dealing with Comrade Koba published by Stalin's predecessors and co-workers. There were pamphlets and books by such prominent Communists as Lenin's widow, Nadezhda Krupskaya; Leonid Krasin, an Old Bolshevik and Lenin's co-worker; Avel Yenukidze and Philip Makharadze; Kote Tsintsadze; Yemelyan Yaroslavsky; and the famous writer and Stalin's friend Maxim Gorky. There were also works by other historians: Karayev, Khandjian and Bubnov, who, describing the workers' movement in the Caucasus, did not overstress—or even mention at all—Comrade Koba's activity as initiator of the Bolshevik organization and his deeds in Azerbaijan, Armenia and Georgia. Biographies and memoirs written by Sergo Ordzhonikidze and Mamia Orakhelashvili dealt more with fact than with idolatry and praise of the new ruler, who was made to look much less important than Lenin. By adopting such a point of view, these two men condemned themselves to oblivion sooner or later, even though they were Stalin's closest comrades and occupied most honorable and responsible posts. By means of his essay, and with Stalin's tacit consent, Beria was going to be their executioner.

Starting the first draft, Lavrenty Pavlovich sketched a preface directing accusations at these two Old Communists, whose protégé Beria once had been, and who had helped him to achieve his present exalted position.

On May 11, 1934, all newspapers announced on their front pages the death of Vyacheslav Rudolfovich Menzhinsky, the victim of a heart attack the day before. From the long obituary notice, the readers could learn that the late Chief of the OGPU was a diplomat and a lawyer, and one of the oldest Bolsheviks, having been involved with the revolutionary idea since 1895; that he had been repeatedly imprisoned by the Tsarist *Okhrana*; that he had fought heroically during the Great October Revolution and had occupied, until the end of 1918, the post of Peoples' Commissar of Financial Affairs. After that he had joined the *Cheka* as one of "Iron Feliks' " two deputies, sharing these responsibilities with Iosif Unshlicht. In 1926, after the death of Feliks Dzerzhinsky, the "Knight of the Proletariat," Menzhinsky inherited the latter's honorable duties, performing them in such a magnificent way that the very next year he had been honored by being made a member of the Central Committee of the All-Union Party of Bolsheviks.

The important post of Security Chief, vacated by the death of that eminent figure, was immediately given to his Deputy, Genrikh Grigorievich Yagoda.

Menzhinsky was the second man to become Chief of the former *Cheka*, later renamed the GPU, and then the OGPU, to die of heart failure.

Although Beria knew Dzerzhinsky had died of a stroke during a quarrel with Stalin, it was generally understood that Menzhinsky had had a heart condition for several years and was under the constant care of the best physicians attached to the Kremlin.

However, Lavrenty, as a well-informed man, was aware that Menzhinsky's Deputy Yagoda was very ambitious and only too happy to take his boss' place. Yagoda was a pharmacist by profession and, thanks to his knowledge of various drugs and poisons, would have been able to accelerate the failure of his superior's heart. But Beria understood that nobody would dare to assassinate the Chief of the Security Police of the USSR without the recommendation, or at least the advice, of someone even more powerful acting behind him. Since the doctors' opinion stated the cause of death simply as "paralysis of the heart," and was not followed by an autopsy, Lavrenty could easily deduce from the date of birth of the deceased, September 1874, that one more Old Bolshevik and one more unwanted witness to the primary events of the Revolution's beginnings had been swept away. On the other hand Yagoda, seventeen years younger than his boss, belonged to the new generation.

Beria's speculation was soon confirmed. A few months later, on December 1, 1934, the whole Sovietland was shaken by the tragic news of Sergey Kirov's assassination.

After the Revolution Kirov, one of the pioneers of the new order, had steadily climbed the ladder to a successful career. In 1919 he was already a leader of the Temporary Military-Revolutionary Committee of Astrakhan and soon after, with the rank of *Komandarm*, was on the Staff of the Headquarters of the Eleventh Red Army, which later conquered Baku and the whole of Azerbaijan, Georgia and Armenia. In 1920 Kirov was nominated the Soviet Representative to Tiflis, and soon after, Deputy Chairman of the Soviet Delegation to Riga for the Peace Conference with Poland. Afterwards, he was promoted to the rank of Secretary of the Central Committee of the Communist Party Bolsheviks for Azerbaijan where, in its capital, Baku, he became absolute master of the population's life and death. He was one of the organizers of the invasion and pacification of Georgia, which he drowned in a sea of blood.

In 1922 Kirov organized the Transcaucasian Federation of the three conquered countries, Azerbaijan, Georgia and Armenia. In 1923, as a reward for his achievements, he reached the summit by joining the Central Committee of the All-Russian Communist Party of the Bolsheviks. From that time on he was Secretary of the Leningrad Committee of the Party in its Headquarters in the famous Smolny Institute, an elegant building, which before the Revolution had been a fashionable school for young ladies. Kirov, a Chief of this Office, was entrusted with the responsible job of Secretary of the North-Western Bureau of the Party's Central Committee as well as of the Executive Central Committee. He became one of the most important personalities in the Soviet Administration. He had never deviated from the Party line; had never been close to Trotsky. When he was appointed to his Leningrad post, he had been called there to replace Zinoviev, who was shortly afterwards expelled from the Politburo. On the contrary, Kirov always staunchly stayed at the side of Stalin, whose faithful follower and bosom friend he was. Now he had been killed in his office by an assassin's bullet.

The whole country was in mourning after the tragic news had been broadcast over the radio.

Stalin rushed from Moscow to Leningrad in order to lead the investigation personally.

Lavrenty Pavlovich Beria was a shrewd and experienced *Chekist* and a smart Chief of the Secret Police. As such, he realized that a killing of this kind could not possibly be undertaken single-handedly. This had to be a wisely prepared scheme, with the plotters themselves being highly placed officials. Like any successful escape from a prison, help always has to come from inside or from guards lending a hand. The killer had been identified on the spot. He was a certain Leonid Victorovich Nikolayev, twenty-nine years old, a former member of the Young Communists League, later a *Chekist* and guard at the Smolny Headquarters, subsequently released from his duties and dismissed because of ill health.

In a period of less than four weeks' time Nikolayev was put on trial, pleaded guilty and had been sentenced to death. Thus, the case was closed, at least for the average man in the street; not, however, for anyone with training in the Secret Police, such as Beria had. He knew very well that a discharged *Chekist* had to surrender to authorities his identity card and his service gun. Without an identity card no one is admitted into Party Headquarters. It is doubtful that anybody could gain admission even by the remotest possibility, since every door to every room in the building is guarded by a Security Police sentinel who inspects the entering person's pass. Above all, every caller is very carefully searched several times, especially if carrying a bag. Nikolayev was carrying a briefcase containing a heavy seven-shot Nagan revolver. The gun was a weapon typical of the *Chekists'* and one that only someone from the Security Police could supply the murderer. Nikolayev managed to reach the door of Kirov's study. The official was absent at the moment, having been called to the telephone. This was a long-distance call from the Kremlin, and the appropriate line was located in the main office. The only witness to the shooting was Kirov's male secretary and personal bodyguard, Borisov.

Immediately after the incident Borisov had been taken by car to a judge for questioning. But there was an automobile accident on the way to the court. The driver and all accompanying persons escaped injury; the only one killed was the secretary, the sole witness to the shooting.

Before Stalin got to Leningrad to start the interrogation, Yagoda flew in from Moscow to arrange for the Leader's comfort and prepare for the investigation proceedings. Beria could predict, therefore, that the days of the present Chief of Internal Affairs were numbered. It was clear that Yagoda, who would direct the investigation, would soon learn too much—if he already didn't know all—of the truth, and that such people were not wanted around. The new post coveted by Beria would be open, if not in the next few months, then in a year or two. Evidently Stalin, by letting Kirov be killed, was liquidating his contemporaries, even if they happened to be those most useful to the Party. It sufficed that, by their very existence, they deprived Stalin of a share of the glory that should have remained his undivided property. Moreover, being intelligent Communists and former fighters, they could at any moment change from followers into foes. They had to be exterminated as a preventive measure.[1]

Now Lavrenty was positive that if he did not hurry with accusations against some Old Bolsheviks, especially the pioneers from Georgia, Stalin, acting quickly, would do it himself, thus making Beria's part in the plan nil. In other words, Beria's work, *On the History of the Bolshevik Organizations in Transcaucasia*, had to be completed and presented as soon as possible.

---

[1] Despite the fact that the murderer was caught red-handed, the ascertainment of his identity, his open trial, his plea of guilty, and his execution, the current official *Great Universal Encyclopedia* published by the Polish Communist Government in Warsaw declared: "[Kirov] was assassinated in Leningrad in the Smolny Palace under circumstances which until now had not been definitely clarified. Kirov's murder was later used to justify the mass repressions in accordance with the distortions of that period." (*Wielka Encyklopedia Powszechna*, Panstwowe Wydawnictwo Naukowe, Warszawa, 1965, Vol. 5, p. 618.) (*Great Universal Encyclopedia*, State Publishing House, Warsaw, 1965, Vol. 5, p. 618.)

21

Midnight Telephone Call from Moscow

IT WAS A WINDY NIGHT in mid-February 1935. The room was sinking into a heavy shadow. A desk lamp with a green globe threw only a white circle of light onto the long pad of paper on which Lavrenty Beria was writing a report.

Across the desk sat a man who was being interrogated. According to the usual rules, he was perched on the very edge of his chair; that way he wouldn't be able to jump to his feet quickly. His hands were on his knees. Behind him stood an armed NKVD[1] guard.

The telephone rang. Beria lifted the receiver. With a gesture of his free hand he ordered the soldier to take the man back to his cell. Then he started to listen attentively to the voice on the telephone. The call was from the Kremlin, and the Great Comrade Stalin in person was speaking. First, he asked Beria whether he had a pen or pencil at hand. After an affirmative answer he began to issue an order.

Holding the receiver with his left hand, Lavrenty Pavlovich took notes with his right. Stalin demanded that the First Secretary of the Transcaucasian Territorial Committee of the Communist Party in Tiflis send a petition addressed to Moscow asking for the honor of having Avel Sofronovich Yenukidze delegated to the Caucasus,

---

[1] NKVD: Narodnyi Komissariat Vnutrennykh Del—People's Commissariat of Internal Affairs. By a decree of July 10, 1934, the OGPU was abolished and its functions were transferred to the NKVD.

where he would become President of the Transcaucasian Republics.[2] The order was to be carried out immediately. The call was over.

Beria lit a cigarette, took off his pince-nez, blew on the glasses and wiped them with his handkerchief. He rang for his orderly and told him to make tea. Of course, he had to prepare the petition at once and mail it by registered express letter the first thing in the morning. But Lavrenty always liked to think twice and consider the reasons behind everything that went on. He tried to find out from which side the wind was blowing: "*Kooda vyeter dooyet*"—as the old Russian proverb says.

Yenukidze was Stalin's bosom friend, whom Stalin once, in 1926, had wanted to include in the Politburo. He had been something of a guardian angel to Nadezhda Alliluyeva, Stalin's late second wife, and was her godfather and best man at her wedding to "Soso." Yenukidze was also a close friend of Nadezhda's father, the Old Bolshevik, Sergo Alliluyev. Yenukidze was the idol of Svetlana, the beloved little daughter of Stalin. To her, Yenukidze was more dear than her own father, of whom she was often afraid. She called Yenukidze "Uncle Avel," and always begged him to tell her the ancient fairy tales and legends about the giants living in the mountains of the Caucasus. Every time Stalin and his wife and children went vacationing to Sochi in the summer, "Uncle Avel," almost a member of the family, went with them.

Yenukidze lived in Moscow, where he and Stalin and "Dear Sergo" Ordzhonikidze formed a trio of Georgians in the Kremlin.

Now Yenukidze was going to be sent to Tiflis as potential President of the Transcaucasian Republics. It seemed that Stalin's best friend was going to be his plenipotentiary in Transcaucasia. This could be a severe setback for Beria, who was disliked by Yenukidze, as well as by Stalin's late wife Nadezhda and her daughter Svetlana. If Yenukidze were back in his native Caucasus as President of the three federated countries—Georgia, Azerbaijan and Armenia—he would undoubtedly push aside Beria, who, until now, had been considered next to Stalin. At first glance, the situation looked dangerous for Lavrenty. But the matter needed thinking over. What would Stalin gain by uprooting Beria from his high

[2] Alexander Orlov, *The Secret History of Stalin's Crimes* (New York: Random House, 1953).

post? Lavrenty Pavlovich was such a good instrument for Stalin's politics in Transcaucasia that it was hard to believe, at least for the present, that somebody more suitable for the job could be found. Besides, Avel Sofronovich was known to be a patron of the arts and a compassionate man, full of understanding for people he knew personally, and he liked to help his friends. He had a soft heart, as far as this is possible for a Bolshevik. It was well known that Yenukidze helped relatives of outstanding Communists in cases where the father or husband had been arrested or sent to Siberia. Stalin, however, never believed in ruling by mildness and compassion. Quite the contrary, he ruled with an iron hand, and wouldn't really wish to entrust Yenukidze with a post of responsibility in Transcaucasia, where national feelings and ambitions still ran high. On the other hand, Avel was not only "Soso's" closest friend, but also his co-worker and comrade from youth, long before the Revolution.

Minootochkoo—just a minute—as the Russian saying goes. Kirov's assassination, which was rather more than mysterious, surely could be interpreted as a sign showing Stalin's co-workers and comrades from early times that they were not entirely welcome. Moreover, even a high post, such as that of President of the Transcaucasian Republics, could be quite the opposite of a promotion, if taking it entailed leaving the Kremlin, where Yenukidze, of the Central Executive Committee of the USSR, sat almost at the right hand of the Dictator.

Lavrenty closed the report on the man he had been interrogating prior to the call from Moscow and put it in his drawer. Then he got up, went to the strongbox and took out the dossier of Yenukidze. Chief of Georgian Security Beria had established that file for his own purpose, and kept it for possible future use.

Here Beria had a very detailed biography: Yenukidze, Avel Sofronovich, born May 7, 1877 in the village of Rastscha, Region of Tskadisy near Kutaisi, Georgia. Joined the Communist Party in 1898. Party pseudonyms: Avel, or Abdul, or Zolotaya Rebka.[3] From 1897 to 1900, a laborer mechanic on the Transcaucasian Railways. Then assistant to the machinist running the locomotive. When in Baku, Yenukidze organized the underground movement and the cells of the Party. He founded the S. D.—Social-Democratic Organization. He also initiated in Baku an illegal clandestine

---

[3] "Golden Fish."

printing shop called *Nina* and directed it until 1906. Yenukidze was one of the most active Bolsheviks in Transcaucasia, carrying on his work there until 1914. Then he went to Rostov on the Don River to continue his political tasks, and later to Moscow and to Petrograd. In October 1914, Yenukidze was arrested by the *Okhrana* and was exiled to Siberia. In 1916 he was drafted into the army.

During the revolution, in February 1917 in Petrograd, Avel Yenukidze took part in the uprising of the soldiers and fought in the streets of that city on the side of the Communists. During the First Congress of the Soviets he was elected to the Central Committee. In 1917 he became a member of the Petrograd Soviet on the Executive Committee of the Party. He was an active member of the Party and fought during the Great October Revolution. After the Revolution, Yenukidze became the Secretary of the All-Russian Central Executive Committee of the Soviets and a member of the Central Committee of the Party.

In that file, among other documents and data arranged in chronological order, Beria encountered a clipping he had cut from a newspaper not long before. It was an open letter to the editor, appearing in the government newspaper *Pravda* on January 16, 1935. In this article Yenukidze corrected and criticized certain Old Bolsheviks who, in relating the history of illegal pro-Communist activities in Transcaucasia in their memoirs, had made several mistakes and distortions. This should be put straight. On this occasion, Yenukidze also confessed that he, too, had made some errors, especially when he had allowed in his biographical note published in the *Great Soviet Encyclopedia* the statement that he, Avel Sofronovich Yenukidze, had directed the underground work in Baku. It was, or at least should be, known to everyone that the leader of the movement at the time had been Comrade Stalin.

This declaration soothed Beria. Now he knew exactly what to think about the new post prepared for his future superior, the proposed President of the Transcaucasian Republics. To the Old Guard Bolsheviks it was common knowledge that Stalin's participation in the revolutionary movement was by no means significant compared to that of the underground workers and other associates of Lenin. It meant even less within the confines of Georgia and Azerbaijan, where Ordzhonikidze, Mikoyan, Yenukidze and the late Kirov had been more active than Comrade Koba. Now Kirov, one of the most important witnesses, was dead. The recent nomination of Yenukidze seemed to be a prelude to his end.

With his indelible pencil, Beria drafted a humble request to the Central Executive Committee of the USSR in Moscow asking that Comrade Avel Sofronovich Yenukidze, Georgia's dear son, be allowed to come to Tiflis to be elected President of the Transcaucasian Federative Republics.

The letter was too important to be given to Beria's male secretary to be typed. Lavrenty Pavlovich called his orderly to bring the typewriter to his office and typed the document himself. He put the copy into Yenukidze's dossier and locked it in the strongbox. He crumpled the carbon paper in his hand, put it in the ashtray and dropped a burning match on top of it. He cleaned the typewriter's platen with benzine, which he used in his cigarette lighter. Then he summoned the soldier again and ordered him to take the typewriter back.

The wish expressed in the petition signed by First Secretary of the Transcaucasian Territorial Committee of the Communist Party, Lavrenty Pavlovich Beria, was granted. On a breezy morning in early March, Avel Yenukidze, a tall, blond, handsome man, alighted from a Pullman car at the station in Tiflis. Beria and several Commissars welcomed him heartily, with typical Georgian friendliness, but also with all the respect due the future President of their country. Lavrenty was especially cordial and affectionate, but at the same time formal, as an obedient subordinate should be. In case this honorable personality should become a successful President, Beria would be able to explain proudly—and even prove— that it was his idea, a result of his own suggestion.

Awaiting his nomination, Yenukidze was resting and enjoying his stay in the capital of Georgia, where he entertained and accepted invitations to the homes of the most influential citizens, and went to theatres and the Opera, where he had a box reserved for him by the officious Lavrenty Pavlovich. But Beria also kept delaying the date of the election, awaiting further instructions from the Big Boss. At last, at the end of May, after several weeks of expectation, a message came from the Kremlin; Comrade Stalin nominated his friend Avel manager of hospitals in Georgia. Offended and ridiculed, Yenukidze left Tiflis and went back to Moscow the same day.

Lavrenty realized this nomination spelled the definite downfall of the Old Bolshevik Yenukidze.

Beria came to the conclusion that the time had come to strike, and to cast the first stone at that outstanding Georgian Communist, once "Soso's" closest friend, on whom he had now turned his back. The sooner Lavrenty attacked Yenukidze and the sooner he could show that he was one of the first to fault him, the better. This would ensure future favors from Stalin. However, while casting blame on Yenukidze, who had chided other writers for their errors and deviations, it would be logical to brand them also. Beria decided to sink some other authors of memoirs or articles, such as Mamia Orakhelashvili and Philip Makharadze, as he intended before, but to leave Sergo Ordzhonikidze alone for the time being. Orakhelashvili had been President of Transcaucasia's Council of Commissars; he was older than Stalin, and one of the first revolutionary pioneers. He had known Stalin from the very beginning of their common activity, and was the author of *The History of the Communist Movement in Transcaucasia.* So it was with Philip Makharadze, former Chairman of the Council of People's Commissars, a historian of the revolution in the Caucasus, author of *The Year 1905 in Transcaucasia* and other works. All three, Yenukidze, Orakhelashvili and Makharadze, when relating in their memoirs the story of the Communist struggles in the Caucasus and of the underground press activity and illegal printing offices, mentioned Stalin only as a lesser activist without special influence. Obviously, these men had been Stalin's comrades and co-workers long enough to know the real truth of the matter. This was a crime, of course. Beria decided to write a new, entirely different version of Stalin's achievements in the Caucasus thirty-five years before. He needed some blank space to create there his own version designed to please the Great Comrade. There should remain no controversial books, memoirs or witnesses of Stalin's real activity.

It was clear that Yenukidze and these two other old comrades of Stalin were losing the favor of "Soso." This trump card had to be properly played by Lavrenty Pavlovich. To the draft of the book he was currently preparing, *Stalin's Early Writings and Activities: On the History of the Bolshevik Organizations in Transcaucasia,* Beria now added this paragraph:

In connection with the struggles of Transcaucasian Bolsheviks as described by Avel Yenukidze, Mamia Orakhelashvili and Philip Makharadze, it should be pointed out it appears they have made several mistakes and distortions of a very important historical nature. Such conscious and deliberate changes of facts and events resulted in great harm for the truth and for the history of the Party.

22

The Retouched Past

FOR THE DAYS OF July 21 and 22, 1935, Beria called a mass meeting of Party functionaries in Tiflis. On the hot, sultry morning of July 21 in the huge, filled hall of the railway repair plant, First Secretary of the Transcaucasian Territorial Committee of the Communist Party Comrade Lavrenty Pavlovich mounted the stage and started to read his essay in the form of a lecture:

Comrades!

A study and understanding of the history of our Party is a most important medium in the Marxist-Leninist education of the members of the Party and the Young Communist League.

Comrade Stalin in his historic article, "Questions Concerning the History of Bolshevism," focused the attention of the Party organizations on the task of studying the history of our Party in a Bolshevik way.

Comrade Stalin wrote at that time of the need:

". . . to raise the questions concerning the history of Bolshevism to the proper level, to put the study of the history of our Party on scientific, Bolshevik lines, and to concentrate attention against the Trotskyite and all other falsifiers of the history of our Party by systematically unmasking them."

This task requires that the teaching of the history of the Party, the study of anti-Party groupings in the history of our Party and of their methods of struggle against the Party line, should be raised to the proper level.

This task requires that Party members know not only how the Party

fought and overcame the Constitutional-Democrats (Cadets), the Socialist-Revolutionaries, the Mensheviks and the Anarchists, but also how
the Party fought and overcame the Trotskyites, the "Democratic Central-
ists," the "Workers' Opposition," the Zinovievites, the Rights, the Rightist-
Leftist freaks, etc.

To raise Bolshevik vigilance to the proper level and arm Communists
against all enemies of our Party it is necessary that every member of the
Party know the heroic experience of how the Lenin-Stalin Party was built
and how it fought; it is necessary that he know and understand not only
the successes and victories of the Party but also how they were won by
the Party in the struggle against all the enemies of Leninism.

Now, with socialism victorious, with the great cultural and political
growth of the broad masses of the working people and the intensification
of resistance on the part of the remnants of the defeated class enemy, it
is indispensable to raise the level of Marxist-Leninist education in every
way, and first and foremost the level of knowledge of the Bolshevik history of our Party.

The study of the history of the Party must not be restricted to a bare
description of events and facts in the heroic history of Bolshevism, but
must explain the economic and political situation of the country, give a
complete picture of the intricate and multifarious struggle of all classes
in pre-revolutionary Russia and of the struggle of the oppressed nations
for national emancipation under the leadership of the working class and
its Bolshevik Party.

The history of the Party must be set forth in such a way as to give the
Marxist explanation of the history of our Party's fight against anti-
Bolshevik trends and factions within the Party and the working class,
demonstrating the supreme importance in principle of this struggle for
Leninism.

What we need now is that the members of the Party and the Young
Communist League study more seriously and acquire a more profound
knowledge of the history of Bolshevism, of the history of the Party's struggle against all anti-Leninist deviations and trends, of the concrete situation in which the Party of Lenin and Stalin worked.

We need a study of the history of our Party such as would ensure the
assimilation of the heroic experience of the Bolsheviks' struggle against
the numerous enemies of Leninism and arm the members of the Party
and the Young Communist League to combat the enemies of the Party,
to combat the survivals of the ideas and views of all the defeated counterrevolutionary, anti-Party groups.

In recent years the Party organizations of Transcaucasia have done
considerable work in the propagation and study of the history of the
Party. But our achievements in this field are obviously inadequate. *We*

are especially behind the Bolshevik treatment and study of the Bolshevik organizations of Transcaucasia and Georgia, in the study of the struggle of the Transcaucasian Bolsheviks for the cause of Lenin and Stalin.

The Bolsheviks of Transcaucasia have acquired enormous historical experience in the struggle to build the Leninist Party, a struggle which went on for decades under the direct guidance of the leader of our Party, Comrade Stalin.

The whole history of the Transcaucasian Bolshevik organizations and the entire revolutionary movement of Transcaucasia and of Georgia have from the very outset been inseparable from the work and name of Comrade Stalin.

These words were rewarded with long applause, which had been organized and staged by Beria's many agents planted in the crowd.

When the "spontaneous" clapping stopped, the speaker continued, but now he launched his well-prepared attack on some of the veteran Bolsheviks:

The Ninth Congress of the Communist Party of Georgia and the Seventh Congress of the Communist organizations of Transcaucasia paid special attention to the questions of treating and studying the history of the Communist organizations of Transcaucasia and of Georgia.

The mistakes and distortions occurring in the works of some Communist historians were severely criticized at these congresses.

In its decisions, the Ninth Congress of the Communist Party of Georgia gave the following instruction:

"Noting the distortions of the history of the Party and the revolutionary movement in Georgia and Transcaucasia occurring in the works of a number of Communist historians, the Congress deems it necessary for all Party organizations of Georgia to concentrate still greater attention against attempts to falsify the history of Bolshevism."

After the Congress our organizations improved their work of collecting and elaborating material on the history of the Bolshevik organizations and the revolutionary movement of Transcaucasia.

However, *what has been done is as yet very little*; there is still a great deal of data and documents to be collected.

The Tbilisi[1] branch of the Marx-Engels-Lenin Institute of the Central Committee of the CPSU (B)[2] has not yet been able to issue a collection

---

[1] Tbilisi: Official name for Tiflis after the October Revolution, but used—in those times—very seldom; presently, capital of the Soviet Republic of Georgia.

[2] CPSU (B): The Communist Party of the Soviet Union (Bolsheviks).

Lavrenty Pavlovich Beria, a heavily retouched and beautified portrait
for official use. (*Bolshaya Sovietskaya Encyclopedia, Moscow*)

Bolshoi Theatre in Moscow. (*Pravda, Moscow*)

Lenin (left) and Stalin about 1910. The photo of Stalin was taken by Tsarist police *Okhrana*. (*USSR in Construction, Moscow*)

Baku, a general view.
(*Progress, Moscow*)

The Old Town of Baku. (*Progress, Moscow*)

A workers' demonstration in Petrograd, 1917.
The crowd is dispersed by the Tsarist
gendarmes. (*The National Archives*)

Moscow after the October Revolution, 1917.
The Cyrillic letters on the banner spell:
"Russian Communist Party (Bolsheviks)
Moscow Committee." (*The National Archives*)

Feliks Dzerzhinsky, "Knight of the Proletariat," founder of the *Cheka*. (*Książka i Wiedza, Warsaw*)

At the Peace Conference in Brest-Litovsk, 1918, the arrival of the Russian delegation. In the center, Trotsky (profile); on the left, Kamenev and Ioffe. (*The National Archives*)

Sergey M. Kirov (S. M. Kostrikov), Beria's protector and the Moscow Representative in the Caucasus in 1919–20. He was assassinated in 1934, supposedly as a result of Stalin's intrigue. (*The National Archives*)

Beria as a young *Cheka* officer.
(*The National Archives*)

The dreary Bailov Prison in Baku—
the first office of Lavrenty Beria
as a *Chekist*. (*The National
Archives*)

A typical street in Tiflis with the ancient Metekhy Castle in the background. (*Private collection of G. K. Coby, Washington*)

The ancient Metekhy Castle in Tiflis—a prison and Beria's headquarters in the Caucasus. (*Private collection of G. K. Coby, Washington*)

A group of Beria subordinates, the *Cheka* executioners and officials in Tiflis. The banner reads: "Commission. Death to enemies!" (*Mishen, Paris*)

A *Komandarm* of the Special Agency in Tiflis. A proud *Cheka* executioner under Beria's orders. (*Mishen, Paris*)

"Dear Sergo"—Grigory K.
Ordzhonikidze, an Old Guard
Bolshevik who died in 1937
under mysterious circumstances.
(*Bolshaya Sovietskaya
Encyclopedia, Moscow*)

A death cell in the State Prison
in Tiflis where executions were
performed under Beria's regime.
(*Mishen, Paris*)

Joseph Pilsudski, Commander in
Chief of the Polish Forces during
the war against Soviet Russia in
1920. (*J. Pilsudski Institute of
America, New York*)

Marshal of the Soviet Union
Mikhail N. Tukhachevsky, the
ruthless suppressor of the Kronstadt
revolt in 1921. He was executed
in 1937. (*The National Archives*)

A group of best friends. Seated (from left): Ordzhonikidze, Stalin, Molotov, and Kirov; standing: Voroshilov, Kaganovich, and Kuybyshev. (*The National Archives*)

Zinaida Volkov, Trotsky's daughter.
She was killed in Berlin by the
Cheka men who staged her suicide.
(*The National Archives*)

Leon Trotsky in his study in exile, in Paris. (*The National Archives*)

Nikolay I. Bukharin, a Bolshevik leader, economist, and theorist, and one of the closest co-workers of Lenin. Later, he was editor of the official newspaper of the Soviet government, *Izvestia*. He was executed in 1938. (*The National Archives*)

of documents and data on the history of the Party organizations and the revolutionary movement of Transcaucasia, nor has it published a single original work on this subject.

Beria stopped his reading for a long, impressive, dramatic pause. Then he returned to his manuscript and scolded the three Old Guard Bolsheviks of the Caucasus, Yenukidze, Orakhelashvili and Makharadze, for distortions and errors of a very important historical nature in their writings, as well as for their negligence in not revising and rectifying their works. Then he continued:

Members of the Party and the YCL,[3] non-Party workers and collective farmers are showing tremendous interest in the study of the Bolshevik organizations and the revolutionary movement of Transcaucasia. The Party organizations are pressing us for literature that will correctly present the history of our Party organizations.

Since the Seventh Congress of the Communist organizations of Transcaucasia and the Ninth Congress of the Communist Party of Georgia, we have already collected some data and documents on the history of our Party organizations.

The Transcaucasian Territorial Committee of the CPSU (B) and the Central Committee of the Communist Party of Georgia have commissioned me to clarify *some questions*—facts and events—concerning the history of the Bolshevik organizations of Transcaucasia and Georgia on the basis of these data and documents.

Since the head of the Transcaucasian Territorial Committee of the Party, as well as of the Central Committee of the Communist Party of Georgia was none other than the speaker himself, his remark about being commissioned to clarify some questions concerning the history of the Bolshevik Organization of Transcaucasia and Georgia was addressed to himself by himself, Lavrenty Pavlovich Beria.

The introduction was over. Now the lecturer could come to his proper subject, to the facts meticulously invented and elaborated to create the mass cult of the Great Leader.

The first chapter of his newly-prepared official textbook of history was titled "On the History of the Inception and Formation of the Bolshevik Organizations in Transcaucasia 1897-1904." Here, when mentioning an eminent pioneer of Communism, Victor Kurnatovsky, "a trained, educated Marxist," Beria called him "a

---

[3] The YCL: The Young Communist League (*Komsomol*).

proletarian revolutionary, a consistent adherent of Lenin's for the rest of his life." Since this man was "a supporter of Lenin," Beria declared:

In the summer of 1900 after his term of exile had expired, the Party transferred Kurnatovsky to revolutionary work in Tiflis. After his arrival in Tiflis, he established close contact with Comrade Stalin and became his intimate friend and co-worker.

In 1900 Stalin was still an obscure activist, a small cog in the underground movement. But since Kurnatovsky, who had died abroad in 1912, had already been dead for twenty-three years and could not deny cooperation with Stalin, there was no danger in publishing such a connection in order to build up the present Dictator. Then, describing the events at the end of 1904 and the beginning of 1905 Beria stated:

. . . in a resolute and uncompromising struggle against Georgian "legal Marxism," against the majority of the "Messameh Dassy,"[4] headed by Noah Jordania, *a revolutionary, Social-Democratic Bolshevik organization supporting Lenin's* Iskra[5] *arose, took shape and grew in Transcaucasia under the leadership of Comrade Stalin.*

Prolonged applauses rewarded these words. When the audience became silent, Beria continued. Now he accused Philip Makharadze of giving "in a number of his works an incorrect exposition of the history of the 'Messameh Dassy' and a false estimation of its role and significance." But, since Makharadze was not yet officially condemned by Stalin and might stay in power for some time, Lavrenty still called him "a Comrade."

Beria turned the page and read as follows:

In 1900, under the leadership of Comrade Stalin, between four and five hundred Tiflis workers celebrated May Day. They gathered outside the city in the Salt Lake district, carrying portraits of Marx and Engels and revolutionary slogans. At the meeting Comrade Stalin delivered a rousing speech and urged the workers to fight against the tsar and the capitalists. Between May and July of 1900 a wave of strikes swept through the factories in Tiflis. In August 1900 a huge strike of the railway shop and depot workers took place under the leadership of Comrade Stalin. . . . About four thousand men downed tools. In 1901 the Tiflis workers paraded the streets in their first public May Day demonstration.

---

[4] *Third Group.*
[5] *Iskra* (*The Spark*): A Russian Socialist newspaper founded by Lenin in 1900.

Under the guidance of Comrades Stalin and Kurnatovsky the leading Social-Democratic group in Tiflis carried on a tremendous amount of agitation and organizational work in preparation for this parade. . . . Comrade Stalin did an enormous amount of work in preparation for the May Day demonstration of the Tiflis proletariat. On his initiative the leading Party group issued a number of leaflets.

The whole chapter was written in this manner, proving that the Communist movement in Transcaucasia was carried out almost entirely by Comrade Stalin.

The speaker was tired and needed some rest. A ten-minute intermission was proclaimed.

After the recess, Beria continued lecturing about the newly created past. The chronological second chapter was titled "On The History of the Bolshevik Organizations of Transcaucasia in the Period of the First Russian Revolution 1905-1907." It began with this paragraph:

Comrade Stalin returned to Tiflis in February 1904 after his escape from exile in Siberia. He took his place at the head of the Bolshevik organizations of Transcaucasia, organizing and directing the struggle against the Mensheviks, who had become especially active after the Second Party Congress during his absence.

Soon after, the speaker revealed the following:

In Chiaturi Comrade Stalin organized a Bolshevik Party Committee of the country, selected a group of propagandists from the foremost worker activists and trained a special group of activists for work among the peasants of the Chiaturi district. . . . On the initiative of Comrade Stalin, the Imeretino-Mingrel Bolshevik Committee was formed in Kutais, which directed the Party organizations of the former Kutais Province.

Comrade Stalin organized a group of propagandists under the Kutais Committee and trained them for Party agitational work.

As the audience could gather from that utterance, if Stalin had not organized such groups and had not trained men for Party agitational work, the Bolshevik organizations in Transcaucasia would never have been initiated. Then Beria announced:

In November 1904 Comrade Stalin left for Baku to intensify the campaign for the convocation of the Third Party Congress and further develop the struggle against the Mensheviks, particularly against the representative of the Menshevik Central Committee, Glebov (Noskov), who was then in Baku.

Comrade Stalin and the Transcaucasian Bolsheviks ruthlessly attacked the nationalist parties: Dashnaks, Federalists, Anarchists and others.

Certainly, when stating that "Comrade Stalin ruthlessly attacked the nationalist parties," Beria in no way criticized the Genius Stalin. Quite the opposite. The word "ruthlessly" was used here as a great compliment to be understood as "consequently, methodically, systematically, with an iron hand" and was meant to be accepted by his listeners in this sense.

". . . In all these debates Comrade Stalin played an outstanding part," the speaker concluded. Then, after a few sentences, Beria declared:

During the first revolution 1905-1907 Comrade Stalin firmly carried out Lenin's line; he was the guide and leader of the Bolsheviks and the revolutionary workers and peasants of Transcaucasia.

Since these words were spoken with special emphasis it was evident that they should be accepted enthusiastically. With his left palm the lecturer inconspicuously rubbed his forehead. This was the sign for applause. Several agents planted here and there in the crowd started clapping their hands "spontaneously." They were joined in loud and long applause by the whole audience. Soon after that Beria revealed:

The leading, guiding force of the revolutionary movement of the workers and peasants in Transcaucasia was the Bolshevik organization, headed by Comrade Stalin, the truest and most loyal comrade-in-arms of Lenin. . . .

. . . The revolutionary struggle of the workers and peasants of Transcaucasia, led by Comrade Stalin, met with warm support, guidance and assistance from Lenin, the Russian working class and the Bolshevik Party.

. . . In the period of 1904-1907 Comrade Stalin, at the head of the Transcaucasian Bolsheviks, did a tremendous amount of theoretical and organizational work. He led and directed the struggle of the whole Bolshevik press. During that time the following newspapers were issued in Transcaucasia . . .

After these words the speaker enumerated in Tiflis, seven newspapers published in Georgian, Russian and Armenian and in Baku, eight newspapers in the same three languages, while one of them was also in Turkish. All of them, according to Beria, were founded and simultaneously directed by Stalin single-handedly, while twelve issues of a paper of the All-Caucasian Committee of the

Party also published in those three languages from 1903 to 1905 were directed by Stalin with the help of two other Comrades. Then Beria continued his elaboration as before stating:

. . . Comrade Stalin constantly advocated and explained what the Party must do to prepare and carry out a victorious armed insurrection.

. . . Comrade Stalin insisted on and propagated the necessity for a general armed insurrection of the working class, and he exposed and stigmatized the Menshevik leaders.

. . . Comrade Stalin proved the necessity for an armed struggle in the revolution on the part of the proletariat and pointed out that its main ally in this struggle is the peasantry. Comrade Stalin urged the peasants to fight tooth and nail against tsarism under the leadership of the proletariat.

Under the leadership of Comrade Stalin the Bolsheviks of Transcaucasia solved the question of unity in a Leninist spirit.

. . . Comrade Stalin proved the validity of the Bolshevik program on the agrarian question.

. . . Comrade Stalin carried on the whole theoretical work with exceptional consistency and adherence to principle, waging a relentless struggle against opportunism in the Russian and international movement. . . .

Beria ended this long chapter of his *History of the Bolshevik Organizations of Transcaucasia in the Period of the First Russian Revolution*, with these words, expressed with special pathos:

During the years of the first revolution the Bolsheviks of Transcaucasia were headed by Lenin's best companion-in-arms, the man who laid the foundations of revolutionary Marxism-Leninism in Transcaucasia and founded the first Social-Democratic organizations there supporting Lenin's *Iskra*—Comrade Stalin.

Loud applause rewarded these words. This time the agents did not have to spur the audience as they had before. Every one in the hall was clapping his hands gladly. This was the end of the first part of the lecture and of the first day of the meeting. The men could now leave the meeting and go home to rest. There were no questions or comments.

The next morning, half an hour before the scheduled nine o'clock meeting, the huge hall of the railway shop in Tbilisi started filling up. The men took their seats, but not at random as they had the day before. They sat in twos or in groups of friends, neighbors or acquaintances. On the second day of that meeting they were able to recognize Beria's agents planted in the crowd, and now they tried not to be close to them.

At nine o'clock sharp Lavrenty Pavlovich mounted the podium. He was greeted with polite applause, loud enough so the public could not be called hostile toward the speaker. From his briefcase the lecturer took out his typescript, opened it to the appropriate page and began to continue the speech he had started the day before.

Chapter Three, "On the History of the Bolshevik Organizations of Transcaucasia in the Period of Reaction and the Revival of the Labor Movement 1907-1913."

From then on, Beria read in a dry, matter-of-fact voice and with the deadpan expression on his face of a prosecutor announcing a bill of indictment. He read that:

. . . Comrade Stalin vigorously combated the Menshevik election tactics of compromise with the Cadets, who wanted to share power with the tsar and the landowners and who dreaded revolution more than reaction.

Time and again Comrade Stalin stressed the enormous danger of the influence of the counterrevolutionary liberal bourgeoisie and of the Menshevik tactics of subordinating the working class to the political interests of the bourgeoisie.

. . . *In the period 1907 to 1912, the Baku Bolshevik Party organization, under the leadership of Comrade Stalin, gained in number, strength and stamina in the struggle against the Mensheviks, winning over the vast majority of the Social-Democratic workers to its side.*

. . . The Bolshevik Baku Committee, headed by Comrade Stalin, stormed and captured every position of the Mensheviks. Besides a great deal of practical organizational work, Comrade Stalin was very active in the sphere of theory and propaganda.

. . . Comrade Stalin unmasked the Menshevik Central Committee, revealing its bankruptcy.

. . . Further on Comrade Stalin discloses a certain inherent law whereby all the opportunist groups and groupings, from the Right Menshevik liquidators to the Trotskyites, consistently unite, and he describes Trotskyism as centrism.

. . . *Comrade Stalin disclosed the social basis of Menshevism, and exposed the tactics of the Mensheviks as the tactics of the semi-bourgeois elements of the proletariat. . . .*

. . . *Comrade Stalin exposed the liquidationism of the Mensheviks and the Menshevik idea of a non-party labor congress.*

. . . Comrade Stalin proved that the idea of calling a labor congress was downright treason to the working class on the part of the Mensheviks, who "by order" of the liberal bourgeoisie, were striving to disband the revolutionary party of the working class and thereby to behead the labor movement.

. . . During the years of reaction, the Baku Bolsheviks, headed by Comrade Stalin, led the class struggles of the Baku proletariat and successfully carried out a big campaign around the conference with the oil magnates at the end of 1907.

. . . *In January and February 1908, the Baku Committee, headed by Comrade Stalin, led a series of big strikes notable for the fact that the workers passed from petty-bourgeois demands (bonuses, etc.) to proletarian demands.*

. . . During his work in Baku Comrade Stalin was arrested and sentenced to exile many times. The tsarist secret police dogged him tenaciously.

. . . Comrade Stalin was confined in the Baku prison from March 25 to the end of September 1908. He succeeded in establishing connections from prison with the Baku Committee and guided its work; he also directed the newspaper *Bakinsky Rabochy* from prison.

. . . Comrade Stalin spoke regularly at district and inter-district Party meetings, and led the work of preparing and conducting strikes. He further developed the relentless struggle to expose and defeat the Mensheviks, Social-Revolutionaries, Dashnaks and other petty-bourgeois parties.

In October 1909 Comrade Stalin arrived in Tiflis and organized and directed the struggle of the Tiflis Bolshevik organizations against the Menshevik-Liquidators.

Comrade Stalin prepared the ground for the calling of the Tiflis Bolshevik Party Conference and the publication of the Bolshevik newspaper, *Tiflisky Proletary.*[6]

The Tiflis Bolshevik Conference took place in November 1909 and worked along the lines of Comrade Stalin's recommendations—to carry on the fight on two fronts.

. . . *Under the leadership of Comrade Stalin the Bolsheviks of Transcaucasia and Georgia, all through their history, carried on a fierce struggle against Menshevism as the principal enemy in the labor movement. At all stages of the history of the Bolsheviks of Transcaucasia Comrade Stalin attacked and defeated the "legal Marxists," the Economists and the Menshevik-Liquidators, in true Leninist fashion. During the period of darkest reaction, as well as during the years of revolutionary revival, he built up and consolidated the Bolshevik Party organizations in a ruth-*

---

[6] *Tiflis Proletarian.*

less struggle against the Mensheviks and Socialist-Revolutionaries.

During his work in Baku, in the period of reaction, Comrade Stalin made Baku a fortress of Bolshevism.

The Party organization, led by Comrade Stalin, "lived right through the period of counterrevolution" and notwithstanding repressions, the reaction failed to smash it. Under the leadership of Comrade Stalin, the Baku organization "took an extremely active part in everything that went on in the labor movement; in Baku it was a mass Party in the full sense of the word."

. . . Under the leadership of Comrade Stalin, the Transcaucasian Bolsheviks organized the preparations for the Prague Conference in a decisive struggle against the Liquidators.

At this time, acting on Lenin's instructions, Sergo Ordzhonikidze arrived in Transcaucasia to assist in the preparations for the Prague Conference of the Party.

With the help and leadership of Comrade Stalin, Ordzhonikidze succeeded in establishing an organization commission in Baku for the convocation of the All-Russian Party Conference.

However, not being an eminent enough personality to be appointed a delegate to the Prague Conference of the Bolsheviks, Stalin was not called by Lenin to represent the Party there. Since the names of all the delegates were recorded and known, Beria decided that he should explain the absence of Comrade Stalin. He announced:

The Prague Conference elected a Central Committee with Lenin as its head. Comrade Stalin was also elected, although he was not present.

During the Prague Party Conference Comrade Stalin was in exile. Comrade Stalin had been arrested in St. Petersburg on September 9, 1911, and exiled to Solvychegodsk in the Vologda Province, but he managed to escape on February 29, 1912.

. . . After the Prague Conference, Comrade Stalin returned to Transcaucasia (Baku and Tiflis), and organized and directed the struggle of the Transcaucasian Bolsheviks for carrying out the decisions of the Prague Conference.

Then Beria declared:

. . . Comrade Stalin gave an excellent definition of the Marxist understanding of unity in the labor movement.

In the tremendous hall where, in the hot July weather, the sweat of more than a thousand perspiring men's bodies spread a heavy odor, the name Stalin . . . Stalin . . . Stalin sounded again and again like the echo of a working treadmill. An atmosphere of boredom and weariness prevailed. The listeners knew that from now on a new political Bible would be in force and anybody careless enough to say a word against the dogmas would quickly find himself behind bars.

Beria ended the chapter with this paragraph:

With Comrade Stalin at the helm, the Bolsheviks of Transcaucasia have at all stages of the revolutionary movement carried on an uncompromising struggle against all enemies of the working class primarily against the Mensheviks, the bourgeois nationalists, the "conciliators" and "compromisers." The historic "Letters from the Caucasus" in which Comrade Stalin tore the mask from the ideologists and builders of the Stolypin "Labor Party," played an extremely important part in the exposure and rout of the Mensheviks.

These words received loud and prolonged applause. The audience was glad that half of that day's meeting was over and they could get a little exercise by clapping their hands. Otherwise, it was easy to doze off, and such behavior, if noticed by any of the agents present, could cause some very unpleasant consequences.

Beria took a big gulp of water from a glass nearby and left the stand. There was a fifteen-minute intermission.

The men hurried to the lavatories or to the courtyard to urinate, and to the street across from the railway shop to buy a bottle of lemonade or *kvas* at the nearest kiosk around the corner.

At noon Beria returned to read the final chapter of his work. It was titled "On the History of the Struggle Against National Deviationism 1913-1924." This chapter did not differ in tone from the earlier three parts. Here Lavrenty Pavlovich revealed again that:

Lenin was the first to appreciate the great importance of Comrade Stalin's theoretical works on the national question.

. . . In his *Marxism and the National and Colonial Question* (1913), Comrade Stalin substantiated the Bolshevik theory on the national question and tore the Menshevik program of national cultural autonomy to pieces.

. . . Comrade Stalin in his report "On the Immediate Tasks of Communism in Georgia and in Transcaucasia," delivered at the meeting of the Tiflis Party organization on July 6, 1921, said that a relentless struggle against nationalism was the main political task of the Communists of Transcaucasia.

Soon after these words the reading was over—at last. There was tumultuous applause. The whole audience arose, giving the speaker a standing ovation. However, it was not for him personally, but through him for Comrade Stalin, who almost single-handedly had won Transcaucasia for Bolshevism. The enormous hall resounded with calls initiated by the Secret Police agents among the audience: "Long Live the Transcaucasian Federation!," "Long Live the Great Stalin!," "Hurrah for Comrade Stalin!," suggested by Beria.

"Hurrah! Hurrah! Hurrah!," answered over one thousand men.

It was 103 degrees outside, that day of July 22, 1935, in Tbilisi, when, at three o'clock in the sunny afternoon, the meeting of the Party workers ended. Beria set his neatly typed papers in order and put them into his briefcase. His throat was dry despite the many glasses of water he had downed during his lecture and his voice was hoarse. He was exhausted indeed. It was hard to convince those sensible men of the leadership of someone who was by no means a leader during the period described, but was just one among hundreds of others. He was also someone whom Beria resented and hated and would be happy to depose from his post, seizing his power after annihilating him without any scruples, exactly as he had done with many other Georgian Communists—even better Old Bolsheviks than Iosif Dzhugashvili—Stalin.

On the same evening Beria mailed a copy of the typescript to the Kremlin, asking Dear Comrade Stalin to peruse it, and, if approving, to be kind enough to direct it to the newspaper *Pravda*, the official organ of the Central Committee of the Communist Party of the Soviet Union, to be printed there.

Lavrenty was sure that due to this procedure his dissertation would be read by his immediate superior, and that the Big Boss would appreciate the efforts of the First Secretary of the Transcaucasian Territorial Committee. Beria, not belonging to Stalin's own, older generation, had no reason to be afraid of falling victim to the Dictator's unique extermination program. On the other hand, if his elaboration were not fully accepted and approved, Beria would not yet start a real, regular purge among the unreliable elements, and especially not against certain Old Georgian Bolsheviks. Anyway, the two-day meeting which Beria staged, and the whole lecture should prove successful.

23

At the Horse Races

THE SUMMER WAS TOO HOT to stay in Tbilisi. Beria decided to take a short leave, and to spend the end of July and part of August with his wife Nina in Abkhazia at their villa in the health resort of Sochi, not far from Sukhumi.

When he returned to his native Sukhumi, Lavrenty visited Nestor Lakoba in his office. The Secretary of the Central Executive Committee of Abkhazia, happy to see his powerful friend, invited him to dinner at his country house in Gudauti, a resort on the shores of the Black Sea near Sukhumi. It was less than half an hour by car.

The food was rich and the Caucasian Kakheti wine was of a vintage year. After dinner, Lakoba told Beria confidentially that he had written a pamphlet he would like to have published. Nestor would be happy to read it aloud to his friend Lara, and to hear his opinion and comments. Beria could not refuse him this small service. There was another bottle of wine; then Lakoba asked his guest to move with him from the dining room to the study. There, seated on the *takhta*, a soft and most comfortable Georgian couch, Lavrenty could listen to his host's melodious voice reading his manuscript. The pamphlet was a paean glorifying the dear Georgian countryman and Great Commander.

It was titled *Stalin and Khashim*, and in it Lakoba praised Iosif Vissarionovich Dzhugashvili as "the greatest man of a whole epoch, such as history gives to humanity only once in one or two hundred years," the "genial leader, unshakable and made of steel, our dear and beloved Stalin."[1]

Lavrenty approved the work in full and advised Lakoba to send the manuscript to Moscow. In his mind, however, a suspicion arose that this man could be a competitor and, since some adversaries already called Lakoba "the creator of the Abkhazian democratic oasis" in Georgia, Lavrenty was thinking that his comrade, by imprudently reading his long eulogy to him, was digging his own grave.

Two days later, from his office in Sukhumi, Lakoba phoned Beria at his summer house at Sochi. The next Sunday there was to be a big attraction at the Gudauti resort: horse races. Nestor Lakoba invited his friend Lavrenty Pavlovich to join him in watching the event as his honored guest.

The race track swarmed with thousands of spectators. Every Georgian is a born horseman, and the races are the most exciting game in the Caucasus. The day was hot, but a breeze from the nearby sea cooled the air.

In the paddock, the parade of the sorrel and black Circassian horses, the most beautiful in the world, was an impressive and magnificent show. Watching them, the Georgians, usually gay, noisy and talkative, were even more excited than ever.

The spacious honorary box, reserved for the Chairman of the Central Executive Committee of Abkhazia, was crowded with eminent persons. Besides the host, Nestor Lakoba, an attractive man with a thin mustache that looked as if drawn on with a pencil, and amiable, informal manners, was his distinguished-looking mother and his wife. There were also present his cousins Basil and Michael, handsome, tall men in their twenties. The lads were so pleasant and open it was hard to believe that in their everyday work they were ruthless *Chekists* and executioners. Now they were serving wine and Pushkin cigarettes, made of the best Caucasian tobacco, to their most honorable guests. Among these were the First Secretary of the Transcaucasian Committee of the Communist Party, dear Comrade Lavrenty Pavlovich Beria, and the People's Commissar of Foreign Trade and former Commander in Chief of

---

[1] Boris Souvarine, *Stalin* (New York: Alliance Book Corporation, Longmans, Green and Co., 1939).

the Soviet Air Force, Arkady Rosengoltz, a pioneer Bolshevik of the old generation, a man with a powerful face and broad shoulders. Rosengoltz came to Abkhazia to spend his summer vacation in Sochi with his daughter, Yelena, who was sitting in the first row. She kept looking through big field glasses lent her by Basil and at the same time nibbled chocolates brought by Michael. Yelena was a joyous and beautiful girl with big, black eyes and natural golden-red hair. It was tied in a heavy knot on her neck, which was white as marble, speckled only by a few freckles. When she laughed, as she did often, she wrinkled her cute little nose, and opened her full scarlet lips, fresh as a Caucasian Georgian cherry, and showed her white teeth. She was plump, but not fat, with small, girlish breasts. She was not yet eighteen and still growing, but looked more mature than most girls her age. Yelena was already a very sexy, bright young woman, probably still a virgin, as is often the case with girls from good Jewish families where the mothers had been brought up in very religious households. Her father was a strong-minded Commissar and known as a splendid administrator. He was an Old Bolshevik who had fought in Moscow during the Revolution. For some years, he had ruled the Donbas[2] with a strong hand. One of the most eminent Communists and a member of the Central Committee, Rosengoltz was later appointed to the Soviet Embassy in London. He stayed there until 1928, when he returned to Russia to work for the Government. He was the father of three children. Yelena, the youngest, was his beloved daughter. He was proud of her and did not let her out of his sight. Not only he, but the two young officers, Basil and Michael, were always at Yelena's side. One did not have to guess that Beria had abnormal inclinations toward very young girls, as rumors about his peculiar tastes circulated freely among his acquaintances. One could be positive that Lavrenty Pavlovich, now trying his best to be interesting and gallant, would not hesitate to do anything to make love to her.

A few days later, Nestor Lakoba invited Beria to his country house for an afternoon cup of coffee, intimating between the lines that this would be a sort of stag party. When Lavrenty arrived at his friend's villa he was surprised to see there were only two other men present. They were Lakoba's two cousins, Basil and Michael;

---

[2] Donbas: Donets coal basin in the Ukrainian SSR. This is one of most important mining and metallurgical areas of the USSR.

the only female guest was the charming redhead, Yelena. Beria did not ask his host what had happened to his previous plans for the party and why this time the girl was not accompanied by her father. Anyway, the party was nice and clean. The gramophone played, the young lady danced waltzes, tangoes and fox-trots, with the two lads taking turns as her partner. The refreshments were also very elegant, with pastries, tea, Turkish delight, candy and wines. But when the girl excused herself and left for a short while "to powder her little nose," one of the young *Chekists* winked at the other men and poured some pure alcohol into her wine goblet. When Yelena returned, the gentlemen toasted her as Queen of Beauty and urged her to drink her goblet in one gulp. Soon afterwards the girl felt dizzy and hot, and asked to go out to get some fresh air. Beria and the two young gentlemen offered to escort her, suggesting a stroll in the garden surrounding the house. Two of the men linked arms with her and went out, led by the third. In one of the shaded alleys the girl felt faint, so her escort helped her to a bench and sat her on it. She was too sick, however, to sit up by herself. They laid her on the grass. One of them started undressing her. At first the girl did not realize what this was about. She probably thought they wanted to loosen her tight clothes to help her breathe more easily. Then, when she understood their intentions, she tried to shout for help. But it was too late. The man on top of her was pressing her to the ground with all his weight. She tried to fight him off, but it was hopeless. She was raped by all of them in turn.

The girl was overpowered and used. But what would happen when she got home and told her father the truth? One of the young *Chekists* put his hands around her throat and pressed. Harder and harder.

Back in the house, Lavrenty went to Lakoba's studio. From there, in a sober and dry matter-of-fact voice, he telephoned the investigations magistrate, ordering whoever was then on duty to come at once with his assistants. In a short time, investigating officials arrived. The Chief of the Secret Police in Georgia, Beria, informed him that, after having had a few glasses of wine, the girl became hysterical and ran away to the garden. They had followed her, calling her to come back, but she did not listen to them. Soon they found her dead. The hysterical girl had committed suicide. No autopsy was needed. A statement by the First Secretary of the

Transcaucasian Committee of the Communist Party, Lavrenty Pavlovich Beria, corroborated by the witness, Secretary of the Executive Committee of Abkhazia, Nestor Lakoba, was sufficient. All the magistrate had to do was to inform at once the deceased girl's father about the accident.

The next day, Beria left Sukhumi for his office in the capital of Georgia.

24

Singing in a Friendly Choir

NESTOR LAKOBA, the Secretary of the Central Executive Committee of Abkhazia, was going to publish his praise of Stalin. He was positive it was good that he had shown it to Lavrenty Pavlovich who, as an intimate friend should, advised him to mail the manuscript to Moscow to be approved and printed. Lakoba, however, did not suspect that Beria, once his protégé, had agents planted in his office and that they informed the NKVD in Tbilisi about his every activity and move. Beria had established a special file with evidence and accusations of all kinds against his former benefactor. Of course, the accident of the rape and murder of Commissar Rosengoltz's daughter, from which the Chief of the Secret Police in Georgia certainly excluded his own part, added to this dossier, was of no consequence. Much more important was the fact that Lakoba, although a Communist, was a Caucasian, or strictly, an Abkhazian patriot, who would gladly become a ruler of that country with Sukhumi as its capital. Beria already had in his files more than one piece of information substantiating the familiar saying that Abkhazia was a "democratic oasis in Georgia," and that under Lakoba's rule many Mensheviks and Dashnaks still enjoyed their freedom. Moreover, Lakoba was Stalin's close friend, and this aspect of the matter was most inconvenient for Lavrenty. Beria was quietly gathering the material needed to liquidate Lakoba, just as he expected to help Stalin with the annihilation of other of his

Caucasian Bolshevik friends: Mdivani, Makharadze, and the closest one of all, Yenukidze, as well as Ordzhonikidze and Stalin's brother-in-law, Pavel Alliluyev. Beria had data about them all carefully stored in his meticulously kept dossiers, and had already denounced some of them in his latest speech delivered at a meeting of Party functionaries.

Lavrenty Beria saw that his career could proceed quickly over the dead bodies of his best friends, sponsors and protectors, and of the Old Caucasian Bolsheviks who remembered that dear Comrade "Soso" Stalin was not the only liberator who had saved the Caucasus from capitalistic oppression, or made sacrifices for the cause of Communism's victory. By eliminating these men Beria paved the surest way to become Chief of the NKVD in Moscow and Stalin's right-hand man. Many individuals after Dzerzhinsky—*Cheka's* creator and organizer, who had died as a result of Stalin's bad humor —had tried to obtain this post of highest power. Some of them, important personalities in OGPU, disappeared sooner than anyone could have envisioned.

Vyacheslav Menzhinsky, who reorganized OGPU into an independent state within a state by rebuilding "Units of Special Purpose—ChON[1]—and a formation of "Troops for Internal Guard" —VOKhR[2]—was a highly educated man and a hardworking official. But, as the inner circle knew, Menzhinsky was poisoned by his Deputy, the little pharmacist Yagoda, who took his place.

One year later Mikhail Trillisser, Yagoda's deputy who, for his own purposes, was carrying on an investigation of his boss' past, found out that Yagoda had given false information about himself, entering in the records that he had been an active Communist long before the Revolution. Trillisser showed his findings to Stalin in the hope that Yagoda would be liquidated and that he, Trillisser, in reward for his good and faithful service, would get the post presently occupied by his superior. Stalin accepted the report but instead of rewarding Trillisser, sent him to a hard labor camp in Siberia as punishment for a subordinate's disloyalty to his boss. There Mikhail Trillisser perished. Yagoda was still needed at that time as an obedient tool for Stalin in preparing the assassination of Kirov.

---

[1] ChON: Chasti Osobnovo Naznachenia—Units of Special Purpose.

[2] VOKhR: Voyska Vnootrennei Okhrany—Troops for Internal Guard.

Beria was too intelligent not to be aware of the fact that one false step would mean his downfall similar to Trillisser's. On the other hand, sitting sheepishly in his corner and doing nothing would not help his career either. He decided to act against someone at the top whose years were already numbered. But Lavrenty did not want to hurry. He had to work step by step, as he was doing with Yenukidze, Orakhelashvili and Makharadze.

From now on Beria concentrated his cunning attack on Grigory "Dear Sergo" Ordzhonikidze. This man had been too close to the late Kirov to be saved. He was a prominent Old Bolshevik, one of the conquerors of Azerbaijan, Georgia and Armenia, and after Kirov's assassination one could predict that he probably was not in Stalin's favor.

Ordzhonikidze, who once was entrusted with the job of writing Stalin's biography—as was Yenukidze—was still one of "Soso" Stalin's closest friends and presently was the People's Commissar of Heavy Industry in Moscow. But so was Avel Yenukidze, who, in 1934 after Kirov's murder, was given a special and most responsible task. On December 1, 1934, on Stalin's personal initiative and demand and without the Politburo's approval, the Secretary of the Presidium of the Central Executive Committee, Avel Sofronovich Yenukidze, signed a most important directive for arrests, deportations and executions of hundreds of thousands of people, and his orders became the basis for mass acts of abuse of social legality.[3]

Yet, a year later, Yenukidze fell so far from favor that Beria had been able to denounce him in his speech in Tbilisi without any fear for his own safety. Soon the turn would come for "Dear Sergo."

On June 18, 1936, the whole Soviet Union was in mourning. Russia's most beloved writer, Maxim Gorky, had died. He was a

[3] "I. Investigative agencies are directed to speed up the cases of those accused of the preparation or execution of acts of terror.

"II. Judicial organs are directed not to hold up the execution of death sentences pertaining to crimes in this category in order to consider the possibility of pardon, because the Presidium of the Central Executive Committee USSR does not consider as possible the receiving of petitions of this sort.

"III. The organs of the Commissariat of Internal Affairs are directed to execute the death sentences against criminals of the above-mentioned category immediately after the passage of sentences." Nikita S. Khrushchev, *Secret Speech Before a Closed Session of the 20th Congress of the Communist Party of the Soviet Union on February 25, 1956* (Washington: United States Government Printing Office, 1957).

good friend of the late Nadezhda Alliluyeva, Stalin's former wife, and of Stalin. While Gorky was ill, Stalin had visited him. Even the day before Gorky's death Stalin had sat at Maxim's bedside. The writer's funeral became a huge national manifestation; the entire country paid its tribute to the author and devoted Communist.

Beria went to Moscow to take part in the last homage paid to the great writer and playwright. In the course of the next few days, Lavrenty submitted to Stalin the draft of a new, tough program in accordance with the Dictator's recent policies regarding the Caucasus. In line with Stalin's plans, the Transcaucasian Federation would have to be abolished, while the three countries, Azerbaijan, Georgia and Armenia, were to be individually incorporated into the USSR as separate Soviet puppet republics. Such an important change could not be achieved without a purge affecting the Old Caucasian Bolsheviks and several of the present leaders. This task had now been given to Lavrenty Pavlovich. Beria also mentioned to Stalin the names of some Old Georgian revolutionaries whom the Dictator had praised years before as his mentors and teachers of Marxism during the course of one of his speeches in Tiflis. Now the First Secretary of the Transcaucasian Committee of the Communist Party, Beria suggested the liquidation of these men, since their names, printed in the text of the speech, would be hard to ignore. Stalin agreed and gave him a free hand in the matter.

During his stay in the capital, Lavrenty learned from his informers that Yenukidze's fall was only a matter of a few months. Now, Beria decided to reveal to Stalin a few details that could be used against this pioneer Bolshevik of the Caucasus. Lavrenty especially criticized the style of Yenukidze's life as one that an exemplary Communist should never lead. Beria also told Comrade Stalin of some crimes committed by Sergo Ordzhonikidze. It was known to Stalin that Sergo's deputy and personal friend, Grigory Pyatakov, although an experienced Communist, showed many shortcomings as an administrator and, by his poor management, had failed to achieve the expected production in his department. However, instead of punishing the culprit, Sergo continued to protect him by falsifying reports. According to the records brought by Beria, Ordzhonikidze was also in constant touch with his bosom friend, Kartvelishvili, a former Chairman of the Georgian Council of People's Commissars, and later the Secretary of the Transcaucasian Federation Committee. But, despite being demoted by Stalin in

order to vacate his post for Beria, Kartvelishvili was still Ordzhonikidze's protégé.

In the evening Stalin invited several of his relatives and friends
to dinner at *Blizhny*, his Kuntsevo villa. The Alliluyevs, parents of
Stalin's late second wife, Nadezhda, came with their other daugh-
ter, Anna. Alexey Svanidze, brother of Stalin's late first wife,
Yekaterina, was also present. Invited also were the always smiling
Anastas Mikoyan, and "Dear Sergo" Ordzhonikidze with his wife,
Zinaida. Even the young Svetlana was allowed to join the guests.

Beria, whom Svetlana in her early girlhood called "Uncle Lara,"
used to play with her when she was a child. He did it not only to
show his warm feelings toward the Dictator's beloved daughter,
but also because of the sexual pleasure he experienced in holding
very young girls on his lap. Now his caresses were limited to kisses
on Svetlana's cheek and to sitting close to her. Svetlana was already
eleven, and Beria realized that showing his taste for very young
females might provoke gossip, so he was careful to behave himself.

The food was excellent and the prevailing atmosphere that of a
family gathering, friendly and gay. All the people present talked
lightheartedly and drank the sweet red Georgian Kakheti wine.
The dinner over, everybody moved to the spacious porch. There,
Stalin's close friend *Komandarm* Semyon Budyonny, who knew
many sentimental and romantic Ukrainian ballads, took his accor-
dion. In a short while all the party, in a wonderful sincere mood
sang in chorus the charming folk songs, while the joyous melodies
sounded clear in the warm night air of the beautiful Russian
June.

25

How to Kill Your Friends

Soon the events in Moscow started rolling with the speed of an avalanche. In the course of a great purge initiated by Stalin, several prominent personalities were put on trial. Lev Borisovich Kamenev and Grigory Yevseyevich Zinoviev, two veteran Bolsheviks active since 1901 and pioneers of the October Revolution, had been arrested and both confessed to crimes such as being Trotskyists, organizers of a terrorist gang, murderers, assassins, traitors and foreign agents. They pleaded guilty, together with fourteen other men accused of being their collaborators or members of their terrorist, subversive organization. The trial started on August 19, 1936, lasted six days and brought a death sentence to the accused. There was no appeal against the verdict and the defendants were executed within 24 hours. Beria had his own ideas about the trials. Of the group of sixteen accused men, the two main defendants, Kamenev and Zinoviev, had once been close friends and worshipers of Lenin. They had been members of the Politburo and were top figures in the Central Committee; in 1920 Zinoviev had been President of the Comintern.[1] In other words, their activity had been at least as honorable and meritorious as that of Stalin. But both were Jews. Grigory Yevseyevich Zinoviev's real name was Hirsh Apfelbaum, while Lev Kamenev was born Rosenfeld. Moreover, Ka-

[1] The Communist International (CI).

menev, educated in Tiflis where he attended high school, was a
fighting Communist in Georgia, where his clandestine work among
laborers was at least as well known as that of Stalin. This weighed
heavily against Stalin's ambition, for he wished to remain the one
and only Communist hero of the Caucasus. Being Lenin's closest
friend, Kamenev later became a member of the Party in Georgia,
representing Lenin's political line in that country, and Lenin's
point of view differed from that of Stalin. Kamenev also used to
go abroad frequently. Once he spent several weeks in London as a
Delegate to the Third International Communist Congress. To Stalin, with his obsession that everybody was a spy, it appeared that
Kamenev could have made contacts with British agents when in
London. Furthermore, he was married to Trotsky's sister and being
a traitor's brother-in-law automatically made him a traitor, too. But
above all else, once when Stalin had escaped from exile before the
Revolution, Kamenev had helped him find a hiding place in Tiflis.
He did it so cleverly that the Tsarist police failed to nab the fugi-
tive, despite a search of Kamenev's flat and interrogation of the
tenants. The performance of such a good deed was sufficient for
Stalin to condemn Kamenev to death, as he hated any sign of char-
ity and unselfish sympathy in people. There was always the danger
that Kamenev might have mentioned this event somewhere in his
memoirs. Stalin hated for it to be revealed that he had been helped
in his underground activities.

As to the confessions of crimes and the general plea of guilty by
the defendants, Beria had no illusions about how such results were
obtained. The NKVD, the successor of *Cheka*, GPU and OGPU,
had their own well-proven methods to get any evidence required
and to prepare the prisoners for trial. The Chief Public Prosecutor,
Andrey Yanuarevich Vishinsky, was sure to get all the evidence
properly documented. This was especially certain because several
of the accused had been arrested soon after Kirov's assassination,
and such a prolonged stay behind bars would have helped make
them more easily bent to the exact will of their inquisitors.

Having staged this spectacular trial, Stalin set out for his native
Georgia for his summer vacation. As usual, he was traveling by his
private, special armored train with a platoon of bodyguards under
the command of Red Army General Nikolay Vlasik. General Vlasik,
the officer in charge of security arrangements for Stalin, was a
simple, crude peasant, illiterate, but endowed with an innate dog's

flair for scenting the direction of danger. Until the last moment, nobody knew in which car the Dictator would ride and, in every town where the train had to stop for coal and water, the local police had been alerted beforehand to empty the station of travelers and circle it with a cordon of troops.

That particular summer, Stalin took as his aide Andrey Alexandrovich Zhdanov, Secretary of the Soviet Communist Party's Central Committee. He chose him not solely for company, but to entrust him with a heavy task he intended to complete while resting on the shores of the Black Sea.

When the train arrived in Tbilisi, the guard detail at the station was under Beria's personal command.

During his short stay in the Georgian capital, Stalin spent most of his time at the bedside of his ailing, eighty-year-old mother.

Two days later Stalin left for his villa at Sochi. That summer, however, there was no time for rest and relaxation. With Zhdanov acting more as male secretary than helpmate and adviser, Stalin decided to put the last touches to the draft of a new Constitution prepared for him by Bukharin, Zinoviev and Radek, all eminent Communists whom he planned to annihilate sooner or later, and by the Chief Prosecutor, Vishinsky; and to pave the way for crushing several Old Bolsheviks who, being open-minded, still stood between him and absolute power.

Officially, however, Stalin was staying at his beautiful Abkhazian health resort for his holiday. In the evenings he invited his countrymen and best friends, Beria, Lakoba and Mdivani. In their company he could talk freely and eat and drink heavily.

To launch a new purge even more perfidious than that against Kamenev and Zinoviev, the Dictator needed somebody even more ruthless than the present Chief of NKVD, Yagoda. Anyhow, Yagoda was no longer wanted. As Chief of the Security Police in the whole USSR he fulfilled his duties in the case of Kirov's assassination, which became a pretext for mass arrests of potential foes of Stalin. This category included the most meritorious and prominent Old Bolsheviks. His useful service began when, thanks to his former position as a pharmacist, Yagoda had been named Head of the Toxicological Laboratory at the Kremlin. This enabled him to speed up the death of Lenin, who suffered a lot anyway after three strokes. His knowledge of drugs and poisons continued to help Yagoda in his career and got him the then vacant post of Chief of the OGPU, when his superior, Vyacheslav Menzhinsky, had died suddenly. His knowledge of drugs also proved useful in stopping forever Maxim Gorky's painful tubercular coughing. Gorky had once rejected Stalin's request to write a book about him and this was enough to make the Dictator decide to annihilate the great writer. Everything Yagoda had ever done was executed on orders from his Master, the Great Comrade Stalin.

Now Yagoda had been used long enough and Stalin did not need him any more. The post could be given to Beria, but Stalin still wanted him in the Caucasus to conduct purges in Georgia, Azerbaijan and Armenia until the final liquidation of the last traces of the nominal independence expressed by the Transcaucasian Federation.

As Yagoda's replacement, Stalin chose Nikolay Ivanovich Yezhov, once Political Commissar in the Red Army, later member of the staff of the Party's Central Committee. Appointed Chief of the Division of Party Cadres, Yezhov was soon elected member of the Central Committee and liaison man between the Politburo and the Security Police. But despite all these honors, Yezhov still resented his poor childhood and his lack of education, and he hated the intelligentsia and anyone who was prominent. This included many Old Bolsheviks, creators of the New Order. Stalin was aware of that hatred and was sure that Yezhov would gladly annihilate anyone who had once been important in the mother country. Therefore, he was the right man for the job.

On September 25, 1936, from his summer house in Sochi, Stalin, together with Zhdanov, sent to Kaganovich, Molotov and other members of the Politburo the following telegram:

We deem it absolutely necessary and urgent that Comrade Yezhov be nominated to the post of People's Commissar for Internal Affairs. Yagoda has definitely proved himself to be incapable of unmasking the Trotsky-ite-Zinovievite bloc. The OGPU is four years behind in this matter. This is noted by all Party workers and by the majority of the representatives of the NKVD.[2]

Immediately after this order Genrikh Yagoda was removed from his office and replaced by Nikolay Ivanovich Yezhov.

---

[2] Nikita S. Khrushchev, *Secret Speech Before a Closed Session of the 20th Congress of the Communist Party of the Soviet Union of February 25, 1956* (Washington: U. S. Government Printing Office, 1957).

The new Chief of Security knew well what his appointment meant. Soon a wave of arrests swept over Moscow. In a short time hundreds of the most prominent Old Bolsheviks, once co-workers and close friends of Lenin, with whom they had built the new fatherland, went to prison.

Stalin had planned to return to the Kremlin in a few weeks. But during the first days of October Beria telephoned from Tbilisi to call him to his mother's home. The old Ekaterina Georgyevna Dzugashvili had died. The funeral became a great ceremony for everyone in Georgia's capital, whose inhabitants, in accordance with Beria's orders, were required to observe official mourning. Schools, factories and shops were closed, while schoolchildren, university students, teachers and professors had to join the procession, following the hearse to the cemetery with lighted candles in their hands.

Stalin's children came from Moscow: Yakov, Vasily and Svetlana. The youngsters became Beria's house guests and stayed in his luxurious apartment in the residential section of the city. Also from Moscow came all the Svanidzes and Alliluyevs, as well as friends. Among these were Bukharin, who was now Editor-in-Chief of the government newspaper *Izvestia*, Malenkov, Bulganin, Khrushchev, Kaganovich, Molotov, Mikoyan and Ordzhinikidze.

When he approached his mother's open coffin and kissed her on the forehead and cheeks, Iosif Vissarionovich was truly and deeply moved although he shed no tears, as he had done so openly at Kirov's funeral.

Immediately after the ceremony relatives and friends returned to Moscow, as did all the officials, including Malenkov. The latter came back with special instructions given him by Zhdanov, as the immediate subordinate of Stalin.

Soon Bukharin was arrested while at work in his editorial office and, by special order of Yezhov, was jailed in the most secure prison, Lefortovo, in a suburb of Moscow.

The next day the Dictator went back to Sochi, accompanied by Zhdanov and his bodyguard, General Vlasik. He took two of his children with him, Vasily and Svetlana, but not Yakov, whom he never could stand.

They were joined by Lavrenty Beria, the best friend of the family and the most faithful disciple of the Leader—the Great Comrade Stalin.

26

Requiem for "Dear Sergo"

THE NEW GREAT WAVE of purges initiated by Yezhov still did not include Ordzhonikidze, who stood in the way of Beria's advancement. Lavrenty decided to attack "Dear Sergo" once again. He realized, however, that this time he had to be more cautious and shrewd than ever before. For Stalin, being extremely suspicious, could easily smell a plot contrived for no other purpose than advancing Lavrenty's climb to the top. This could end the career of Beria, whom the Great Dictator would destroy exactly as he had many of his other immediate subordinates.

Weaving the plot against Grigory Ordzhonikidze took Beria many days of exhausting work and several sleepless nights. Finally Lavrenty built a most cunning trap which at the same time was the safest one for its constructor. In a few months Ordzhonikidze was going to be fifty years old. Since he was the People's Commissar of Heavy Industry and officially Stalin's bosom friend, it was obvious that his birthday would be marked by a national celebration. Beria decided to write and publish a long essay in which he would praise Ordzhonikidze as one of the most eminent of Old Guard Bolsheviks, but only as a capable and obedient disciple of the Great Stalin. By this strategy Lavrenty would avoid being an author who raised someone over the Big Boss. Quite the contrary: Beria, while availing himself of one more means of expressing his admiration for the Genius Stalin, would direct the whole fury of the Chief against Ordzhonikidze as a man who supposedly claimed a share of the

Dictator's laurels. In his writing Beria would remind his Superior that Ordzhonikidze was another famous Georgian who had contributed much to the Revolution and was one of Stalin's meritorious contemporaries. And such individuals the Dictator could not stand.

On October 28, 1936 there appeared in *Pravda* an article "Staunch Fighter of the Cause of the Lenin-Stalin Party."[1] It started with a joyous sentence: "Comrade Ordzhonikidze is fifty years of age!" This lucubration, which filled almost the whole second page, was adorned with a big photograph of Grigory Konstantinovich "Sergo" Ordzhonikidze, while above the title of that article the name of its author, Lavrenty Beria, was underlined. In this panegyric for the Genius Stalin and eulogy for Ordzhonikidze, the Muscovites could read such declarations as: that Comrade Ordzhonikidze, who just celebrated his fiftieth birthday has devoted thirty-three years of his life "to the heroic revolutionary struggle of the working class," and also that "the first teacher and instructor of Comrade Sergo was the Initiator of the revolutionary Marxism-Leninism, the Founder of the Bolshevik Party in Georgia and Transcaucasia, the Great Stalin." After such an introduction Beria could emphasize the notion that "during the period of tsarist autocracy Comrade Sergo was one of the builders of the Bolshevik Party," and that "he earned a place among the outstanding fighters of the Old Guard Bolshevik." This so positive and impressive a phrase, as Beria rightly calculated, would place a nail in Ordzhonikidze's coffin rather than bring "Dear Sergo" an award from the hands of the Great Stalin.

The article, as well as the whole intrigue, was a real masterpiece of perfidy. After reading Beria's lucubration Stalin became so angry with Ordzhonikidze that he rescinded his previous decision to award Sergo with the Order of Lenin, a decoration usually given to outstanding Bolsheviks on their fiftieth birthday.

On December 6, 1936, Stalin's Constitution was officially announced, having been voted into law the preceding day. It was a great holiday for the nation which had received "the most democratic Bill of Rights in the world." The new Constitution promised the people freedom of expression by freedom of the press, speech, assembly and demonstration.

Certainly everyone realized that such freedoms were in fact lim-

---

[1] Appendix 7.

ited to freedom in the meaning of the interests of rulers of the USSR, which was well guarded by the Secret Police.

Within the framework of Stalin's new Constitution, which transformed the USSR into a paradise on earth, there was no place for any separatist groups. In other words, such organizations as the Transcaucasian Socialist Federated Soviet Republic were to decide for themselves whether or not their existence was needed for the welfare of the Caucasian peoples. A convention of representatives of the three Transcaucasian countries, Azerbaijan, Georgia and Armenia, had been called on December 27, 1936, in Baku. The meeting took place in the building of the Central Committee of the Azerbaijan Communist Party, located in the heart of the town not far from a broad avenue recently renamed Kirov Avenue. The delegates were addressed by Old Caucasian Bolsheviks, who had fought for the liberation of Transcaucasia from the clutches of the capitalists. These were the good comrades Anastas Mikoyan and Sergo Ordzhonikidze. Among the Georgian delegates were Charkviani, Bakradze and Dekanozov. The head of the delegation was Lavrenty Pavlovich Beria.

After three days of debating and discussing the new situation, the Assembly voted unanimously on December 30, 1936, to disband the Transcaucasian Federation. Azerbaijan, Georgia and Armenia were to be incorporated into the USSR as three separate republics. The resolution was voted unanimously, as was the suggestion of sending a telegram to Comrade Stalin, Caucasus' favorite son, asking him to accept the three countries into the family of Soviet Republics.

Beria had no doubt whatsoever that the decision had been adopted under pressure originating from his presence in his capacity as Chief of the Caucasian NKVD and from Malenkov's arrival in Baku. He had been sent from Moscow, purportedly as an observer. The Presidium consisted of Mikoyan and Ordzhonikidze, the two who once had initiated the ruthless bloodbath in Baku and in Georgia; their presence was also quite significant.

Now Beria started to prepare a new purge in Transcaucasia. He realized that, if he failed to liquidate all Caucasian Bolsheviks who believed in the benefits of Communism in their own countries but rejected the notion of being the Kremlin's vassals, he would never obtain a post as Stalin's aide in Moscow.

It was no secret that almost all the leading Caucasian Communists were nationalists. Such a point of view had no place in the Soviet Union. These men had to be annihilated. Beria understood, however, that it would be risky to begin with the small, unimportant cogs while one of the most eminent personalities in the Caucasus was still in full power. Accordingly, Beria decided to convince Stalin of the great danger of keeping Sergo Ordzhonikidze in his post.

Shortly after the Russian New Year's Day, Lavrenty went to Moscow and spent the two-day holiday in talks with the Dictator in his *dacha* at Kuntsevo. Beria reminded his Boss that, since Ordzhonikidze had dared to contradict Stalin and defend his protégé, the recently arrested former Deputy Commissar of Heavy Industry Grigory Pyatakov, paying him friendly visits in jail, he became guilty of all the crimes against the Soviet industry committed by Pyatakov, and the crime of lowering industry's productivity was tantamount to sabotage. This was an act directed against the Country, the Government and, finally, a crime against Stalin.

On the other hand, reasoned Beria, as long as Ordzhonikidze was alive, it would be hard even to begin breaking down the stronghold of Transcaucasia's leaders, where many of the People's Commissars were Sergo's men.

Lavrenty returned to Tbilisi feeling sure the days of "Dear Sergo" were numbered. This suited his private plans, as he knew Ordzhonikidze had some objections to Beria's occupying his present post of First Secretary of the Transcaucasian Committee and was voting for his pal Kartvelishvili for that position; sooner or later he would try to undermine Beria's career in Moscow. Moreover, it was Ordzhonikidze who had interrupted Beria's education to become an architect, nominated his spy Snegov as Lavrenty's deputy in Azerbaijan, and later delayed Beria's transfer from Baku to Tbilisi after his appointment by Stalin. For this, Ordzhonikidze should be punished.

On January 23, 1937, Ordzhonikidze's deputy, Grigory Leonidovich Pyatakov was brought before a court. With him were seven prominent Bolsheviks: Mikhail Boguslavsky and Yakov Drobnis, heroes of the Civil War; Yakov Lifshitz, a former Deputy Commissar for Railways and Head of the Southern Railways; Nikolay Muralov, a former Inspector General of the Red Army and former Military Governor of Moscow; Karl Radek, an eminent journalist and editor of the newspaper *Izvestia* who had worked on the draft of the new Stalin Constitution; Grigory Sokolnikov, former Commissar of Finance and Ambassador to London; and Leonid Serebryakov, former Commissar of Transportation. There were also nine other defendants, persons of lesser importance.

Pyatakov was accused of sabotage in the railway, coal and chemical industries. The Chief State Prosecutor of the USSR, Andrey Vyshinsky, was Public Attorney for the case. The trial lasted seven days. The verdict was announced on January 30, 1937. The death sentence had been voted for Pyatakov and the other defendants, with the exception of Radek and Serebryakov. They each received ten years of hard labor in Siberia.

As soon as the trial ended, Ordzhonikidze went to Stalin and asked for mercy for the devoted Communist, Comrade Pyatakov. He begged for his life to be spared. The Dictator answered, however, that this would be disastrous for the prestige of the Soviet judiciary which now, thanks to the new Constitution, had become absolutely free and independent from any outside efforts to interfere with and influence its decisions. All Soviet citizens were equal in the face of justice, so nobody should enjoy special privileges and favors.

The same night, the condemned were executed.

The death penalty for Pyatakov, deputy of Commissar Ordzhonikidze, meant the downfall of his chief and protector. Ordzhonikidze fully realized this, because months earlier, shortly after Pyatakov's imprisonment, Sergo had defended his actions before Stalin, and Soso had promised "Dear Sergo" his protégé would not be sent before a firing squad.

Two weeks later, when Ordzhonikidze, still a member of the Politburo, was working late in the evening, as he often did, in his office of the People's Commissariat of Heavy Industry, NKVD functionaries entered his private apartment. They forbade his wife Zinaida to phone her husband and started searching the flat. They even tore the mattresses apart and confiscated some private letters, notes, family photographs and documents.

When Ordzhonikidze returned home he tried to phone Stalin, but to no avail. He was only able to reach Yezhov, the Chief of the NKVD, and he furiously berated him. Of course, this was an act of helpless despair. This event had been kept from public knowledge, but not from Beria, for whom it became a signal to begin taking an active part.

On February 17, 1937, "Dear Sergo" had a long, personal talk with "Soso." The conversation was friendly, as befits a talk between two comrades who had been close to each other for so many years, and two countrymen both hailing from Georgia, which was so dear to them. Then, Sergo went to his office, where he worked until two o'clock in the morning.

When he came home two high-ranking NKVD officers were waiting for him. They asked him for a few words in his study, without his wife's presence. The next morning Ordzhonikidze did not go to his office, but tried to talk to Comrade Stalin on the phone. Unfortunately, the Dictator could not be reached. Later, Sergo was visited by Alexander Poskrebyshev, Stalin's personal secretary and aide for special commissions. Soon after, Grigory Konstantinovich Ordzhonikidze was dead. His widow Zinaida phoned Stalin, who came immediately. Four doctors, G. Kaminsky, People's Commissar for Health, USSR; I. Khodorovsky, Chief of the Kremlin Medical Administration; L. Levin, Consultant to the Kremlin Medical Administration, and S. Mets, Duty Physician of the Kremlin's Clinic, performed a quick autopsy and issued and signed an official report giving paralysis of the heart as the cause of death. That night in Tbilisi Ordzhonikidze's older brother, Sergo-Papuli, an outstanding Georgian Bolshevik, was secretly arrested by Beria, underwent several hours of interrogation and beating, and was then shot to death.[2]

The next day, on February 19, *Pravda* reproduced on its front page a photograph showing Stalin, Molotov, Zhdanov, Mikoyan and other comrades standing in front of Ordzhonikidze's coffin. All were in deep grief.

After the great and never-to-be-forgotten "Dear Sergo's" funeral, Beria hastened to show Stalin that everybody having doubts about the cause of Ordzhonikidze's death and daring to whisper any rumor about the matter would be liquidated. The Georgian Commissar Mirzabekyan, a close co-worker of Sergo-Papuli Ordzhonikidze, disappeared one day from his office, was brought to the Tbilisi prison in Metekhy Castle, and at night was shot in its cellar. Later, Beria signed an arrest warrant for Gvakharia, an active and meritorious organizer, promoter and administrator of a huge Geor-

---

[2] N. S. Khrushchev, *Secret Speech Before a Closed Session of the 20th Congress of the Communist Party of the Soviet Union on February 25, 1956* (Washington: U. S. Government Printing Office, 1957).

gain ironworks. After a prolonged session of beatings with a club administered by Beria personally, the prisoner, who for several years had been Lavrenty's close friend, was taken to the basement and shot.

By coincidence, Gvakharia was a nephew of the late "Dear Sergo."

In a few days' time the families of those three executed men, Sergo-Papuli Ordzhonikidze, Mirzabekyan and Gvakharia, some of their associates, as well as immediate subordinates, were arrested by Beria and disappeared behind the bars of the State jail on Olginskaya Street in Tbilisi.

27

The Teachers of Practical Communism

IN HIS MEMORABLE AND MONUMENTAL SPEECH delivered at the meeting of Party Functionaries on July 21 and 22, 1935, in Tbilisi, while defending the still existing Transcaucasian Federation, Beria accused Mamia Orakhelashvili, Philip Makharadze and other Caucasian Old Bolsheviks of national deviationism. Lavrenty attacked them because previously they had been against the Federation.

Before March 1922 this group of Georgian Communists had been in fact against the Federation, since they were afraid their country would lose its national character in the amalgam of the three countries. Instead, they suggested that each of these countries, Georgia, Azerbaijan and Armenia, should separately join the USSR.

Being proud Georgians, they preferred that their country enter the union of Communist Republics as an equal member with its own banner. This idea of nationalism, however, although accepted by Lenin, was against the harsh line of politics represented by Stalin, Dzerzhinsky and Ordzhonikidze. There was no place for any nationalism whatsoever. But since Stalin's recent Constitution, the new times were different from before. There was no question of a separate Federation being a state within a state. When, on December 30, 1936, in Baku at a specially called session, the delegates of these three Transcaucasian countries decided to disband the Federation in order to join the USSR separately, it seemed that the dream of the Old fighters, Mdivani and his comrades, had come true. But it only seemed to be so. Indeed, it was a trap. This time the three countries were to be only small cogs in the tremendous machine, recognizable only by their names, mere puppets with no significance at all. Their role in the USSR was to be reduced to nothing. They would be vassals toiling for Russia by supplying it with corn, fruits and wine from Georgia, oil from Azerbaijan and cotton from Armenia, at the expense of the Caucasian peoples.

The Old Georgian Bolsheviks realized this. But they were unable to vote for retaining the status quo and continuing the present form of the Transcaucasian Federation, and to oppose the annexation of the three Caucasian countries to the Soviet Union. They felt caught because some years before when they had fiercely advocated the very same idea, they had been later branded "national deviationists" by Beria in his speech. Moreover, they still occupied top positions as Commissars, so they should be aware that the Kremlin was always right in its decisions about what was best for the Sovietland as a whole. Now if they were to express any hesitation about accepting this suggestion from Moscow, they would appear once more to be Georgian nationalists—which they indeed were, despite their Communist beliefs. They realized that their Caucasian country was losing its last trace of independence. By creating at first a Federation of three separate Transcaucasian Republics on March 12, 1922, Stalin used their own idea, and then soon after, on December 13, of the same year, he reshaped that new Federation of the three independent countries into one Transcaucasian Socialist Federation, so that these three countries lost their individual character and at last were incorporated into the USSR. If Stalin planned it so from the very beginning, it was really a devilishly cynical plot.

During a period of fourteen years, the pioneers of Communism in the Caucasus were watched by the shrewd Chief of the Georgian *Cheka*, Stalin's henchman, Lavrenty Pavlovich Beria, so well remembered there for his merciless, bloody purge of thousands of Georgians in the aftermath of the 1924 uprising.

During the trial of Kamenev, Zinoviev and others, one of the defendants, Ter-Vaganyan, Chief of the Armenian Bolsheviks and leader of the Soviet revolutionary movement in Armenia, former Editor in Chief of the Party newspaper, *Under the Banner of Marxism*, testified that a group of Georgian deviationists planned to assassinate Stalin, Kirov, Ordzhonikidze, Kaganovich, Voroshilov, Beria and other dignitaries. Ter-Vaganyan mentioned only one name: that of Mikhail Okudzhava, but it was well known that one of the most prominent Georgian deviationists was Budu Mdivani. Later on, in the course of the Pyatakov trial, Mdivani's name had again been mentioned repeatedly, this time in connection with his purported planning of terrorist acts against Yezhov and Beria. Although such false depositions were usually extorted from defendants by torture, or they confessed to anything at all to please and mollify the prosecutor, it was a good pretext for Beria to start new mass arrests.

Soon after Ordzhonikidze's sudden death and imprisonment of his relatives, hundreds of persons suspected of being nationalists were arrested at night, loaded into trucks and brought to jail.

About the end of February 1937 Beria arrested Budu Mdivani, Stalin's friend from boyhood times, and a fighting Bolshevik who once, leading a small detachment of Communists, had seized the city of Kutais. Later, Mdivani became Prime Minister of Georgia and Chairman of the Council of People's Commissars. Years before, however, he had been opposed to Stalin's ruthless method of dealing with the Georgian nation, and had sought protection from Lenin. Above all, he knew very well the real activities of Stalin in the Caucasus during his youth. He surely remembered that he was by no means the great and glorious hero described by Beria in his speech in Tbilisi.

Next, Mikhail Okudzhava was arrested. He was an Old Bolshevik who had the misfortune of being befriended by Trotsky. Stalin, however, had once been Trotsky's associate too, when they worked together in the same administration, in 1917. Stalin was then Commissar of Nationalities, while Trotsky was Commissar of Foreign Affairs, holding a much higher post in the hierarchy of the Administration than Iosif Vissarionovich Dzhugashvili.

Mdivani and Okudzhava were tried *in camera*; that is, in jail, since the word *kamera* means in Russian, "prison cell." They were called to Chief of the Secret Police Lavrenty Pavlovich Beria's office in the prison, where, without trial or counsel, they were read the bill of indictment. They were accused according to Article 58, Paragraphs A, B, and W[1] of the Soviet Penal Code. This Article

---

[1] In the Cyrillic alphabet the letter *W* is the third one, as *C* is in the Latin alphabet.

Commissar

describes the defendant as the "enemy of the people, a traitor of the country and a parasite."

On July 10, 1937, despite their fierce denial of any guilt during their last interrogation in the prison, both Mdivani and Okudzhava were sentenced to death. They were immediately taken to the "death cell," the prison's cellar and shot.

Soon after their execution, Vano Bolkvadze and A. Khumarian were arrested without warrants, beaten and shot without trial. They were Old Communist conspirators who, in 1902, before the Revolution, had worked as compositors in an underground printing office in Baku. They had to be liquidated by Beria, since they knew quite well that at that time the real organizer of the illegal press in Azerbaijan was not Comrade Stalin, but Avel Yenukidze.

On a different occasion five elderly men were arrested before dawn and brought to the Metekhy Castle.[2] Having been taken straight from their beds in the middle of the night, they were just in their overcoats and long underwear.

They were lined up in the prison corridor and told to stand against the wall, with their foreheads touching it and their hands behind their backs.

One by one, they were called into the office of the First Secretary of the Transcaucasian Committee of the Communist Party, Lavrenty Pavlovich Beria, who liked working at night till very late.

Lavrenty asked each arrested man to sit down on a chair in front of his desk and, in a calm, soft voice, read to him a passage from a speech Comrade Stalin had delivered in 1926 at a meeting of Tiflis railroad workers.

The paragraph, which Beria had used once before, in his own *Stalin's Early Writings and Activities: On the History of the Bolshevik Organizations in Transcausia*, ran as follows:

I recall 1898, when I was first given a circle of railway depot workers. That was 28 years ago. I remember how I received lessons in practical work at Comrade Sturua's house in the presence of Sylvester Jibladze— at that time, he, too, was one of my teachers—Zakro Chodrishvili, Mikho Bochorishvili, Ninua and other leading workers of Tiflis.[3]

---

[2] Vano Sturua, Sylvester Jibladze, Zakro Chodrishvili, Mikho Bochorishvili and G. Ninua.

[3] *Zarya Vostoka* (*Dawn of the East*), June 10, 1926; *vide* L. P. Beria, *On the History of the Bolshevik Organizations in Transcaucasia* (Moscow: Foreign Languages Publishing House, 1939).

Then Beria politely asked his listener whether he agreed with this text, in which his own name was mentioned, and if he accepted its contents. Nobody refused to do so, because it was true; some smiled happily and proudly volunteered to add details omitted from the description. Lavrenty Pavlovich put down their words, inquired whether the man had spoken that way before to some of his relations, friends or neighbors, and if so, what their names and addresses were. He then handed his colloquist a pen with which to sign his testimony. The man was glad to put his signature to a declaration of this kind, which in his opinion could only bring him a reward. But the contrary was true: to state that someone had taught practical Communism to the Great Stalin was a crime.

After the whole group of men had been interrogated they were brought downstairs to the cellar one by one and killed by a shot in the backs of their skulls.

Every night for a week, a truck loaded with arrested men taken from their homes under guard of eight NKVD functionaries with rifles with fixed bayonets arrived in the courtyard of the prison on Olginskaya Street or Metekhy Castle.

Soon the captives were standing in line, their foreheads touching the whitewashed wall of the prison's corridor, and the tragic farce started once more. The men were called separately into Beria's office, where the Chief of the Transcaucasian NKVD politely read to them a paragraph from his *History*, as if entertaining a child with a fairy tale. The story went as follows:

In the period of 1898-1900, the Central Social-Democratic group of Tiflis did an enormous amount of revolutionary propagandist and organizational work for the formation of an illegal Social-Democratic Party organization. The members of the Central Party Group carried on intensive revolutionary propaganda work. All of them were in charge of workers' study circles. Comrade Stalin alone conducted more than eight Social-Democratic workers' circles.

In 1896 and 1897, Comrade Stalin conducted two revolutionary Marxist circles of students in Tiflis' Seminary.

The first revolutionary Marxist circle, called the "Senior" circle, was attended by the following students of the Tiflis Seminary: . . .[4]

Here Beria would pause dramatically, and then read some eight

---

[4] L. P. Beria, *On the History of the Bolshevik Organizations in Transcaucasia* (Moscow: Foreign Languages Publishing House, 1939).

names from a list.[5] Among them was the surname of his listener. The Chief of the Georgian Secret Police, Lavrenty Pavlovich Beria, then asked whether the whole story was true and accurate. He scrupulously added to his historical files any details or amendments made by the interrogated person, and asked for a signature. That was all. The inquest was over. The man being investigated was allowed to leave the half-dark room, lighted only by an electric lamp with a green shade, which stood on the desk of Lavrenty Pavlovich, a really nice fellow, with whom a chat in their native Georgian was such a pleasure. The problem of being released from the gloomy jail was, according to Beria's assurances, to be resolved in a matter of minutes.

Indeed, while the next Old Georgian Bolshevik was being ushered into Beria's office, the one whose questioning had been completed was left in the care of Mikhail Moodry and a sergeant on duty, both of whom escorted him downstairs. They passed by the ground floor door and descended one floor, where they entered a corridor with a few small cells at its end. In a short time, the officer and the sergeant on duty emerged from the cellar, alone.

The men brought to the basement did not realize that by signing a statement that they had met Stalin in the past and under the circumstances described, they put their names on their own death warrants. Beria knew as well as did the interrogated men that in reality Stalin never conducted even one Social-Democratic Workers' circle, let alone eight of them; he only participated in some of them occasionally. And Beria intended to annihilate all witnesses to the truth.

When the eight men connected with the first, "Senior" circle had been executed, then came the turn of the veteran conspirators from the second circle, the "Junior," as it was called. This one had been attended by seven Communists mentioned specifically by name. However, only six of them had been arrested,[6] since one of them, Alexander Svanidze, brother of Stalin's first wife, was in Moscow as Head of the Bank for Foreign Trade.

The former members of the third circle were next to be ques-

---

[5] Misha Davitashvili (pseudonym: Davidov), Archil Dolidze (pseudonym: Rostom), Gutsa Parkadze, Grigori Glurjidze, Simon Natroshivili, Guigo Razmadze, Laddo Akhmetelov and Joseph Iremashvili.

[6] Georgi Yelisabedashvili, Dimitri Gurgehidze, Datiko Suliashvili, Vasso Berdzenishvili, Vanno Ketskhoveli and D. Oniashvili.

tioned and immediately executed. These were six old revolutionaries.[7]

It was almost dawn when Beria completed his readings of the historical passages to the six former members of the third circle, to the four former conspirators of the fourth circle[8] and to the three men of the fifth.[9]

Shortly after the "Helper of Death"—Mikhail Moodry—reported that the last execution was completed, Chief of the Georgian Secret Police Beria cleaned up his desk meticulously, locked all dossiers in the strongbox, switched off the lamp on his desk and left the office. He was pleased with his performance. His aim was to liquidate all potential rivals of Stalin's glory, even the most unimportant ones.

Lavrenty Pavlovich entered his limousine and told his chauffeur to drive him home. He was sleepy and tired, much in need of some rest in his country house, with its beautiful garden, in the residential section of Tbilisi, where he was spending the summer with his young wife, Nina, and his little boy, Joseph, named after the Great Comrade, Joseph Stalin.

[7] D. Guldedava, Pyotr Khurtsilava, K. Shengelia, N. Tomaradze, R. Sturua (brother of Vano Sturua) and Sandro Merabishvili.

[8] Alexey Zakomoldin, V. Razhanov, Leonti Zolotaryov and Pyotr Montin.

[9] Dombrovsky, Y. Kochetkov and P. Skorobogatko.

28

A Methodical Slaughter

THERE WERE NOT only small fry to be eliminated like the veteran members of the revolutionary Marxist circles of forty years before. These men, who once belonged to the underground cells where Stalin was just one of them rather than their organizer or leader, could contradict the new history. But they had no influence on the future of the three Transcaucasian countries which had to be cleansed of any important personalities with patriotic feelings.

Beria could predict that after the annihilation of Kirov, Gorky, Kamenev, Zinoviev, Ordzhonikidze and others and after the disgrace of Yenukidze, who now was imprisoned, there would be more victims among the Old Bolsheviks, Stalin's friends and close comrades. Lavrenty came to the conclusion that, in order to further his own career, he should purge Transcaucasia once more. Being Stalin's junior rather than his contemporary, Beria was not afraid of becoming his victim as long as he was just Stalin's instrument in liquidating unwanted people.

In his office at Metekhy Castle Beria made lists of those persons who had committed or could commit the crime of being nationalists.

These men were arrested at their homes the following night, after a warrant was issued, and were dragged out of their beds. They were brought to the prison in covered trucks, as well as other vehicles. So as not to arouse the suspicions of other politicians, who might then hide themselves or manage to escape, the arrested men were taken to the jail in an ambulance, by Post Office van, or if they were eminent personalities who might be invited to Lavrenty Pavlovich's home for a reception, even by Beria's limousine. The arrests were not limited to Tbilisi or other Georgian cities, but were also carried out in Armenia and Azerbaijan as well. However, all detained people were brought to Metekhy Castle or to the prison on Olginskaya Street.

The jailed men were the most outstanding Caucasian Bolsheviks. Soon the cells of the two prisons in Tbilisi were filled with such personalities as a chairman of the Executive Committee of Soviets in Transcaucasia, two Chairmen of Councils of People's Commissars, and three Deputy Chairmen of the Councils of People's Commissars.

All these prisoners had to be destroyed individually soon after being detained. They were kept in their cells and called for interrogation separately at night when, being sleepy, they were less careful in answering questions. The questioning took hours. Lavrenty Pavlovich, who conducted the investigation himself, was not in a hurry. Having time, he liked to remind each victim of the slightest personal abuse or affront that he had received from the present prisoner. Every reception that any of these men had given without inviting Lavrenty, at the time when Beria was just a tyro, every one of his "good mornings" which had not been answered properly, was now recalled to the arrested man by the inquisitor, who talked with a calm voice and sometimes with a smile. This was the power which Lavrenty, the student of the Technicum, had dreamed about during his school days, as he wandered through the streets of Baku. There was no greater pleasure in the world than to listen to the apologies of such men, once important, honorable personalities, now aware that their lives depended on the mercy of Beria. They explained with regret their earlier behavior, corrected offenses which they had never intended and at last, seeing that they could not convince their tormentor, started begging for mercy in the name of their wives and children, ready to kneel in front of him and to kiss his shoes.

It was a paramount joy for Lavrenty Beria, like a sexual one, almost capable of causing a climax. The more the man humiliated himself, apologizing and asking for compassion and naming his family, the more he doomed himself, since for the inquisitor there was much more satisfaction in annihilating someone who worried about himself for the sake of his dear ones. Listening patiently to his victim, Beria let him speak without restraint until the man was exhausted and had nothing else to reveal except to repeat his words. Then the First Secretary of the Transcaucasian Committee of the Communist Party, Lavrenty Pavlovich Beria, who was now prosecutor and judge in one person, announced to the victim that he was accused under the Article 58, Paragraph A, of the Penal Code, as "an enemy of the people," and since his case was not yet closed, he would be called once more for examination. In the meantime, he was told to sign the transcript of his inquest.

As soon as the man wrote his signature, the interrogation was over. By signing, the prisoner confessed his guilt. In the report it was stated that the arrested man pleaded guilty of being "an enemy of the people." Now, in a calm voice, Lavrenty called the man the most dirty names. Such a list took quite a while. Then he rang the bell and ordered the guard to take the prisoner "downstairs." This was the last walk for the imprisoned man, since "downstairs" meant the cellar.

All of those condemned were executed without any trial, but just *in camera*. Each one was read Article 58, Paragraphs A, B and W, and afterwards was taken to the death cell, where a soldier tied his hands behind his back with his belt, and told him to face the wall, touching it with his forehead. Then Mikhail Moodry who stood by took his Nagan revolver out of his holster, put the barrel to the victim's neck and pulled the trigger.

There was only one exception to this routine. During an interrogation of the First Secretary of the Armenian Communist Party, Agasi Khandzhyan, Beria, instead of sending him to the death chamber, shot him personally in his office. The man being investigated did not ask for mercy, but called his inquisitor the same dirty names which Lavrenty used against him. Khandzhyan was even ready to hit his tormentor. Beria took out the revolver that he kept in his desk and shot the man on the spot. This killing ignited the liquidation of some other too bold Communist dignitaries in Armenia.

To get a free hand for a new great purge in Transcaucasia, Beria staged an attempt on his own life. This pretext was aimed at smashing the intellectuals. Lavrenty always hated the intelligentsia, whom he identified with the bourgeoisie. To him this meant anyone born in a residence with servants, and thus never had to engage in manual work. Soon after he had staged a plot against himself by shooting his gun and killing one of his bodyguards on night patrol at his summer house in the suburb of Tbilisi, Beria ordered three men arrested. From them he extorted all the needed confessions. These three eminent personalities were a Georgian bacteriologist and a researcher Georgy Eliva, and two Armenian writers, Balcunts and Zabel Esazan. The first two were executed *in camera* after admitting under coercion that the conspiracy was initiated and staged by the former Chairman of the Georgian Concil of People's Commissars, Kartvelishvili, presently on a prominent post in Moscow and a bitter foe of Beria. The writer Esazan, after admitting obediently that he intended to kill the first Secretary of the Transcaucasian Committee of the Communist Party, Lavrenty Pavlovich Beria, was tried as an example by the Military Collegium of the Supreme Court in Erevan—the Armenian capital—to show the whole population of Armenia that in their country nothing was more respected than objective justice. The sentence for Zabel Esazan was ten years' hard labor. However, his, as well as the two other confessions obtained by beatings, initiated mass arrests and liquidation of hundreds of Armenians, among them many professors, architects, writers and other intellectuals, because the plot was supposed to have been arranged by the intelligentsia. This purge was not just an expression of blind hatred by Beria against the intellectuals. Lavrenty knew very well that in this circle nationalistic and patriotic feelings were most strongly preserved and that these people could become at any time the leaders of the patriotically-minded Caucasian peasants, fishermen and highlanders.

The purge served the Soviet cause, enhanced Beria's career in the eyes of Stalin, and satisfied Lavrenty Pavlovich personally.

When purifying Transcaucasia of the nationally-oriented Commissars, Beria had no doubt that his good friend Nestor Lakoba, under whose administration Abkhazia was called "An Oasis of Democracy," was one of the most fervent Georgian patriots. A policy such as his was a serious enough crime to justify the liquidation of the ruler of Abkhazia. According to the general line, Lakoba had to be executed. Moreover, Nestor was aware that Beria's previous achievements in Baku were not as impressive as Lavrenty Pavlovich wished them to be. Lakoba also knew the truth about Beria's stay in the Kutaisi prison, where Lavrenty had behaved very sheepishly and had never intended to stage a hunger strike. It was clear that Nestor Lakoba should not live any longer.

One day his dear schoolmate "Lara" wrote a sincere letter to Nestor asking him to come down to the Georgian capital, where they could spend a few evenings together in bachelor style. Lakoba accepted the invitation gladly and soon arrived in Tbilisi. Beria awaited him at the station. They kissed each other's cheeks and embraced publicly like two brothers. Then Lavrenty, in his chauffeured limousine, took Nestor to the best hotel in town, where he had reserved a luxurious suite for his old pal.

The reunion of these two friends after such a long period of time was more than cordial. Lavrenty took Nestor to a dinner with good wine. Then they went to the opera where Beria, a lover of classical music, had his box. After the theatre, they stopped at a cabaret for a floor show and supper, with vodka and a bottle of champagne and coffee with liqueurs.

It was late when Lavrenty took Nestor to his hotel. Since his tipsy friend had trouble keeping his balance, Beria helped him get the key to his suite at the reception desk. Singing a frivolous ditty together, they climbed the stairs.

Being more sober than his companion, Lavrenty helped him find the right suite and open the door. He even undressed his comrade and put him to bed. Then he turned off the light and left.

The next morning People's Commissar Nestor Lakoba, leader of Abkhazia and the first citizen of its provincial capital Sukhumi, was found dead in his bed. Notified by the hotel's manager, Beria rushed immediately to the spot and ordered the door of the suite to be sealed. Soon a telegram was sent to Abkhazia revealing that Comrade Nestor Lakoba had died suddenly of angina pectoris. In such a case no investigation was necessary. The diagnosis of angina pectoris had to be accepted, despite the fact that Lakoba, a young and healthy man in the prime of life, had never complained of any heart trouble. If Lakoba had been strangled with a pillow, a towel, or was hit in the back of his head with a little iron ball on a short strap—a so-called blackjack or knuckle duster—which Beria always kept in the drawer of his office desk, or sometimes carried in his pocket, it was never revealed. No legal specialist was called nor was an autopsy performed. The case was closed.

The funeral of Commissar Nestor Apollonovich Lakoba became a great official mourning. The coffin was transported to the railway station with all honors due such an outstanding personality. In Sukhumi an immense throng was awaiting the train with its red flags and crêpe-draped engine. Then a long funeral procession with a military band followed the hearse drawn by six black horses. At the cemetery Beria, who had accompanied the remains of his bosom friend from the capital to their mutual native Sukhumi, delivered a moving eulogy. Then the coffin was buried and the grave covered with hundreds of wreaths and bouquets with scarlet sashes with golden inscriptions. The whole ceremony was at the expense of the State of the Georgian Soviet Socialist Republic.

Three days after the flowers were taken away, the coffin with the corpse was secretly exhumed and disappeared, while the grave was leveled to the ground. Lakoba's widow, who might ask for some explanation, was arrested and deported to an unknown destination. There were even more arrests. Lakoba's two cousins, Mikhail and Boris, were also detained and soon after were executed.

In the files for Security use only, Beria enclosed declarations extorted from two women, who knew the late Nestor Lakoba. These witnesses testified that Lakoba, a Georgian nationalist, had planned to assassinate the Great Comrade Stalin. In Beria's dossier it was stated beyond any doubt that Lakoba was a traitor and an enemy of the people.

Beria annihilated people according to his meticulously prepared plan, which had two objectives: to purge all Transcaucasian nationalists who had or could have any patriotic feelings contradictory to the general Soviet line, and to liquidate all witnesses of Stalin's early activities. These executions were performed unemotionally, but only for a certain purpose. Beria did no less and not very much more than was needed for his own political career. In Moscow, however, Chief of the NKVD Yezhov liquidated people throughout the whole country with the tremendous frenzy of a mad monster. Due to the directive signed by Yenukidze, which was ordered by Stalin after the assassination of Kirov, thousands of people—men, women and children—were arrested and shot or deported to the concentration camps. The most eminent Old Bolsheviks were put on trial and sentenced to death.

On June 11, 1937, at 2:30 in the morning, in the Lefortovo Prison in Moscow a special firing squad of the NKVD executed Marshal Mikhail Nikolayevich Tukhachevsky, the hero of the Soviet-Polish war in 1920 and the memorable victor of Kronstadt. He was the highest ranking officer who, while fulfilling the orders of Lenin, Trotsky and Dzerzhinsky, massacred more than 15,000 Russian sailors.

Together with Tukhachevsky seven other Red Army generals were executed. Their wives and children, as families of political criminals and traitors, were deported to hard labor camps in Siberia. Also shot to death were many other Generals, Commanders, and the People's Commissars, as well as the Presidents of the Ukrainian and Byelorussian Soviet Socialist Republics.

On December 20, 1937, a short notice in the press announced that Avel Yenukidze, Orakhelashvili and several others had been tried by a Secret Military Court for espionage and terrorist activities, condemned to death and executed. The "Secret Military Court" meant no regular trial was held but a sentence read to the prisoners in the jail by the chairman of three Secret Police Officers, a *Troyka*, and then the execution *in camera*.

After enclosing in his dossiers the notice of Yenukidze's death from the government newspaper, *Pravda*, Beria decided that he should make some changes in his book, *On the History of the Bolshevik Organizations in Transcaucasia*, which was going to be printed in its fourth edition for 1938. On a copy that he intended to send soon to the printing office, Lavrenty crossed out the sentences about admonishing Yenukidze and Orakhelashvili for their errors, and wrote some entirely new paragraphs which said:

It must be admitted that the history of the Party organizations of Transcaucasia and Georgia is still far from having been fully investigated and adequately treated.

As for the expositions of the struggle of the Transcaucasian Bolsheviks given in the writings of Philip Makharadze (*The History of the Labor Movement in Georgia, The Year 1905 in Transcaucasia, The Thirtieth Anniversary of the Tiflis Organization, Outlines of the Revolutionary Movement in Transcaucasia* and others), they contain a number of errors in principle and of a historical nature, distort historical facts and events and present a number of points in the history of the Party *dishonestly*.

So far Comrade Makharadze has not taken the trouble to revise his works and correct the mistakes and distortions they contain.

A. Yenukidze and M. Orakhelashvili, since exposed as enemies of the people, smuggled deliberate distortion and falsification of the history of the Transcaucasian organization into their books.[1]

And further:

A. Yenukidze, later exposed as a mortal enemy of the people, deliberately and with hostile intent falsified the history of the Bolshevik organizations of Transcaucasia in his authorized biography and in his pamphlet, *Our Illegal Printing Shops in the Caucasus*, cynically and brazenly distorted well-known historical facts, crediting himself with alleged services in the establishment of the first illegal printing shop in Baku.

As we know, in view of the imminent danger that these fallacies and distortions of his would be exposed, A. Yenukidze was obliged to admit these "mistakes" in the columns of *Pravda* on January 16, 1935.[2]

By this annunciation Beria revealed the only real crime of Avel Yenukidze was that he dared to publish the truth that not the Genius Stalin, but he, Yenukidze, was the organizer of the illegal printing office in Baku.

These three new paragraphs were added to the text book in December 1937, dealing entirely with a speech delivered in July 1935.

In checking the ending of his lecture the author realized that in the meantime many changes had occurred in the USSR; the new Stalin Constitution had been introduced and, subsequently, the Transcaucasian Federation had been abolished. In this latter case the slogan, "Long Live the Transcaucasian Federation!" shouted by the audience after Lavrenty finished his speech, and recorded by him in his manuscript, had to be deleted. With one stroke of his pen Beria cut that exclamation out. But it was not enough. Lavrenty, who was determined to please his Boss by all possible means, did not want to ignore in his writing the Stalin Constitution even though it was proclaimed over a year after the memorable meeting in Tbilisi. For the same reasons Beria did not want to omit the event of the abolishing of the Transcaucasian Federation.

After a short consideration, Lavrenty Pavlovich, a strong believer in the power of imprisoning people as the best method of convincing them and keeping them quiet, decided to write a few new paragraphs for his disquisition. On these pages in Chapter Four of

---

[1] L. P. Beria, *On the History of the Bolshevik Organizations in Transcaucasia* (Moscow: Foreign Languages Publishing House, 1939).

[2] *Ibid.*

his historical essay dealing with the period 1913-1924, Beria, with a cold cynicism described events that had happened in 1936 as a part of his speech delivered in 1935.

This passage went as follows:

. . . In 1936, with the adoption of the Stalin Constitution of the USSR, the Transcaucasian Federation was dissolved, and the republics of Transcaucasia—Georgia, Azerbaijan and Armenia—entered the Union of Soviet Socialist Republics directly, as Union republics with sovereign rights.

The abolition of the Transcaucasian Federation was a direct result of the achievements and victories of the general line, and in particular of the national policy of our Party, achievements and victories won in the years of the revolution in the process of socialist construction in the republics of Transcaucasia.

The Transcaucasian Federation had performed a historical rule, completely solving the tasks set before it. The Republics of Transcaucasia have become industrial-agrarian republics. The collective farm system prevails in the agriculture of Transcaucasia. Enormous progress has been made in developing national culture. The Republics of Transcaucasia have produced Bolshevik national cadres that are wholly devoted to the Party of Lenin and Stalin.

Having broadened the economic and cultural ties of Georgia, Azerbaijan and Armenia with the other Republics, Territories and Regions of the Soviet Union, the victories of socialist construction prepared the conditions for the abolition of the Transcaucasian Federation and the direct entrance of the Transcaucasian Republics into the Soviet Union.

The new Constitution of the USSR ensures the further strengthening of the friendship between the nations of Transcaucasia and the whole Soviet Union, it ensures great new achievements on the part of the national policy of Lenin and Stalin. . . .[3]

Then Lavrenty Pavlovich stated:

Loud and prolonged applause. All rise. The hall resounds with shouts of "Long Live the Great Stalin!," "Hurrah for Comrade Stalin!," "Long Live the Central Committee of the Bolshevik Party!"[4]

No word about the slogan, "Long Live the Transcaucasian Federation!," because the Transcaucasian Federation did not live anymore. But from this revised report the readers could learn that the

---

[3] L. P. Beria, *On the History of the Bolshevik Organizations in Transcaucasia* (Fourth Edition, Moscow, 1939).

[4] Appendix 8.

whole audience rose and applauded the great Stalin Constitution a year and a half before it was written.

To change his own oration, delivered a few years before, was for Beria a trifle.

Eventually, on behalf of his superior, Joseph Stalin, as well as for his own sake, Lavrenty Pavlovich Beria changed the past history of the entire Communist Party in the Soviet Union.

PART TWO

MOSCOW

29

Surprise

IN THE FIRST-CLASS COMPARTMENT of his own private Pullman car, with two bodyguards stationed at the front and the rear, Beria was on his way to Moscow. Just the previous night, July 28, 1938, during one of his lonely late work sessions in his murky office at Metekhy Castle, he had been ordered to come to the nation's capital. Calling him personally on the telephone, Stalin summoned his subordinate to appear in Moscow immediately. That was all. No reason was given.

Before his morning departure, Beria told his wife that he was leaving for a routine trip, just like those he took quite often. He did not say where he was going or for how long. His duties were always confidential. He mentioned his new trip with a casual air, as was his custom. However, in case Lavrenty was arrested in Moscow, he left one of his closest associates, Bogdan Kobulov, an order to destroy instantly the archives of the Top Secret dossiers so meticulously collected by Beria and containing testimonies extorted from false witnesses, fabricated documents and other evidence against several persons still holding high posts in the Party.

Once on the train, Lavrenty seethed with conflicting feelings. He could hardly expect a pleasant reception at the Kremlin. Stalin was not the type of man who liked to make people happy, especially when he called a subordinate to show up at once without adding a word of explanation.

The wheels of the train clicked against the rails rhythmically, banging the same short, monotonous tune over and over. And in the same way, Beria's brain repeated a single thought, asking again and again one question, booming it against his temples. What was the reason for that call to report to the Leader?

Beria tried to examine his conscience. He could not find any sin, crime, guilt, deviation or fault for which he should be punished. But you did not have to commit any trespass to be arrested and liquidated. Beria knew this perfectly from his own practices as well as from almost all the big show trials staged against the most devoted Communists and Old Guard Bolsheviks, who inevitably were sent to face the firing squad in the prison yard, or to get a bullet in the head in the death cell. He remembered that especially bloody purges had occurred two years earlier when Nikolay Yezhov, the present Chief of State Security for the Soviet Union, had taken his post. Lavrenty knew too well that Yezhov hated him as his equally powerful counterpart in the Caucasus. Just a few months before, Beria had learned that his name was on Yezhov's proscriptive list of men to be arrested. Yezhov had ordered one of Lavrenty's deputies, Sergey Goglidze, to arrest Beria. In that confidential person-to-person memorandum Yezhov let Goglidze understand that after imprisoning his superior he would take his position. With his primitive mentality, however, Yezhov did not consider that Beria and his pals represented such a close clique that for every one of those individuals it was more profitable to stick together than to plot any intrigue against each other. Goglidze felt that as Beria's deputy he would possess more power and wealth with less risk to his life than if he were at the top.

With this in mind, instead of arresting his boss, Goglidze showed him the warrant. Lavrenty immediately rushed to Baku on the pretext of an official inspection of the local NKVD under its chief, Mir Djaffar Bagirov, while Goglidze telegraphed back to Yezhov that he was unable to carry out his order because Beria was not in Georgia.

From Azerbaijan Lavrenty phoned Mikoyan and Molotov, both in Moscow, to intervene with Stalin and to persuade him that Beria was in the process of preparing some papers for inclusion in the proposed publication of Stalin's *Collected Works*. In this case Beria's liquidation would be a disservice to the Great Comrade Stalin.

The day after receiving word from Mikoyan that the Dictator had spared Beria's life, and that Lavrenty Pavlovich was in his favor, Beria went to Moscow to see the Leader and to submit his project of an edition of Stalin's *Collected Works.* The incident of Beria's arrest was conjured away and Lavrenty returned to Tbilisi as powerful and bossy as he was before.

The only unpleasantness that Beria had to accept was the new deputy sent to him from Moscow. The watchdog set on him was Stanislav Redens, one of the most cruel and brutal NKVD chiefs, who often executed people senselessly in a blind fury. This method, or rather lack of method, was alien to the cunning politics of the systematic Beria, who liquidated only those people who could be really dangerous to Stalin, to the regime, or to Lavrenty himself. Beria realized that Redens was assigned to his office not because the Kremlin and Yezhov doubted that Lavrenty was not peremptory and merciless enough, but because they wanted to plant their spy there. Stanislav Redens was dangerous for Beria not because he was an old, experienced *Chekist* and former close associate of the late Feliks Dzerzhinsky, but because being the husband of Anna Alliluyeva, the older sister of Stalin's second wife Nadezhda, he was himself a relative of the Dictator.

Beria, accordingly, had to be very diplomatic in his relations with both of the Redenses. Treating them with the respect due to relatives of the Great Comrade Stalin, Lavrenty found for them a comfortable house with a garden in the suburb of Tbilisi and the most luxurious villa at the Caucasian health resort Sochi. He also frequently sent them complimentary tickets for the honorary box at the Opera. Being aware that every human being has his weakness, Lavrenty discovered that Stanislav Redens liked girls and vodka. Soon Beria introduced him to some of his friends, bachelors who shared the same tastes. Needless to say, these fellows were Lavrenty's agents who, being supplied with special funds, spent that money with Redens in cabarets, where Beria's new deputy, in the company of call girls, drank like a sailor and brawled, smashing mirrors, breaking furniture and demolishing the premises. All these scandals were arranged by his new pals to discredit Redens, so he would be recalled as soon as possible to Moscow, to become the subject of a trial and a purge.

The nomination of Redens was not the first trap that Lavrenty had had to escape in his career. Just a year and a half before,

Commissar of Health Dr. Grigory Mikhailovich Kaminsky, in a meeting of the Central Committee in Moscow, had denounced Beria as a former undercover agent working for the Azerbaijan nationalist group, Mussavatists. But Kaminsky was a scholar and Stalin did not like highly educated people, whom he called *oomnye doorake*—educated fools. The same day he delivered his speech against Beria, Kaminsky was arrested and shot. In his sincerity as a loyal Old Bolshevik Kaminsky did not suspect that Stalin was aware not only of Beria's membership in the Azerbaijan nationalist party as well as the Mensheviks, but that Lavrenty had joined them as a spy and provocateur with the full approval and blessing of Ordzhonikidze, Kirov and Mikoyan. Moreover, in his youth Stalin himself had served occasionally for the Tsarist *Okhrana*, so he was not shocked by the revelation that someone else had been an agent working in the enemy camp. For his courage in attacking Beria Dr. Kaminsky paid with his naivete. Kaminsky also had to be annihilated because, as Commissar of Health, he was the Chairman of the collegium of physicians who had signed Ordzhonikidze's death certificate declaring the cause as paralysis of the heart, in spite of the fact that there could be a quite different cause. To prevent Kaminsky from expressing any other opinion at a later time, he had to be silenced forever.

But now maybe Beria was not as lucky as he had been with the two previous cases. Perhaps this time Yezhov would be able to succeed. Who knows? Beria would be executed on Stalin's order because of a false denouncement, or to make room for someone else—for Malenkov or Khrushchev, for instance?

With every mile bringing him closer to the end of his journey Beria saw himself nearer the death cell in one of Moscow's prisons: Lubyanka, Lefortovo, or Butyrki. Lavrenty decided not to give up docilely.

Beria had always hated Stalin as a rude boor with no manners, culture, civilization or education, a dropout from theological school, an invariable cad whose breath stank of the cheapest black tobacco, garlic and the scent of indigestion, while the odor of his feet could be smelled from a distance. And it was enough to fail to look straight at his dark pockmarked face, or his small wicked eyes all the time when talking or listening to him, to be suspected of conspiracy and condemned to death by that maniac who saw plots against himself everywhere.

From the very first time he heard about Stalin, Beria could not stand him. He envied his position, fame and power. He also despised the Great Comrade Stalin because he licked the Dictator's boots by praising him in the *History of the Bolshevik Organizations in Transcaucasia*. In this lucubration Beria built up Stalin and made him a hero of the Revolution and a god of the new era of Communism, knowing well enough that the whole essay on the greatness of Stalin was nothing other than one big lie from the very beginning to the very end.

Now probably he was going to be jailed and executed. When contemplating such a fate, he touched his bulky briefcase on his lap. In that heavy old-fashioned bag of black leather, among many papers and documents, Beria carried his Nagan—the duty revolver. There was nothing wrong in the Chief of the Security Police for Georgia carrying a weapon with him, even when dressed as a civilian, as Lavrenty preferred to be. Now he was determined that if the conversation with his superior should be switched into a kind of inquest, which would of course be nothing but a prelude to arrest and execution, he, pretending to produce some papers, would take the gun out of his briefcase and shoot his inquisitor.

At least, before being sent to the firing squad, he would have his satisfaction by killing that dirty *sooken-sen*—that son of a bitch. Then he would be executed himself. Never mind. Anyhow, what is man's life if one stupid shot—paff!—can change his whole world? All fears, troubles and problems are solved quickly, once and forever. Beria regained his usual balance and cold-bloodedness.

It was a long journey. At last, after three days the train reached the spacious terminal, the Kazan Railway Station, at the Soviet capital. Beria and his two companions descended from their cozy and safe Pullman. The gray dawn greeted them with its Moscow chill. The three travelers from the warm Caucasus rushed toward the station, but just as they started they were approached by an NKVD officer. Saluting snappily, he reported himself as Colonel Bobrov and asked Comrade Beria to follow him to the car. Lavrenty dismissed his guards, ordering them to report in the afternoon at the Select Hotel, where he usually stayed when in Moscow. Then he hurried off with his guide.

They left the huge station and crossed the street. Far away, a black limousine was parked. Colonel Bobrov opened the door and let Beria in. Then he took his seat next to the civilian uniformed chauffeur and they started off.

In the spacious automobile Lavrenty found a small fat man

awaiting him. In his black coat over a white tunic, a black cap and high boots, the man reminded him of a penguin. With a solemn look on his round face the man extended his little hand, greeting the newcomer.

They shook hands like two acquaintances. Beria knew this character indeed. He was Stalin's famous confidential secretary, General Alexander Poskrebyshev—the same man who had come immediately to the spot where Stalin's wife, Nadezhda, a victim of acute appendicitis according to official account, was in reality found shot and left to die. Poskrebyshev had not allowed a doctor to be called although the wound was not a deadly one. He picked up the revolver and ordered that the stains of blood on the floor be wiped out. Soon after, Nadezhda died. Later, together with Stalin, Poskrebyshev visited the ailing writer Gorky, a few moments before the great author died. Poskrebyshev also accompanied Stalin to Leningrad to investigate the assassination of Kirov, staged by Stalin, as assumed by the innermost circle. And the same fat little Poskrebyshev went to see "Dear Sergo" Ordzhonikidze in his flat, and soon after he left, Ordzhonikidze was found dead. To meet Poskrebyshev was always significant and never hopeful. This officer was not only Stalin's personal secretary but also Chief of the Special Section for Secret Department of the Party Secretariat. Thus, being the most trusted man in liquidating eminent people without trial, he was more powerful not only than Beria, but even Yezhov, Chief of the Secret Police.

Beria and Poskrebyshev, sitting next to each other in that big limousine in complete silence, rode through the streets of Moscow. Stalin's secretary was a taciturn person and did not care for small talk. Beria felt great relief when at last at Red Square the car was driven straight on and not directed to Dzerzhinsky Street, which led to Lubyanka Prison.

They crossed the Kremlin's Spassky Gate and stopped in front of the main building. Led by Poskrebyshev, with Colonel Bobrov just behind, Lavrenty entered the hall. A lieutenant helped them take off their overcoats and, under the watchful eye of General Pyotr Kosynkin, Chief of Security of the Kremlin, the man responsible for guarding Stalin's life, politely but firmly took Beria's briefcase.

Poskrebyshev walked upstairs to report their arrival to Stalin. Beria, accompanied by Colonel Bobrov, entered the anteroom. They didn't stay there long. Soon the telephone in the hall rang, and a moment after, the guard appeared in the doorway and announced that Comrade Stalin would like to see First Secretary of the Transcaucasian Party Committee, Lavrenty Pavlovich Beria.

Beria got up and followed the guard to the second floor. There he knocked on the door and entered the huge study of the Russian Dictator. Against the opposite wall Stalin was seated behind his old-fashioned desk, busy filling his pipe with tobacco from a yellow oilcloth pouch. Next to him stood Poskrebyshev, ready with a match and box in his hands to give him a light.

With a nod Stalin beckoned for Beria to approach him, and pointed to the chair in front of his desk. He accepted a light from his secretary and took a puff. He asked Beria about his trip to Moscow, mentioned the discomfort of a three-day-long journey, and made a remark about the pleasant climate in their wonderful Georgia. Lavrenty answered with the humble smile of a subordinate being favored by an informal talk with the Boss. He knew, however, that the polite mood of his superior had no significance. Then, with the same courteous air, Stalin announced that he had decided to transfer Beria from his high post in Tiflis to Lubyanka Prison—to the front office. He would become the first deputy of Yezhov, the present Commissar of Internal Affairs and the head of the NKVD, the Soviet Security Police.

Lavrenty Pavlovich was to start his new job the next morning. The audience was over.

30

Next to the Big Boss

AFTER BEING FURNISHED with a limousine by Colonel Bobrov, Beria
arrived at the Select Hotel, where he had a room reserved. He told
his two bodyguards to return to Tiflis and that he would follow
soon.

Sitting by himself at a small table in the corner of the hotel
restaurant, and enjoying his lunch, Lavrenty thought about his recent talk at the Kremlin and tried to solve the secret of his unexpected promotion. Why did Stalin decide to nominate Beria deputy
to Yezhov who not long before was going to arrest and annihilate
him? Such a move was evidently not a fleeting whim of the Big
Boss, but the result of a deeply studied conclusion in the light of
the political situation in the world.

Munching his roast beef, lavishly washed down with beer and
vodka, Beria scrutinized the events during recent months. Only a
few months ago, in March 1938, Hitler's military forces had entered Austria and taken it over with no resistance.

Hitler had shown quite openly that he would not stop his march
over Europe and that after this bloodless victory he would push
further. Recently, through his agents in Poland, Stalin had surely
obtained reports of the defense plans of the Polish Government in
the event of attack by the Third Reich. It was evident that Poland
did not intend to be swallowed by Germany and was determined to
fight for her independence.

One of Stalin's personal informers was a Pole, Vladislav Gomulka, a member of the underground illegal Polish Communist Party, KPP. He had previously spent two years, 1934 and 1935, on special subversive political courses in Moscow. From him the Soviet Dictator had a sober and true picture of the political atmosphere in Poland and of the general patriotic mood prevailing in that determined nation. It was clear that a war in Europe was inevitable and its outbreak was only a matter of months. Stalin would not idly accept such events with detached neutrality. He realized that he should be ready to face the fact that after smashing Poland, Hitler would cross her Eastern borders and strike the Soviet Union. Russia, however, was not prepared for war. Yezhov, with his great purges, had decimated the cadres of the most eminent members of the Communist Party, the political Brain Trust, as well as of the People's Commissars with their deputies and other high executives in the Soviet Government. Just a few months before, Yezhov had staged a spectacular trial against such outstanding Bolsheviks as Bukharin, Rykov and Krestinsky, the Old Guard Communists and members of Lenin's Politburo, as well as against Yagoda, former Chief of Internal Affairs, and several others. Among them was the former Commissar of Foreign Trade, Arkady Rosengoltz, father of that pretty Yelena who was raped and murdered in Nestor Lakoba's villa in Abkhazia.

All of these defendants, accused of being Trotskyites, Mensheviks, spies, traitors and agents for the Western countries, were sentenced to death and executed.

When recalling the execution of Rosengoltz, whom he had met at the horse races in Sukhumi, Beria could not restrain a smile. Once a powerful Commissar, and the only person who could seek revenge for the killing of his daughter, he was silenced forever.

The execution of Rosengoltz solved Lavrenty's personal problem. When thinking of the country's difficulties Beria recalled that with his lunatic purges Yezhov had annihilated many leaders of the Red Army. Dozens of Marshals, hundreds of Generals and thousands of Colonels and Majors were arrested and either executed against the wall of the prison yards, or deported to hard labor camps in Siberia. The best specialists and the most talented strategists were eliminated. Among those executed were Marshal Tukhachevsky and his comrades in arms, Marshals Kork, Uborevich, Yakir, Feldman, Primakov, Eideman and Putna, who were accused of being Fascists. A short time later, Chief of the Red Air Forces, Alsknis, and the Commander in Chief of the Red Navy, Admiral Orlov, were condemned to death, as was Marshal Yegorov, while Marshal Rokossovsky and Army Commander Belov and General Gorbatov, along with many other leading officers, were deported to Siberia.

The insane purges in the Red Army reduced the Soviet military forces by at least 30 percent. For the men who were familiar with the situation it was no secret that 60 to 70 percent of the officers were arrested; that 11 Adjutant Commissars of War, and 71 out of 80 members of the High Council for War disappeared, being deported to hard labor camps in Siberia. They knew also that 90 percent of the generals and 80 percent of the colonels were eliminated. All told, between 30,000 and 35,000 men, including the Specialist Officer Corps, were exterminated.

The Soviet Army was practically without a head. The High Command and the troops were neither trained nor disciplined. Obviously, these two years of Yezhov's rule, called *Yezhovshchina*, were nothing but a period of terror.

Of course, all this was not done without Stalin's approval. But, having an obsession about plots against his life, the Dictator could be quite easily influenced by that mad dog Yezhov, who took the greatest pleasure in exterminating the most important personalities.

However, why did Stalin suddenly decide to place Beria next to Yezhov? It was evident that the Leader planned to deprive Yezhov of playing the role of guardian of the Dictator's safety. But what was the reason? Beria was calculating, trying to find a key to that puzzle.

How would Stalin figure? The Civil War in Spain had now been accelerated to full speed and the lack of good, high-ranking Soviet officers who could serve as advisers for the Spanish partisan army would strengthen the Fascists under General Franco. It would also provoke Mussolini. The so-called Berlin-Rome Axis was a pact between Hitler and Mussolini, signed over two years before to fight Communism. Soon after, the Nazi regime signed a similar alliance with Mikado Hirohito. With Japan, the Third Reich established an anti-*Comintern* Pact to fight the *Comintern*—the International Communist Laborer's Association. Afterwards, Hitler's invasion of Austria, and the slow but constant concentration of Nazi troops near the Polish border, under the pretext of maneuvers, would create a real danger for the Soviet Union.

From now on, if Stalin wanted to survive, and for the sake of the USSR, he could not afford any further weakening of the Red Army. Beyond any doubt, Stalin had to halt the purges in the ranks of the military forces, the arrests and exterminations of the officers, while some of those who were deported to the Far North had to be released and rehabilitated. To save his face, the Big Boss would dismiss Yezhov shortly. Stalin probably would not put him on trial as he did Yezhov's predecessor, Yagoda, because by such a move he would condemn all Yezhov's purges. But it did not mean that Yezhov would not sooner or later be liquidated.

Of course, Stalin had not ceased suspecting that his closest friends intended to get rid of him, so he still needed someone like Beria as the new Chief of Security to guard his safety. But the mass executions should be limited and carried out with cold calculation. They should be more methodically organized, geared to accomplish more than just forcing people to confess crimes that they never had plotted. For this purpose Stalin quite probably brought Beria to Moscow from their native country, Georgia, where Lavrenty, according to the Dictator's directions, had uprooted and destroyed the weeds of any opposition in the Caucasus.

Now he would be doing the same throughout the whole vast Soviet Union.

31

The Purger of the Purgers

AFTER REPORTING TO YEZHOV as his deputy Beria began his new job
soberly and pedantically, as if nothing had ever happened between
him and his new superior, who not long before had planned to lock
Lavrenty behind bars. With the obedience of a perfect subordinate
Beria carried out every investigation he was assigned. By a special
order of Yezhov, Lavrenty raided the flat of Kosarev, the president
of the Young Communist League—*Komsomol*—who was accused
of some deviations, and personally arrested him. Beria performed
this task as if he were a mere policeman. It was the first time
Lavrenty had done this kind of duty. But he did not regard it as a
dishonor or beneath his high rank. Beria did not feel degraded.
He knew very well that shortly his present situation must be
changed. Stalin, for certain, had not called Beria from Tiflis to
make a small cog of him.

Beria's calculations proved to be right. In a few months Yezhov
was deposed from his position as Lavrenty predicted and received
a new assignment as People's Commissar of Water Transport. It was
one step in an inevitable fall, because the Department of Water
Transport was a minor agency, really a blind alley. Yezhov's predecessor, Yagoda, before being put on trial and executed, also had
been transferred to another post. The vacant desk of Chief of the
Secret Police was given to Beria.

His new office in Moscow was installed in Lubyanka Prison on

Dzerzhinsky Street. Beria took five adjoining rooms there. The first was for typists, the second and the third for the offices of Beria's deputy, Merkulov. The fourth was the office of Merkulov's assistant, Mamulov, who was also Beria's personal secretary. In Mamulov's office were two side doors, the left one leading to Merkulov's office and the right the entrance to the room of the Commissar of Internal Affairs, Lavrenty Pavlovich Beria.

Lavrenty's office was huge. It was lighted mainly by a powerful electric floor lamp standing in the corner. There were no windows, and the walls were hung with thick rugs to deaden sound. The air entered through a ventilator.

In the middle of the room stood a massive green-topped desk and a reading lamp with a green glass shade. There were also three telephones, the first a direct line to Stalin, the second to Commissars and Government offices and the third for long-distance calls to any part of the USSR. Behind the desk was a big armchair covered with leather. The office was also furnished with a wardrobe, a tall strongbox for files and two regular chairs. A big portrait of Stalin in a golden frame hung high on the wall behind the armchair, and beneath the picture was a large brown oilcloth-covered sofa.

Within six weeks after taking his new post as Head of State Security, Beria had organized his work efficiently enough so the Russian people could see changes for the better and breathe more freely.

One of the first steps the new Chief of the Secret Police took was the arrest of almost all the deputies of his predecessor and several NKVD officers who worked immediately under Yezhov. This move was received by the whole nation with great relief. The people believed that the era of the horrible *Yezhovshchina* was ended forever. In that light Beria, soon called the "Purger of the purgers," appeared to be a savior. However, as a matter of fact, Lavrenty sent those functionaries to jail because, being Yezhov's men, they were his potential enemies as long as Yezhov was alive. Nor could he count on them to work for him wholeheartedly. The purging of the purgers was primarily Beria's self-defense, so he did not arrest or even dismiss Andrey Vyshinsky, the Prosecutor-General who had performed such an excellent job in accusing the Old Guard Bolsheviks in their show trials. This Russian lawyer, a brilliant mentality, but an extremely cruel character, could be helpful to any Chief of Soviet Security. It was then advisable to keep him on his post and also to befriend him. Beria also spared the life of Victor Abakumov, a very experienced high ranking "Old *Chekist*," and of the Secret Police General, Sergey Nikiforovich Kruglov, the chief hangman, who during the Great Purges had executed several outstanding Soviet personalities, Marshal Tukhachevsky included. Such men as Abakumov and Kruglov could always be useful to the new Commissar of State Security.

Soon after, in Moscow, in Leningrad and in Kiev, as well as in several other cities, there were a number of exemplary trials against dozens of former high ranking NKVD Security Police officers who, when fulfilling Yezhov's orders, had extorted confessions from many innocent people. Their trials, which were open to the public, proved them guilty beyond any doubt and, to the satisfaction of the Russian population, the defendants were sentenced to death and executed.

In the meantime, Beria was checking the files of the prisoners who had been deported to hard labor camps in Siberia as well as in other parts of the extensive Soviet Union during the past two years. Among others were thousands of innocent people, poor illiterate peasants from remote villages, and harmless inhabitants of small towns and communities from all over the country. These nobodies were imprisoned and sent to compounds in exile just because they failed to greet a local militiaman with enough respect, or because they were seen talking to a relative of someone already arrested, or because, being a little tipsy, they were singing loudly at night. Such victims of Yezhov's functionaries were now released from their hardship and allowed to return home.

Beria also exonerated and freed from the concentration camps hundreds of Red Army officers and almost all the security agents and high ranking functionaries deported by Yezhov for being trusted supporters of his predecessor. Now they were freed, even though some of them had been condemned to years of hard labor because they really had committed crimes. Beria not only decided to liberate those policemen and agents, but even reappointed them to their former posts. By that action Lavrenty made these men the most devoted subordinate element in his cadres and the mortal enemies of Yezhov's regime. Beria personally scrutinized every file with the meticulous pedantry of an industrious former student of the Mechanical-Construction Technical School.

The relations of the new Chief of State Security with the Dictator differed from those of his predecessor. While Yezhov was just a subordinate, narrow-minded policeman who sent dry, matter-of-fact military-style reports to the Kremlin, Beria was much less formal, although full of respect. Preferring to deliver his memoranda personally, Lavrenty went to see the Great Comrade Stalin from time to time. But not so often as to be annoying. During their talks, Beria proposed action rather than asking for instructions. However, he managed to make his suggestions sound as if they came from his Superior.

Stalin liked this Georgian countryman much more than the gloomy, fanatical dwarf Yezhov, who took everything extremely seriously, even an order to imprison and liquidate a personal enemy. Such a pleasant assignment should bring a smile to one's lips.

With Beria, the Big Boss could not only give orders but make jokes and ask for an opinion. Stalin still remembered that dinner in Tiflis where the only person who enthusiastically answered his remark about using a red-hot iron for the opposition was the young apprentice and servant, Lavrenty Pavlovich.

And Beria knew how to ingratiate himself with the Dictator. His liberal activity on behalf of the thousands of nameless people whom he released from prisons and concentration camps did not mean that Lavrenty discontinued entirely arrests and night interrogations in his office. Besides the imprisonment and executions of Yezhov's deputies and henchmen, Beria still could find a scapegoat to show his Superior that he, Lavrenty, was taking care of the safety of the Great Comrade and Leader of the nation. Beria was constantly aware of Stalin's fear of being assassinated, and he did not intend to cure him of that obsession.

Despite the great burden of his new duties, which often required him to work an eighteen-hour day, Beria did not neglect his own private affairs. He found time to return to Tiflis, not only to complete his official work in the Caucasus, but also to transfer his family and his possessions to their new home in Moscow. Still keeping his villa in the suburbs of the capital of Georgia, as well as his comfortable apartment in the center of that city, Lavrenty chose for himself a large, two-story house at 28 Katchalov Street in the heart of Moscow, and a luxurious *dacha* near the capital.

His two homes in Tiflis had previously belonged to two rich Georgians whom Beria annihilated to obtain their property. His present villa near Moscow was acquired the same way.

Not far from Stalin's home at Kuntsevo, in the outskirts of Moscow, was a house inhabited by Vlas Yakovlevich Chubar, a former Bolshevik leader in the Ukraine. His house, a huge and beautiful estate in the middle of a spacious park, was erected by the same builder who had created several villas for Stalin. Beria decided to take this residence for himself. It was true that Chubar was a devoted Bolshevik, who soon after the Revolution became Commissar of Artillery, then held several important posts in the Ukraine, and later, when transferred to Moscow, became a candidate member of the Politburo. But he had one shortcoming. He was one of the cadre of Old Guard Bolsheviks, and having been an active Communist more than ten years before the Revolution, he knew the truth about the real part Stalin had played in the Communist achievement. Such knowledge could not please the Dictator. Beria didn't have much difficulty in convincing his Superior that Chubar was a dangerous character who was leading a movement against Stalin within the Central Committee. Chubar was arrested at night and brought to Lubyanka Prison where he was questioned personally by Beria in his office. There, the man heard that he was a traitor and learned about a crime that he had never even considered. However, he was neither shot *in camera* nor put on trial. He was still too eminent to be executed on the spot or to be brought to a spectacular trial. Beria, a newly-created liberal "Purger of purgers," did not yet want to imitate Yezhov. It was much better to take Chubar out of circulation quietly and inconspicuously. So, in 1938, he simply disappeared, having been whisked to Siberia. His family was arrested the next day and deported to a different remote place.

Soon after, Beria moved into the vacant estate, and brought his wife Nina and their little son from Tiflis.

32

The Slaveholder

REPORTS THAT HAD STARTED flowing into Beria's Moscow Headquarters at Lubyanka Prison from the commanders of all the hard labor camps from Siberia on the north to the Chinese border on the south were more than gloomy.

While it was possible to liberate those people who had been deported shortly before Beria's order to free them reached their compounds, those prisoners sent there about two years before were mostly already dead. As a result of that unofficial amnesty, fewer than 30 percent of the convicts were released. The phenomenon of such a high death rate caused Beria to be concerned about life in those camps. Not that Lavrenty Pavlovich was sorry for the prisoners, but he detected the wasting of the manpower.

Still working on the reorganization of his office of Internal Affairs, Beria started studying with great care the rules and the treatment in the three prisons in Moscow: Lubyanka, Lefortovo and Butyrki. He found the conditions there were miserable. Soon, Lavrenty ordered that all the jail cell windows, which Yezhov had ordered sealed up, be immediately reopened. Beria also improved the nourishment which, under his predecessor's regime, consisted only of a little bread and a soup smelling like hogwash. However, all these liberal changes were by no means due to his compassion for the captives. Beria calculated that if the prisoners had to be deported to the labor camps later, they should not just be living corpses, but convicts strong enough to be able to work. Otherwise, it would not pay to feed them at all. The places of exile were not compounds for exterminating people as were the Nazi concentration camps with their gas chambers, but they were areas where the slaves had to work to build a better and stronger Sovietland. If they were weak and died like flies, there would be no profit in sending them there. It would not make sense to deport to those places more and more batches of prisoners if they were not able to work properly and their achievements were almost nil. Their slave labor should be the most important consideration, because the camps were located in the Siberian forests where the men cut down the trees for the use of the whole country and even for export. Or the prisoners were sent to other remote corners of the USSR to work in coal and other mines such as iron, copper, asbestos, silver and gold. They also worked in the oil fields or built railroads so more inmates could be delivered more quickly and not in so exhausted a state as those who were herded on foot. In short, it behooved the Administration, for its own advantage, to take care of those human beings.

Beria studied this problem chronologically from its very beginning. The first concentration camps under the Communist regime were ordered by Lenin. They were established on Solovetsky Island in 1922. There, in that Arctic climate, especially during the wintertime, without proper barracks and clothes, thousands of men who had survived the transports perished in less than a year. From the practical point of view of the Administration this policy was entirely wrong. If someone wanted to annihilate those people, he could execute them in the prison. It was much less complicated, took less time, required fewer guards and was cheaper, since a bullet costs only three kopecks. It was strange that such a bloodthirsty beast as Dzerzhinsky, who liked so well to send people before the firing squads, using machine guns to kill the condemned more quickly, was also determined to exterminate captives by the time-consuming method of deportation.

The situation did not change under the rule of his successor Menzhinsky. It was true that the tremendous White Sea-Baltic Canal was built, and that it was created entirely by slaves. But they were treated so badly that thousands more of them had to be sent there as replacements.

The conditions in the camps during Yagoda's rule were really most cruel. If during his shift someone failed to work efficiently enough, he was punished later by not being allowed to enter the so-called *zone*, the living quarters of the camp with barracks and kitchen encircled by tall and strong fences with barbed wire. He was left outside until the next day, when he had to work well enough to deserve the benefits of the *zone*. However, the prisoner almost never proved anything the next day, since during the night he either met the white death of the frost or was torn to death by the wolves.[1]

The news of the horrible circumstances in the camps was revealed to the world when a desperate convict cut off one of his fingers with the ax with which he cut trees in the tundra. With his blood he wrote a short note on a cloth, wrapped the finger with that nightmarish message and smuggled it among the logs to Finland, which used to buy the exported lumber believing in good faith that it was produced by volunteers of the Communist Youth League.

The Finnish press published that news and made a lot of stir about the event. By public demand Finland discontinued her import of Russian lumber. It was the first time that the free world had learned about the slave camps in the Communist paradise. Such things must never happen again and the unbearable conditions in the hard labor confinements should be improved for the sake of the nation. However, under Yagoda's successor, Yezhov, nothing was done for improvement. Now Beria decided that the slave labor system, on which the whole wealth of the USSR was based, should be scientifically reorganized.

From that time on Lavrenty spent most of his office hours planning and adjusting the entire new labor system according to the real needs of the Soviet Union. The main Agency for that great branch of Soviet labor and economics, which played such an immensely important part in the life of the whole country, was called GULAG.[2] Beria decided to shake it up, to change its high executive and to re-do it completely.

Beria faced a tremendous job, especially as he had other work to attend to first—the Security of the country as well as of Stalin and

---

[1] As related to the author by an experienced inmate who survived Yagoda's regime and later was transferred to the Vorkuta camp, where the author was confined in 1942.

[2] GULAG: Glavnoye Uprovlenye Lagerey—Chief Administration of Hard Labor Camps.

of the members of Politburo. Then there were such related functions as arrests, interrogations, preparations for trials and participation in the Collegium of *Troyka*, sentencing the accused to exile or to execution *in camera*. There was the equally important job of Intelligence Service: planting spies in foreign countries, giving them instructions, receiving their reports, listening to their debriefings, or masterminding the secret liquidation of some of them abroad when they did not seem trustworthy enough.

The reorganization of GULAG, however, was extremely exciting for Beria, the architectural engineer, who found fulfillment in the building of a tremendous project. Lavrenty worked out everything to the smallest detail. He designed individual camps with a specific number of barracks, describing the size of every one of them; the kitchen, steambath, laundry, latrines, and warehouses. He prescribed food rations for the deportees during the transport from prison to their destination. On their way to the hard labor camps they were given twice as much bread as they had been given in jail, as well as raw fish, butter, margarine, sugar and salt, which they had never received when behind bars.[3] After they reached the camps they were fed according to their efficiency.

With a pedantic exactness Beria also established the hierarchy of the administration in the labor camps, the special rules and regulations, as well as norms of productivity for every camp in each area. From the commanders of these camps he demanded reports about how many physicians, engineers, specialists and skilled laborers were needed there. In accordance with those demands, Lavrenty looked for supplies. A doctor who was not of peasant or worker origin, but practiced in Moscow or any other big city in the USSR, would be summoned at night to his local Security Police NKVD station. There he was asked politely by a high ranking officer if he was a Soviet-minded person and a good patriot. When the man confirmed that he was, he was told that he would go immediately to a certain labor camp, where medical help was badly needed. The officer persuaded him that to a good Soviet doctor it should make no difference where he practices, in Moscow or in Siberia, because both places are in the same Sovietland. Also, it should not matter where he cures people as long as he is bringing help to his coun-

[3] Thaddeus Wittlin, *A Reluctant Traveler in Russia* (New York: Rinehart and Company, Inc., 1952).

trymen, and the help of a good physician is needed even more in the camps than in a big city where all medical facilities are available.

A truck driver who had an accident, instead of losing his license for a period of time, would be told at the police station that he should learn to be a better chauffeur. In order to get some training, he was going to be sent to a correction camp where he would be busy working at his profession. Then he was whisked to a camp where there were more trucks than men who knew how to operate them.

The same thing happened to cobblers, carpenters and masons, as well as other skilled laborers who were involved in a drunken brawl or arrested for other minor trespasses. The interrogating officers of those men arrested as hooligans, after sentencing them to three or five years of forced labor, usually consoled them by saying, "Don't be afraid, my friend, nobody is going to kill you there. You will only be sent to a correction labor camp where you will be busy in your own profession." If the person was fearful, and the police functionary happened to be a humane individual, he cheered up the captive by saying, "You will get your food and board free of charge, and some good, warm clothes, too. You will be allowed to write letters to your family and to receive correspondence, as well as parcels from them. You will have a bathhouse there, a theatre, movies, radio, books, newspapers and lectures. The Russian soil is the same everywhere, and useful workers are needed everywhere for the glory and the building of our country."

The hardest jobs—cutting trees in the tundra and working in the mines—were left to the simple peasants and Gypsies arrested for vagrancy, as well as farmers who were too rich, so-called *kulaks*, unskilled men, the intelligentsia, political criminals, the youths and the old men.

Beria also prescribed norms of achievement for individual brigades working on specific projects in the mines, in forests, erecting barracks, or constructing railroads and highways. There were also strictly designated norms for every man in each brigade. The brigades that worked efficiently received bonuses such as better lodging and better clothes. For each individual there were fourteen categories of cuisine, called kettles. The fourteenth, the best, was for "champions," those men who fulfilled double the norm prescribed for a day. Besides the regular ration of bread for everyone, these men received soup, a piece of fish, or a meat cutlet, and sweetened tea. The first kettle, a punitive one, consisted of only a small piece of bread and a bowl of watery fish soup. And between the first kettle and the fourteenth there existed a gradual improvement in menu. By such feeding, Beria cunningly destroyed any friendship among the inmates, because when struggling for better food everyone worked only for himself. Nobody could afford to help his not-so-strong pal who could not fulfill the daily norm.

On the other hand, by designating the punitive rations on which it was impossible to work properly the next day, Beria was not much more humane than Yagoda, who left such poor beings outside the camp as the prey of frost or wolves. On the punitive diet Beria's victims soon lost their strength and died of malnutrition.

But, in general, the new system worked perfectly and soon the productivity of Soviet industry proved to be higher in quality as well as in quantity.

Now, from the hundreds of camps spread over the whole Soviet Union all kinds of goods were flowing to the central points. Timber came from the Siberian forests, and iron, nickel and copper from Vorkuta; coal from Donbas; coal, cement, asphalt and bricks from Karaganda; petroleum from Ukhta and asbestos, silver and gold from Kolyma, while thousands of miles of railroads and highways were built all over the vast USSR. And all of it was constructed by millions of deportees: men, women, and teen-agers distributed by GULAG, which was supplied with the manpower by the Soviet Security Police.

The dream that Beria had as a student at Technicum in Baku had come true. Now he was building towns, and dams, and canals, and mines, and factories, and foundries, and paper mills, and highways and railroads. That desire was realized with horrifying exactness. Until now, in the whole history of mankind, there had never existed such a powerful Roman Caesar or even Biblical Pharaoh who could rule so many millions of working slaves as had been mastered by Chief of Internal Affairs and Commander of the Soviet Security Police: Commissar Lavrenty Pavlovich Beria.

33

"We Live More Joyfully"

BERIA NOT ONLY RELEASED from hard labor camps and restored to their ranks in his Department hundreds of Security functionaries who had been imprisoned and deported into exile by his predecessor. He also freed many Red Army officers and soldiers and incorporated them into his regiments of NKVD Forces and the so-called Special Purpose Divisions, which he was building up. As their Commander in Chief Beria strengthened these units, armed them with the most modern equipment and supplied them with the best uniforms, billets and food. In this way he obtained men who would be most faithful to him.

To the key positions Beria appointed his friends and reliable supporters. His old trusted subordinate, Colonel Sarkisov, became his aide-de-camp. Besides Merkulov and Kruglov as his deputies in Moscow and Mamulov as his secretary, Beria established as chiefs of the Secret Police in Georgia, Azerbaijan and Armenia, as well as in several big Russian cities like Leningrad, Kiev, Kharkov and Odessa, his comrades and fellow students from the Technicum in Baku, like Goglidze, Dekanozov, Gvishiani, Meshik and others. Bagirov, the Chief of Secret Police in Baku, became also the Head of the Party in Azerbaijan. These men could advance their own careers only by serving him obediently.

To make the way clear for his close associates in Georgia, Beria decided definitely to get rid of Stanislav Redens. One more drunken brawl provoked by Lavrenty's agents and performed by Redens in Tbilisi was enough to declare him a hoodlum and hooligan. After a report from Beria, Stalin called back Redens to the NKVD Headquarters in Moscow. Soon after Stanislav Redens got a new assignment in Kazakhstan, and with his wife Anna left Moscow for the town of Alma-Ata. But he did not stay there for long. By special order of Beria, Redens was summoned back, arrested and jailed in Butyrki Prison.

By such a policy of establishing his own followers and destroying his adversaries Beria held the whole country in check.

The great purges and the show trials staged previously against eminent Party members and high ranking Red Army officers were discontinued. After two amnesties, suggested to Stalin by Beria, resulted in the release and return home of thousands of prisoners and after many of Yezhov's henchmen were arrested and executed, the nation started believing that at last better times had come. A newly composed ditty with an inspiring lyric, "I don't know any other country where a man breathes so freely," became instantly popular on the radio and was sung at schools by children organized in the units of Pioneers, or Red Scouts, by members of the Young Communist League, and in the Red Army, as well as by millions of ordinary citizens.

At the beginning of his reign in Moscow, Lavrenty Pavlovich Beria became a visible symbol of liberalization and of a golden era, while the Great Comrade Stalin who had demoted that monster Yezhov and appointed Beria as Commissar for Internal Affairs and Chief of Security Police in his place, was praised as the savior of the people. There was nothing more astonishing to Beria than unexpectedly becoming a righteous person, a humane and forbearing personality, and a true benefactor in the eyes of the people who, in fact, he held by the throat. His new role as a reluctant idol instead of a chief hangman really amused him.

Bearing in mind that his Big Boss hated any trace of competition and wanted to grab all credit for himself, Beria did not ask for much recognition. From several unknown, but well paid artists, Lavrenty ordered paintings showing Stalin all in smiles surrounded by loving children, or happy workers, or beautiful and neatly dressed peasant girls. Soon after, huge colored posters depicting these idyllic scenes were designed and hung on the fronts of factories, movie theatres, and youth clubs.

Sonetchko Sovietskey Vlaste—"A Little Sun of the Soviet Country," was a new nickname for the Great Comrade Stalin, started by Beria's men scattered around the nation.

Lavrenty was not only a policeman and a functionary, but a shrewd individual. He was aware that for his popularity he could pay with his life. Beria never cared for fame and he preferred to stay in the shadows; his only ambition was not the glory, but the power. He constantly kept in mind that the only person who should be beloved by the people must be *Sonetchko*-Sun Stalin. As if he were Stalin's ghost writer, Beria attributed to his Superior the slogan, *Zhyt' stalos veseley*—"We Live More Joyfully," although he himself had proposed it for use by the nation as an expression for the new era.

When not in public, Beria's and the Dictator's manner of speech was neither so poetic nor lofty, but rather quite coarse. Lavrenty, who had his summer house in the neighborhood of Stalin's home *Blizhny* at Kuntsevo, frequently joined the dinner parties held by the Big Boss for an exclusive circle of his best comrades and the members of the Politburo. The guests were different from those when Beria had visited his Superior while in Moscow on duty from the Caucasus. There was no more "Dear Sergo" Ordzhonikidze, the generally liked Avel Yenukidze and the clever and witty Bukharin. They had been executed, and Bukharin's wife was imprisoned, as were Alexander Svanidze, the brother of Stalin's first wife, and his wife, Maria. The atmosphere of the previous mood had changed. But the dinners at Stalin's home were still attended by his closest friends, Marshal Voroshilov and Commissars Mikoyan, Molotov and Kaganovich, with their wives. There were also two of Stalin's three children, Svetlana and Vasil, and some other members of the Dictator's family, like the old Sergo and Olga Alliluyev, parents of Nadezhda, Stalin's late second wife. There was also Stalin's mistress, the dark, big-bosomed, sexy Rosa Kaganovich, sister of Commissar Lazar Kaganovich.

In this company, after several drinks, Stalin often became as drunk as a cobbler and amused himself by using gutter language and calling his guests dirty names. He cursed Jews with the most filthy abuses, in spite of the presence of Molotov's wife, Paulina, who was Jewish, as was his mistress, Rosa, and her brother, Lazar. The exclamation *"Yob tvoyou mat'!"*—"F . . . your mother!"—was the expression most frequently used by the Soviet Leader. His favorite pranks at these parties included putting a tomato on the chair of someone who stood up for a moment, or forcing people to drink pure alcohol with pepper with one gulp as if it were ordinary vodka.

Beria accepted this kind of humor eagerly and was not far behind his master in vocabulary. Lavrenty was the only one whom the Boss did not abuse, calling him "my prosecutor." Having a strong head for liquor, and being able to stay almost sober even after heavy drinking, Lavrenty was not afraid to amuse Stalin when the Dictator called for his most beloved game at the table. After asking some of the men present about the temperature outside, the Big Boss checked it, and then the person who had been asked had to drink as many glasses of vodka as he had been off in degrees.

The era of free breathing for the Soviet people was not so joyful as it seemed to be at the beginning of Beria's new order, either.

Teams of specialists, engineers, and technicians assigned by Beria as the new Commissar for Internal Affairs to scientific expeditions, explored many beds of coal, ore and petrol in the remote parts of Siberia and on the European side of the Ural Mountains. The exploitation of these areas resulted in the establishment of a number of new mines. In other words, new concentration camps were needed to provide more manpower. For furnishing more laborers there was GULAG, the Agency reorganized by Beria to supply slaves. His objective, however, was not to destroy them in a mad frenzy as his predecessors had, but to use them to the best advantage, rationally and methodically, according to local needs. Slowly, the whole economic life of the Soviet Union became based on the forced labor camps as the main supplier of goods. The delivery of human material was constant. Whole contingents of Army recruits were drafted in several villages and towns far distant from each other. After the military physical examination and other typical army procedures, they boarded trains, but instead of being sent to their units, they were directed to Siberia.

There they learned that they were bound for "temporary" duty. Soon after, for any small trespass or disobedience one could easily get a disciplinary sentence of five or ten years of hard labor in that encampment. They were unable to communicate with their relatives, who did not guess what had happened to those boys.

GULAG had demands for women, too. They were needed as

nurses, seamstresses and cooks, as well as to work in fields and in the factories, or even to build highways together with men.

Any sign of dissatisfaction with the farm collectivization resulted in deportations of entire villages. After extinguishing a brief uprising of Kuban Cossacks in the Caucasus, Beria transferred almost the whole tribe from its sunny country to the frozen Siberian tundra. During a roundup lasting four days and four nights, over 2,000 men, women and children were surrounded by units of Beria's Special Purpose Divisions with machine guns and half-wild Alsatian hound dogs, and were herded into cattle cars of long trains and deported to the far north. In those massive deportations from Georgia some 130,000 people were sent to Siberia.[1]

According to the new rules introduced by Commissar of Internal Affairs Lavrenty Pavlovich Beria for hard labor camp policy, it was not permissible to keep families in the same compound. When a whole community was exiled, husbands were directed to different places from their wives, children were taken from their parents and sisters and brothers were separated. This cruel method was dictated not just because of the viciousness of a tyrant, but to make impossible any kind of mutual aid among people close to each other. In accordance with the same policy, convicts never stayed longer than six months in one camp. They were shuffled and switched from one compound to another, from one end of Russia to another. This prevented the establishment of real friendships and mutual reliance, which led to escapes, plots and riots. In the Soviet Union there were constant transports of prisoners by trains, barges, trucks and on foot. And in GULAG there was a special Department of Transportation with an elaborate timetable, and a map of special bases and stations with supplies of food, clothes, and guards equipped with weapons and German shepherd dogs.[2]

While the humble masses of peasants and workers were terrorized by the enormous deportations, the staged show trials and great purges were halted and the intellectuals—writers, poets, dramatists and artists—saw the new regime as a period of relative freedom of expression.

Nonconformist writers could publish their essays, articles, short stories and poetry in some literary magazines. Artists and sculptors

---

[1] *Encyclopaedia Britannica*, Vol. 10, 1958.

[2] From the own experiences and observations of the author, who was deported by such a transport to a hard labor camp in Vorkuta in the Far North.

were allowed to exhibit their modern works, and the avant-garde dramatists and stage directors produced experimental plays.

Unfortunately, they did not realize that the new wave of freedom was nothing but Beria's sly provocation to lure the so-called subversive elements. Under the Communist regime men of letters should serve the masses and build their morale, as well as praise the Soviet Union and its achievements, or unmask the traitors and ridicule the capitalistic countries. But they should not experiment and follow the example of the decadent West.

Beria was aware that Stalin would never allow anything in art except "Soc-realism," Socialism in content and realism in form.

Soon the creative intellectuals paid for their carelessness when the omnipotent Chief of Internal Affairs entered the action. Lavrenty initiated a unique shake-up among the men of letters. One of his first victims was a forty-five-year-old writer, Boris Pilnyak. He was an outstanding novelist and storyteller whose books were quite popular in the Soviet Union and had been translated into several languages. Pilnyak was a devoted Communist, but that did not mean very much. More devoted Bolsheviks than he had been annihilated. Pilnyak had committed several sins. He was the author of a book, *Red Wood*, which was published abroad, namely, in Germany, and for this trespass he was told to step down from his post as President of the All-Russian Writers' Union. He also traveled abroad a lot. This was never liked by the Soviet Administration because one could bring home some undesirable ideas. Because in addition to Western Europe the writer had also visited Japan and the United States, it was not hard to accuse him of being a spy for these countries. It was true that Pilnyak described his experiences in the United States in his book *Okay*, which was anti-American propaganda, but it could be just a camouflage of his real attitude. Pilnyak had already been summoned to the NKVD office several times under the Yezhov regime, but now he was arrested. Beria knew that the destruction of this writer would be especially pleasing to Stalin, not only because Pilnyak, whose real name was Vogau, was a Jew, but because he once wrote a book of fiction, *The Story of the Unextinguished Moon, or the Death of the Komandarm*. The novel, about a *Komandarm* named Gavilov, was based on the death of the real great Soviet hero Mikhail Frunze, who was supposedly poisoned on Stalin's order. The book was confiscated instantly, but the writer was not disciplined. The authorities realized that his immediate persecution would prove that his work hit the target. But now, several years later, it was a different matter. The right time had come and Lavrenty knew that by liquidating this author he would please his Boss.

Awakened in the middle of the night and brought to the Lubyanka Prison, Pilnyak was immediately taken to the office of the Chief of State Security. The crime of spying for the United States and Japan was too serious for the case to be given to anyone other than Beria himself. Moreover, Lavrenty was glad to meet an outstanding writer and feel that he could dominate him. The talk between these two individuals did not resemble an inquest. Quite the opposite. It sounded like a pleasant conversation between two gentlemen. Beria graciously offered cigarettes. He asked the writer what he was going to publish next and how he found the literary circles in the West. Then, when their long, amiable conversation was almost over, the chief policeman asked the writer to admit that he was a spy for Japan. Pilnyak denied this most emphatically. The investigator accepted the answer with the remark that if the writer would like to change his mind he could be brought back to the office at any time to make his declaration. Then Beria pressed the bell and ordered the guard to escort the guest upstairs to the fourth floor, Room 16. Stalin had already legalized torture as a method of obtaining information or pleas of guilty from victims, and Beria was a good organizer of that system, too. On the fourth floor were located the prison's medical facilities: clinic, hospital, pharmacy, and other related sections. Room 16 was the Dentistry Department. The person in charge there was a young Georgian girl, Vera. She was a graduate of the University in Tiflis, a beautiful lass, whom Beria had forcibly made his mistress and later brought with him to Moscow. She was tall, slim, had large, brilliant black eyes and a peachlike complexion, but she never smiled. She worked on the medical staff of Lubyanka Prison, where she lived. She had a small apartment there, and Beria sometimes visited her at night. After her office hours Vera could go out in a government-chauffeured limousine with a guard, but she was practically a prisoner herself, and Beria's slave. Besides her regular practice as a dentist, Vera also had to execute some of the perverted and cruel tortures introduced by Beria. When a new victim was on his way to her office, she got a phone call from Beria, personally ordering her to apply his invention. The method looked harmless. The quiet handsome young lady, with her melodious voice, asked the patient to take a seat for a routine checkup of his teeth.

As soon as the man was in the chair and opened his mouth, the guard held him firmly while the dentist started drilling a hole in healthy teeth, one after another. The dentist stopped only when the man nodded "yes" to the question asked by the guard: would he like to go back to the investigator's office and plead guilty? If the prisoner was still obstinate, the drilling continued.

In fifteen minutes Boris Pilnyak was indeed back in Commissar Beria's office confessing every crime he was accused of. Beria accepted his declaration with polite understanding. The case was over. Lavrenty realized that a quick execution of Pilnyak would not please Stalin as much as condemning to slow death the author of a book that had smeared the Dictator. Without a trial, Boris Andreyevich Pilnyak was sentenced to ten years' hard labor in the mines of Kolyma, in northeast Siberia.

Certainly the Pilnyak case was not unique. There were several other writers, poets, playwrights and artists who followed him.

Richard Stande, a Polish poet who emigrated in 1931 from his native Warsaw to the Soviet Union, where he established and edited the magazine, *The Literary Monthly*, was arrested by Beria just because he was a close friend of another Polish writer, Bruno Yasenski, already imprisoned for almost two years. Yasenski, after being expelled from France where he published his novel, *I Burn Paris*, a book translated into several languages and highly acclaimed by critics, went to Russia, where he accepted Soviet citizenship and joined the Communist Party. Soon he became a member of the Board of Directors of the Society of Soviet Writers and was nominated Editor-in-Chief of *International Literature*, a magazine published in four languages for circulation abroad. Richard Stande was his deputy. Yasenski also edited the magazine, *The Culture for the Masses*, published in Polish as a Communist propaganda organ to be smuggled into Poland, where the Communist Party was banned by law. Having been arrested by Yezhov on unsubstantiated information, Yasenski was still awaiting trial. For Beria, it was enough that both of these individuals, Yasenski and Stande, were Polish intellectuals, whom he despised. Officially they were accused of being Polish spies. Stande, who, during the interrogation realized he had nothing to lose, did not behave sheepishly but boldly fought back. He was condemned by Beria to death *in camera* and was executed the very same night in the basement of Lubyanka Prison. Yasenski, a fragile poet with highly advanced tuberculosis contracted in jail, received fifteen years in a concentration camp near Vladivostok. Lavrenty knew that the hardship of transport to the train, the journey in a cattle car and on a prison barge, and then the long, exhausting walk to the camp would be murderous enough for the Polish man of letters, for whom death by bullet would only be an act of mercy.

Beria also focused his attack on the theatre. The living word from the stage was always considered in the Soviet Union to be one of the best tools of Communist propaganda. Consequently, it should be examined most carefully by the State Security. Soon Vsevolod Meyerhold, one of the most eminent figures in the Russian theatre, became the target of Beria's anger. An outstanding disciple of the great stage director and pillar of the Moscow Art Theatre after the October Revolution, Konstantin Stanislavsky, Meyerhold joined the Communist Party, left Stanislavsky's Art Theatre and organized a new one under his own direction. Shortly, his playhouse became an avant-garde theatre despite the fact that the Soviet regime believed only in social realism in art and disapproved of that trend. However, knowing that he was one of the most popular figures in Moscow artistic life, Meyerhold hoped that he would be able to manage it. He had been a friend of the late Gorky, whose plays he performed, and like Gorky, Meyerhold could not be annihilated like a mere nobody. But in Soviet art in general, and in its drama in particular, there is no place for experimentation. In a Communist country, art should educate and entertain the masses and lift their spirits in the Marxist way of thinking without any dangerous innovations. The theatre should teach the masses and lead them. But it should not lure the people into a dark labyrinth. In the course of the years, Vsevolod Meyerhold became a more and more controversial person, but he was still at liberty. This continued until Beria came to power. Lavrenty visited theatres not only to inspect them as part of his duties, but for his own pleasure, as well as to spot young actresses with whom he could later become acquainted. He saw several of Meyerhold's productions and was not satisfied with them. In his opinion, this kind of theatre did not represent culture for the masses. Lavrenty had no doubt that by destroying Meyerhold, a Jew, he would please Stalin, who hated the elite in general and the Jewish in particular because, in his opinion, the Jewish intelligentsia was always creating a ferment. The shutting of Meyerhold's theatre would satisfy the Dictator, who persecuted any kind of art other than social realism, and could not stand having a Jewish director of a leading playhouse in Moscow.

In 1939, Vsevolod Meyerhold was arrested after the closing night performance of *Don Juan*, by Moliere. Meyerhold, heading for home, was walking alone. He was the last to leave the theatre. His wife Zina, a noted actress, did not play in that show and had not come to the theatre that evening. On an empty street he was pushed into a police car and driven straight to Lubyanka Prison to be interrogated by Commissar Beria.

At the same time, Meyerhold's front doorbell rang. Zina opened it and saw a Secret Police officer with two functionaries. During their house search for weapons and anti-Communist propaganda documents, as they said, the NKVD agents destroyed all Meyerhold's personal memorabilia: autographed photographs of his colleagues, posters, playbills, and press clippings—the most precious gems to every artist. When they found the manuscripts of Meyerhold's diary, Zina begged them to seize and confiscate them, to at least preserve them. Her pleas had no effect. The memoirs were torn page by page. Meyerhold's large library was ruined in the same way, with the destruction of many rare editions and valuable autographed books by such authors and personal friends as Anton Chekhov, Maxim Gorky, Konstantin Stanislavsky, and poets Vladimir Mayakovsky and Sergey Yesenin.

If the functionaries did not arrest Meyerhold's wife and if they did not seize his papers it was evident that they acted strictly by order of the Chief of Security, Commissar Beria.

During this time Lavrenty Pavlovich carried on a sophisticated discussion with the theatrical director, ending the conversation by telling him that his playhouse had to be closed. Then Beria also asked the detained man to sign the protocol and accept a sentence of fifteen years at hard labor in the concentration camp in the Archangelsk region.

The agents left the Meyerholds' apartment entirely destroyed. The mattresses on the beds were ripped, the pictures painted by famous artists were cut, the desk was hacked up, the chairs were broken, the lamps were smashed. In the studio the only piece of furniture that was untouched was a sofa on which Zina lay dead, killed by a bullet in her forehead.

A similar fate was met by one of the most gifted writers and dramatists, Babel. He was an Old Bolshevik, a member of the Communist Party, and a brave officer of the Soviet Army during the Civil War. His books were widely read, and some of them, like *Red Cavalry*, were translated into English. Such facts as his popularity in the Western countries and his short trip to France, were enough pretext to arrest him under suspicion of being a Western spy. Besides, Babel, whose first name was Isaak, was a Ukrainian Jew from Odessa. In a few articles printed in the state newspapers, *Pravda* and *Izvestia*, some little-known critics and second-rate writers accused Babel of being alien to Soviet art and to the Communist line. They demanded that his works be banned from the Soviet stage and libraries. Such public voices, inspired by Beria, were enough to produce action. During his interrogation Babel had no choice but to admit his crime. He was sentenced to ten years in a concentration camp.

The new Commissar of Internal Affairs, Lavrenty Beria persecuted not only Jewish or Polish men of letters, but Russian ones as well. He was aware that otherwise the non-Jewish and domestic writers would feel safe, and he intended to keep all intellectuals in suspense. Besides Pilnyak, Meyerhold and Babel, he arrested the Russian novelist Panteleymon Romanov, known in the West for his novel, *Three Pairs of Silk Stockings*, adapted later for the stage and performed abroad with great success. Jailed by Beria on the accusation of having contacts with foreigners and of being of aristocratic origin which, in the eyes of Communist justice, was a crime, Romanov was sentenced to death *in camera*. Nikolay Ognyov, the author of two charming novels translated into English under the titles, *The Diary of a Schoolboy*, and *The Diary of a College Student*, was too much beloved by young readers to be left alone. Being an intelligent man, Beria liked to read. But he also liked to show his power over an individual. It was enough to warrant punishing Ognyov that his recently published book, *The Three Dimensions*, seemed to Commissar Beria to be not in accord with the general line. It was a great pleasure and a triumph for Lavrenty to drag such a person out of his home at midnight and, after a short conversation, to bend him and make a nobody of someone who, only a few hours before, had been a celebrity. Kept in Lubyanka Prison in a solitary cell in the basement without a light, Nikolay Ognyov died in a few weeks.

During the period when the Red Army officer corps was being rebuilt, the Security Police NKVD troops were strengthened, and the ranks of the Politburo and the outstanding members of the Communist Party were no longer annihilated by senseless purges. But the Russian intellectuals who shaped the mentality of the nation, were caught by the throat.

Now Beria had under his thumb millions of nameless slaves in the hard labor camps, as well as the artistic elite of the vast Soviet Empire. It was not too bad a progress in a year after he had been transferred to Moscow from his native Caucasus.

34

Work and Pleasure

BERIA REMEMBERED the beautiful white villas of the rich people living in Baku before the capture of Azerbaijan by the Bolshevik Eleventh Army. He could recall the interiors of those charming houses that later were ransacked by the victorious Russian soldiers, who shot to death the owners of the residences. Beria himself had confiscated the possessions of some of those bourgeois. Then, as an officer of the local *Cheka* in Baku, he inspected the houses of the people already arrested by his order. He could observe how such homes were decorated. He saw the expensive editions of French, German and English books in their libraries. He saw the exquisite china, the silver and chandeliers in their dining rooms, and the valuable paintings on the walls in their salons.

Now Beria owned the same: a magnificent house in Moscow and a villa with a charming garden near the Soviet capital, a summer house in the neighborhood where Stalin lived. This house was already fully furnished, as it was confiscated by Beria complete with silver and antiques. It also contained canvases painted by the foreign masters, all of them taken from the estates of the Caucasian noblemen whom he had persecuted during his reign in Tiflis. Through the Soviet embassies abroad, Beria purchased books of the best contemporary French, German, English and American writers banned in the Soviet Union. He also hired tutors to teach his son foreign languages. Beria converted one of the rooms in his lavish

villa into a projection room, where foreign films unavailable to the
public were shown. It was great entertainment for Lavrenty's
guests, for his family and his son's friends. For himself, Beria built
a shooting gallery in a corner of his garden. He liked to practice
shooting with different pistols.

In the study of his house in Moscow on Katchalov Street, in a
locked drawer of his desk, Beria had a tremendous collection of
pornographic photographs and films. These were supplied by his
many agents from abroad, mostly from Germany, France, Sweden
and Denmark. He also kept in that room a cupboard with rows of
bottles full of vodka and cognac. The more powerful he felt, the
more he found pleasure in drinking, especially since no matter how
much he drank, he was always still half sober and aware of what he
was doing or saying. He never uttered a word he would be sorry for
later.

As a companion in drinking the best foreign liquors and in the
pleasure of watching the pornographic pictures, Lavrenty Pavlovich used to invite Vasily Stalin. Vasily was the beloved son of the
Dictator, who made him Chief of Aviation of the Moscow Military
District and, at twenty-four, nominated him General of the Red Air
Forces. To befriend such a personality was a big opportunity for
Lavrenty. He knew well that Stalin Junior liked women and alcohol, so a place like Beria's house in the city, with a study furnished
with drinks, obscene photographs, pornographic movies, and from
time to time, with call girls, was a real heaven. Lavrenty also gladly
lent money to General Vasily Stalin, who permanently was short of
cash. No wonder this young man soon became his pal and often
praised Lavrenty to his omnipotent father.

Beria had almost everything: a lavish residence, a quiet wife
whom he could call dirty names if he liked, and an obedient mistress near him at his office. He was a master of millions of slaves
working in mines and forests, or building canals, roads and tunnels,
according to his orders. He was Chief Censor of the press and
dictator of the arts, theatre and literature. He was Commander-in-
Chief of a strong and well-disciplined Security Army, equipped
with all of the most modern weapons, including tanks and air-
planes. He could arrest and bring to his office at Lubyanka Prison
anyone he wished, and shoot him to death, if he pleased.

Commissar of Internal Affairs and Chief of Security Police of the
Soviet Union Lavrenty Pavlovich Beria possessed power, title,

money and women. But he was still not entirely happy. He was not yet at the top, not the Number One he intended to become. There was no reason to relinquish this idea. If this could be achieved by Stalin, his Georgian countryman, that stinking cad from the village of Gori, a boor whom Lavrenty hated and despised, it could be done by Beria, too.

All Beria had to do now was to be careful to maintain good relations with some of the other highly influential people, like Georgy Malenkov who, although three years younger than Lavrenty, had already become a member of the Party's Central Committee, or Nikita Khrushchev, First Secretary of the Ukrainian Central Committee. Those men were presently too powerful to be annihilated, so, until the right time came, it was safer to be friendly with them. Some others, however, not so strongly situated, who were potential enemies or obviously disliked him, Beria would liquidate, wisely playing them against Stalin's vanity and suspiciousness, which had developed into an obsession.

Beria constantly kept in his mind that the main principle of a good statesman should be to serve his Boss in the best possible way as long as that man is in power and can award favors to his faithful subordinate. But such a good and humble disciple, helpful and available at any time, should be simultaneously patient and alert for the right moment to cut his Superior's throat and take his job.

Besides being the master of the enormous system of concentration camps, the Chief of the Special Divisions of the NKVD Forces, and the whip of the intellectuals, Commissar Beria was also Chief of an agency, the Administration of Special Task—the net of so-called Residents and their subordinates; in other words, the web of spies spread all over the world. Beria was also head of that Agency's unit called *Mobile Group* which, according to need, was sent abroad to murder the leading foreign Trotskyites and to kidnap or kill Soviet defectors. These offices, inherited from his predecessor Yezhov, Lavrenty reorganized and perfected. Their activities, especially kidnaping or assassinating Soviet enemies on foreign soil, had to be done with as little fuss as possible and with all precaution, using the appearance of suicide or a fatal accident. The earlier kidnaping in 1937 by Yezhov men of two Russian generals, Miller and Kutepov, in Paris, was too big an international scandal to allow such blunt methods to be repeated.

When he received a message in the diplomatic pouch from the

Soviet Embassy in Belgium telling him that Georges Agabekov had
arrived in Brussels from Paris, Beria decided to liquidate him
quickly without the publicity of a kidnaping. Georges Agabekov, a
former Chief of the Eastern Section of the OGPU, was the same
eminent *Chekist* who several years earlier had visited Lavrenty in
his room at the Select Hotel in Moscow and had given him instructions for abducting Commissar Miasnikov, and then had accompanied Beria on the trip to Tiflis. Later, as the OGPU Resident in
Turkey, Agabekov turned his back on his masters in Moscow and
left Istanbul for Paris. There, he joined Miasnikov, whom previously he had planned to return alive by force to the USSR. In
France, these two defectors became friends and used money they
had embezzled from the Soviet Government.

In Paris, Agabekov had written his memoirs, *OGPU, The Russian
Secret Terror*, in which he described the methods of Soviet espionage in the Orient as well as in Germany, France and the United
States. He revealed the most confidential and unpublicized secrets
of the OGPU's organization. Moreover, when recalling his trip to
Georgia with Lavrenty Beria, Agabekov portrayed him as a narrow-
minded policeman who knew very little about the Communist
Party and the problems of the Central Committee, while only "the
petty doings at Tiflis absorbed him to the exclusion of grand politics."

This book, written in Russian in Paris in 1930, was soon translated into French, German and English and published in Paris, Berlin and New York. For almost ten years an intensive chase after
Agabekov was conducted by the men of the OGPU in Paris, but the
defector always succeeded in avoiding their traps. At last Agabekov
was tracked down in Brussels, where he was living in a small hotel
under a different name and with a fake passport. In spite of the fact
that it would be the best revenge and the greatest satisfaction to
bring Agabekov back to Moscow alive, where Lavrenty could kick
his teeth out and break his bones one by one, the Chief of Soviet
Security decided to sacrifice the pleasure of an hour or two of
personal joy for the sake of the reputation of the Soviet Secret
Police abroad, in case an attempted kidnaping were not entirely
successful and leaked into the foreign press.

The execution of Agabekov, according to Beria's order, had to be
done in such a way that it would not attract attention in the West.
Moreover, among the employees of the Soviet Embassy in Belgium,
as well as their Russian colleagues in the diplomatic service all over

the world, it would be a good warning that sooner or later every defector would be assassinated, even if it took a decade.

When Agabekov did not appear in the hotel lobby for two days, the manager called the police, who unlocked his room. He was not in but on the small night stand next to his bed they found a letter to the authorities. In his note, the mysterious visitor from Paris wrote that his real name and title was Georges Agabekov, former Chief of the Eastern Section of the Soviet Security and Secret Resident of OGPU in Istanbul, and that he was the author of the book *OGPU, The Russian Secret Terror*. Further, he informed the local authorities that for a long period of time he had suffered from mental depression, and had decided to commit suicide by drowning himself in the river.

The Belgian police did not call any expert to check whether the letter was really in the suicide's handwriting. But when, in a few days, the body of an unidentified man, well-dressed but without any documents, was taken out of the Senne River, there were traces of several blows on his skull.

The assassination of Agabekov was a small achievement of Beria's liquidators from the Mobile Group of the Administration of Special Task. It passed entirely unnoticed by the public in the Soviet Union, where the death of Georges Agabekov, an obscure person, was not published in the press. However, the staffs of all the Soviet diplomatic posts abroad were left without any doubt as to whose hand had deprived Agabekov of his life. A few days after his assassination, Evgeny Dumbadze was found dead in Paris. He was the same disenchanted ardent Communist and Red Army volunteer who was also a former *Chekist* in Tiflis and who later escaped to France. He supposedly killed himself by gas from the kitchenette in his cold-water flat on the Left Bank. Like Agabekov, the suicide left a note to the French police explaining that, being fed up with his poor existence as an émigré, he had decided to shorten his misery. Like Agabekov, Evgeny Dumbadze when in Paris published his memoirs entitled, in Russian, *Na Sluzhbe Cheka i Kominterna—On the Service of the Cheka and the Comintern—*in which he described Beria as a bloodthirsty mass murderer. The People's Commissar of Internal Affairs of the USSR, Lavrenty Pavlovich Beria, would never leave unpunished such a crime as making those revelations.

❉   ❉   ❉

Beria kept a bottle of vodka in his office. He liked to drink moderately with his lunch, which was brought to him from the NKVD Officers' Mess. This lavish restaurant was located in the nearby former Select Hotel, which Beria converted into the offices of several sections of his Security Department.

A few glasses of vodka used to give him more vitality for working from early morning until very late at night. The vodka even cleared his mind and let him figure more easily how to entrap the person he was going to interrogate that day with sudden questions. It also brightened his imagination when he was planning a mass hunt for occupants for a recently established hard labor camp, or workers for a new railroad construction project or for building a mine. It gave him more passion for questioning a man he had arrested, and for hitting him with the iron rod he usually kept in his desk drawer. Sometimes the alcohol made him feel amorous. In such cases, if he did not have any important meeting scheduled in the afternoon, Lavrenty called his aide, Colonel Sarkisov, for an escapade. They took Beria's government car, a huge black Packard limousine, driven by a uniformed chauffeur, and went to town.

They usually stopped near the Soviet Army Theatre. In that neighborhood was Dostoyevsky Street, where the Fyodor Dostoyevsky High School was located. Soon after two o'clock the school day was over and the students were leaving the building for their homes.

From behind a curtain half covering his car's greenish windows, Beria observed the young people like a prowling black panther which, hiding in a bush, watches a herd of young does and stags. He watched the students going through the main door of the dark school building like a flock out of the dark wilderness. He sat in ambush quietly and patiently. He was not in a hurry; he had plenty of time.

At last, when he spotted a plump girl about fourteen or fifteen years old, with a round face, rosy pink cheeks like a peach, big innocent eyes, lips moist as the morning dew, revealing white teeth when parted in a carefree smile, Beria pointed at her with a jerk of his chin.

Colonel Sarkisov would leave the car and start toward the chosen girl. He was a tall slim man in his forties; in his navy-blue NKVD officer's uniform he looked impressive and dangerous.

Approaching the girl with a snappy salute he asked her to follow him. It was not an order of arrest, or a taking into custody, but a nicely expressed wish. However, it was done with an air that did not permit rejection. From his car, often using field glasses, Beria could see terror flash into the eyes of the horrified victim as if she had been shot straight through her heart. It pleased him.

The lass realized there was no escape or rescue. She had to leave the group of her stunned friends and classmates and, with her head bowed like a slave girl, follow her tormentor. She was aware of her fate. When the girl entered the limousine and took her seat next to him, Beria did not even glance at his captive. He was sure she would beg him to let her go free, she would cry with big childish tears flowing over her rosy cheeks, and would try to kiss his hands and shoes asking for mercy. This sensual pleasure he wanted to save until they were alone.

Shortly the car passed the gate of the Lubyanka Prison and stopped in the yard at the rear entrance to Beria's office. Firmly held by her arm by Colonel Sarkisov, the girl was dragged through the long, dark and narrow corridor, through the interior lighted with only a few electric bulbs. Finally she was pushed into the office of Beria, who stepped in behind her and locked the door.

He took his seat at his desk and with a quiet, indifferent, almost expressionless voice, told the girl to undress. If she stood rooted to the floor, sobbing and trembling, and did not begin to obey his order, Beria took a horsewhip out of his drawer, left his desk, faced the girl and hit her on the calves of her legs. The girl could shout as loudly as she wished. The walls and the door of Beria's office were padded with thick rugs that deadened the sound. And even if one of the guards should hear crying, so what? Beria did not care. Anyhow, in his office almost everyone cried; nobody laughed.

If the girl sank to her knees begging, Beria let her sob and plead. Then he hit her over her shoulders once or twice, and in a quiet formal voice repeated his order. At last, the defeated girl started undressing. When she was naked and barefoot, Beria took her to the sofa and threw her onto it, crushing her with his weight. If she kept her legs tight instinctively, she had to be taken by force. Beria, embracing her firmly with his left arm, grabbed her hair with his right hand and beat her head against the wooden frame of the settee. Soon the girl was overwhelmed completely. Now came the most thrilling sensual joy for Beria when, as he entered the young and innocent body and raped it as if he would tear it apart, the small, helpless, adolescent girl suddenly gave a mad shriek from the pain of being deflowered. It was the end of her defense and of everything. She was crushed by that heavy bully of a man who, lying on top of her with his broad, hairy chest on her little bosom, pressed her body into the harsh couch and kissed away the tears from her young, innocent eyes.

Shortly everything was over. The man was fully satisfied. His main desire was the rape itself, to submit to his power a girl who resisted being taken by him, and had to be subdued against her will. The joy was to smash her and to destroy her. To defile that clean body, never touched before, was the utmost pleasure for Lavrenty Beria, much more exciting than just making love, which any man can do.

With her face rubbed raw by the chin of a man who hadn't shaved since early morning, and chilled all over her body, the girl was left alone and could get up. She was still dizzy with pain, and nauseated from the smell of vodka, garlic, rotten putrid teeth, and sweat from his hairy armpits. She was told to pick up her underwear and wipe her belly, which was wet with her virgin blood, and get dressed.

Then Beria phoned Colonel Sarkisov to come in and to take the girl away.

Sometimes Lavrenty was more generous to his victims. When they were alone in his office, he smiled benignly at the captive girl, treated her with chocolates, persuaded her that she had no reason to be frightened, and promised to let her go free at any moment. Then, when the girl was calmed, he asked her if she had brothers or sisters, what her father's occupation was, and if her parents were a loving couple. When the girl told him that she was perfectly happy at home, he assured her that she would join her family shortly if she submitted to his will. He explained to her that she should take her dress off and satisfy him physically in the way that he liked. If not, her parents would be arrested that very night and sent to concentration camps on opposite sides of Russia, while her brothers and sisters also would be deported to other hard labor compounds. The fate of her loved ones depended upon her.

She had a few seconds to make her decision. When the defeated girl was kneeling entirely naked at his feet, forced to commit sodomy, the man watching her young face all in tears felt a peculiar pleasure in debasing and sullying the innocent young girl.

Often this was not enough, and the man, being highly excited, threw his victim to the floor and raped her to destroy her virgin body.

Sometimes, instead of taking her to his office in Lubyanka Prison, Beria brought the girl to his house in Moscow at Katchalov Street. There he treated his involuntary guest with a glass of wine. After drinking it the girl fell asleep and then Laventry possessed her. The presence of his wife at home did not stop Beria from these excesses. The house was large, with many rooms and two entrances, and his wife had been told once and forever not to come to Lavrenty's study.

Later, many of those girls, after being driven out of Lubyanka Prison in Colonel Sarkisov's car and left on a secluded street in a suburb of Moscow, were too ashamed to return home to their parents, and were terrified at the thought of going to school the next day. The only escape they saw was death. And they committed suicide by throwing themselves from a bridge into the Moscow River, or by jumping from a window in the hallway of a tall apartment house chosen at random. There was no solution. There was nothing that could be done to prevent this horrible game that the richly-decorated Commissar of Internal Affairs and of the Soviet Union Lavrenty Pavlovich Beria liked to play.

Certainly, nobody knew when Beria would have a whim for a good time, or which day and which school he would choose as the terrain for his hunt. There were many schools in the nation's capital, and all youngsters had to attend them. Keeping a child out of school and away from regular education was a crime in the enlightened USSR. For such a trespass the parents could be punished with deportation to a hard labor camp.

Even if a girl were accompanied by her mother or father it would not be any protection, because the parents would be as helpless in front of a colonel of the NKVD as the girl herself.

And above all, Beria enjoyed himself in that way with the mute approval of his immediate Superior. Stalin knew everything about the taste and philanderings of his subordinate and he did not pay any attention.

Stalin even laughed loudly when he learned some details of this or that escapade of Beria's. The Dictator needed him, and understood that after having a good time Beria was more vigorous and worked better and more efficiently. In Stalin's opinion Lavrenty

Beria, as the People's Commissar of Internal Affairs of the Soviet Union and Chief of the Security Police of the USSR, was an exceptionally productive high executive and useful personality to the country. He solved many problems of state, and this was much more important than his little weakness, which every human being has of one kind or another. So if a silly teen-age girl can satisfy the senses of an individual who is such an outstanding personality and who works so hard for the Government, a dignitary and a Commissar, then she should not dramatize. Sure enough, every girl loses her virginity sometime, so the sooner the better. At least the Soviet Union had the profit of that monkey business, which, in Stalin's mind, was too meaningless a trifle to be bothered with.

35

Tasks and Rewards

IN THE HUGE, almost empty room at the Kremlin, Stalin was sitting behind his low, old-fashioned desk. In front of him stood Commissar Lavrenty Pavlovich Beria, at attention like a soldier before his superior.

It was a gray, dark and gloomy morning, and so was the mood of the Dictator.

Stalin had just phoned Beria in his office, demanding his immediate presence. When Lavrenty arrived at the Kremlin he did not have to wait in the anteroom, as he usually did before he was called in. As soon as he reported to the chief of the guard, he was sent upstairs.

Stalin fumed in anger. From the top of his mail he picked up a telegram in diplomatic code addressed to the Kremlin. The cable was from Mexico and said that Judas Iscariot had seen his doctor again.

Judas Iscariot was a cryptonym by which Stalin and the Soviet Embassy in Mexico City described Leon Trotsky.

Beria stood mute, waiting for orders or some explanation. When Stalin was in a rage, all that his subordinate should do was keep his mouth shut and look straight into the Dictator's eyes. Avoiding Stalin's gaze could result in a death sentence. Beria knew well that that maniac had an obsession about the eyes of his men. If someone failed to look into his eyes it meant he was contriving a plot, and soon he would be arrested and executed. So, you had to watch your Boss like a dog watches its master. That was all you should do. One awkward question, or the wrong word, could be no less dangerous.

It was really difficult to determine the reason for Stalin's anger. Judas Iscariot was Trotsky. All right. The message that he "saw his doctor again," did not mean anything other than what it said. In other words, Trotsky was sick again. So what? It was well known that Trotsky, who recently had been living in Mexico, had suffered from high blood pressure for a year or even longer and his health was very poor. It seemed that Stalin, Trotsky's mortal foe, should be happy to get such news. Instead, he was furious. Now a long silence prevailed. Evidently Stalin wished to hear a response from the Commissar of Internal Affairs. Beria, who now had to say something, muttered a short expression, that that *sooken-sen*—son-of-a-bitch—Trotsky could die at any moment, and it was too bad. Beria was conscious that it was the only remark he could make safely. He quickly concluded that if that cable were not in conflict with some of Stalin's plans, he would not raise such hell.

His answer was the right one. Stalin quite agreed with his man. That lousy Jew Trotsky, Judas Iscariot, could die at any moment. There was no time to lose. That bastard should not die from a natural cause. He had to be punished for all his crimes against Stalin, so he must be killed. It was a matter of Stalin's ambition and prestige that Trotsky should be liquidated. It was too important to be neglected. The extermination of Trotsky would also be the best warning for other traitors of the Sovietland that the arm of Stalin's power could reach them everywhere. The *Mobile Group*, the unit specializing in assassinations abroad, should act at once—quickly and effectively.

Beria eagerly echoed that order. Those few words of his Chief gave him enough of a hint to grasp the whole idea. Lavrenty assured Stalin that as soon as he returned to his office he would take all the steps necessary to perform the Trotsky liquidation, and he, Beria, as Commissar of Internal Affairs, would work untiringly until he finished the task that his predecessors, Menzhinsky, Yagoda and Yezhov had initiated and developed, but were unable to bring to a successful end.

When leaving the Kremlin Beria realized that from now on he and Trotsky were bound together in life and death. The whole career, if not the very existence, of Lavrenty depended on Trotsky's death by assassination. If that scoundrel died as a result of his high blood pressure, Beria's future would be over. He had to act in a hurry.

Trotsky's dossiers were tremendous. It was really a whole literature and a library in itself.

Soon after being expelled from the USSR to Turkey in 1929 with his wife, Natasha, his daughter, Zinaida, and his son, Lev Sedov, Trotsky established contacts with his followers in Russia and continued his fight against Stalin and his policy. He wrote pamphlets and brochures which were printed in the underground typesetting offices and smuggled into Russia. Copies of each of those subversive writings were in the files of the Soviet Secret Police.

Several attempts to assassinate Trotsky, staged by Stalin's agents, were unsuccessful. The OGPU Resident in Istanbul, Yacob Blumkin, the infamous killer of the German Ambassador in Moscow, Count Wilhelm von Mirbach-Harff, was assigned to slay Trotsky in Turkey. But instead of murdering him, Blumkin became his trusted courier, and under several pretexts, circulated between Istanbul and Moscow to be in touch with the Trotskyites in the USSR.

When caught, Blumkin was sentenced to death, and by Stalin's personal order was executed *in camera.* Trotsky realized that while living in Turkey he was in constant danger. He was too near the Soviet Union, and if he were not assassinated on the spot he could be kidnaped back to his homeland. There, after a long period of torture, he would confess all the crimes he had committed and many more that he had not. Then he would stand trial before at last being sentenced to death and shot.

After publishing his autobiography, *My Life,* in which he described Stalin in the worst light, and after writing other anti-Stalinist books, Trotsky decided to leave Istanbul for Paris. However, it was not so easy to obtain entry there. Finally, in 1933, France granted him asylum and a visa.

When in Paris, Trotsky undertook his anti-Stalinist activity again. There he published his pamphlets: *A Defense of Terrorism, The Terrorism and Communism, The Kirov Assassination, Soviet Economy in Danger, The Suppressed Testament of Lenin* and most important, *The Revolution Betrayed: What is the Soviet Union and Where is it Going?*

In his writings Trotsky stated that Stalin was not a leader at all, but just a "small-time propagandist and organizer." During the October Revolution of 1917, when all the Old Guard Bolsheviks "went around with cracked voices" from delivering fiery speeches to the people, Stalin had no power to attract the throng. "He emerged from the Civil War as unknown and alien to the masses, as he had from the October Revolution."

Such remarks could not be left unpunished.

Trotsky's political work in exile was not limited to his writings only. While in France he organized a small but extremely vigorous "Fourth Communist International," directed against Stalin and his policy.

Trotsky fought Stalin in spite of all kinds of repression. The agents of the Secret Police OGPU tried to assassinate him several times but, well guarded by his men, Trotsky evaded all their attempts. However, he could not protect his family, which he had left behind in Russia, and Stalin did not hesitate to wreak his vengeance upon those innocent people. Trotsky's first wife, Alexandra Sokolovskaya, and his younger son, Sergey, were arrested and executed in prison. Then Trotsky's daughter, Nina, her husband, Man Nevelson, and their two little children, Trotsky's grandchildren, were exterminated. Later, Platon Volkov was incarcerated and shot. He was the husband of Trotsky's daughter, Zinaida, who had left Russia with her parents and with her brother, Lev Sedov. Unlike her parents and brother, Zinaida lived in Berlin rather than in Paris, and in 1933 she was slain there by Soviet agents from the *Mobile Group*, who arranged the killing as a perfectly staged suicide.

Trotsky, with his wife, Natasha, their son, Lev Sedov, and their only grandson, Sevushka, the late Zinaida's little boy, left Paris and hid themselves in a remote village near Grenoble. But even there they were soon spotted by Stalin's ferrets. Since there was no safe place for them in France, the Trotsky family decided to part. Their son Lev Sedov went back to Paris where, in a big city, a single man would find it much easier to hide. The Trotskys, with their grandson, smuggled themselves into Norway and tried to live in Oslo, from where they planned to go overseas. In 1938 they were at last granted a resident visa to Mexico, where they expected to be joined by their son from Paris. However, just before his departure from France, Lev Sedov was murdered by Stalin's agents, who this time did not even bother to simulate suicide.

All that were left alive from the large family were Trotsky, his wife and their grandchild.

However, to stretch an arm from Russia to the Western Hemisphere and to reach the Trotskys in their new location was not an easy task. Trotsky settled with Natasha and little Sevushka in a tiny place in Mexico called Coysacan, living in an unapproachable house converted into a kind of fortress. The estate was surrounded with high walls topped with barbed wire, with a heavy gate at the entrance. At two corners of the walls were turrets with sentries with field glasses and machine guns. The house itself was equipped with strongly built doors and had bars in the windows. A platoon of Trotsky's followers, armed with rifles and pistols, guarded the place twenty-four hours a day, while the whole vicinity was constantly patroled by Mexican police.

Under such circumstances, the order for the annihilation of Trotsky given by Stalin to Beria seemed unfeasible. Still, that order had to be fulfilled, and the People's Commissar of the USSR Internal Affairs and Chief of the Secret Police in the Soviet Union, Lavrenty Pavlovich Beria, realized that he absolutely had to accept the challenge.

At the beginning of March 1939, Beria was proposed as a candidate to the Politburo. He was the first Chief of the Secret Police in the USSR ever introduced to that Brain Trust. It was a great promotion for Beria since the Politburo was the board ruling the USSR. This body, established by Lenin in 1917 just after the October Revolution, was created for the making of prompt decisions, and it was the governing organization of the Communist Party and of the Soviet State. To join it even as a candidate and a potential full member in the near future meant joining the highest collegium of the Party elite.

In 1939 the Politburo consisted of Stalin, Molotov, Voroshilov, Kalinin, Kaganovich, Andreyev, Mikoyan, Shvernik, Zhdanov and newly-appointed Khrushchev, with only a few alternates, among whom was Malenkov. The organization, previously the central policy-making board, later became just a tool in the hands of Stalin, the Dictator and the Supreme Boss. Having that fact in mind, Beria realized that the speech that he would deliver as every new candidate had to do, should be nothing but one great panegyric to the glory of the genius, Comrade Joseph Stalin. Lavrenty remembered well that he owed his present career mainly to his elaborate *Stalin's Early Writings and Activities: On the History of the Bolshevik Organizations in Transcaucasia.* Therefore, if he wished to be successful again he should use the same stratagem once more. On March 15, 1939, the official Communist Party newspaper, *Pravda*, published the inaugural speech that the People's Commissar for Internal Affairs and Chief of the Secret Police of the Soviet Union, Lavrenty Pavlovich Beria, had delivered the day before to the members of the Politburo at the 18th Congress of All-Union Communist Party. The oration, which *Pravda* adorned with a photograph of Beria, was one big ode to the glory of Comrade Stalin, the "beloved Leader," "the Greatest Genius of Mankind," and to his magnificent achievements for the progress of the Soviet Union.[1]

After that paean worshiping his Boss, Beria had no doubt he was riding the best horse for advancing his career. From now on, all it depended on was his ability to stay in the saddle and run the race to final victory, solving his main problem—the liquidation of Trotsky—early on the course. Lavrenty remembered well that he was twenty years younger than Stalin, who was already about sixty, and at such an age, time works against a man but not for him. Stalin needed a successor. Nobody lives forever, but some live longer, some shorter, and eventually someone close to the Dictator would be able to make the Boss' life shorter. The other members of the Politburo could also be eliminated after a time. Kalinin was sixty-four, so he was already an old goat. Kaganovich was a Jew, and Molotov was the husband of a Jewess. So, by some careful intrigues it should not be too difficult to make use of Stalin's hatred of Jews to eliminate both of them. Even Kaganovich's sister, Rosa, Stalin's mistress, would not be able to protect her brother against a cleverly framed plot, especially since Stalin would sooner or later tire of her and be glad to get rid of her as well. Andreyev, although much younger than the others, had been a member of the Party since 1914 and an active participant in the October Revolution. Thus, he knew what part Stalin had really played in the Bolshevik movement, and that would not help him to walk on this earth for a long time—besides, his wife, Dora Khazan, was Jewish. Then there was Mikoyan, who had helped Beria several times. It would be easy enough for Lavrenty to dump Mikoyan. There was also Zhdanov,

---

[1] Appendix 9.

who had just become a full member of the Politburo, so he should be counted as having good backing from Stalin. But Zhdanov, who had joined the Bolsheviks in 1913 and was active during the October Revolution in the Urals, was an Old Guard Bolshevik. Later he took the office of Chief of the Party in Leningrad after Kirov's assassination, and it was not a very lucky post. Among the others who remained was Voroshilov, an active Communist since his youth. In 1906 and 1907 he was a delegate to the Social Democratic Party Congresses in Stockholm and in London. After the Revolution he became Commissar of Military Affairs, and was promoted to the rank of Marshal of the Soviet Union. Voroshilov was very popular in the Army and in the nation. That was against him, because Stalin could not stand popular personalities for long.

There remained only Khrushchev and Malenkov, who had just been nominated as the alternate to the Politburo. Both of them were young and unscrupulous. It was advisable to be on good terms with them, since they were dangerous. But all intrigues against those members of the Politburo, as well as against the Great Boss, were dreams of the future, part of a long-range plan. Before doing anything in their direction Lavrenty decided first to exterminate enemies and adversaries who were less powerful, but still in his way.

Beria did not forget his predecessor, the former Chief of NKVD, Nikolay Ivanovich Yezhov, who had been appointed by Stalin as Commissar of Water Transport. The post was next to nothing and now Yezhov was helpless. But Beria remembered that once Yezhov, when on the top, had intended to arrest him, and beyond any doubt to execute him, and for this that bastard should be punished.

In less than three weeks after delivering his address to the Politburo extolling the great Stalin, Beria convinced his Superior that Yezhov was mentally ill and, as a frustrated man, could be as dangerous a lunatic as was Nikolayev, who assassinated Kirov. Yezhov was dismissed from his post as Commissar of Water Transport. Then, in the middle of the night an ambulance stopped in front of his apartment. Two hospital attendants got out and entered Yezhov's home. Soon they brought the former "bloodthirsty dwarf" out in a straitjacket, put him into the ambulance and whisked him to Moscow's Serbsky Psychiatric Institute where he was locked up in an isolation cell.

Yezhov, however, did not stay there for long. One morning a

nurse, on entering his solitary cell, found him dead, hanging from the window bar with a noose made from his underwear around his neck. His death was stated officially as suicide. How, in a mental hospital, where the patients are watched constantly, Yezhov could tear his clothes, make a noose and kill himself was never investigated or revealed.

The political situation in Western Europe indicated that Germany would not stop her expansion with Austria, Sudeten and Czechoslovakia only. It was evident that the Third Reich was going to carry on her new *Drang nach Osten*—March to the East—and would try to conquer the countries located to the east of Germany. The first target was Poland, from whom the Third Reich demanded Pomerania, Danzig and the Polish Corridor, which had been part of Germany before the Versailles Treaty. However, on March 31, 1939, Great Britain and France guaranteed officially the independence of Poland. In the face of the new formation of powers, Stalin decided to act.

After the great purges in the ranks of the Red Army carried out during the period of the *Yezhovshchina*, Soviet military forces were too weak to be involved in a world war. However, by the wise maneuver of standing aside while Hitler fought England and France, the Soviet Union could gain a lot. A few weeks later, Stalin dismissed his Commissar of Foreign Affairs, Maxim Litvinov, and replaced him with Molotov. In Berlin this move was rightly understood as a gesture of goodwill toward the Third Reich, since Maxim Maximovich Litvinov was a Polish Jew from Bialystok whose real name was Meer Genokh Moissevitch Wallach. Soon after, in Berlin the German Undersecretary of State von Weizsaecker invited to his office the Soviet Chargé d'Affairs Astakhanov to advise him that the Fuehrer would be glad to start negotiations not only about trade policies but also about political ones. In the meantime, Molotov was negotiating with Great Britain and France. The two Western powers were ready to guarantee the Soviet Union their help in case the USSR was attacked by Germany. As a result of that proposed alliance, the British Government sent William Strong, a high executive of the Foreign Office, to Moscow.

Lavrenty Beria, as the People's Commissar of Internal Affairs and Chief of the Secret Police of the Soviet Union, received the most delicate assignment from Stalin. The British and the French diplomats in Moscow should by no means learn that the Kremlin was simultaneously negotiating with the Nazis. From now on, the number of Beria's agents around the French and British embassies was doubled. The janitors in the apartment houses where the members of the French and British staffs were living were called to the Secret Police Office every other day for interrogations and briefings, especially since they were not mere watchmen but professional plainclothesmen. The same requirements were made for the Russian cooks and maids and the children's nurses employed by the embassies and the diplomats.

Telephone conversations were intercepted constantly, and every foreigner was always followed by an agent.

Beria isolated the Western colony perfectly. On August 11, 1939, the British-French Military Mission arrived in Moscow to begin the conference about a mutual defense against Germany. The next day, the representatives of the three powers, England, France and the Soviet Union, went to their first meeting at the Kremlin to discuss with Marshal Voroshilov their common action against the Third Reich in the event of her attack on Poland. At exactly the same time, Molotov was expressing to Hitler Stalin's eagerness to sign a treaty of mutual friendship between the Soviet Union and Nazi Germany. He also proposed an agreement for Poland's partition between these two countries and invited Hitler's representative to Moscow.

Such double negotiations on opposite fronts lasted for almost three weeks. Under Beria's twenty-four-hour-a-day vigilance, the Kremlin could prolong its talks with the British-French military delegates and simultaneously arrange its alliance with Germany in absolute secrecy. It took until August 23, 1939, when the German Minister of Foreign Affairs, Joachim von Ribbentrop, arrived in the Soviet capital. At Moscow's Sheremetyevo Airport, decorated with Nazi flags with swastika and Soviet banners with hammer and sickle, von Ribbentrop was serenaded by the Red Army military band playing the Nazi and Soviet anthems,—the *Horst Wessel Lied* and the *Internationale*—and was welcomed by the Vice-Commissar of USSR Foreign Affairs.

The same day William Strong and the British and French Military Mission left the Soviet Union. At the Kremlin, the representative of the Third Reich and the Soviet officials accepted the newly created ten-year German-Soviet Treaty of Nonaggression, as well as the Secret Supplementary Protocol. Both documents, signed by von Ribbentrop and Molotov, cut Eastern Europe into Soviet and German spheres and meant a new war. The Nazis would invade Poland at any time, and after defeating it, there would be a partition of that country between Germany and Russia.

In the evening a gala dinner was held at the Kremlin in honor of the German representative. At that banquet, Stalin delivered his historical toast saying, "I know how much the German nation loves its Fuehrer. I wish to drink to his health."

Later, during the informal part of this reception, Stalin jokingly introduced Lavrenty Pavlovich to Ribbentrop saying, "Beria— Chief of my Gestapo."

The next day, after von Ribbentrop returned to his fatherland, Commissar of Internal Affairs Lavrenty Pavlovich Beria was decorated by Stalin with the Order of the Red Star for the excellently executed job of keeping the governments of Great Britain and France in absolute ignorance about what happened in Moscow concerning dealing with the Nazis.

36

"The Soviet Soldier Never Retreats"

On September 1, 1939, at six o'clock in the morning, the Nazi army attacked the Polish border, while the German Luftwaffe dropped incendiary bombs on the open city of Warsaw. Soon, several hospitals, orphanages and schools, as well as churches, where women with children sought shelter, were in flames.

But Poland was prepared for such an assault and her troops had been kept on the alert for several months. The Polish infantry and artillery stopped the German foray, while the Polish Air Force audaciously fought the foe. On September 3, 1939, England and France, to fulfill their guarantee of March 31, declared war against Germany.

The Poles tried to resist the aggression until relief could come. The British and French warplanes, as well as their fleets of destroyers, were expected at any moment. But the rescue did not appear. Instead, on September 17 Stalin, to honor his treaty with Hitler, threw the masses of his forces across the Polish border from the east.

Thousands of Polish officers and soldiers were taken prisoner by the Soviet Union. But the USSR and Poland had been bound by a mutual ten-year nonaggression pact since July 25, 1932. In breaking it now, to save her face, the Soviet Union declared that she had entered the Eastern Polish territories to keep order against marauders and the panic caused by the war with the Germans. Marshal Semyon Timoshenko, the Commander in Chief of the Red

Army that invaded Poland, assured the captured Polish officers and soldiers that they would be freed and, according to individual wishes, would be able to return home or to go to France, where a new Polish Army against the Nazis was being created. The promise was confirmed by Marshal Timoshenko's assistant, Nikita S. Khrushchev, who served in the Red Army on Polish-occupied soil as a member of the Politburo of the USSR and representative of the Soviet Ukrainian Government.

In a few weeks the Poles, divided into groups of several hundred men, were taken to trains supposedly destined for the Rumanian or Hungarian border.

However, every car was guarded by eight Soviet soldiers with machine guns and rifles with fixed bayonets. The insignia on the guards' uniforms and caps showed that they were not from the regular Red Army regiments, but from the crack troops of the NKVD, the Special Forces, whose Commander in Chief was People's Commissar of Internal Affairs and Head of the Secret Police of the Soviet Union, Lavrenty Pavlovich Beria.

The procedure of moving out the Poles took several weeks. Altogether, about 15,000 soldiers from the regular army, as well as reserve officers, were deported. They were men representing the best Polish intelligentsia and the most patriotic element so undesirable to the suppressor. Beria decided that with these people something drastic must be done.

After a long journey by cattle trains, trucks, and in some cases, by barges, they were placed in three widely separated concentration camps in Central Russia, at the opposite corners of the country. All of these compounds were under the personal surveillance of Lavrenty Beria. During a conversation with Stalin Beria asked how he should solve the difficult problem of the fate of those 15,000 men. It was true that Lavrenty Pavlovich was the Chief of the Secret Police, but still, being only the faithful and obedient lieutenant of the Great Dictator, he did not want to take such an important step without a mutual agreement. Beria's first suggestion was to let the Poles go home from their POW camps and later, arrest them one by one and send them to hard labor camps. But there was a danger that before being rearrested many of them could manage to escape to France or England, where the new Polish Army was being organized to fight for a free and independent Poland.

Beria remarked that the war was still continuing in the West, and nobody knew if the Polish Forces abroad would not be used at some time against the USSR. "One bird in the hand is worth two in the bush," as the old adage goes. So, the sooner the Poles were made quiet once and forever, the better. Stalin had no scruples, especially since the Poles in the Soviet POW camps were not useful, but just were eating the Russian bread, so valuable for the Red Army. The Commissar of Internal Affairs should take this matter into his own hands. It was his job.

Beria approached his new task carefully. From the commanders of three POW camps in Russia, Kozelsk, Ostashkov—the so-called "Devil's Island Camp"—and Starobelsk, all administered and guarded by the NKVD, Beria obtained lists of the Polish prisoners of war, with all particulars about each one. After very detailed interrogations of every Polish officer, as well as reports of agents planted in those camps, Lavrenty had complete information about the political orientation of each of the prisoners.

Among those Poles there was a handful of Communists who, for their own interests, would be glad to convert their country into another Soviet Republic. These men were released from their camps by Beria's special orders and transferred to Malakhovka, a place near Moscow that soon was nicknamed "Haven of Bliss" or "Villa of Delight." There Polish fellow-travelers got the best food and accommodation, as well as schooling in how to convert the future Red Poland into the Seventeenth Soviet Republic.[1, 2]

For the rest of the Poles, about 15,000 men, Beria prepared a different fate. In the camp of Kozelsk, containing about 5,000 prisoners of war, from the beginning of April 1940 on, a few hundred names were called out almost every day. Those men were told they were being released from their compound to be sent, in accordance with their wishes, either back home or to the Hungarian or Rumanian border. From there they would be able to go to the new Polish Army in France or in Great Britain. The lucky ones bade good-bye to their friends and hurried to waiting trucks to ride to the nearest railway station, where special trains would take them to their destination, dreamed of for so long.

Soon such a train, consisting of several prison cars, took them to the station at Smolensk.

---

[1] Facts and Documents Concerning Polish Prisoners of War Captured by the USSR during the 1939 Campaign. (For private circulation only), February 1946.

[2] Supplementary Report of Facts and Documents Concerning the Katyn Massacre. (For private circulation only), October 1947.

A few miles beyond that town the train stopped, and the passengers were told to alight. There, after a military roll call the Poles were taken in small groups in a black bus to somewhere in the woods—a kind of summer resort called Katyn. After their arrival, they were ordered to stand in line abreast, and were carefully searched. Money, watches, rings and gold wedding bands were confiscated. Under a heavy guard of the Secret Police NKVD functionaries with rifles with fixed bayonets, and half-wild bloodhounds on leashes, the prisoners had their arms pinioned behind their backs. Soon the execution started.

At 6:30 A.M. in the Katyn forest about 5,000 Polish officers and soldiers were massacred by the firing squads of the People's Commissar of the Soviet Internal Affairs, Lavrenty Pavlovich Beria.

In the meantime, other units of the NKVD exterminated the Polish prisoners of war in the two remaining camps in central Russia, then the one at Kozelsk. From the approximatly 4,000 Poles locked up at Starobelsk Beria selected about 400 men who were transferred to another compound at Grazovets. Among these officers and cadets, the Soviet authorities expected eventually to find a few who would join the group in the "Villa of Delight." The rest of the Poles from Starobelsk, almost 3,500 persons, were sent to the firing squads of Beria's troops, as had been the Poles in the Katyn woods.

The more than 6,500 Polish prisoners of war from the third camp, Ostashkov, with its chilling nickname, "Devil's Island Camp," met an entirely different fate.

After being assured by an NKVD colonel that they were going to be set free, they were ordered to form ranks and were led to the shore of the nearby Seliger Lake, which covers approximately 100 square miles and discharges into the waters of Volga River. Here the Poles boarded several giant barges to sail home. Singing carefree ditties, the men started their happy journey. When the barges arrived in the middle of the vast lake, the NKVD unit of light artillery, hidden until that time behind a column of trucks, opened fire on the big brown boats.

That was the last group of Polish prisoners of war. The next day, Beria reported to his Superior, the Great Comrade Stalin, that the "Polish problem" had been solved.

The September campaign was over and Poland was conquered and divided between Germany and the USSR. From the eastern part of Poland, which was occupied by Russia, thousands of arrested men, women and children were herded into cattle cars and sent to Siberia, Kazakhstan, Turkestan and other parts of the Soviet Union. These Poles—priests, regular army and reserve officers, government employees, social workers and their families—were arrested by the Soviet Security Police as so-called "dubious elements." Without any trial they were sentenced to live in exile; some in the hard labor camps and some, mainly women with little children, were separated from their husbands and sent to remote Russian villages and communities where they had to work either in the fields or in the plants for small wages.

In the Russian-occupied part of Poland, all factories and private enterprises were confiscated by Beria's functionaries and nationalized, while their owners with their families were arrested and deported to Siberia or executed. The same fate met the clergymen and rich peasants. The whole action was prepared and organized by Beria as the Chief of GULAG—Main Administration of Corrective Labor Camps and Labor Settlements. The journeys usually took weeks, since military trains had priority. The locked cars with the arrested people were halted at the stations or crossroads for several days. Their nourishment, according to the prison regulations established by Beria, was two cups of boiling water, called in Russian, *keepyatok*, a quarter of a pound of dark bread and a little raw fish. Hundreds of children, women and old people who could not survive the hardship of such a trip died during transport. Each day, the guards who came to take a roll call to check that no one had escaped, removed the corpses and threw them into a ditch near the railroad track.

At the end of September 1939, following the Molotov-Ribbentrop agreement in Moscow, the USSR forced Estonia to accept Russian bases on her soil. Soon after the Red soldiers were sent in as occupation forces, Beria brought in his Special Troops of the Secret Police. They started to make mass arrests of whole families living in those areas as being dubious elements against the Soviet Union. The long trains of hundreds of cattle cars full of people were directed to the Ural mountains and to villages near the Chinese border.

Less than two weeks later, the same fate met another Baltic country, Latvia. This small nation also had to give up its army, air and naval bases to the Russians under the Soviet-imposed pact of mutual assistance. And again, the People's Commissar of Internal

Affairs of the Soviet Union, Lavrenty Pavlovich Beria, sent his troops to do their job of arresting and deporting thousands of innocent people. Old and sick men and women, mothers and children, were exiled to northern Kazakhstan as being dangerous to the Russian Empire.

The USSR, the best ally of the Nazis, did not waste any time in swallowing one small Baltic country after another that lay within the sphere of the Russian interests. Soon after, the same tragic farce was played with Lithuania, which was forced to sign a treaty of mutual assistance with the Soviet Union and to accept Russian land and air bases on her territory. Once again Beria's regiments of NKVD in their dark uniforms and pink and blue caps followed the regular Red Army to herd thousands of inhabitants into the cattle cars and whisk them to the Ural region.

Beria's troops did not leave Bessarabia in peace either. Whole villages of peasants in the light clothing worn in September in that sunny country were deported to the far north. They were arrested so suddenly that they could not even take warmer clothes with them. Once in Siberia, they died by the hundreds.

By taking the land, air and naval bases in Latvia, Estonia and Lithuania, whom the USSR forced to sign treaties of mutual help, the Soviet Union in the guise of assuring assistance, put a foot in the doors of the Baltic countries. In a few months, Russia sent more troops to the bases in Latvia and soon after spread the Red Army troops all over the Latvian territories, ending the independence of that country. A week later, the same method was repeated with Lithuania. In the following month, Estonia was occupied and lost her freedom. These three small countries, after being overwhelmed by Red military forces, had to be cleansed of any patriotic young element eager to carry on an underground movement and uprising. Therefore, they would become the victims of a planned-in-advance incorporation into the USSR.

This important task belonged among the many duties of Beria, as the People's Commissar of Internal Affairs and Chief of the Security Police of the Soviet Union. Beria ordered the new Communist editorial staffs of the local newspapers in these Baltic countries to print on the front pages long articles explaining that the Soviet Union had not conquered their lands, but had liberated them from the oppression of fascism and capitalism. The USSR, herself a socialist country ruled by the workers and peasants, was happy to bring a new and better life to the Latvian, Lithuanian and Estonian workers and peasants who, until now, had been cynically exploited by the bourgeois, who made fortunes from the poor and drank their sweat and blood. These liberated Baltic countries were promised their own independent socialist governments and their own People's Armies.

Soon such socialist administrations were established, but they consisted of Soviet "yes men" and puppets. Citizens were drafted into the Free Peoples' regiments and compulsory conscription from the age of eighteen was proclaimed. Equipped with new uniforms with red bands and insignia and with Soviet weapons, the armies, after a month of training went on maneuvers that ended in several sports contests, for which valuable trophies were awarded. Then the boys were told to return their rifles. The Free Independent Peoples' Armies were encircled by the Special Soviet troops of NKVD carrying machine guns. They were then herded into cattle cars and sent to Siberian hard labor camps. By this cunning stratagem, Lavrenty Beria deprived these countries of their young generation, which would have been capable of an army uprising.[3]

Besides the young people, over 30,000 families of Lithuanians, about 20,000 of Latvians and more than 40,000 of Estonians—politicians, statesmen, professors, clergymen, government employees, bankers, factory and store owners and farmers—were arrested by Beria's Soviet Secret Police functionaries and deported to the region of the Ural mountains.

When the job was over and the terrain cleaned out by Beria, the three overpowered countries were ripe to be brought into the USSR. First the Soviet Union incorporated Lithuania. Within two weeks, Estonia met the same fate, while Latvia was wiped off the map of free nations the following month.

In the meantime, on November 30, 1939, the Soviet Union invaded Finland. But this time the move was not accepted without a shot. Quite the opposite. Like Poland against Germany, Finland decided to fight the USSR for her independence. The defending Army was small but brave. Platoons hidden in the thick pine woods lured the Russian troops in and there, in the darkness of the northern polar night, they encircled them and, without a sound, stabbed them to death one by one with their famous long Finnish knives. Other nests of Finns, clad in white sheets, white overalls, white

---

[3] The author met some of those Latvian troops, still in their light summer uniforms despite the winter weather, in a hard labor camp in the Far North of Russia.

tunics and white hoods as a camouflage in the snowy landscape suddenly darted on white skis from behind the numerous hills and opened fire with their white-painted machine guns, decimating the enemy.

All that Soviet Headquarters could do against Finland was to throw in thousands of troops. But even these masses were overwhelmed by panic and quickly retreated, dropping their weapons as they withdrew in rout. Moreover, the Red Army as a fighting power was of very poor quality at that time. It still suffered a lack of good commanders, marshals and generals, as well as other high ranking regular army officers, most of whom either had been executed or had died in Siberia when they were deported by Yezhov. The new amnesty for those in the hard labor camps, which had been proclaimed in accordance with Beria's policy, could not fully repair the losses. Besides, the soldiers were badly trained and undisciplined. And above all, the regiments thrown against Finland consisted mostly of men drafted in Uzbekistan, Turkmenistan, Tadzhikistan, Azerbaijan and Armenia—warm, sunlit countries, where snow was almost unknown. These Soviet soldiers, sent to the northern country during the severe winter weather, had never been in a climate that exposed them to the white death.

The war of the Soviet Union against tiny Finland extended from weeks into months. October, November and December passed, and the war was still on. The legend of the unbeatable Red Army became a joke; the prestige of the USSR as a great power was at stake.

Lavrenty Beria realized that if smartly played, the present political situation of the unsuccessful war could strengthen his personal career. During one of his sheepish talks with Stalin, while explaining his new plan of action against Finland, Beria asked for more troops and modern equipment for his own Special Forces of the NKVD. The Boss promised to discuss that plea soon at a conference with the board of Commanders.

Two days after, at a meeting with a group of generals at the Kremlin, Stalin introduced the demand of his Commissar of Internal Affairs, who had asked for several units of the best storm troops to be shifted from the regular Red Army to his Security Police Forces. Present at that meeting, Beria revealed his project. His idea, however, seemed so strange and horrible to the regular army officers that they could not approve it. Besides they understood that, having their best picked troops under his control, Beria would grow to such power that he would dominate them. They hesitated to give their consent. But Beria, who felt that Stalin was supporting him, no longer had to be the polite, civilized man he liked to appear to be. For a long time he had been aware that it was not he who had nominated Stalin, but Stalin who had chosen him and appointed him Chief of Internal Affairs because he appealed to Stalin's nature. The purpose of transferring the select regular army regiments to Lavrenty's Special Forces, as the Chief of the Security Police suggested, pleased Stalin very much. Beria was sure that he would get what he wanted. If Lavrenty stayed at his post it was because he appeared to be a reader of Stalin's thoughts. He then made them a reality for the Dictator's and his own profit. Now the opinion of the officers, which Stalin had requested from his subordinates, was only a pure formality, and they seemed not to realize it. But Beria felt strong enough to show these stupid military blockheads what they meant to him. His usually pallid face turned purple, and with his lips tight, blinking his cold, watery, blue-green, staring eyes, he barked at them, "I will get it from you with your guts."

This vulgar expression, quite popular in the Russian language, could be taken literally when used by that arrogant but powerful man. Beria received what he demanded.

Soon after a new slogan for the Red Army was invented by Commissar Beria: "The Soviet Soldier Never Retreats." This catchword, introduced into practice, was supported by Beria's new storm troops, which were sent to the Finnish border.

The Red Army in Finland was still suffering losses. The majority of the Soviet soldiers, if not killed in ambush by the Finnish white devils on skis, experienced third-degree frostbite, resulting in gangrene, or were frozen to death.

Now the new Select Special NKVD Forces approached the regular troops, not to support or replace them on the battlefield, but to stay far behind the front lines. With this slogan, "The Soviet Soldier Never Retreats," and fulfilling Commissar Beria's personal order, the picked troops, with their rifles aimed at the backs of the regular army men, followed the fighting regiments. Any soldier who tried to retreat or give up was shot by the members of Beria's Special Forces.

Despite the barbarous method applied by Beria and his troops to their own Russian soldiers, the USSR still could not achieve a quick victory over that courageous Scandinavian country.

In the middle of the following February the war was still in full swing, and it continued for another month, when at last, on March 12, 1940, it was settled by a peace treaty, by which the USSR grabbed only a small piece of Finnish territory.

On March 15 Stalin decorated Commissar Beria with the medal "For Valor." It was evidently in appreciation of Lavrenty's part in the victorious war.

If after the experience in Finland the gigantic Soviet Union avoided discredit in the eyes of the world, and especially of its ally, Nazi Germany, it was mostly thanks to the merit of Lavrenty Beria and his slogan, "The Soviet Soldier Never Retreats."

37

Handsome Jacques Mornard and the Flying Dutchman

Besides annihilating the captive enemies and cleansing the newly-occupied territories of dubious and dangerous elements to the USSR the Security Police of the Soviet Union kept a constant vigil over its inner foes. Since, potentially, every person could turn from a good Soviet citizen or even an ardent Communist into a corrupted traitor and a renegade, every individual had to be watched closely. This policy was the equivalent of putting everybody in the Soviet Empire under surveillance.

Keeping an eye on the people was the responsible task of Lavrenty Pavlovich Beria, as Chief of the Secret Police, the Counter-intelligence Service and of no less importance, the spy ring abroad.

The Communist espionage system established by Lenin even before the Revolution and improved later by the consecutive chiefs of the *Cheka,* GPU and OGPU, Dzerzhinsky, Mezhinsky, Yagoda and Yezhov, was perfected by their heir, Beria. Every Soviet Embassy, Trade Delegation, Consulate, Legation and Mission on foreign soil was a well-organized spy cell, which worked under detailed instructions from Lavrenty's Headquarters of People's Commissar of Internal Affairs. To every such Soviet agency abroad there was sent an NKVD Resident who had his own special code for direct communication with Moscow and who often gave orders to the ambassador. However, even Beria could make a mistake by failing to be cautious enough in a certain country or by underestimating the perspicacity of the local authorities. But in case of a scandal, the only culprit was the unsuccessful Soviet Foreign Service functionary who was either punished abroad on the spot, or later in his own fatherland. This happened to the Soviet ambassador to France, Yacov Suritz, who was personally involved in spying on the French military sources. Discredited by the French authorities, the ambassador was recalled to Moscow where, after being debriefed by Beria, he was sent to a concentration camp in Siberia, where he soon died.

The Soviet radio, press, literature and theatre were also still kept under strict control so no one would be able to spread a word that could undermine the official way of thinking. The dramatists and writers were in constant terror of being arrested and deported to the Far North, even those who previously had been awarded Lenin and Stalin prizes for their service to Soviet culture. In 1940 the famous Soviet novelist, Mikhail Bulgakov, author of *The Master and Margarita* and several other books, and a playwright whose dramas were staged by the Moscow Art Theatre, was arrested by Beria.

Imprisonments, deportations and executions *in camera* without a public trial, or the threat of detaining someone dear to the trespasser—mother, wife or child—were not the only methods the Commissar of Internal Affairs used to keep the people in awe. Beria applied beatings, which he administered in his office either through one of his men, or personally. It was popularly known that in his desk Lavrenty had a horsewhip and bludgeons of several lengths.

Just as in his suburban Moscow villa where he trained his eye in using a pistol in a shooting alley, in Lubyanka Prison Beria practiced his hand in using a blackjack. This weapon, a small ball of lead covered with leather and attached to a spring with a loop, he always had at hand.

Sometimes, after sentencing a prisoner to death *in camera*, Beria followed the condemned man and his guard to the door of the execution cell in the basement. There he told the guard to bring the man to the cell, face him against the wall and leave him there. Just after the soldier left Lavrenty entered the death chamber and closed the door. With his hand in the pocket containing a blackjack Beria stopped before the victim at a distance of two or three steps.

Then with a flash he took out his weapon and with the accuracy of a swift marksman hit the man behind his right ear. The victim fell dead instantly. Beria left the cell and ordered the guard to come in and shoot the prone man in the back of his head. Officially, executions were to be performed by a bullet.

To attain such an exact blow Beria trained by using his blackjack on a dummy, which he had in his study at home. Lavrenty tried his skill only occasionally on a living person, to prove that he had not lost his accuracy and that his shot could kill on the spot.

During investigations Beria also applied some tortures that were not limited to the drilling of healthy teeth by the pretty dentist Vera in her prison office. There was quite a list, with a big choice of different kinds of cruelty. There were some that seemed innocent and harmless. In his office, Beria only told the interrogated person, man or woman, to stand in the corner with hands raised while a guard watched. That was all. The moment the tired victim tried to lower his hands, the guard reminded him not to move with a blow of his gun under the arm. In the meantime, Commissar Lavrenty Pavlovich Beria, at his desk, was busy with routine paper work. After several hours, the exhausted victim was ready to admit to any crime of which he was accused.

Sometimes, to break the monotony of such interrogations, there was another version of the exercise. The prisoner, instead of holding his hands up, was ordered to stand in a half straddle, neither upright nor sitting on his heels. There were also interrogations in a special darkroom similar to a photographer's laboratory. It was equipped with an apparatus with an electric lamp, covered on one side by a black metal sheet. The interrogating officer stood behind that shield while the prisoner was ordered to sit before the electric bulb with his hands behind his back. When the guard switched on the lamp, the prisoner found himself directly in front of a light of four or five hundred candle-power. There was also a threat of putting the prisoner's fingers into the doors, and if the man remained obstinate Beria told his officer to do it.

At other times Beria told the guard to put the metal wastebasket on the prisoner's head and to bang against it with a bayonet. This noise was continued until the questioned person confessed his guilt.

There were also some atrocities that Lavrenty liked to administer personally. Since Commissar of Soviet Internal Affairs Beria was too dignified to climb on top of his desk and then jump down on his victim's chest, as he used to in his twenties when he was just a *Chekist*, he enjoyed himself with a different game. After ordering the prisoner to open his trousers and put his penis on the desk, Beria would hit it with his fist with all his strength.[1] Subsequently, when the prisoner, holding his lowered pants and guarded by an NKVD soldier, stood next to the Chief of the Secret Police, Beria opened a desk drawer, put in the man's testicles and suddenly shut the drawer. Then he slowly continued to open and close the drawer. The cry of the fainting prisoner and the expression on his terrified face seemed so funny in the eyes of the Commissar and his subordinate that they could hardly stop laughing.

But in the middle of 1940 Beria's main job and the most important task to be accomplished was that special one given to him by Stalin some months before. The Chief of the Secret Police worked scrupulously on that problem for several hours every day and night.

The task was the liquidation of Leon Trotsky in Mexico.

It was high time to end his life because Trotsky, in the process of writing Stalin's biography for over a year, had almost finished it and might send the manuscript to his publisher any day. Since Stalin was his mortal enemy there was no question that Trotsky's book would be an entirely negative account revealing all the crimes Stalin had committed. It would also throw light on the really small part Stalin played before and during the October Revolution, a role obviously not significant at all, contrary to the myths about Stalin built up by Beria in his elaborate *Stalin's Early Writings and Activities.*

Lavrenty planned to destroy Trotsky in either one of two ways: by a raid with machine guns on his stronghold; or, if that failed, which was rather dubious, by a more laborious plot, which a year before had proved to be quite successful against a different target. That time it was an assignment to kill a Soviet ambassador to a Near Eastern country who, according to reports of the NKVD Resident there, had decided to defect. For this secret task, which had to be performed with perfection, an NKVD clerk named Bokov, a former sailor, was assigned. After calling Bokov to his office, Beria asked him if he could kill a man with one blow of an iron bar. When

---

[1] This method of Soviet interrogation was also described by General Wladislav Anders in his book, *An Army in Exile* (London: Macmillan and Co., Ltd., 1949).

Bokov confirmed that he could, he was supplied with credentials and sent to see the ambassador on a special mission. Before that conference Bokov met the NKVD Resident who armed him with an iron club short enough to be hidden under a coat. Then Bokov, with his aide, went to see the ambassador. During the conference, when the diplomat turned his head to answer a question asked by the other visitor, Bokov hit him over his head, killing him instantly. The two men, with the help of the NKVD Resident, drove the corpse beyond the town, where they buried it in a previously prepared ditch. The whole job was done so quickly and neatly that nobody in the office could become suspicious. Even the bloodstained rug in the ambassador's office was taken away. The doorman was told the men were taking it for dry cleaning. In fact, the body of the murdered man was wrapped in that carpet. The wife of the ambassador was informed that he had been called to Moscow on duty, on such an emergency that he was even unable to let her know about his departure, but had asked one of his deputies to tell her that she and their two children should follow him by train immediately. On their way to Moscow the woman and children were arrested by the NKVD. From their sleeper they were transferred to a cattle car en route to a hard labor camp in Siberia. The ambassador and his family disappeared without a trace, while Bokov was congratulated by Beria and then awarded a silver medal and a promotion for his service.

While preparing the assassination of Trotsky, Beria decided to stage a similar trick, only instead of an iron club, to use an Alpine-pick. But this was not as simple as it sounded. Quite the opposite. This plot was very complicated. It demanded a lot of work and a meticulously designed plan, studied deliberately in every detail for several months, then kept in reserve if the raid proved unsuccessful.

On the hot Mexican night of May 23, 1940, there was a big fiesta in the town of Coyoacan, not far from the private Trotsky fortress. A few attractive village girls in their colorful folk costumes invited the young men of Trotsky's guard to escort them to the dance, where there would be plenty of wine and beer. The pretty lasses did not seem to be very hard to get and one could guess that after a few drinks they would not object to making love somewhere under a tree. Several of the young guards could not resist, and went to the dance.

At two o'clock in the morning a military truck with a platoon of Mexican policemen, led by an army officer, stopped in front of Trotsky's stronghold. The officer asked for the commander of the guard. When the American Trotskyite Robert Sheldon Harte appeared, he was shown an official document introducing additional Mexican troops to strengthen the post.

When the gate was opened and they were admitted, the officer killed Harte with a single shot, while his men overpowered the sentries. Soon the wires of the alarm system, the telephones and the electricity were cut off. The attackers pushed their way into Trotsky's bedroom and opened fire from a machine gun. The whole assault took only a few minutes. The truck drove away carrying the dead body of Harte and the conspirators with their Mexican Army "officer," an artist-painter named David Alfaro Siqueiros, a Mexican Communist and Stalin's follower.

The attack, however, was not successful. In the darkness the awakened Trotsky and his wife managed to crawl under the bed and hide. They were slightly wounded, and so was their little grandson Sevushka.

The failure of that assassination plot did not mean that it was the only and last attempt. Trotsky realized that, and his fortress was strengthened with real enforcements. The warning system was also improved and electrified high-voltage wires encircling the outside walls and doors were installed. Trotsky, anxious to finish his work about Stalin as soon as possible, concentrated all his time on writing and turned away any visitors except a handful of his best friends and worshipers. One of the most ardent disciples was an American young lady of Russian descent, Sylvia Agelov, who had met Trotsky and his wife in Paris and had even followed them when they fled from France to Norway. The entire Trotsky family was very fond of her and trusted her implicitly, especially since Sylvia had helped them organize their escape overseas.

When in Switzerland, Miss Agelov met a young alpinist, Jacques Mornard, a Communist and, as she learned with joy, of Trotskyist orientation. She fell in love with the mountaineer, and soon they were married. Sylvia proudly informed her best friends, Leon and Natalia Trotsky, about her wedding.

After her return to New York, Sylvia took her husband to Mexico to introduce him to the Trotskys. From that time on, the young couple paid several visits to the armed home in Coyoacan, spending long evenings in carefree chats on the patio or in the living room. Jacques Mornard was a bright, sincere man, eager to listen to Trotsky and to learn as much as possible from him. They used to sit in Trotsky's study, which was full of books, photographs, newspaper clippings, notes, manuscripts and memorabilia.

One day the two men were in that study and the host was reading a manuscript of an article written by his young guest, who stood behind him looking over his shoulder. Suddenly Mornard took from inside his jacket an Alpine ice-axe with a short shaft, especially cut for his purpose. He struck Trotsky over his bowed head. The blow, however, was not instantly mortal. Screaming for help, Trotsky managed to step on the button of the alarm-bell under his desk. The assassin was caught by the sentries and, under heavy guard, transferred to prison. Trotsky's manuscript was saved. But Leon Trotsky died in the hospital the next day, August 21, 1940.

Jacques Mornard, also supplied by Beria with a forged Canadian passport for a certain Frank Jacson, was in reality a Spanish Stalinist, Ramon Mercader, whose mother had worked for the NKVD as a Russian spy during the Spanish Civil War. Shortly after the murder of Trotsky she was invited to Moscow as Beria's guest of honor and at the Kremlin the proud mother, Señora Caridad Mercader was awarded a medal for Ramon's achievement.

At that special reception there was a memorable moment when, for his masterpiece of international intrigue which he had engineered with the precision of a really great architect, People's Commissar Lavrenty Pavlovich Beria received the highest government award, the Order of Lenin, from the hands of the dear Great Comrade Stalin.

Being responsible for the Security, Beria had to keep an eye on every Russian diplomat, even those at the top level. This duty of invigilating every statesman, no matter what his assignment, Lavrenty Pavlovich often used to cloak his own purposes. When Molotov, as Commissar for Foreign Affairs, was invited to Berlin for a conference with Hitler on November 12 and 13, 1940, Beria did not miss the opportunity to spy on that Soviet envoy. Molotov was too close to Stalin, too wise a psychologist and too open-minded not to be dangerous to Beria, whose intrigues Molotov could see through. Now Beria had a chance to check on Molotov while in Berlin. During one of his conversations with Stalin, Lavrenty suggested the nomination of Vladimir Dekanozov as Molotov's deputy in Berlin. He was a well-trained high ranking Secret Police officer who would be at the same time Molotov's chief bodyguard and could observe events in the German capital. After Stalin accepted that suggestion, Beria was sure that Dekanozov, his co-worker and most faithful subordinate, would report to him Molotov's every step and word, which eventually would lead this diplomat to his untimely end.

Soon after Molotov returned from Germany, Dekanozov, thanks to Beria's sponsorship, was nominated Soviet Ambassador to Berlin, while another of Beria's friends and agents, Kobulov, was sent to that Embassy, officially as Counselor, but in fact as the Secret Police Resident, chief of the Soviet Intelligence Service and watchdog of the whole Russian diplomatic staff in Berlin. By this move Lavrenty planted in Germany two of his best informants.

Beria's invigilation of Molotov was not discontinued after the Commissar for Foreign Affairs came back from his mission to the Third Reich. Using his influence on Stalin, Beria succeeded in arranging the appointment of Molotov's First Deputy, Andrey Vyshinsky, the Prosecutor-General. Vyshinsky, now Lavrenty's confidant, was a man whose further career depended more on Beria than on anybody else.

Besides initiating and proceeding with his own plans and tasks, Beria also had to complete several important cases begun by his predecessor, particularly liquidations of outstanding Soviet executives who had defected abroad, but who were not destroyed because their liquidator, Yezhov, had himself been annihilated. Among those persons was Walter Krivitsky, former Chief of Soviet Intelligence in Western Europe, the NKVD Resident in Paris and a master Soviet spy. He also traveled often to Austria, Italy and Holland. Despite his extensive trips to Moscow and back, he was careful never to be caught by the local intelligence authorities of those foreign countries. In Vienna Walter Krivitsky organized an important network of Soviet agents; in Rome, thanks to his connections with a Fascist Navy officer, he obtained blueprints of the newest Italian submarine. In Paris, where he had his headquarters as Chief of Soviet Military Intelligence in Western Europe, Krivitsky lived simultaneously in several places under several different names. At the same time, he also operated an expensive bookstore of rare volumes in The Hague and worked there disguised as a quiet Austrian antique dealer. He lived there with his pretty wife, Tanya, and their little boy, Alex. During one of his numerous trips to Berlin Krivitsky procured documents of top secret German-Japanese negotiations, and then, through his antique shop in Holland, sent them to the Soviet Union. In that rare bookshop, which served as a camouflage for smuggling secret papers and microfilms, Krivitsky's aide and close friend was a young, handsome Dutch Communist, Hans Bruesse. Krivitsky was sure that he could trust the devoted lad entirely and left to him many of his confidential assignments, which the enthusiastic Dutch idealist fulfilled brilliantly.

During one of his numerous stays in Paris, Krivitsky was approached by the chief of the NKVD Special Mobile Group. These were men who were sent abroad to kidnap or liquidate the persons marked by Yezhov or Stalin personally. That time they had not come for Krivitsky, but for his former co-worker, Ignace Reiss, who refused to return to Moscow when summoned, and broke with his masters. The agents appeared in order to give him such a good lesson that it would also be an exemplary punishment and a warning for every Soviet dignitary abroad who denied to obey orders from the Main Office in Moscow. Krivitsky, however, was not any help to them and warned his hunted friend, who then escaped from Paris to Switzerland. But he did not enjoy his freedom for long. Soon Krivitsky learned that Reiss had been found dead not far from Lausanne. He had been shot with a series of machine gun bullets. Krivitsky realized that shortly it would be his turn and decided to escape with his wife and child. But before their flight two attempts to murder him were made in Paris. Fortunately, Krivitsky managed to save his life. In both cases the would-be assassin was one and the same person, the handsome, sincere, and so faithful aide, the young Dutchman Hans Bruesse, who appeared to have been a watchdog of the NKVD headquarters from the very beginning. Krivitsky understood that not only he but also his wife and their son would be annihilated in the very near future. He had connections important enough to be able to present his plea to the French Prime Minister, Leon Blum, and asked him for asylum. Not long before, French public opinion had been shocked by the scandal of the kidnaping in Paris of two Russian Generals, Miller and Kutepov, by Soviet agents. The French Ministry of Foreign Affairs, through the Soviet Embassy in Paris, made a strong protest to the Kremlin, stating that such excesses would not be tolerated in France.

In 1938 Krivitsky and his family arrived in New York. In the

United States he and his family felt safe. Here, the former Chief of Soviet Intelligence in Western Europe, who once knew Stalin personally, tried to help the American authorities fight Communism, but it was a thankless job. Talk against the Soviet Union was not very popular in America at that time. Russian spies in the United States had an easy field for their operations.

Krivitsky made his living from his articles, which were published in some magazines. When at the end of 1938 Yezhov was removed from his post as Chief of Internal Affairs, Krivitsky breathed a sigh of relief. He learned that the new head of the NKVD, Lavrenty Beria, had introduced a kind of amnesty for the high ranking functionaries persecuted by Yezhov. But this time the shrewd Krivitsky was mistaken. He was condemned to death anyway, not only because he was a defector, but because he had been too important a personality in the Soviet Intelligence. He knew too much about the Russian spy network abroad, overseas especially, and he was eager to sing about it in Washington and had already published in the American press several articles revealing Soviet methods.

In a few months Krivitsky finished his memoirs, which were not just an account of his defection but stated facts about the Kremlin as well as about Stalin's crimes, which were unknown to the free world. The chapters covered several sensational events such as: "Stalin Appeases Hitler," "Stalin's Hand in Spain," or explained "Why Stalin Shot his Generals." A copy of this book, *In Stalin's Secret Service, An Exposé of Russia's Secret Policies*, published by Harper, was purchased by the Soviet Embassy in the United States and mailed to Moscow. To his *Mobile Group* for the Administration of Special Tasks in New York, Beria coded the order to liquidate Krivitsky. *In Stalin's Secret Service* shortly became an American best seller, bringing its author and his family enough money to survive for at least a year. However, one day when on Broadway, Krivitsky spotted two men whom he remembered as professional assassins from the NKVD. They had just left a cafeteria on 42nd Street. The huge self-service restaurant off Times Square was at that time a popular hangout for Soviet agents. In its spacious rooms, anyone could carry his tray to a vacant seat at any of the more than one hundred tables, even if the other chairs at the table were occupied by strangers. Then he could start a conversation during his meal. This custom created a good opportunity for meetings and the confidential exchange of information without awakening suspicion. The two agents who were after Krivitsky noticed him from their post. On crowded Broadway, in the daylight, they could not do him any harm, but they followed him. The Russian defector was aware of this. Crossing a street one of the two agents acquainted with him as Sergey Bassov approached the hunted man and let him know that Krivitsky's mother, and the mother of his wife in Moscow had been arrested and executed as the family of a criminal who had committed treason. Krivitsky managed to lose his tormentors this time, but he knew that they would not give up their hunt. He went to Washington, asking for help and protection and volunteered to serve the American authorities with his knowledge of the Soviet subversive activity in the United States. But nobody there was eager to listen to him.

At any moment Krivitsky could be killed, or his wife murdered, or their little son kidnaped. One day the former Soviet dignitary was informed by a friend that the young Dutchman, Hans Bruesse, had flown to America and had arrived in New York. Krivitsky decided that from now on it would be a mortal, jungle-style battle between him and his former friend, especially since a professional assassin who had already failed twice must fulfill his assignment by any means possible. Otherwise he would be liquidated himself. So each of them would be fighting for his own life.

From New York the defector went to a small town in Virginia where he could buy a gun and bullets without a permit. On his way home he had a short stopover in Washington to change trains. But he did not board. The next day, February 10, 1941, Walter Krivitsky was found dead in a second-class hotel, the Bellevue, near Union Station in Washington. He was shot to death. On the floor was his newly purchased revolver, and in one of his pockets the police found some letters. They revealed that the refugee had decided to commit suicide. His widow, however, knew her husband's style of expression and could read between the lines. She announced that those notes were written under coercion, particularly since he would never deprive her and their child of his protection. She also stated to the Washington police and to the American press that her husband had told her several times not to believe it was suicide if he were ever found dead.

Undoubtedly, while waiting for his train, Krivitsky was approached by the Dutchman and told that if he would not write the notes dictated to him and then shoot himself, his beloved wife and son would be murdered. He made his choice.

The mysterious death of the author of *In Stalin's Secret Service,* the former Red Army General, and Chief of the Soviet Intelligence in Western Europe, defector Walter Krivitsky, was filed in the NKVD Moscow archives as just another case of the routine work completed in the office of Commissar of Internal Affairs, Lavrenty Pavlovich Beria, who not long before, on January 31, 1941, was officially appointed by Stalin, General Commissar of State Security.

38

Death to Spies!

On June 22, 1941, Germany attacked the Soviet Union. The impact was so strong and the Russian defenses so vulnerable that the offensive swept across the Soviet borders and ran into the interior like a hurricane. Finland joined the Germans three days after they attacked the USSR.

Stalin nominated himself Supreme Commander and Commissar of Defense, as well as Chief of a new body, immediately called by him the State Committee on Defense of the Soviet Union. This board—the Big Five—consisted of four members besides Stalin: Voroshilov, Malenkov, Molotov and Beria.

The war front, stretching from the White Sea to the Black Sea, was over 2,000 miles long, and Hitler's forces, with their allies, Italians, Hungarians, Rumanians and Finns, represented over 3,000,000 men. In less than two weeks the German armies captured Minsk, the capital of Byelorussia; Grodno; Brest-Litovsk; Vilna; and Riga, the capital of Latvia, the remainder of Latvia, as well as Lithuania and the western Ukraine. Soon after, they reached the Luga River, took Smolensk, ended the "Battle of Kiev" and began the siege of Leningrad. The entire operation was completed in less than three months. Stalin asked the Western powers for help. Great Britain responded to that plea immediately and signed a pact of mutual assistance with the USSR. Stalin, in panic, asked for a second front. As a consequence of this request, on July 30, 1941, the

Soviet Ambassador to Great Britain, Ivan Maisky, signed an agreement in London with the Prime Minister of the Polish Government in Exile, General Wladislav Sikorski. It stated, among other things, that the Soviet Union recognized that the Soviet-German treaties of 1939 relative to the territorial changes in Poland had lost their validity, and that the USSR expressed its consent to the formation on her territory of a Polish Army with a Polish Commander appointed by the Government of the Republic of Poland. In the Protocol signed the same day it was stated that "the Government of the Union of Soviet Socialist Republics will grant amnesty to all Polish citizens who are at present deprived of their freedom on the territory of the USSR, either as prisoners of war or on other adequate grounds."

Soon after, in the gloomy prison of Lubyanka in Moscow the Polish General Wladislav Anders, who had been jailed there, was called from his cell to the office of the Commissar of Internal Affairs and State Security, Lavrenty Pavlovich Beria. About this meeting General Anders writes in his memoirs, *An Army in Exile*, describing in detail how he was shown into that luxuriously furnished office where he met Beria and his deputy, Merkulov, who told him that he had been appointed by the Polish authorities, with the consent of the Soviet Government, Commander of a new Polish Army, which soon should be formed.

A few days after, General Anders was visited at his home in Moscow by some callers. They were a few of the high ranking Polish officers who, as Soviet-oriented fellow travelers, were living in a suburb of Moscow in the "Villa of Delight." During their conversation they mentioned the 15,000 Polish officers and men confined to the three POW camps at Kozelesk, Starobelsk and Ostashkov. These men would be a great suport for the newly-created Polish Army. However, General Anders learned shortly that before visiting him the officers had had a talk with Beria who, being responsible for those camps, was now obliged to release all the prisoners of war. But despite the Soviet-Polish agreement creating a new independent Polish Army, Lavrenty Beria planned the organization of an Army consisting of Poles, but under Russian command.

For that purpose, he had called the leaders of the group from the "Villa of Delight." During the conference, when they mentioned that there were large numbers of staff officers fit for active service in the camps at Kozelsk, Ostashkov and Starobelsk who could be excellent cadres for the army, Beria answered evasively: "Well, make a list of them, but there are not many left, because we made a great mistake."[1] And Beria's deputy Merkulov, who was present at that conference, confirmed the words of his superior by saying, "No, not those. We made a great mistake with them."[2]

This puzzling answer could be interpreted that Commissar Beria hesitated to have a strong foreign army on Russian soil. At that time nobody was yet aware of either the massacre in the Katyn forest or on Seliger Lake.

The Nazi invasion had been developing with tremendous speed. In September the Germans penetrated Donbas. Within a few days they captured eight big key cities, Orel, Tula, Vyazma, Rostov, Kaluga, Odessa, Taganrog and Kharkov and declared the siege of Moscow. These easy victories resulted not so much from the superiority of the German soldiers over the Russians as from the Red Army's morale, which was almost nil. Nazi propaganda was more successful at that time than anything else. Through their field radios and loudspeakers, talking in Russian day and night, the Germans called on the Soviet soldiers to come over to their side. They promised them the best conditions, good food and liberation from those bloody tyrants and oppressors, Stalin and Beria, with their prisons, misery and hard labor camps. The Soviet soldiers who remembered the mass deportations of millions of Russian peasants during the years of farm collectivization, the exile of hundreds of thousands of Russian workers to the mines in Siberia, as well as the role which Beria's NKVD Special Troops played during the war against Finland, listened to this propaganda gladly. Whole platoons, units, even regiments of the Red Army, with all their equipment, artillery, tanks and machine guns, joyously crossed the front lines, and with their banners and their military bands playing gay music, surrendered to the enemy, joining him as their savior.

This situation meant disaster for the Soviet Union. The Red Army had to be reorganized by any means and as soon as possible. For this task, Lavrenty Beria, as Commissar of State Security, was

---

[1] Lt. General Wladislav Anders, *An Army in Exile, the Story of the Second Polish Corps* (London: MacMillan & Co. Ltd., 1949). Reprinted by special permission of Gen. W. Anders.

[2] *Ibid.*

responsible. His life was now at stake. If he were not successful, he would either be torn to pieces by the hordes of escapees from demolished prisons and hard labor camps, or would likely be shot by the Gestapo, which followed the victorious Nazi Army.

Beria asked Stalin to transfer more troops and weapons to the Special Task Forces. This time he needed them for a different purpose than the method used during the war with Finland. He also wanted more soldiers to reinforce the guards in the hundreds of concentration camps to prevent any revolt of the prisoners. To the commanders of the NKVD units guarding the jails throughout the Soviet Union, Beria sent an order that the night before the evacuation of the town, they should take all inmates out of their cells into the prison yard and execute them with machine guns.

To all Soviet soldiers who were giving up to the enemy, voluntarily or not, even when encircled and outnumbered by German troops, Generalissimo Stalin and Commissar Beria decided to be merciless. On Beria's suggestion a new order released by Stalin was to be read to every Red Army detachment. However, this time, the Supreme Commander did not appeal to the patriotic feelings of his subordinates. He just stated dryly that every soldier who was taken prisoner of war, even if he had been wounded, would be considered as surrendering voluntarily to the enemy, and when recaptured would be treated like a traitor and a deserter. Court-martial and execution by an NKVD firing squad would be the punishment. Besides, everyone should keep in mind that the family of any Red Army soldier who surrendered to the Germans would be arrested immediately and either imprisoned or deported to Siberia.

This order, effective immediately, did not exclude Stalin's own son, Yakov, who, after graduation from the Frunze Military Academy, left for the front the very next day after Germany attacked his country. Wounded while fighting in the first line of the front, he had been taken prisoner of war. Just after the news of his capture reached the Kremlin, Beria was glad to get Stalin's permission to inform Yakov's wife, Yulia, of that new rule. He then arrested her and, without trial, condemned her to three years in prison, despite the fact that she was the only support of her four-year-old child, Gulya, Stalin's granddaughter. Beria received permission for Yulia's arrest from his Boss quite easily because she was Jewish, and that was enough to make Stalin detest her. The imprisonment of that woman was a secret sweet triumph for Beria, who always experienced a peculiar joy when he could make someone miserable. And this time, it was not only Yulia, but Stalin's son to whom Lavrenty delivered a blow. If Beria could cut the throat of Joseph Stalin, whom he so glorified in his book and speeches, he certainly would do it even more eagerly. But it was not yet the right moment. For that chance, the Commissar of Soviet Internal Affairs and State Security decided to wait.

In pursuing Stalin's order to persecute any Russian soldier captured by the enemy the NKVD platoons became busier than ever. There were arrests and deportations of thousands of relatives and children of officers and soldiers who became POW's, while all their belongings were confiscated. In his office Beria created a new Department with the special purpose of watching over the morale in the Red Army. For the chief of this Agency Lavrenty nominated his aide, Victor Abakumov. This new organization was called SMERSH—an abbreviation of two Russian words, *Smert Shpionam* —"Death to Spies." However, counterespionage played only a minor part in SMERSH. The main role of SMERSH was to shoot retreating Russian soldiers, to execute the recaptured ones and to supervise the spirit in the political orientation of the army men by infiltrating into every unit through a network of agents. According to a very detailed regulation, outlined by Beria personally, in every detachment of the Red Army, Navy and Air Force there should be an officer designated by SMERSH who should have several informers of every rank. The slightest delation against someone in the ranks, even though unproven, was enough to cause arrest and deportation to a hard labor camp, or even execution.

The regiments of the Security Police of Commissar Beria, safe from the fights in the first line of the battlefields, were busy deporting to the Far North whole villages of Volga German colonists who had been living in the Saratov Region for generations—since the times of Tsaritsa Catherine the Great. Now these people were taken from their homes, husbands separated from wives, parents from children, and transported to the opposite corners of the Soviet Union. In Beria's opinion these people, being Protestants and still proficient in the German language, could be a potential Fifth Column for the enemy approaching their communities. The Commissar of State Security therefore decided to transfer them to hard labor camps and to keep them there behind barbed wires.[3]

All these precautions, however, did not stop the German ad-

---

[3] The author met such deported German colonists in the hard labor camp in Vorkuta.

vances, which were still successful. Their armies took one Russian city after another.

In November 1941 the Germans besieged Leningrad, and captured two cities in the Moscow region, Klin and Istra. The latter was located about sixteen miles from Moscow.

The Soviet government was hurriedly evacuated from the capital to Kuybyshev, a town on the left bank of the central Volga River. In the stronghold shelters in Moscow where their Headquarters were, there remained only "the Big Five," Stalin with the four statesmen, Molotov, Malenkov, Voroshilov and Beria.

In his office, now located in an air-raid shelter in the basement of 2 Dzerzhinsky Street, Beria, with a handful of his aides, was busy collecting the archives of NKVD to burn all dossiers and documents of the Soviet Secret Police if the Germans took Moscow; then he planned to try to escape.

In bloody battles the Red Army kept the Nazis from further advancing toward their capital. This heroism was due not so much to the SMERSH action as to the mad stupidity of Hitler, who did not keep his word about giving the Soviet prisoners of war liberation and good living conditions. On the contrary, Hitler ordered his SS and Gestapo troops to murder the Russian boys in mass executions by machine gun, poison gas, or electrocution. The Russian prisoners of war in Germany also died of starvation after being denied bread or any other food. Facing such a fate, every Red Army man was fighting to the utmost for his own survival and did not have to be watched by the Soviet Security Police troops pushing him to the front. Simultaneously, behind the German lines in the villages, towns and cities, the Russian partisans voluntarily and spontaneously organized a vast and highly patriotic underground movement. This home army consisted of soldiers of all ages, from boys and girls barely out of childhood to oldsters who had fought in the First World War a quarter century before.

In spite of suffering gigantic losses the Russians defended Moscow successfully. The Nazis' attack on that city was beaten back and the danger of capture of the capital of the Soviet Union by the Germans vanished.

With the help of Great Britain, which, besides supplying the USSR with large quantities of food, ammunition and all kinds of weapons—ships and planes included—opened an offensive in the

Western Desert, the face of the war was reversed and the Red Army began a counterattack.

Toward the end of 1941 the image of the war changed significantly. Supported by the exceptionally severe winter, the so-called "General Frost," the Russian partisans and the bitterly fighting Soviet soldiers recaptured the city of Rostov, and the Moscow counteroffensive began. They also liberated several towns, small communities and important outposts. Some part of those victories was still due to Beria and his Security troops which, with their machine guns, herded the regular units forward. Lavrenty again enforced Stalin's new order to the Red Army, "Not one step back," with the exactness of a blindly obedient subordinate. Soon after a township or a village was regained, a unit of the NKVD troops entered. They arrested all persons who had any contact with the enemy or, knowing just a few words of German, could communicate with them. A groundless report against a neighbor was sufficient excuse to arrest the denounced one and to beat him until all his teeth were knocked out. These people were deported to Siberia in batches of 200. Any Russian girl who had relations with a German soldier was shot on Beria's personal order to his troops.

The Security as well as the Police NKVD SMERSH units, under command of Beria's deputy, Victor Abakumov, still kept the Soviet Forces in their usual iron grip. Lavrenty and his men were no longer afraid of being exterminated themselves, either by a victorious Gestapo or the Russian masses liberated from conquered hard labor camps.

The NKVD platoons also convoyed the German prisoners of war to the far north. In the midst of the Russian winter the captured soldiers, according to Commissar Beria's order, had to be stripped of their uniforms and shoes and left only with their light cotton shirts, trousers and socks. Then, guarded by NKVD troops armed with machine guns, they were herded to Siberia on open cars of freight trains.[4] Since the military transports carrying Soviet troops, cannons and ammunition to the front had priority, the open trains with the prisoners of war were halted on sidings for several hours at night. In spite of the delays in the journey, no extra food was

---

[4] These transports of prisoners of war, deprived of their uniforms and riding on open platforms directed to Siberia in the winter 1941, were seen by the author, who, being released at that time from the hard labor camp in the Far North, was on his way to Buzuluk to the Headquarters of the Free Polish Army under General Anders.

distributed to the prisoners. At dawn, whole batches of prisoners on every car no longer had to be carried farther to their destination of concentration camps, because they were dead or critically ill. They were disposed of in a strange way. A train, which was running through snow-covered steppes and forests, was halted there. The guards threw the corpses off the cars onto the ground and poured buckets of water on them, changing the dead bodies instantly into blocks of ice. Lavrenty Beria, Chief of the Red Secret Police, and one of the best disciples of Stalin, was no more humane toward the prisoners of war than his counterpart, Heinrich Himmler, Chief of the Gestapo and one of the best disciples of Hitler. No wonder that, when in a gay mood, Stalin called Beria "My Himmler." Besides, not long before, Stalin and Hitler were the best of allies for better or for worse.

The more the war situation changed, the more Beria, as a member of the Big Five, was involved in high echelon politics and the less with his regular job as chief policeman. At their regular daily meetings, besides the routine agenda, the Committee of Defense had to solve two problems of the utmost importance. One of them was the question of the necessity of keeping two million Soviet troops on the far north to prevent a potential attack by Japan. If, as a partner of the Axis, Japan would decide to fulfill her obligation to Hitler and support him by striking at the USSR in Siberia, the victory of the Fascist bloc over the Soviet Union would be more than certain. However, if the Japanese government would stay off, the Soviet troops stationed in Siberia could be removed from there to reinforce the Red Army on the European front.

The second point the Committee of the Big Five had to discuss was that the balance of Germany's overwhelming power over Russia could be changed only if America would become involved in the war. At that time the United States only supplied the Soviet Union, Great Britain and France with war materials.

The Committee of Defense at the Kremlin came to the conclusion that for the USSR it was a matter of life and death to draw the United States into the war, and that it could be done only by a cunningly prepared provocation.

The accomplishment of both of these tasks, to obtain information as to whether Japan was going to attack the Soviet Union, and to lure America into the war was given primarily to Lavrenty Beria.

In Japan Beria had a well-organized network headed by the top

Red spy, Dr. Richard Sorge. This German Communist, whose grandfather, Adolf Sorge, had been a private secretary of Karl Marx, was a doctor of political science and had been working as a Far East correspondent of the newspaper, *Frankfurter Zeitung.* He was a member of the Nazi Party and a personal friend of Joseph Goebbels, the Minister of Nazi Propaganda, who had introduced him to the Fuehrer. Richard Sorge was a thoroughly trusted man when he was sent to Japan. In Tokyo, Sorge became a frequent guest in the German Embassy and a good friend of German Ambassador Dr. Herbert von Dirkesen. Later, when von Dirkesen was replaced by the Nazi Air Force General Eugen Ott, a friend of Richard Sorge, the new Ambassador nominated Dr. Sorge as Press Attaché of the Embassy. There Sorge was the last man apt to be suspected as a Soviet spy.

Supplied with money by Beria, Dr. Sorge soon masterminded a ring of the best-qualified men, a young Japanese professor and journalist, Hozumi Ozaki, and a Japanese artist, Yotoku Miyagi, both from high society in Tokyo. Through these two individuals Sorge had access to members of the Japanese Cabinet and even to the Prime Minister, Prince Fuminaro Konoye. Dr. Sorge transmitted his intelligence to Beria from his villa in a suburb of Tokyo, where he had a clandestine radio operated by a German Communist, Max Klausen, supposedly a rich businessman. From this spy ring Beria obtained most valuable reports. On October 15, 1941, Moscow received from Dr. Sorge a coded message that Japan would not attack the USSR. Sorge also transmitted to Moscow the further intelligence that the Japanese troops stationed in the north, in Manchuria, were to be withdrawn from their post on the Siberian border and thrown against Burma, Indonesia and the Philippines.

The next day Commissar Beria was able to report to Generalissimo Comrade Stalin and to the whole body of the State Committee on Defense that Japan definitely would not go to war against the USSR.

Richard Sorge personally, with the help of Professor Ozaki, supported the Japanese military authorities in the idea of attacking the United States. In constant contact with Beria, Dr. Sorge forced this policy to involve the United States in the war. Finally, Sorge tried to transmit to Beria the long awaited message letting him know that Operation *Tora! Tora! Tora!*[5]—the Japanese attack on Pearl Harbor—was going to be launched, probably on December 6. In the meantime, however, Sorge was arrested by the Japanese.

On December 7, 1941, the Japanese bombed Pearl Harbor and raided British Malaya. The United States and Great Britain declared war on Japan. On December 11, Hitler declared war against the United States.

Lavrenty Beria, who had been on the board of Stalin's advisers, plunged into several new tasks of international significance. The United States, as a new partner in the war, had to be watched more closely and her politics had to be penetrated and influenced according to the aims of the Kremlin. Previously, soon after July 12, 1941, when the USSR and Great Britain signed the Anglo-Soviet Agreement of mutual friendship and support against the Nazis, Beria established a larger and more effective network of spies with access to the Foreign Office in London. Among these recruits were members of exclusive English society, such as Harold Adrian Russell, "Kim" Philby and two other refined and well-educated young gentlemen, Donald MacLean and Guy Burgess. These three men were denounced by the Russian defector, former Red Army General Walter Krivitsky, as Soviet agents, but the British government ignored that information.

Beria also organized a widespread net of spies in America, which infiltrated even the White House. Even before the United States entered the war Beria, through his agents, managed to establish connections with one of President Roosevelt's advisors. In 1940 this individual, Alger Hiss, was recognized as an informer and denounced to American authorities by Walter Krivitsky. But at that time in the United States there was no office such as the Central Intelligence Agency, and the Federal Bureau of Investigation was then almost exclusively occupied with watching the Nazi emissaries in the country. The information given in Washington by Krivitsky about Alger Hiss was neglected and laughed off, and shortly afterward Krivitsky was liquidated by Beria's agent, while American authorities declared that defector's death to be a neurotic suicide and soon entirely forgot the whole case.

There was another defector in the United States even more important than Krivitsky. He was an outstanding former Soviet per-

---

[5] "Tiger! Tiger! Tiger!"

sonality, a man who had already escaped to America in 1938. But his life was not in danger, even if he became an informer to the American authorities. It was secured thanks to a unique deal. Alexander Orlov, who was Stalin's plenipotentiary in Spain during the Civil War in 1938, flew to the West after learning that he had become the subject of a purge staged by Yezhov. After escaping his tormentors, Commissar Orlov reached Washington by way of France and Canada and asked for political asylum. Beria would annihilate that man even more gladly than anybody else, for he hated Orlov personally. Orlov once was Deputy of the OGPU and was later nominated Commander of NKVD in Transcaucasia for the frontier troops on the borders of Persia and Turkey. As an important personality in the Caucasus, Orlov stood in the way of Beria's career. But when Orlov defected, Lavrenty was helpless. Although by assassinating Trotsky in Mexico Beria proved he had no difficulty in liquidating a defector abroad in either hemisphere, in the case of Orlov he was unable to exercise his skill. It was a special order of his Boss, the Great Comrade Stalin, that kept Beria off Orlov.

After landing in America, Orlov, who knew Stalin personally, decided to blackmail him. In a letter to the Kremlin, he announced that he had deposited some documents in his lawyer's office that would discredit Stalin in the eyes of the whole world. Orlov warned his former superior that in the event of his murder by Soviet henchmen from SMERSH, the papers would be published immediately. Orlov was too experienced an NKVD official himself, and knew the Dictator well enough. The stratagem worked perfectly. Stalin let him alone.

The establishment of a large, strong and productive ring of spies in the United States demanded from Beria a lot of exhausting labor and a meticulous, long-range plan, worked out in advance in every detail. It required a lot of energy, slyness, ability to find the right men for special training, and plenty of money. Beria realized that the job had to be performed so efficiently that there would not be the slightest error which could evoke any international scandal or even unpleasant repercussions which could ruin the relations between the United States, Great Britain and the Soviet Union. The first target was bugging and intercepting the telephone calls and other personal conversations in the American and British Embassies in Moscow. Then Soviet agents must be planted there so they could check the diplomatic pouches to decipher the codes and investigate the private lives of the embassy staffs. This was accomplished by placing NKVD Majors and Colonels as janitors, chauffeurs and cooks, as well as maidservants, tutors for the children and nurses, all of whom made weekly reports of their observations. They had to report everything that happened at the homes of their employers, including the contents of letters they received.

At Bykovo, forty miles from Moscow, Beria established a special Academy for spies, where the most talented officers of the Secret Police, as well as the most brilliant students of Moscow University and handsome stage and screen actors were housed and received their schooling. The curriculum was also prepared by Beria. Besides physical culture, map reading, radio operation, ciphering and sabotage, it offered an intensive course in English in two classes. One was with the British accent and the other with the American. There were also such subjects as British and American customs, their way of living and even their sense of humor. The students were initiated into all kinds of subversion and were taught the skill of discovering the weaknesses of people who could be useful: their inclination for gambling, drinking, girls or homosexuality. They also studied the art of luring and seducing women employed by the U.S. Government for subsequent use as tools for spying and learned how to contact other agents and smuggle information to the USSR. Such men, furnished with forged passports in false names, were later sent to Great Britain and to the United States through England and Canada. The problem of the immense amount of money required for these activities was solved by Beria in two ways. After convincing Stalin that the USSR needed good propaganda, and that it would be expensive, Beria received a huge budget running into nine figures for this purpose. In addition, as Chief of the NKVD Lavrenty had at his disposal a special *Valuta Bureau*—Currency Office—organized sometime before by the OGPU. The responsibility of the *Valuta Bureau* was to collect as much hard foreign currency as possible. Beria's functionaries in that agency were performing a so-called "Dollar Inquisition," which meant the extortion of dollars hidden by Soviet citizens. The methods were imprisonment, beating, torture and blackmail by the threat of sending to the hard labor camps members of the family of a person suspected of possessing American money. The office also operated a laboratory where counterfeit $100 bills were produced. This procedure had been accepted by Stalin several years before.

The shrewd enterprise of Soviet propaganda abroad proved to be fruitful in a short time. Beria's men successfully infiltrated the most exclusive circles in Great Britain and the United States. The style of life in the Soviet Union became most fashionable among some professors and brilliant students in Oxford and Cambridge universities in England, as well as at Yale and Harvard universities in the United States. Many of them were eager to discover the wonderful, exciting and stimulating new Red World. The same atmosphere prevailed in literary and artistic societies, and among rich intellectuals who liked to display their Communist ideas, as well as among scholars, writers, poets, journalists, and stage and film directors. Everything that was imported from the USSR was wonderful and a person who did not accept this point of view was branded as a reactionary, a fascist or simply a blockhead.

Generalissimo Stalin, the former best ally and supporter of Hitler, became the "Sun of the Nations" and "Good Uncle Joe." This success he owed mainly to his Commissar of Internal Affairs and Chief of State Security, Lavrenty Pavlovich Beria.

Beria now had no doubts that, since he had in his hands all the strings of international espionage and all media of the Soviet propaganda in the West, he was irreplaceable to his Boss, who would not purge him or execute him as he had Bukharin or Zinoviev, nor would he be arrested and liquidated in the basement of a prison as Yenukhidze had been, nor would he be the subject of an assassination as had Kirov, nor of a staged suicide like Ordzhonikidze, nor removed from his post as Yezhov had been. Beria was especially confident because he did not make any of the mistakes those men had committed. He was wise enough not to object to staying in the shadow of his Master, who, thanks largely to Lavrenty, became the dear friend of the British Prime Minister, Sir Winston Churchill, and of President Franklin Delano Roosevelt and afterwards of President Harry S Truman.

International fame as second in power after Stalin did not mean very much to Beria, now Vice Chairman of the State Committee on Defense—the Big Five. Lavrenty's ambition was to jump into his Boss' shoes at the first opportunity, which he was preparing and timing with the precision of an architectural engineer. But for the time being Lavrenty Pavlovich Beria was Chief of his own, almost private army of one and a half million men and officers who were highly trained, well fed, uniformed and paid, and equipped with all kinds of modern weapons. These men knew that their Commander took the best care of them, so they supported him and served him sincerely, while simultaneously being aware of the hatred of the whole Russian population, they were the more united and ready to stand behind their protector. On the other hand, Beria was conscious of the sentiment prevailing in his troops and knew that he could depend on his NKVD Forces even more than Stalin could depend on his Red Army.

So why shouldn't Beria let Joseph Stalin be "Good Uncle Joe" in the eyes of the Western world, which had become so crazy about everything from the Soviet Union—from caviar and vodka and Astrakhan fur caps for American and European men to the *babushka* kerchiefs used instead of ladies' chapeaux, to high Russian-style boots which sophisticated and elegant women wore in London, Paris and New York to the tunes of Soviet songs suddenly so popular everywhere.

It was understood that in comparison with these great achievements of Commissar Lavrenty Beria a little thing like his kidnapings of schoolgirls from time to time for a half hour of pleasure on a couch in his office as an afternoon pastime was a trifle that did not count, and Stalin, "Sun of the Nations," did not bother to ban it or even to reprimand his disciple. Anyhow everybody has his hobby, and a person working so hard and efficiently for the sake of the USSR and its Leader, the Great Comrade Stalin, as Beria did, needed a little relaxation and some fun. Didn't he?

39

The Greatest Show in the World

IN THE SPRING of 1943 an international scandal exploded that almost undermined the alliance between the Western powers and the USSR. Near the town of Smolensk, still occupied by the Germans, the men of the so-called Todt Organization were busy repairing the railroad and highway, both badly damaged by bombs. The battalions of the Todt, attached to the German combat engineer divisions for the building of trenches, bridges and other construction work in Russia, consisted of forcibly recruited laborers from the Nazi-occupied countries of Rumania, Czechoslovakia, Hungary, Poland, Denmark, Holland and France.

In April 1943, not far from Smolensk, a few men from the Todt Organization, while working in the Katyn Forest at the Dnieper River, accidentally encountered during their diggings a mass grave of officers and soldiers. All of them wore uniforms which were neither Russian nor German. The Nazi officials summoned to the spot initiated an investigation. It was revealed that the dead men were about 5,000 Polish prisoners of war captured by the Red Army after the USSR invaded Poland. They were the missing Poles who, because of the "great error," according to Beria, were unable to join the Free Polish Army created on Russian soil.

Beria's NKVD Secret Police troops had liquidated these men. The executions had been performed with the typical precision of all operations directed by the Chief of Soviet Security. The hands of the dead servicemen had been tied behind their backs and every one of them was shot in the back of the head.

The Nazis did not hesitate to use the discovery of the massacre for their own purpose. On April 13, 1943, Radio Berlin announced that a large common grave full of men massacred by the Soviet Secret Police NKVD had been discovered in the district of Smolensk.

The Polish Government in Exile in London and the British authorities suspected that the Nazi broadcast was a lie and just another cynical propaganda trick. However, the Germans were ready to prove its truth and asked the International Red Cross in Geneva to appoint a commission to take part in the exhumation of the bodies. The Red Cross in Switzerland accepted the suggestion to participate in the autopsies of the corpses near Smolensk, but under the condition that all three of the involved parties—the Polish Government, the USSR and the Third Reich—would agree that the examination be performed. The British Administration and the Polish Government in London were certain that Stalin would be glad that the event of international importance would be investigated by such an objective institution as the Swiss Red Cross. Only a week earlier Radio Moscow, controlled by Commissar of Internal Affairs, Lavrenty Beria, had denied the accusation as a slander, and had promulgated a quite opposite version, calling it a crime committed by the Nazis as a provocation against the Soviet Union. However, when the Kremlin was asked for its agreement, the letter from Geneva was disregarded by Moscow. Instead of answering the request, Stalin sent a sharp note to the Polish representatives in London announcing that the USSR had decided to break diplomatic relations with the Free Polish Government.

Hitler was happy to show the world that Stalin's Red terror was no less ruthless than his own Brown one, and that Nazi Germany should not be considered to have a monopoly on inhumanity. Soon the Germans brought to the Katyn Forest an international committee of forensic professors, physicians and other experts. These scientists, after meticulous examination and research came to the conclusion that the length of time the corpses had been buried, the bullets they had been killed with and the shape of wounds, which were typical of a certain model of Russian triangular-shaped bayonet all proved beyond doubt that this particular mass murder had been done by the Soviet Special Troops. Among the witnesses to the autopsies were several American and British officers: U.S. Army Lt. Colonel John H. Van Vliet, Jr., U.S. Army Captain Donald B. Stewart and, from the British Army, Captain Dr. Stanley B. Gilder and others who, being German prisoners of war, had been forcibly taken there from their POW camps. Contrary to their original strong opinion that the execution was staged by the Nazis, whom they rightly considered the enemy, and that their ally, the USSR, could never commit such a horrible atrocity, they were finally convinced that the crime had been committed by Stalin and his Commissar of State Security, Lavrenty Beria.

A few months later, in September 1943, when the Soviet Army recaptured Smolensk and the Katyn Forest, the Kremlin attempted to hush the worldwide scandal and to save face. This assignment Stalin left to his Commissar of Internal Affairs. Beria ordered Radio Moscow to announce the establishment of a "Special Commission for Ascertaining and Investigating the Circumstances of the Shooting of Polish Officer Prisoners by the German-Fascist Invaders in the Katyn Forest."

This new commission which consisted entirely of Russians, members of the Communist Party and high ranking officers of the Red Army, even before it began its investigation was given notice by the controlled Soviet radio and the press that the mass murder in the Katyn Forest had been committed by the Germans. In other words, the obedient commission had nothing to do but confirm what had been decreed by the Chief of State Security.

Before the Soviet Special Commission went to the scene of the mass murder, Beria sent to Smolensk a group of his highly trained Secret Police officers whose task it was to stage the forthcoming performance. First, a platoon of the NKVD forces rounded up all the peasants, men and women alike, from the neighboring village. Some, who looked bright enough to be used, were told that a commission was coming soon and that the villagers should serve it as volunteers who had been accidental witnesses when the Germans brought the prisoners to the forest to be shot. However, the Secret Police officers told their captives word by word exactly what they were to say and ordered them learned by heart.

Then the commission under the chairmanship of Nikolay Shvernik, a member of the Politburo, left Moscow for Smolensk. After a few days spent in the Katyn Forest, where it mainly interviewed the previously trained villagers, the commission returned to Moscow. Soon the Medico-Legal Experts Investigation Protocol was concocted and, after it was checked and approved by Beria, the findings were publicly announced.

Beria's next step was to invite foreign correspondents accredited in Moscow to a well-prepared show. These were eleven American reporters: Henry Clarence Cassidy, Chief of the United Press Bureau, also broadcasting for NBC; William H. Lawrence of *The New York Times*; James Fleming of CBS; Henry Shapiro for UP; Ralph Parker of *London Times* and *The New York Times*; Jean Champernois, Harold King, Edward Angly, H. Lauterbach, Alexander Worth and Edward Stevens.

The United States Ambassador to the USSR, William Averell Harriman, asked his daughter, Kathleen, to join the group of journalists and he designated John F. Melby, Third Secretary of the American Embassy in Moscow, for this trip to Katyn. The Ambassador, in a strictly confidential telegram of January 25, 1944, informed President Franklin D. Roosevelt and the Secretary of State about this visit. In that message Mr. Harriman revealed that, "None of [the] party was able to judge scientific evidence of autopsies which were performed in their presence. Moreover, they were not permitted to make independent investigations except for formal questioning of few witnesses made available. Correspondents filed reports telling what they saw without expressing opinions, but for some reason censor has held up these stories . . . [1]

After her journey to Smolensk, Miss Kathleen Harriman, despite the fact that she was not a newspaperwoman nor an experienced person who could easily recognize the deception and Beria's slyness, prepared a detailed report in which she wrote:

On January 23, 1944, members of the foreign press were taken to Smolensk to get first hand the evidence compiled by the Commission on the Katyn incident.

The party was shown the graves in the Katyn Forest and witnessed post mortems of the corpses. As no member was in a position to evaluate the scientific evidence given, it had to be accepted at its face value.

The testimonial evidence provided by the Commission and witnesses was minute in detail and by American standards petty. We were expected

---

[1] Hearings before the Select Committee of the U.S. House of Representatives, 82nd Congress, Part 7, Exhibit 24 (Washington, D.C.: United States Government Printing Office, 1952).

to accept the statements of the high ranking Soviet officials as true, because they said it was true.[2]

And further:

The witnesses themselves were very well rehearsed, and they appeared subdued rather than nervous, their pieces having been learned by heart.

When the last witness had been heard general questions were asked, some of import to the Katyn incident, others not. Shortly, however, the representatives of the Foreign Office Press Department got up and said we'd better break up as our train was due to leave shortly. I got the distinct impression that the Committee was relieved. They had been told to put on a show for us—the show was over—and they did not want to be bothered any further. The meeting broke up without any informal chatting.[3]

The statement written by the Third Secretary of the American Embassy in Moscow, John F. Melby, was even more skeptical. He declared:

During the evening the Commission held a session devoted to questioning the witnesses. . . . It soon became apparent that the session was staged for the benefit of the correspondents and that the witnesses were merely repeating stories they had already given the Commission. The show was staged under hot and blinding klieg lights and motion picture cameras. In all, five witnesses were produced who added nothing to what had been said at the press conference. Attempts by the correspondents to question the witnesses were discouraged, and finally permitted reluctantly only through the members of the Commission. All witnesses were shunted out of the room as rapidly as possible upon finishing their statement.

The atmosphere at the session grew progressively tense as the correspondents asked one pointed and usually rude question after another. At midnight it was announced abruptly that our train would leave in one hour.

Certainly the members of the Commission were not at all pleased when leading questions were asked. On the return trip the Foreign Office officials who accompanied us were almost unduly anxious . . . to be assured that we were convinced. It is apparent that the evidence in the Russian case is incomplete in several respects, that it is badly put to-

---

[2] Hearings before the Select Committee to Conduct an Investigation of the Facts, Evidence and Circumstances of the Katyn Forest Massacre. 82nd Congress Second Session, Part 7, June 3, 4 and November 11, 12, 13, 14 (Washington, D.C.: United States Government Printing Office, 1952).

[3] *Ibid.*

gether, and that the show was put on for the benefit of the correspondents without opportunity for independent investigation or verification. On balance, however, and despite loopholes the Russian case is convincing.[4]

This method of staging facts to fool the West was typical of the Soviet Propaganda Office, one of several agencies in the People's Commissariat of the USSR Internal Affairs under Lavrenty Pavlovich Beria. Under such circumstances in spite of the fact that the plot was not faultless it is no wonder that for "extraordinary service rendered to the Soviet Union" Beria was awarded the honorable title, Hero of Socialist Labor, by his superior, Generalissimo Stalin.

---

[4] Hearings before the Select Committee to Conduct an Investigation of the Facts, Evidence and Circumstances of the Katyn Forest Massacre. 82nd Congress Second Sessions, Part 7, June 3, 4, and November 11, 12, 13, 14 (Washington, D.C.: U.S. Government Printing Office, 1952).

40

The Soviet Purchasing Commission in Washington

THE UNEXPECTED ATTACK by Hitler's army on his Soviet ally in 1941 caused the change of the entire policy of the Kremlin. From that time on, Stalin and his Brain Trust of four advisors had to seek the help of the West. This event, however, did not at all alter the general attitude. The idea of conquering the whole world and putting it under the Communist yoke, as depicted on the Soviet emblem of the hammer and sickle against the blue background of the globe, still prevailed.

Joining the camp of the Western Allies—Germany's enemies— was an act of necessity for the Soviet Union. But it did not change its feelings of hatred for and inferiority to Western culture, civilization and wealth into a sudden outburst of love, or even friendship.

The USSR simply needed very badly the support of the Western powers. Consequently, the Soviet Union now approached the United States, Great Britain and France solely for that purpose. These new pacts of mutual assistance gave the Russians one more advantage. They made it easier for them to infiltrate the countries of their new allies and to obtain their military and economic secrets and other important information which they would be able to use later for their own purposes against their present blood brothers.

Remembering the basic maxim expressed by Lenin in his speech delivered at the Ninth Party Congress on April 3, 1920, that "a good Communist is, at the same time, a good *Chekist*," Commissar Lavrenty Beria organized, in addition to his academy for spies at Bykovo, a highly programmed course for Soviet diplomats, ambassadors, attachés and other foreign service employees. The newly opened areas of international relations—political, economic, social, cultural and artistic—would enable the Soviet Union to send abroad officials and to establish a number of different commissions. In addition to their abilities as expert politicians, scholars, writers and musicians, these men, according to Beria's regulations, had to join and pass certain examinations to become highly trained spies. With their easy access to the most influential figures in the Western countries when abroad, and being, moreover, above suspicion, their activities would be of great value.

One such spy cell created and designed under the guidance of Lavrenty Beria was sent to the United States as early as 1943, when the Soviet Union pretended to be a faithful comrade-in-arms to America. This was called the Soviet Purchasing Commission, and it consisted of highly educated men as well as intensively trained agents. After a conference with Anastas Mikoyan, his old friend and protector since their days in Baku, Beria achieved yet another goal. Through Mikoyan, then People's Commissar of Foreign Trade and also in charge of lend-lease for the Soviet Union, Beria ordered the Chief of the Purchasing Commission, Red Army General Leonid Rudenko, and his staff to search out all secret information about United States industry, especially the military industry. The Commission had more than 1,000 employes, all of them schooled in Beria's unique academy to obtain as many American production secrets as possible. They were instructed to observe new military devices such as bombs, artillery and tanks; new industrial processes and developments; and United States policy. The Soviet Purchasing Commission operated in America according to Commissar Beria's directions, in a wartime rush atmosphere and on the basis, "Who cares what the Russians get? They are our allies, and Mr. Stalin is the Good Uncle Joe and our sincere friend."

Commissar of Internal Affairs Beria was above all interested in what the Kremlin called "Super-Lend-Lease." This consisted of America's secrets. Such stolen information was sent to Beria's office by air and sea. It was whisked away in suitcases designed to be protected from search under diplomatic immunity, and contained photographs, maps, photostats, charts, and meticulous descriptions of American devices and machines. Just a few months after the Soviet Purchasing Commission arrived in Washington in 1943, when the USSR was still the staunch ally of America, the members of that Commission obtained the most secret data, which they sent to the Commissariat of Lavrenty Pavlovich Beria. The information was about uranium, a vital component of the atomic bomb. It passed through the U.S. Air Force base at Great Falls, Montana, en route to the Soviet Union.

On April 4, 1944, thousands of Americans read sensational news under the headline, "Soviet Official Here Resigns," which appeared on the front page of *The New York Times*. In this article the newspaper revealed that an official of the Soviet Purchasing Commission in Washington, Victor Kravchenko, who had asked for political asylum in the United States, accused the Soviet Government of a "double-faced" foreign policy with respect to its professional desire for collaboration with the United States and England. He also denounced the Soviet Administration for failure to grant political and civil liberties to the Russian people, who are "subjected . . . to unspeakable oppression and cruelties while the NKVD—Soviet Secret Police—acting through its thousands of spies, continues to wield its unbridled domination over the people of Russia."

The same day the announcement of his defection appeared in *The New York Times*, the personal files of Victor Andreyevich Kravchenko were demanded by the Commissar of Internal Affairs and Chief of State Security, and were put on his desk. Lavrenty Beria scrutinized the papers and then decided upon the same fate for the escapee that he had previously decreed for another high ranking Soviet official, Walter Krivitsky, who had fled to the United States in 1938. The sentence for Krivitsky was "suicide," and it was carried out less than three years after it had been pronounced.

This new case, however, was much more difficult to execute. From the very day of his escape to New York, where Kravchenko called a press conference and declared that he now placed himself under the protection of American public opinion, he became a prominent figure. Although protected by American detectives, Kravchenko hid himself most of the next year in the apartment of an elderly lady, Mrs. Norman Hapgood, the widow of an American diplomat. At her home the Russian refugee found a shelter from

Beria's agents, who, as he stated, had been ordered to murder him for revealing Soviet espionage activity in America, as well as everywhere in the world.

In his new home Kravchenko wrote his memoirs, which Mrs. Hapgood, being a linguist, translated from the original Russian into English. Two years later, in 1946, his autobiography was published. The title of that book, *I Chose Freedom*, initiated a popular expression used from that time on to apply to everyone who determined to leave a Communist country for the West.

In his account the author recalled the thoughts that tormented him on the night of his escape, when, deciding to flee from the Soviet Embassy in Washington to New York, he fully realized the danger of revenge by Beria's henchmen, located all over the world.

Kravchenko was aware of the consequences of his step when he wrote that the USSR regime "will pronounce a sentence of death upon me. Always its secret agents will haunt my life. They will trace my steps and keep vigil under my windows, and if ordered by their masters, will strike me down."[1]

The book soon became a best seller. Victor Kravchenko rapidly became too famous on both continents to be liquidated immediately; his sudden death would be very suspicious and could arouse an international scandal. The execution of the verdict had to be delayed. Lavrenty Beria had time, was patient, and did not mind waiting.

From the royalties he received from his memoirs, Kravchenko lived in a comfortable apartment in one of the most fashionable districts of New York City, near Central Park. Years passed, but the sentence of death by suicide had never been revoked.

Later Victor Kravchenko appeared before the House Committee on Un-American Activities and testified about Soviet espionage agents, including diplomats on the highest level, who had stolen "tons" of U.S. secrets. Kravchenko even confessed that once he personally had had to help pack some suitcases filled with stolen information to be sent to Russia in a pouch, under diplomatic immunity. He also admitted that Soviet diplomacy was indivisible from espionage. "Every Soviet diplomat," assured Kravchenko, "whether it be Yakov Malik, Russian delegate to the United Nations, or Alexander Panyushkin, Soviet ambassador in Washington, or their col-

---

[1] Victor Kravchenko, *I Chose Freedom* (New York: Charles Scribner's Sons, 1946).

leagues in Paris or London, has passed through extensive training in this activity and has had wide experience."[2]

Asked by one of the members of the Un-American Activities Committee, Representative Francis E. Walter, Democrat of Pennsylvania, if the Soviet diplomatic agents in the United States were engaged in espionage, Kravchenko answered: "Absolutely. That is part of the system."[3]

It was part of the system initiated by Lenin, who created the *Cheka* under Feliks Dzerzhinsky, which later became OGPU, and then the NKVD. Under Dzerzhinsky's successors, particularly the most effective one, People's Commissar of Soviet Internal Affairs and Chief of State Security of the USSR, Lavrenty Pavlovich Beria, it was also part of the system to murder everyone who decided to choose freedom.

Finally, Victor Kravchenko met the fate he predicted in his memoirs. On the dreary morning of February 25, 1966, he was found dead in his New York apartment. His death and its attendant evidence of suicide was similar to the circumstances that surrounded the supposed self-murder of the other Russian defector, Krivitsky. In the same month, February, that Krivitsky died, Kravchenko, exactly like Krivitsky, left a note declaring that he had decided to take his own life and shot himself through the right temple with his own gun.

The difference was that while Krivitsky's revolver lay near the dead body, the revolver with which Kravchenko took his life was in the pocket of his sports jacket. The cause of Kravchenko's death was officially declared a suicide. But it was a strange one, requiring acceptance of an incredible fact: that the self-murderer, after shooting himself in the right temple, carefully returned the weapon to the pocket of his sports jacket.

From the time he chose freedom until his death twenty-two years later, Kravchenko had lived in constant fear. Neighbors described him as "scared all the time and distrustful of everybody, especially strangers; very fearful, very secretive, and seemed to look over his shoulder, as though he felt somebody was following him."[4] The persistent Commissar of Internal Affairs in Moscow, Lavrenty Beria, ordered the staging of several attempts on the life

---

[2] *The New York Times*, March 8, 1950.
[3] *Ibid.*
[4] *New York Herald Tribune*, February 26, 1966.

of the Russian defector, and Kravchenko claimed that in 1949 alone, four such attempts were made by Communist agents to murder him; then three times in California and twice in New York agents broke into his home only to find he was not there. Some years later he fought off two intruders who forced their way into his New York apartment. Kravchenko reached for his revolver, for which he had a permit, and shot and wounded one of his assailants, while the other ran away.

Victor Kravchenko managed to outlive Beria for almost thirteen years, but the sentence of suicide the late General Commissar of State Security had pronounced on this man was still in effect. And it had to be executed.

41

The Brotherly Slavic Russian Army

THE POLISH FORCES under General Anders, organized from prisoners of war in the USSR, did not represent the whole number of captives. The exact list of imprisoned Poles detained in hard labor camps throughout Russia, which was delivered to Beria on his demand, was never disclosed by him. In 1943, after the Polish troops left the Soviet Union to join the British Eighth Army of Marshal Montgomery for the Italian campaign, Beria ordered GULAG to release the Poles who were still behind barbed wire.

After diplomatic relations between the Polish Government in London and the USSR were severed, Beria was no longer obliged to transfer more regiments of discharged Poles to their own authorities. These stateless men, neither Soviet citizens nor free Poles on foreign soil, were at the mercy of their captors and could be sent back at any time to the mines of Siberia or executed as were their compatriots in the forest of Katyn. But Beria had no intention of repeating that "big error," as he termed the massacre. The Commissar of Soviet Internal Affairs designed a different plan for the proper use of these prisoners, having at his disposal Colonel Zygmunt Berling, who on the eve of the evacuation of the Free Polish Forces from the USSR abandoned his unit and deserted to the Red Army. This action was the result of Berling's previous training in the Russian Academy for Polish defectors in the "Villa of Delight," or "Haven of Bliss," at Malakhovka, near Moscow. Now that schooling, created by Commissar Beria to prepare cadres of Red Poles, was going to show a profit. According to Beria's project, the recently released Poles could take their choice: they could join a new Polish Communist Army which, under Soviet Command, would take Poland after the Germans were defeated and fight against the brotherly units under General Anders should he, with the Western Powers, enter Poland first.[1] Or, if any of these at long last liberated men did not like that idea, they would be sent back to Siberia.

This ultimatum was not presented as obviously, harshly and openly as it would appear. The shrewd Beria's policy was almost never an open or obvious one. In this case Lavrenty Pavlovich decided to use subtle politics and a sly stratagem to convince the Poles that they were going to fight for their own good—to liberate their native land.

Despite being so opposed to nationalism that he tried to uproot it even from his native Georgia and other Caucasian countries, Beria was determined to play on the nationalistic feelings of the Poles, who traditionally were known as deeply devoted to their country, their ancient customs and their Roman Catholic faith. As Commissar of Internal Affairs, Chief of State Security and head of the censorship of the press and other mass media, Beria gave his permission to publish a new paper for the Poles in the USSR. This weekly magazine, under the title, *Nowe Widnokregi*,[2] was printed in the Polish language and edited by a group calling itself the "Union of Polish Patriots." Among several nationalistic articles and poems, strictly censored in Beria's office, the magazine called upon its readers to join the ranks of the new Polish Kosciusko Division. Kosciusko, the great Polish hero of the eighteenth century who had always fought the Russians, and had sailed to America where he became a personal friend of George Washington and Thomas Jefferson, was for the Poles a national symbol of liberty, independence and democracy.

The cunning stratagem worked perfectly. The Polish officers and soldiers who had no choice other than to join the Kosciusko Division anyhow, if they did not want to perish in the far north, were now full of enthusiasm, eager to fight the Germans to liberate their

[1] Zygmunt Berling, *"Pamietniki"* ("Memoirs"), (Warsaw: *Kultura*, April 16, 23, 30 and May 7, 21, 1967).

[2] *New Horizons.*

country under the auspices of Kosciusko's name. Some Polish Roman Catholic priests, released from jail, were allowed to celebrate holy mass every Sunday, and the Poles, who were supplied with Soviet weapons and equipment, received their own Polish uniforms with their national emblem, the White Eagle, on their caps, and had their own Polish commanders. Their headquarters, however, was under high ranking Polish officers previously indoctrinated in the "Haven of Bliss." After extensive training, these units were ready to be sent to the battlefield. They were impatient to fight the Nazis and to take their revenge, as was every Pole equally, not only those from the Polish troops of General Anders' Free Corps, or from the Polish Underground Forces in the occupied fatherland—the Home Army.

The Commander in Chief of the Kosciusko Division, Colonel Zygmunt Berling, was even invited to the Kremlin for a special audience with Stalin, who promoted him to the rank of General in appreciation of Berling's usefulness to the Soviet Union in preparing his troops to take Poland as a Russian satellite. Stalin also, in the presence of the whole body of the Soviet Committee of Defense —Molotov, Voroshilov, Malenkov and Beria—decorated Berling with one of the highest Soviet awards: the Order of Suvorov.

But then a most unexpected reaction to that ceremony occurred; it was a response which until that time had never happened in the history of the Sovietland, or even within the walls of the ancient Kremlin. The Polish traitor Berling asked Generalissimo Stalin not to give him the Order.

Great consternation prevailed. Berling, however, explained to Comrade Stalin that this decoration could anger the whole Polish Kosciusko Division, the men who had been so cleverly cheated. Suvorov, one of Russia's most gifted field marshals during the reign of Tsaritsa Catherine the Great, fought against the Polish Army under Kosciusko and became famous for the massacre of Polish women and children in a suburb of Warsaw. It would seem suspicious, if not ironic, if the Commander in Chief of the Kosciusko Division in Russia were decorated in the name of Suvorov.

The gloomy atmosphere which hung over that ceremony for a moment changed immediately. All the Soviet dignitaries, Stalin included, started roaring with laughter, as only Russians can. The newly promoted General Berling received an order not of a lesser class, but more suitable. Then the entire party moved to an adjoining room, a special one for such occasions, for an informal social reception with plenty of caviar and vodka.

Berling's troops, attached to the Soviet regiments under Marshal Konstantin Rokossovsky, Commander of the First Byelorussian Front, were shortly sent to the battlefield.

The war was drawing rapidly to its end. The Nazis were beaten in Europe; in Italy, as well as in North Africa at Tobruk; in the Middle East at Al Alamein; in the Atlantic and Pacific; and in their own land, where Berlin, Munich, Frankfurt and Hamburg were bombed by the American and British Air Forces.

In the still German-occupied Polish capital, Warsaw, the Underground Resistance Army was ready for an uprising. This Home Army of over 40,000 men consisted of officers and soldiers who were well trained and equipped with British weapons dropped by parachute from England or smuggled in by boat through the Channel and the Baltic Sea, as well as with German rifles and machine guns captured during the night raids of the partisans on Nazi transports, garrisons and armories. Rokossovsky's army was pushing the Nazis from the east. It was evident that in a few weeks the Reds would approach Warsaw. There was a possibility, however, that if the German forces were to abandon the Polish capital without a shot, the Poles, fearing a new danger from the Bolsheviks, would start fighting them, as they had five years before when Stalin was Hitler's ally. They also would be supported by the Poles from the Kosciusko regiments in the rear of Rokossovsky's troops. Of course they would not have any chance to win. But the Poles were commonly known as Don Quixotes and bravados who, according to Stalin's and Beria's opinions, were always and everywhere troublemakers; before they could be defeated they might fight the USSR for several weeks and involuntarily help the Germans.

This phenomenon must be avoided at any price. In a meeting of the State Committee of Defense, Lavrenty Beria proposed to provoke a Polish uprising against the Germans, so the Home Army would be choked to death and destroyed by them. Later, the Nazi troops, after being bled out as a result of that suppressed Polish national movement, would be weakened in battle and could be easily defeated by the Red Army. By this stratagem the Russians would gain a double success: they would win an easy victory over the Nazis on Polish territory, and they would get rid of the unfriendly Polish Home Army, smashed for them by the Germans.

After the cleansing of the Underground Forces at the hands of Hitler's regiments, and after defeating the Nazi troops on the outskirts of Warsaw, the Red Army, under Marshal Rokossovsky, would enter the Polish capital, playing the role of liberator of Poland. The key posts would be closed off by Berling's regiments, obedient to the Red Commandment, and by the small but always useful Fifth Column of a unit calling itself The People's Army and consisting of Polish Communists organized in Poland, but independent of the underground resistance force, the Home Army.

Beria's plan was accepted by Stalin and responsibility for its realization assigned to the Commissar of Internal Affairs and Chief of State Security, the master of all kinds of provocation. This task was a trifle for Beria. Lavrenty summoned to his office the editors of the two leading Soviet newspapers, *Pravda* and *Izvestia*, and ordered them to draft an appeal to the Underground Resistance Forces in Warsaw, calling upon them to initiate an uprising against the German occupants. The address, promising support from the Russian Forces, after being censored and approved by Lavrenty Beria would be translated into Polish and, at the proper time, broadcast to the Poles by Radio Moscow.

In early July 1944, Rokossovsky's army started its march toward Warsaw and on July 29 of that year Radio Moscow broadcast the official Soviet Appeal, as edited by Beria, urging the Warsaw resistance to begin an armed uprising against the Third Reich. This message was repeated several times.[3]

The next day the Soviet Army under Marshal Rokossovsky appeared on Praga on the right bank of the Vistula River across from Warsaw. Now the Soviet artillery could begin its cannonade, while the Red Air Force could drop bombs on the German garrison in the Polish capital. But nothing like that happened. The Russian forces were silent and inactive. They were waiting until the Polish Underground Army began the uprising that the Soviet Union had promised to support.

In less than forty-eight hours, at six o'clock in the morning of August 1, 1944, the soldiers of the Home Army attacked the Germans. On the roofs of thousands of apartment houses throughout Warsaw, Polish national flags bloomed. Heavy fighting burst out on

---

[3] Appendix 10.

a number of streets, avenues and squares. Some buildings occupied by the Third Reich offices were soon in flames. Nazi tanks appeared on the streets and Luftwaffe planes circled over the city. But the Soviet troops, on the other bank of the river according to the plan of Generalissimo Stalin and Commissar Beria, were still as quiet as if they were not there. Marshal Rokossovsky and his staff, with field glasses at their eyes, observed the fights and sent reports to Moscow. The entire city stood in flames, while the heroically fighting young Polish partisans were killed by the hundreds. Beria's provocation was working perfectly.

The Russians, however, did not anticipate that the resistance of the Poles would be so strong and the fights so bitter. The days and nights passed by and the Underground Resistance Army was still in action, taking German prisoners of war, capturing their equipment and ammunition, shooting down Nazi planes and blowing up German tanks. They still believed that the Red forces under the Pole Rokossovsky, born in Warsaw himself, now with its Kosciusko Division commanded by another Pole, Zygmunt Berling, would come to reinforce them at any moment. But the hope was in vain. The attitude of the Reds resting on the right bank of the Vistula River was entirely opposite to that which was promised by them in their broadcasts, and which was expected.

Radio Moscow, which previously was broadcasting in the Polish language, stopped its appeals, and the Soviet official press agency, TASS, also controlled by Beria, stated definitely that the USSR had nothing in common with the uprising. On August 16, 1944, in his personal telegram to the British Prime Minister Winston Churchill, Stalin declared: "Things being what they are, Soviet Headquarters have decided that they must dissociate themselves from the Warsaw adventure since they cannot assume either direct or indirect responsibility for it."[4]

In the meantime in Poland, many detachments of partisans from other cities and towns, rushing to Warsaw to join their fighting compatriots, were stopped at the right bank of the Vistula River by Rokossovsky's forces, and disarmed by special NKVD units. These Security Police battalions, following Beria's personal order, herded the Poles into railroad box cars destined for concentration camps in Siberia.

---

[4] Dr. Bronislav Kusnierz, *Stalin and the Poles* (London: Hollis and Carter, 1949).

The British Air Forces, as well as the Polish Squadrons stationed in England, and the American, New Zealand and Australian pilots, were eager to fly over Warsaw to fight the Nazis with bombs in Poland, as they had in Germany, or at least to drop by parachute military gear, weapons, ammunition, food, first aid and medical supplies, and some paratroopers. All they needed was the permission of the Commander of the Soviet First Byelorussian Front to make use of the airstrip on the right bank of the Vistula.

But Rokossovsky denied permission, while the Kremlin, to which the request was dispatched from London, answered that the planes of the Western Powers not only would not be allowed to land on the Russian airfield from where they could support the Polish Home Army, but would be forbidden to land even in a case of emergency. The Western Allies also were warned that Soviet anti-aircraft artillery had already received the order to shoot any foreign plane approaching Warsaw. The only help from outside that the Resistance Army received was some supplies dropped by American and British planes that, in defiance of the Soviet threat, managed to fly over the heroic city and some platoons of the Kosciusko Army that at night deserted their unit, swam over the river and joined their countrymen.

The uprising lasted two months. The city, methodically burned down by the Nazis, street by street and building by building, was wholly in ruins. The decimated inhabitants were exhausted to the utmost and half starved to death; the only soldiers of the Home Army who were still alive were the wounded.

When the fire was extinguished, the smoke hanging low, and the Germans gone from the city, the brotherly Slavic Russian Forces crossed the Vistula River over a pontoon bridge and "victoriously" entered the Polish capital.

Soon the Soviet Administration was announced by proclamation of Commissar of the USSR Security, Lavrenty Beria. All members of the former Polish Home Army—soldiers, officers, doctors, nurses, and even little boys and girls who had worked as messengers—were called upon to register themselves at special precincts.

These men and women were to be eligible for rewards and honors for their fight against the Nazis. However, anyone who refused to obey the instruction and hid himself, when caught would be treated as a potential enemy of the legal new rulers.

As a result of this proclamation, thousands of young Polish patriots, went to the precincts and disclosed their names, addresses and ranks in their disbanded army. They were promised good jobs according to their individual abilities, or scholarships to continue their disrupted education.

The next night, in front of the flat of every one of those Poles, there stopped a truck of NKVD troops. They took the arrested person into the trucks and thence to prison. The next step was transport to Siberia. This fate was allotted to the youths who had fought in the ranks as privates, while many of those who were officers and commanders had their homes suddenly entered at night by Beria's NKVD functionaries, and were shot to death in their beds.

42

Marshal of the Soviet Union

THE FATE OF THE NAZIS was sealed. While the Western powers were focused only on finishing the war and nothing else, at the Kremlin the Committee on Defense, with Stalin as its head and Beria as its Vice President, was working systematically on a plan for organizing conquered Europe and the countries grabbed by the Soviet Union.

Under Beria's reign the forced labor camps in Siberia, in Soviet Central Asia, and in many other remote places in the USSR were still the main sources of all Soviet ore and goods production. GULAG—Hard Labor Camps Administration—supervised by State Security General Maltzev, the immediate subordinate of Beria, was responsible for delivering prescribed quotas of timber, coal, fuel and mining ores. The inmates there also built roads and railroad tracks and dug canals. Since living conditions in those camps were deplorable and the climate was killing, the death rate was very high and GULAG continuously asked for more manpower, if the national productivity was not to be decreased. In charge of delivering new quotas of manpower, batches of forcibly working people, was NKVD General Nedosekin, another Beria subordinate.

During the gradual cleaning out of the Nazi occupants from Russian terrain, Beria's Secret Police Forces followed the ranks of the regular Red Army, performing mass arrests of real or suspected

Commissar

German collaborators, traitors, anti-Soviet elements and other persons described as enemies of the people, and sent them to the hard labor compounds.

Some entire Soviet nationalities were herded to the mines, forests and factories to work under the bayonets of the Security Police.

Under the pretext that they had failed to resist the Nazi forces, or had even collaborated with them, Beria did not hesitate to destroy several tribes, following the Kremlin's policy of international power, which was against any separatist patriotic feelings other than the Soviet one.

Surrounded by Beria's NKVD troops armed with machine guns and supported by half-wild bloodhounds, they were deported to the slave camps. The whole populations of Tatars from Crimea, Kuban Cossacks, Chechen and Ingush from Stalin's and Beria's native Caucasus, and Kalmyks, whose whole Republic was liquidated, shared their fate with over 700,000 Balkars, Karachai, Uzbeks, Tadzhiks, Ossetians and Ukrainians, along with thousands of Moldavians, Bessarabians, Rumanians, Latvians and Lithuanians.

Immediately after the Red Army entered Berlin, the Special Unit of the Secret Police, personally led by Beria's deputy, General Merkulov, rushed to fulfill the most important order Beria had issued since becoming Commissar of State Security. It was a top secret task and no one could perform it other than one of his few substitutes. Merkulov, whom Beria had known since their school days in Baku, was a most intelligent and reliable man. The job was really too serious to be neglected; every minute counted. It was one of the reasons Stalin asked President Truman and British Prime Minister Churchill for a friendly favor—to let the Soviet troops be the first to enter Berlin. Through his agents Beria learned that the Americans were going to perform the same trick he had in mind, so the member of the three Allies who was first in Berlin would be the winner.

When the Red Army marched into Berlin and was still kept in order and under arms, and before the Soviet soldiers were allowed to get their first meal and have some rest on the squares of that defeated German capital, the officers of the Selected Unit of Soviet Security Police, furnished with the private addresses of sixteen German civilians, visited them at their homes. Politely, but without allowing any opposition, they asked in fluent German that the tenants follow them out. In front of every house was awaiting a Mercedes-Benz limousine chauffeured by a civilian driver. Soon they were at the airport, where a plane was ready for takeoff. A few hours later they landed at the Sheremetyevo airfield in Moscow. There, four Packards were ready to receive the reluctant guests, who soon found themselves in the lobby of the luxurious Hotel Metropol on magnificent Sverdlov Square.

In the spacious elevator operated by a liveried liftboy, they were taken to the top floor. There, every one of the involuntary visitors was assigned to a comfortable private suite. In every apartment there were shelves with books in original German: poetry by Heinrich Heine, novels by Thomas Mann and Stefan Zweig—the best German poetry and prose that the arrivals could desire, literature unavailable after Hitler came to power and banned these authors, publicly burning their books. In the vases were fresh cut flowers, and nearby on a table stood a bottle of a good German Rhine wine and a box of the best German brand of cigars. A note in German informed the guests that a German-speaking valet or maid would answer their ring. Big windows and a balcony overlooked the spectacular center of Moscow, with its Bolshoi and Academic Maly Theatres.

Soon someone knocked on the door of each suite. It was a good-looking young woman, who inquired in fluent German whether "Herr Professor" would like to go to dinner; if so, she would be happy to lead him to the restaurant.

In a reserved banquet room the guests from Berlin were received by several Russian scientists and a few officials, all high ranking officers. Both the civilians and the military dignitaries wore medals and decorations. The orchestra played Strauss waltzes and tunes from German and Viennese operettas.

A Soviet general greeted the guests in the name of the Great Comrade Stalin, who had won the most horrible war and liberated the German intellectuals from the nightmare of Nazism and that monster, Hitler. From now on the German intelligentsia, the inheritors of the famous culture represented by such geniuses as Marx and Engels, Beethoven and Wagner, Goethe and Schiller, Kant and Hegel and many others, would enjoy their stay on the friendly soil of the Soviet Union where everyone could work freely, according to his vocation, for peace and a wonderful future. Soon the newcomers would be followed by more of their compatriots— colleague scientists and professors. They would receive private vil-

las and chauffeured cars, clothing and books and many other lux-
uries. All free of charge. Their families would be able to join them
and would be brought by plane at the cost of the friendly Russian
Government. Just a word from any one of the guests, and Commissar of Soviet Internal Affairs Lavrenty Pavlovich Beria would
arrange a trip for their dear ones. On the outskirts of Moscow,
newly erected laboratories furnished with the most modern equipment awaited the honorable personalities, who would be encouraged to continue their experiments in atomic energy. Everything
they would need would be at their disposal, and they would be
able to exploit their discoveries as much as they wished. Among the
German scientists honored at that memorable banquet were Professors Max Steenbeck, Gustav Hertz, Fritz Volmer, Manfred von
Ardenne, Karl Bernhardt and Dr. Kurt Mie.

On May 7, 1945, the Third Reich was finally defeated and signed
the act of unconditional surrender at General Eisenhower's Headquarters at Reims. The next day they signed a surrender at General
Zhukov's quarters near Berlin. On the Western Front the Allies
achieved full victory. But for the United States there was still the
war with Japan. The United States tried to make the USSR join the
war against Japan as an ally, but Russia refused with the excuse
that she was bound to Japan by a mutual nonaggression pact. In
truth, however, the Soviet Big Five had decided to push the United
States into an adventuristic war in the Far East. It seemed to the
Kremlin a good chance to institute a new and effective anti-American propaganda drive, which the USSR had had to discontinue
during the war in Europe.

Provocation was the method in which Lavrenty Beria was a
champion. Now Stalin, with his master of plots, Commissar Beria,
was going to use this weapon and provoke Washington to take a
desperate step.

Facing the danger of long and exhausting fights against Japan
before the American soldiers would be able to land in Tokyo after
being decimated by the thousands by the enemy, President Franklin Delano Roosevelt ordered "Operation Manhattan," which meant
using atomic weapons. Later, on August 6, 1945, under Roosevelt's
successor, Harry S Truman, the American B-29 bomber dropped
the first atomic bomb on Hiroshima; and three days after, another
atomic bomb was dropped on Nagasaki. Japan capitulated.

The same day, August 9, 1945, the USSR *at last* declared war against Japan, to be cleared of any suspicion of intrigue.

The provocation worked perfectly. Later, the former American Ambassador to Russia, William Averell Harriman, announced that:

On the strong recommendation of our Chiefs of Staff every effort was made to get Russia to come into the war against Japan. The quick and complete collapse of Japan took everyone by surprise because we thought the American armies would be forced to land on the plains of Tokyo. Post-war revelations proved that Japan sought out Russian help about six months prior to the end of the war, pleading with Russia to act as a peace intermediary.[1]

The war was over. At the Potsdam Peace Conference, which met July 17, 1945, rumors about Beria ran through the corps of Western representatives. Stalin, head of the Soviet delegation, was accompanied by Molotov, while Chief of State Security Lavrenty Pavlovich Beria did not appear, although he was expected by some Americans and Britishers. The bodyguard of the Soviet Leader was the same NKVD Colonel General Sergey Nikolayevich Kruglov, who was already known to the Allies since he had previously chaperoned the Great Boss at the Conferences in Teheran and Yalta in 1943, and had escorted Molotov on his trips to London and Washington in the spring of 1942, as well as in April 1945 to San Francisco at the Conference of the Representatives of Fifty Countries when the United Nations Organization was established. General Kruglov was a popular character with the Western dignitaries. This bodyguard of Stalin's resembled the image of the symbolic Russian bear, as drawn by a sharp-eyed cartoonist.

Sergey Kruglov stood six-feet three-inches and weighed about 250 pounds. Each of his palms was like a big steak. He was round-faced and was always in a good humor. He smoked one cigarette after another, which he used to bite, spitting out flakes of tobacco from both sides of his mouth. When he was not smoking, he eagerly chewed gum, which he begged from every American he met. He always had a number of packages of chewing gum in the pockets of his military tunic. He did not know how to chew it properly and swallowed the gum as if it were candy. At any gala dinner, Kruglov consumed plenty of food and a lot of vodka and drank innumerable

---

[1] Union Calendar No. 792, 82nd Congress 2nd Session House Report No. 2505 (Washington: United States Government Printing Office, 1952).

glasses of tea so boiling hot that civilized Western people would find it impossible to touch. He roared with laughter, often without any reason, and then his big stomach shook as if he were a male belly dancer.

He seemed very amusing. At the Potsdam Conference, President Truman liked him so much that, besides several cartons of American cigarettes and boxes of chewing gum, he gave that harmless Russian house pet his autographed picture and even decorated the Soviet cop with the American Legion of Merit. At the same conference in Potsdam Kruglov was also decorated with the title of Honorary Knight of the British Empire despite the fact that he had been an executioner of the SMERSH Agency and previously, during the purges, he personally had shot to death many high ranking Red Army officers.

However, the Western delegates were curious to see Lavrenty Beria who, as Commissar of Soviet Security, they had expected to meet in the role of Stalin's personal bodyguard. They did not take into consideration the possibility that Beria preferred to stay in the shadows, at least until he could step into Stalin's shoes, or the fact that he was by no means a mere policeman, but a clever politician and statesman. Beria had kept under his reign all the vital branches of the Soviet Union and had a power practically equal to that of the Great Dictator Joseph Stalin.

As the People's Commissar of Internal Affairs, Beria was a member of the Cabinet; as Commissar of State Security, he was the Supreme Commander of his own NKVD army of over 1,500,000 officers and soldiers. His troops consisted of divisions with infantry, cavalry, motor corps, artillery, tanks and an air force. His men were equipped with the most modern weapons, their uniforms were from the finest fabrics, and they received the best provisions and many other privileges. With these troops Beria kept in line all the countries, nationalities and tribes in the orbit of the Soviet Union, as well as the Red Army, Navy and Air Force. As Chief of the Militia, which in the USSR is the equivalent of the police, Beria controlled every individual in Russia and the lives of the whole civilian population, members of the Communist Party included.

As Chief of Intelligence, Counterintelligence and the Espionage Department, Lavrenty Beria supervised the entire Soviet diplomacy, ambassadors included. Since all members of the Soviet foreign service in embassies, chambers of commerce, consulates, and the United Nations had in addition to their regular posts some specific espionage duties and had to be graduated from a special academy for secret agents, Beria nominated, or at least approved, each of them.

As Chief Censor, Beria was at the helm of all the press, radio, theatre and film industries, book publishing, and controlled the entire communications system: telegraph, telephone and postal service, all of which were under constant surveillance inside the country and from and to abroad. Beria was also Chief Supervisor of religion, suppressing churches and clergymen as so-called nests and distributors of opium for the masses, a superstition fought mercilessly by Marx.

As Chief of the system of so-called correction camps of hard labor that supplied the Soviet Union with all kinds of goods, especially timber, coal, iron, steel, asbestos, platinum, gold, silver and oil, Beria controlled the main branches of USSR industry and the economic life of the country. As the Head of GULAG, the administration of the forced labor camp system, which continuously demanded more manpower and new condemned people, Beria controlled the courts, the judges, the prosecutors, the lawyers, and in fact, the whole judiciary apparatus.

As Head of the transport of those hundreds of thousands of deportees to their destination by trains and boats, as well as their transfer from one camp to another, and as designer of plans for new railroad tracks and canals to be built by the prisoners, Beria, in practice, was Chief of Transportation, Communications and Road Construction.

As Head of propaganda Lavrenty Beria ruled the Communist parties in foreign countries, primarily the United States, Great Britain, France and Italy. He also controlled all kinds of international meetings, the Red Front formations, and directly or indirectly, many foreign leftist organizations of writers, pacifists, intellectuals, students, workers and housewives, as well as some militants, Fascists, racists, right-wing parties, and factions that by fighting or demonstrating in their own countries against their own governments, or for their own ideals, caused disturbances and violence that weakened the strength of those nations and made them morally and physically less resistant to any pressure from outside.

As a controller of vast lands in Siberia and other uninhabited parts of the country used only as concentration camp sites, Beria was also supervisor of all atomic research projects, of uranium mines, territories for atomic bomb tests, and was the Chief of the Special Intelligence Service for Atomic Energy.

As Chief of SMERSH—Death to Spies and Diversionists—which he himself had organized, Beria controlled the whole Red Army, Navy and Air Force. This unit, directly under Beria's aide-de-camp, Victor Abakumov, was less interested in spies in the literal meaning of that word than it was in suppressing any sign of opposition and also any free thought in the Red Forces. The activities of SMERSH were not discontinued even after the war was over. Among the victims of SMERSH, which annihilated or sent to concentration camps thousands of Russian officers, real heroes and patriots, was Alexander Solzhenitsyn, a university graduate, who during the war was commander of a battery, took part in combat against the Nazi army, and had been awarded the Order of the War of the Fatherland and the Order of the Red Star. As a result of reports from some informants, Solzhenitsyn was arrested by SMERSH, accused of violating Article 58 of the Criminal Code, and as an enemy of the people, was court-martialed and on July 7, 1945, sentenced to a hard labor camp for eight years.

After serving his term and being released from confinement, Solzhenitsyn, a great writer, awarded the Nobel Prize in 1970, published his autobiographical novel *One Day in the Life of Ivan Denisovich.* Only in 1957, four years after Beria's death, did the USSR Supreme Court decide to rescind the condemning sentence, announcing that his accusation was entirely groundless.[2]

Beria's agents abroad were also very efficient. In 1945, just after the war ended, U.S. Colonel John H. Van Vliet, Jr. was liberated from a prisoner of war camp in Germany; he went immediately to Washington. At the Pentagon, Colonel Van Vliet reported to Major General Clayton Bissell, Army Assistant Chief of Staff in charge of U.S. Army Intelligence. Colonel Van Vliet had much to testify to. As a German prisoner of war he was forced to witness the exhumation the Germans performed at Katyn Forest. At first Colonel Van Vliet was convinced that the massacre of thousands of Polish officers and enlisted men was committed by the Germans, but after

---

[2] Appendix 11 is the original text of the USSR Supreme Court decision rescinding the sentence against Alexander Solzhenitsyn.

thoroughly examining the evidence at the place of execution he changed his mind and became positive that the mass murder was done by the Russians. Supplied with documentary photographs, Colonel Van Vliet described his observations to General Bissell, who immediately labeled the report TOP SECRET. This report was prepared in a single, original longhand copy without duplicates, and locked in the Pentagon's strongbox.

The only eyewitness to the shooting and killing of the Polish prisoners by Beria's troops was a Russian peasant, Ivan Krivosertsov, who escaped to the West. He also reported his experience to the Allies, and later emigrated to Great Britain where he lived under the name of Michael Loboda and worked in a small town near London. The evidence of the two men, Colonel John Van Vliet in Washington and Ivan Krivosertsov before the British authorities, was too critical of the Soviet Union to be ignored by Lavrenty Beria. These reports, if preserved in the West, sooner or later could be used against the USSR. Beria decided that the documents must be destroyed promptly, as was the duty of the Commissar of State Security.

Soon it was revealed in Washington that Colonel Van Vliet's TOP SECRET report was missing from the files of the Pentagon, and since it was a single manuscript without copies, it was lost forever. The Russian peasant, Ivan Krivosertsov, who lived in England, was simply found dead one morning, hanged in the dilapidated workshop of an old deserted orchard.

The circumstances of the theft of the TOP SECRET document in the capital of the United States, as well as the mysterious death of Krivosertsov near the capital of Great Britain, were never disclosed.

For all these and other activities of the far-reaching and efficient agents performing their job abroad under Beria's orders, as well as for his exemplary performance for the Country and its Leader, the Great Comrade Stalin, the Chief of Soviet Security and of the People's Commissariat of Internal Affairs, Lavrenty Pavlovich Beria, was elevated to the military rank of Marshal of the Soviet Union.

After establishing closer relations with the West and with British and French statesmen, Prime Ministers and Ministers, the titles of the Soviet Commissars sounded rude and primitive to Stalin. Having this in mind, the Dictator decided to rename his Commissariats

Ministries, and their chief Commissars, to become Ministers. In March 1946, after this change was proclaimed, Commissar Marshal Beria, besides becoming Head of the Ministry of Internal Affairs and of the Ministry of State Security, was also nominated Vice Chairman of the Board of Ministers of the USSR.

43

Friendly Planes

THE PROCEEDING ACTION in several areas in foreign countries did not divert Beria's attention from domestic affairs in his own country. Beria realized that after every war there is a reaction against bloodshed and atrocities. There are voices calling for peace on earth forever and for the brotherhood of all nations. But such a trend was not in keeping with the Soviet Union line which, according to the text of her anthem, the *Internationale*, beginning with the words "It will be the last battle," remains at war with the capitalist world until Communism conquers the whole globe. Until that final moment the Communist revolution is still on, and the Soviet Union should be prepared and alert. There was no time for any songs of doves and peacemakers, or for fraternization with Americans and Britishers that would soften the hearts of the Russian fighters and weaken their will for the victory of Communism in the world.

Since feelings of peace and brotherhood are usually expressed primarily by poets and novelists, Lavrenty Beria once again turned his eyes toward the Russian literary world. Among the victims of a new wave of repression against Russian men of letters were Anna Akhmatova and Mikhail Zoshchenko. Akhmatova was the leading Russian poetess whose verses were filled with love and lyricism expressed in a uniquely mystical way. The first collection of her poems, which she published even before the Revolution, brought

331

her instant fame. From that time on, Akhmatova published several volumes of poetry. She stopped writing for some years, after her husband, also a poet, was arrested and executed for supposedly expressing anti-Soviet ideas and her son was sent to a hard labor camp in Siberia. Later she returned to her poetry, in which she found her only consolation. In 1946 Beria ordered the editors of *Pravda* and *Izvestia* to initiate a campaign against Akhmatova. Soon, both of these newspapers, as well as some literary magazines, published several articles in which Akhmatova was severely criticized for the lack of ideological content in her poems. This outcry signaled her downfall. In the middle of the night Anna Akhmatova was arrested and brought to Lubyanko Prison. Beria demanded from Soviet poetry that it be strong and stirring, so as to cause the blood to boil, or that it hail Communist heroism and its will and power, but did not praise friendship, love and forgiveness or express any romanticism or lyricism. Lavrenty realized, however, that if Akhmatova, the idol of students and of the whole young Soviet generation were executed, he, Beria, would be thought of as a brutal beast and an ignorant savage who had devastated a most wonderful Russian soul. But if he saved Akhmatova's life, he would be praised as an understanding and good statesman.

After a night in detention, the 58-year-old woman was called from her cell to Lavrenty's office, where Marshal Beria personally told her that in spite of her crime of writing verses that were not Soviet-minded, her life would be spared. She would be allowed to go home, but must write no more nonsense.

Another prominent writer also arrested at that time was the internationally famous short story teller, Mikhail Zoshchenko. He was an outstanding satirist, who by his vignettes made his readers laugh until they cried. Although he satirized every sign of bureaucracy and the laziness of some workers—in other words, the shortcomings branded by the State—he had too critical a mind to be trusted for long. Besides, it was not good to make people laugh and be excessively merry. Such a good mood would make them tolerant of many other aspects of life, and tolerance is a kind of indifference wrong for the Soviet Union. Especially in Zoshchenko's later works one could notice that the author, from his former fervent enthusiasm for the achievements of the new order, was revealing some sense of doubt and pessimism. After a short campaign against Zoshchenko in the press, his books and phonograph records with recitations of his humorous stories were confiscated in all shops in the USSR and destroyed. Finally, Zoshchenko and Akhmatova were expelled from the All-Russian Writers' Union. This decision, taken by the board of that association on Beria's demand, was equal to their civil death, because being removed from the Writers' Union, they were unable to publish their works anywhere in the USSR.

Beria's policy against the literary world also had another aim besides persecuting independent minds. Lavrenty wanted to please Andrey Zhdanov, an eminent member of the Politburo and a powerful personality. Before the end of the Second World War Zhdanov, an Old Guard Bolshevik, had been engaged in a personal struggle with Malenkov for second-in-command status, and had recently achieved his victory. As a result of that friction, Malenkov lost his post as Secretary of the Central Committee of the Party. Beria hated Malenkov—that puffy double-chinned eunuch. Malenkov, three years younger than Lavrenty, had become Stalin's protégé—in Beria's opinion, hell knew why—a long time before Stalin noticed Beria, who had to spend all his effort, wit and energy to advance his career.

Besides being such a great figure in the Soviet hierarchy, Zhdanov was a personal friend of Stalin, and being much younger than the Dictator, was apparently intended as Stalin's heir. It was commonly known that Zhdanov's son, Yuri, had always liked Stalin's daughter, Svetlana, his childhood playmate. Now, since Svetlana had married Grigory Morozov, who happened to be a Jew, it was evident that because of Stalin's blind anti-Semitism this marriage would sooner or later be dissolved and Yuri Zhdanov would have every chance to become Stalin's son-in-law. All these factors proved that it would be wise for Beria to please Andrey Zhdanov until the right time to destroy him arrived in Lavrenty's pursuit to the highest power. The best way to please Zhdanov was to lay a strong hand on the literary and artistic circles. Zhdanov, a political leader very close to Stalin, became the Politburo and Party spokesman in all fields of the arts. He demanded from all writers and artists a decisive use of their talents for pro-Communist education and anti-Western propaganda. Everyone who failed to answer to that appeal, even including some of Stalin's former award winners, had to confess his faults and correct his line of creativity if he did not want to land in Siberia. The new regime was so harsh that it did not exclude sculptors or even composers. The famous sculptor,

Eduard Neizvestny, known for his abstract work, was accused of being "a formalist" and had to admit his deviation and promise to mend his ways after his one-man show was closed by the authorities on its opening day. Some composers also had to confess their faults, such as Aram Khachaturyan, the famous Armenian creator of *Danse Suite*, Stalin prize winner. Now Khachaturyan had to admit that his music was bourgeois, "formalistic," and did not serve the Soviet people properly; although it is hard to imagine how to determine whether music is bourgeois or not. The internationally known composer, Dmitry Shostakovich, creator of several symphonies, piano concertos and operas, experienced an even harsher time. Some years before, one of his operas had been condemned by the reviewer of the official newspaper, *Pravda,* and the critique appeared in an editorial entitled "Confusion Instead of Music." Later, his ballet suite, *Limpid Stream,* was condemned by Zhdanov as anti-Soviet and soon was suppressed by the Soviet Administration for being more sensational than Socialist. Only fear of the reaction of the whole free world and of protests by Shostakovich's personal friends, Arturo Toscanini and Leopold Stokowski, who used to conduct his works, stopped Beria from imprisoning Shostakovich. However, his music was banned in the whole USSR Imperium.

But merely pleasing Zhdanov, who was expected to be Stalin's eventual heir, was beneath the level of Marshal Beria. Lavrenty had much higher ambitions. He decided to use the setback Malenkov had recently suffered from Zhdanov as a chance for himself. For several years there had been a race between Malenkov and Beria to the Politburo—Political Bureau of the Central Committee of the Communist Party. It was the main goal of each of their careers. From 1939 on, Beria was a candidate member; Malenkov became a deputy member two years later. Zhdanov's attack on Malenkov could be a good opportunity for Beria. But Lavrenty realized that his success would not come easily, because Stalin still liked Malenkov very much and would not lend his ear to any intrigue against him. Beria was smart enough to understand that Malenkov's education as a technical engineer and his devotion as a dedicated fighter of all anti-Stalin oppositionists, and Beria's education as an architectural engineer and his achievements as Commissar of State Security, was playing them against each other to keep them in balance, so neither would outgain his opponent. The only way to win Stalin's favor when Malenkov received his setback by

Zhdanov, was to do something that would make Stalin seem even greater than he appeared to be after winning the Second World War.

Beria dug into his arsenal of old tricks, which years before had helped him in his career in Tiflis to become master of life and death in Georgia, and later in the whole of the Caucasus. When, after collecting, or rather, inventing, Stalin's heroic deeds and publications, Beria created a new Soviet history which he revealed in his memorable speech, *Stalin's Early Writings and Activities: On the History of the Bolshevik Organizations in Transcaucasia.*

Besides his duties as Vice Chairman of the Board of Ministers and his routine office work, usually done at night, Beria still found time to reread his work *On the History of the Bolshevik Organizations in Transcaucasia,* which was going to be sent to the typesetter for a new edition. Lavrenty did not intend to issue just another consecutive printing of that volume, which for several years had been designated for use as a textbook in the schools. It had to be delivered to the coming generation of Soviet high school students as a revised and enlarged edition, in which the October Revolution appeared to be successful thanks entirely to the achievement of Stalin, the Great Leader of the country. In the new volume Stalin's role was emphasized even more than in those previous editions.

While working on his latest editorial revisions, Beria discovered that he could still find some paragraphs to be improved from the angle of building up the Soviet Dictator.

In the chapters dealing with the early revolutionary movement in the first decade of this century, where originally Beria had mentioned the texts of some underground leaflets and brochures distributed secretly among the workers in the Caucasus, he now announced for the first time that the contents of those publications were prepared and written by Stalin personally, solely and entirely. Also, many other descriptions were now enriched by the name of Stalin as the Initiator, Author and Leader. The new enlarged edition, with a "Chronology of Comrade Stalin's Arrests, Exiles and Escapes," was to be illustrated with a front-page photograph of the Great Comrade Joseph Stalin and a small reproduction of a pencil drawing of Lavrenty Beria. Needless to say, both of those portraits were retouched and beautified to look much younger and more handsome than their models.

Boumagha vsyo teerpet—The paper is patient—as the old Russian adage says, which means that the blank sheets of paper wait for and accept everything written or printed on them. Beria therefore was able to complete and update his essay delivered originally in 1935. He altered several pages by praising some new deeds the Great Comrade Stalin had supposedly effected. Even achievements performed by Beria himself the author preferred to ascribe to his Big Boss. All the Old Guard Bolsheviks who had published their own memoirs describing their efforts and successes had been liquidated. Commissar of State Security Lavrenty Pavlovich Beria knew it well, because he, and no other, had sentenced most of those men to death *in camera* and, directly or indirectly, was responsible for their execution by a bullet in the back of their skulls in a prison basement. It was much wiser to stay in the background, to give all credit to the Chief, to please him, and thus, to outlive him. This material, as well as some from other sources about Stalin's activities that Beria had gathered—or rather falsified and fabricated during his research but did not include in his book—he completed meticulously and delivered to his Superior. When presenting these well-prepared documents, Lavrenty asked his Chief to publish them as the first two volumes of *Stalin's Collected Works* so they would not be lost to posterity.

Beria had already made such a suggestion to the Boss just after the Moscow newspaper, *Pravda*, of July-August 1935 printed in installments the text of Beria's lecture, *On the History of the Bolshevik Organizations in Transcaucasia*, which had been delivered in Tiflis a few days before. This essay, more invention than fact, pleased Stalin so much that it speeded Beria's promotion. Later, Lavrenty repeated his suggestion when his life was threatened by Yezhov. At that time Beria was eager to give away to his principal all his data for use in the future edition of Stalin's *Collected Works*. The material was almost ready for printing, and the farseeing and faithful Lavrenty Pavlovich had even supplied the title for his elaborate history of the Transcaucasian Bolshevik Organizations: *Stalin's Early Writings and Activities*. The Leader therefore had every right to use that work as his own. Beria proved once more that he was nothing but a mere Stalin worshiper and servant. However, Stalin hesitated to take advantage of the manuscript and the project had to be postponed for the time being. The main reason was that, at that time there were still too many people alive who were either the real authors of the brochures and leaflets Beria mentioned as being written by Stalin, or were at least witnesses to the events, and remembered the true mediocrity of his role before the Revolution. Under such circumstances, even a whispered criticism of his *Collected Works* would undermine the prestige of the Dictator. First, all those embarrassing individuals had to be wiped off the surface of the earth. Simultaneously, all their writings had to be withdrawn from the libraries and from circulation. Also, the citizens in the whole Soviet Empire must be required to take their own copies of those books to the nearest precinct of the militia to be destroyed. And the appropriate parts of the *Great Soviet Encyclopedia* and the previous editions of *History of the Communist Party of the Soviet Union (Bolsheviks)* had to be changed. With Stalin's permission and encouragement, Beria was glad to take in hand the task of exterminating the old activists and many of their supporters. The burden of rewriting the *Great Encyclopedia* and *The History of the Party* was given to a group of obedient scholars who were to submit their work to Beria for censorship and approval after all the inconvenient names of the Old Bolsheviks were either stricken out, ignored, or presented as anti-Soviet or simply "enemies of the people." Under Beria's surveillance, *History of the Communist Party of the Soviet Union (Bolsheviks)*, edited in 1939, did not mention the deeds of Leon Trotsky, despite the fact that after the October Revolution Trotsky became Commissar of Foreign Affairs and his popularity was second only to Lenin's; that later from 1918 to 1925 he was People's Commissar of War, the organizer and Commander in Chief of the Red Army; and that until October 23, 1926, he was an outstanding member of the Politburo. All that edition says about him is that "Trotsky attempted to deflect the Party from the path of Socialist Revolution." But if searching for the merits that caused Trotsky to become a member of the Party and to attract so many followers, the reader of the edition of the official *History of the Communist Party of the Soviet Union (Bolsheviks)* would fail to find any trace.

In 1943 Lavrenty had suggested to Stalin that he publish his *Collected Works*. But the Boss did not then accept the idea. He realized that the materials were too poor, too doubtful and too insignificant to be sufficient, and that they were not representative enough for the Ruler of the Soviet Union. But now, in 1946, after the Second World War, before its outbreak and during it, when Stalin made so many speeches and announcements, the time was right in Beria's opinion for publishing. Stalin's early writings preceding the Revolutionary struggles, his speeches, leaflets and articles, real, or concocted by Lavrenty, would be only a prelude to the Leader's later pronouncements. This time Stalin accepted the notion.

For several months, in addition to his regular duties in his office at Lubyanka Prison, Beria checked the material that he had painstakingly gathered, clipping Stalin's every utterance printed in the press, as well as making copies of all of Stalin's messages, telegrams and letters to which he had access in the archives. At last he brought to his Superior a huge typescript consisting of over one thousand pages. In a few weeks the material, checked and approved by the Dictator, was sent to the printing office to be published on November 2, 1946, when the first volume of Joseph Stalin's *Collected Works* should be released.

His cunning move worked well: shortly Marshal Lavrenty Pavlovich Beria became a full member of the ruling Politburo.

Together with his new elevation to membership in the Politburo, Beria was appointed Chief of Atomic Energy Development. This post was given to him as the man responsible for top secret projects, and as Chief of Intelligence, who planted spies in the United States, Great Britain and France to steal confidential atomic research information, and lured liberal and left-oriented scientists in those Western countries to escape to the USSR, or at least to cooperate with them. In his new role, Beria reorganized the Atomic Energy Program, attaching it to the seldom mentioned and less important Ministry of Medium Machine Building in order to avoid recognition. He nominated as heads of this department his immediate subordinates—two high ranking Secret Police officers, NKVD General A. P. Zavenagin, and NKVD General Boris Vannikov—and also Vassily Yemelyanov, Chief of the State Committee. While the latter directed the laboratories, Security General Zavenagin controlled the whole Ministry of Medium Machine Building, and General Vannikov became the supervisor of installations concerned with weapons production and other war operations. A military drill which Beria introduced there made of those areas a kind of concentration camp, although the scientists had most comfortable homes and the best conditions for their work and relaxation.

The new regime, however, demanded their utmost efficiency, since Marshal Beria wished to obtain the explosive device as soon as possible. For all these achievements Lavrenty Pavlovich Beria was decorated with the Medal for Labor Merit.

Among the Air Forces attached to the NKVD Army of State Security, Beria had some squadrons of British Wellington bombers and Spitfire fighters, and American Dakota bombers. These planes were given to the USSR by the Western Allies in 1943 in the lend-lease program. Hundreds of these aircraft had been shipped to Iran, where on the outskirts of Teheran they were repainted. After the Red Soviet Star was substituted under their wings for the British Royal Air Force and the U.S. insignia, they were delivered to Russian pilots, who flew them to the Soviet Union. Some of those planes Beria spared for his State Security Air Forces, to be used for intelligence service duties.

Soon Beria decided to make use of a few of these aircraft in a very delicate mission. Their destination was Yugoslavia and their aim was to establish Josip Broz Tito in his position as Dictator in Yugoslavia and a puppet of the Kremlin. Tito, the leader of the Yugoslav Communist Party, obeyed everything he was ordered by Moscow. During the time Stalin was Hitler's ally, the leader of the illegal Yugoslav Community Party, Josip Broz Tito, was Hitler's ally too. Later, after the Nazis attacked the USSR and the Luftwaffe bombed Yugoslav Communist headquarters, Tito escaped to Italy, and from there went to the Soviet Union, where he stayed until the Red Army under Marshal Fyodor Tolbukhin, entered the Balkans.

In the meantime, the Yugoslav Patriotic Underground Army of so-called *Chetniks*[1] General Draza Mikhailovich, fought the German occupants. They attacked German garrisons and Nazi troops, demolished bridges and railroad tracks, destroyed German tanks with hand grenades and blew up German transports, supplies and ammunition. When the Russians approached Yugoslavia they captured thousands of these resistance units. Beria immediately sent his Security Police who, with the assistance of Tito's Communist troops, executed the national Yugoslav officers, while the captured soldiers were deported to hard labor camps in Siberia. Finally, General Mikhailovich, with his staff and some of his men, withdrew to the mountains, where they hid themselves in caves. Getting

[1] Ex-soldiers and peasant volunteers in the Yugoslav National Guerrilla.

them out of there became a new priority task for Commissar of
Soviet Internal Affairs Lavrenty Beria. It had to be done intelli-
gently and concisely, without a mistake. The plot Beria invented
was really a devilish one.

First, Beria had to discover where the Yugoslav heroes were
located. The reconnaisance of his regular Russian planes was unsuccessful. The caves in the mountains were numerous, and probably many of them were used as hideouts.

Beria decided to put into action his squadrons of British Well-
ingtons and American Dakotas. He ordered them to cover the Soviet star under the wings so the planes would appear to be flown
either by British or American pilots, but would be unidentifiable as
evidently English or American. The Commissar cunningly realized
that such an obvious act as he planned, if done by any of the
supposed Western Allies, would look too suspicious to work successfully. It was much better strategy to render the planes' identity
impossible to pinpoint, except as of either English or American
origin.

It was in the last week of February 1946 when these aircraft first
appeared over the mountains in the vicinity of the caverns where
Colonel Mikhailovich, with his staff officers and several men, were
thought to be hidden. At exactly high noon the unidentified, but
surely Western and undoubtedly friendly, planes began circling
over a nearby plain, where they dropped some parcels by parachute. Soon after they flew away the Yugoslav patriots went out to
examine the unexpected transport. They found invaluable supplies:
American canned food and cigarettes, Scotch whisky, medicines
and first-aid supplies from the Swiss Red Cross and British rifles,
guns and ammunition. The war was over but the Yugoslav patriots
needed weapons for their self-defense against the Communists.

Three days later the same planes once more appeared, and at
noon in the same place over the plain, they dropped more supplies.

These wonderful lifesaving visits were repeated every two days.
At last, on March 13, 1946, when General Mikhailovich and his
officers heard the roar of the friendly approaching planes, they
emerged from their caves, and standing in front of their hideouts
waved a greeting expressing their appreciation and gratitude.

This time supplies were again bestowed by parachute. When the
men ran out to take them from the middle of the plain, the planes

dipped down and spread a stream of sleeping gas. Several fliers parachuted out; they were paratroopers from the Combined Operation Unit of the NKVD Soviet Security Forces. They bound the gassed men's hands behind their backs and laid them on the ground in a row. The whole operation took only a few minutes.

After leaving some guards to watch the captives, the commander of that operation and his aides went down to the nearest village to bring mules and carts to transport the still unconscious prisoners.

This plot, worked out by Lavrenty Beria, was unknown to the free world until April 18, 1946, when the Italian newspaper, *Il Giornale della Sera*, in Rome announced that, on March 13, after an unexpected air-ground attack during which a poison gas was used, General Draza Mikhailovich and his eleven followers were captured. They were all that remained of his force of several thousand men.

On July 15, 1946, in Belgrade, the trial opened against the captured twelve leaders of the Yugoslav Patriotic Underground Army. On the second day of the hearing, General Draza Mikhailovich said in his last words, "I wanted much, I started much. But the wind of the world carried me and my work away." The fate of the defendants was sealed.

By Tito's order, all the captured men were sentenced to death. There was no appeal, and the executions were performed the next morning, July 17, 1946.[2]

Lavrenty Beria was a real master at setting traps.

---

[2] The *Great Universal Encyclopedia* published in 1966 in Warsaw, Poland, under the Communist regime describes Mikhailovich as follows: "Mikhailovich Draza born 27 of June 1893, died 17 July 1946. General, a Yugoslavic Monarchist. Before World War II among other posts he was in diplomatic service (Bulgaria and Czechoslovakia). After the German occupation of Yugoslavia in 1941, Mikhailovich became the organizer and leader of the Underground Army "Chetniks" fighting against the occupants as well as against the partisans led by Communists. Mikhailovich was the Minister of War in the Yugsolavian Cabinet in Exile; after the war he was arrested, condemned and executed by the sentence of the People's Court." (*Great Polish Universal Encyclopedia*, Volume 7, Warsaw, 1966.)

44

Happy Anniversary

THERE WAS A GREAT TASK assigned to Marshal Lavrenty Pavlovich Beria, Minister of Security of State of the USSR, by his Superior, Joseph Stalin. The assignment, which was of fundamental value for the Soviet Imperium, was to hold Czechoslovakia in the Soviet bloc.

Czechoslovakia, with her highly developed heavy industry, especially of automobiles, machines, weapons and tools, was of great importance to the USSR. However, that small West European country, which during the Second World War suffered so much under German occupation, never had any tendency to link with Communism. A few weeks before the end of the war, when the American Forces were liberating Europe, General Eisenhower sent some of General Patton's troops to reinforce the Czechoslovak Underground Army, igniting a national uprising against the Nazi suppressors. Indeed, on May 6, 1945, several American tanks appeared in the suburbs of Prague and a message was wired from General Patton's Headquarters that his armored units were prepared to enter Prague the next day. The whole Czechoslovakian nation was full of enthusiasm. Thousands of women were waiting to welcome the Americans with flowers. However, Eisenhower's decision to liberate Prague caused an instant protest to Washington by Stalin. As a result, President Truman ordered Patton's troops to halt. This prolonged the Czech uprising for two days and resulted in the killing and wounding of thousands of Czech patriots fighting against the Nazis. At last, on May 9, the Red Army, instead of the Americans, entered the Czechoslovakian capital, exchanging the Nazi occupation for a Soviet one.

After the regular Russian troops, Beria's NKVD Secret Police followed; a wave of arrests and deportations of the valiant soldiers and officers of the Czech Resistance began.

From that time on the peace in Czechoslovakia was maintained by the bayonets of the Russians. Although in 1946 the Kremlin planted its puppet Prime Minister, Klement Gottwald, in Prague, it was hard to subdue that small but brave nation, which was still run by President Eduard Benes, a great Czech patriot. His government consisted of several members truly devoted to their country. Among them was the Minister of Foreign Affairs, Jan Masaryk, a brilliant statesman and a son of Thomas Masaryk, one of the greatest Czech statesmen and patriots. Jan, who held the entire Czechoslovak population's highest esteem during the Second World War, was living in London, where he was active as a prominent personality in the Free Czech Government in Exile. After the war he returned to his fatherland, where he became Minister of Foreign Affairs.

From his agents Beria had information that Jan Masaryk was going to prepare a movement aimed at breaking with the Soviet Union and with the bloc of the Communist countries, and joining the Free Western world to which Czechoslovakia, by her culture and civilization, had always belonged. The apartment that Masaryk occupied in the building of his Ministry was bugged and his conversations were taped by Beria's Secret Police. Being aware of this, Masaryk either talked with his aides in the garden, or exchanged ideas in his office by writing short notes, which were burned immediately.

In spite of all those precautions, Beria learned that Masaryk planned to escape to London where he would organize a new anti-Communist bloc and launch a broad attack against Soviet influence in the West. As a diplomat who for several years before the war had been an envoy to England, Jan Masaryk, with his fluent English and French, was highly respected by the British, American and French authorities, and could be harmful to the politics of Soviet expansion in the West.

Beria determined to prevent Masaryk's trip to England by any means, although this was not easy, since the Minister of Czech Foreign Affairs could leave his country any time under the pretext of going to an international conference.

To imprison Masaryk would not be a wise step; it would create a bad reaction in the Western world and would anger the whole Czechoslovak nation, making the people even more stubborn and hostile than before.

On March 9, 1948, Jan Masaryk visited President Benes at his residence; they had a short, quiet talk during which Masaryk whispered his plan to fly to London the next day.

However, either the microphones hidden by the Soviet agents in the walls of the President's home were supersensitive, or someone from the President's household worked on Beria's payroll, because that news was cabled immediately to the Commissar of State Security in Moscow. Beria decided not to waste any more time, especially since Masaryk's death would not only liquidate that troublesome man once and for all, but also would break the morale of his whole obstinate nation.

That very night, when Masaryk was in his lonely study on the top floor of the Czernin Palace, the residence of the Ministry of Czech Foreign Affairs, the sentry at the main gate was removed suddenly and the apartment of the diplomat was entered by a couple of NKVD executioners, called in Soviet slang, "Beria's gorillas."

In the quiet, empty palace there began a life-and-death struggle. Jan Masaryk was a tall, heavy, strong man, and to overcome him was not easy. It was complicated by the fact that the murderers had been ordered to simulate suicide. During the long and exhausting fight the assassins dragged Masaryk to the bathroom, put him in the bathtub, and started to suffocate him with two pillows. Then, when he was unconscious they pushed him out the window overlooking the palace yard.

The next morning, March 10, 1948, the Soviet Security-controlled Radio Prague announced the death of Jan Masaryk by suicide. Nobody in the country believed the self-killing. This notion of the Czechs was confirmed shortly by a new wave of arrests of dozens of people who had been close to the late diplomat, as well as of some officials, who according to their duties, had to examine the corpse at the scene of the accident. Ten of these prisoners were executed—shot without trial—while several of the rest were tortured to death in jail or died soon after being released; blind obedience in the country was soon restored.

Marshal Beria proved once more that he was irreplaceable in that kind of job and that no one else would be able to keep the subdued countries in the Soviet bloc in line as he could.

Lavrenty realized his great value to the USSR Imperium; not only for his own high ambition but also for the sake of his country, he saw himself as the only rightful inheritor of Stalin's power.

Beria could not stand the friendship and favoritism that the Great Leader bestowed on the crude and narrow-minded Zhdanov. For a long time Lavrenty had been working to undermine gradually Stalin's confidence in the man whom the Dictator had nominated Chief of the Leningrad Party Organization after the murder of Kirov. Zhdanov had been a Party member since 1913, a member of the Central Committee since 1930 and later a member of the Politburo as well; he also belonged to the victorious Military Board of the Leningrad Front during the Second World War. Zhdanov had defeated Malenkov in a personal struggle for power and influence, was the tamer of the "Cosmopolitans," a fanatic "anti-Western" militant, and was still second in command to Stalin. As long as this powerful individual existed he was Lavrenty's mortal enemy, and had to be annihilated.

It took Beria almost six months of cunning and diplomatic remarks dropped into his conversations with his Big Boss. In front of Stalin, Lavrenty always praised Zhdanov as a great individual who had taken part in the October Revolution in the Urals. Between the lines Beria let his Superior know that Zhdanov could have some objections when reading Stalin's *Collected Works* and the newly edited *History of the Communist Party of the Soviet Union.* His doubts about several facts and events could be of the same kind as those of Yenukidze, Bukharin, Zinoviev, Trotsky and dozens of other Old Guard Bolsheviks. But of course, Beria was positive that Zhdanov was far too devoted to Stalin to utter a word that would undermine the legend of the Great Dictator. Beria also expressed his opinion that, as the leader of the Leningrad Regional Party Organization, Zhdanov and his followers were planning their own economic policy, different from Comrade Stalin's. Since he was practically designated as Stalin's heir, Zhdanov, similar to every successor, would probably be eager to receive his heritage as soon as possible. This last remark of Beria's was also used very cautiously and rather seldom, but it was one of his most efficacious innuendos. With Stalin's obsession about assassination, even by one of his closest friends, such insinuations, administered in microscopic doses wisely and systematically, were bound to bring about the inevitable result.

At last Marshal Beria received a free hand from his Boss. To accomplish his goal, Lavrenty chose the same method that was used by one of his own predecessors, Yagoda, for destroying his immediate superior, Chief of the OGPU Menzhinsky. A few drops of a medicine in a glass of tea worked perfectly in a couple of hours.

On August 31, 1948, Andrey Zhdanov died of a heart disease of which he had had no previous symptoms. He was in the prime of health, a man fifty-two years old and at the height of his power when he suddenly died. There was no doctor's post mortem examination performed. There was no question that Zhdanov's fate, staged by Beria, was previously decreed by Stalin. Proof that Zhdanov's death was demanded by Stalin and executed by his hangman Beria was evident in the eulogy which Molotov delivered at the funeral. In an unexpectedly short and cold speech Molotov described the deceased, one of the most devoted and meritorious Bolsheviks, as just "a skilled worker for the Party."

The death of Andrey Zhdanov, the future successor to Stalin, was too important an event not to be exploited by Beria in his drive toward his goal of taking power after Stalin. All of Zhdanov's associates who could be potential enemies when Beria became the highest Boss at the Kremlin had to be eliminated as soon as possible. It was not too difficult for Lavrenty to convince his Superior that if Zhdanov was condemned to death, the same fate should meet his followers.

The leaders of the Leningrad Party Organization evidently had bad luck. The first one, Zinoviev, was arrested on Stalin's order, and after a public trial in Moscow, was sentenced to death and executed. His successor, Kirov, as a result of Stalin's masterfully prepared plot, was assassinated. Now the same happened to Zhdanov, who had replaced Kirov. Every time it was the same play, only the scenery and props were different. Zinoviev was condemned officially, Kirov was killed by a hired psychopath, and Zhdanov died suddenly of an unconfirmed heart attack.

In every one of these cases several people around the victim had to lose their lives, too. Together with Zinoviev, some of his close co-workers were liquidated as Trotskyites; after Kirov, his devoted male secretary was killed in a staged car accident, and a few other men vanished without a trace. The same happened to Zhdanov's friends, who composed a clique of known and important personalities in the Party and even in the Politburo, in expectation of governing the country when Zhdanov replaced Stalin. They had to be annihilated, but their liquidation was not a simple or easily solved problem. It had to arrive on the wave of a new purge.

For this task Beria assigned his deputy, Victor Abakumov. However, Lavrenty was too cunning to carry out this action with only the mute consent of Stalin; there were other people who were still powerful, and if they were against the action they could be dangerous. They had to be asked to join his side. The most important one was Malenkov. Although Beria hated Malenkov as his competitor, he decided to invite him to participate in his plot. It was not very hard to convince Malenkov, who being once defeated by Zhdanov, was his enemy; by Zhdanov's death and the elimination of his associates, Malenkov would get his revenge and could expect to gain a lot in power. Now, Beria had done everything to befriend Malenkov.

Abakumov fabricated the so-called "Leningrad Case" and prepared a list of proscribed names on various charges. Soon, in the middle of the night, the NKVD officers knocked on the doors of the branded men, the supporters of the late Zhdanov. Among them was a member of the Politburo and Chief of the State Planning Commission, Nikolay Voznesensky; his brother, Alexey Voznesensky, Rector of Leningrad University; Alexey Kuznetzov, a Secretary of the Central Committee; M. I. Rodionov, Chairman of the RSFSR—Russian Soviet Federated Socialist Republic Council of Ministers; Colonel General I. V. Shikin, Chief of the Red Army Political Directorate; Major Rahov, Director of the Museum of the Defense of Leningrad while the Museum was closed; Peter Popkov, Secretary of the Leningrad Party Organization and several others. As administrator of this purge of the Leningrad Party Organization, Beria appointed Vasily Andrianov, the right hand of Malenkov, and after Popkov was ousted, Lavrenty suggested to Stalin the nomination of Andrianov to the vacant post of First Secretary of the Leningrad Party Organization. By this move Beria won the favor of Malenkov and his followers.

All the arrested personalities were jailed or sent to concentration camps in Siberia. They were not annihilated immediately, but were preserved temporarily in case they would be needed eventually for other purposes. Besides, it was no problem to shoot someone already behind bars. It could be done any time.

This new great purge, inspired by Marshal Beria, authorized by Great Comrade Stalin and executed by the Minister of State Security Beria, was managed differently from the shake-up under Beria's predecessor, Nikolay Yezhov. During those years the "show" trials took place in the representative Hall of Columns in the House of Unions Building. At those monstrous trials, carried out by the Military Collegium of the Supreme Court of the USSR in Moscow, the defendants confessed their crimes and the State Prosecutor, Andrey Vyshinsky, delivered a smashing indictment, while the Soviet press was loaded with articles and write-ups from the courtroom.

On the contrary, the purge managed by Beria had no publicity, was held in secret, and was kept from public knowledge as far as possible. Lavrenty also did not seek any praise or profit for his activity, at least before he succeeded his Big Boss. Until that time he preferred to play the part of "Comrade Nobody" in behalf of Stalin. In this particular fabricated purge, the "Leningrad Case," Beria supposedly worked entirely for the sake of the Dictator and to introduce Malenkov as Stalin's heir, rather than anyone else, including himself.

There were very hard days at the Kremlin that year: the Communist Party was undergoing a more difficult crisis than appeared on the surface. Stalin became much more restless and nervous than during the times of the Great Purge Trials. Those cases Stalin had staged himself, and he had enjoyed the personal pleasure of liquidating Old Guard Bolsheviks like Bukharin and Rykov, or like Kamenev, Zinoviev, Radek and Rosengoltz as Trotskyites, and above all—as Jews.

The "Leningrad Case" had been suggested to him rather than initiated by him. Since he was growing old and had an obsession about his own death, Stalin would have preferred to topple his younger co-workers, causing their violent deaths, rather than having constantly before his eyes his potential successor: a visual reminder of Stalin as a past figure in the near future.

During the days of the purges of Zhdanov's followers, Stalin was more morbid, impatient and rude than at any time before, and except for his bodyguards, Voroshilov, Beria, Malenkov, Khrushchev and a few members of his Cabinet, he could not stand anyone. Especially bothering him were the old women, the wives of some members of his own family, mostly Jewesses or friends of his late wife Nadezhda. These women, who joined him at the table for dinner, talked constantly and were getting on his nerves. They reminded him of his first wife, Ekaterian Svanidze, or of his second one, Nadezhda Alliluyeva. The sight of those old relatives who were still with him displeased the Dictator and made him mad.

Stalin's bad humor was used by Beria for his own purpose, as it had been before. While some minor purges and executions of functionaries of less importance had been carried out by Lavrenty mostly for political reasons, now, to pave his way to the Kremlin's "room at the top" Beria found a new opportunity to liquidate people who were or could become his personal foes. Using Stalin's extreme anti-Semitism, Lavrenty liberated the Great Comrade from several of his noisy and unpleasant house guests. This was the result of a short and sly conversation with his beloved Superior, hinting that he be allowed to rid his home of those people.

In due course, a few weeks later, Beria arrested Lozovsky, Secretary-General of the *Profintern*—International of the Communist Trade Unions—and former Vice Commissar of Foreign Affairs. This Old Guard Bolshevik, a frequent guest at Stalin's home and a friend of his relatives, was a witty character, always in a good mood. His constant laugh got on the nerves of the humorless Dictator, who could not stand the Jewish jokes that Solomon Abramovich Lozovsky liked to tell.

Beria had no difficulty imprisoning this man after accusing him of being a "Cosmopolitan."

Soon after, another frequenter of Stalin's home was put in jail. She was Lina Shtern, who, after receiving her diploma from the University of Geneva, became a Professor and Director of the Institute of Physiology in Moscow. To imprison her was also a trifle, because Lina Solomonovna Shtern was a Latvian Jewess. By accusing her of "Cosmopolitanism," Beria had an excuse to arrest her two best friends, Anna and Evgenia Alliluyeva, who had introduced Lina Shtern into Stalin's household. Anna, a sister of Stalin's second wife Nadezhda, was formerly married to Stanislav Redens, the same *Cheka* dignitary and foe, whom Beria after an intrigue denounced to Stalin, had locked in Butyrki Prison and executed in the basement of that jail. Having no doubt that Anna hated him, Lavrenty was glad to annihilate her.

The imprisonment of Evgenia Alliluyeva, widow of Pavel Alliluyev, Stalin's brother-in-law, who was executed some years before, was a personal triumph for Beria. Lavrenty loathed Evgenia because she talked too much about his love affairs with schoolgirls, whom the Commissar kidnaped on the streets. Having a very sharp tongue, Evgenia laughed at Beria's escapades, calling him a lothario. Evgenia recognized Beria's complex about being ugly and teased him about it, saying he was a romantic and a most handsome Don Juan. Such ridicule Beria would never forgive or overlook; Evgenia had to be punished.

All these arrests were made with Stalin's silent consent, and so they proceeded as smoothly as the previous ones, when Beria had imprisoned Alexander Svanidze, the brother of Stalin's first wife, and Alexander's wife Miriam—Maria. Stalin hated that couple as bores who constantly complained, and who by their presence reminded him of both his wives—the first, Ekaterian, to whom they were related, and the second, Nadezhda, whom they loved so much. And Maria, whose maiden name was Korona, was a Jewess from a very rich family to boot. So the Dictator gave a free hand to Beria. They were arrested and each sentenced to ten years hard labor. Soon Alexander and his wife were deported to concentration camps at opposite ends of the country, Alexander to the Far North and Maria to Kazakhstan. Stalin was very glad not to be bothered by them anymore and Beria was always happy to destroy his Superior's family.

In the same sweep that persecuted Lozovsky, Lina Shtern, and the two Stalin relatives Anna and Evgenia Alliluyeva, Beria struck a blow at Molotov, who would be Stalin's successor should Malenkov fail.

Beria reasoned that before anything else happened, Molotov's present strong position should be shaken a little. His wife, Paulina, was a confidante of the late Nadezhda Alliluyeva Stalin, of her sister Anna, of Maria, the Jewish wife of Alexander Svanidze, of Lina Shtern, and of Zinaida Bukharin, also a Jewess and the widow of Nikolay Bukharin, the Old Guard Bolshevik and editor of *Izvestia*, later accused of being a Trotskyite and executed. Paulina Molotov was a Jewess herself. Although she had been a member of the Communist Party even before the October Revolution, and later was distinguished with the highest Soviet decoration, the Order of Lenin, she had to be condemned. This slight, dark, not very attrac-

Arkady Rosengoltz, one of the most important Soviet leaders and an outstanding member of the Central Committee, ruler of Donbas and People's Commissar of Foreign Trade. Executed in 1938. (*The National Archives*)

Nina, the girl who was kidnapped by Beria and later was forced to marry him. (*The National Archives*)

Stalin with his beloved daughter, Svetlana, on the porch of his dacha, *Blizhny*, at Kuntsevo near Moscow. (*The National Archives*)

A typical meeting in a Soviet factory. Workers are "unanimously" voting for Stalin. The Cyrillic letters above Stalin's portrait spell: "Long Live our Great Leader and Teacher, Comrade Stalin!" (*Soviet Union Magazine, Moscow*)

Little Svetlana Stalin during her summer vacations at Sochi in the Caucasus and Lavrenty Beria, whom she called "Uncle Lara." (*The National Archives*)

A Politburo meeting. Beria sits at Stalin's left.
(*Painting by Nalbadyan, Gospolizdat, Moscow*)

December 21, 1949, Stalin's seventieth birthday. According to Beria's order, a slide of Stalin was projected on a cloud over the Kremlin and Red Square. (*Ogoniok, Moscow*)

Happy smiles. Stalin and Joachim von Ribbentrop, Hitler's Minister of Foreign Affairs, at the Kremlin after signing the Nazi-Soviet Treaty of mutual assistance, August 23, 1939.
Later, during the banquet, Stalin delivered his historical toast: "I know how much the German nation loves its Führer. I wish to drink to his health!" (*The National Archives*)

Slave workers in one of the Soviet hard labor camps in Siberia installed by Commissar Beria. (*USSR in Construction, Moscow*)

FORCED LABOR CAMPS IN SOVIET RUSSIA

The Soviet slave camps in the USSR under Beria's rule.
(*The Library of Congress*)

A group of American and British officers, German prisoners of war at Katyn Forest, where 5,000 Polish officers and other ranks were massacred by Beria's troops. (*Polish Cultural Foundation, London*)

General W. Anders (right), Commander in Chief of the Polish Forces created from the former prisoners of War in the USSR and later Commander of the Second Polish Corps in Italy shakes hands with King George VI. (*Private collection of General W. Anders, London*)

Warsaw uprising, 1944. The Polish Home Army in action.
(*Private collection of A. Pomian*)

On their way to the platform to watch the May 1 Parade, 1945. Stalin
in the company of his closest associates (left to right): Beria, Malenkov,
and Kalinin. (*The Library of Congress*)

General Draza Mikhailovich,
leader of the Yugoslavian Home
Army, trapped by Beria in 1946,
executed by Tito.
(*Private collection of Adam
Schmidt, Washington*)

At Stalin's casket, March 9, 1953 (left to right): Molotov, Voroshilov, Beria, and Malenkov. (*Soviet Union Magazine, Moscow*)

Mourners at Stalin's funeral in Red Square. At right: Beria and Khrushchev. (*Pravda, Moscow*)

The new duumvirate: Malenkov and Beria. (*The National Archives*)

Marshal Ivan S. Konev, twice Hero of the Soviet Union, Deputy of the Supreme Soviet of the USSR, and President Justice of the Special Judical Session of the Supreme Court of the USSR, the court which sentenced Lavrenty Beria to death by a firing squad. (*Gospolizdat, Moscow*)

Lavrenty Pavlovich Beria, First Deputy Premier, Minister of Internal Affairs, and Chief of State Security. (*The National Archives*)

tive female, who had been a frequent visitor at the Dictator's home when Nadezhda Stalin was still alive, was too vivacious, always making remarks, knowing everything under the sun better than anybody else, and always had to be right. Paulina was not like Rosa, the sister of Commissar Kaganovich, a vulgar woman who kept her mouth shut and worshiped Stalin, whose senses she satisfied.

Beria did not have much trouble framing Paulina Molotov. Some years before the Second World War, as Head of the Soviet Union's Cosmetic Trust, she went to the United States to study the American cosmetics industry. During her American tour Paulina Molotov was even received by the First Lady, Eleanor Roosevelt, with whom she spent a whole afternoon in the White House. After her return to the Soviet Union, Paulina used to praise American women for their good taste in clothing and their skill in applying makeup.

It was sufficient to accuse Paulina Molotov of being anti-Socialist and pro-Western, a dangerous element, a bourgeois Zionist, and an enemy of the people to arrest her and deport her to a concentration camp in Siberia. However, her husband was still too important a statesman and world figure to be liquidated. As Minister of Foreign Affairs, Vyacheslav Molotov was doing a remarkable job and was a representative of great value. Stalin did not mind retaining him in his post, particularly when the day after Paulina's imprisonment Molotov came to Stalin to thank his Leader for arresting her and for administering the treatment that she undoubtedly deserved. Such behavior allowed Molotov to keep his post for a short time. But he lost prestige, and he was no longer invited to private parties or dinners at Stalin's home as he had been. From that time on, the usual group of regular guests at Stalin's table consisted of Beria, Malenkov, Khrushchev, Mikoyan, Bulganan and Kaganovich. Beria hated Molotov, a man with good Western manners, and seeing his fall from favor as well as his humiliation gave him double satisfaction.

A few months after the arrest of his wife Molotov was removed from his post as Minister of Foreign Affairs. He became Vice Chairman of the Council of Ministers; his portfolio of Minister of Foreign Affairs was given to Andrey Vyshinsky, Beria's protégé.

The wave of anti-Semitic action against the so-called "Zionist Center" initiated by Lavrenty Beria was carried on quickly, systematically and without any publicity.

Among other purged personalities arrested, imprisoned and later executed in connection with "anti-Cosmopolitan" action was Solomon Mikhoels, Director of the Yiddish State Theatre in Moscow and a great Shakespearean actor. Mikhoels was neither arrested nor put on trial nor executed. He was simply liquidated. According to one story, he was attacked by hoodlums while walking on a deserted street. In another account it was said he was run over by a truck. The real truth, apparent to everyone, was that he had been killed by Beria's agents.

Mikhoels was also a member of the Presidium of an "All-World Jewish Anti-Hitlerite Committee," which previously, in 1941, Beria had suggested be established. The main goal of this organization was to appeal to the Jews abroad, especially in the United States and England, to aid the Soviet Army with money and medical supplies. With this mission Mikhoels was delegated to London and New York and soon he had returned with quite a success. However, the All-World Jewish Anti-Hitlerite Committee was Beria's trap to lure and then catch the Russian Jews who revealed their national "Zionist" feelings. As co-chairman of this Committee Lavrenty put Victor Alter and Henrik Ehrlich, two Polish Jews who before the war were leaders of *Bund*—the General Jewish Workers Union in Poland, a Socialist-oriented organization. When the Red Army invaded Poland in 1939, Alter and Ehrlich were arrested by the Soviet Secret Police and shipped to Moscow and jailed in Lubyanka Prison. When the amnesty for all Polish citizens in the USSR was proclaimed, these two men were released by Beria who asked them to create the All-World Jewish Anti-Hitlerite Committee. They accepted and went to Kuibyshev, where the Polish Embassy in the Soviet Union was located, together with the whole Corps Diplomatique after the evacuation of Moscow. Soon the new organization started its activity and was joined by many eminent Soviet Jews, Solomon Mikhoels among them. A few months after, however, in 1942, Alter and Ehrlich were kidnaped on the street by four NKVD functionaries, and then, according to Beria's personal order, were murdered in the prison's execution cell.

Now came Mikhoels' turn. Soon after Beria jailed Joseph Morozov, a Jew despite his typically Russian name. This man happened to be the father of the first husband of Svetlana, daughter of Generalissimo Joseph Stalin.

                              *   *   *

On December 21, 1949, there was a great holiday in the whole USSR: the anniversary of Stalin's seventieth birthday. Although there was no amnesty for any political or regular criminal detained in prisons and hard labor camps as was expected by the inmates, there was a day off in the factories and plants, where the workers held joyous meetings. After appropriate speeches delivered by the political guides attached to every factory, there were entertainments and receptions. Theatres and movies were free for the workers and members of organizations, among whom tickets were distributed. The press was full of articles and poems praising Stalin's achievements as the Founder of the Soviet Union and as the immortal hero who had defeated Hitler and won the Second World War. All these stories and poems, as well as numerous photographs and paintings of the Dictator, carefully retouched and beautified, were closely scrutinized by Lavrenty Pavlovich Beria himself.

In the evening, for the celebrities, there was a gala performance in the Bolshoi Theatre, attended by Stalin, his daughter Svetlana and all members of the Cabinet and the Politburo and the Corps Diplomatique in the honorary boxes. The show was followed by an official reception at the Kremlin. During the lavish banquet several toasts were proposed, wishing the Dictator a life of one hundred years in health, happiness and prosperity. The dinner over, telegrams were read aloud extending congratulations and paying homage to the Leader of the USSR from Kings, Presidents and Prime Ministers from all over the world. Then Marshal Lavrenty Beria took the stand and began to deliver a paean to the honor of his beloved superior.

. . . The name of the Great Stalin is being pronounced with fervent love by the workers in every country of the world, connecting it with the realization of their century-old hopes and aspirations.

The name of Comrade Stalin is being pronounced with a feeling of great gratitude by the workers of the countries of people's democracies who entered upon the path of building Socialism. The name is also revered by the workers and peasants of China who threw down the yoke of colonial oppression. The name of Comrade Stalin inspires the workers of Europe and America in their fight against capitalism. The name also inspires the peoples of subjugated colonial and semicolonial countries in their just struggle for national freedom and independence.

The whole life of Comrade Stalin is inseparably linked with the struggle for the creation and strengthening of the Bolshevik Party, for the victory of proletarian Revolution, for the well being of the workers, and the victory of Communism. . . .[1]

In this tone Beria carried on for over fifteen minutes, and finished his eulogy with the exclamation: "Glory to Comrade Stalin! Forward towards new victories under the leadership of the Great Stalin!"[2]

Outside the Kremlin walls the entire city was brilliantly illuminated, and according to Beria's special order, the enormous crowd on the streets saw an unusual performance. High in the sky of the frosty, winter Moscow night there appeared the image of the Father of the Country, the greatest personality of all times: Joseph Vissarionovich Stalin. A slide showing the bust of The Boss in his military cap and uniform and with his Generalissimo insignia on his epaulettes projected onto an enormous beam of an antiaircraft searchlight, was thrown against the background of a dark cloud over Red Square.

From the heavens high above the onion domes of St. Basil Cathedral and the Kremlin Castle, the Dictator of Soviet Russia looked down at his people as if he were the merciless new god of millions of his slaves.

---

[1] Appendix 12.
[2] *Ibid.*

45

One Little Oversight

As CHIEF OF THE GREATEST worldwide spy ring in history, Lavrenty Beria proved to be a real genius of evil. It was due to Beria's expertise that espionage activity in the United States and Soviet penetration into almost all United States government agencies had been increased and was so effective. Through his contact men in the United States, Colonel Boris Bykov, a Red Army officer of military intelligence at the Soviet Embassy in Washington, and Whittaker Chambers, an American Communist courier, Beria received valuable information. Chambers was in touch with Harry Dexter White, assistant to the Secretary of the Treasury, and with some other high ranking Administration personnel. Classified material from the Department of State purportedly came from Alger Hiss, a special attorney in the Department of Justice and later aide to Assistant Secretary of State Francis B. Sayre. Hiss was also one of the bright young men around President Franklin D. Roosevelt, whom he accompanied at the conference with Churchill and Stalin in Yalta.

Beria had information about the United States Air Force from Abraham George Silverman and about the American War Production Board from Edward Fitzgerald and John Abt. From Major William Ludwig Ullmann of the War Department Beria obtained information about United States Army Intelligence war plans and FBI reports.

Beria also had lured some other personalities who became his informants. Among them were Robert T. Miller from the Department of State; Harold Ware in the Department of Agriculture; Donald Niven Wheeler from Counterintelligence of the Department of War; Philip Keepey in the Foreign Economic Administration; Norman Burster from the Department of Justice; Hellen Tenney and Duncan Lee in the Office of Strategic Services and Joseph Greeg, Coordinator of Inter-American Affairs.[1]

Thanks to these and some other persons Lavrenty Beria could infiltrate the American Government, and was well informed about its secrets.

In England, Beria's top spies were two Britishers of great value: Guy Burgess and Donald McLean. Later, when their subversive activity was disclosed, Beria arranged a safe escape to Russia for both of them.

In the field of atomic research in the West, Beria organized a spy ring on a grand scale: in America he had such important agents as the famous Italian scientist, Bruno Pontecorvo, whom finally in 1949, Beria helped to escape to the USSR through France and Finland. Beria also managed to recruit as professional Soviet agents some Americans working in atomic laboratories, such as Julius and Ethel Rosenberg, Harry Gold and David Greenglass; in England his contacts were two nuclear researchers, Dr. Allan Nunn May and Dr. Klaus Fuchs; in Paris he was in touch with the French scientist and ardent Communist, Frederick Joliot-Curie. These were just a few members of several large spy rings established by Beria's office throughout Western Europe, Canada and the United States. But above all, the most valuable spymaster for Lavrenty Beria was the cynical Englishman, Harold "Kim" Philby, the Communist agent who managed to become Chief of British Counter-Soviet Intelligence in the United States and also was one of the organizers of the Central Intelligence Agency in Washington. From the time he assumed his post in 1945 until his successful escape to Moscow several years later, Philby supplied Beria with a great deal of information in complete detail.

Thanks to Beria's great talent for organizing top value spy rings in every foreign country, an art that enabled him to supply the

---

[1] James Burnham, *The Web of Subversion: Underground Networks in the U. S. Government* (New York: The John Day Company, 1959). See also David J. Dallin, *Soviet Espionage* (New Haven: Yale University Press, 1955) and Ronald Seth, *Unmasked!* (New York: Hawthorn Books, Inc., 1965).

Kremlin with detailed and accurate information of tremendous importance, including stolen data about American atomic research, Beria was an irreplaceable man for Stalin. Since Lavrenty always fulfilled any assignment he had been given, never looked for any publicity, and was building up the ego of the Dictator in every way he could, as well as keeping him informed about potential personal enemies, Stalin trusted Beria more than anybody else. As a result of his Superior's confidence Lavrenty was called upon to install a special net of security around Stalin's private life.

After he was summoned by Stalin to Moscow to take the job of Commissar of Internal Affairs, Beria introduced his spies into the closest entourage of his Chief. Among these agents there was a certain Alexandra Nakashidze, a Security Officer holding the rank of Major in the Secret Police, who became a housekeeper in Stalin's private apartment at the Kremlin. Alexandra was a Georgian from a village not far from Tiflis. After studying for some time in the Tbilisi Industrial Institute she became a Security agent. She was an attractive, dark, medium-sized woman of twenty, and Beria made her his mistress. Later, when he was transferred to Moscow, he took her with him.

In Stalin's house, Alexandra Nakashidze kept an eye on the personal life, friends, letters and telephone conversations of Stalin's children, Vasily and Svetlana, whose property she searched, even examining their textbooks and school copybooks. She also spied on other of Stalin's relatives and denounced them to Beria, who later made use of that information. Along with Alexandra Nakashidze, Beria planted his other agents, Ivan Krivenko, Alexander Volkov and Mikhail Klimov as Svetlana's watchdogs. All of them supplied Beria with the smallest details about the private life of Stalin's family and completed the files which Lavrenty maintained for his own purpose. Those were the dossiers of all his potential enemies, Stalin himself included.

These three agents and Alexandra Nakashidze carried out their assignment successfully until they were fired by Stalin when Svetlana got married. Svetlana's first husband, Grigory Morozov, was a Jew. Stalin blamed the housekeeper and Svetlana's constant guard for failing to prevent her falling in love with a Jew.

The loss of his informants did not do very much harm to Beria, since the person who next took the post at Stalin's home, Ivan Borodachev, was also a Major of Security and Beria's man. Later, by skilfully playing upon Stalin's obsessive fear of being encircled by traitors and potential assassins, Lavrenty managed to imprison Stalin's much trusted head bodyguard, General Nikolay Vlasik, who, since he did not serve in the NKVD, was independent of Beria. The deposed General Vlasik was replaced by Beria's trusted follower, Vasily Khrustalov, who became chief of Stalin's personal guard.

Being well aware that irreplaceable people truly do not exist anywhere for long, especially in the Soviet Union, Lavrenty, in his goal to take his Boss' chair at the earliest opportunity, decided to remove everyone who stood between him and Stalin politically, as he had Zhdanov and Molotov. Besides them there were a few other important personalities to be eliminated, like Poskrebyshev, the personal secretary of the Dictator and his most trusted man, as well as Kaganovich, Mikoyan, Bulganin, Malenkov and Khrushchev.

Bulganin knew what he was talking about when he remarked that after a party at Stalin's home none of the guests was sure if he would finish the evening back home or in jail. However, Beria was still not powerful enough to be able to liquidate these personalities by his own will. He still depended upon the Dictator—the Supreme Despot. It was Stalin who made plans; Beria could only make suggestions. And these suggestions had to be submitted in such a way that they would not turn against the initiator. The cunning Kaganovich was a Jew and an Old Guard Bolshevik, so he was logically the first target. His sister Rosa, however, was the Chief's mistress, and as long as Stalin was taking her to his bed it would be impolitic to attack her brother. Mikoyan also belonged to the Old Guard Communists. But Stalin had a kind of weakness for this easily smiling modest Armenian who had never mentioned his contribution to the revolutionary movement. Beria realized that it would be hard to undermine the position of that man. But Anastas Mikoyan had a brother, Artem, ten years his junior, an aircraft designer who invented the famous MIG fighter plane. Beria decided to fabricate, at first, a case against Artem, accusing him of treason and contacts with the British Intelligence Service during the time he had studied jet technology in London. As part of his plan Lavrenty intended to arrest the noted mathematician, Mikhail Gurevich, the co-designer of that aircraft. The model MIG took its name from the surnames of Mikoyan and Gurevich. Since the latter was a Jew, Stalin would not mind his imprisonment. In jail Gurevich would admit all his and Artem Mikoyan's crimes. Beria knew how to carry on an inquest. He even boasted about it. Once, when he was in a good mood, he said, "Give me somebody for twenty-four hours and I will make him confess he is the King of England."[2] The arrest of Artem Mikoyan and Gurevich would undermine the position of the famous revolutionary Bolshevik, Anastas Mikoyan. Such an intrigue had worked perfectly once before against Molotov when his wife, Paulina, was imprisoned. However, his plan for Mikoyan Beria left for the future.

Bulganin already knew what he could expect, so he was warned to stay in line and created no problems. Khrushchev also was considered a small fry by Beria; he planned to vanquish first those presenting the greatest threat. The most dangerous for Lavrenty could be Malenkov, who was even younger than Beria. Malenkov was a very dutiful, obedient and silent worker, popular among the high rank officers of the Red Army, and a personal friend of Marshal Voroshilov. Beria had no illusions that he himself was despised by the military men of the Soviet Forces. He realized they had reasons to hate him. It was Beria, and no other, who had installed Secret Police troops to follow the Russian infantrymen in order to shoot everyone who tried to take one step back in retreat; it was Beria who had initiated the organization SMERSH—the units which decided the fate of every officer in the Army, Navy and Air Force; it was Beria who planted his so-called *politrooks*—political guides and spies—in every regiment, every garrison and every platoon; it was Beria who suggested to Stalin the imprisonment and deportation to Siberia of the families of every Russian soldier and officer captured by the enemy during the Second World War, and the confiscation of all their possessions; it was Beria who supplied his own NKVD troops with the best uniforms, food and housing, along with other privileges, in spite of the fact that they did not fight on the battlefield. And it was Beria, no other, of all the Politburo members of the State Committee of Defense, who showed his contempt so openly against the regular army staff officers, letting them know that he had a very low opinion of their mentality.

Lavrenty Beria was aware of the Soviet Army's hostile attitude toward him, but still, as Commander in Chief of Security Forces equipped with artillery, tanks and planes, and with agents in every

---

[2] *Khrushchev Remembers* (Boston: Little, Brown & Co., 1970).

military unit of the Red Army, he was sure that he would always be informed in sufficient time about any movement against him and would be able to master the situation. Beria was not only powerful enough, but also too needed by the Dictator to be destroyed by him. It was Beria who edited the new *History of the Communist Party*, in which he proved that during the October Revolution Lenin played an almost secondary role to Stalin's. It was Beria who collected Stalin's works and prepared them for publication.

There was only one weak point in Lavrenty's calculations. He overlooked Stalin's realization that the false history of the Party, where he became such a hero, was fabricated by Beria, and that as the inventor of the great Stalin's splendid past, replete with deeds the Dictator never committed, Beria became a dangerous witness to that hoax and thus exposed himself as a subject for liquidation.

46

The Last Conversation

BERIA'S MAIN TASK for the government was the atomic research program, which Stalin entrusted to him as a top priority project. Besides this job he had other responsibilities as a Marshal of the Soviet Union, First Deputy Chairman of the Council of Ministers, a member of the Presidium of the Central Committee and Minister of Internal Affairs (MVD). Under such a weight of duties Beria delegated his responsibility as Chief of the Ministry of State Security (MGB) to one of his trusted men, Vsevolod Merkulov.

This stocky, dark man, who held the rank of general, thanks to Beria's support, was later sent abroad and his post given to Victor Abakumov, whose career also depended on the Minister of Internal Affairs, and on whom Beria could also fully rely.

The development of the atomic weapon was deemed so important by the Dictator that he demanded weekly reports. The war had been over for more than five years, but it seemed as if the Great Comrade Stalin was in a hurry to obtain the most deadly weapon of all. There was some speculation in Stalin's inner circle about his anxiety to have the bomb: would he then not hesitate to provoke a new war against the free world, unprepared as it was for another holocaust? The progress of the atomic research, however, was not as speedy as the Dictator wished and Beria stood in danger of becoming a victim of his Superior's impatience.

Over the course of years, especially after he passed his seventieth birthday, Stalin's obsessive fear of being assassinated, perhaps by his closest co-workers, grew tremendously. Fearful of being poisoned, he ate only at his suburban home *Blizhny* at Kuntsevo. But even then, despite the fact that his food was prepared by his old cook, Matryona Petrovna, and served by an old chambermaid, the housekeeper, Valentina Istomina—"Valechka"—both of whom were faithful and devoted to him, Stalin demanded that every dish and every piece of bread brought to him be previously examined by a physician. The most trusted medics, like Dr. Dyakov, were assigned to this task, while the physician who for many years took care of the Dictator's health was the famous professor, Dr. Vladimir Vinogradov.

These physicians, as well as the specialists in poisons who tested Stalin's food and wrote reports, were under constant surveillance by Beria's special duty Security agents who watched carefully every facet of the doctors' private lives. Since that investigation had been left in the hands of the Minister of Internal Affairs, Beria drew the obvious conclusion that the Big Boss had not lost his great confidence in him.

However, the Dictator's paranoiac symptoms were making alarming progress and it was evident that Stalin would eventually be replaced by someone not mentally ill. This successor would come from the younger generation rather than from the Old Guard Bolsheviks who belonged to the waning world era, so it would be either Khrushchev, Malenkov or Beria. The race would be won only by the one who was the quickest, the most unscrupulous and the best prepared. Lavrenty was a cunning strategist with a good knowledge of the way his colleagues in the Politburo thought, and of the psychology of his nation.

As an experienced statesman, Beria realized that a power grab could not be a goal in itself. The man who would take the Dictator's chair at the Kremlin should start his regime with a program, an already prepared project that would capture the imagination of the country, as well as the whole otside world.

The plan Beria worked out encompassed problems of industry, agriculture and foreign policy. On the internal market front, Beria had no doubt that the goods produced by the inmates in hard labor camps should no longer be utilized as the basic supplies for the country. Factories and plants were needed throughout the nation in addition to those that existed in the campland. He proposed that the production of heavy industry, weapons and war materials could be reduced for light industry and the production of everyday goods such as better candies, soap, or stationery. In this area private initiative, to a certain extent, should be allowed. Even if it were a reversion back to the NEP—New Economic Policy of 1921, later so ruthlessly persecuted by Stalin as a crime—so what? At least, under the NEP there was production of more consumer goods and the man in the street did not suffer shortages of everything.

As to agricultural marketing, Beria decided that something must be done to change the deplorable situation. It was a shame that Russia, by tradition a rustic country with the best soil, had a bread problem and was forced to import grain from abroad by exchanging timber and ores produced by the exploited slaves in hard labor camps.

The rule of periodic delivery of grain quotas by the peasants from the collective farms was nothing other than a requisition, and a most brutal one, since, if in a certain collective farm a prescribed quota failed, the foreman and some workers were arrested and exiled to Siberia. This method also had to be changed. The Russian villagers had never become accustomed to that collective and state farm system which Stalin had introduced by force in the form of the execution of all so-called *kulaks*—the well-to-do peasants—and the liquidation of private rural households so that villagers, deprived of their soil, died of starvation by the thousands.

Much later, after the Second World War, facing another food crisis with the collective farm system, the aging Stalin, who was ignorant about farming, had decided to introduce a new idea. He planned to level all the collective and state farms and to fuse them into big "agro-towns," more a kind of grain factory than a countryside. This project would make the bread situation in the Soviet Union even more severe than the already existing system, poor as it was. The initiator of this program was Nikita Khrushchev who, in spite of being a Ukrainian peasant himself and well aware that this idea would be disastrous for Soviet agriculture, promoted the project to please Stalin.

Beria planned to stop any attempts to realize that program of the agricultural cities and the amalgamation of the *kolkhozes*, and to moderate the collective farm system. He also calculated that if the Soviet Union was really to be shifted from an agricultural country to an industrial one no longer based on the productivity of the camps, it should have enough bread for the workers in the cities. And if it would exchange its grain for foreign machines and tools, such transactions must not be made to the detriment of the population as was being done under Stalin's regime. And last, but not least, there also existed in the Soviet Union a tremendous class that was not productive at all, but had to be fed well before any other: these were the divisions of the Secret Police, Militia, and the Red Army, Navy and Air Force. A resolution of the food and agriculture problem was the main aim and Beria proposed to solve it by returning to the approach of the pre-Stalin era, the NEP, with some modification according to the circumstances of modern postwar times.

When it came to foreign policy, Beria also had his own point of view, one entirely different from that of his Big Boss. Primarily, he wanted to abandon Stalin's maniacal idea of becoming the greatest power as soon as possible equipped with an arsenal of atomic weapons with which to blackmail the disarmed free world into surrendering without a single shot. Quite the opposite, Lavrenty Beria, as the would-be leader at the Kremlin, would like to have good diplomatic relations with Western countries, which could then be reshaped into Communist ones gradually, from the inside, by their own Communist groups and parties. They would follow instructions and receive support from the Soviet Union, as does the French Communist Party with its headquarters in Paris, the Italian one in Rome, the biggest Communist Party in the world outside Russia, and the American Communist group in the United States. This project Beria had already started to actualize without any delay. Through his men abroad, in the United States as well as in Great Britain and other Western countries, he secretly began some preliminary steps. With the slogan, "Better international relations with the West," Beria's emissaries abroad approached the most influential and responsible personalities in Washington and London. Among Beria's "Residents" in the foreign countries were Vladimir Petrov, real name Shorokhov, and his wife, Evdokia, who was working under the name "Tamara," in the Soviet Embassy in Sydney; Yuri Rastorov, Second Secretary of the Soviet Mission in Tokyo, who was also a Colonel of the NKVD; Pyotr Deryabin, a "Resident" in the Soviet Embassy in Vienna; and Nikolay Khokhlov in Germany.[1]

---

[1] Later, after Beria's fall, these people, facing recall to Moscow to be arrested and executed, defected. Vladimir and Evdokia Petrov asked for asylum in Australia, Rastorov in Japan, Deryabin in Austria, and Khokhlov escaped to West Berlin.

Beria also intended to restore relations with Tito and was against the Stalin policy of Russification of non-Russian nations and republics such as Ukraine, Uzbekistan, Tadzhikistan, Kazakh SSR and others.

Of course, the accomplishment of all these guidelines made in 1951 Beria left until the death of the Dictator and the moment when he, Lavrenty Pavlovich, as a winner of the race to power would leap into the Great Comrade's shoes. Stalin was 72 years old; he should not last long. And if despite his age he continued in the prime, vital, active and full of energy, it would be possible eventually to help Mother Nature take him back to her womb. If Lenin's existence was shortened by his disciple, Stalin, why should not the same fate meet Stalin from his disciple, Beria?

But it was still music of the future and until that day when he would replace the Dictator and become the Big Boss himself, Beria had to play the role of the most faithful subordinate. On the thirty-fourth anniversary of the October Revolution, November 6, 1951, Marshal Lavrenty Beria delivered an oration. From this long and idolatrous lecture, later published in *Pravda* and reprinted by other newspapers all over the country, millions of people throughout the Soviet Union could learn that in the entire history of the world there was no greater individual than "the bright Genius of mankind, the Standard-bearer of peace, the Great Leader and Teacher Joseph Vissarionovich Stalin."[2]

To please his Boss, Beria adorned this speech with many anti-American and anti-British remarks and slogans stating that: "the United States of America are at the head of the camp of imperialism, as a center of attraction for all the aggressors and reactionaries of the whole world, striving to unleash a new war with the view of plundering and enslaving other peoples"; that "the United States of America are stubbornly trying to convert the United Nations Organization into an instrument of war"; and that the American-English bloc is embarked upon the road of preparing and unleashing a new war.[3]

However, nothing could satisfy the Dictator. The first sign of the bad mood of the Big Boss against his Minister of Internal Affairs, who was not proving efficient enough with his atomic research

---

[2] Appendix 13.
[3] *Ibid.*

program, was the removal of Beria's man, Abakumov, from the post
of Chief of Ministry of State Security and the nomination to that
job of Semyon Denisovich Ignatyev, a member of the Party since
1926 and Stalin's man acting in Byelorussia, Uzbekistan and Mon-
golia. By this nomination, for the first time since Beria had moved
to Moscow from Tiflis, the Chief of Ministry of State Security became an official independent of the Minister of Internal Affairs.

Semyon Ignatyev, a never-smiling fanatic, with a bald head and
prominent cheekbones that gave him a somewhat Asiatic look, was
an experienced Bolshevik. He understood well that his nomination
was a kind of warning for Lavrenty Beria, if not a whip on him. As
a once indirect follower of the line represented by the late Zhdanov, he was a bitter enemy of Beria. One could predict that with
Ignatyev's arrival on the scene a new wave of purges would soon
start. The nomination of Ignatyev could easily mean the beginning
of the end for Lavrenty Pavlovich.

The first target for the attack on Beria's position was the terrain
of Czechoslovakia. All the key posts there had been given by Beria
to his associates. Positive that he could fully rely on his staff, Beria
thought of that small but tough country as a kind of personal
stronghold. After the assassination of Jan Masaryk and the death of
President Benes, Beria ruled that highly industrialized and civilized nation through his men of the Czechoslovak Secret Police
and a puppet government of his creatures, according to his needs.

Just after Ignatyev took the State Security office, he struck at
Beria's bastion. A sudden wave of arrests swept through the Soviet
apparatus in Prague, including high ranking officers of the Czechoslovak Secret Police working under Beria's orders. The main victims of that purge were the accomplices of the Minister of the
Soviet Internal Affairs. These officials were arrested for alleged
espionage, sabotage, diversion and high treason, but being Beria's
men, the accusation hit indirectly at him, as their patron. But one
striking feature characterized the whole action. Almost all the imprisoned high ranking officers, along with the leaders Rudolph Slansky, whose real name was Zaltzman, and his associates, Bedrich
Geminder, Rudolph Margolius, Andre Simone, Artur London, and
nine other protégés of Beria, were Jews. The arrested men were accused also of being Zionist and "Cosmopolitan" elements.

The interrogation of the accused was carried out in such a way
that the imprisoned dignitaries were not aware of their real tor-

mentor, Stalin's new henchman, Ignatyev. Because of this stratagem they felt abandoned and betrayed by their former sponsor,
Lavrenty Beria, whom they blamed for their present ordeal.

The new purge had a typical anti-Semitic flavor, and was evidently managed by Stalin. Commissar Ignatyev, as an immediate
performer of the Great Dictator's orders, was now too strong to be
liquidated by Beria.

Lavrenty Pavlovich, however, was still powerful enough not to
feel too threatened by a mere Chief of Security. He was used to
dangerous situations, and sooner or later had always mastered
them. The best strategy in such cases was to sit back, observe and
wait; then to strike back quickly and surely.

But now the situation was grave. Soon Beria suffered a blow on
the other cheek. Simultaneously with Ignatyev's first arrests of the
Czech leaders in Prague, he aimed an attack at another of Beria's
personal strongholds: his native Georgia. There Ignatyev ordered
the arrest of the First Secretary of the Georgian Communist Party,
Kote Charkviani. Beria had put him in this post, which he had held
since 1939, and he was one of his closest and most devoted co-
workers in Tiflis. Charkviani also controlled the Secret Police in the
Caucasus. Now he was arrested after being kidnaped in Tiflis at
night on the way home from his office.

This event initiated a new action in Georgia, this time against
the Mingrelian people, inhabitants of the western part of Georgia
on the shores of the Black Sea. Stalin, although a Georgian himself,
did not mind decimating his countrymen if it served his purpose.
Years before, he called upon his followers to plow up the weeds
from the Georgian soil with a red-hot iron, and Beria, then a young
apprentice, swore to translate these words into action. Now, Stalin
used the same maneuver again. His new State Security Chief, Ignatyev, staged a Mingrelian nationalistic conspiracy, a trumped-up
plan for an uprising in Georgia under the leadership of Charkviani.
The final aim of that rebellion was supposedly secession from the
Soviet Union and alliance with capitalistic Turkey. Of course, the
whole so-called "Mingrelian Plot" was mainly directed against
Beria and his Georgian followers, and had been fabricated by Chief
of State Security Ignatyev, exactly as the "Leningrad Case" was
fabricated by Beria's Security against Zhdanov and his devotees.

In the Georgian Security Office Beria had his own creatures,
with Charkviani at the top. No uprising of Mingrelians nor of any

Caucasian tribe against the USSR could occur. But Beria's motherland, Georgia, where he had risen to power, was his strongest bastion, almost his own little sovereign principality where his immediate subordinates enjoyed a nearly free hand. Beria's deputies ruled
there as if they were independent overlords. But Stalin would never
accept such freedom. If his attack was chosen against no other
people but the Mingrelians it was because they were known as a
very patriotic and liberty-loving ethnic group, so such an accusation made sense, and was even probable. Besides, it was significant
that Beria was a Mingrelian himself, while his mother, who was
born near Merkheuli village, in a community called Uria Sopeli,
mostly inhabited by Jews, could be partially Jewish. Lavrenty, by
inference, just might have some Jewish blood in his veins.

This was another stone thrown at him. Together, these two
blows, one in the west against the Jews in Czechoslovakia and one
in the east against the Mingrelians in the Caucasus, could smash
Lavrenty Pavlovich Beria.

The new Chief of State Security, Ignatyev, worked patiently.
Beria was still Marshal of the USSR, Head of Atomic Research and
chief of the greatest worldwide spy ring in the history of mankind,
as well as Minister of Soviet Internal Affairs and the highest executive of GULAG, the Administration of Hard Labor Camps, which
were the main nerves of Soviet industry. And he was still a member
of the Politburo. In other words, Lavrenty Pavlovich Beria was, not
nominally but in fact, perhaps even more powerful than Stalin, and
for the sake of the Soviet Union solidity he must not be liquidated
abruptly or quickly. His fall had to be brought about gradually,
almost imperceptibly.

The purge in Tbilisi which followed the arrest of First Secretary
of the Georgian Communist Party Charkviani, and the annihilation
of members of the nonexistent nationalistic organization of Mingrelians in Georgia, took several months. During this period of time
Ignatyev arrested the most trusted of Beria's officials, like the Second Secretary of the Central Committee of Georgia, I. M. Bara-
miya; the General Attorney of Georgian Republic, B. Y. Shoniya;
Georgian Minister of Justice, A. M. Rapava; and the leader of the
Georgian Young Communist League, Zodelava, as well as several
high ranking officers of the local Secret Police, and many others
who belonged to the so-called "Beria Gang."

Besides them there were imprisoned hundreds of innocent people who were not interested in Moscow politics and whose only guilt was that they were real patriots who deeply loved their sunny motherland, the Caucasus.

The Mingrelian problem was dragged out by Ignatyev for over half a year, in contrast to Beria's method; he had fabricated and liquidated the "Leningrad Case" in a quick strike. However, in Georgia there were more arrests than executions, and after several months some of the imprisoned were released from jail and even restored to their former posts.

Lavrenty Beria was wise enough to interpret this as a sign of improvement in the situation of his "gang" in Georgia since it had happened without his personal intervention in that direction, it could be nothing else but a part of Stalin's cunning trap. Anyhow Beria, still Minister of Internal Affairs, was the highest Commander of the NKVD Forces, which would back him. Lavrenty could count on his officers; they would stand behind him not because they were devoted to their Chief, but because they knew that with the fall of Beria, hundreds of his men would be executed, while other thousands would be sent to Siberia. Above all, Beria realized that his end would not be immediate. He must be kept on as long as he was the watchdog of the atomic development program which Stalin was so eager to see brought to fruition, and as long as he held all the strings of the foreign espionage network in his hands. But if he were going to lose his power little by little, retention of his high position was only a matter of time. A wise statesman, Beria foresaw that Stalin's new tactic could change its course any day. To survive, he had to act quickly.

After Zhdanov's assassination and the "Leningrad Case," Beria drew closer to Malenkov. He was motivated by Malenkov's popularity among the generals and the support from the Red Army that would accompany his friendship. That way, a Beria-Malenkov duumvirate created a new power which could face even the Dictator. On the other hand, Stalin also might have nominated Ignatyev for Beria's sake, to save his image in the eyes of the Georgian people. As a purger of the Caucasian patriots and the Mingrelians, Stalin might prefer to assign someone else, an executive independent of Beria, so that Lavrenty would not be called the hangman of his own countrymen and kin. The purge of the Jews in Czechoslovakia might also be just another outbreak of the pathological anti-Semitism from which Stalin suffered more severely as he grew older. But since it would be nonsensical if Beria were to start persecuting his own men in Czechoslovakia, the Dictator might prefer to delegate this job to the new Chief of State Security. Beria based this speculation on one very important fact: Stalin still apparently trusted him one hundred percent, for he always took Lavrenty's remarks under consideration.

On October 5, 1952, Stalin called the Nineteenth Congress of the Communist Party. Among the several speeches delivered, three were very significant. One was by Malenkov, who warned that negligence had penetrated the Party, and that its members were not sufficiently alert, had lost their self-control and become conceited by their successes, forgetting the interests of the country; this behavior should be certainly branded and punished.

Such criticism, emphasizing that some high executives were not as efficient as they should be and that they were not completely Soviet-minded men, was always gladly accepted by the Superior.

The next lecture was given by Khrushchev. Although, like Malenkov, he did not mention any particular names, Khrushchev scolded those members of the Party for not being watchful enough, showing laxness in carrying out their duties, and for becoming careless of Party and State secrets. Khrushchev did not specify in his attack what kind of secrets were disclosed, nor to whom and by whom. He simply reminded the Party Congress that enemies of the USSR abounded and that the Soviet Union was encircled by hostile capitalist countries that plant their agents everywhere, even into Party ranks, so any Russian Communist who was not careful and talked too much would have to face the consequences.

This speech was prepared in a style calculated to please the Dictator, who was a most suspicious character and everywhere smelled traps, agents, spies, plots, rebellions, coups d'état attempts and assassinations.

However, this time nothing could satisfy the Big Boss, who was sitting gloomy and severe, looking about darkly. During the entire Congress he did not say a word. Neither did Beria, who preferred to use the tactic of waiting and observing.

Speaking for the Dictator was Alexander Poskrebyshev, Stalin's secretary, known as his shield-bearer or just his loudspeaker. Extolling Stalin, the Great Leader and Teacher, the speaker equated economic errors and deviations with treason and espionage against the Soviet country, and between the lines he signaled a new and chilling move in the Party, designed by Stalin.

It was hard to discern exactly what the Dictator had up his sleeve, but it was evident to the audience that some terrible event would occur in the near future.

The last item on the agenda was the election of the central organs of the Party. Then, on October 14 the Congress ended.

The members of the convention left for home with hearts full of deep concern and anxiety.

Two days later, the Plenum of the Party's newly elected Central Committee was called. This time Stalin took the floor. At the lectern in front of the members of the Presidium—Malenkov, Beria, Molotov, Voroshilov, Khrushchev, Bulganin, Kaganovich, Mikoyan and a few others—standing on tiptoe to make himself appear taller and less paunchy and squat than he really was and raising his voice, Stalin lashed his subordinates for their real and imaginary deviations, guilts and crimes. Unlike Malenkov, Khrushchev and Poskrebyshev, who at the previous meeting spoke in generalities, the Big Boss did not beat around the bush. He mentioned one name after another. Speaking in a limited Russian vocabulary with a heavy Georgian accent, Stalin accused Molotov of several crimes, charges not far from the definition of an enemy of the people. Just after he finished with Molotov, the Dictator looked at Mikoyan sitting in the front row and began to whip this Old Guard Bolshevik, one of the most devoted workers of the Party, with the harshest words, announcing his trespasses, crimes and subversive activities and making such fantastic and groundless accusations that it would have been laughable had it not been so frighteningly macabre.

Nor was this all. Lifting his right arm, which was visibly much longer than his left, Stalin leveled it and with his index finger pointed at Marshal Voroshilov. With a mad grimace at his dark, pockmarked face, now gray with rage, Stalin aimed thunderbolts at the head of that Old Communist from days long before the Revolution, an ardent Stalinist and the defender of Leningrad during the Second World War. Now, in the words of his superior, Voroshilov was a stupid British spy and an awkward moron who was even unable to stop the Nazi blockade of Leningrad. His activity with the Sovietization of Hungary, where he was later sent, was also unsatisfactory, Stalin declared, and so was Voroshilov's current work as Deputy Chairman of the Council of Ministers. In short,

Voroshilov was good for nothing, an old gelding, a piece of rug ready for the trash can.

Nor was Voroshilov the last in line for a lesson, the Big Boss continued. There was someone else, too, another Marshal of the Soviet Union, the Minister of Interior Affairs, Lavrenty Beria.

It was true that Beria was not as narrow-minded as that clumsy regular army man, Stalin admitted. But the bald head of Lavrenty Pavlovich seemed to be turned by his high position. Beria evidently felt himself a chieftan in Georgia and Czechoslovakia, as if they were his own states. And the Soviet Union had no room for such landlords. Besides this crime Beria was also blamed by the Big Boss for the betrayal of that Yugoslavian traitor, that scoundrel Tito, who broke with the Soviet Union.

At the end of his speech, the Dictator said that the four men named, along with a few others not specified, but smart enough to understand that some of the remarks applied to them too, could still reform their errors and deviations. But if they did not want to be sorry, they must begin their correction immediately.

Stalin finished his oration and stepped down from the lectern. All present rose and applauded him loudly. The meeting was over. Followed by his secretary, General Alexander Poskrebyshev, Head of Kremlin Security, Major General Pyotr Kosynkin and the chief of his bodyguard, Vasily Khrustalyov, Stalin left the auditorium. There was no doubt that the words of the Dictator were not just empty threats, and that in a short time a new terror, probably another tremendous wave of purges, would sweep over the highest posts in the Administration, destroying some of the best co-workers of the Great Comrade.

Soon the conjectures, guesses and fears were fully proved true, although as is usual in such cases, the terror took an entirely different direction than anyone had expected. It was probably only a prelude to a great new bloody purge, but at that time it was limited to another outburst of Stalin's hatred for the Jews.

In November 1952, after a long time in prison, the thirteen Czech leaders and the First Secretary of the Communist Party in Czechoslovakia and Deputy Prime Minister, Rudolph Slansky, were brought to court. The staged trial of "Slansky and his accomplices" took several days, and was broadcast and filmed, although Western newspapermen were barred from the session. By decision of the State Court, Slansky and ten of his closest co-workers were sentenced to death on the gallows, while the other three defendants received life prison terms.

In the same month, presumably on Stalin's order, Lydia Tima-shuk, a medical worker of dubious professional ability, even though on the payroll of the Ministry of State Security under Ignatyev, wrote to the Kremlin denouncing several doctors; the great major-ity of them were Jews. They supposedly were arranging a plot against the lives of the most eminent personalities, among them Marshal Alexander Vasilevsky and Marshal Ivan Konev. According to her information, some other outstanding Bolsheviks who had died not long before, such as Andrey Zhdanov, were victims of a poison administered by these physicians, who had taken care of their health. The group of fifteen "Kremlin physicians," among whom was Stalin's family doctor, Professor Vladimir Vinogradov, were, by the Dictator's order, arrested by Ignatyev. The case of these jailed men was given to Ignatyev's deputy, General of State Security Ryumin, Chief of the Section for Investigating Special Important Cases of State Security.

With beatings expressly ordered by the Big Boss, Ryumin ex-torted from these detained physicians confessions of committing all of the alleged crimes. Soon after their statements were procured for Stalin, the Soviet press revealed on its front pages that State Secur-ity had unmasked a terrorist gang of doctors who, using their pro-fessional knowledge maliciously, had killed several outstanding figures from the public and political world of the USSR. The major-ity of those criminals admitted having connections with the inter-national Jewish nationalist organization *Joint*, formed by American Intelligence, which financed sabotage and espionage in the Soviet Union. The other non-Jewish arrested doctors confessed that for a long time they had been British and American agents. Their trials were to be announced shortly.

This news was published simultaneously in the two leading So-viet newspapers, *Pravda* and *Izvestia*, on January 13, 1953.[4] One week later, the informer, Lydia Timashuk, was rewarded by Stalin for her service with the highest Soviet decoration, the Order of Lenin.

Beria was wise enough to realize that the whole affair of the

---

[4] Appendix 14.

"Doctors' Plot" was aimed against him—to accuse him of a lack of vigilance as Commissar of State Security. In accordance with Soviet law for such carelessness Beria should be imprisoned and tried as an accomplice of these criminals.

In the middle of February the formal bill of indictment against the defendants was still in the process of preparation when an alarming new event occurred—a sign that the senior members of the Politburo and Stalin's closest comrades were doomed. It was the arrest and execution of Colonel General Lev Mekhlis, Stalin's former secretary and later Deputy Commissar of Defense and Political Commissar of the Red Army. If now Mekhlis became a victim of the Big Boss, it was either the Dictator's unreasoning anti-Semitism, increasing with his years until he could no longer stand a Jew, even one who was his most ardent worshiper, or a piece of cunning stratagem to confuse the members of the Politburo.

Beria understood the execution of Mekhlis as another personal warning for himself, because General Mekhlis, Head of the Army Political Administration, was his very effective co-worker.

After the annihilation of a man as close to Stalin as Mekhlis, there was no doubt that soon other disciples of the Big Chief and Old Guard Bolsheviks would be liquidated: the Jew Kaganovich; Mikoyan, who already had been condemned in the recent Plenum; Voroshilov, who was married to a Jewess, Ekaterina Davidovna, as was Molotov, whose Jewish wife, Paulina, was still in a concentration camp. Yet another member of the Politburo, Andrey Andreyev, was married to a Jewess, Dora Khazan, while Khrushchev's son-in-law was a Jew.

In a few days Khrushchev's male secretary was arrested, obviously for the purpose of extracting information from him about political crimes supposedly committed by Khrushchev, which would lead to his imprisonment. Since Beria was also said to have some Jewish blood in his veins, it was clear to him that shortly he might be locked behind bars and shot. After the purge of his men in Czechoslovakia and Georgia as traitors and saboteurs, he could now be accused quite easily of dangerous negligence while acting as Commissar of State Security. Evidence of his crime would be his failure to discover the plot of the Kremlin doctors and other conspiracies. Another failure would justify his removal from his posts and replacement by a successor, Ignatyev.

Beria was well aware that among Stalin's immediate subordinates not only Poskrebyshev was his master foe; so also was General Kosynkin, the Chief of Security of the Kremlin. If a new purge were to begin, Beria would be the first of its victims.

Of course, that prognosis was only a guess. It was quite logical, however, to assume that if Stalin were not halted by an unexpected event, he would execute his new purge with the same method with which he had accomplished others before. On February 17, 1953, the sudden death of Major General Kosynkin was announced. Supposedly, he had died of a heart attack.

Although now seventy-three years old, Stalin did not look weak or senile and his health apparently gave him no cause for complaint. He also was in an exceptionally good frame of mind, which did not seem to portend any attempts against his old pals. Quite the opposite. He attended operas with them at the Bolshoi Theatre, although previously he had seldom had patience enough to stay until the end of the performance. Including them as guests, he gave receptions at the Kremlin for foreign diplomats and representatives and dined with the members of his Cabinet in his villa at Kuntsevo.

It was just about two weeks after the portentous death of Mekhlis was disclosed that Stalin, back from the movie theatre at the Kremlin with a few members of his Cabinet and after a dinner with them at his country home, *Blizhny* at Kuntsevo, was left alone except for Beria, who had his villa nearby, within walking distance. They talked informally in Stalin's study as they did often after a good meal. It was the beginning of March; the snow in the park beyond the windows was still piled high and the bare branches of the trees waved in the wind. In the room the logs in the fireplace in the corner crackled, their flames glowing red and blue. It was warm, quiet and cozy. With his usual slow but firm steps, the Great Comrade was pacing the room to and fro between his devoted disciple Lavrenty, who remained standing with proper respect, and the window. The view of the darkening garden behind the pane looked like a blue canvas, a landscape behind the glass framed by the thick brown wood. For a moment Stalin turned around, stopped and glanced at that living picture. Standing with his back to his subordinate, the Dictator displayed his short neck and above it the weak spot just under the right ear and the bone behind. One swift, precise stroke with the blackjack Beria always carried in his pocket could cause the same effect he had achieved so many times when practicing on victims in the cellars of Lubyanka Prison.

The right and perhaps the only moment came. Did Beria seize this chance? Nobody can tell for certain.

47

The Dictator Is Dead

ON THE MORNING OF March 2, 1953, Stalin's daughter Svetlana rushed to Kuntsevo in response to a phone call letting her know that Malenkov asked her to come as soon as possible. When she arrived she saw her father on the couch, dying. In the room were Malenkov, Khrushchev, Bulganin and Beria. She was told that Stalin had been found the previous night in his library, lying on the carpet near the couch, and was then carried from there to his bedroom. In the country house were several physicians, but since the best family doctors attached to the Great Comrade Stalin had been imprisoned by him, their deputies, now present at the villa, *Blizhny*, were only some inexperienced young medics who did not even know how to operate the artificial-respiration machine that had been brought in. All they did was administer some injections and apply leeches to the Big Boss' neck, a primitive treatment used in Russian villages for ages. The whole household, as well as Khrushchev, Bulganin and Malenkov, pretended to be crying. Only Beria did not. Although extremely agitated, he stood at Stalin's bed watching him intently, speculating whether the Big Boss was really dying and whether he was too paralyzed to be able to utter a few words that could reveal the true cause of his impending death. But even in that moment Beria was wise enough to assume an expression of sorrow gloomy enough to convince the expiring man that Lavrenty Beria, and no other, was his most faithful follower.

In the same moment Stalin sank into a coma; there was no more reason for Beria to play games. He intended to grab power and become master instantly. Excited to the utmost, he ordered Stalin's daughter taken from the room. Then he left the villa, sending the chief of the late Dictator's bodyguard, Khrustalyov, for his limousine, as if from now on this man was to be his servant. Beria hurried to his office to organize and take the tumultuous situation in hand. He knew very well that if he were not the first to take over the reins, he would be pushed aside by Malenkov or Khrushchev.

Stalin was dying; he appeared to be unconscious. The stroke he had suffered was murderous. But all of a sudden he opened his eyes, and peered at the faces of those around him, as if he were looking for someone whom he intended to punish. He lifted his left arm as if in an effort to point out the culprit. However, he did not find him in the crowd and was unable to express himself. But his gesture was full of anger and passion against an enemy. In a moment Stalin was dead.

At his desk in Lubyanka Prison Beria immediately phoned the Ministry of Health and the Moscow Academy of Medical Science of the Soviet Union, demanding the medical report signed by the consultation of professors and specialists. Lavrenty then ordered a car to be sent at night to Kuntsevo to take the body of the late Dictator for an autopsy. Afterwards the corpse was to be secretly transferred to the Kremlin. Lest there be any clues to the cause of the unexpected accident at the *Blizhny* villa at Kuntsevo, Beria decided to change the setting for the public, implying that the Great Comrade Stalin's stroke occurred while he worked alone in his headquarters in Moscow. Lavrenty also called the commanders of several regiments of armored divisions for tanks and cars with machine guns, and ordered the battalions of his Secret Police stationed in nearby towns to reinforce the Moscow garrison in case of any unrest.

Afterwards, Beria warned the press against displaying any sign of mourning, even by withdrawing light or humorous articles from their daily columns, while the radio station was forbidden to broadcast any funeral music. The theatres and movies were instructed to carry on as usual until the official news was announced.

These and other instructions and memoranda took Beria several hours, until at last he found time to summon to his office Alexander

Poskrebyshev, whom he had ordered arrested just after he returned to Lubyanka. The interrogation did not consist of many questions. Beria told Stalin's personal secretary to be seated, and while the guard held his arms behind the chair, Beria hit Poskrebyshev in the mouth, again and again, calling him the dirtiest of names. By the time the berserk Lavrenty had exhausted himself by shouting and hitting, the face of the beaten man looked like a piece of raw meat. He was bleeding from cut lips, and his jaw and nose were broken. Finally, Beria told the guard to take the prisoner to the solitary cellar in the basement.

The present Chief of State Security, Ignatyev, was also put under arrest. Since he was Malenkov's protégé, however, his life was spared. The same applied to his deputy, Ryumin. But the separate Ministry of State Security lost its independence and was shuffled back under Beria's control.

During the night of March 2-3, Beria called to his office all the professors of therapeutics and neuropathology who had been summoned to Stalin's deathbed. At this meeting Lavrenty declared that until the time a new Administration at the summit was established, the death of the Great Comrade was, for the sake of the country's security, to be a top secret. Then he ordered the physicians to prepare a bulletin announcing the serious, but not yet critical, illness of Stalin. Such a communiqué, previously presented to Beria for approval, would be broadcast and released to the Soviet press and to foreign correspondents in two days, on March 4. Subsequently it would be followed by several other bulletins, gradually expressing less hope for Stalin's recovery and preparing the Soviet population and the whole world for the tidings of his death. The exact date was to be determined immediately after the newly constituted regime was finally formed. The State apparatus then would work efficiently enough to master the situation, and to lead the country without any disturbances.

On March 4, 1953, Radio Moscow announced the tragic news that two days before, in the late hours, in his apartment at the Kremlin, Comrade Stalin had suffered a cerebral hemorrhage. The Great Teacher and Father of the nation had lost consciousness and the right side of his body was paralyzed. He also had lost his speech, and respiration was poor. This medical bulletin was signed by nine physicians, whose names were read by the speaker.

Thanks to Beria's precaution, Stalin, dead since March 2, was in the mind of the whole world still alive, when the broadcast revealed the illness that in reality had happened a few days before. The first bulletin was followed by two more, while, in the meantime, the new government was formed. Beria allowed the official announcement of the demise of Great Comrade Stalin on March 5, 1953, three days after the Dictator actually died.

The new Administration consisted of Malenkov as Premier, Beria and Molotov as Vice-Chairmen of the Council of Ministers, and Voroshilov, Kaganovich, Bulganin, Mikoyan and Khrushchev as members of the collective leadership.

Realizing that as the chief executioner, hangman and master of concentration camps, he was not popular in the nation, Beria decided to avoid unrest by pushing forward Malenkov as the leader immediately after Stalin's death. For the time being Lavrenty preferred to give priority to his involuntary friend and companion, Malenkov, who also was in opposition to the new purge prepared by Stalin just before the tyrant died. Why not let Malenkov enjoy the leadership for a short time, until the new order was firmly established? At any rate Beria, as Minister of Internal Affairs and State Security was still Commander in Chief of the Secret Police and in practice held all the power in his own hands. From now on it depended entirely on Beria to choose the right moment to overthrow that fat, owl-eyed eunuch Malenkov, together with that self-glorifying conceited Ukrainian churl, Khrushchev, and to imprison both of them as dangerous characters. Then, along with Mikoyan, who had been so helpful to Lavrenty in his Baku times, and therefore was so hated by Beria, these three imbeciles would be jailed in Lubyanka where in the solitary cellars they would be cured permanently of their stupidity with an injection of an ounce of lead in each of their heads. Molotov would become Lavrenty's man forever, because Beria had ordered the release of Molotov's wife from Siberia and her return to Moscow and because, thanks to Beria, Molotov again became Minister of Foreign Affairs.

On the night of March 5, when returning to his estate from the office, Beria's car passed by the neighboring Stalin villa *Blizhny* at Kuntsevo, and Lavrenty decided to erase the house of his late superior, the home where he, Beria, had been forced to listen thousands of times to the same dull jokes made by that bore Iosif Vissarionovich Dzhugashvili-Joseph Stalin, and to laugh at them, pretending enjoyment, while simultaneously aware that if he did

not look straight into the eyes of the tyrant, the Boss would annihilate him. This place, witness to Beria's shame and humiliation,
should vanish once and forever.

The next morning Beria appeared at Kuntsevo and called together all of Stalin's former civilian servants, cooks and maids. In a
shrill voice he told them to pack all their late master's belongings,
which were to be taken away, and to hurry, because the military
trucks he had ordered by phone were due to arrive at any minute.
Soon a few lorries stopped at the front door and several functionaries of the Secret Police started loading them with the furniture
and other possessions of the late Great Comrade and Sun of the
Sovietland, Joseph Stalin. These things were destined for a warehouse in a suburb of Moscow, where the confiscated belongings of
all imprisoned, exiled or executed persons were stored. Then Beria
called the household together again, and shouting, let them know
that they were not needed anymore, and could go to hell, for he did
not care for them at all. The military unit at Kuntsevo, the sentries
and bodyguards were all under arrest, except those who had been
planted there by Beria to spy on Stalin.

Finally, when the villa was stripped down to the last picture on
the walls and all the electric bulbs and rugs in the home had been
removed, Beria ordered his men to lock the empty abode and to
nail up all the doors and windows with planks.

When the job was finished the loaded trucks sped to the warehouse, the household dispersed, and Beria entered his Packard and
went to his office as usual.

That afternoon, with due honors and pomp, Stalin's coffin was
transferred to the Hall of Columns in the House of Unions Building, which had been draped in black. There the body was displayed
for three days and nights so the masses could pay homage. Prior to
that ceremony the face of the deceased Dictator had been em-
balmed. Under Lavrenty's supervision the makeup of the dead man
was so heavy that not only were his pockmarks invisible, the expression on the always gloomy face was uncharacteristically serene.
The job was done so expertly that even Stalin's daughter Svetlana
could scarcely recognize the features of her own father. Now nobody would be able to imagine that he saw any sign of a violent
death. Thousands of Beria's militiamen, standing side by side like a
living fence, prevented the mourners from stopping in front of the
casket even for a moment. The people were kept moving so they

could have only a short, superficial glance at the waxed face and the corpse, which looked like a fallen mannequin in the window of a second-rate clothes shop downtown.

The line of Muscovites was over a mile and a half long. At the casket the guard of honor was kept by the members of the Cabinet. This vigil was held for the press photographers, with Malenkov and Beria standing at each side of the head of the casket, as if Beria would like to emphasize that they were two equally powerful members of the leading duumvirate. A small military orchestra was playing old Georgian folk melodies. The music was soft and mournful.

The next day the official autopsy was published, citing, among other reasons for death, a massive hemorrhage in the brain of Comrade Joseph Stalin. The document, signed by nine doctors and professors, was revealed March 7, although the autopsy had been performed four days before with the vigilant Beria present. The announcement, an exact and detailed diagnosis, was prepared in such a way that it excluded any possibility of assassination. It read so smoothly that Lavrenty began suspecting that—Hell knows— perhaps those damn veterinarians smelled something wrong and then had faked the report and were only pretending to believe that Stalin's death was caused by some normal and natural phenomenon. The opinion was written too well to be rejected by Beria for release to the press, but he decided to remember the names of those doctors who were being helpful to him.

March 9, 1953, was designated as the date of the historic funeral. From the Hall of Columns the casket was carried out on the shoulders of the members of the new Cabinet led by Malenkov and Beria and by General of the Red Air Forces Vasily Stalin, son of the deceased Dictator. He was strategically located just behind Malenkov and in front of Molotov, who would support him should he stumble or fall, for Stalin junior was an alcoholic in a permanent state of drunkenness. They placed the coffin on the gun carriage, then formed lines and the tremendous funeral processesion started into Red Square. In the first row behind the casket, marching abreast were the pallbearers, the eight representatives of the new power, and Vasily Stalin. This line was headed by Khrushchev, who was made Chairman of the Commission for the Organization of the Funeral, with Beria next to him.

When the procession arrived at the Red Square, near the Lenin

Mausoleum, speeches were delivered by Malenkov, Beria and Molotov. While the first eulogy, by Malenkov, was a typical funeral oration full of clichés praising the deceased as the Most Eminent Citizen of the Country, Beria's sounded more like the political oration of a new ruler delivering an inauguration speech from the throne, expounding his program to his subjects.[1]

On that gray, wintry March day in Moscow, Beria's hoarse, nasal voice fell on the clear air monotonously and colorlessly. The fat, bespectacled Commissar in his big black hat and heavy black overcoat looked like a monstrously gigantic cockroach standing on its back legs and humming to itself.

The solemn silence of the listeners was interrupted from time to time only by Vasily Stalin who, after repeated gulps of vodka from a pocket flask, drunk and in a fighting mood, stood at a distance and shouted at the speaker, calling Beria *svolotch, blad'* and *sookenseen*—a scoundrel, a whore and a son of a bitch, and the murderer of his father, the Great Joseph Vissarionovich Stalin.

This disharmony with the majesty of the Leader's death was not the worst phenomenon hanging over the mournful ceremony, however. Much more depressing was the general mood created by Beria who, as Commissar of Internal Affairs responsible for the safety of the people present at this historical funeral, had taken some unusual steps. For the sake of State Security, Beria had mobilized his Special Forces with tanks and armored cars and infantry with machine guns and flamethrowers on all streets on the route of the funeral procession. By this action Beria intended also to present a kind of a military parade demonstrating his own strength, thereby warning his associates and anyone who had any doubts that Marshal Lavrenty Pavlovich Beria was the most powerful man in the Soviet Union and the personality who would run the country in the near future.

However, this particular order of his was a great mistake. Instead of impressing and frightening his enemies, it opened their eyes to the danger his power posed. In his self-assurance Lavrenty forgot the old maxim that underrating your foes is the first step to defeat. By displaying his military force, Beria showed his co-workers that he thought of them as just a bunch of his potential prisoners, with whom he was following the dead Dictator to the mauso-

---

[1] Appendix 15.

leum. His troops not only seized the streets, avenues and squares but they even encircled the whole city, cutting off the nation's capital from the entire country. By this move Lavrenty was evidently letting his partners in the Cabinet know that the military parade of his Security Army was nothing else but a dress rehearsal before the opening night of the performance that Beria was going to stage. And the title of that show would be: *Coup d'Etat.*

The third and last speaker at that grand, ceremonial funeral was Molotov, whose oration was a typical routine tribute from an Old Guard Bolshevik to his Superior. But for this eulogy, nobody cared.

48

Two Days Before Coup d'Etat

SOON, NORMAL TIMES PREVAILED AGAIN, as if nothing unusual had happened in the colorless and dull life of the Soviet citizens. Again, there was exactly the same work, with its iron discipline and stiff regulations, the same shortages of everything in groceries and other shops, the same boring propaganda in the press, radio and movies as had predominated during Stalin's era.

At the Kremlin the newly reigning triumvirate, Malenkov, Beria and Molotov, did not change by a hair the previous line of domestic politics. While Malenkov was still busy struggling with economic problems, Beria, with the exactness of an architectural engineer, constructed his last few steps to the top.

The system of concentration camps had to be reorganized. After the news of Stalin's death millions of convicts expected their hardship to be relieved and the general mood of optimism decreased their efficiency. Mostly they had believed their misery to be caused by Stalin, and after he was gone, they looked for an amnesty, or at least a review of their long sentences. Of course, not all inmates were innocent people, political prisoners and sheepishly behaving peasants. There were also professional criminals, murderers, burglars, rapists, thieves and hooligans. These men were waiting for any sign of a softening of the severe rules in the camps, expecting that some convicts would be allowed to return home. It would be the right time to start a revolt, to disarm and kill the guards, and then to murder the intelligentsia and Jews to seize their possessions needed for the journey back from exile.

According to reports from GULAG, the camp commands asked desperately for reinforcements and equipment, and for the issuance of some new rules and regulations to increase the low productivity. Beria had to solve this problem as soon as possible.

To calm the tension in the hard labor camps Lavrenty proclaimed a small amnesty of petty criminals—hoodlums, drunkards and pickpockets serving sentences under five years. The political prisoners, however, and the intelligentsia could not expect any mercy. Beria also was busy with several important changes on the international scene. In spite of the fact that Molotov was Minister of Foreign Affairs, it was Lavrenty Pavlovich Beria who had the last word on the recommendation and approval of Soviet ambassadors and the diplomatic staff abroad, since all these people worked as Security agents and spies for Beria's Ministry of Internal Affairs and of Security of the Soviet Union. Beria also decided that his man Vyshinsky, who recently was told to step down from his post as Minister of Foreign Affairs, should be elevated to the rank of Head of the Soviet Delegation to the United Nations and transferred from Moscow to New York. There Vyshinsky became chief of the Red spy net in America.

Beria now recalled several of those men who had been Stalin's protégés and whom Lavrenty had been forced to accept even though they were not his blind followers. This reshuffling Beria handled with cunning and so discreetly that it neither attracted the attention of the free world nor shook the structure of the Soviet Foreign Service. Nor did it provoke too many defections among the higher echelon of Soviet personnel abroad.

The ranks of his Security Police and the top functionaries of the Militia were also checked by Beria and cleansed of any unreliable elements, especially the henchmen of the recent Minister of State Security, Semyon Ignatyev, who although removed from his post was still at large as a personal friend of Malenkov.

There was still the question of the autopsy performed on Stalin by the nine doctors. Despite the fact that their postmortem report was written in such a way as to please everybody, Beria above all, it was hard to believe that these wise and skilled professionals had not been able to discover the main reason for Stalin's cerebral hemorrhage and paralysis of his right side. Such witnesses were always dangerous, especially if by chance one of them, choosing freedom, managed to escape to the West. This information could ruin Beria's position as ruler of the USSR. It was not long after Lavrenty Pavlovich came to that conclusion that one of the doctors who signed the postmortem, Professor Rusakov, died suddenly. A few days later the chairman of the team of those professors, the Minister of Public Health in the Soviet Union, Dr. Tretyakov, disappeared from his home at night and was brought to Beria's office at Lubyanka. There the physician learned of his new assignment as Chief Doctor of the enormous two-thousand-bed hospital newly built in Vorkuta, one of the biggest hard labor camps in the far north. On the very same night, Dr. Tretyakov was driven to a prison train where, in a cattle car with sixty inmates, he met Professor Kuperin and two of the other eight colleagues with whom he had examined Stalin's body. The remaining four doctors of the autopsy commission were less important scientists and Beria decided he would leave their fate for the future.

This whole operation Lavrenty performed quickly under the shade of a few nights, without any fanfare, unlike Ignatyev and his right hand Ryumin who had initiated the "Doctors' Plot" ordered by Stalin. However, the removal of such personalities as Dr. Tretyakov, the Minister of Public Health, and Professor Kuperin, Chairman of the Medical Health Council, and two other scholars, members of the Academy of Medical Sciences in Moscow, plus the unexpected and rather mysterious death of the fifth doctor, could not pass unnoticed by the people. All these physicians, whose names were mentioned by the press and radio with the announcement of the autopsy, had become known to the masses. Something had to be done to prevent a panic in the nation's medical circles and to alleviate any fear that a new purge among doctors was being instituted or that the Ignatyev-Ryumin anti-physicians' action still continued.

The "Doctors' Plot" was promulgated by the former Ministry of State Security, which at that time was not under Beria, but it could be ascribed to him by the people, because Beria was the Minister of Internal Affairs. He decided, therefore, to denounce the entire doctors' affair as a fabricated frameup and a hoax with which he had no connection and which should be unmasked and condemned. Beria also had no doubt that if Stalin had lived longer, the anti-Jewish and anti-American "Doctors' Plot" staged by him would have ignited a great new purge in which he would have been one of the first and main victims. By the stratagem of announcing that the doctors were innocent victims, Lavrenty would also undermine the myth of Stalin as the beloved Father of the Country, a Genius who should be worshiped by his people; it would denigrate as well Stalin's aggressive foreign policy against the West, the United States and Great Britain primarily.

However, since Ignatyev was still under Malenkov's wing, the scapegoat would have to be Ignatyev's deputy, Ryumin. This functionary, once Chief of the Security Section in Stalin's personal Secretariat and Poskrebyshev's man, could be presented as the late Dictator's creature who had stood behind Ignatyev and was nothing but a puppet in his hands. Ryumin, who according to Stalin's explicit order to "beat, beat, and beat the Kremlin doctors until they confess all their crimes,"[1] had personally tortured the victims. But he was a mere policeman and nobody would care about his fate, particularly not his former superior Ignatyev, who would be more concerned with saving his own neck. So Ryumin was arrested and locked up in Lefortovo Prison.

On the night of April 3, 1953, Lydia Timashuk, the medical worker who, as Ignatyev's agent, had written the letter to Stalin provoking the arrest of the Kremlin doctors, was brought to the main office at Lubyanka Prison, where Beria told her to take off the Order of Lenin Stalin had awarded her for her information. She was then sent to a solitary cell in the basement to wait for transport to a hard labor camp.

The next morning *Pravda* published the official statement of the Ministry of Internal Affairs of the USSR. In this announcement Beria rehabilitated all the persecuted doctors, presenting them as baselessly accused. He also denounced the former Ministry of State Security, which at that time had not been under his control, as an agency that used impermissible methods of inquest forbidden by USSR law.

Pravda also announced Lydia Timashuk's deprivation of her decoration; nobody now would have any doubt of the fate Beria had prepared for this provocateur who had once been Stalin's protégée.

---

[1] Nikita S. Khrushchev, *Secret Speech Before a Closed Session of the 20th Congress of the Communist Party of the Soviet Union on February 25, 1956* (Washington: United States Government Printing Office, 1957).

Day after day *Pravda* brought one sensation after another to its readers. In the editorials, inspired and virtually dictated by Beria, his enemy Ignatyev was denounced as a politically ignorant man who was taken in by his deputy Ryumin, a criminal character.

Soon after, the arrest of Ryumin was publicly revealed. He was presented as the main culprit, the individual responsible for the frameup and imprisonment of the Kremlin doctors. Among them had been the most prominent medical figures in the Soviet Union, including the famous seventy-one-year-old Doctor Vladimir Vinogradov, whom Ryumin had put in chains and beaten and tortured until he lost consciousness. This, despite the fact that such atrocious methods during inquiries are not allowed by the Soviet Constitution. In this *Pravda* article thousands of Soviet citizens could read Beria's announcement that ". . . a group of doctors accused of sabotage, espionage and terrorist activities directed against active statesmen of the USSR . . . have been arrested wrongfully by the former Ministry of State Security of the USSR, without any legal justification whatsoever."[2]

In the meantime, during an interrogation Ryumin was beaten by Beria, who, with true satisfaction and both of his fists, knocked out all the teeth of Stalin's former secretary, despite the fact that such methods of interrogation supposedly horrified the good Lavrenty Pavlovich. Ignatyev, Ryumin's former boss, was removed from the post he still held as Secretary of the Central Committee of the Communist Party of the Soviet Union.[3] However, thanks to his two powerful protectors, Prime Minister Malenkov and Khrushchev, Ignatyev was saved from Beria's fists and beatings with blackjacks, but exiled by him far from Moscow, to the remote Bashkir Soviet Republic in the Urals.

Nor did Lavrenty forget his other personal foes. He never did. He still remembered the behavior of Vasily Stalin at the funeral, and although he had not himself heard what the drunkard had shouted at him, his agents' reports were enough.

Beria had a friendly talk with his partner in the Cabinet, Minister of Defense Bulganin, telling him that it was unbearable that an alcoholic like Vasily was still a General of the Red Air Forces. Bulganin, who for years had feared Beria, agreed eagerly. Soon

[2] Appendices 2 and 3.
[3] Appendix 16.

Vasily Stalin was called to the Ministry of Defense where he was told to return his military papers and learned that he was being kicked out, dishonorably discharged from the Red Army and Air Forces. This was not all, however. Beria's ferrets followed Vasily wherever he went for a glass of vodka, and in a few weeks arrested him; when in a drunken state the young Stalin got involved in a barroom brawl. The scuffle was staged and provoked by his agents and Beria got what he was waiting for. Stalin Junior was branded a hooligan, and now could be so handled. While an average Soviet citizen arrested for a drunken fracas in a tavern was sentenced to three years at hard labor, Stalin's son was to be treated more severely.

The trial of the former Chief of the Red Air Forces of the Moscow Military District, General Vasily Josephovich Stalin, was brief and uncomplicated. After hearing the testimony of a few witnesses, the judges, as instructed by Beria, sentenced Vasily Stalin to eight years in prison. Under guard the condemned son of the late Dictator was driven straight from the courtroom to an ancient jail, a dark and damp one, in the small town of Vladimir, far from Moscow.

After this victory over the son of the beloved Great Comrade Stalin and after smashing Ignatyev and Ryumin, Marshal Beria started to redress the damage those two adversaries had done him by purging his trusted men all over the Soviet Union and in the countries of Eastern Europe. Beria flew to Tbilisi, where Ignatyev's fabricated "Mingrelian uprising" had been aimed against him and his associates. There, without using any frameup to justify a new purge, Lavrenty Pavlovich removed all the new functionaries and restored his followers, installing his personal friend, Kote Charkviani, First Secretary of the Georgian Communist Party.

Back in his main office in Moscow, Beria introduced the same method he had used in Georgia into other Soviet republics. In the Ukraine, Byelorussia, Latvia, Lithuania and Estonia, Lavrenty renominated men from his followers and tightened the Security Departments in the conquered countries: Bulgaria, Albania, Rumania, Czechoslovakia, Hungary and Poland. Of the loyalty of East Germany Beria could be quite certain, knowing he would never have any trouble with that country. He ruled it through his most devoted disciples: Otto Grotewohl, the puppet Premier of the German Communist People's Republic; Vladimir Semyenov, who was

Lavrenty's man and a Soviet High Commissioner; and Wilhelm Zaisser and Bogdan Kobulov. A colonel in the German Army, Wilhelm Zaisser was an Old Communist who fled from his fatherland to the USSR where he attended a Military Academy for Soviet Espionage. When Beria was transferred from the Caucasus to Moscow, Zaisser worked for him from the first and became his confidant. After Hitler's defeat, Beria sent Zaisser to East Germany, and helped him win the nomination for Minister of Defense. Lavrenty was sure that Zaisser, his subordinate and drinking companion, was a German on whom he could rely. To be one hundred percent certain, Beria kept in East Berlin his Russian subordinate, Bogdan Kobulov, one of the most trusted members of the infamous "Beria Gang."

On his toilsome road to supreme power at the Kremlin, Lavrenty Pavlovich Beria was now preparing his final step. This path he paved meticulously, as should a farseeing statesman, a wise strategist who, during the victorious war against the Third Reich, was Vice Chairman of the Big Five USSR Defense Committee, and above all, as a pedantic architectural engineer who realized that one little error could ruin his long-planned structure. Like a gigantic spider, Beria spun his murderous cobweb over Moscow, over the heads of the other Ministers of the ruling Government, preparing for his triumphant entrance on Red Square in front of the Kremlin, which soon would become his own palace.

The members of the Cabinet were aware of what was going on, but they were helpless. Beria, with his own military forces, was too powerful; he was also as ruthless as Stalin and more sober-minded as well as colder and more calculating than the late psychopathic Dictator. At night, chilled with terror, Malenkov, Molotov, Mikoyan, Voroshilov, Kaganovich, Bulganin and Khrushchev listened to every rumble on their streets, to every hum before the windows of their homes, knowing that if a car stopped in front of their houses, and if someone knocked on their doors, it would be a Secret Police officer with two armed guards, to arrest them and bring them to Lubyanka Prison. There Beria would "interrogate" them by knocking out their teeth and beating them unconscious, until at last they would be taken to a cellar to be executed *in camera*.

The Secret Police garrison in Moscow seemed to them to be waiting only for a sign to start their procedure. Some perspicacious high ranking officers of the Ministry of State Security predicted the Zero hour of Beria's coup d'état as 6 o'clock in the morning of June 19, 1953.

Two days before, on June 17, in East Berlin, an uprising against the Soviet occupation broke out.

49

Beginning of the End

AFTER MASS MEETINGS in several East Berlin factories on June 16, German workers, angered by increased production quotas, protested against poor working conditions and proclaimed a general strike the next morning. Demanding higher wages, more food and lower prices they poured into the streets and squares. Soon the crowds rose to over 100,000 people; demonstrations began against the Communist regime. The windows of the Soviet Propaganda Office in Potsdamer Platz were smashed and the building was set on fire. Several cars of German Communist dignitaries were overturned. The big Soviet red flag with hammer and sickle, waving on top of the high pole above the Brandenburg Gate, was pulled down, ripped into shreds and perished in flames.

Russian troops stationed in the Soviet Zone of Berlin, unprepared for such riots, were entirely disoriented. The few Soviet tanks that appeared in Potsdamer Platz were met by a hail of stones and bricks; there was danger that soon the rocks would be followed by Molotov cocktails: bottles of benzine. The revolt threw all of East Berlin into chaos. It was not until two o'clock in the afternoon that the surprised Russians pulled in reinforcements from nearby bases. Then, over 200 heavy tanks and 10,000 troops rushed into the city. Fire from the Soviet machine guns killed dozens of demonstrators and wounded hundreds. The main streets, avenues and squares— Stalin Allee, Marx-Engels Platz and Unter den Linden, where the

Soviet Embassy was located, were blocked by military trucks and armored cars and the Volkspolizei—the German People's Police— began making mass arrests. Martial law was declared over loud-speakers.

But the situation still was not contained. On the contrary, in spite of the ruthless steps of the Soviet occupants, the revolution spread to several other cities and towns of East Germany; in Dres-den, Leipzig and Magdeburg the workers proclaimed strikes, burned official buildings and red banners, and demolished any visi-ble signs of Russian bondage.

The revolt lasted several days before it was entirely subdued and extinguished. Nobody realized that the riots were a blessing for the Soviet rulers at the Kremlin, whose existence and lives were endan-gered by Beria. In view of the situation in East Germany, where the ashes of many buildings and factories were still smoldering, any coup d'état in Moscow was impossible. If the German uprising were carried on by other countries enslaved by the USSR, like Czechoslovakia, Hungary, Poland, Rumania and Bulgaria, and if they were supported by the Western Allies, it would be disastrous for the Soviet Union, which was not yet prepared for resistance against the United States and its atomic weapons. Under these conditions Beria's dictatorship would be shortly put to an end. At the moment his main task was to restore order in East Berlin and in the whole Soviet Zone of Germany. It was also necessary to send reinforcements to all East European countries occupied by the Russians. The uprising in East Germany, the only West European country of over 18 million people under Russian rule, was too great a discredit to the USSR, a shame that could weaken the Soviet policy with the Western powers. The riots in East Berlin destroyed the legend of happiness in the Socialist People's German Republic, a myth built by Soviet propaganda for the consumption of the West.

To quell the unrest in East Germany Beria sent more Secret Police troops and replaced several high ranking officers and func-tionaries of the Ministry of State Security MGB stationed there, as well as commanders of the Red German Police indirectly subordi-nate to him. Lavrenty also called to step down from their posts such personalities as his protégé, the Soviet Security General Ko-bulov and the High Commissioner in East Germany, Vladimir Semyenov, although he did not arrest any one of them.

But the revolution in East Germany was not the only event that undermined the reputation of the Soviet Union. The whole free world was still shocked by the affair of the Kremlin doctors staged by the late Stalin and recently revealed by Beria as a frameup, and also by the attempted assassination of Premier Malenkov on May 31, which had stirred some interest. Until the dust from these events had settled and they had been forgotten by the international press and the general public of the Western countries, Beria had to put aside any steps toward his own career.

On June 26, 1953, Lavrenty Beria went to the Kremlin to a joint meeting of the Presidium and the Politburo Party Secretariat. It is hard to say for certain if he was shot to death there by General Moskalenko, or by Khrushchev, or strangled by his colleagues of the Cabinet, Mikoyan and Molotov, with the help of three Red Army Generals who jumped him and took him by his throat, as it was also rumored. It is also impossible to state positively whether Beria was arrested when on his way to the Bolshoi Theatre on June 28, or whether he was apprehended after a reception in the Polish Embassy in Moscow, or at the meeting of the Presidium at the Kremlin, as was related in the book *Khrushchev Remembers*; or whether it was truly Beria himself who stood in the defendant's dock when his trial was announced officially on December 18, 1953; or whether it was he who, on December 23, listened to the sentence condemning him to death, to be executed that same night. Perhaps it was his double exhibited in the courtroom to the public, while the real Beria lay dead, liquidated five months before, in July, according to the *Great Universal Polish Encyclopedia* passed by the Communist censor in Warsaw. Since Khrushchev gave several versions of the death of Lavrenty Pavlovich Beria and every story differed from the one before, it is hard to believe any of his tales. However, the first hint of Beria's disappearance from the political scene came in the form of a note in *Pravda* of June 28, when the newspaper published the exact list of all eminent political personalities who attended the gala performance of the opera, *The Decembrists*, but omitted the name of the first Deputy Premier of the Soviet Union, Marshal Lavrenty Pavlovich Beria.

The first official announcement of the fall of Beria was published on the front page of *Pravda* July 10, 1953. It read as follows:

Information Bulletin on the Plenary Session of the Central Committee of the Communist Party of the USSR.

A Plenary Session of the Central Committee of the Communist Party of the USSR was held a few days ago.

Having heard and discussed a report of the Presidium of the Central Committee delivered by Comrade G. M. Malenkov concerning criminal activities against the Party and the State; undermining the security of the Soviet Union, being in the interest of the foreign capital, perpetrated by L. P. Beria, and manifested by his treacherous attempts to place the Ministry of the Internal Affairs of the USSR above the Soviet Government and the Communist Party of the USSR, the Plenary Session of the Central Committee of the Communist Party of the Soviet Union resolved to expel L. P. Beria from the ranks of the Communist Party of the Soviet Union, for being the enemy of the Communist Party and of the Soviet Union.

At the Presidium of the Supreme Soviet of the USSR.

In view of the recently uncovered criminal activities against the State, directed towards undermining the Soviet State, and being in the best interest of foreign capital, committed by L. P. Beria, the Presidium of the Supreme Council of the USSR, after due deliberation on the report made by the Soviet of the Ministers of the USSR concerning this matter, resolved to:

1. remove L. P. Beria from the position of the First Deputy Chairman of the Council of the Ministers of the USSR, and from the position of the Minister of Interior of the USSR;

2. to submit the matter of criminal activities of L. P. Beria for consideration by the Supreme Court of the USSR.

In the same issue *Pravda* printed a long and exhaustive commentary on this proclamation under the headline:

INDESTRUCTIBLE IS THE UNITY OF THE PARTY, GOVERNMENT OF THE SOVIET UNION.[1] It was followed by a communiqué: COMMUNISTS OF MOSCOW AND THE MOSCOW REGION UNANIMOUSLY APPROVE THE RESOLUTION PASSED BY THE PLENARY SESSION OF THE CENTRAL COMMITTEE OF THE COMMUNIST PARTY OF THE USSR,[2] while the other newspaper, *Izvestia*, of July 10 published an editorial: THE UNITY OF THE PARTY, GOVERNMENT AND OF THE SOVIET NATION IS UNSHAKABLE.[3]

The next day the attack on Beria continued. *Pravda* published an editorial entitled, THE VOICE OF THE PARTY IS THE VOICE OF THE NATION.[4]

[1] Appendix 17.
[2] Appendix 18.
[3] Appendix 19.
[4] Appendix 20.

Then Malenkov let the masses cool off for four weeks until August 9 and 10, when the press again reminded the nation of that enemy of the Soviet people, Lavrenty Beria, provocateur and secret agent of the corrupt, capitalistic West.[5]

Behaving as if Beria were still alive awaiting his trial, the Public Attorney of the Soviet Union, announced on December 17, 1953, in both *Pravda* and *Izvestia* the official report of his investigation of Beria and his closest co-workers and disciples, popularly known as "Beria's Gang," although described in the press as his accomplices. This was a really dramatic document. It stated:

IN THE OFFICE OF THE PUBLIC PROSECUTOR
OF THE USSR.

On June 26, 1953, the Presidium of the Supreme Council of Ministers of the USSR reviewed the report of the Council of Ministers of the USSR pertaining to the criminal activities of L. P. Beria, an agent of foreign capital, aiming to undermine the Soviet Government, resolved to: remove L. P. Beria from the position of the First Deputy Chairman of the Council of Ministers of the USSR and from the position of Minister of Internal Affairs of the USSR: furthermore to put him on trial. On August 8, 1953, the Supreme Council of the USSR approved the decree issued by the Presidium of the Supreme Council of the USSR on 26 of June.

Presently, the Office of the Public Prosecutor of the USSR has completed the investigation concerning the case of L. P. Beria, traitor to his Country.

The investigation has shown that Beria, taking advantage of his position, organized a group of conspirators, hostile to the Soviet Government, with the criminal intent of using the central as well as the local organs of the Ministry of Internal Affairs against the Party and the Government of the USSR, serving the interests of foreign capital, attempting in their treacherous plans to place the Ministry of Internal Affairs above the Party and Government, aiming to seize the power and to abolish the Soviet Workers' and Peasants' system, in order to restore capitalism and establish the rule of the bourgeoisie.

Active participants of the treacherous group of conspirators, collaborating with Beria in the course of several years in their joint criminal activities within the organs of the People's Commissariat of Internal Affairs or Ministry of Internal Affairs, are the accused: V. N. Merkulov, former Minister of the State Security of the USSR, and recently the Minister of State Control of the USSR; V. G. Dekanozov, former Head of one of the Departments of the People's Commissariat of Internal Affairs of the USSR

---

[5] Appendices 21 and 22.

and recently the Minister of Internal Affairs of the Georgian Soviet Social-
ist Republic; B. A. Kobulov, former National Commissar of the Internal
Affairs of the Georgian Soviet Socialist Republic, later Vice-Minister of
the State Security of the USSR and recently Vice-Minister of the In-
ternal Affairs of the USSR: S. A. Goglidze, former National Commissar of
Internal Affairs of the Georgian Soviet Socialist Republic, and recently
Head of one of the Departments of the Ministry of Internal Affairs of the
USSR; P. Y. Meshik, former Head of one of the Departments of the State
Security of the USSR, and recently Minister of Internal Affairs of the
Ukrainian Soviet Socialist Republic; and finally L. E. Vlodzimirsky,
former Head of the Investigation Section for extremely important matters
of the Ministry of Internal Affairs of the USSR.

Beria and his collaborators carefully camouflaged and hid their hostile,
treacherous activities over a period of many years. After J. V. Stalin's
death, when reactionary imperialist powers activated their covert moves
against the Soviet Government, Beria intensified his subversive work
aiming to accomplish his criminal goals primarily by using organs of the
Ministry of Internal Affairs to seize power; this, however, led in a short
time to the unmasking of the foul face of the traitor to his Country, and
to undertaking decisive measures toward suppressing his hostile activities.

Succeeding to the post of the Minister of Internal Affairs of the USSR
in March 1953, Beria began his efforts of upgrading and placing participants of the group of conspirators in executive positions in the Ministry
of Internal Affairs. The conspirators subjected the honest employees of
the Ministry of the Internal Affairs to persecution and victimization, because of their refusal to carry out Beria's criminal orders.

Aiming to undermine the collective farm system and to create difficulties in the Country's food supply system, Beria sabotaged in every
possible way, and impeded the implementation of the most important
measures of the Party and the Government, designed to improve the
economy of collective and state farms as well as measures directed
towards a steady rise in prosperity in the Soviet Nation.

It has been determined also that Beria and his accomplices undertook
criminal measures aiming to revive the remnants of the bourgeois and
nationalistic elements in the Soviet Republics, to spread hostility and
misunderstanding among the nations in the USSR and in the first place
to undermine the friendship of the nations of the USSR with the grand
Russian Nation.

Lacking any sort of social support within the USSR, Beria and his accomplices counted in their criminal designs on the support of their
conspiracy by the reactionary, imperialist powers from abroad.

It has been established now by the investigation, that Beria made connections with the foreign Intelligence service during the period of Civil

War. In 1919, Beria, while in Baku, perpetrated a treachery by becoming a secret agent in the counterrevolutionary services of Mussavat government in Azerbaijan, which was acting under the control of the British Secret Service. In 1920, Beria was in Georgia, where again he committed a treacherous act, by establishing a clandestine communication with the Menshevik Secret Political Police Department in Georgia, the latter being a branch of the British Intelligence Service.

The investigation has proven that during the following years Beria continued and widened his clandestine criminal connections with the foreign Secret Service through spies who were sent from abroad and whom he always managed to save from being caught and subjected to well-deserved punishment.

Acting as a spy and traitor, who sold out to foreign Intelligence Service, Beria with the help of his accomplices, continued also to communicate secretly with the counterrevolutionary Georgian Menshevik émigrés, agents of several foreign Intelligence Services through the entire period of his criminal activities.

Cleverly concealing and camouflaging his criminal past, and hostile connections with Intelligence Service of foreign countries, Beria chose slander, intrigues, various provocations, and the basic method of operation against the honest members of the Party and Soviet workers, who stood in his way in implementing the hostile designs against the Soviet Government and interfered with his climb to power.

Having reached positions of responsibility by means of these criminal methods, in Georgia and in the whole Transcaucasia, and subsequently in the Ministry of Internal Affairs of the USSR, furthermore attempting to seize power in order to fulfill his treacherous goals, Beria and his accomplices dealt summarily with people unfriendly to them, never being deterred by acts of arbitrariness and lawlessness, thus deceiving the Party and the Government in a vile manner.

The investigation has revealed a number of criminal intrigues of Beria, directed towards achievement of his career-climbing goals and frustrating the unmasking of his hostile designs. Indeed, the investigation has established that Beria, over a period of several years with the aid of accomplices was conducting a criminal, underhanded campaign against Sergo Ordzhonikidze, a prominent figure in the Communist Party and Soviet Government, recognizing him as the man who was standing in the way of his further advancement and implementation of his hostile plans. As it has been now determined, Sergo Ordzhonikidze nurtured a political distrust toward Beria. After Sergo Ordzhonikidze's death, the conspirators continued to practice a cruel vengeance against the members of the latter's family.

The investigation has also determined the facts that conspirators committed terrorist murders of persons from whom they feared exposure. Thus, Beria and his conspirators murdered M. S. Kedrov, a member of the Communist Party since 1902, former member of the Presidium of the All-Russian Extraordinary Commission for Combatting Counterrevolution and Sabotage, and of the staff of the OGPU under F. E. Dzerzhinsky. The conspirators had reason to believe that Kedrov possessed materials concerning the criminal past of Beria. Other facts have also been established concerning terrorist murders committed by conspirators with the criminal intent of destroying the honest cadres devoted to the cause of the Communist Party and Soviet Government.

The investigation has shown also that Beria and his accomplices committed a number of treacherous acts, attempting to weaken the defense capability of the Soviet Union.

Evidence brought by the investigation shows that the members of the treacherous group, the defendants: Merkulov, Dekanozov, Kobulov, Goglidze, Meshik and Vlodzimirsky, being tied together with Beria in criminal activities throughout many years, carried out every criminal order given by Beria, thus helping him to hide and camouflage his criminal past, committing several very grave crimes against the State, as shown above.

Hence, it has been determined that defendants Beria, Merkulov, Dekanozov, Kobulov, Goglidze, Meshik, and Vlodzimirsky, by betraying their Country, worked as secret agents for international imperialism, as the worst enemies of the Soviet Nation.

The investigation revealed also the facts concerning other crimes perpetrated by Beria, which testify to his extreme moral degradation, also facts concerning his criminal mercenary activities and abuses of power.

Having been exposed by the testimony of numerous witnesses during investigation and shown genuine documented data, the defendants confessed their guilt in having perpetrated a number of very grave state crimes.

Beria, handed over to justice, under charges of treason against the State for organizing anti-Soviet conspiracy, perpetrating terrorist acts, for active opposition against the working class, as well as against the revolutionary labor movement, manifested by him while he was serving as a secret agent in the Intelligence agencies of the counterrevolutionary Mussavat government during the period of Civil War, i.e., acts specified by the articles 58-1B, 58-8, 58-13, 58-11 of the Criminal Code of the Russian Soviet Federated Socialist Republic.

Merkulov, Dekanozov, Kobulov, Goglidze, Meshik and Vlodzimirsky, handed over to justice under charges of treason against the Country, for perpetration of acts of terrorism, and for participation in the counterrevolutionary, conspiratorial group, that is, for the crimes specified by the articles 58-1B, 58-8, 58-11 in the Criminal Code of the Russian Soviet Federated Socialist Republic.

In compliance with the Decree issued by the Presidium of the Supreme Council of the USSR, the case concerning the charges against Beria, Merkulov, Dekanozov, Kobulov, Goglidze, Meshik and Vlodzimirsky is submitted for consideration of the Special Court in Attendance of the Supreme Court of the USSR, instituted in accordance with the Statute of December 1, 1934.

Thus was the stage set for the next step in the case of Lavrenty Pavlovich Beria.

EPILOGUE

Voice of the People

THE BILL OF INDICTMENT against Beria was followed by a general
action involving the masses of workers and peasants throughout the
Soviet Union, as during former great purges. The late Stalin never
wanted to appear in the eyes of his nation as a terrible tyrant who,
at his fancy, executed the best patriots. He wished to seem to be the
savior of his country and the sentinel of his compatriots, whom he
protected from their mortal enemies. Before sentencing his close
friends to death, he accordingly ordered in every factory and collective farm in Sovietland the watchdogs, officially called, the *politrooks*—political guides and propaganda officers especially attached
or sent there—to call mass meetings where speeches were delivered
explaining how villainous the accused men were. At the end of the
speech the orator urged the audience to issue a declaration condemning the victim. Such an announcement had to be signed by
everyone present as the wish of the nation. The workers or peasants
herded to those meetings had to comply with everything the
speaker demanded, even if they sometimes sympathized with the
victim or had never before heard of him. Of course, any attempt at
opposition was out of the question. In this way the accused were
condemned publicly, not by Stalin but by the entire worker and
peasant class of the USSR who all of a sudden were told to demand
death for Old Guard Bolsheviks, many Fathers of the Great Revolution, best patriots. and marshals, generals, and heroes of the Red
Army.

In the case of Beria, the same method was applied. In hundreds of Soviet cities, towns, regions, villages, farms and plants meetings were called to condemn Lavrenty Pavlovich. But this time the accused was not a stranger to the people. In almost every family there was at least one person who had been Beria's victim, either imprisoned by him and sent to a hard labor camp or executed. Now the audiences at these meetings were really glad to listen to the speaker's official declaration that the persecutor of their beloved ones was a low character, a traitor and a scoundrel, who at last was going to be rightly punished for his mean activities. They expressed their approval of his penalty eagerly and hurried to sign the resolution, hoping that that satrap would receive the punishment he had deserved for such a long time.

Their applications were dispatched to the two leading Moscow newspapers, *Pravda* and *Izvestia,* which published them with emphatic introductions. On December 20, 1953, on the front page of *Pravda* was an article headlined, PEOPLE'S WRATH,[1] which declared Beria guilty while he was still being tried. *Izvestia* was even more aggressive against Beria in its editorial of December 23 under the headline, THE ANGRY VOICE OF THE SOVIET PEOPLE,[2] in which the utterances of several citizens were quoted along with preface and comments.

On the same date, December 23, *Pravda* also published similar messages sent to its editorial office by the paper's corespondents from several corners of the country. These writeups were headlined, ALL NATIONS OF THE USSR ARE UNANIMOUS IN THEIR DEMAND FOR SEVERE PUNISHMENT OF THE TRAITORS TO THEIR COUNTRY, THE SPIES—BERIA AND HIS GANG.[3]

All quoted voices of anger were undoubtedly sincere, not because Beria was accused of being a British agent, a spy and a traitor, crimes in which almost nobody believed, but because he had persecuted millions of innocent Russian people.

The entire action of the people's wrath bursting out all over Sovietland was summarized in *Pravda* in an article printed the following day under a crushing headline:

---

[1] Appendix 23.
[2] Appendix 24.
[3] Appendix 25.

NO MERCY FOR TRAITORS AND SPIES—SUCH IS
THE UNANIMOUS DEMAND OF ALL SOVIET PEOPLE

Yesterday, meetings were taking place at establishments, collective and
State farms, on construction projects and in institutions. The Soviet Nation
angrily censures Beria and his accomplices, demanding that these sworn
enemies be banished from the face of the earth.[4]

All of these expressions of the Soviet masses' anger sealed the
already foreordained fate of the fallen, once-omnipotent Commissar Beria. In the meantime, for a week, from December 18 to 23,
there supposedly was a trial in Moscow of Beria and six of his
alleged accomplices, Merkulov, Dekanozov, Kobulov, Goglidze,
Meshik and Vlodzimirsky.

According to information given by Alexey Yakushev to the
West German weekly magazine, *Der Spiegel,* published in Hamburg on December 8, 1969, the trial began earlier. Yakushev, Professor of Philosophy of Natural Science in Moscow and later in
Warsaw, a Russian who defected to the West, stated that the trial
of Beria and some of his subordinates, which that scholar witnessed,
took place in the Building of the Trade Unions in Moscow, and
started on December 14, 1953.

In an interview for *Der Spiegel* Yakushev declared that he obtained a pass to enter the courtroom for the first day of the trial,
where he saw Beria and the other defendants in the dock. It is hard
to believe in the truth of this informant, however. He said that
there were over 120 people in the courtroom and he added that
there was not one Western or even local journalist among them.
Besides, as the opening date of the trial, Yakushev gave December
14, while *Pravda* on December 24 announced officially the trial
began December 18.

Possibly the quiet man in a gray civilian suit and necktie whom
Yakushev described as Beria, could have been a double of the already liquidated Lavrenty Pavlovich, playing in the court the deposed Commissar among the other real codefendants. But for what
reason would the court stage such a performance, since the trial
was not for show, and neither the press nor photographers were
present? This was not logically documented or explained in the
interview. However, Yakushev stated that in addition to all the
accusations of a political nature, Beria was indicted for his immoral

---

[4] Appendix 26.

behavior: for the orgies he had staged with the teen-aged girls he enslaved in his villa in Georgia, and the perverted and sadistic excesses he performed on girls whom he used to kidnap on the streets and later rape in his office or in his house at 28 Katchalov Street in Moscow. These charges, also specifically included in the formal official bill of indictment, were common knowledge, and they were directed against the former Chief of Secret Police, Beria, at his trial, whether it was in the courtroom of the Trade Unions or *in camera* without any witnesses or audience.

On December 24, 1953, *Pravda* announced the formal indictment and the sentence, as well as the execution of Beria and his code-fendants as follows:

IN THE SUPREME COURT OF THE USSR

From the 18th to the 23rd of December 1953, the Special Judicial Session of the Supreme Court of the USSR consisting of:

I. S. Konev, Marshal of the Soviet Union, Presiding Justice of the Special Judicial Session of the Supreme Court, and Members of the Special Session: N. M. Shvernik, Chairman of the All-Union Central Council of the Trade Unions; E. L. Zeydin, First Deputy Chairman of the Supreme Court of the USSR; K. S. Moskalenko, General of the Army; N. A. Mikhaylov, Secretary of the Moscow Region Committee of the Communist Party of the Soviet Union; M. I. Kuchava, Chairman of the Council of Trade Unions in Georgia; L. A. Gromov, Chairman of the Moscow Municipal Court; K. F. Lunev, First Deputy Minister of Internal Affairs of the USSR sitting in a Secret Session *in camera* duly constituted according to procedure established by law of 1 December 1934, examined the criminal case of L. P. Beria and others.

In accordance with the indictment, L. P. Beria was brought to trial under charges specified by Articles 58-1B, 58-8, 58-13, 58-11 of the Criminal Code of the Russian Soviet Federated Socialist Republic; V. N. Merkulov, V. G. Dekanozov, B. Z. Kobulov, S. A. Goglidze, P. Y. Meshik, L. E. Vlodzimirsky under the indictment for crimes specified by articles 58-1B, 58-8, 58-11 of the Criminal Code of the Russian Soviet Federated Socialist Republic.

The judicial investigation fully confirmed the findings of the preliminary investigation, presented to all defendants in the indictment.

The Court has determined that having betrayed the Country and acting in the interest of foreign capital, Beria organized a treacherous group of conspirators, hostile to the Soviet State, consisting of defendants V. N. Merkulov, V. G. Dekanozov, B. Z. Kobulov, S. A. Goglidze, P. Y. Meshik, and L. E. Vlodzimirsky, tied with Beria in joint criminal activities in the course of several years. The criminal intent of the conspirators was to use the organs of the Ministry of Internal Affairs against the Communist Party and the Government of the USSR; to elevate the Ministry of Internal Affairs above the Party and the Government in order to seize power; to destroy the Soviet Workers' and Peasants' System; to revive capitalism and to restore the rule of the bourgeoisie.

The Court has found that the beginning of the criminal, treacherous activities of L. P. Beria and the establishment of secret communication with foreign service dates back to 1919, the time of Civil War, when L. P. Beria, residing in Baku, committed treason by working as a secret agent for the Intelligence of the counterrevolutionary Mussavat government in Azerbaijan, operating under the control of the British Intelligence network.

In 1920, L. P. Beria was living in Georgia, where again he committed treason by establishing a clandestine communication with the Secret Political Police of the Georgia Menshevik government, the latter being also a cell of the British Intelligence.

In the following years, L. P. Beria continued and widened his secret connections with the foreign Intelligence until the moment of his arrest.

In the course of several years, L. P. Beria and his accomplices carefully concealed and camouflaged their hostile activities.

Following the death of J. V. Stalin, counting on the intensification of efforts against the Soviet Government by the reactionary imperialist forces, L. P. Beria increased his efforts in order to accomplish his anti-Soviet treacherous designs, which facilitated in a short time the unmasking of Beria as well as of his accomplices, thus putting an end to their criminal activities.

When he became the Minister of Internal Affairs of the USSR in March 1953, the defendant L. P. Beria, preparing for a seizure of power, began to promote intensely the members of his conspiratorial group to positions of leadership in the Central as well as in the local organs of the Ministry of Internal Affairs. L. P. Beria and his accomplices persecuted the honest employees of the Ministry of Internal Affairs who refused to carry out criminal orders of the conspirators.

To achieve their anti-Soviet treacherous goals, L. P. Beria and his accomplices undertook a number of criminal measures in order to revive the remnants of the bourgeois and nationalist elements in the Soviet Republics, to spread hostility and mistrust among the nations of the USSR, the first before all to undermine the friendship of the nations of the USSR with the great Russian Nation.

Acting as a foul enemy of the Soviet Nation, and intending to create problems in the Country's food supply system, the defendant L. P. Beria sabotaged and hampered the implementation of important measures undertaken by the Party with the view of improving the economy of collective and State farms and constantly raising the prosperity of the Soviet people.

It has been established that by concealing and camouflaging their criminal activities, defendants L. P. Beria and his accomplices perpetrated acts of terror upon persons by whom they feared to be exposed. Slander, intrigues, and various forms of provocation were among the basic methods used by the conspirators against honest Party and Soviet Government workers who stood in the way of the hostile designs against the Soviet State of L. P. Beria and his accomplices, and who were hindering their thrust for power.

The Court has determined that defendants L. P. Beria; V. N. Merkulov; V. G. Dekanozov; B. Z. Kobulov; S. A. Goglidze; P. Y. Meshik; and L. E. Vlodzimirsky, using their official positions in the organs of the People's Commissariat of Internal Affairs, NKVD; the Ministry of State Security, MGB; and the Ministry of Internal Affairs, MVD; perpetrated a number of grave crimes with the intention of destroying honest cadres who were dedicated to the Communist Party and the Soviet Government.

The Court has also established that L. P. Beria committed crimes which testify to his moral degeneration; and that he committed acts of criminal greediness, self-aggrandizement and an abuse of power.

Guilt of all defendants was proven in Court on the basis of genuine documents, material evidence, records in their own handwriting, and testimony of many witnesses.

Being exposed by the evidence in Court, defendants L. P. Beria, V. N. Merkulov, V. G. Dekanozov, B. Z. Kobulov, S. A. Goglidze, P. Y. Meshik, and L. E. Vlodzimirsky, corroborated the evidence with which they were confronted during the preliminary hearing and confessed being guilty of perpetrating a number of acts of high treason.

A Special Judicial Session of the Supreme Court of the USSR has found L. P. Beria guilty of treason against the Country for organizing the anti-Soviet group of conspirators aiming to seize the power and to restore the rule of bourgeoisie; for committing acts of terror against political leaders devoted to the Communist Party and to the Nations of the Soviet Union; for actively opposing the revolutionary workers' movement in Baku in 1919, when Beria was a secret agent working for the Intelligence of the counterrevolutionary Mussavat government in Azerbaijan, where he made connections with the foreign Intelligence Service, and subsequently for maintaining and expanding his contacts with the foreign Intelligence until the time of his exposure and arrest, that is for the offenses specified by Articles 58-1B, 58-8, 58-13, 58-11 of the Criminal Code of the Russian Soviet Federated Socialist Republic.

The Court established the guilt of defendants V. N. Merkulov, V. G.

Dekanozov, B. Z. Kobulov, S. A. Goglidze, P. Y. Meshik, and L. E. Vlodzimirsky, committing treason against the Country; committing acts of terror; and for participating in the anti-Soviet treacherous group, that is for offenses specified by Articles 58-1B, 58-8, 58-11 of the Criminal Code of the Russian Soviet Federated Socialist Republic.

The Special Judicial Session of the Supreme Court of the USSR decided: to sentence L. P. Beria, V. N. Merkulov, B. Z. Kobulov, S. A. Goglidze, P. Y. Meshik, L. E. Vlodzimirsky to the highest degree of penalty—execution by firing squad, confiscation of their personal property, forfeiture of military titles and decorations.

The Sentence is final, without right of appeal.

EXECUTION OF THE SENTENCE

Yesterday, on 23 of December, the Sentence passed by the Special Session of the Supreme Court of the USSR, condemning L. P. Beria, V. N. Merkulov, V. G. Dekanozov, B. Z. Kobulov, S. A. Goglidze, P. Y. Meshik and L. E. Vlodzimirsky to the highest degree of punishment— execution by a firing squad, was carried out.

This was the official version of Beria's end.

The next morning, December 25, 1953, *Pravda* published an editorial on its front page under the headline:

SENTENCE OF THE COURT—THE VERDICT OF THE NATION[5]

It declared that the Soviet citizens fully accepted the court's sentence and announced publicly the death of Lavrenty Pavlovich Beria.

In the meantime, the new Commissar, Sergey Nikiforovich Kruglov, the same harmless-looking Russian house pet so much liked by President Truman and Sir Winston Churchill at the Potsdam Conference, now Beria's successor as Chief of the Security Police, ordered Beria's wife, Nina, and their son to be arrested and immediately transported from jail to a cattle car of a freight train to be sent to a hard labor camp in Siberia. Their house in Moscow, on 28 Katchalov Street, and the suburban villa were sealed, and all possessions from both of those buildings—the antique furniture, oriental rugs, silver, china, paintings, the library with the projectors

---

[5] Appendix 27.

and movie cameras, as well as Lavrenty's cupboard with various kinds of liquors and albums full of pornographic photographs— were confiscated and loaded on trucks to be stored in the warehouse for the belongings of convicted criminals. The same action was carried out in Beria's three other houses in Georgia, the two in Tbilisi and the one at the summer health resort of Sochi.

Commissar Kruglov also forwarded a memorandum to all public libraries in the Soviet Union stating that the book, *On the History of the Bolshevik Organizations in Transcaucasia*, by L. P. Beria, should be withdrawn from the shelves and destroyed, as well as all other of Beria's writings and photographs. There also should be a change made in the fifth volume of the *Great Soviet Encyclopedia* under initial *B*. The pages with the Lavrenty P. Beria biography, illustrated with his portrait, were to be removed and destroyed, and replaced with a picture of the Bering Strait and exhaustive information about it and a biography of an obscure eighteenth-century statesman, Berholtz. The new pages were enclosed with the memorandum.

Simultaneously there was a demand sent to all mayors of cities, towns and other communities to change the names of places dedicated to Beria. Especially concerned was his native Georgia, where many lanes and gardens had been named in his honor. As a result of this order, the most beautiful spot in the center of the Georgian capital, Tbilisi, Beria Square, was renamed Lenin Square, and the main avenue in that city, Beria Street, became Kalinin Street.

If Beria was not killed during the Politburo meeting at the Kremlin six months before, as some versions of his death hold, but was executed in the routine way as a result of a sentence proclaimed by his judges either in secret chamber or after an open trial in the court in December, the procedure was the same.

As with every highly important convict, Beria himself became the responsibility of the First Special Department of the MVD, and Security Lieutenant-General Blokhin undertook the usual action. From the courtroom, Lavrenty was transferred in an armored police car to 11 Dzerzhinsky Street—Lubyanka Prison—the building so familiar to him in every detail. There he was escorted to the basement, which housed the cells for those condemned to capital punishment. In one of those cellars Beria was ordered to take off his clothes and put on a long white shirt, which was given to him.

Then he was taken to the cell of death. There he had to stand facing the wall, with his forehead against it. Soon he was shot in the back of the skull between his ears by an executioner, a certain "Comrade T," formally assigned to liquidate eminent convicts. As his weapon "Comrade T" used an eight-shot automatic pistol. If, after the first shot, the victim was still alive, "Comrade T," repeated his action until the last, eighth bullet.

Then came the prison's physician who confirmed the death and signed the death certificate. A charwoman appeared with a bucket full of warm water, soap and a piece of rug to clean the whole mess. At last came two guards carrying a tarpaulin. They spread it on the floor and wrapped the corpse in it. They picked it up and took it out to the back yard, where a truck was waiting. They drove away and buried the body on the outskirts of the city in an anonymous common grave, really a ditch, which was then leveled with the ground so that no sign remained of the body's hiding place.

The doctor's death certificate of the convicted Minister of Internal Affairs and of Security of State of the USSR and Soviet Marshal, now erased from the surface of the earth, was sent to the files of the victim.

It was the final document. The case of Commissar Lavrenty Pavlovich Beria was closed.

APPENDICES

Appendix 1

THE DECEMBRISTS OPERA IN THE BOLSHOI THEATRE

The second performance of *The Decembrists*, a new opera of Y. Shaporin (libretto by V. Rozhdestvensky) took place on Saturday, June 27, 1953, at the Bolshoi Theatre of the Union of the Soviet Socialist Republics.

The opera was under the direction of A. Melik Pashayev. The play was staged by N. Okhlopkov, the scenery was produced by artists A. Petritsky and T. Starzhetskaya. The choreography was by L. Lavrovsky, the leader of the chorus was M. Shorin.

In the main roles appeared: A. Ivanov (Ryleyev), A. Krichenya (Pestel), G. Nalepi (Kakhovsky), N. Petrov (Bestuzhev), P. Selivanov (Trubetskoy), V. Ivanovsky (Shchepin-Rostovsky), N. Pokrovskaya (Yelena), A. Ognivtsev (Nikolay I), P. Volovov (Yakubovich), P. Chekin (Rostovtsev), N. Shchegolkov (Old soldier), Y. Verbitskaya (mother of Shchepin-Rostovsky), V. Borisenko (Gypsy Stesha) and others.

The basis for the opera constituted events connected with the uprising of the Decembrists on the Senatskaya Square at Petersburg in the year 1825.

The presentation of the opera scored a great success. The audience applauded in particular the following scenes: the uprising on the Senatskaya Square, the meeting of Ryleyev and Pestel at the Peter and Paul Fortress as well as the finale of the opera.

The performance was attended by the leaders of the Communist Party and of the Government, Comrades: G. M. Malenkov, V. M. Molotov, K. Y. Voroshilov, N. S. Khrushchev, N. A. Bulganin, L. M Kaganovich, A. I. Mikoyan, M. Z. Saburov, M. G. Pervukhin, N. M. Shvernik, P. K. Ponomarenko, and V. A. Malyshev.

(*Pravda*, June 28, 1953)

Appendix 2

ANNOUNCEMENT OF THE MINISTRY OF INTERNAL AFFAIRS OF THE USSR

The Ministry of Internal Affairs of the USSR conducted a thorough verification of all materials of the preliminary investigation and other evidence concerning the case of doctors accused of sabotage, espionage

417

and terrorist activities directed against the active leaders of the Soviet Government.

The results of the verification have shown that the detained, in this case, Professor M. S. Vovsi, Professor V. N. Vinogradov, Professor M. B. Kogan, Professor B. B. Kogan, Professor P. I. Yegorov, Professor A. I. Feldman, Professor Y. G. Etinger, Professor V. K. Vasilenko, Professor A. M. Greenstein, Professor V. F. Zelenin, Professor B. S. Preobrazhensky, Professor N. A. Popova, Professor V. V. Zakusov, Professor N. A. Shereshevsky and Doctor G. I. Mayorov were unlawfully arrested by the former Ministry of State Security of the USSR, without any legal basis.

The verification has shown that accusations made against the above mentioned persons were false and the documentary evidence which served as the basis for personnel conducting the investigation, groundless.

It has been established that the testimony given by the arrested persons, allegedly confirming the crimes with which they were charged, had been obtained by the personnel of the Investigative Department of the former Ministry of State Security by using unacceptable means, which are strictly forbidden by the Soviet Law concerning methods of investigation.

On the basis of the conclusions reached by the Investigative Commission, specially established by the Ministry of Internal Affairs of the USSR for the purpose of verification of this case, the arrested M. S. Vovsi, V. N. Vinogradov, B. B. Kogan, P. I. Yegorov, A. I. Feldman, V. K. Vasilenko, A. M. Greenstein, V. F. Zelenin, B. S. Preobrazhensky, N. A. Popova, V. V. Zakusov, N. A. Shereshevsky, G. I. Mayorov, and others arrested in this case have been fully exonerated of the crimes of which they were accused, that is of sabotage, terrorist and espionage activities; and consequently, in accordance with the Articles 4 and 5 of the Criminal Legal Code of the RSFSR,* they were released from custody.

(*Pravda*, April 4, 1953)

Appendix 3

THE SOVIET SOCALIST LAW IS INVIOLABLE

Our press published the announcement of the Ministry of Internal Affairs of the USSR on the results of a careful checkup of all materials concerning the preliminary investigation as well as other data pertaining to the case of a group of doctors accused of sabotage, espionage and terrorist bearing directed against active statesmen of the USSR.

The completed checkup permitted the establishment of the fact that

---

* RSFSR: Russian Soviet Federated Socialist Republic.

the professors and doctors accused in the above case have been arrested wrongfully by the former Ministry of State Security of the USSR, without any legal justification whatsoever. As it has been stated in the communication of the Ministry of Internal Affairs, the undertaken verification of the case has proved that accusations brought against these persons were faked and the documented data on which the officers of the preliminary investigation were basing their case were without foundation. It has been established that the admissions of guilt on the part of the arrested persons, which supposedly confirmed the accusations of committed crimes, have been obtained by the officers of the Investigation Section of the former Ministry of State Security by applying inadmissible measures which are explicitly forbidden by the Soviet Law concerning the investigation.

Based on the conclusions of the Committee of Inquiry, specially created by the Ministry of Internal Affairs of the USSR for the purpose of checking into this case, the arrested professors and physicians were fully exonerated of the accusations made against them and released from custody.

All persons who were guilty of irregular conduct of the investigation have been arrested and accused of criminal offense.

How could it have happened that within the Ministry of State Security of the USSR, expected to defend the interests of the Soviet State, a provocative case has been concocted, whose victims were honest Soviet citizens, eminent representatives of Soviet science?

This happened primarily because the leaders of the former Ministry of State Security were derelict of their duties. They were alienated from the people and from the Party and forgot that they were the servants of the People and should defend the Soviet Law. The former Minister of State Security S. Ignatyev gave an example of a political blindness and gullibility and was led by such criminal adventurers as Ryumin, the former Deputy Minister and Chief of the Investigation Section, who was personally responsible for the conduct of the investigation and who is now under arrest. Ryumin was acting as a secret enemy of our State, of our People. Instead of working towards unmasking the true enemies of the Soviet State, the actual spies and saboteurs, Ryumin embarked upon the road of deceiving the Government, on the road of criminal adventurism. Flouting the lofty vocation of the officers of the State apparatus and their responsibility before the Party and the People, Ryumin and some other workers of the Ministry of State Security in their criminal aspirations committed the most flagrant violations of the Soviet Law, even including a crude falsification of the corpus delicti, and they had the audacity to trample the inviolable rights of Soviet citizens, stipulated in our Constitution.

The Commission of Medical Experts, organized in connection with the accusations against a group of doctors, was also unequal to the occasion by reaching a wrong conclusion as to the methods of medical treatment which were adopted in the past towards A. S. Shcherbakov and A. A. Zhdanov. Instead of analyzing the history of the illnesses as well as other materials with a scientific conscientiousness and objectivity, this Commission let itself be influenced by the materials fabricated by the investigation and lent its authority to support the slanderous falsified accusations against a number of prominent personalities in the field of medicine. At this point it has to be noted that the investigation authorities withheld from the experts some important facts in the medical procedure testifying to the correctness of the adopted treatment.

The Soviet people learned with satisfaction that the accusations directed against numerous prominent personalities in the field of Soviet medicine proved to be absolutely false, that it was a vile slander of honest and honorable personalities in our State. Only individuals who lost Soviet consciousness and human dignity could have come to lawlessly arresting Soviet citizens, prominent personalities in the field of Soviet medicine, to a crude falsification of the investigation process, to a criminal abuse of their civic obligations.

The contemptible adventurists of the Ryumin type tried to foment in the Soviet society, welded together by a moral and political sense of unity and by the ideas of proletarian internationalism, sentiments of national hostility which are completely alien to the Socialist ideology by the expedient of a case fabricated during the investigation. In their provocative aims they did not stop at shameless slander of Soviet citizens. A careful verification established, for example, the fact that in a like way was slandered a well-known popular figure—Mikhoels, the nationally famous actor of the USSR.

As it can be seen from the communication of the Ministry of Internal Affairs of the USSR, the Agencies of the former Ministry of State Security crudely violated the Soviet Law and committed acts of arbitrariness and abuse of power. Criminal acts of such dimensions could not remain for long without being uncovered and punished, since the Soviet Government stands guard of the rights of the citizens of our Country, takes great pains to preserve these rights and severely punishes all those, notwithstanding the personality or the position, who are guilty of an act of arbitrariness.

The Communist Party and the Soviet Government were constantly insisting and they continue to demand that the operation of all our organizations, of the whole State machine remain under the watchful control of the leading authorities and the whole Soviet community. At the present time, when the Soviet people are particularly aware of the significance and enjoying the victory of Socialism in our Country, we should exert extreme vigilance and be very demanding in the observing of our Soviet, Socialist Law.

The Soviet Government openly and straightforwardly informs the people about acts of abuse of power and lawlessness committed by individual workers in the State apparatus, fearlessly disclosing wrongdoings in the State machinery in order to weed out these deficiencies with the utmost resoluteness and implacability. This constitutes a testimony to the great strength of the Soviet State and of the Socialist system. The source of this strength derives from the fact that our Government is closely and unshakeably united with the Nation and relates to the people in all its actions as well as it resolutely and consequently pursues policies that correspond to the vital interests of the Nation.

The Country of Socialism, imbued with an unbreakable strength and creative forces is resolutely advancing on the road leading towards Communism. The exploiting classes have long since been liquidated in the Soviet Union. This is why the reactionary forces abroad in their efforts to conduct a sabotaging activity against the Soviet State cannot count on finding any meaningful social support inside our Country. But the Soviet people is well aware of the fact that as long as the capitalist encirclement exists there are and necessarily will be further efforts made to plant among us saboteurs and spies. Efforts will be also undertaken to use in anti-Soviet activities some isolated renegades, individuals following the bourgeois ideology, and degenerates. Against all these real, open or hidden enemies of the people, enemies of the Soviet State, we have always to remember to keep our powder dry. The Party teaches us to be vigilant at all times.

The extensive rights of the citizens of the Soviet Socialist State are established in the Constitution of the USSR. Article 127 of the Constitution of the USSR guarantees personal immunity to USSR citizens. Nobody can be put under arrest without the decision of the court or without the sanction of the Public Prosecutor.

Socialist Law, the protection of the rights of Soviet citizens as outlined by the Constitution of the USSR, is the most important foundation for a further development and strengthening of the Soviet State.

Nobody will be allowed to break the Soviet Law. Every agricultural or industrial worker, every Soviet intellectual can peacefully and resolutely work, being convinced that his citizen's rights are being securely protected by the Soviet Socialist Law.

The citizen of the great Soviet State can be assured that his rights, which are guaranteed by the Constitution of the USSR, will be strictly honored and protected by the Soviet Government.

This fact constitutes one of the most important conditions of a further close relationship of all nations of the USSR with their Soviet Government, of a continuous strengthening of the power of our Nation and of a steady increase of the international prestige of the Soviet Union.

(*Pravda*, April 6, 1953)

Appendix 4

In his book, *On the History of the Bolshevik Organizations in Trans- caucasia* (Moscow: Foreign Language Publishing House, 1939) Lavrenty P. Beria described the Social-Federalists of his native Georgia as follows:

Social-Federalists—A Georgian nationalist party consisting of intellectuals from the bourgeoisie and nobility. It was formed at a conference in Geneva in 1904. Among the founders of the party were A. Jorjadze, K. Abashidze, G. Laskhishvili and G. Zdanovich-Mayashvili.

The main demand of the Social-Federalist program was for the national autonomy of Georgia within a Russian bourgeois and landowner state.

In the years of the first Russian Revolution the Federalists preached national autonomy, supported the liberal bourgeoisie and fought rabidly against the Bolsheviks.

In the years of reaction they completely gave up the struggle against tsarism, and during the imperialist war occupied a defensist position.

After the victory of the Great Proletarian Revolution in Russia the Federalists joined the Georgian Mensheviks, Dashnaks and Mussavatists in a counterrevolutionary bloc, which, with the support of the Germano-Turkish interventionists and, later on, of the Anglo-French interventionists, cut off Transcaucasia and Georgia from Soviet Russia.

After Soviet rule was established in Georgia, the Social-Federalist Party fell to pieces.

The sorry survivors fought viciously against Soviet rule and took an active part in the Menshevik putsch of 1924.

The leaders, who are in emigration, are in the intelligence services of foreign states, together with Menshevik and Whiteguard counterrevolutionaries.

About the Armenian Dashnaks, Beria wrote in the same volume:

Dashnaks (*"Dashnaktsutyun"*)—An Armenian nationalist party which arose in the early nineties. Its program (socialization of the land, state federation, and terrorism) closely resembled that of the Russian Socialist-Revolutionaries.

Its main slogan was for the emancipation of the Armenian nation from the tyranny of Imperial Turkey and the formation from Turkish Armenia and the Armenian regions of Transcaucasia of a "Great Armenia" under the protection of tsarist Russia.

In the beginning of 1900, under the influence of the movement for national emancipation, the Dashnaks went Left for a time and came out in opposition to tsarism.

In the period of the first Russian Revolution, the Dashnaks made open cause with the interests of the Armenian bourgeoisie and fought against the revolutionary movement of the workers and peasants. At the behest of the tsarist authorities they organized an Armenian-Tyurkic massacre in Baku, Tiflis, Elizabethpol (Kirovabad) and other parts of Transcaucasia.

In a letter to Stolypin, Vice-Regent of the Caucasus, Vorontsov-Dashkov characterized the activity of the "Dashnaktsutyun" as follows:

In this period the Dashnaktsutyun organization acquired a special, leading influence in Baku after the Armenian-Tatar disorders and the turbulent period of 1905-06. This is due to the fact that at that time in the eyes of the influential and wealthy part of the Armenian population this organization was an armed bodyguard against the Mussulmen and the anarchistic organizations engendered by the revolution, and they generously supported the Dashnaktsakans financially, which explains why the latter were so well armed; besides using them as bodyguard, the wealthier Armenians used the Dashnaktsakans to guard their property and property interests, so that it would happen that in the oil fields the Dashnaktsakans would break strikes by means of intimidation and, on contrary occasions, when they had it in for some industrialist who had turned down their demands for money, they made the workers on his site go on strike. (*Krassny Arkhiv*,* Vol. 34, p. 206)

During the years of reaction and in the first imperialist war the Dashnaks served as the militant vanguard of the Armenian bourgeoisie, open defenders and servants of tsarism. During the war the Dashnaks (the Armenian National Bureau headed by Dashnaks) publicly petitioned Nicholas II to seize the Dardanelles. They formed volunteer companies and sent them to the Russo-Turkish front.

After the victory of the Great Socialist Revolution of Russia the Dashnaks joined the Georgian Mensheviks and Mussavatists in a counterrevolutionary bloc and severed Transcaucasia from Soviet Russia.

In 1918-20 the Dashnaks headed the bourgeois Republic of Armenia which had been set up by the Turkish General Staff, and made Armenia a *place d'armes* for the Anglo-French interventionists and Russian Whiteguards in their war against the Soviet Government.

The Dashnaks, together with the Mensheviks and Mussavatists, transformed Transcaucasia into an arena of bloody strife between the nationalities; with the Georgian Mensheviks and Mussavatists they organized

---

* Red Archives.

the Armenian-Georgian and Armenian-Tyurkic wars, and engineered raids and pogroms on the Tyurkic population of Armenia.

After Soviet rule was established in Armenia, the Dashnak Party was broken up. On the instructions of the intelligence services of the imperialist states, the surviving Dashnak scum continued to carry on a rabid struggle against the Soviet Government through espionage and wrecking.

As to the Mussavatists, here is how Beria defined them in his book:

Mussavatists (*"Mussavat"*)—A nationalist Tyurkic bourgeois—"democratic" party. It was established in 1912 and was called the "Mussulman Democratic Party"—"Mussavat" (which means *equality*). The founders of the Party were representatives of the Tyurkic bourgeoisie and the bourgeois intelligentsia: M. E. Rassul-Zadeh, G. R. Sharif-Zadeh, A. K. Kyazim-Zadeh and K. V. Mikhailov. The program of the "Mussavat" was permeated with both Pan-Islamism—the ideology of Turkish, Tatar and the like khans, landowners and Mussulman mullahs, who sought to unite all the peoples professing the Mussulman religion—and Pan-Tyurkism, which sought to unite all the Tyurkic Mussulman nationalities under the rule of the Ottoman government.

During the imperialist war the Mussavatists were ardent supporters of tsarism. One of the leaders of the Mussavatists, M. E. Rassul-Zadeh, wrote:

Touching upon the fate of our common native land, Russia, we too, together with all other citizens, wish primarily for Russia's success and victory . . .

During this war the nationalities inhabiting Russia have been cleared of all doubt, and by their sincere attitude have shown that they have honest aims and feelings of ardent patriotism. (Newspaper *Achyg-Soyuz**)

After the second Russian Revolution, in 1917, the "Mussavat" merged with the Tyurkic Federalist Party of the Bek landowners and adopted the name of the Tyurkic Federalist Party, "Mussavat," demanding autonomy for Azerbaijan, and the formation of a Russian democratic republic on federative principles.

During 1918-20 the "Mussavat" constituted the main counterrevolutionary force in Azerbaijan, fighting against Soviet rule and the Bolshevik Party.

In May 1918, the Mussavatists organized a so-called "independent" bourgeois-landlord government with its center in Gyandzeh, and waged a savage fight against the Baku Commune, enlisting the aid of the Turks and later of the British.

In 1920, on the instructions of British imperialism, the Mussavatists gave direct armed assistance to Denikin's retreating Whiteguard bands and fought against the Red Army.

---

* *A Clear Word.*

In 1920 the Mussavatists and Dashnaks organized a Tyurkic-Armenian war.

When Soviet rule was established in Azerbaijan, the "Mussavat" Party was smashed and lost all influence. The émigré leaders of the Party are acting as spies for foreign states.

Appendix 5

Years later, when Dumbadze, a *Cheka* officer, feared a purge and execution, he managed to escape to France. In Paris, he wrote memoirs which were published in 1930. In his book, *Na Slushbe Cheka i Kominterna* (*In the Service of the Cheka and the Comintern*), Evgeny Dumbadze described the "Week of Suppression of the Bourgeoisie" from the point of view of an eyewitness.

Appendix 6

In a mass meeting on March 2, 1921, the sailors of the Kronstadt garrison and of the Baltic Fleet stationed there announced:

"We joined the Communist Party to work for the good of the people and stand for the help of the workers and peasants. Therefore at the present hard time which our Country is surviving, when all our efforts have to be turned to the struggle with the misery, cold and hunger, we state that we do not stand for power, but for the interest of the workers . . .

"The worker instead of becoming the master of the factory, became a slave. He can neither work where he would like to, nor can he reject work that is beyond his physical strength. Those who dare to say the truth are imprisoned to suffer in the torture-cells of *Cheka*, or are shot. . . .

"Therefore as honest men, standing for the defense of the interest and rights of the workers, we declare that we call ourselves under the Temporary Revolutionary Committee, which takes the task of creating Soviets entirely from the proletarian masses . . .

"We are fighting for the liberation of the workers from the despotic power of the usurpers.

"Long Live the Soviet Power, the true defender of the workers!"
(*Izvestia Vremennogo Revolutsionnogo Komiteta Matrosov, Krasnoarmeytsev i Rabochikh Goroda Kronstadta,*[*] March 3-14, 1921)

---

[*] *News of the Temporary Revolutionary Committee of Sailors, Red Army Soldiers and Workers of the City of Kronstadt.*

Appendix 7

STAUNCH FIGHTER FOR THE CAUSE OF
THE LENIN-STALIN PARTY
by Lavrenty Beria

Comrade Ordzhonikidze is fifty years of age! Of this time span he devoted thirty-three years to the heroic revolutionary struggle of the working class for the cause of the Lenin-Stalin Party and for the victory of the Proletarian Revolution and Socialism in the USSR.

From the very first days of his participation in the workers' movement Comrade Sergo, a young and fiery revolutionary, placed himself squarely on the side of Lenin and Stalin, on the side of the Bolshevik Party.

The first teacher and instructor of Comrade Sergo was the Initiator of revolutionary Marxism-Leninism, the Founder of the Bolshevik Party in Georgia and Transcaucasia, the Great Stalin.

Comrade Sergo was shaped by the Bolshevik Party and was brought up by the Great Leaders of the Proletariat, by Lenin and Stalin.

During the period of tsarist autocracy Comrade Sergo was one of the builders of the Bolshevik Party. Having graduated from the rigorous school of the Bolshevik underground movement he earned a place among the outstanding fighters of the Old Guard Bolshevik.

In the Civil War era Comrade Sergo under the direct leadership of Lenin and Stalin became an organizer of victories of the Proletarian Revolution over the hordes of the Russian Whiteguard counterrevolution and of international imperialism.

The work performed by Comrade Sergo was tied in with the defeat of the bourgeois-nationalistic government and with the victory of the Proletarian Revolution in Transcaucasia.

Comrade Sergo was the instructor in organizing the Soviet Republics of Transcaucasia over a period of several years. Under his leadership the Bolsheviks strengthened the Soviet rule on the Eastern borders, organized the Transcaucasian Federation, laid solid foundations for a Socialist reconstruction of the national economy, achieved a stable national peace and brotherly cooperation among the nations of Transcaucasia.

Comrade Sergo is one of the leaders of the Lenin-Stalin Party and of the Soviet State, as well as one of the leaders of the Socialist heavy industry of the Union of the Soviet Socialist Republics, the closest comrade-in-arms and friend of Comrade Stalin, the Great Genius of mankind and the Leader of the peoples.

The name of Comrade Sergo is being pronounced with love and admiration by the Bolsheviks and by the toilers of our Socialist homeland.

Already on the school bench Comrade Sergo manifested a great interest in social and economic problems.

He joined the ranks of the Russian Social Democratic Workers' Party (RSDPR) in the year 1903, in Tiflis.

When the Tiflis Bolshevik organization took shape towards the end of 1904 and at the beginning of 1905, under the direct leadership of Comrade Stalin, Comrade Sergo joined the Bolshevik faction of the Russian Social Democratic Workers' Party.

The first Russian revolution broke out in Transcaucasia at the beginning of 1905. The revolutionary struggle of the workers and peasants in Georgia as well as the entire Transcaucasia against autocracy assumed large proportions. At the head of the revolutionary movement stood the Transcaucasia Bolshevik organization and its Creator and Teacher, the Great Leader of the Bolshevik Party, Comrade Stalin.

Under the leadership of Comrade Stalin the Bolsheviks of Transcaucasia, armed with the Leninist strategy and tactics, organized the struggle of workers and peasants for the victory of the revolution, for the abolishment of the autocracy and for the establishment of the revolutionary democratic dictatorship of the proletariat and peasantry.

The young Sergo, who completed in Tiflis the Stalin Bolshevik schooling, was successful in his work to organize a revolutionary propaganda in Sukhumi and Gudauti among the peasants and to lead their revolutionary activities against the autocracy.

After the proclamation of the tsarist manifesto of October 17, 1905, Comrade Sergo organized an armed action at Gudauti on December 24, 1905, during the unloading of weapons from a long boat in the village Bombori, not far from Gudauti. The weapons were shipped from abroad and in that connection Comrade Sergo was arrested for the first time, together with a group of Red fighters, by a detachment of Cossacks.

Comrade Sergo under arrest was then spirited away to the Sukhumi prison where he remained four months.

In Baku in 1907, under the leadership of Comrade Stalin, Comrade Sergo took active part in the work of the Baku Bolshevik Organization and became a member of the Baku Committee of the Party.

In the course of the same year Comrade Sergo was arrested for the second time during the First of May demonstration at the Stepan Razin Hill and was detained at the Baku prison under the name of Kuchkhishvili.

After he was released from prison he continued active Party work in Romany of the Balakhansky region.

In the spring of 1909 Comrade Sergo was deported to the Angara River area.

Two months later he escaped and came back to Baku from where, on the instructions of the Baku Committee of the Russian Social Democratic Workers' Party, he moved to Iran where he continued revolutionary work in the fall of 1909.

From Iran Comrade Sergo established a connection with Lenin through the intermediary of Nadezhda Krupskaya, maintaining a correspondence with him and organizing deliveries of Bolshevik literature from abroad and their subsequent shipments to Russia by way of Baku.

At the end of 1910, Comrade Sergo left Iran for Paris where he took part in Bolshevik activities.

During the period of a new revolutionary upsurge (1910-1912), the basic decisive problem for the workers' movement was the strengthening of the Party and the intensification of the revolutionary work among the masses. The Mensheviks and Trotskyites then took definitely to the road of surrender, treason and betrayal. Under these circumstances it was of particular importance to call a Party Convention that would map out the tactics in the preparation of a new revolution and which would rid the Party of the quitters and Trotskyites.

Lenin then organized the struggle to call in an All-Russian Party Conference. On Lenin's instructions Comrade Sergo went to Russia in August 1911 as a plenipotentiary of the Organizational Committee in the Foreign Countries for the Convocation of the All-Party Conference in Prague.

During the same period Comrade Stalin, in accordance with Lenin's planning, conducted in Russia and in Transcaucasia a large-scale action with the view of convocation of the Prague Conference. Comrade Stalin purposely came to Baku and Tiflis in 1911 in order to organize the struggle for the convocation of the Bolshevik Conference in Prague.

Under the leadership and with the help of Comrade Stalin, Comrade Ordzhonikidze succeeded in assembling the Organizational Committee for the Preparation of the All-Russian Party Conference. The first session of this Committee took place in Baku with the representatives from the Ural area, Kiev and Yekaterinoslav being present. The delegates from Moscow and some other areas were arrested on their way to Baku. The Committee after its first session, in connection with the conspiratorial mishap in Baku and in order to preserve the secrecy of its deliberations, moved to Tiflis where it finished its work.

At the Conference in Prague Comrade Sergo delivered a report on behalf of the Russian Organizational Committee dealing with the necessity of holding the Conference in Prague and he was elected to the membership of the Central Committee of the Russian Social Democratic Workers' Party (Bolsheviks).

After the Conference Comrade Sergo Ordzhonikidze, on Lenin's instructions immediately returned to Russia and traveled to Vologda to meet with Stalin who, at that time, was living there in exile at Solvyche-godsk. At this point Lenin charged Comrade Stalin with the task of organizing the Russian Bureau of the Central Committee of the Russian Social Democratic Workers' Party (Bolsheviks).

Shortly thereafter Comrade Stalin succeeded in escaping from the place of his banishment.

After the escape Comrade Stalin, together with Comrade Sergo, arrived in Transcaucasia (Baku and Tiflis) where he organized the struggle for the acceptance of the decisions approved at the Conference in Prague and to lead the fight of the Transcaucasian Bolsheviks against the Menshevik quitters.

In 1912, on orders from Lenin, Comrade Stalin together with Comrade Sergo went to Petersburg to continue their Party work. Here Comrade Sergo was soon arrested under the name of Guseynov. The Petersburg Secret Political Police succeeded in determining his real identity and he was placed before the court for his escape from the place of exile. After being kept in prison under a temporary arrest order, Comrade Sergo was sentenced to three years of hard labor, which he served at the Shlissel-burg Fortress.

In the fall of 1915 Comrade Sergo was deported to Siberia and kept in the Aleksandrovsk Transitory Prison until the spring of 1916, when he was sent to the place of his banishment in Yakutsk.

When the bourgeois democratic revolution broke out in February 1917 Comrade Sergo was still in the remote Yakutia, in the Pokrovskaya village.

As soon as river navigation opened Comrade Sergo, together with Andreyev, Petrovsky, Yaroslavsky and others who were also banished to Yakutia, boarded the first steamer and arrived in revolutionary Petrograd in 1917.

Comrade Sergo was then chosen as a member of the Executive Committee of the Petrograd Council of Workers' Deputies and became a member of the Petrograd Executive Commission of the Petrograd Committee of the Russian Social Democratic Workers' Party (Bolsheviks). He was also chosen to the membership of the Petrograd Committee of the Russian Social Democratic Workers' Party (Bolsheviks).

Comrade Stalin remained in Petrograd and he directed the overall work of the Bolshevik Party. On Comrade Stalin's instructions Comrade Sergo traveled to meet with Lenin, first in Sestroretsk, and then in Finland. He kept him informed about the state of affairs in Petrograd and received from him instructions, which he then conveyed to Comrade Stalin.

The historic Sixth Congress of the Bolshevik Party took place in Petrograd from July 26 to August 3, 1917. Lenin was not present at the

Congress. The work of the Sixth Congress was directed by the Great Leader of our Party, Comrade Stalin.

At this Congress Comrade Sergo reported on the problem of the appearance of Lenin at the court of justice of the provisional bourgeois counterrevolutionary government. Comrade Sergo firmly supported the point of view of Stalin in that matter.

As is well known, the Sixth Congress accepted the motion of Comrade Stalin to the effect that Lenin should not present himself before the court.

In September 1917, Comrade Sergo arrived in Georgia, according to directives received from Lenin and Stalin, where he remained until October 17, 1917.

On October 24 Comrade Sergo returned to Petrograd and took an active part in the October Socialist Revolution.

The intervention of the Entente against Soviet Russia started in the spring of 1918. A Civil War broke out in the Country.

The leadership in the struggle against the counterrevolution in the South of Russia and in the first-line defensive battle at Tsaritsyn was given to Comrade Stalin, in accordance with Lenin's instructions, and in fulfillment of the mission entrusted to him by the Central Committee of the Russian Communist Party (Bolsheviks).

Comrade Stalin was in command of the Tsaritsyn Front beginning in June 1918. He created the Revolutionary Military Council, organized a regular Red Army and dealt crushing blows to the counterrevolutionary and hostile elements behind the front line of the Red Army.

Under the leadership of Comrade Stalin, the Red Army, commanded by Comrade Voroshilov, the illustrious military comrade-in-arms of Comrade Stalin, crushed the Whiteguard armies of Krasnov and Mamontov in August 1918, and threw them far back towards the Don River.

During this period of the fiercest struggle against the bourgeois counterrevolution Comrade Sergo proved to be an untiring, fearless organizer and instructor of the Armed Forces of the Proletarian Revolution in the Northern Caucasus area.

Comrade Sergo accomplished a tremendous job in the Northern Caucasus. He was strengthening the defenses of the revolutionary movement, he was liquidating all breakthrough attempts of the enemy and he was responsible for the victories of the Red Army over the Whiteguard bands of Serebryakov, Bicherakhov, Shkuro and Pokrovsky. Beating back the attacks of the counterrevolutionary forces he at the same time strengthened the organs of the Soviet authority under exceptionally difficult and complex circumstances existing in the multi-national area of the Northern Caucasus.

The operations of the Red Army against the Whiteguard bands were also directed by S. Kirov, Gikalo, Levandovsky and others along with Comrade Sergo.

Towards the end of 1918, General Denikin succeeded in uniting under his command numerous White units. Sorokin, the commander of the Red Armies in the Northern Caucasus area defected from the Soviet side and as a result the White units began to crowd the Red Armies. The 11th Red Army was lacking ammunition, equipment and food while at the same time spotted fever was taking its toll and the ranks of the Army were shrinking with every passing day.

During these bleak days of mortal danger Comrade Sergo mobilized all Bolsheviks, revolutionary workers and peasants, organized guerrilla units, strengthened the discipline and boosted the morale of all units.

After the main units of the 11th Army departed for Astrakhan, Comrade Sergo, together with a group of leading workers of the Party Organization and of the Soviet Government, fled to the mountains of the Ingush and the Chechen regions where the poor highlander population, under the leadership of Bolsheviks was gathering its combat strength in order to resume the fight against the Whiteguard counterrevolution.

In the spring of 1919, Comrade Sergo sneaked illegally into Baku, traversing the snow-clad Caucasus range and then crossing Georgia, at that time occupied by the Mensheviks. From Baku he sailed on a Turkmen fishing boat to Astrakhan, from where he reached Moscow.

From Moscow Comrade Sergo was sent to the Western Front, to Comrade Stalin, where he was nominated to membership of the Revolutionary Military Council of the 16th Army.

After the Southern Front was pierced by Mamontov, Comrade Sergo, at the head of a Latvian Division, was transferred to the Southern Front and made a member of the Revolutionary Military Council of the 14th Army.

A significant impact on the Southern Front was caused by the change in military tactics proposed by Stalin, who suggested the use of a striking force.

During that period of operations Comrade Sergo was put by Comrade Stalin in command of a striking force composed of units from the 13th and 14th Red Armies.

Together with Comrades Kirov and Tukchachevsky Comrade Sergo was directing actions that resulted in further defeats of the remnants of the Denikin armies in the northern Caucasus.

In the whole northern Caucasus area Comrade Sergo very strictly implemented the Lenin-Stalin national policy. Under the direct leadership of Comrade Stalin, Comrade Sergo organized the Soviet National Autonomous Republics in the Northern Caucasus area.

In April 1920, the Baku proletariat, led by the Bolsheviks, started an insurrection against the Mussavatist government and against the English and French interventionists.

Following the direct orders from Lenin and Stalin the heroic 11th Red Army, directed by Comrade Sergo Ordzhonikidze and S. M. Kirov, came to the assistance of the workers and peasants of Azerbaijan. During that time the Army was under the command of Comrade Levandovsky.

After the victory of the Soviet Government in Azerbaijan, Comrade Sergo remained in Baku and continued to direct the operations leading to the total defeat of the remnants of the Whiteguards in the Northern Caucasus. He was responsible for liquidating the landing of General Ulagay in the Kuban area and of several other landings of Whiteguard bands in the Northern Caucasus area.

The Soviet rule in Armenia was established on November 29, 1920.

After the victory of the Great October Socialist Revolution the Georgian Mensheviks, in alliance with foreign imperialists, tore Georgia away from Revolutionary Russia and converted the country into a bridgehead of foreign intervention as well as the bourgeois Whiteguard counterrevolution.

The Menshevik dictatorship brought Georgia to complete economic ruin and cultural degradation and exposed the workers and peasants to unspeakable deprivations and sufferings.

The Mensheviks were responsible for bloody massacres of the national minorities in Georgia, among them those of Ossetia, Abkhazia and Adzharistan. Together with the Dashnaks and Mensheviks they instigated the bloody Georgian-Armenian war, which pitted brother against brother.

The toilers of Georgia started to intensify the struggle against the domination of the Mensheviks and interventionists.

Following Lenin's instructions, and being under the direct leadership of Comrades Ordzhonikidze and Kirov, the workers and peasants of Georgia started an uprising against the Mensheviks and interventionists in February 1921 and, with the help of the heroic Red Army, established Soviet rule on February 25, 1921.

During the 1921-1926 period Comrade Sergo became the leader of the Party in Transcaucasia in his capacity as Secretary of the Caucasus Bureau of the Central Committee of the Russian Communist Party (Bolsheviks) and later as Secretary of the Transcaucasian Committee of the All-Union Communist Party (Bolsheviks).

Under the direct leadership of Comrade Sergo the Bolsheviks of Transcaucasia were steadfastly following the instructions of Lenin and Stalin in their merciless struggle against the remnants of anti-Soviet parties, i.e., Mensheviks, Dashnaks, Mussavatists, as well as in their fight against nationalism and all nationalistic tendencies. They were strengthening the dictatorship of the proletariat in the Transcaucasian Republics of Georgia, Armenia and Azerbaijan. They were also organizing the Transcaucasian Federation, which insured peace among the nationalities and friendship between all peoples in Transcaucasia.

The correct implementation of the Leninist-Stalinist national policy by the Bolsheviks of Transcaucasia with Comrade Ordzhonikidze at their head constituted the decisive factor in strengthening the Proletarian dictatorship, making the National Republics of Georgia, Armenia and Azerbaijan flourish, and in developing a Socialist economic and cultural construction.

The Transcaucasian Federation played an important role in the struggle of the Republics of Transcaucasia to achieve victories in Socialist construction and it solved all the encountered problems to complete satisfaction.

An important share of all these achievements of the toilers of Transcaucasia belongs to Comrade Ordzhonikidze, the closest comrade-in-arms of the Great Stalin.

At the Tenth Congress of the Communist Party Comrade Ordzhonikidze was elected to membership in the Central Committee of the Russian Communist Party (Bolsheviks).

In 1926, at the Plenary October Session of the Central Committee and of the Central Control Commission of the All-Union Communist Party (Bolsheviks), Comrade Ordzhonikidze was elected Chairman of the Central Control Commission of the All-Union Communist Party (Bolsheviks) and nominated People's Commissar of the Workers' and Peasants' Inspection.

In November 1930, Comrade Ordzhonikidze was nominated Chairman of the All-Russian Council of National Economy and later on, after the reorganization of the Council, he became the People's Commissar for Heavy Industry.

Beginning with 1930, Comrade Sergo continuously has been a member of the Political Bureau of the Central Committee of the All-Union Communist Party (Bolsheviks).

The contribution of Comrade Ordzhonikidze as Commander in Chief of Heavy Industry is enormous.

Heavy industry, under the command of Comrade Sergo, is leading victoriously the entire Socialist economy of the USSR.

In heavy industry Comrade Sergo is implementing steadily and systematically the instructions of the Great Stalin and he is organizing and assembling the best economists in the Central Committee of our Party.

Comrade Sergo is a man of action who is able to overcome all difficulties in the development of our Socialist attack on a problem, and is a prominent expert in Bolshevik leadership.

Comrade Ordzhonikidze is the closest, most loyal and devoted comrade-in-arms of our Great Leader, Comrade Stalin.

He is also one of the most popular leaders of the Lenin-Stalin Party.

Under the leadership of the Central Committee of the All-Union Communist Party (Bolsheviks) and the Great Stalin, Comrade Sergo is devoting his entire Bolshevik wisdom, his inflexible will power, energy and enthusiasm to the struggle for the victory of Communism in the USSR as well as for the victory of the Socialist Revolution in the entire world.

(*Pravda*, October 28, 1936)

Appendix 8

EXCERPTS FROM *ON THE HISTORY OF THE BOLSHEVIK ORGANIZATIONS IN TRANSCAUCASIA*

by L. P. Beria

Thus:

1. *National deviationism in the ranks of the Bolshevik, Communist Party of Georgia represented a Right-opportunist trend, which reflected the pressure of bourgeois-nationalist Menshevik elements upon certain sections of our Party organization.*

Having entered upon the path of struggle against the Party, the national-deviationist opposition lapsed into the position of Georgian Menshevikism.

2. *National deviationism represented aggressive chauvinism, reflecting the Great-Power bourgeois nationalism of the Georgian Mensheviks and national-democrats.*

Having entered upon the path of struggle against the national policy of Lenin and Stalin, the national deviationists fought furiously against the Transcaucasian Federation and the autonomy of Abkhazia, Ajaristan and South Ossetia for the perpetuation of the oppression of the national minorities in Georgia.

3. *On the agrarian and peasant question the national deviationists reflected the interests and demands of the Georgian noblemen and kulaks.**

In defending the kulak agrarian policy, national deviationism acted

---

* Rich farmers.

as the mouthpiece and champion of the capitalist path of development for our countryside.

4. The national deviationists adopted an openly liberal, conciliatory position on the questions of the struggle against counterrevolutionary Menshevikism. They substituted a policy of "peaceful reeducation" and collaboration with the Mensheviks, the bitterest enemies of the workers and peasants of Georgia, for the ruthless struggle of the Party and the Soviet Government against the Menshevik counterrevolutionaries—the direct agents and accomplices of international imperialism.

5. The danger of national deviationism lay in the fact that if it had been victorious it would have strengthened the survival of serfdom in the countryside, would have reinforced the position of kulaks, would have made Georgia and Transcaucasia an arena of friction and bloody conflicts among its nationalities, would have undermined the united inter-national front of the Soviet Republics against imperialism, would have unleashed the reactionary forces of the Mensheviks and bourgeois nationalists, and in this way would have paved the way to imperialist intervention and the restoration of capitalism.

6. The national deviationists lapsed into a Trotskyite-Menshevik position at the very start, fighting tooth and nail under the banner of Trotskyism against the Party of Lenin and Stalin and degenerating in the ranks of counterrevolutionary Trotskyism into hired agents of fascism, a rabid gang of spies, wreckers, diversionists, murderers, vile betrayers and enemies of the people.

7. Armed with the national program of Lenin and Stalin, the Bolsheviks of Transcaucasia and the Communist Party of Georgia (Bolsheviks) defeated and crushed the national deviationists, raised the indestructible edifice of the fraternal collaboration of the peoples of Transcaucasia, established and consolidated the Transcaucasian Federation, a "model of peace among the nationalities unprecedented under the bourgeoisie and impossible under the bourgeois system" (Lenin).

8. After forming a strong Transcaucasian Federation, under the leadership of the Party of Lenin and Stalin, the Bolsheviks of Transcaucasia succeeded in attaining enormous achievements in socialist construction and great victories for the socialist system in the Republics of Transcaucasia, thereby making conditions ripe for the abolition of the Transcaucasian Federation and the incorporation of the republics of Georgia, Azerbaijan and Armenia into the Union of Soviet Socialist Republics in accordance with the great Stalin Constitution.

Appendix 9

EIGHTEENTH CONGRESS OF THE ALL-UNION
COMMUNIST PARTY (BOLSHEVIKS)

Speech of Comrade Beria

Comrades, our glorious Communist Party presents itself at the Eighteenth Congress as a monolithic, unified Party rallied closely to its Leader, the Great Stalin. (Long-lasting applause.)

Comrade Stalin in his report summarized the historic achievements of Socialism in every field in our Country and staked out the path for a continuous victorious onward-rush towards Communism.

The Bolshevik Party, and all peoples of the Soviet Union have every right to be proud of achievements obtained under the wise leadership of Comrade Stalin.

Our Country became powerful, prosperous and highly cultured. Our people have led a life enhanced by freedom, happiness and prosperity.

For the first time in the history of mankind a new society has been built where all exploiting classes have been eliminated, where exploitation of man by man has been rooted out and the workers themselves have become sole recipients of all material and cultural blessings.

Liberated from oppression and exploitation, from lawlessness and destitution, the people developed forces theretofore hidden in their midst. Fearless heroes have arisen from the ranks of the people, performing remarkable feats for the glory of their country.

The true national Soviet culture experienced a rapid growth. A big army of intelligentsia has arisen from the ranks of the working class and during the years of the Soviet Administration, successfully absorbing the fundamentals of the Marx-Engels-Lenin-Stalin teachings and making significant strides in all fields of science and technology, arts and literature.

Our intelligentsia, which has been given every support and attention by the Party and the Soviet State, and which constitutes the bone and flesh of all workers of our Country inspired by the Soviet patriotic feeling, is selflessly devoted, heart and soul, to the cause of Lenin-Stalin.

The Stakhanovites'* movement based on the new up-to-date technology developed, breaking old standards and lifting the productivity of the Socialist worker to a higher level. The Bolshevik Party groomed and trained numerous cadres of Party, Soviet and economic leaders, whole-

---

* Stakhanovite: an exemplary worker.

heartedly devoted to the Party of Lenin-Stalin and successfully mastering the skills of Bolshevik leadership.

The Bolshevik Party, unflinchingly realizing the wise instructions of Comrade Stalin on raising revolutionary vigilance and having the unanimous support of the entire nation, destroyed the basic hostile nuclei of the Bukharin-Trotskyite and other brands of saboteurs, wreckers, murderers as well as spies of foreign intelligence agencies.

The foundation for the victory of Socialism in the USSR was laid by the unheard of in history moral and political unity of the Soviet people leading to the strengthening of the Stalin friendship of all USSR peoples.

The Stalin Constitution of victorious Socialism raised even higher the political activity and consciousness of the masses of workers and strengthened even more the power of Soviets.

The Soviet Union became a powerful Socialist State.

These achievements of our Country were brought about by our wise Leader, Comrade Stalin. (Prolonged applause.)

The Bolshevik Party, all toilers in our Country, have every right to be proud to call all our achievements Stalin victories. (Storm of applause.)

At the time when the Soviet Country steadfastly and victoriously marches on towards a new development of economy and culture, in the capitalist countries poverty and unemployment are on the increase and the crises of the capitalist system assume progressively larger proportions.

Our Bolshevik Congress maps out and discusses far-reaching plans for continued Socialist construction and for a further rise of the material and cultural level of the toiling masses. At the same time all efforts of the bosses in the bourgeois states are directed towards unleashing imperialist carnages.

The leaders of the capitalist countries meeting in Munich and Paris, in London and Rome, are weaving nets for a new aggressive war for repartition of the world, are plotting to determine the next victims of fascist aggression, are cheating each other and selling countries down the river.

Entangled in its internal and external contradictions, capitalism looks for solution through further aggressions against the vital interest of the workers, by stepping up the exploitation as well as by making war.

Thus for more than two years the combined forces of the German and Italian fascist interventionists, with the help of the so-called democratic countries—England and France—are tearing to pieces the heroic Spanish people.

Japan with the connivance of other capitalist countries tries for almost two years to enslave the great Chinese nation and to take away from the Chinese people its independence and freedom.

The struggle of the Chinese people against Japanese imperialists in the defense of its liberty and independence will serve as an object lesson and a terrible warning for all imperialist predators, who, in the heat of their predatory efforts discount in their calculation the great strength of the people.

In its heroic struggle the Chinese people are overcoming national separatism foisted by the feudal militaristic generals and, at the same time, they are consolidating into a strong invincible power which is inflicting crushing blows to the enemy, thus upsetting the plans not only of the Japanese imperialism but of the worldwide one as well.

The admiration and fellow feeling of the entire Soviet nation, as well as of the workers in the entire world, is on the side of the freedom-loving heroic Chinese people.

The Stalin policy of peace, conducted steadfastly and without deviations by our Soviet State, opposes the diplomatic bargaining and machinations of the bourgeois fascist governments.

The peaceful policy of the USSR is unmasking the intentions of the imperialist states, is wrecking their plans, provoking a rabid animosity and hatred of the ruling classes in the capitalist countries towards the Soviet Union. Enemy provocations are foundering on the power and strength of our Soviet State.

On guard of our Socialist Country are the invincible Red Army of workers and peasants, the Red Navy, our glorious Aviation and our Soviet Intelligence Service. (Prolonged applause.)

The Khasan lesson should be memorized not only by the Japanese generals but by all the aggressors from the so-called anti-Comintern Bloc as well.

Comrades, great indeed are our achievements in all fields of the Socialist economy and culture, but the tasks remaining ahead of us are equally great. The fulfillment of the goal set for our Party and our Country by Comrade Stalin—to equal and surpass the leading capitalist countries of Europe and America in the economic field during the next ten to fifteen years will require not only the mobilization of all our forces and skills, but also a control and correction of all committed errors and shortcomings in our work.

It is a well-known fact that a great deal of harm was done by the Bukharin-Trotskyite saboteurs, wreckers and spies of foreign intelligence agencies which crept into our Soviet, Party and economic organizations. But it would be an error to explain the breakdowns which occurred in various segments of our national economy solely by the subversive activity of our enemies. These breakdowns are due, to a certain degree, to the unsatisfactory, unskilled work of a number of our Soviet economic leaders who have not yet mastered adequately the fundamentals of the Bolshevik management.

Comrade Stalin, criticizing the work of some People's Commissariats, stated earlier, during the Seventeenth Party Congress:

"They are solving problems but do not think to check on the implementation of their decisions, to call to order those who break the regulations and instructions of the leading agencies and to promote honest and conscientious workers."

Instead of the concrete operational solutions of problems, some of our economic People's Commissariats and in particular some of the Main Directorates convoke not always necessary conferences of various sorts, often with the participation of a large number of workers from faraway places. Problems for the conferences are badly prepared, the conferences themselves last too long and the called-in comrades have to stay in Moscow for weeks. Nobody checks the implementation of the resolutions and decisions approved by the conferences; in a number of cases they are put aside for months by the management of the economic organizations and are finally forgotten. Some People's Commissariats are issuing an enormous amount of decisions and instructions but they are not instituting any active control for the implementation of these instructions and decisions. That is why it often happens that in the same matter a number of orders are issued with the same wording, sometimes even containing an opposite meaning. For example, the People's Commissariat of Agriculture issued over 1,500 orders and instructions in 1938, not counting the appointment and transfer orders, while the People's Commissariat of Water Transportation issued 900 orders.

In view of such an irresponsible, I would say, attitude of some chiefs of the economic People's Commissariats and their Main Administrations towards their own orders and instructions, these documents are losing force and authority and are ignored and broken with impunity.

This state of affairs can, in a large degree, be explained by the fact that these comrades do not acquaint themselves with, nor satisfactorily study the problem entrusted to them; they are unfamiliar with their cadres and local conditions.

We have to draw all necessary conclusions from what Comrade Stalin was telling us in his speech at our Congress about a conscientious study of a given assignment, about the proper study and use of the cadres, about the resolute promotion of the tested young workers, devoted to the Party and to the Soviet Fatherland, about the effectiveness and decisiveness in the management, about keeping in touch and being close to local conditions.

There are conditions present in our Country for the fulfillment of the grandiose plans of the Third Stalin Five-Year-Plan period, but we have to remember the wise remark of Comrade Stalin who said: "Victory never happens, it has always to be earned. . . . The success of an endeavour depends upon the organizational work, upon the organization of the struggle to put in operation the Party line, upon the correct selection of people, upon checking on the implementation of the decisions of the authorities."

The discussion of the theses of Comrade Molotov on the Third Five-Year-Plan for the Development of the National Economy of the USSR, which took place in advance of the Party Congress, showed a unanimous approval by the Soviet nation of the Stalin line of our Party with regard to the continued development of the Socialist economy and culture in our Country as well as people's readiness to fight for the implementation of the outlined plans.

Comrade Stalin in his speech presented a firm foundation of the steadily increasing role of the Soviet State in the task of fulfilling the future far-reaching plans of building Communism, in the task of a continuous strengthening of the military power of our Country, which is subjected to a capitalist encirclement.

Contemptible Bukharinites, putting forward the counterrevolutionary theory of laissez-faire and slurring the decisive organizational role of the Soviet State as well as all "leftists" of various description with their anti-Lenin theory of the withering away of the State of the working class through gradual weakening of its role, all served the single counterrevolutionary purpose of restoring capitalism in our Country by weakening the Soviet State.

Striking crushing blows against the enemies of the people, Comrade Stalin unmasked and abolished hostile theses with regard to the Soviet State and with a brilliant perspicacity outlined the goals in the task of strengthening the Dictatorship of the Proletariat.

"A strong and powerful Dictatorship of the Proletariat," said Comrade Stalin at the Joint Plenary Session of the Central Committee and the Central Control Commission in 1933, "this is precisely what we need in order to disperse the last remnants of the dying classes and destroy their thievish connivances.

The withering away of the State will be accomplished not as a result of the weakening of the State power but through its maximum intensification, which is indispensable in order to liquidate the remnants of the dying classes and organize the defense against the capitalist encirclement which has by no means yet been destroyed and will not yet be destroyed for a long time."

Not even for a moment should we forget the wise instructions of Comrade Stalin about the necessity of fortifying our Soviet State in every possible way. The strengthening of all segments of the Soviet State apparatus with well-tested, strong cadres and the elimination from them of all not yet unmasked and still hiding enemies of the people, constitutes a task of primary importance.

Comrade Stalin emphasized in his speech that in our State system an important role belongs to the Soviet Intelligence Service.

The Soviet Intelligence Service has been created as a result of the initiative of Lenin and Stalin and it was developed and strengthened under the leadership of the Bolshevik Party, the Stalin Central Committee of the All-Union Communist Party (Bolsheviks).

In the cause of the further victorious forward movement of our Country on the road towards Communism the People's Commissariat of Internal Affairs is entrusted with very important tasks, since our Country exists and is developing in conditions of encirclement by hostile capitalist states, who smuggle in spies, saboteurs and murderers. These foul enemies of the people will also try in the future, with an even increased determination, to harm us, play dirty tricks on us and to thwart the realization of our future plans of building Socialism.

The workers of the People's Commissariat of Internal Affairs, enjoying the consideration and support of the Party and the Nation, are wholeheartedly devoted to our Party, to the Stalin Central Committee of the All-Union Communist Party (Bolsheviks), to our own beloved Leader —Comrade Stalin. Having cleansed their ranks from hostile elements who succeeded in creeping in, and having strengthened their ranks with checked-out cadres, the workers of the National Commissariat of Internal Affairs will insure the unmasking, defeat and purge of all enemies of the people. (Prolonged applause.)

Our invincible Communist Party of Bolsheviks, led by its Great Leader —Stalin—is the organizer of the victory of Socialism in our Country.

All victories, all changes which have taken place in the political, economic and cultural life of our Country are reflected in the life of our Party, in its growth and in its development as if it were a mirror.

Comrade Stalin explained to us the meaning of changes that are being introduced in the statutes of the All-Union Communist Party (Bolsheviks), which derive from the changes which have taken place in the class structure of our society based on the liquidation of the exploiting classes and from the fact of the moral and political unity of the Soviet people based on the friendship between the working class, the peasantry and the intelligentsia, each of which is equally loyal to the cause of Communism, equally imbued with the feeling of Soviet patriotism and wholeheartedly devoted to their Socialist Country.

The speech of Comrade Stalin at our Congress, which gave a brilliant explanation of problems of international politics and of the ways leading to the victory of Communism in our Country under conditions of capitalist encirclement, which outlined the problems connected with a further development and strengthening of the Soviet State as well as the methods of training, employment and indoctrination of the Party members, the Soviet and economic personnel, and the Soviet intelligentsia cadres, constitutes the most important contribution to the ideological treasure house of Marxism-Leninism, a program of action for our entire Party as well as for the entire Soviet nation. (Storm of applause.)

Executing the instructions of Comrade Stalin our Party will continue to strengthen its unbreakable bonds with the broadest masses of workers while the peoples of the Soviet Union will close their ranks even tighter around the Lenin-Stalin banner and strengthen the Stalin friendship, which is the foundation for the power and invincibility of the Soviet State.

Let our enemies know that our great Soviet Union is impregnable, that our heroic Red Army of workers and peasants, the object of Stalin's care, is invincible and still being developed, that equally invincible is our people, constituting with its Army a single indissoluble and mighty power, ready to crush and destroy any given enemy who would dare to strike against the happiness and liberty of the Soviet nation or the sacred frontiers of our Socialist Country.

The historic instructions of Comrade Stalin and the resolutions of the Eighteenth Congress of the All-Union Communist Party (Bolsheviks) will be realized by our Party nurtured by Lenin and Stalin and hardened in the struggle for Socialism as well as by our Nation, which rallied closely around the Party of Bolsheviks. This is because our Party and our Nation is led from one victory to another by the Greatest Genius of Mankind—Stalin. (Storm of applause. Everybody stands up. Exclamations are heard: "Long live the Soviet Intelligence Service! Hurrah!")

(*Pravda*, March 15, 1939)

Appendix 10

Broadcasts from Moscow Radio continuously urged the Warsaw population to begin an armed rising against the Germans. On July 29, for example, at 8:15 P.M., the following message went on the air from the Union of Polish Patriots:

"Calling Warsaw. Fight against the Germans! Warsaw undoubtedly hears already the artillery guns engaged in a battle which will bring freedom to the city. Those who had never yielded to Hitler's violence will once again, as in 1939, join in the fight against their oppressors, but this time it will be a decisive battle! A Polish Army trained in the USSR which is just now entering Polish territories will join the People's Army to form a Polish Army Corps—an iron-clad hand of the Nation wrenching back its independence!

"Tomorrow, the citizens of Warsaw will also find themselves in the ranks. They will join our Allied armies in chasing the enemy westward in

order to clear Polish soil of the Nazi pestilence and to deal a mortal blow
to the monster of Prussian imperialism.

"For the city of Warsaw, which has never yet capitulated and has
never stopped the struggle, the hour for action has struck."

On July 30, the Russian-sponsored broadcasting station *Kosciusko*
repeated the following message in Polish several times (at 3 P.M., 8:55
P.M., 9:55 P.M. and 11 P.M.):

"Warsaw is quivering from the rumbling of artillery fire. Soviet troops
in their violent attack are approaching the gates of Praga.* They are
heading towards you, bringing you freedom. The Germans repelled from
Praga will try to put up a defence in Warsaw. They will endeavor to
destroy everything behind them. It took them six whole days to destroy
the city of Bialystok. They murdered thousands of our brothers. Let us
do our uttermost to stop them from repeating the same in Warsaw.

"Citizens of Warsaw! To arms! Let the whole population stand as one
man around the Home National Council. All must report to the Underground Army. Strike against the Germans! Prevent them from destroying
our buildings. Help the Red Army crossing the Vistula. Send us all
information, show us the way! Let the million inhabitants of Warsaw
turn overnight into a million soldiers to chase the aggressors and win
freedom again!"

Bronislav Kusnierz, *Stalin and the Poles* (London: Hollis and Carter,
1949).

Appendix 11

THE USSR SUPREME COURT
DECISION NO. 4N—083/59

The Military Collegium of the USSR Supreme Court consisting of the
Presiding Justice Counselor Borisoglebsky and members—Justice Colonels Dolotsov and Konev, have examined at the Session of February 6,
1957.

The Appeal of the General Military Prosecutor against the decision of
the Special Board of the USSR People's Commissariat of Internal Affairs
(NKVD) of July 7, 1945, on the basis of which Aleksander Isayevich
Solzhenitsyn, born in 1918 in Kislovodsk, a college graduate, has been
committed to a labor correction camp for eight years, according to Articles 58-10, Paragraph 2, and 58-11 of the Criminal Code of the Russian
Soviet Federated Socialist Republic. Until his arrest he was the com-

---

* Praga: suburb of Warsaw.

mander of a battery, took part in combat against German Fascist forces and has been awarded the Order of the War of the Fatherland, 2d Class, and the Order of the Red Star.

Having heard the report of Comrade Konev and the closing statement of the Deputy General Military Prosecutor, Justice Colonel Terekhov, submitting to sustain the protest, the Military Division established the following:

Solzhenitsyn was charged with conducting an anti-Soviet propaganda and was taking steps to create an anti-Soviet organization among his acquaintances, from 1940 to the day of his arrest.

In his protest the General Military Prosecutor raised the question of repealing the mentioned decision of the Special Board and closing the case against Solzhenitsyn in the absence of a corpus delicti on the following grounds:

From the materials of the case it is evident that Solzhenitsyn in his diary and in letters to his friend N. D. Vitkevich while writing about the rightness of Marxism-Leninism, about the progressiveness of the Socialist Revolution in our Country and its inevitable victory in the whole world, declared himself against the Stalin personality cult, wrote about the artistic and ideological weaknesses in the literary works of art of Soviet authors, about the lack of realism of many of them and about the fact that in our works of art the historical inevitability of the victories of the Soviet people and the Soviet Army is not being explained totally and from every angle to the readers in the bourgeois world and that our belles lettres cannot withstand the cleverly manufactured slander against our Country.

These statements of Solzhenitsyn do not contain any corpus delicti.

In the process of verification of Solzhenitsyn's complaints Reshetovskaya, Simonyan, Simonyants, who supposedly have heard Solzhenitsyn utter anti-Soviet lies, were questioned. The enumerated persons, however, described Solzhenitsyn as a Soviet patriot and denied that he was making anti-Soviet speeches.

From Solzhenitsyn's war record and from the testimonial of Captain Melnikov, who served with him in the Army, it is evident that Solzhenitsyn, beginning with 1942 and up to the day of his arrest, that is until February 1945, was in the front lines of the Great Patriotic War, fought valiantly for his country, many times performed personal acts of heroism and carried with him the staff of the subunit of which he was the commander. Solzhenitsyn's subunit was first in the unit inasmuch as discipline and combat performance is concerned.

Based on this account the General Military Prosecutor believes that the conviction of Solzhenitsyn is an error and in that connection he raises the question of closing his case on grounds of Article 4, Paragraph 5 of the Code of Criminal Procedure of the Russian Soviet Federated Socialist Republic.

Having examined the materials of the case and of the supplemental verification and furthermore concurring with the arguments presented in the Appeal and taking into consideration that in the activities of Solzhenitsyn there is no *corpus delicti* and consequently his case is subject to discontinuance for lack of *corpus delicti*, the Military Collegium of the USSR Supreme Court determined:

> to rescind the decision of the Special Board of the NKVD of the USSR People's Commissariat of Internal Affairs of July 7, 1945, relative to Aleksander Isayevich Solzhenitsyn and to close his case because of lack of *corpus delicti*, based on Article 4, Paragraph 5 of the Code of Criminal Procedure of the Russian Soviet Federated Socialist Republic.

The original with the proper signatures.
Certified true copy: Senior Officer of the
Military Collegium
Major Degtyareva
(Translated from a copy smuggled to the West.)

Appendix 12

THE GREAT INSPIRER AND ORGANIZER OF COMMUNIST VICTORIES

by L. Beria

After the great Lenin, no name in the entire world is as close to the hearts of millions of workers as that of the Great Leader, Comrade Stalin.

The name of the Great Stalin is being pronounced with fervent love by the workers in every country of the world, connecting it with the realization of their century-old hopes and aspirations.

The name of Comrade Stalin is being pronounced with the feeling of great gratitude by the workers of the countries of people's democracies who entered upon the path of building Socialism. The name is also being revered by the workers and peasants of China who threw down the yoke of colonial oppression. The name of Comrade Stalin inspires the workers of Europe and America in their fight against capitalism. The name also inspires the peoples of subjugated colonial and semicolonial countries in their just struggle for their national freedom and independence.

The whole life of Comrade Stalin is inseparably linked with the struggle for the creation and strengthening of the Bolshevik Party, for the victory of Proletarian Revolution, for the well-being of the workers and the victory of Communism.

Activities of Comrade Stalin are so sublime and multi-sided, that it would require many years to describe them adequately.

The entire activity of Comrade Stalin is inspired with such theoretical power, linked with an enormous organizational sweep, the ability to inspire the Party and the multimillion masses of workers with a single strong will to direct their efforts towards the fulfillment of important tasks and to set forth for the Party the true course leading towards victory.

It is a well-known fact that the Socialist social system differs basically from all other social systems in the way it came into being. While the latter developed their economic programs spontaneously, Socialism can be formed only through a conscious action of the masses according to scientifically worked out plans. Remarking on the peculiar complexity of the problem of building Socialism Lenin said:

"It was not difficult to chase away the tsar—this task required only a few days. There will be no special difficulty in chasing away the land-lords, this can be done in a few months. Neither is there any problem in removing the capitalists.

"But it is immeasurably more difficult to liquidate the classes: the division into workers and peasants still remains . . .

"It is imperative that everyone should work according to one single overall plan on common land, in communal plants and factories based on the same regulations. Is this easy to accomplish? You can see that a solution cannot be reached here as easily as with the removal of the tsar, landlords and capitalists." (*Works*, Volume 30, p. 411.)

The Stalin era is therefore an era during which a new Socialist society is being created. The genius of Comrade Stalin appeared before the eyes of the nations of our Country and before the entire forward looking and progressive mankind in all its grandeur under the conditions of a new historic situation.

The name of Comrade Stalin ranges next to the name of the sublime geniuses of mankind—those of Marx, Engels and Lenin. Mankind is indebted to Marx and Engels for the creation of scientific Communism. Mankind owes the victory of the Proletarian Revolution and the creation of the Soviet social and state system to Lenin and to his faithful disciple —Comrade Stalin. Mankind is indebted to Comrade Stalin for the victory of Socialism in the USSR and for the saving of its civilization from the fascist barbarity.

I

Comrade Stalin, during Lenin's lifetime and under his guidance, beginning with a preparatory period of organizing the Bolshevik Party, came forward as the closest disciple of Lenin, as his most faithful successor and as the greatest, after Lenin, theoretician, organizer and architect of our Party.

Among all men of the Lenin era nobody, except Stalin, was able to fully comprehend Lenin's greatness, his historic role as a creator of a new type Proletarian Party.

Stalin has said, "Familiarity with the revolutionary activity of Lenin beginning with the nineties and in particular after 1901, that is after the publication of *Iskra*, gave me the conviction that in the person of Lenin we have an unusual personality. In my opinion he was at that time not only the Leader of a Party, but he was its creator, since he alone understood its internal nature and the urgent needs of our Party. When I was comparing him with other leaders of our Party, I was at all times under the impression that Lenin's comrades—Plekhanov, Martov, Akselrod and others—were far below his level and that Lenin, by comparison, was not one of the leaders, but a higher-level Leader, a soaring eagle, without fear in the battle and boldly leading the Party along the untried path of the Russian revolutionary movement." (*Works*, Volume 6, pp. 52-53.)

From the very beginning of his revolutionary activity Comrade Stalin unswervingly ranged himself under Lenin's banner, being his faithful and devoted follower in the great work of an overall preparation for the creation of a genuine revolutionary Marxist Party in Russia. He contributed a very important share of preparing, in a Lenin way, the ideological, organizational, political and theoretical foundations of the Marxist Party.

In the drive to prepare the victory of the October Revolution, in the fight against capitulators and traitors of various breeds Comrade Stalin stood steadfastly, shoulder to shoulder with his great teacher Lenin and at the head of the military headquarters of the Party—the Central Committee of the Party.

During the difficult years of the Civil War Lenin and Stalin led the Party, the State, the Red Army and the total defense of the Country.

The change to a peace economy after the reestablishment of the national economy following the Civil War, required a new concentration of all forces of the Bolshevik Party in order to overcome great difficulties in stopping violent and malicious attacks on Lenin's policy on the part of the Trotskyite, Kamenevite, Zinovyevite and Bukharinite gang.

Stalin came forward then and together with Lenin organized the forces of the Party for the defense of the Lenin Party line and thus saved the Party unity.

One of the great merits of Comrade Stalin was the important work performed under the leadership of Lenin with the view of creating and strengthening the Soviet People's Republics and organizing the Union of Soviet Socialist Republics.

Lenin made the motion at the Central Committee of the Party to elect Stalin to the post of General Secretary of the Central Committee. Beginning April 3, 1922, Comrade Stalin continuously performs the functions of this position, the highest in the Party.

Thus, when in January 1924, the Bolshevik Party, the peoples of the USSR and the workers in the entire effort sustained a severe loss—Lenin, the creator, leader and teacher of the Party, died—the Party closed its ranks around Comrade Stalin and followed him on the path of Lenin, crushing all his enemies.

Along the difficult and complex path leading towards the victory of Communism and under the conditions of a fierce class struggle the Party, under Stalin's leadership, beat back numerous attacks of enemies of Leninism, smashed all and sundry opportunistic groups, and eliminated from its ranks all skeptics, opportunists, capitulants and traitors.

In this struggle our Party entered in full possession of Leninist ideology. Stalin provided the Party with the sharpest arms of Leninism.

II

Comrade Stalin defended Leninism against its enemies, he generalized the experience of class struggle of the proletariat under the conditions of the dictatorship of the proletariat, the experience of the era of the victory of Socialism in the USSR, he developed and moved forward the Marxist-Leninist theory in all its fields.

The classic work of Comrade Stalin, *Fundamentals of Leninism*, provided the Communists with the weapon of Marxist-Leninist theory in problems of the Proletarian Revolution, Dictatorship of the Proletariat, the victory of Socialism in a given country, the national liberation movement in colonial and semi-colonial countries and others.

Substantiating and developing Leninism and basing on Lenin's instructions, Comrade Stalin worked out conditions for the Socialist industrialization of the Country. Based on their implementation the historic task of the collectivization of agriculture has been solved. The effects of this collectivization constituted an achievement equal to the revolutionary upheaval in October of 1917.

Comrade Stalin provided a solid theoretical basis for the necessity to strengthen the State under the conditions of the Dictatorship of the Proletariat, created a doctrine on the Socialist State, thus filling a gap in the Marxist theory of the state, substantiated theoretically and developed the Leninist thesis on the advantages of the Soviet social and state system as compared with any given non-Soviet social system, threw light on the sources of power of the Soviet State, worked out the problem of legality in the coexistence and struggle of the two systems, i.e., the Socialist and the capitalist in international relations.

Comrade Stalin developed Lenin's doctrine concerning the Party, provided a solid and well-developed characteristic of the peculiarities of the Bolshevik Party as a new type of party, determined the decisive role of the Party under the conditions of a Dictatorship of the Proletariat and the building of Socialism, the ways of training, ideological preparation and political hardening of Party cadres, the importance of the education of the masses in the spirit of revolutionary vigilance and the role of self-criticism in the life of the Party.

Self-criticism constitutes a continuously active weapon of Bolshevism, inseparably linked with its nature and revolutionary spirit.

"I believe, Comrades," said Stalin, "that we need self-criticism the same as we need air or water. I believe that without it, without self-criticism, our Party would be unable to move ahead, it would not be able to uncover our ulcers, it would not be able to liquidate our shortcomings. We have plenty of shortcomings. This we should admit openly and honestly.

"The self-criticism slogan is not a new slogan. It is imbedded in the very foundations of the Bolshevik Party. It is imbedded in the foundations of policy of the Dictatorship of the Proletariat. Since our Country is the country of the Dictatorship of the Proletariat and the dictatorship is led by the only party, the Communist Party, which does not and cannot share power with other parties, it should be clear that we ourselves should uncover and correct our mistakes, if we want to move forward, since it is equally clear that there is nobody else who would uncover and correct them. Is it not clear, Comrades, that self-criticism should constitute one of the most important forces which would further our development?" (*Works*, Volume 11, p. 29.)

In the *Short Course of History of the All-Union Communist Party (Bolsheviks)* Comrade Stalin summarized the development and the overall experience of the Bolshevik Party, and added up the results of its historic path. Stalin's deductions, continued in the conclusions of the *short Course of History of the All-Union Communist Party (Bolsheviks)* constitute a further expansion of the Marxist-Leninist doctrine on the Party of the working class and are a combat weapon in the actions of our Party, to be used by all Communist and genuinely Marxist parties in their fight for the victory of Communism.

Comrade Stalin developed Lenin's instructions concerning the international significance of the Great October Socialist Revolution in Russia and of the victory of the Socialist building in the USSR, and demonstrated the unity of the national and international tasks in the revolutionary struggle of the proletariat. Comrade Stalin was unmasking the contemporary social-democracy as an ideological support of capitalism and demonstrated that "it is impossible to finish off capitalism, without eliminating social democracy in the working class movement." (*Works*, Volume 10, p. 250.)

Stalin's definition of the tasks of Communist Parties which he gave in the article, "On the International Posture and Tasks of Communist Parties," constitutes also at the present time an action program for Communists.

Comrade Stalin explained that the tasks of the Communist Parties consist in:

"1. Exploiting to the hilt all and sundry contradictions in the bourgeois camp with the view of demoralizing and weakening their forces and strengthening the position of the proletariat.

2. Outlining definite forms and methods to draw together the working class of the leading countries with the national revolutionary movement of colonial and dependent countries with the view of supporting this movement in every possible way against imperialism, the common enemy.

3. Developing and bringing to a successful conclusion the struggle for unity in the trade union movement, remembering that this act constitutes the best way to take control of the working class, numbering millions of people.

4. Outlining definite forms and methods to bring together the working class with the small peasantry, oppressed by the bureaucratic machine of the bourgeois state, and by the exorbitant prices of omnipotent trusts and bearing in mind that the fight for the defense of the small peasantry constitutes the immediate task of the Party which would lead towards the Dictatorship of the Proletariat.

5. Supporting the Soviet Administration by thwarting interventionist intrigue of imperialism against the Soviet Union, remembering that the Soviet Union constitutes the bulwark of the revolutionary movement of all countries and that the preservation and strengthening of the Soviet Union draws nearer the victory of the working class over the world bourgeoisie." (*Works*, Volume 7, pp. 57-58.)

Under the leadership of Lenin and Stalin the international Communist movement has developed and become firmly established; new Communist Parties were transformed into parties of the masses of the working class, cadres of staunch Communist fighters were raised who, during the years of war with the Hitlerite aggressor, defended the national interests of their countries and the vital interests of the working masses and who were leaders in the defense of peace and of the independence of nations in the postwar era.

The historic service, which Comrade Stalin as a Leader of our Party performed for the peoples of our Country and for the whole of mankind, consists of his wise guidance, which insured the achievement of victory for Socialism in the USSR and the victory of the Soviet people in the Great Patriotic War.

These victories constituted historic landmarks, indicative of all subsequent development of human society.

III

The USSR was transformed into a powerful industrial and Socialist kolkhoz state from a backward agrarian country in less than a quarter of a century of peaceful Socialist construction by the heroic effort of the working class and all working people, under the leadership of the Bolshevik Party and its Leader, Stalin.

In the vast territories of the USSR there were built new large cities, plants and factories, electric power plants, *sovkhozes,** and machine tractor stations, as well as *kolhozes.*** High schools, technical schools, universities, institutes, theatres, clubs and libraries sprouted all over the Country.

After the end of the Great Patriotic War the Soviet State in a short period of time achieved the prewar output level in industry and agriculture and already, in 1948, exceeded this prewar level. The production of industry increased 18% and the gross national product 16%, as compared with the 1940 level.

The goals set by the postwar Five-Year Plan are being met in the area of industry, railroad and water transport as well as in the area of agriculture, national culture, public health and development of the material well-being of the workers.

The rapid growth of the national economy considerably increased the USSR share in the industrial production of the world with the result that in the gross output and in such important fields as iron smelting, steel melting, coal mining, production of electric power, production of tractors, trucks, agricultural combines and cement the Soviet Union actually ranks second in the world.

Our Soviet industry is able to build the most complex machines, machine tools and instruments, all types of industrial products necessary for the national economy and the population, which constitutes a firm guar-

---

* Sovkhoz—a state farm.
** Kolhoz—a collective farm.

antee for the economic independence of the USSR from the capitalist countries.

The Soviet Union was in a position to solve successfully and in a short period of time the problem of obtaining atomic energy. This success is due exclusively to the wise Stalin policy of the industrialization of the Country and the creation and development on this basis of such important branches of industry as metallurgy, chemistry, precision machinery and instrument manufacturing and others.

Our Socialist rural economy numbers over 246,000 kolhozes and 4,500 sovkhozes and constitutes the most extensively mechanized agriculture in the world, equipped with the most up-to-date machinery as compared with the rural economy of any given country.

Providing modern equipment for the whole USSR national economy represents one of the most important victories of the building of Socialism.

An achievement of no lesser importance is the creation and training of cadres able to utilize fully the capacities of this machinery and insure their continuous improvement.

In order to create and elevate large numbers of the Soviet intelligentsia, to achieve a substantial rise in the cultural level of the working class and peasantry, a cultural revolution had to be initiated. This cultural revolution has been carried out by the Bolshevik Party under the leadership of Comrade Stalin.

The victory of the Soviet system in all branches of the USSR national economy permitted the establishment in our Country, for the first time in the history of mankind, a new Socialist economy "which is not subjected to crises and unemployment, poverty and ruin and which guarantees the citizens the opportunity for a prosperous and cultural life." (J. Stalin. *Problems of Leninism*, p. 510.)

USSR is the first and so far the only country in the world where all exploiting classes have been liquidated. The victory of Socialism in the USSR lifts the spirit of the working class in the capitalist countries and strengthens the confidence in its forces, confidence in the victory of Socialism in the whole world.

One of the most significant achievements of Socialism is the creation of a friendship of nations in the multi-national Soviet State, unprecedented in the history of mankind.

In the brotherly family of USSR nations, all enjoying equal rights, the Russian nation is the most prominent nation.

The Russian working class under the leadership of the Lenin-Stalin Party carried the main burden of the fight for the success of the Great October Socialist Revolution.

In its fight for the success of the building of Socialism the Russian nation constitutes the leading edge among the nations of the USSR, serving as an example for all other nations in the industrialization of the country, collectivization of the rural economy, in the work of building a Socialist way of life.

During the years of the Great Patriotic War the Russian nation with its clear mind, staunch character and intelligent patience has won universal recognition as the leading force of the Soviet Union among all nations of our Country.

Comrade Stalin made the significant remark that "the faith of the Russian nation in the Soviet Government constituted the decisive factor which insured the historic victory over Fascism, the enemy of mankind." (J. Stalin, *The Great Patriotic War of the Soviet Union*, fifth edition, p. 197.)

The brotherly cooperation of nations in our Country, properly adjusted by Comrade Stalin under the conditions of the Soviet system, on the basis of an economic, political and military mutual aid in the system of a single union state, changed radically the aspect of USSR nations. On the ruins of old, bourgeois nations new Socialist nations developed and took shape.

In the new Socialist nations powerful creative forces of the Russian people developed, as well as the inexhaustible creative forces of all nations of the USSR.

In the People's Republics of the Soviet Union there were created important centers of Socialist industry, sovkhozes and kolhozes, provided with up-to-date equipment, 78,000 primary and secondary schools (not counting those of the RSFSR) with the native tongue as the language of instruction, hundreds of higher education establishments, scientific research institutes as well as hundreds of national theatres.

The development of the People's Republics of the Soviet Union is particularly striking if it is compared with conditions existing in states that are neighbors of the USSR.

Let us take, for example, the Azerbaijan and Uzbek Soviet Socialist Republics and the neighboring states of the USSR—Iran and Turkey. It is understood that in this instance we shall limit ourselves only to some isolated comparisons of indices pertaining to the state of the economy and culture.

Actually it is well known that the Uzbek and Azerbaijan people long ago chased away all their one-time exploiters—khans, beks and bais, merchants and capitalists. The most able sons and daughters of the working people in Azerbaijan and Uzbekistan are now managing the affairs of the state, the plants, the kolhozes, the schools and institutes of their republics. The workers of Azerbaijan and Uzbekistan, like the entire Soviet nation, are no longer exposed to the yoke of exploitation, horrors of poverty, hunger and unemployment. The cultural and material standard of life of the people is increasing from one year to another.

The nations of Iran and Turkey continue to vegetate under the power of landowners—the khans, capitalists and foreign oppressors.

The Azerbaijan SSR and the Uzbek SSR were transformed during the period of Soviet Administration from backward, agrarian states into republics with a highly developed industry, taking a predominant place in the national economy.

Iran and Turkey remained backward agrarian states, where rural economy with primitive machinery remains the basis of the whole national economy. Furthermore in Iran two-thirds of all peasants do not own land, while 62% of all arable land belongs to landowners. In Turkey an overwhelming majority of peasants are without land and work on farms of landowners.

In Azerbaijan and Uzbekistan 90% of the population were illiterate until the take-over by the Soviet Administration; by 1946 illiteracy was already completely wiped out. At the present time illiterates constitute 85% of the population of Iran and about 66% in Turkey, where about 70% of villages have no schools.

The Azerbaijan SSR has 19 establishments of higher education, attended by 29,000 students, with one establishment per 163,000 of population, while Iran has only five institutions of higher education, with about 4,500 students, or one establishment of higher education per 3,400,000 people.

In the Uzbek SSR there are 36 institutions of higher education attended by 38,000 students, or one establishment of higher education per 175,000 people. Turkey has 10 institutions of higher education, where there are about 11,000 students, or one establishment of higher education per 1,950,000 people.

In the Azerbaijan SSR there are 13 theatres and 2,100 Houses of Culture and clubs. In the Uzbek SSR there are 23 theatres, 3,011 Houses of Culture and clubs. A motion picture industry has been created in each of these Republics. In Iran and Turkey there are only a few theatres, which belong to private companies, and eke out a pitiful existence. These states do not have their own motion picture industry; their motion picture theatres show chiefly Hollywood banalities.

In the Azerbaijan SSR there are 5,902 doctors, that is one doctor per 525 people; in Iran—1,500 doctors, or one doctor per 11,333 people; in Uzbek SSR—6,612 doctors, or one doctor per 953 people; in Turkey—2,181 doctors, or one doctor per 8,941 people. The number of hospital beds in the respective countries is as follows: In the Azerbaijan SSR—one bed per 183 people; In Iran—1 bed per 3,400 people; in the Uzbek SSR—1 bed per 186 people; in Turkey—one bed per 1,400 people.

In the Azerbaijan SSR 48 cities and city-type townships have a water supply system. Not a single city in Iran has a water supply system, including the capital, Teheran, which incidentally, has no sewage system, either.

In the rural economy of the Azerbaijan SSR more than 5,000 tractors, 600 agricultural combines and 77,000 attachments and other agricultural machines are at work. In Iran the basic agricultural tools are still a primitive wooden plough, the *azal* and *omach*.

In agriculture in the Uzbek SSR there are engaged more than 24,000 tractors, 1,500 agricultural combines and 280,000 tractor-drawn implements and other agricultural machinery. In an Iranian village, on the other hand, the basic earth-working tool is still a wooden plough, *karaspan*. There is one karaspan for every two farms and one steel plough for every 16 farms, while there is only one agricultural machine per 220 farms.

These few comparisons reflect the economic and cultural growth of the People's Republics of the Soviet Union which was achieved as a result of introducing the Lenin-Stalin national policy and is also due to the fatherly concern of Comrade Stalin in the development of nations of the multi-national Soviet Union.

The victory of the Great October Socialist Revolution, our Soviet social and state system, the victory of Socialism in the USSR, achieved under the leadership of Comrade Stalin—these are the foundations of the unprecedented uplift and flourishing of the economies and cultures of all nations of the USSR under the leadership of the working class and the Bolshevik Party, paving the way to Communism.

IV

During the most brutal and severe war ever fought in the history of our Country the entire Soviet nation recognized once more how wise and farsighted was the policy of the Bolshevik Party carried out under the leadership of the successor of Lenin's cause—Comrade Stalin—the policy of industrialization of the Country, collectivization of agriculture, concern for the strengthening of the Armed Forces of the Socialist State and of increasing the vigilance of the Party and the people against the intrigues of all and sundry enemies of the Soviet State.

The greatness of Comrade Stalin has been unveiled with a new force during the years of the Great Patriotic War. From the first days of the war, when a mortal danger loomed over our Country, when the Red Army under the monstrous pressure of Hitlerite armies was abandoning cities and villages so dear to us, Comrade Stalin was the Head of the State Defense Committee and the Chief of the Armed Forces of our

Country and he inspired the nations of the USSR with faith in the victory of our just cause and gathered all under the banner of Lenin for the task of routing the enemy and achieving victory.

Under the direct leadership of Comrade Stalin and with his personal participation, plans were worked out of all the most important combat operations of the Red Army, problems were decided of supplying the front lines with replacements of men, armaments, ammunition and foodstuffs as well as problems of aid to Leningrad, Sevastopol, Odessa, Caucasus and Stalingrad, beleaguered by the enemy. Measures of a colossal range were prepared to relocate the war and civilian industries to the eastern parts of the Country and to develop their production at the new places, as well as measures pertaining to the evacuation and resettlement of workers of the relocated plants, measures to insure railroad transportation, to increase the area under grain crops in the east, to increase the work discipline at the plants, sovkhozes and kolhozes, and measures to supply the workers with consumer and industrial goods.

All activities of our Party and of the Soviet State have been directed by Comrade Stalin. His brilliant perspicacity, his ability to quickly grasp and solve the meaning of oncoming events, of the characteristics of each stage of the war, his skill in aiming and directing the efforts of the Party and the Nation towards the fulfillment of the important and decisive tasks, his indomitable will, steadfastness and persistence in carrying out decisions insured for our State the victory over the enemy.

The military genius of the creator of Soviet military science, Comrade Stalin, guided our Soviet Army towards victory in the battles of the Great Patriotic War.

The defeat of the German armies at Moscow, at Stalingrad, in the Caucasus, at Orel, Kursk and Leningrad, the unusually powerful thrust, which crushed the German defense along a 1,200 kilometer* front line from the Baltic Sea to the Carpathian Mountains in January of 1945, the conquest of Berlin, effected by Soviet troops under the leadership of Comrade Stalin, were examples of the excellence of the Stalinist strategy, tactics and military operational skill in a contemporary war.

During the years of severe battle ordeals the Soviet people became even more intimately linked with their beloved Leader, Comrade Stalin. The Soviet nation even more clearly and distinctly recognized in Comrade Stalin the features of his great teacher—Lenin. They realized that our Army and our Nation is being led against a brutal enemy by an experienced Leader; like Lenin, fearless in battle and pitiless towards the enemies of the nation; like Lenin, devoid of any simile of panic; like Lenin, wise and daring in solving complex problems; like Lenin, clear

---

* 744 miles.

and articulate, true and honorable and loving its nation in the same way as did Lenin.

The Soviet nation by its selfless struggle not only defended its independence and liberty. It saved European civilization from Fascist barbarians.

The leading personalities in the whole world know and understand the preponderant role played by the Soviet Union in the defeat of Hitler's Germany. They are perfectly aware of the fate which would await the peoples of Europe in the event of the victory of fascist Germany.

Recently one of the eminent English scientists, Professor Bernal, excluded from the membership of the Council of the British Association for the Development of Science for his criticism of the English government in his letter to the press declared:

A few years ago the Soviet nation was our ally, and if it were not for its sacrifices, which were much greater than our own, all decent people in England would now be either in concentration camps or dead.

An important share in guaranteeing the victory of Socialist building in the USSR and of the victory of the Soviet people in the Great Patriotic War was due to the wise Stalinist policy of the Soviet Government. From the first day of existence of the Soviet Administration its policy was and remains a consistent policy for peace and a policy directed toward uncovering the aggressors and war instigators, toward insuring a peaceful Socialist building in the USSR, as well as insuring peace in the whole world, and to support nations which became the victims of aggression and who are struggling for the independence of their countries.

At present, when American and English imperialists are preparing a new world war, when a new danger is threatening peace-loving nations, civilization and culture, the eyes of the whole progressive and advanced mankind, the eyes of hundreds of millions of simple people in every country of the world are turned towards Comrade Stalin—the Inspirer and Organizer of the innumerable forces of the camp of peace and democracy.

The forces of the antiimperialist camp, the forces of peace, democracy and Socialism, grew and became stronger in their fight for peace. A testimonial to this is the continuing growth of the power of the Soviet Union, the political and economic strengthening of countries of the People's Democracy—Poland, Czechoslovakia, Rumania, Bulgaria, Hungary and Albania, their success in building Socialism, the creation of the German Democratic Republic. The increase of forces of the camp of peace and democracy has been proved by the historic victory of the Chinese People's Republic, achieved by the Chinese people under the leadership of their famous leader, Mao Tse-tung.

The strengthening and the increase of influence of Communist Parties in France, Italy, as well as of Communist Parties in other countries, the growth of the democratic movement in the capitalist countries, the mighty sweep of the movement of the peace supporters, all this is proof of the increasing power of the democratic camp.

The Anglo-American imperialists will not be able to stop all people's movements for peace growing in every country of the world, by terrorist actions against democratic organizations, nor by persecutions against the defenders of peace. The betrayal of the Anglo-American hireling Tito and his fascist gang who sold out their own country into the bondage of American and English imperialists, will not be able to throw into confusion the ranks of the democratic camp.

The Soviet nation marches resolutely and confidently towards Communism. At the present time a powerful upsurge of all branches of the USSR national economy is taking place.

There is no power in this world that would be able to force the Soviet nation to abandon its path, staked out by Lenin and Stalin.

Comrade Stalin is holding firmly in his hands the leadership controls in the struggle for the victory of Communism. The genius of our Leader harmonizes with his simplicity and modesty, with the exceptional sense of duty so peculiar to him, while his implacability towards the enemies of Communism combines with his sensitiveness and fatherly concern for the nation. His distinctive features are an utmost clarity of thought, a quiet grandeur of character, contempt and intolerance of all sensationalism and outward effects.

The entire life of activity of Comrade Stalin constitutes one big inspiring example of loyalty towards Leninism and limitless devotion to Lenin, an example of selfless service for the working classes and the entire working nation, for the cause of liberating mankind from suppression and exploitation.

The splendid Seventieth Anniversary of Comrade Stalin was a memorable event in the life of the Soviet nation. The workers of our Country express their deep gratitude and limitless devotion for their Great Leader and Teacher, Joseph Vissarionovich Stalin, by their renewed powerful national and patriotic effort. The nation honors its Inspirer and the Creator of its victories by new achievements of a free and joyous labor in all sectors of Socialist construction.

The workers of the countries of people's democracies are marking the Seventieth Anniversary of Comrade Stalin by a new labor upsurge and by closing their ranks tightly in their struggle for Socialism.

Millions of fighters for peace and democracy in all countries of the world are today closing their ranks even tighter around Comrade Stalin, their Standard-bearer.

On this memorable day greetings are heard in every language of the world addressed to our Leader: "Glory to Comrade Stalin!"

"Forward, towards new victories under the leadership of the Great Stalin!"

(*Pravda*, December 21, 1949)

Appendix 13

THIRTY-FOURTH ANNIVERSARY OF THE
GREAT OCTOBER SOCIALIST REVOLUTION

Address of L. P. Beria at the Solemn Session of the Moscow Soviet on November 6, 1951

Comrades!

The nations of the Soviet Union are celebrating today the Thirty-fourth Anniversary of the Great October Revolution, illuminated by the genius of Lenin, which opened to mankind the road to the new socialist world. Every year that we move along this road brings new gains for our Country.

The entire activity of the Bolshevik Party and of the Soviet Government during the time period from the Thirty-third to the Thirty-fourth Anniversary of the October Revolution, as well as all the years after the death of the great Lenin, took place under the wise leadership of our Leader, Comrade Stalin. (Long-lasting applause.) Comrade Stalin is guiding the Party and the Nation with a brilliant insight in the most complex situations of internal and international events and he is establishing goals for a continuous development. The inexhaustible energy of Comrade Stalin in the everyday leadership in important as well as routine affairs, his wise determination in defining the main tasks of the Soviet State and in directing all our efforts towards their fulfillment, are guaranteeing the nations of the Soviet Union great achievements in the building of Communism. (Applause.)

This past year of 1950 has been the concluding year of the first postwar Five-Year Plan period. The Soviet nation, as well as all our friends abroad, have learned with pleasure that the postwar Five-Year Plan of reconstruction and development of the USSR economy has been successfully fulfilled. For this fulfillment our nation had to fight under difficult conditions while healing its wounds inflicted by the war. This constitutes, without any doubt, a new great victory of the Soviet nation, having as a result a still greater increase of the power of our Socialist State. The achievements of this peaceful construction lead to further gains in the material and cultural living standards of the workers.

In the realm of foreign affairs the Soviet Union continued to fight for peace, as it did before, which raised still higher its international standing.

In the whole world two foci became even more polarized during the last year, and two centers of attraction were in evidence. On one side there was the Soviet Union at the helm of the camp of Socialism and Democracy as a center of attraction for all progressive forces fighting to avert a new war, to strengthen the peace as well as defending the right of nations to organize their lives by themselves. On the other hand there is the United States of America at the head of the camp of imperialism as a center of attraction for all the aggressors and reactionaries of the whole world, striving to unleash a new war with the view of plundering and enslaving other nations.

In the camp of Socialism and Democracy, the last year has been a year of further growth and strengthening of forces, of development of the economy and culture and of increase in the living standards of the workers. The nations of the countries of the new democracies, the great Chinese nations, having retaken their fate from the hands of the imperialist oppressors, are joyfully and resolutely building a new Socialist life with the brotherly help of the nations of the Soviet Union. (Applause.)

In the imperialist camp, the past year was a year of continued aggravation of internal and external contradictions, of a further increase of the general crisis and of weakening of the capitalist system as well as of subordination of the whole economic life to the criminal goal of preparation for war and of a pitiless attack on the life interests of the workers.

New achievements of the peaceful construction in the USSR

For our own Country the year 1951 constitutes a year of a continued upturn of the Socialist economy and culture. The industrial and agricultural workers, as well as the intelligentsia who are engaged in a peaceful creative work for the good of their country, are striving with great fervor to fulfill and exceed the State production quotas. A striking testimony to this fact are the patriotic letters, addressed to Comrade Stalin, which are being published in the press and in which workers engaged in industry, agriculture, transportation and construction are reporting their production achievements and informing us about new pledges undertaken within the framework of the Socialist competition.

The Bolshevik Party is inspiring and organizing our nation for heroic production deeds, it is directing its creative energy towards a single goal—that of the victory of Communism. With every passing day the grandiose ideas of Lenin-Stalin are sinking deeper and deeper into the consciousness of the broad masses of workers, multiplying their strength and illuminating their road of struggle and victory. This fact finds its expression in a conscientious attitude towards work, in an inexhaustible initiative and in the fulfillment of its duty towards society and towards the State. In this lies the source of the invincibility of our system, and the source of unceasing achievements in our work.

The results of work in the field of agricultural construction for the ten months of this year show that the 1951 economic plan will be fulfilled and exceeded. (Applause.) Industrial production increased more than 15% as compared with the preceding year and is double that of the prewar year 1940. The basic production funds of industry increased 12% as compared with 1950.

The increase in technical capacity and in qualifications of workers, as well as the improvement in the organization of production, permitted the raising of labor productivity by 10%, as compared with the past year. Almost two-thirds of the increase of industrial production this year will be due to the increase in labor productivity. This means that industrial production is increasing in our Country, basically as a result of the increase in labor productivity.

The decrease in production costs, as Comrade Stalin often stated, constitutes the quality index of industrial production as well as one of the most important sources of savings in the national economy. At the same time it is also an indispensable condition for the reduction of prices and consequently also for the increase in the material well-being of the workers. In the current year the planned decrease in production costs will be exceeded, which in the field of industrial production alone will result in 26 billion rubles of savings.

All branches of heavy and light industry succeeded this year in considerably increasing their production.

The production of ferrous metals registered a significant growth. The increase in pig iron smelting alone will amount to 2.4 million tons; that of steel ingot melting, to about 4 million tons and of rolled steel, to 3 million tons as compared with the production of the last year. The Soviet Union is now melting, for example, as much steel as England, France, Belgium and Sweden combined. (Applause.) Our metallurgists are at the present time much more efficiently utilizing their blast and open hearth furnaces. This increased efficiency will alone contribute some 1.3 million of additional tons of pig iron and 1.35 tons of steel in 1951.

The increase in the output of nonferrous and rare earth metals achieved this year is not less significant.

In ferrous and nonferrous metallurgy, remarkable cadres of workers, technicians, engineers as well as managers were trained who now know well their profession and are constantly improving production technology.

The scheduled coal production quota is being successfully met. During the past few years the annual average increase in coal production amounted to 24 million tons. The coal industry of the USSR at the present time not only satisfies the needs of our Country but it has also insured the establishment of the necessary reserves.

The reequipment of the coal industry that has taken place during the last years enabled the full mechanization of such difficult and labor-consuming operations as cutting, breaking and delivery of coal at the benches, and also its underground transport and loading on railroad cars.

The Soviet Government, and Comrade Stalin in particular, are evincing constant care to facilitate the work of the miners and to better the conditions of their life in every possible way. In contradiction to the capitalist countries, where the miners are the most downtrodden and unfortunate people, in the Soviet Union the miners enjoy attention and respect. The workers of the coal industry are first among workers of other branches of industry inasmuch as wages are concerned. As a result we have stable, qualified cadres of miners, which is insuring the successful development of the coal industry.

The achievements of our petroleum industry are even more impressive. For a number of years now the annual increase of crude oil in our Country amounted to 4.5 million tons. In the current year the planned production quota of oil has been overfulfilled. As a result of a successful completion of an extensive exploratory drilling campaign, rich oil deposits have been discovered in new areas and the volume of the industrially explored oil reserves increased considerably.

Large-scale construction of new oil refineries and an expansion of the old ones is under way. The new plants alone, all of them equipped with first-rate machinery of domestic production which are being put in operation this year, will be able to process six millions tons of oil annually.

It can be stated with confidence that the goal designated by Comrade Stalin to bring oil production up to 60 million tons per year will be fulfilled according to schedule. (Applause.)

Considerable gains have been made in developing the electrification of our Country. During the current year some 104 billion kilowatt-hours of electric power will be produced, thus surpassing the electric power output of England and France combined. The annual increase of electric power production alone amounts in our Country to more than 13 billion kilowatt-hours, which exceeds seven times the total electric power output of prewar Russia.

In the current year the construction of new electric power plants is assuming even larger proportions. The aggregate output of electric power plants and new power units put into operation during 1951 will have attained some three billion kilowatts which, for example, would equal five large electric power plants such as the Dnieper Hydroelectric Power Plant.

Our chemical industry increases from one year to another. The production of chemical fertilizers rose significantly and the output of new organic toxic chemicals used in combatting pests and weeds of agricultural crops almost doubled.

The production of synthetic rubber registers a 20% increase as compared with the past year. The workers of the chemical industry, in close cooperation with Soviet scientists, attained a notable success in solving important technological problems in the field of chemistry.

Our economic growth would be unthinkable without the uninterrupted growth and perfecting of our domestic machine-building industry, which is the basis of the technological progress of the whole national economy.

The overall output of the machine-building industry increased 21% as compared with the previous year. The production of the main types of electrical equipment for the electric power plants increased two- or threefold. This year a steam turbine is under construction which has a 150,000 kilowatt capacity. A turbine of such capacity is being built for the first time in the world, which is a testimony to the maturity of Soviet science and technology. The construction of oil machinery almost doubled as compared with 1950. Our machine-building industry is putting on the market more than 400 new types of machines and mechanisms this year.

Our machine construction workers are justly proud of their achievements in the production of the most complex modern machinery, as well as of geophysical, electromechanical, electronic, electrovacuum and other types of precision instruments.

Due to the successful development of industry and as a result of the increase in the production of agricultural raw materials, the output of consumer goods is on the increase. Following the initiative of Comrade Stalin the Government took measures this year to increase the production of foodstuffs and industrial goods above the initially scheduled annual quotas. Compared with 1950 the amount of foodstuffs and industrial goods the population will receive as a result of measures taken will be increased as follows: textiles—by 24%; knit goods—by 35%; footwear —by 12%; meat and meat products—by 20%; fish products—by 8%; vegetable oil—by 35%; butter—by 8%; sugar—by 24%; tea—by 38%; watches— by 11%; photographic cameras—by 30%; sewing machines—by 28%; and furniture—by 44%. Our industry has already started to produce television sets, refrigerators, washing machines as well as other machines for home use.

As you can see, our industry is registering very significant gains. We should not forget, however, that there were also deficiencies in the work of individual enterprises which, because of poor organization and insufficient use of modern equipment, are not accomplishing their goals of increasing their productivity of labor and of lowering their costs, are guilty of squandering raw materials and fuel and are also sustaining losses due to rejects. The elimination of these mistakes would permit the achievement of further important savings.

Some individual enterprises, even though fulfilling and even exceeding their overall production quotas, often do not meet goals set for some important production items by the Stalin plan. The managers of these enterprises evidently want, as it appears, to make the work easier for themselves by concentrating on the production of those items that require less effort and care. It is time for them to understand that the State cannot accept the fulfillment or production above the plan in a haphazard way, but only in such a way that would insure the national economy of the products it needs.

In our Socialist economy each manager, whether he is in charge of a more or less important work, should place the interest of the State above everything else and strictly observe State discipline. It is imperative to get rid of the narrow, bureaucratic approach to work, which can still be seen to exist in some managers, an attitude that inflicts losses to the interest of our planned economy.

The current year was marked by a further upswing of our Socialist agriculture. The increased equipment of our agriculture together with a better organization of work permitted this year the harvesting of grain crops in a much shorter period of time and with a considerable decrease in grain losses. The kolhozes and sovkhozes harvested grain of a higher quality, they were on time with their deliveries of grain to the State and they set aside in storage reserves of seed grain. For the past few years the overall grain harvest had exceeded seven billion pounds annually.

We shall harvest more cotton and sugar beets this year than the year before. Our Country is now producing more cotton than the well-known cotton-producing countries—India, Pakistan and Egypt—put together. (Applause.)

The kolhozes and sovkhozes are successfully striving to fulfill the Stalin plan for the development of animal husbandry. The commonly owned sovkhoz and kolhoz livestock now constitutes the major part of the overall cattle population of the Country. The most important task in the field of animal husbandry remains the expansion of its fodder base.

Agriculture is being supplied every year with a large number of up-to-date machinery by the State. During the current year agriculture is scheduled to receive 137,000 tractor units, calculating 15 hp for each unit; 54,000 grain harvesting combines, of which 29,000 are self-propelled, as well as two million other agricultural machines and implements. Large-scale operations are under way to electrify agriculture. All these projects will permit the further mechanization of the basic agricultural operations to lighten the work of kolhoz workers and to increase their productivity. The machine tractor stations are at the present time fulfilling two-thirds of all field work in the kolhozes. In 1951 almost all ploughing in the kolhozes has been mechanized, about three-fourths of all sowing is being done by tractor-driven seeding machines, while more than 60% of the grain crops area has been harvested by combines. All basic agricultural operations in the state farms have been almost completely mechanized.

The common wealth of the kolhozes is growing constantly. The indivisible funds of the kolhozes alone increased 11% during the past year. It is imperative, however, that the kolhoz workers should continue to strengthen and develop in the future the common economy which is the foundation for the further growth of the kolhozes and for the increase in the material well-being of the kolhoz workers themselves.

Together with industry and agriculture our railroad, river and maritime transport also is growing steadily. During the current year the freight turnover on the railroads is increasing at a rate of 11%. It would be, of course, appropriate to mention that these 11% of increase are almost equal to the aggregate annual freight turnover of England and France put together. (Applause.) The carriage of freight on inland waterways is increasing at the rate of 12%, while on the ocean lines it shows a 7% increase. A still remaining task for the multi-thousand army of our transportation workers will be the speedup in the turnover of railroad cars and a better utilization of the whole rolling stock of the railroads as well as the inland waterways and oceangoing vessels.

Our Country is in the process of putting into effect a broadly conceived construction plan. The overall volume of capital construction rises each consecutive year. The amount of State capital investments during the current year is two-and-one-half times greater than the amount in the prewar year 1940.

The construction enterprises are receiving a steady stream of machines and equipment and they were also much better supplied with construction materials. The existing inventory of excavators, scrapers and bulldozers increased considerably during 1951. Cement production increases annually at the rate of two million tons. The output of brick, slate, cast iron and ceramic tubing and other construction materials rose considerably.

Our construction workers have notable achievements to their credit in the field of lowering costs and shortening the time of construction. There still remains, however, a great deal to be accomplished. It is necessary, first of all, to introduce a proper order in the organization of work at construction sites, to utilize more effectively the construction equipment, to better organize the labor and to reduce considerably the overhead expenses. The excesses that still exist in projects and estimates and that are adding costs to construction should be eliminated.

A special place in our construction projects, as you well know, is taken by large hydroelectric projects, which are under construction on the Volga, Don, Dnieper and Amu Darya rivers. The construction projects have no peer in the whole world inasmuch as their volume and speed of construction are concerned. Work schedules established by the Government for the year 1951 with regard to all construction projects are being successfully met and even exceeded.

Already in 1952 the first of these installations, the Volga-Don Waterway, will be put in operation. With the opening of this Waterway all seas of the European part of the USSR will be linked to form a single transportation system. (Applause.)

As a result of the completion of these grandiose hydroelectric projects important goals of the national economy will be solved. The new electric power plants alone will produce 22½ billion kilowatt-hours of low-cost electric power per year, which is almost the total annual electric power output produced in Italy. The increase in the irrigated and watered areas will permit the production of three million tons of raw cotton annually, which constitutes more than one-third the annual average cotton production in the United States of America, as well as one-half billion pounds of wheat, thirty million pounds of rice and six million pounds of sugar beets. The number of large cattle in these areas will increase by two million heads, while the number of sheep will increase by nine million heads.

The construction of these projects has been started as the result of the initiative of Comrade Stalin, who shows a never-ending concern about the common good and prosperity of our Country, about the lightening of work and improvement in the living conditions of the Soviet nation. The initiative of Comrade Stalin is meeting enthusiastic support on the part of our entire nation, which correctly called all these projects of the Great Stalin "Constructions of Communism." (Continued applause.)

Unlike the capitalistic countries, where production serves the purpose of profit and enrichment of a handful of exploiters, in our Country the interests of the workers are at the basis of development of the whole national economy. The national income increases from one year to another and on that basis the income of workers, employes and peasants is also increasing. In 1951 the national income of the USSR is increasing at the rate of 12% as compared with the year 1950.

The Soviet Government is conducting a policy of a systematic reduction of prices of articles of mass consumption. A new one, the fourth during recent years, reduction in the State retail prices for industrial and consumer goods, took effect in March of the current year, which will insure a further rise in the real wages of workers and employes and the reduction in the expenses of peasants by buying industrial articles at lower prices.

In the current year the overall turnover of goods is increasing at the rate of 15% as compared with the past year. It has to be noted, however, that there are a great number of shortcomings in the work of trade organizations. The demands of the population are very poorly investigated, mistakes are being committed in deliveries of goods according to requirements of the individual regions and Republics and the stocks of goods are not always satisfactorily utilized. The workers of the trade organizations should substantially improve the servicing of the Soviet consumer.

The Party and the Government are continuously showing their concern for improving the living conditions of the workers. During the current year houses with about 27 million square meters of living area will be released for occupancy in the cities and worker settlements, while in the countryside locations there will be 400,000 houses built by the collective farm workers themselves.

Very gratifying is the fact that as a result of the increase in the well-being of the people and of the achievements of the Soviet Government in the protection of public health, the mortality rate diminished by one-half as compared with the prewar year 1940 (applause) and children's mortality rate decreased even more. (Applause.)

At the same time, when the imperialist cannibals in the capitalist camp are busying themselves with inventing various "scientific" means of destroying the better half of all mankind and of decreasing the birth rate, in our Country, as Comrade Stalin stated, the most valuable asset constitutes the people, while the well-being and happiness of the people constitute the main task of the State.

The problems of preparation and training of cadres of specialists in all fields of economy and culture were and still are taking an important place in the system of measures that were put into effect by our State. There are 2,720,000 people studying this year at institutions of higher learning and in technical schools. During 1951 alone, 463,000 young specialists graduated from institutes of higher learning and from technical schools. At the present time there are over five million specialists at work who have their higher or technical education completed and not a smaller number of qualified and experienced specialists who learned their profession on the job, and who got their education at courses without interrupting their work.

In all our achievements a great role has been played by Soviet science. During recent years our scientists solved a number of important problems that were of particular value to the national economy and to the defense of the Country. In a number of scientific fields Soviet scientists led the development of science on an international scale. A significant fact, which has manifested itself during the last years, is the very real broadening and strengthening cooperation of Soviet scientists with the industrial workers. This fact not only is conducive to a better application of scientific achievements in the process of production but it also benefits science by incorporating the experience and inventive activities of the numerous ranks of innovators in the realm of industry, transportation and agriculture.

One of the more striking manifestations of the cultural upswing in our Country is the flowering of art and literature. Presenting in vivid pictures the great ideas of Communism, they constitute a potent means of elevating the masses in the spirit of Communism, in the spirit of Soviet patriotism and internationalism. The current year, similar to preceding years, has been marked by the appearance of a number of highly artistic works of art and belles lettres, truly presenting the high moral values of the Soviet people, their life and struggle for a further growth of the power of their Country, for peace and friendship between nations and for the happiness of all the peoples in the whole world.

Directing the main forces and assets of the Country towards a further growth of the national economy and culture, the Party and the Government do not lose sight of the necessity of strengthening the Country's defenses. Historic experience fully vindicated the repeated warnings of Comrade Stalin to the effect that the Country of victorious Socialism that finds itself in a capitalist encirclement should be always ready to beat off a possible aggression of the imperialist states. During the current year, as always, the Party and the Government have done everything in their power in order that the heroic Soviet people, in its enthusiasm of labor in creating the grandiose edifice of Communism could rest assured of the future fate of the Country. (Applause.) The Soviet Army and Navy, imbued with the unmatched morale and fighting qualities which are well known to the whole world, are in possession of all types of modern weapons and are ready to inflict a crushing blow on anyone who, disregarding the persuasive lessons of history, would dare to attack our Country. (Long-lasting thunderous applause.)

As is well known, the decisive factor of our achievements is the qualities of our social and state system created by the October Revolution. One of the expressions of these qualities is the fact that the Soviet system liberated and developed for the first time the great forces of our people, called to life a powerful activity and a never-ceasing creative initiative of the masses, liberated from capitalist exploitation. Precisely this activity and initiative of the masses constitutes the source of the invincible power of Communism. A further improvement of the work of the Party and Government organs, as well as public organizations, which are mobilizing and organizing this creative activity of our people, remains a constant concern of the Party and Government.

The work of the Soviet nation is without fail crowned with success because the Soviet people are not conceited and they are never satisfied with what they have reached and are always measuring their achievements primarily in the light of the great tasks of the future. Criticism and self-criticism, as it is being taught by our Comrade Stalin, constitute the law for our development, a decisive means to overcome all routine and stagnation, all that is old and decaying and that is hindering our victorious surge forward. The level of consciousness of the masses, the theoretical and ideological training of the cadres in many instances determine the effectiveness of Bolshevik criticism and self-criticism. As always, the full attention of the Party is centered on the problem of the Communist education of the masses and on the problem of a further increase of the ideological and political levels of the cadres and the mastering by them of the great teachings of Marx, Engels, Lenin and Stalin.

Concurrently with our new achievements in the Communist construction, the moving forces in the development of a Socialist community are steadily growing and becoming stronger at the same time. Every day of life and work of the workers, peasants and intelligentsia of our Country produces strong new manifestations of patriotism, of moral and political unity of the Soviet community, and of the friendship of nations in the USSR. The unbreakable unity of the will and aspirations of the peoples of our Country, the unity of its material and moral forces constitutes one of the basic foundations for the power of our Country. Precisely because of this unity our Country has the necessary strength to solve such important problems, the solution of which was out of reach even for the keenest intellects of mankind.

The Soviet Union in the fight for peace

The broad range of peaceful construction taking place in our Country is a convincing testimony to the peaceful external policy of the Soviet Union and it undercuts the slanderers who were profusely talking about the aggressive designs of our Government.

"Not one single state," announces Comrade Stalin, "including our own State, is able to significantly develop the consumer goods industry; to begin great construction projects of the kind of those hydroelectric power plants on the Volga, Dnieper and Amu Darya, which require tens of billions of budgetary outlays; to continue a policy of a systematic reduction of prices of mass consumption articles, which also require tens of billions of budgetary outlays; to invest hundreds of billions for the restoration of the national economy destroyed by the German occupants; and on top of that and at the same time to increase its Armed Forces and develop war industry. It is not difficult to understand that such a foolish policy would bring about the bankruptcy of the State."

The peaceful policy of the Soviet State originated during the October Revolution. The more than twenty-year-old history of the Soviet Administration has shown that the October Revolution is a revolution of creativity and of a planned construction of a new, Communist Society. The wars that have been forced upon us by enemies only hindered us in accomplishing this great goal.

Comrade Stalin in his address on the occasion of the Fourteenth Party Congress with utmost clarity defined the external policy of the Soviet Union: "The basis of the policy of our Government, its external policy, rests on the ideology of peace. Our task is to fight for peace, to fight against the occurrence of new wars and to unmask all those steps that are being taken with the view to preparing a new war."

There was not a single international conference or meeting that took place with the participation of the Soviet Union, where the representatives of the Soviet Government would not advance constructive proposals towards avoidance of international conflicts and towards insuring peace and security. Our efforts, however, in this direction in the majority of cases met with direct counteraction of the ruling circles in a number of bourgeois states. This situation changed little after World War II, from which, as it would seem, statesmen of various countries should have drawn appropriate conclusions.

The peoples made enormous sacrifices and suffered privations while the destruction of the fascist bloc was being accomplished, all the time hoping that after victory they would be assured of conditions for peaceful development. While World War II was still in full swing Comrade Stalin was warning that it was not enough to win the war, it was also necessary to insure a secure and long-lasting peace among nations. With the blood of the millions of victims, however, still fresh on the battlefields the American and English imperialists already began planning a new war. Immediately after the war ended the ruling circles in the United States of America, England and France embarked upon the road of an outright breach of the major agreements reached by the Big Powers during the war, and embarked upon the road of sabotaging international cooperation by organizing a new bloc in order to plunge the peoples into the disaster of a new world war.

There is no need to enumerate here all the facts, which are well known. Suffice it to point out that the United States of America are openly restoring these two hotbeds of war, one in the West in the area of Germany and the other in the East, in the zone of Japan. The liquidation of these hotbeds in the last war cost the freedom-loving nations millions of human lives and required on their part colossal material sacrifices and unspeakable suffering.

Recently a remilitarization of Western Germany has begun to be carried out at an accelerated pace and with the participation in this undertaking of Hitlerite war criminals. Furthermore, contrary to logic, in this restoration of German militarism the most active part is being played by the present-day rulers of France, whose people, during the span of one human generation had twice experienced all the horrors of German aggression. It is easy to understand why the American bosses find it more convenient to spin their plans with regard to Germany in the form of the "Schuman Plan," the "Pleven Plan" and others, using helpful hands from among the French people. However, the peoples of Europe cannot but understand that this creates a real danger to peace. The Soviet Government could not overlook the fact of the serious violation not only of the Potsdam Agreement but of the Franco-Soviet Agreement of Alliance and Mutual Aid concluded in 1944, as well. The Soviet Government in special notes drew the attention of the French Government to the dangerous consequences of its present policy and to its responsibility for the presently created situation.

Not long ago the American-English bloc forced through the so-called peaceful agreement with Japan and the United States of America and in addition concluded a military covenant with Japan, thus openly embarking upon the restoration of Japanese militarism. World opinion is indignant because of the fact that the great Chinese people were excluded from participation in the peaceful agreement with Japan, that the people who suffered most from Japanese aggression and who had a tremendous share in the defeat of Japanese imperialism while the Americans are flaunting the signatures of the representatives of Honduras, Costa Rica and similar small semicolonial states who not only did not participate in the defeat of imperialist Japan but in the persons of their merchants and landlords, profited during that war. It is no secret to anyone that the separate agreement with Japan serves not the purpose of peace but helps to prepare for war. The Soviet Union, which many times insisted on the conclusion of a genuine, just peace treaty with Japan based on the declarations of Cairo and Potsdam and on the Yalta agreement, would have to change its traditional policy of peace if it would put its signature under such a "peace" treaty. The importance of this treaty is further depreciated by the fact that in its conclusion India, the second biggest state in Asia, also did not take part.

Inspirers of the restoration of German and Japanese militarism, as it appears, do not want to take into consideration the German or the Japanese people who suffered no lesser losses than the other nations as a result of a war which was foisted upon them by their recent rulers. These peoples cannot expect anything good from a new war and are not likely to consent to be cannon fodder for the American billionaires.

The aggressive policy of the American bloc is very clearly demonstrated by the military intervention of the United States in Korea. The representatives of the United States of America were rejecting all proposals of the USSR and other peace-loving nations aiming at the cessation of the American aggression in Korea and now they are dragging out in every possible way the negotiations which are under way in Kaesong.

We are convinced that the valiant Korean people will find an honorable solution to the bloody conflict, which was provoked by the Americans, and at the same time they will show once more to the whole world that there is no force that could enslave a nation imbued with the spirit to fight and to win. (Applause.)

The United States of America is stubbornly trying to convert the United Nations Organization into an instrument of war. Under the pressure of the United States of America the United Nations lent its flag to cover the American aggression in Korea and then, violating the primordial law of nations, they declared the Chinese People's Republic as the aggressor. Honest people in the whole world cannot but agree with the correctness of the statement made by Comrade Stalin that "as a matter of fact the United Nations Organization constitutes at this moment not so much an organization for the whole world as an organization for the Americans, acting on behalf of the American aggressors."

During the last years the speed of preparations for war in the imperialist camp has been intensified. The United States of America are enlarging the aggressive Atlantic bloc in every possible way, by pressure, by various promises, dragging in new countries, among them also those that are not geographically connected with the Atlantic zone, creating new military bases in all parts of the world and feverishly expanding the production of all types of weapons and at the same time looking for cannon fodder in all corners of our globe.

Even the smallest manifestations of antiwar sentiment are pitilessly suppressed, particularly in the United States of America, and fascist and police methods are being introduced in all agencies of the state system. Sorry ruins only remain of the advertised "American democracy." This fact is admitted even by the American press. Chester Dempsey, Senator from the State of Wisconsin, stated recently in the newspaper, *Capital Times*:

We were astonished in the past by the servility of the Germans who were under the influence of the propaganda of Hitler and Goebbels. Today we find ourselves in an even worse situation than the Germans ever were. In our country there exists full control over our thoughts; we are in the hands of militarists and their slanderous clique.

The statesmen of the United States of America have been carried away to the point where they are transferring their police methods to the international forum. Certainly the Hitlerite political manipulators could indeed envy the fraudulent methods of the American diplomats headed by Truman at the Conference in San Francisco. (Applause.)

In the United States the absorption of the state apparatus by the capitalist monopolies is being intensified. Where the actual rulers of the country, the financial and industrial barons, formerly kept themselves in the background, leaving it to their political clerks to defend their interests in the field of politics, now they are laying their hands directly on the administrative, political and diplomatic apparatus of the United States. It is well known that the more important affairs of state are directed by the smart dealer from the Morgan group—Charles Wilson, who without qualms is placing at the most important controls of the state apparatus persons from the largest trusts of billionaires—those of Morgan, Rockefeller, Mellon, Du Pont and others who are closely knit together not only by economic but also by family ties. They are using the economy of the country without scruples in the interest of the billionaires.

Precisely at the time of such a debauch of plutocracy and police oppression in its own country, President Truman has the audacity of shamelessly expounding on the "absence of democracy" theme in the Soviet Union, in the same Soviet Union where, as it is well known, police oppression and plutocracy has been abolished long ago and where the whole power belongs to the people. (Continuing applause.)

These, Comrades, are the facts. They are testifying to the fact that the American-English bloc embarked upon the road of preparing and unleashing a new war.

Under these circumstances the Soviet Union, faithful to its peaceful policy, is waging a continuous struggle to avert a war and preserve the peace. At every assembly of the Organization of United Nations, at the meetings of the Security Council, at the sessions of the Council of Ministers of Foreign Affairs, the Soviet Union by every available means is unmasking the plans of the war instigators and puts forward definite proposals directed toward securing peace, while it altruistically defends the rights and the sovereignty of nations. Everybody is familiar with the Soviet proposals of recent time about the conclusion of a peace treaty among the five great powers, about the reduction of armed forces of the

Appendices

big powers by one-third during one year, about the prohibition of atomic weapons, about a speedy conclusion of a peace treaty with Germany, with subsequent withdrawal of all occupation forces, about the creation of an all-German democratic government. One of the most significant examples of the struggle for peace waged by the Soviet Union constitutes the Peace Defense Law promulgated by the Supreme Soviet on March 12, 1951, according to which all persons guilty of war propaganda will be handed over to a court as criminal offenders.

Our foreign policy is based on the power of the Soviet State. Only naive politicians could judge its peaceful character as lack of confidence in our strength. The Soviet people demonstrated many times to the whole world how they are able to defend their Country. There was a time when our young, not yet solidified Soviet Republic was forced to defend its existence against a military array of 14 bourgeois states headed by the imperialist sharks of England, the United States of America, France and Japan. The enemies were attacking from the north and from the south, from the east and from the west. The Country was suffering an economic dislocation, there was not enough bread for the workers, nor equipment for the Army. The interventionists were convinced that the days of the Soviet State were numbered, that they would quickly finish it off by their military might. The affair, however, took a different turn. "The whole world knows," wrote Comrade Stalin on the results of this campaign, "that the English interventionists and their allies were ignominiously thrown outside the borders of our Country by our Victorious Army. This lesson should never be forgotten by the gentlemen instigators to new war."

When in June of 1941, Fascist Germany, armed to the teeth, and having at that time at its disposal the military potential of almost the whole of Europe, treacherously attacked our Country, not only the Hitlerite generals, intoxicated by their easy successes in the West, but also many in the camp of our contemporary allies were convinced that the Soviet Army would be able to hold on a few weeks or at the best a few months. Nevertheless it was precisely the power and strength of the Soviet Army against which the military machine of the Hitlerite Germany ran asunder.

We are persistently struggling for peace not only because we have no use for war but also because the Soviet nation, having created at home under the Lenin-Stalin banner the most just social system, considers an aggressive war to be the gravest crime against humanity, the greatest calamity for the simple people in the whole world. However, should the imperialist plunderers interpret the love for peace of our Nation as its weakness, then an even more shameful downfall awaits them than the one that was experienced by their predecessors in their military adventure against the Soviet State. (Tremendous applause.) There is a good proverb coined by the Italians: "He who does not want to believe a lesson, will have to learn it on his own hide." (Applause.)

The ruling circles of the United States of America and England are trying to deceive world public opinion by assertions that they are forced to rearm in the face of the danger of military aggression on the part of the Soviet Union.

Lies concerning the Soviet danger and the insincerity of the Soviet peaceful proposals are not new. Against the background of such talks the imperialists of Europe and America were rearming fascist Germany, for which many nations during World War II had to pay in blood. The honorable diplomats from the American-English bloc are, however, wrong if they think that the peoples have a short memory and that they are easily confused by lies.

The peoples of this world are judging the policy of a government not by its words but by its deeds. The Soviet Union was never avoiding the scrupulous fulfillment of accepted responsibilities. This constitutes the unity of word and deed in practice. It sounds at least strange in the mouths of the ruling circles of the United States of America that they accuse others of insincerity while they themselves rudely destroyed the historic decisions taken at the Teheran, Yalta and Potsdam conferences. In the face of the peoples of the world it is impossible to hide whose words are at odds with deeds.

In order to justify their aggressive policy towards the Soviet Union, the leaders of the imperialist states slanderously attributing to the Soviet nation the denial of the possiblity of a peaceful coexistence of the two systems.

During the first years of the Soviet Administration Lenin, the founder of our State, already put forward the principle of peace and agreements with the capitalist states. "Our course is true," said Lenin, "we are for peace and agreement, but also against servitude and against shackling agreements." This Lenin principle is at the base of the policy of the Soviet State. "The foundations of our relations with the capitalist states," states Comrade Stalin, "rest on the admission of coexistence of the two diametrically opposed systems." Comrade Stalin also defined the real base of agreements between the USSR and the capitalist countries. "Exports and imports," pointed out Comrade Stalin, "constitute the most appropriate grounds for such agreements. We need equipment, raw materials, for example cotton, and semi-finished products such as metals and others, while the capitalists want to export these articles. There you have a ground for agreement. The capitalists need oil, timber, grain products while we want to export these products. There you have grounds for an agreement."

This was stated in 1927. Today we have considerably more possibilities for business relations with the capitalist countries. We are not averse to substantially increased business cooperation on the basis of mutual profit with the United States of America, England and France as well as with other bourgeois states both in the West as also in the East. It is no fault of the Soviet Union if the ruling circles of these countries, contrary to the interests of their states, embarked upon the road of undermining and curtailing economic relations with the USSR.

The peaceful coexistence of the two systems presupposes also political agreements. "We are conducting a policy of peace," stated Comrade Stalin, "and we are ready to sign with the bourgeois states mutual non-aggression pacts. We are conducting a policy of peace and we are prepared to make agreements with regard to disarmament up to a complete abolishment of regular armies, which we declared to the entire world as far back to the Geneva Conference. There you have a ground for agreement along diplomatic lines."

However, the imperialists do not want agreements. They are afraid to make agreements with the Soviet Union, since these agreements could undercut their aggressive plans, make the armaments race unnecessary, which brings in billions in additional profits. The imperialists want war. They need it for robbing and enslaving the peoples; it is needed in the first place by the American monopolists in order to obtain colossal additional profits.

The preparation for war is being conducted by the American imperialists and still the leaders of the United States do not stop talking about their supposedly peaceful intentions. They are, it is evident, not against the "preservation" of peace, but on "conditions" which will be dictated by the United States. And what are these "conditions"? The nations of the world should remain on their knees before American capital, renounce their national independence, accept such form of government which will be imposed by the American "counselors," introduce in their countries the "American way of life," develop only these branches of economy and only to such an extent that is welcome and advantageous to the American monopolies. In one word, the peoples should renounce their political sovereignty and economic independence, their cultural and other interests and become subjects of the newly formed American empire. And this is being called the "preservation" of peace! As a matter of fact, why would the ringleaders of American imperialism risk a war if they could succeed in subjecting the peoples under their dictate by way of threats and by blackmail alone? As is well known, even the raving Hitler was agreeable to such "conditions of peace." However, precisely these imperialist "conditions of peace" led to World War II. It is evident that Truman, by advancing analogical "conditions of peace" embarks upon the road taken by Hitler, having as his aim dragging the nations into a third world war.

Every honest man asks this legitimate question: What is the basis for the United States of America to claim a privileged position among other nations? Are not the peoples of the world all equal? Could it be possible that gold constitutes the basis for this claim, all this gold acquired through sufferings and blood of millions and which is being used for bribery? The peoples, however, do not trade their freedom. The American gentlemen capitalists should not deceive themselves into believing that if they succeeded once in buying some rulers in the bourgeois countries for their gold, they also bought by the same token the peoples of these countries.

The leaders of the United States of America cannot hide the fact that they need the arms race in order to dictate to other nations, under the threat of power, their imperialist, predatory "conditions of peace."

As you can see, these gentlemen everywhere and always talk about peace but at the same time they are preparing a new war, they are openly letting us hear their saber rattling and are bragging about having some "fantastic weapons." They should not think that they will be able to scare anyone with this behavior. Inasmuch as the Soviet people cannot be intimidated by threats. If up till now every military attack on the part of militarist states on our Country invariably ended with a failure, it is obvious that at the present time our State is even stronger and more powerful and our nation even more united and confident of its strength. (Applause.) These gentlemen, intoxicated by war hysteria, should know that if they attack our Country now the Soviet people will be able to meet them in such a way that they will lose forever their desire for the senseless attempts on the freedom and independence of our Socialist Country. (Storm of long-lasting applause.)

If there is anyone who should be afraid of the consequences of a new world war, these are in the first place the capitalists of America and of other bourgeois countries, since the new war will put before the peoples the question of the harmfulness of the capitalist system, which cannot exist without war, and the question of the necessity to replace this bloody system by another one, the Socialist system (long-lasting applause), in the same way that it happened in the countries of the People's Democracies of Europe and Asia after World War II.

At first sight one might think that the imperialist camp constitutes a powerful agglomeration of aggressive forces. Naturally we should not underestimate these forces. On the other hand, however, the camp of peace is much stronger. While the camp of peace is knit together by a unity of purpose, in the war camp we can observe considerable divergencies of interests and many countries have been drawn into this camp by taking advantage of their economic dependency on the United States of America resulting from the notorious "Marshall Plan."

The outward unity of the imperialist front cannot conceal its far-reaching internal contradictions, mainly connected with the struggle for raw materials, for markets and for spheres of capital investments. These contradictions intertwine, involving all countries in the capitalist camp, but the most important contradictions are in existence between the United States and England, both in Europe as well as in Asia.

There can be no doubt that these contradictions in the capitalist camp cannot but increase more and more with the passage of time.

An even more significant factor is the weakness of the home front in the imperialist countries. Try as the imperialists may to deceive their people with lies, even with the persistent help of the socialists of the right—those cringing servants of imperialism in the betrayal of the interests of the workers—the fact remains that right in the imperialist camp, on the home front of the imperialists, there are significant forces of the partisans of peace in the person of millions of honest people, who place the interest of preserving the peace above the miserable pittance sometimes offered by capitalism. The antiwar sentiments of the masses are bound to intensify in view of the fact that the enormous expenses for the preparation of war constitute a heavy load for the workers to carry.

The weakness of the home front of imperialism is also personified in the increase of national liberation movements in the colonial and dependent countries. The people in Vietnam are fighting heroically for their liberation, the peoples of the Philippines, Burma and Malaya are also struggling, the people of Indonesia did not lay down their arms, the forces resisting imperialism are on the rise in the countries of the Near and Middle East as well as in those of north and south Africa.

The economies of the leading imperialist countries, in the first place the United States of America, are facing constantly the danger of perturbations. The observed militarization of the economy in the United States, England and other capitalist countries which is an abnormal expansion of the war industry as well as of those branches which serve this industry at the expense of a reduced production of articles needed by the civilian population, cannot but bring about an economic collapse in a short period of time. We are not even mentioning the existence of millions of unemployed in the United States of America.

This is what the camp of imperialism and war looks like.

A different situation can be observed in the camp of democracy and peace. The strength of this camp, devoid of any internal contradictions, is rising and solidifying with every passing day. I have already mentioned the achievements of the Soviet Union, representing the main, leading force in the camp of democracy and peace. From one success to another are also moving the countries of the people's democracies. Having liquidated the serious consequences of the last war in a short period of time, thanks to the qualities of the new social system, the peoples of these countries are rapidly developing their own economies. At the end of the first half of the current year the industrial production level in Poland and Hungary increased more than two-and-one-half times; in Bulgaria, more than three times; in Czechoslovakia, more than one-and-one-half times; in Rumania, more than twice and in Albania more than four times as compared with prewar industrial output. As in our own Country, the development of industry in these countries serves the needs of the workers and promotes further peaceful development. Concurrently with the development of the economy, changes are also noticeable in the cultural life of these countries, the sciences, literature and art are flourishing, new men are being raised who understand the vital interests of their countries and who are able to defend these interests. The new public and political system has definitely solidified, thus ensuring a relentless movement of these countries along the road toward Socialism.

The Chinese People's Republic achieved significant successes and occupies one of the leading places in the struggle for peace. During the short period of its existence the Chinese People's Republic, under the leadership of the Communist Party of China, was able to strengthen the system of the dictatorship of the people's democracy and solve a number of important economic and political problems in their struggle for a complete economic independence from the capitalist world, in their fight for the industrialization of the country and for the development of the culture.

The German Democratic Republic is successfully developing its peaceful construction and took a durable place in the camp of democracy and peace. It is fighting persistently for the vital interests of the entire German nation, for an independent, democratic, united peace-loving Germany, for the conclusion of a just peace treaty that would insure the German people an honorable place among the peoples of the world.

In contrast to the countries of the imperialist camp, which are savagely competing with each other and cannot help but continue this competition, the countries of the democratic camp are developing their economies on the basis of close cooperation and mutual assistance.

Thus the camp of Democracy and Socialism constitutes a unified indestructible force both from the moral and political as well as from the economic point of view. The power of this camp is being increased even more by the fact that it is defending the just cause of freedom and independence of all nations. This means that if the ringleaders in the imperialist camp will, after all, risk the unleashing of a war, then there is no doubt that it would end with the downfall of imperialism itself. (Applause.)

Comrades! One of the greatest movements of the people in our times constitutes the movement for peace. Notwithstanding all the obstacles and the oppression that the partisans of peace have to suffer on the part of the ruling circles of an imperialist state, the movement for peace assumed enormous proportions, encompassing all countries of the world and all classes of the population, without regard to political, religious and other convictions. The fighters for peace in the whole world are inspired by the words of the Great Standard-bearer of the peace movement, Comrade Stalin, who said: "Peace will be preserved and strengthened, if the peoples will take the cause of safeguarding the peace into their own hands and will defend this cause until the end." (Applause.)

The initiators and the leading force in the fight for peace in all countries are the Communist Parties. Due to their complete lack of fear and because of their selflessness in the fight for the vital interests of the workers, for the defense of peace and sovereignty of nations, the Communist Parties have won the confidence of the broad masses of peoples.

Comrades! By the Thirty-fourth Anniversary of the October Socialist Revolution our Country took another step on the road toward Communism. The successes that we have achieved prove once more that the policy of the Bolshevik Party constitutes the only correct policy, insuring a steady increase of the power of our Country and an improvement in the well-being of workers. (Applause.) In the struggle for realization of the grandiose program of Communist construction the Soviet nation will close its ranks even tighter around its own Communist Party, as well as around the Inspirer and Organizer of our achievements—the Great Stalin (Frenetic applause.)

Conscious of its strength and of the correctness of its path the Soviet nation, with an unruffled calm and confidence in the future, is continuing its great creative work. No power in this world can interrupt the victorious march of the Soviet people towards the final victory of Communism. (Applause.)

Long live the great invincible banner of the October Socialist Revolution! (Applause.)

Long live our powerful Country, the indestructible bulwark of freedom in the world! (Applause.)

Long live the Party of Lenin-Stalin, our famous Bolshevik Party! (Long-lasting applause.)

Onward toward the victory of Peace and Democracy in the whole world! (Long-lasting stormy applause. The ovation to honor the Organizer and Inspirer of the gigantic historic achievements of the Soviet people, the bright Genius of mankind, the Standard-bearer of peace, the

Great Leader and Teacher, Joseph Vissarionovich Stalin, lasts several minutes.)

(Pravda, November 7, 1951)

Appendix 14

FOUL SPIES AND MURDERERS UNDER A
MASK OF PROFESSORS AND PHYSICIANS

A news item is being published by TASS today about a group of physicians-saboteurs. This terrorist group, exposed some time ago by the organs of State Security, had as its goal to shorten the lives of the active personalities in the Soviet Union by harmful medical treatment.

It has been established by an investigation that the participants of the terrorist group, using their profession as doctors, had abused the confidence of their patients with premeditation, criminally ruined their health by making wrong diagnoses and consequently killing their patients by improper medical treatment. Hiding behind the honored and noble titles of physicians, men of science, those monsters and murderers trampled the sacred banner of science. Following the road of monstrous crimes, they defiled the honor of scientists.

Comrades A. A. Zhdanov and A. S. Shcherbakov were the victims of this gang of anthropoid animals. The criminals confessed that, taking advantage of the illness of Comrade Zhdanov, they deliberately concealed his condition of infarction of the miocardium and ordered a treatment contraindicated in the case of such a serious illness, thus causing the death of Comrade Zhdanov. These doctors-murderers shortened the life and brought death to Comrade Shcherbakov by an improper application of a strong medication and by recommending a noxious routine.

First, these criminals attempted to ruin the health of the leaders of the Armed Forces, eliminating them from active duty, hence weakening the defense posture of the Country. The arrest of the criminals stopped their perfidious plans, and put an end to their monstrous goals.

Whom were these monsters serving? Who was directing the criminal, terrorist and saboteur activities of these foul traitors of the Country? What goal were they attempting to achieve by killing the active leaders of the Soviet Government?

It has been established that all members of the terrorist physician group worked for foreign Intelligence agencies to whom they sold their bodies and souls and were their paid hirelings and agents.

The majority of the terrorist group—i.e., Vovsi, B. Kogan, Feldman, Greenstein, Etinger and others were bought by the American Intelligence. They were recruited by a branch of the American Intelligence—

by the international Jewish bourgeois-nationalist organization *Joint*. A disgraceful image of this Zionist spying organization, concealing its foul activities under the pretense of charitable activities, has been fully exposed.

Relying on a group of corrupt Jewish bourgeois nationalists, the professional spies and terrorists of *Joint* conducted their sabotaging activities in the Soviet Union as instructed and directed by the American Intelligence service.

Arrested Vovsi indicated during the investigation that he received directives from the United States concerning "the annihilation of leading personalities of the USSR." This directive was passed on to him on behalf of *Joint*, a spy and terrorist group, by Dr. Shimelnovich and Mikhoels, a well-known Jewish bourgeois nationalist.

Unmasking of the gang of doctors-murderers constitutes a major defeat for the international Jewish Zionist organization. Now, everybody can see what kind of "do-gooders" and "friends of peace" are hiding behind the sign of *Joint*.

It has been established by now that the other members of the terrorist group: Vinogradov, M. Kogan, Yegorov, had been old agents of British Intelligence, working for the latter for many years and committing for it the worst crimes and dirtiest tasks.

Shifty Americans and their English "junior partners" know that it is impossible to take over the government of other nations by peaceful means. While preparing feverishly for another world war, they are planting their spies behind the front lines of the USSR and of the countries of national democracy, attempting to accomplish what the Hitlerites failed to achieve in the USSR, that is, to create a subversive "Fifth Column." It suffices to mention an open and cynical appropriation of one hundred million dollars by the American government for subversive, terrorist and spying activities in the countries within the Socialist camp, not to mention the fact that additional hundreds of millions of dollars are being secretly spent for that purpose by the Americans and the British.

The Soviet people should not for a minute forget to intensify their vigilance in every possible way; to be on the alert for all manifestations of the warmongers and their agents, and continuously strengthen the Armed Forces as well as the Intelligence Service of our Country.

Comrade Stalin warned many times that our achievements have also a dark side; that they create an atmosphere of satisfaction and complacency among many of our workers. We have not yet succeeded in changing the frame of mind. We still have many gullible people. Precisely this gullibility of our people creates a fertile soil for the scoundrelly sabotage.

Socialist attitudes have complete dominion in the USSR. The Soviet nation has won a victory unprecedented in history during the Great Patriotic War. Heavy damages caused by the war have been erased in a short time, never recorded before. We are registering achievements in all phases of our economy and culture. From these facts some of our people draw the conclusion that by now the danger of sabotage, diversion and espionage has been removed, that the leaders of the capitalist world decided to renounce their efforts of continuing their undermining activities against the USSR.

But this line of reasoning may be followed only by true opportunists, seeing things from an anti-Marxist point of view, believing in the "attenuation" of the class struggle. They do not or cannot understand that our achievements lead to an intensification of the struggle and not to its attenuation. Consequently, the more successful is our development, the more intensified will become the struggle on the part of the enemies of our Nation, who are doomed to destruction, led to despair.

So teaches immortal Lenin, so teaches Comrade Stalin.

Lenin indicated that "our Revolution, more than any other, confirms the law stating that the power of the revolution, the power of pressure, the energy, determination and its triumph caused an intensification of the resistance on the part of bourgeoisie."

Exposing the opportunistic theory about "the attenuation" of the class struggle, as related to our successes, Comrade Stalin had warned:

"It is not only a rotten theory, but also a dangerous one, since it lulls our people, and leads them into a trap, while giving the class enemy a chance to prepare for war against the Soviet Government."

The exploiting classes were crushed and liquidated in the USSR a long time ago; however, vestiges of the bourgeois ideology, psychology and morality, as well as of private ownership, have survived. The carriers of this bourgeois mentality and bourgeois morality are living people, who are the hidden enemy of our Nation. Precisely these secret enemies of our Nation, supported by the imperialist world, will continue their sabotage.

All this obligates the Soviet people to intensify in every way the revolutionary vigilance, and diligently watch for underhanded plotting by the enemy. The fact that a group of contemptible degenerates among the "men of science" could act unpunished for some time indicates that some of our Soviet organs and their leaders abandoned vigilance and became infected by gullibility.

The Agencies of State Security did not detect in time the existence of a saboteur, terrorist organization among the doctors. These Agencies, however, should have been particularly vigilant, since history has already known cases of foul murderers and traitors of the country hiding behind the masks of doctors; like those "doctors" Levin and Pletnev, who, following orders of the enemies of the Soviet Union, killed the great Russian writer, Maxim Gorky, and the prominent functionaries of the Soviet Government, V. V. Kuybyshev and V. R. Menzhinsky by way of deliberate application of improper medical treatment.

The exposure of the gang of doctors-poisoners constitutes a major blow to the American and British warmongers. Their agents have been caught and rendered harmless. The true image of slavedrivers and cannibals from the United States of America and England appears again before the whole world.

The Soviet Nation angrily and indignantly brandishes the gang of murderers and their foreign bosses. The Nation will crush the hirelings who sold themselves for dollars and pounds sterling like despicable reptiles. Inasmuch as those are concerned who inspired the hirelings-murderers, they can be sure that retribution will not bypass them. A way will be found to punish them.

All this is true, of course. However, it is also true that besides those enemies there is also among us still another enemy—that is the gullibility of our people. There need be no doubt that as long as there is gullibility among us, there will be also sabotage. Consequently: In order to liquidate the sabotage it is essential to eradicate gullibility from our midst.

(*Pravda*, January 13, 1953)

Appendix 15

FUNERAL OF JOSEPH VISSARIONOVICH STALIN

Speech of Comrade L. P. Beria

Dear Comrades and Friends,

It is difficult to express in words the great sorrow being felt by our Party and the peoples of our Country as well as the whole of progressive mankind during these days.

Stalin, the Great Companion in arms and the brilliant Continuator of the work of Lenin, has passed away. The man who was the closest and dearest to all Soviet people and to the millions of workers of the whole world is no more.

The whole life and activity of the Great Stalin constituted an inspiring example of allegiance to Leninism, an example of selfless service to the working class and to all working people as well as to the cause of liberation of the workers from oppression and exploitation.

The great Lenin organized our Party and led it to the victory of the proletarian revolution.

Together with the great Lenin, his brilliant comrade-in-arms, Stalin has been strengthening the Bolshevik Party and organizing a Socialist State, the first one in the whole world.

After Lenin's death Stalin led our Party and our Country along Lenin's path for almost thirty years. Stalin defended Leninism against many enemies, developed and enriched the Lenin doctrine in new historic conditions. The wise leadership of the Great Stalin insured for our people the possibility of developing Socialism in our Country and secured the victory of the Soviet Union in the Great Patriotic War, a fact of worldwide importance. The Great Architect of Communism, the brilliant Leader, our dear Stalin equipped our Party and our people with a grand program of building Communism.

Comrades! There is an inconsolable grief in our hearts and our loss is incredibly great, but under its weight the strong will of the Communist Party is not going to bend, its unity and steadfast resolution to fight for Communism will not be shaken.

Our Party, armed with the revolutionary theory of Marx-Engels-Lenin-Stalin, enriched by a half-century of experience in the fight for the interests of the working class and all workers, knows very well how to proceed in order to insure the building of a Communist society.

The Central Committee of our Party and the Soviet Government finished the great school of Lenin and Stalin in the problems of state leadership.

The Central Committee of our Party and the Soviet Government, leading and directing the heroic battle of the Soviet nation, acquired enormous experience in the leadership of the Party and of the Country amidst the fires of the Civil War and intervention, during the difficult years of the fight against hunger and devastation, in the fight for the industrialization of the Country and collectivization of agriculture, during the difficult years of the Great Patriotic War, when the fate of our Country and the fate of all mankind hung in the balance.

That is why the peoples of the Soviet Union can also in the future depend with full confidence on the Communist Party, on its Central Committee and on their Soviet Government.

The enemies of the Soviet State are hoping that the heavy loss we have sustained will lead to disorder and to dissolution in our ranks.

All their calculations will come to naught and they will be sadly disappointed.

Anyone who is not blind can see that our Party in these difficult days closes its ranks even tighter and that it is united and firm.

Anyone who is not blind can see that during these sorrowful days all peoples of the Soviet Union, in brotherly unity with the great Russian nation, are rallying even closer to their Soviet Government and the Central Committee of the Communist Party.

The Soviet nation unanimously supports the internal as well as the foreign policy of the Soviet State.

Our internal policy is based on the unbreakable union of the working class and the collective farm agricultural workers, on the brotherly friendship between the peoples of our Country, on the close association of all Soviet National Republics in the system of a single, multi-national State—the Union of Soviet Socialist Republics. This policy is directed towards a further strengthening of the economic and military potential of our State, towards a further development of the national economy and towards a maximum satisfaction of material and cultural requirements of the entire Soviet society.

Industrial and collective farm workers as well as the intelligentsia of our Country can work peacefully and confidently, knowing full well that the Soviet Government will continuously and with great care protect their rights established in the Stalin Constitution.

Our foreign policy is clear and understandable. Beginning with the first days of the Soviet Regime Lenin determined the foreign policy of the Soviet State as that of peace.

This policy of peace has been steadfastly pursued by the Great Continuator of the work of Lenin, our wise Leader Stalin.

In the future the foreign policy of the Soviet Government will be also the Lenin-Stalin policy of maintaining and strengthening of peace, fighting against the preparation and unleashing of a new war, a policy of international cooperation and development of business relations with all countries on the basis of reciprocity.

The Soviet Government will strengthen even further the brotherly union and friendship as well as cooperation in the common fight in the cause of peace in the whole world and broad economic and cultural cooperation with the great Chinese People's Republic, with all the countries of people's democracies and with the German People's Republic.

Our brothers and friends abroad can rest assured that the Communist Party and the peoples of the Soviet Union, faithful to the banner of the proletarian International, faithful to the banner of Marx-Lenin will also in the future develop and strengthen friendly connections with the workers in the capitalist and colonial countries fighting for Peace, Democracy and Socialism.

A deep feeling of friendship unites our people with the heroic Korean people fighting for independence.

Our great leaders Lenin and Stalin taught us constantly to increase and sharpen the vigilance of the Party and the people towards the intrigues and machinations of the enemies of the Soviet State.

Now we will have to increase our vigilance even more.

Let no one be mistaken that the enemies of the Soviet State will be able to catch us unawares.

Our valiant Armed Forces are equipped with every type of modern weapon for the defense of the Soviet Country. Our soldiers and sailors, officers and generals, enriched by the experience of the Great Patriotic War, will know how to meet any given enemy who would dare to attack our Country.

The strength and indestructibility of our State is not based on the fact alone that we have an Army which is steeped in glory and hardened by experience.

The power of the Soviet State rests on the unity of the Soviet nation, on its faith in the Communist Party, the leading force of the Soviet society and on the faith of the people in its Soviet Government. The Communist Party and the Soviet Government value highly this trust of the people.

The Soviet nation met with unanimous approval the Decree of the Central Committee of our Party, of the Council of Ministers and of the Presidium of the Supreme Council of the USSR concerning the implementation of important decisions to insure an uninterrupted and sound leadership of all activities of the Country.

One of these important decisions is the nomination of the talented pupil of Lenin and a faithful companion in arms of Stalin—Georgy Maksimilianovich Malenkov—to the post of Chairman of the Council of Ministers of the USSR.

Decisions taken by the highest Party and State organs in our Country represent a striking expression of complete unity and solidarity in the leadership of the Party and State.

This unity and solidarity in the leadership of the Country is a guarantee for a successful implementation of the internal and foreign policy worked out through many years by our Party and Government under the leadership of Lenin and Stalin.

Stalin, the same as Lenin, left for our Party and our Country an important legacy, which we will have to protect as an apple of our eye and which we will continuously increase.

The Great Stalin raised and kept close to himself a cohort of leaders tested in battle, who acquired the Lenin-Stalin mastery of leadership and who are now charged with the historic responsibility of bringing to a victorious end the great work initiated by Lenin and successfully continued by Stalin.

The peoples of our Country can rest assured that the Communist Party and the Government of the Soviet Union will not spare their efforts nor lives in order to protect the strong unity in the ranks of the Party and in its leadership, to strengthen the unbreakable friendship of the peoples of the Soviet Union, to increase the power of the Soviet State, to protect, without any alterations, the loyalty to the principles of Marxism-Leninism and, following the advice of Lenin and Stalin, lead the Country of Socialism into Communism.

Eternal glory for our dear, cherished Leader and Teacher—the Great Stalin.

(*Pravda*, March 10, 1953)

Appendix 16

AT THE GENERAL COMMITTEE OF THE
COMMUNIST PARTY OF THE
SOVIET UNION

According to the decision taken by the Plenary Session of the Central Committee of the Communist Party of the Soviet Union, Comrade S. D. Ignatyev was relieved of his post as Secretary of the Central Committee of the Communist Party of the Soviet Union.

(*Pravda*, April 7, 1953)

Appendix 17

INDESTRUCTIBLE IS THE UNITY OF THE PARTY,
GOVERNMENT AND THE SOVIET UNION

The Soviet Union, fully aware of its indestructible power and creative capabilities, confidently moves forward along the path of building Communism. Implementing the decisions of the Nineteenth Congress of the Communist Party of the USSR, under the leadership of its Central Committee, the Communist Party has insured a tremendous advancement in all areas of the National economy. Carrying out ambitious plans of building Communism, the Soviet nation has rallied still closer behind the Party and Government. The economic and defensive potential of our Country has achieved a noteworthy progress; higher living standards have been achieved for factory workers, collective farm workers, intelligentsia and all Soviet peoples.

We have powerful Socialist industries, well-developed all-around heavy industry, which constitutes the basis for the Socialist economy. Our machine-building industry, which supplies modern equipment to all branches of the national economy, grows steadily. Impressive successes had been achieved by our food and light industries. They possess presently a capability of fulfilling the growing needs of our urban and rural population, consistent with the Party policy of reducing consumer prices. The agriculture, reconstructed during the postwar period, has been supplied with the newest equipment in greater numbers than before the war.

All these successes are the result of a lasting union between the working class and peasantry of our Country; the result of solidifying friendship among the nations within the USSR and the persistently growing morale and political unity of our society; the result of the consistent implementation of the policy formulated by the Communist Party.

The Soviet Government, persistently and consequently pursuing a peaceful policy, has stated that all disputed problems of international relationships can be resolved through discussions between the interested parties. This statement of policy meets with unqualified support and approval by all nations. The new peace initiative manifested by the Soviet Government has led to the strengthening of the international standing of the Soviet Union; to elevating the prestige of our Country; toward intensification of worldwide efforts to preserve and to secure peace.

A different picture is presented by the capitalist camp. One can see there a continuing aggravation of the overall capitalist crisis, an unrestrained expansion and a policy of insolent dictation on the part of American imperialism, and an intensification of contradictions among the capitalist countries, all these factors increasing impoverishment of the working masses.

Hence, such a course of world events witnesses the inevitable growth of Democracy and Socialism on the one hand, and a general weakening of the capitalist camp on the other hand. This situation causes great concern among the imperialists and generates renewed activity by the reactionary imperialistic powers, attempting feverishly to restrain the growing power of the international forces of Peace, Democracy and Socialism, with its leading power, the Soviet Union. Imperialists are seeking support from various renegades and destructive elements in the Socialist and Democratic countries, thus increasing subversive activities by its Secret Service.

A statement made by the Plenary Session of the Central Committee of the Communist Party of the USSR is being published today in *Pravda*. It reads as follows:

"Having heard and discussed a report of the Presidium of the Central Committee, delivered by Comrade G. M. Malenkov, concerning criminal activities against the Party and the State, aiming to undermine the security of the Soviet Union, benefiting the foreign capital, perpetrated by L. P. Beria, and manifested by his treacherous attempts to place the Ministry of Internal Affairs of the USSR above the Soviet Government and the Communist Party of the USSR, the Plenary Session of the Central Committee of the Communist Party of the Soviet Union resolved to expel L. P. Beria from the ranks of the Communist Party of the Soviet Union for being the enemy of the Communist Party and of the Soviet Union.

Having considered the statement made by the Council of Ministers of the USSR, the Presidium of the Supreme Soviet of the USSR decided the following concerning this matter:

1. To remove L. P. Beria from the position of First Deputy Chairman of the Council of Ministers of the USSR, and from the position of Minister of Interior of the USSR.

2. To submit the matter of the criminal activities of L. P. Beria for an inquest by the Supreme Court of the USSR.

The presently exposed enemy of the people, Beria, wormed himself into confidence and gained access to leadership by various self-promoting schemes. While his earlier criminal anti-Party and anti-State activities were carefully concealed and masked, Beria has become recently bold, throwing aside all restraints and showing his real political image, i.e., the image of a malicious enemy of the Party and the Soviet Nation. The increased criminal activities of Beria are a corollary of an all-out intensification of subversive, anti-Soviet activities of hostile international reactionary powers directed against our Government. Both the international imperialism as well as its secret agents are becoming more active.

Beria began his foul manipulations, designed to take over power by attempting to place the Ministry of the Interior above the Party and Government, using for this purpose the central and local Agencies of the Ministry of the Interior against the Party and its leaders, and against the Government of the USSR: furthermore, he had promoted those employees of the Ministry of the Interior who were personally subservient to him.

As has already been established, Beria persistently impeded the solution of important and urgent problems in the area of agriculture by means of many pretexts. This was done in order to discredit collective and State farms and to create problems in supplying the Country with foodstuffs.

By devious means, Beria attempted to undermine friendship among nationalities of the USSR, the very basis of the multiple nationality Socialist State and the main basis of all achievements of the brotherly Soviet Republics; he attempted to sow the seeds of discord among the nationalities of the USSR, and to reactivate bourgeois and nationalistic elements in the Union Republics.

Although obligated to carry out specific directives issued by the Central Committee of the Party and the Soviet Government intended to uphold the Soviet Law and to eliminate certain cases of lawlessness and willfulness, Beria deliberately hampered the implementation of such directives; moreover, in many instances he attempted to distort them.

Undisputed facts indicate that Beria discarded the image of a Communist and changed into a bourgeois renegade, serving the agents of international imperialism. This adventurer and mercenary of the foreign imperialist forces planned to take over the leadership of the Party and the Country, his objective being the actual destruction of our Communist Party and the replacement of the policy worked out by the Party through many years by a policy of a subservience, which in the final analysis would lead to the restoration of capitalism.

Thanks to timely and decisive measures taken by the Presidium of the Central Committee of the Communist Party of the Soviet Union, approved unanimously and in their entirety by the Plenary Session of the Central Committee of the Party, the Criminal, anti-Party and anti-State plans made by Beria were exposed. A liquidation of Beria's criminal adventure shows time and time again that as in the past, anti-Soviet plans of foreign imperialist forces will be crushed by an indestructible power and complete unity of the Party, Government and the Soviet Nation.

In connection with Beria's case, a political lesson should be learned and undisputable conclusions made. The strength of our leadership lies in collectivity, solidarity and monolithic character. The collective leadership constitutes a higher form of leadership of our Party. This principle is totally consistent with the renowned Marx's position pertaining to detriments and rejection of the cult of personality. 'Because of my dislike for any kind of the cult of personality'—wrote Marx—'I never permitted giving any publicity to the numerous addresses during the sessions of the International, in which credit was given for my contributions and with which many people annoyed me everywhere; I never responded to them, except perhaps, occasionally to rebuke them. The very first time Engels and I joined a secret Communist society, it was on the condition that from its rules would be eliminated all features which permit superstitious adulation of authority.'

Only the collective political experience, the collective wisdom of the Central Committee based on the scientific principles of Marx-Lenin theory, insures the proper leadership of the Party and the Country, an immovable cohesiveness and solidarity among the Party ranks and a successful development of Communism in our Country.

Every worker, regardless of his position, should be under an active Party surveillance. The Party organizations should inspect regularly the work of all organizations and agencies, and the work of all labor leaders. It is vital that, among others, the activities of the agencies of the Ministry of the Interior be under a systematic and never weakening control. This is not only a right, but the basic obligation of the Party organizations.

It is imperative that the revolutionary vigilance grows more vigorous among the Communists and all workers, permeating every endeavor of the Party and Soviet organizations. As long as the capitalist encirclement exists, it sends and will continue sending its agents to us to carry out their subversive activities. One must remember that, never forget it, and always keep our weapon sharp against imperialist intelligence and their hirelings.

It is essential that in matters concerning the hiring of workers, the Party principle of political and professional qualifications be observed with a firm determination.

The power and invincibility of our Party rests on its close and unbreakable ties with the masses, with the Nation. This objective demands that these ties be strengthened and expanded; it calls for everyday concern for improving the standards of living for the industrial and agricultural workers, intelligentsia and all Soviet peoples.

The sacred duty of the Party calls for a continued cementing of the amity among the nations of the USSR; strengthening of our multi-national Socialist Government; educating the Soviet peoples in the spirit of proletariat internationalism; and continued, uncompromising struggle with all and every type of manifestation of bourgeois nationalism.

Having mobilized the creative power of our Nation, Party, Soviet, Trade Unions, Youth Organizations, they should be directed in such a manner as to fully utilize our reserves and potential for successful accomplishment of the aims set forth by the Nineteenth Congress of the Party.

It is imperative that the task of Party propaganda and political-educational work of the masses be drastically improved. Teaching of the Marxism-Leninism theory should not emphasize its dogmas, nor single precepts or citations, but the essence of the Marx-Engels-Lenin-Stalin theory, i.e., its all-conquering, revolutionary remaking of the world—this is the aim of our propaganda.

The resolution made by the Plenary Session of the Central Committee of the Communist Party of the Soviet Union meets with unanimous and warm approval by the entire Party, and by the whole Country. Yesterday, the joint Plenary Session of the Moscow Region and Moscow City Committees of the Communist Party of the Soviet Union, together with the Party activists of the city of Moscow and the Moscow Region, expressed their deep and angry indignation because of Beria's treacherous activities. Furthermore, they unanimously approved the resolution of the Plenary Session of the Central Committee of the Communist Party of the Soviet Union. Similar decisions were made by the joint Plenary Session of the Kiev Region and Kiev City Committees of the Party together with their activists, as well as a number of other Party Organizations.

The Communist Party of the Soviet Union, created 50 years ago by the genius of Lenin, has grown into a gigantic power, battle-hardened under the leadership of Lenin, the latter's student and follower, the great Stalin, and their companions-in-arms.

The Soviet Nation, under the leadership of the Communist Party, rallied around its war banner, is fulfilling its great historical mission. Our Country, the Party, Government and Nation, in close unity, is confidently and steadfastly moving forward along its way—the glorious way of building a victorious Communism."

(*Pravda*, July 10, 1953)

Appendix 18

COMMUNISTS OF MOSCOW AND THE MOSCOW REGION UNANIMOUSLY APPROVE THE RESOLUTION PASSED BY THE PLENARY SESSION OF THE CENTRAL COMMITTEE OF THE COMMUNIST PARTY OF THE USSR

A Joint Plenary Session of the Moscow Region and Moscow City Committees of the Communist Party of the USSR, together with the Party activists of the City and Moscow Region

Yesterday, July the 9th, a joint Plenary Session of the Moscow Region and Moscow City Party Committees, together with the activists of the City and Moscow Region, was held in the Hall of Columns at the Union House, for the purpose of discussing the conclusions of the Plenary Session of the Central Committee of the Communist Party of the USSR. Some 2,000 persons were present at the meeting of the Plenary Session.

The report, delivered by Comrade Mikhaylovich, Secretary of the Moscow Committee of the Communist Party of the USSR, containing the resolution of the Plenary Session of the Central Committee of the Communist Party of the USSR, concerning the criminal, anti-Party and anti-State activities of Beria, was heard with great attention by those present at the Plenary Session.

Expressing the common will of the entire Moscow Party organization, the participants of the Plenary Session responded with sustained bursts of applause to the decisions made by the Plenary Session of the Central Committee of the Communist Party. They also approved in its entirety the timely and solely correct measures taken by the Central Committee of the Communist Party of the USSR, aiming to put an end to the criminal, anti-Party and anti-State activities of Beria.

The resolution passed by the Plenary Session of the Central Committee of the Communist Party of the USSR, to exclude L. P. Beria from membership in the Communist Party of the USSR, as the enemy of the Party and of the Soviet Nation for his treasonous activities, aiming to undermine the Soviet Government, and the resolution passed by the Presidium of the Supreme Council of the USSR to submit the matter of the criminal activities of L. P. Beria for an inquest by the Supreme Court of the USSR, were met with total unanimity, warm approval, and a burst of applause.

The joint Plenary Session of the Moscow Region and the Moscow City Committees of the Communist Party of the USSR, together with the Party activists gave expression of the unity of the Moscow Party Organization and its close solidarity with the Central Committee of the Communist Party of the USSR. The speaker and all who participated in the debates voiced the opinion that the resolution passed by the Plenary Session of the Central Committee of the Communist Party of the Soviet Union has an enormous significance for the Party, as well as for the Soviet Nation. The participants of the Plenary Session declared that the resolution of the Plenary Session of the Communist Party of the USSR will have the full approval and backing of all Party organizations.

The participants of the Plenary Session declared unanimously that the Central Committee of the Party has provided a continuous and sound leadership of the entire Country during the past four months following the death of Joseph Stalin, performed a great work in uniting the Party and the people behind the task of building Socialism; strengthened the economic and military potential of our Motherland; improved the standard of living of industrial workers, collective farm workers, intelligentsia and the entire Soviet population.

Implementing the decisions made by the Nineteenth Congress of the Communist Party of the USSR, the Party has achieved great progress in all branches of the national economy. The policy of peace, followed consistently by the Soviet Government, brought about a further strengthening of the international position of the USSR, growth of prestige of our Country; and gave an impetus to the international movement for the preservation and protection of peace. The Central Committee of the Party has shown particular concern for achieving unity in the Party and Government leadership, in order to successfully solve the fundamental goals of building the Communist Society.

The participants of the Plenary Session expressed their anger and indignation because of the perfidious activities of Beria, a base enemy of the Party and the Soviet Nation, and an agent of international imperialism.

Comrade Gulyayev, Secretary of the Lenin District Committee of the Communist Party of the USSR in the City of Moscow, stated the following: "The foul activities of Beria, this bourgeois renegade, aroused the outrage and indignation of the entire Party and the entire Soviet Nation. The timely and appropriate measures, approved by the Central Committee of our Party for ending the criminal anti-Party and anti-State activities of Beria, are being wholeheartedly accepted."

Comrade Kopenkin, Secretary of the Naro-Fominsk City District Committee of the Party, stressed in his address the deep meaning and the tremendous importance of the decisions made by the Plenary Session of the Central Committee of the Communist Party of the USSR. Comrade Kopenkin criticizes shortcomings in the ideological work and talks about indispensability of more extensive application of criticism and self-criticism, stressing also a need for greater vigilance in this work.

Comrade Severyanova, Director of the *Trekhgornaya Manufactura** group of plants, has stated that our Party teaches us to hold on to the fundamentals and exercise political acuity, everywhere and in everything; to be always on guard against capitalist encirclement and to be vigilant. We should learn a political lesson from the Beria case. This renegade and traitor embarked on the road of monstrous crimes, attempting to obstruct the efforts of building Communism in our Country. We are deeply grateful to our Central Committee of the Party for detecting and exposing this traitor.

Comrade Azhirkov, Chairman of *Borets*** collective farm has stated that no enemies shall ever succeed in undermining the further expansion of the collective farms in the USSR. Collective farms' peasantry, educated by the Communist Party, will welcome necessary measures taken against Beria, workers' enemy.

Comrade Vasilyev, Chairman of the Council of Moscow Region Trade Unions, and Comrade Khaldeyev, Secretary of the Moscow Region Committee of the Young Communist League, representatives of organizations of the working masses, expressed the thinking of millions of members of the Trade Unions, and of the Young Communist League as well as of youth at large when they talked with indignation about the base, hostile activities of Beria. The speakers had declared that all workers are rallying around the Communist Party; that they are ready to contribute all their efforts towards the task of successful development of Communism.

Academician Topchiyev, Professor Vovchenko, writer Simonov—participants of the Plenary Session, speaking on behalf of the Soviet intelligentsia, the scientific community, literature and arts, talked about successes of science and culture in our Country achieved under the leadership of the Communist Party. Academician Topchiyev has stated that the

---

* The Three Hills Factory.
** The Wrestler.

Soviet scientists and those employed in the arts field are holding up to shame the anti-Party and anti-State, criminal activities of Beria, the enemy of the Nation; furthermore, they are contributing all their potential and knowledge toward a swift implementation of the historic tasks set forth by the Nineteenth Congress of the Party.

Responding to the appeal by the Plenary Session of the Central Committee of the Communist Party of the USSR, to learn a political lesson from the Beria case, and to draw the necessary conclusions for their continued efforts, the Communists of the City and Moscow Region were uncovering and criticizing inadequacies in the work of the Party and Soviet Organizations in the areas of economic development and Communist indoctrination.

Concrete facts were cited at the Plenary Session showing that in the City of Moscow and Moscow Region there still exist industrial enterprises that are lagging behind; that some collective farms are in a state of neglect. The participants of the Plenary Session put forward practical suggestions aiming to remedy these shortcomings.

A great attention was given at the Plenary Session to the tasks of the Party Organizations in the area of improving the organizational and ideological work of the Party. As was already mentioned at the Plenary Session, serious shortcomings exist in the Moscow Party Organization pertaining to the adherence to the Bolshevik principles of leadership, worked out by Lenin. Some Region and City committees of the Party are not conforming to the regulations made by the Communist Party of the USSR, requiring that Plenary Sessions be called periodically, and principles of collective leadership applied; furthermore, they fail to cultivate an indispensable criticism and self-criticism.

Major shortcomings were noted in the area of Party propaganda. In recent years, a departure from the Marx-Lenin conception of the role of an individual in history was noted in the Party propaganda in the Moscow Party organization. Instead of the correct interpretation of the role of the Communist Party as the leading force in the building of Communism in our Country, the Party propaganda had often strayed toward the cult of personality, which leads to minimizing the role of the Party itself, and its leading center, as well as to decreasing the creative activity of the rank and file Party members and broad masses of workers. A creative approach to the matter of the teachings of Marx-Engels, Lenin and Stalin in many instances is being substituted by dogmatism. Inadequate attention is given to the need of ideological hardening of the Party, Soviet and economic cadres, and to educating them in the spirit of a strict Party and State discipline. It has been noted also that the Party organizations give inadequate attention to propaganda concerning the concept of Soviet patriotism, friendship among the nationalities of the

USSR, and to educating the workers in the spirit of political vigilance, Socialist approach to labor and to Socialist property.

The Joint Plenary Session of the Committees of the Moscow Region and Moscow City of the Communist Party of the USSR, in its resolution passed unanimously and unequivocally, has approved the decision of the Central Committee of the Communist Party of the Soviet Union as a guideline totally, in its entirety, for strict compliance and execution. The decisions contain practical measures by which the Moscow City and Region Organizations are to implement the tasks set by the Plenary Session of the Central Committee of our Party.

The resolution reads: "The joint Plenary Session of the Moscow Region and the City of Moscow Committees of the Communist Party of the USSR together with the activists—assures the Central Committee of the Communist Party of the Soviet Union that the Moscow Party Organization in the future shall continue to give faithful and reliable support to the Central Committee.

"The Moscow Party Organization with its members shall rally even closer behind the Central Committee of the Communist Party of the USSR; and under its experienced leadership shall lead the workers in the City of Moscow and Moscow Region in the efforts aiming to implement the policy laid down by the Party; to achieve the grand program of building Communism in our Country."

(*Pravda*, July 10, 1953)

Appendix 19

THE UNITY OF THE PARTY, GOVERNMENT AND
THE SOVIET NATION IS UNSHAKEABLE

The Soviet Nation, united in its support of the Communist Party and the Soviet Government, is confidently building Communism. Having accomplished worldwide achievements of historical significance of building a Communist Society, the Soviet Nation prevails, because of the correct leadership of the Party, because of the inexhaustible creative power of our Socialist system. The Soviet Country has at its disposal a powerful Socialist industry, all-around developed heavy industry, which is the very foundation of the basis of our Socialist economy. Our machine-building industry, supplying all branches of the national economy with modern equipment, makes steady progress. Impressive successes have been achieved by progressive Soviet science. Our consumer and food industry has reached a high level of development. It is in a position to fulfill the growing needs of the rural and urban population, thanks to the policy of lowered prices established by the Party and Government. Our agriculture has been revitalized in the postwar period. Sovkhozes and kolhozes have been better supplied with modern equipment than prior to the war. Highly qualified cadres of specialists have been trained in all branches of the national economy.

All these achievements have been made possible thanks to the fact that the building of a Communist Society in our Country is being carried out on the principle of a solid union between the working classes and the collective peasantry, as well as on the principle of ever growing, stronger friendship among the nations of the USSR; finally, a steady solidifying of the moral and political unity of the Soviet Nation, based on the principle of a strict and persistent implementation of the policy formulated by the Communist Party.

At the same time, the general crisis of capitalism in the capitalist camp grows progressively worse, and the entire capitalist system becomes weaker, economic problems become more acute, unemployment is on the increase, prices go up, and workers become more destitute.

Two courses, two clearly distinguishable lines characterize the entire course of contemporary development in the world. On the one hand, an inevitable, powerful increase in the power of Democracy and Socialism takes place, and on the other, a general weakening in the strength of the imperialist camp. This is an inevitable course of history.

A new peace initiative undertaken by the Soviet Government has led to further strengthening of the international position of the Soviet Union, the prestige of our Country, strengthening the worldwide movement for the protection and preservation of peace.

The Communist Party constitutes the inspirational and organizational force in the Soviet Society. The Party leadership constitutes the decisive factor of the strength and stability of the Soviet State. Hence, it is no accident that the enemies, cleverly masked as Communists, attempted and shall attempt to infiltrate into the ranks of the Party, pursuing their hostile objectives for the sake of their career as well as to carry on their undermining activities in their capacity as agents of the imperialist states.

Today, *Izvestia* is publishing an informational report on a recently held Plenary Session of the Central Committee of the Communist Party of the Soviet Union. This report reads:

Having heard and discussed a report of the Presidium of the Central Committee, delivered by Comrade G. M. Malenkov, concerning the criminal activities against the Party and the State, aiming to undermine the security of the Soviet Union, benefiting foreign capital perpetrated by L. P. Beria, and manifested by his treacherous attempts to place the Ministry of Internal Affairs of the USSR above the Soviet Government and the Communist Party of the

USSR, the Plenary Session of the Central Committee of the Communist Party of the Soviet Union resolved to expel L. P. Beria from the ranks of the Communist Party of the Soviet Union, for being the enemy of the Communist Party and of the Soviet Union.

Having considered the statement made by the Council of Ministers of the USSR, the Presidium of the Supreme Soviet of the USSR, decided the following concerning this matter:

1. To remove L. P. Beria from the position of the First Deputy Chairman of the Council of Ministers of the USSR, and from the position of Minister of the Interior of the USSR.

2. To submit the matter of the criminal activities of L. P. Beria for an inquest by the Supreme Court of the USSR.

As has now been established, Beria, the enemy of the Country, by means of various self-promoting schemes gained the confidence and reached one of the leadership positions. While his earlier criminal, anti-Party and anti-State activities were well hidden and camouflaged, recently Beria, being pressed for time, cast aside all restraints and began revealing his real image, an image of a malicious enemy of the Party and of the Soviet Nation. There can be only one explanation for Beria's criminal activities: the international imperialism is being activated—and so is its secret service.

Beria, a foul provocateur and enemy of the Party, has started by attempting to place the Ministry of Internal Affairs above the Party and Government, using central and local organs of the Ministry of Internal Affairs against the Party, its leadership, as well as against the Government of the USSR. Unlawfully violating Party Rules pertaining to hiring of the cadres according to their professional and political qualifications, Beria promoted those employes of the Ministry of Internal Affairs who were his staunch followers.

It has been determined that using various pretexts, Beria obstructed the solution of important and urgent problems relating to the improvement and development of agriculture. Now, it is beyond any doubt that this foul enemy of the Nation set for himself the goal of undermining the kolhozes and creating difficulties in the food supply system of the Country. Beria attempted by devious means to sow the seeds of misunderstanding among the nations within the USSR; attempted to activate bourgeois and nationalistic elements; to undermine the friendship among the nationalities of the USSR, the latter being the very foundation of the multi-national Socialist State and the main condition of all achievements of the brotherly Soviet Republics.

Although being obligated to implement direct instructions of the Central Committee of the Party and the Soviet Government concerning the strengthening of the Soviet Law, and putting an end to certain instances of lawlessness and arbitrariness, Beria deliberately obstructed the implementation of such directives, and in several cases attempted to reverse them.

The Plenary Session of the Central Committee of the Communist Party of the USSR has established beyond any doubt that Beria cast aside the image of a Communist, turned into a bourgeois renegade, became an agent of international imperialism, nurturing plans to take over leadership of the Party and the Government for the purpose of destroying the Communist Party and changing the policy worked out by the Party through many years into a policy of surrender, which would inevitably lead in the final analysis to the restoration of capitalism.

Thanks to the timely and decisive measures undertaken by the Presidium of the Central Committee of the Communist Party of the USSR, approved unanimously and in full by the Plenary Session of the Central Committee of the Party, Beria's criminal, anti-Party and anti-State plans were unmasked and stopped.

It is imperative that a political lesson be learned and necessary conclusions drawn from the case of Beria's criminal, anti-Party and anti-State activities.

It is essential that the Party leadership be strengthened in all Party and Government agencies and a precise adherence to the principles of the Party leadership, worked out by Lenin, be insured and that directives of the Statutes of the Communist Party of the USSR be strictly observed.

The higher principle of the Party leadership in our Party is a collective form of leadership. This principle is in full agreement with the known position taken by Karl Marx concerning the harmfulness and inadmissibility of the cult of personality. "Because of my dislike for any kind of the cult of personality"—wrote Marx—"I never permitted giving any publicity to the numerous addresses, during the sessions of the International, in which credit was given for my contributions and with which many people annoyed me everywhere; I never responded to them, except perhaps, occasionally to rebuke them. The very first time Engels and I joined a secret Communist society, it was on the condition that from its rules would be eliminated all features which permit superstitious adulation of authority."

Only a collective political experience and wisdom of the Central Committee, based on the scientific principles of the Marx-Lenin theory, insures the proper leadership of the Party and Country, firm unity and cohesiveness within the Party's rank and file; and a rapid building of Communism in our Country. It is essential that the principle of collective leadership be strictly observed in the work of all Party organs.

The Party organizations should regularly check the work of all Organizations and Departments as well as of every worker, regardless of the position he occupies. A Party leadership of all organizations constitutes the main condition for their successful functioning. The Party controls fulfill a function of training the cadres in the spirit of a high degree of responsibility to the Party and the Nation. On the other hand, a laxity of the Party controls leads inevitably to failures in the work and dissatisfaction among the workers.

The Party teaches the Soviet peoples to constantly remember and never forget about the encirclement by the capitalists who were sending and will continue to send their agents to carry on subversive activities among our ranks. The task of the Party and Soviet Organizations is to increase the revolutionary vigilance among Communists and all workers in every way possible, in all their activities. It is essential to cast away a narrow-minded attitude in the selection of cadres, and to adhere strictly to the Party principle of hiring workers according to their political and professional competence.

The power and invincibility of the Communist Party lies in its unbreakable union with the Nation. The Party organizations should continuously develop and strengthen the ties of the Party with the masses, be sensitive to the workers' inquiries, demonstrate everyday concern for the improvement of the material well-being of the industrial and collective farm workers, of the intelligentsia and of all the Soviet peoples.

It is a sacred duty of our entire Party to continue strengthening the friendship among the nations of the USSR; strengthening the multi-national Socialist State; educating all Soviet peoples according to the ideology of proletarian internationalism; and resolutely combating all manifestations of bourgeois nationalism.

The Soviet Socialist system enjoys an indisputable advantage over the capitalist system and has a significant potential for a further, even more impressive progress of our economy and culture, for a continued improvement of material prosperity of our Nation. The Party, Soviet, and Komsomol organizations, as well as the Trade Unions should mobilize and organize the inexhaustible powers of our Nation, in order to achieve an optimum utilization of our resources and our potential, for not only a speedy fulfillment but even for surpassing the Five-Year Plan of development of the USSR, and the tasks set forth by the Nineteenth Congress of the Party.

Vital interests of the Party urgently require an improvement of the entire Party propaganda, and of the work related to the political education of the masses. Our propaganda is called to educate the Communists and the entire Nation in the spirit of conviction in the invincibility of the great cause of Communism; in the spirit of selfless devotion to our Party and Socialist Motherland.

The resolution of the Plenary Session of the Central Committee of the Communist Party of the USSR meets with the unanimous and warm approval of the entire Party and the whole Soviet Nation. A joint Plenary Session of the Central Committees of the city of Moscow and of Moscow Region of the Communist Party of the USSR, together with the Party activists of the City of Moscow and of Moscow Region held yesterday, expressed their indignation because of Beria's treacherous activities; and with a complete unanimity gave its approval of the resolution passed by the Plenary Session of the Central Committee of the Communist Party of the USSR. The same kind of decisions were adopted by a number of other Party organizations.

The Communist Party of the USSR, formed 50 years ago by the genius of Lenin, has grown into a gigantic power and became hardened in struggles under the leadership of Lenin and of the great Stalin, the pupil and successor of Lenin, as well as their collaborators. No bourgeois renegade and bureaucrat career-climber shall succeed in wrecking the unity and diminish the role of the Party as the leading force of the Soviet Society. No intrigues of enemies will be able to block the progressive development of our Nation, which is building Communism. Our Country, closely united with its Party, Government and Nation, shall confidently and steadfastly march forward, under the invincible banners of Lenin and Stalin, on its way to building Communism.

(*Izvestia*, July 10, 1953)

Appendix 20

THE VOICE OF THE PARTY IS THE
VOICE OF THE NATION

The announcement published yesterday on the Plenary Session of the Central Committee of the Communist Party of the USSR, as well as the decision made by the Presidium of the Supreme Soviet of the USSR, are focusing the attention of our Nation. The Communist Party, the entire Soviet Nation, warmly and with a complete unanimity approves the decision of the Plenary Session of the Central Committee of the Communist Party of the USSR. Moreover, they approve the measures undertaken by the Presidium of the Central Committee of the Party, designed to put an end to criminal, anti-Party and anti-State activities of Beria as singularly timely and decisive. The Soviet people received with a deep satisfaction the decision of the Presidium of the Supreme Soviet of the USSR to refer the case of the criminal activities of Beria for an inquest by the Supreme Court of the USSR.

Communications coming in from various regions of the Country regarding the plenary sessions of the Party committees, the Party activists, meetings of workers and functionaries at establishments in Moscow, Kiev, Leningrad, and in other cities constitute a new, clear proof of an unshakable unity of the Party, the Government and the Soviet Nation. The common will of the Party and the entire Soviet Nation is reflected in ardent speeches of orators and in the unanimously approved resolutions. Millions upon millions of the Soviet people angrily hold up to shame the criminal activities of Beria, a sworn enemy of the Party and Nation, and call for an intensified revolutionary vigilance.

Joint plenary sessions held recently by the Region and City Party committees, together with the Party activists in the Moscow, Kiev, Leningrad, Minsk and many other organizations of our Party called in to discuss the decision made by the Plenary Session of the Central Committee of the Communist Party of the USSR, turned into a powerful demonstration of a rock-hard unity of the rank and file of the Party, and of a close solidarity of the Party with its Central Committee.

Comrade Baykov, Senior Master of a rolling mill shop at the Kirov Plant, declared at the joint plenary session of the Leningrad Region and City committees of the Communist Party of the USSR:

"The Communists and all workers of the Kirov Plant warmly and unanimously approve the decision of the Plenary Session of the Central Committee of the Party concerning the exclusion of Beria, contemptible enemy, an agent of international imperialism, from the Party, as well as the decision of the Presidium of the Supreme Soviet concerning handing him over to justice. The unmasking of Beria shows once more that all the plans of our enemies, all of their designs, had been shattered in the past and shall be shattered by the indestructible unity of our Party, Government and the Nation. We will intensify even more our vigilance, and close our ranks around the Central Committee."

The discussion concerning the resolution of the Plenary Session of the Central Committee of the Communist Party of the USSR by the Party organizations is being conducted in the spirit of a complete unanimity and close solidarity, demonstrating a high level of activity of Communists. Expressing the will of the Party organizations, the joint plenary sessions of the Region committees and City committees, as well as the plenary sessions of District committees together with Party activists, approve the resolution of the Central Committee of the Communist Party of the USSR in its entirety and adopt it as a strict guidance for implementation in the future.

Being guided by the instruction of the Central Committee concerning the necessity of learning a political lesson and of drawing the indispensable conclusions from the Beria case as a guidance in future activities, the Plenary Session of the Party committees are analyzing the work of the Party organizations, are bringing up for criticism the shortcomings and are outlining concrete measures designed to accomplish the goals set forth by the Central Committee. The attention has been focused on the following tasks: the strengthening of the Party leadership in all Party cells and the State machinery; a strict adherence to the principles of the Party leadership and to the norms of the Party way of life; the compliance with the Party Rules; and a strict adherence to the supreme principle of the Party leadership—i.e., collective form of leadership.

The Party organizations are called upon to intensify in every way possible the revolutionary vigilance among the Communists and all workers. The Party is teaching that one should keep in mind and never forget the encirclement by capitalism, which has been sending and will continue to send its agents to infiltrate our ranks, in order to carry out subversive activities. Taking this fact into consideration, the Party organizations are mapping out concrete measures designed to improve the process of selection, advancement and education of the cadres, and of organization of the mass political work, among all strata of the population. The necessity of a considerable improvement of the entire program of the Party propaganda and of a far-reaching creative mastery of the all-conquering, world remaking, revolutionary teachings of Marx-Engels-Lenin-Stalin, is being stressed with a renewed energy. The Party, Government, Trade Unions and Komsomol organizations should manifest an everyday concern for the improvement of the material well-being of industrial and kolhoz workers, intelligentsia, and of all Soviet peoples. They should mobilize and organize the creative power of the Nation, in order to utilize our potential and capabilities to the fullest extent for the sake of a swift fulfillment and overfulfillment of the Fifth Five-Year Plan for the development of the USSR, for the sake of implementation of the historic goals set forth by the Nineteenth Party Congress.

Our Party is the organizational and inspirational force of the Soviet Society. The Soviet people speak with a feeling of rightful pride about the Great Communist Party of the Soviet Union. Our Communist Party, created by the genius of Lenin half a century ago, has grown to become a colossal power. The Party has a long road of struggle and victory to its credit and it became hardened in the struggle under the leadership of Lenin, as well as under his pupil and successor—the great Stalin, and their companions-in-arms.

The strength and invincibility of the Communist Party rests on its indissoluble bond with the Nation. The Soviet Nation looks upon the Party as its experienced leader and teacher, an inspiration and organizer of all our victories. The Communist Party of the Soviet Union is surrounded by the love of the entire Nation. Our Nation trusts its own Communist Party implicitly, knowing well that the Party will reject and cut down every attempt aimed at shaking its unity and at decreasing its role as the leading force in the Soviet Society. The feeling of millions of the Soviet people expressing a deadly hate for the enemies of the Nation and their love for the Communist Party, was well formulated at a meeting of workers and employees of the *Serp i Molot** plant, by Comrade Romanova, a worker of the plant, by saying:

"Beria, the worst enemy of the Party and of the Nation, attempted to undermine the unity of the Party, and to create a hostility among the nations of our Country. However, the Central Committee of the Party exposed this foul enemy, a hireling of capitalists. Our Nation loves the Communist Party, its own Soviet Government. The Party and the Government gave happiness to our children and insured cultural and prosperous living conditions for the Nation. Let the enemies know that what has been gained and won by our Nation will never fall into their filthy hands. Let the enemies and their accomplices know that none of them will escape severe punishment. The Nation will pull out their snake's sting with roots! In response to all underhanded plotting of enemies, we will close our ranks in solidarity with the Communist Party, its Central Committee and our own Soviet Government.

"Criminal activities and treacherous designs of Beria, an agent of international imperialism, aimed at undermining the Soviet Government for the benefit of capitalism. Beria, the foul provocateur and enemy of the Party, cleverly disguised, gained confidence by various schemes and succeeded to a position of leadership. Having reached the position of the Minister of Internal Affairs, he made treacherous attempts to place the Ministry of Internal Affairs of the USSR above the Government and the Communist Party of the USSR. In his attempt to accomplish his criminal schemes, designed to seize power, this arch career-climber and adventurer selected those employees who were his staunch followers. Using various pretexts, Beria obstructed, by any means, the solution of important and urgent problems relating to the improvement and development of agriculture; set for himself a goal of undermining the kolhozes, and of disrupting the food supply system of the Country."

Comrade Trushkevich, Chairman of the administration of the *Sovetskaya Byelorussia*** kolhoz, stated as follows at the Plenary Session of the Minsk Region and City committees of the Party:

"We, collective farm workers, have learned with indignation and anger that Beria, the enemy of the Country, having attained a position of leadership, wanted to hold back the rapid growth of our Socialist agriculture, to take away our happy life as collective farm workers.

---

* Sickle and Hammer.
** Byelorussian SSR.

"Beria, the sworn enemy of the Party and Nation, attempted to break the friendship among the nations of the USSR—the basic foundation of multi-national Socialist State. Under the false pretext of combating violations of the national policy of the Party, he attempted to sow the seeds of discord and hostility among the nations of the USSR and to activate bourgeois and nationalistic elements in the Union Republics."

Comrade Semenenko, Vice-president of the Academy of Science of the Ukrainian Soviet Socialist Republic, declared at the joint Plenary Session of the Kiev Region and City committees of the Party, the following: "Beria, the enemy of the Country, encroached upon the most sacred, that is, on the friendship of the Soviet nations, created by the efforts of our great Party over a period of many years. The friendship of nations constitutes the foundation of our multi-national Soviet State, the main condition of all successes of our brotherly Soviet Republic. Consequently the contemptible enemy directed his attack toward this area. However, nobody will ever succeed in breaking the great cause, which is the friendship of nations. Soon, we will celebrate an important date, i.e., the tercentenary of the union of the Ukrainian Nation with the great Russian Nation. Our Ukrainian Nation will never forget the brotherly aid from the great Russian Nation and will strengthen the friendship with the Russian and other nations of our Country in the future."

Having approved the resolution of the Plenary Session of the Central Committee of the Communist Party, the Party organizations, the entire Soviet Nation closes its ranks even tighter in its solidarity with the Communist Party, its Central Committee and the Soviet Government, and intensifies its efforts in the struggle to implement the policy set forth by the Party.

The Soviet Nation, lead and inspired by the Communist Party, devotes all its energy to peaceful development, to the promotion and intensification of the competition designed to fulfill and to exceed the Fifth Five-Year Plan, increasing in every way possible the power of its Socialist Country, an indestructible stronghold of peace in the entire world.

Engaged in constructive, peaceful work, it watches closely any underhanded plotting by imperialists and their contemptible hirelings and deals crushing blows to the organizers of provocations and adventure. Our Nation constantly promotes friendship with the great Chinese People's Republic. There is no power in the world that could hold back a continuous progressive forward movement of Soviet Society on its way toward Communism.

(*Pravda*, July 11, 1953)

Appendix 21

ON THE MATTER OF APPROVAL OF THE DECREES OF THE PRESIDIUM OF THE SUPREME SOVIET OF THE USSR

Report of the Deputy N. M. Pegov, Secretary of the
Presidium of the Supreme Soviet of the USSR

Comrades! Deputies! The Presidium of the Supreme Soviet of the USSR submits for your consideration the decrees passed after the Fourth Session which are subject to approval by the Supreme Soviet of the USSR.

The Decree of the Presidium of the Supreme Soviet of the USSR of June 26, 1953, concerning the criminal anti-State activities of L. P. Beria, is being submitted for the approval of the Supreme Soviet of the USSR.

The Presidium of the Supreme Soviet of the USSR having considered the report of the Council of Ministers of the USSR concerning the criminal hostile activities of L. P. Beria directed against the Soviet State, the Communist Party, and the Nation, has unseated L. P. Beria from the position of Deputy of the Supreme Soviet of the USSR, has dismissed him from the position of First Deputy Chairman of the USSR Council of Ministers and also lifted all titles and decorations bestowed upon him. At the same time the Presidium of the Supreme Soviet of the USSR has decided to submit the case of the criminal activities of L. P. Beria for the consideration of the Supreme Court of the USSR.

Upon the recommendation of the USSR Council of Ministers, the Presidium of the Supreme Soviet of the USSR at the Session of June 26, 1953, adopted the decree for the establishment of a new All-Union Ministry of Medium Machinery Construction. By the same decree to the newly formed Ministry of Medium Machinery Construction enterprises and organizations have been transferred according to a list which has been approved by the USSR Council of Ministers. The Presidium of the Supreme Soviet of the USSR submits the Decree about the Establishment of the All-Union Ministry of Medium Machinery Construction for the approval of the Supreme Soviet of the USSR.

The Presidium of the Supreme Soviet of the USSR nominated Comrade Maxim Zakharovich Saburov to the post of Chairman of the State Planning Commission of the USSR, relieving him at the same time from the duties of Minister of Machinery Construction of the USSR. Comrade Grigory Petrovich Kosichenko, who occupied previously the post of the Chairman of the State Planning Commission of the USSR, has been relieved from this duty by a Decree of the Presidium of the Supreme Soviet and nominated by the USSR Council of Ministers to the position of the First Deputy Chairman of the State Planning Commission of the USSR.

The Presidium of the Supreme Soviet of the USSR by its Decree of June 30, 1953, relieved Comrade G. N. Safonov from his duties as the General Prosecutor of the USSR and designated Comrade Roman Andreyevich Rudenko to this position. In nominating Comrade Rudenko to the position of General Prosecutor of the USSR the Presidium of the Supreme Soviet of the USSR took into account his sustained work in the capacity of Prosecutor of the Ukrainian SSR, as well as his active participation in State and Public Affairs.

After the Fourth Session (of the Supreme Soviet), the Presidium of the Supreme Soviet decided, upon recommendation of the USSR Council of Ministers, to nominate several Ministers of the USSR.

Comrade Sergey Nikiforovich Kruglov has been nominated to the position of Minister of Internal Affairs of the USSR by the Decree of June 26, 1953.

The Presidium of the Supreme Soviet of the USSR nominated Comrade Vyacheslav Aleksandrovich Malyshev to the position of Minister of Medium Machinery Construction of the USSR, relieving him from the functions of the Minister of Transportation and Heavy Machinery Construction of the USSR.

Comrade Ivan Isidorovich Nosenko has been nominated to the position of Minister of Transportation and Heavy Machinery Construction of the USSR by the Decree of June 29, 1953.

The Presidium of the Supreme Soviet of the USSR introduced some changes in the composition of the Supreme Court of the USSR during the period between the Fourth and the Fifth Session (of the Supreme Soviet). On the basis of the recommendations of the President of the Supreme Court of the USSR the Presidium of the Supreme Soviet nominated to the bench of the Supreme Court of the USSR as members Comrades Nikolay Zakharovich Danilov, Piotr Ivanovich Bardin and Fedor Arkhipovich Belyayev. All above mentioned Comrades have higher law studies to their credit as well as great experience in leading positions of the organs of the Soviet Judiciary. Comrade N. Z. Danilov was active in the agencies of the judiciary since 1932 and lately was a member of the Supreme Court of the Russian Soviet Federated Republic. Comrade P. I. Bardin worked in the Prosecutor's Office from 1936 until 1951 and subsequently was the head of the Law Department of the former Council for Kolhoz Matters for the Government of the USSR. Comrade F. A. Belyayev has been working in the organs of the judiciary for the past twenty-five years and during the last four years was holding the position of Minister of Justice of the RSFSR. The Presidium of the Supreme Soviet of the USSR is submitting the motion to nominate Comrades Danilov, Bardin and Belyayev as members of the Supreme Court of the USSR.

These are the problems which are being submitted for consideration to the Supreme Soviet of the USSR.

The Presidium of the Supreme Soviet of the USSR submits the drafts of respective decrees and asks for their approval.

(*Pravda*, August 9, 1953)

Appendix 22

THE DECREE OF THE PRESIDIUM OF THE SUPREME SOVIET OF THE USSR WITH REGARD TO THE CRIMINAL ANTI-STATE ACTIVITIES OF L. P. BERIA HAS BEEN SUSTAINED

As a result of uncovered criminal anti-State activities of L. P. Beria, which were directed towards the undermining of the Soviet State in the interests of foreign capital, the Supreme Soviet of the Union of Soviet Socialist Republics decrees:

To sustain the Decree of the Presidium of the Supreme Soviet of the USSR relative to his unseating as a Deputy Member of the Supreme Soviet of the USSR, his dismissal from the position of First Deputy to the Chairman of the USSR Council of Ministers, as well as his removal from the post of Minister of Internal Affairs of the USSR with the simultaneous lifting of all titles and decorations bestowed upon him and the submittal of the case of the criminal activities of L. P. Beria for consideration to the Supreme Court of the USSR.

K. Voroshilov, Chairman of the Presidium of the Supreme Soviet of the USSR.

N. Pegov, Secretary of the Presidium of the Supreme Soviet of the USSR. Moscow, Kremlin, August 8, 1953.

(*Pravda*, August 10, 1953)

Appendix 23

PEOPLE'S WRATH

The whole Country took cognizance of the communication of the USSR Prosecutor's Office with regard to the completion of investigation into the case of Beria, traitor to the Country, as well as his accomplices, active participants of the treacherous group of conspirators—Merkulov, Dekanozov, Kobulov, Goglidze, Meshik and Vlodzimirsky. Everywhere in the enterprises, in the offices and educational institutions, on construction sites and in public transportation, in collective farms, machine and tractor stations, crowds are gathering at meetings. The Soviet people angrily brands the traitors to their Country as spies and murderers, and demands a most severe punishment for their most serious crimes.

Monstrous and loathsome are the crimes of these corrupt characters who lost all semblance of being human. There was no evil deed which they would not commit, there was no baseness to which they would not stoop. They sold out and were continuing to sell out the interests of our Country to its worst enemies and planned to restore the capitalist system so obnoxious to the people. They were spying and sabotaging the defense capacity of the Soviet State. They treacherously and inhumanly killed honest Soviet people. In their vile crimes they reached the lowest point of moral decay.

Beria and his accomplices carefully camouflaged their hostile treacherous activity over a period of many years and were deceiving the Party and the Soviet State in a vile manner. The conspirators established as their criminal goal the use of the Agencies of the Ministry of Internal Affairs against the Communist Party and the USSR Government in order to seize power, liquidate the Soviet Workers and Peasants system, restore capitalism in our Country and bring back the rule of the bourgeoisie.

The despicable and base traitors did not and could not have any kind of social backing inside the USSR. All their hopes and plans were resting on the support of their conspiracy by the reactionary imperialist forces abroad.

As the investigation has shown, the organizer of the treacherous group of conspirators had already sold his soul and body to the foreign Intelligence agencies during the years of the Civil War. Having enlisted as a secret agent in the service of the Mussavatist Intelligence Agency in Azerbaijan, which was under the control of English Intelligence, and having established contact with the Menshevik Secret Political Police Department in Georgia, which was also a branch of English Intelligence, Beria was sinking lower and lower on this dirty criminal road. He maintained through all those years secret contacts with counterrevolutionary Georgian Menshevik emigrants, agents of a number of foreign Intelligence agencies. He was also extending collaboration with foreign Intelligence agencies into other fields and protected spies sent into the USSR from the foreign countries from being unmasked and justly punished.

In order to attain these goals—to grasp power and to save himself from being unmasked—Beria did not stop at any means, be they the meanest and vilest. He was using infamous calumny, dirty intrigues, all types of provocations against honest Party workers and Soviet people who were standing in the way of his hostile plans. In this way, and over a period of many years, Beria used intrigues to fight Sergo Ordzhonikidze, a prominent leader of the Communist Party and the Soviet State who, as it now becomes known, nurtured political suspicions insofar as Beria was concerned. After the death of Sergo Ordzhonikidze the conspirators continued to be vindictive towards the members of his family. A coarse arbitrariness and lawlessness, terroristic murders—all these means were applied by Beria and his gang against persons whom they suspected of being in a position to unmask them. In liquidating people objectionable to them they set for themselves the goal of the elimination of cadres who were honest and loyal to the cause of the Communist Party and the Soviet State.

After the demise of J. V. Stalin, the reactionary imperialist forces activated their undermining efforts against the Soviet State. The agency that represented these forces—Beria and his gang of spies—equally increased their activity.The bosses were urging and impatient, and as a result Beria began to redouble his efforts in using the Agencies of the Ministry of Internal Affairs for the seizure of power. He tried very hard to promote to leadership positions in the Ministry of Internal Affairs participants of his conspiratorial group, and the honest workers of the Ministry of Internal Affairs who refused to follow the criminal orders of Beria were subjected to persecution and purge.

Beria used every available means to sabotage the implementation of important decisions of the Party and the Government intended to raise agricultural output and continuously increase the material well-being of the Soviet people. The goal of this sabotage was the undermining of the collective farm system and the creation of production difficulties in the Country. Beria and his accomplices tried to animate anti-Soviet, bourgeois-nationalistic elements in the Union Republics, to sow misunderstanding and hostility between the peoples of our Country and in the first place to undermine the friendship between the peoples of the USSR and the great Russian nation.

When the presumptuous, insolent conspirator Beria redoubled his activities in order to attain his criminal goals the opportunity soon presented itself to unmask him and show the true face of the traitor. As a result of decisive measures taken by the Central Committee of the Party as well as by the Soviet Government his hostile activity was brought to an end. The mask has been torn from the traitors. Unmasked by the testimony of numerous witnesses and by the presentation of genuine documentary evidence, they all pleaded guilty to committing a number of acts of treason.

The announcement of the USSR Prosecutor's Office stating the facts about the monstrous crimes of Beria and his accomplices gave rise to a powerful and violent wave of national wrath, which engulfed the whole Country from one end to another.

"The foul deeds of the traitor Beria and his gang of conspirators," said steel melter Comrade Grebeshkov at a meeting of the Moscow Plant, *Serp i Molot*, are evoking in the heart of every honest Soviet toiler a deeply felt indignation. We are holding up to shame Beria and his accomplices, the hirelings of international capital. The restoration of the capitalist system in our Country, the restoration of rule of the bourgeoisie—this is what the scoundrels were dreaming of accomplishing! Let them now feel the full impact of the popular indignation! We are convinced that Soviet justice will punish the criminals with the utmost severity. And furthermore that this sentence will constitute the true verdict of the entire Nation, the expression of its feelings and its indignation. We will close our ranks even tighter around the Central Committee of the Party and the Soviet Government and we will not spare our efforts in order to continuously strengthen the power of our Country."

"Our people understand perfectly well that the criminal activities of Beria and his gang were directed against the greatest achievements of workers of all countries—against the Soviet Social and State system, against the inviolable union of the working class and the peasantry, against the life in freedom of the Soviet people." Comrade Chapygin, a collective farm worker of the Agricultural Cooperative *Pushkin* of the Fatezhsky District in the Kursky Region in this way started his speech at the collective farm meeting—by telling the story of his life and his work.

In conclusion he said: ". . . And now the vile traitor Beria planned to undermine the collective farm system which constitutes the basis of a prosperous and cultural life of Soviet peasants. Having set this as his aim he was damaging agriculture, he was preventing the Party from improving the collective and farms, and prevented us, the collective farm workers, from increasing productivity; simultaneously he strived also to create production difficulties in the Country. There is no mercy and there will be none for the enemies of the people, for spies and saboteurs!"

The voice of Soviet intelligentsia is merging with the voices of the working class and collective farm workers. During a speech at the Academy of Sciences of the Georgian SSR its President, Comrade Muskholishvili, declared:

"I am expressing everybody's thoughts and feelings when I say that no perfidious intrigues of our enemies are able to shake our love and trust of the great Russian people. The intelligentsia of the Georgian SSR together with the working class and peasantry demands the most severe punishment of the contemptible conspirators, traitors to their country, sworn enemies of the people."

The workers are declaring at their meetings that they will raise even higher their revolutionary vigilance, this tested weapon of the Soviet people against all and sundry enemies of our Country and that they will multiply their efforts in their struggle to strengthen the power of the Soviet State. The unanimity, which reigns at all meetings of industrial workers in the cities, collective farm workers and intelligentsia, the angry indignation, which accompanies the branding of the criminal deeds of the contemptible conspirators by all the nations of the USSR, show again and again the extent of the solidarity of the Soviet people with the Party and the Government, and the immense force of the great and inviolable unity of the Party, the Government and the Nation.

Expressing its anger and indignation about the monstrous misdeeds of Beria and his gang, the Soviet people at the same time are stating with the greatest satisfaction that the criminal group of conspirators has been unmasked and disarmed. The Party and the Government took decisive measures insuring the unflinching observance of the Soviet Socialist Law, the establishment of a continuous and systematic control by Party organizations of all the segments of the Soviet structure, among them also the Agencies of the Ministry of Internal Affairs. By adoption of these measures an end has been put once and for all to a situation where all sorts of adventurers and career-climbers as well as hostile scouts would be able to sneak inside the Agencies of the Ministry of Internal Affairs and use the apparatus of the Ministry of Internal Affairs for their criminal ends, that is, against the Party and the Government, against the honest cadres of the Party and the Soviet State which were devoted to the cause of Communism.

The Soviet people threw away from their path, as a bunch of venomous snakes, this band, of contemptible traitors, agents of international capitalism. The powerful surge of the Nation will sweep away from the face of the earth these anti-Soviet mean wretches, these pitiful pygmies, who dared to lift their hand against our Party, against our dear Country. The great Communist Party of the Soviet Union, united like a monolith, with ranks rallied closely around its Central Committee, unbreakably connected with the Nation and with the working masses through blood ties, continues to resolutely and steadfastly lead the Country forward along the glorious path of building Communism. And there is not a single power in this world that could stop this victorious movement of the great Soviet nation, the builder of Communism!

(*Pravda*, December 20, 1953)

Appendix 24

THE ANGRY VOICE OF THE SOVIET PEOPLE

During these days at the industrial and transportation enterprises, at the collective farms, machine tractor stations and across the entire Country, worker meetings are taking place with large crowds being present in connection with the announcement of the USSR Prosecutor's Office on completing the investigation into the case of the foul traitor Beria and his associates—Merkulov, Dekanozov, Kobulov, Goglidze, Meshik, and Vlodzimirsky. The industrial and collective farm workers, the Soviet intelligentsia and the entire Soviet nation are holding up to shame the infamous traitors and conspirators and are unanimously demanding a severe punishment for this band of spies and murderers.

Nursing a base hate towards our people and the Communist Party, the conspirators established the seizure of power as the goal of their criminal activity, as well as the liquidation of the Soviet Worker and Peasant System, the restoration of capitalism and reestablishment of the bourgeois supremacy in our Country. Deprived of any social support inside the USSR, Beria and his associates based their perfidious plans on the support of their conspiracy by the foreign reactionary imperialistic forces.

The investigation completed by the Prosecutor's Office established the fact that the organizer of the group of conspirators, Beria, first became a hireling of foreign Intelligence during the time of the Civil War. In the year 1919, Beria, during his stay in Baku, was guilty of an act of betrayal by accepting the post of a secret agent in the service of the Intelligence of the counterrevolutionary Mussavat regime in Azerbaijan, which was acting under the control of English Intelligence agencies. In the year 1920, Beria, during his stay in Georgia, again committed a traitorous act by establishing a secret contact with the Menshevik Secret Political Police Department in Georgia, which was representing the English Intelligence Service. Following the path of treachery and betrayal Beria continued to expand his spy contacts with foreign Intelligence agencies in the following years. He established and maintained secret contacts with counterrevolutionary Georgian Menshevik émigrés and with Intelligence agents of capitalist countries. The despicable lackey of the bourgeoisie, the hireling of the foreign capital, Beria shielded the foreign spies sent into the USSR from being unmasked.

Acting in the interest of the foreign capital the traitorous group of conspirators, hostile to the Soviet State, established as their goal the use of the Agencies of the Ministry of the Interior, both the central as well as the local ones, against the Communist Party and the USSR Government, as well as for the seizure of power and the reestablishment of the supremacy of the bourgeoisie in our Country.

Beria and his associates were painstakingly masking and hiding their hostile treacherous activity over a period of years, deceiving the Party and the Soviet State. In order to capture power and avoid being exposed, the conspirators did not shrink from using any available means. They used the most vile slander, dirty intrigues of any kind and provocations against honest Party members and Soviet workers. The investigation has shown that Beria, over a period of years, with the aid of his associates was conducting a criminal intrigue against Sergo Ordzhonikidze, the prominent leader of the Communist Party and the Soviet State. As it has now become known, Sergo Ordzhonikidze was imbued with political distrust of Beria. After Sergo Ordzhonikidze's death the conspirators continued to persecute members of his family with their vindictiveness.

Beria and his band dealt cruelly with men on whose part they feared exposure, perpetrated acts of crass arbitrariness and lawlessness against them, even committed terroristic murders. The investigation also disclosed other facts of crimes committed by Beria, which bear testimony to his deep moral degradation.

After the death of J. V. Stalin the reactionary imperialist forces initiated their subversive activity against the Soviet State. Obedient to the command of his lords Beria accelerated his activity in order to achieve his criminal goals. Striving to place the Agencies of the Ministry of Internal Affairs above the Party and Government and to use these Agencies for the capture of power, Beria started to promote members of the conspiracy group to a number of leading positions, at the same time victimizing and persecuting honest workers of the Ministry of Internal Affairs who would not execute his criminal orders.

In order to undermine the collective farm system and create food supply difficulties in the Country, Beria used every means to sabotage and interfere with the implementation of the important measures taken by the Party and the Government directed towards development of collective and State farms and the continuous improvement of the well-being of the Soviet people. Beria and his co-participants undertook criminal measures with the view of bringing back to life the remnants of the bourgeois nationalistic elements in the Union Republics, to sow hate and dissension between the peoples of the USSR and in the first place to undermine the friendship between the peoples of the USSR and the great Russian nation.

The high-handed and insolent enemy Beria, striving to take over power, activated his hostile actions which eventually permitted the unmasking of this traitor and showed his true face. As a result of drastic measures taken by the Central Committee of the Party and the Soviet

Government, an end has been put to the hostile activity of Beria. Beria and his associates pleaded guilty to having committed very grave State crimes when they were faced with the testimony of witnesses and factual documented data during the investigation.

At crowded meetings workers express their boundless anger towards the gang of conspirators that were caught redhanded and unmasked.

At the meeting of the collective of the Kiev *Karl Marx* Factory, old-time worker Comrade Rozhkova, who worked at this enterprise for 30 years, made a speech. She declared:

"The monsters of the human race who sold themselves out to the foreign capital planned to commit a terrible crime. The traitor Beria and his assistants strived to deprive us of the possibility of living and working in freedom by handing us over into the serfdom of the bourgeoisie. This did not and will not succeed! The gang of spies and murderers has been unmasked and disarmed. We will unite even more closely around our own Communist Party and the Soviet Government."

The Soviet citizens in their passionate, emotional pronouncements declared that no enemy will succeed in depriving the Soviet people of the great achievements brought by the October Revolution—that is, of our Social and State system, the most progressive in the whole world, the unbreakable union of the working class with the peasants and a life in freedom of the Soviet people. The union of the working class with the toiling peasants constitutes an immovable base of the Soviet system, the source for every achievement in the economic and cultural development of our Country and in the building of Communism.

Collective farm worker I. Ziborov said at the meeting of the agricultural cooperative *Probuzhdenye*:* "The foul criminals Beria and his associates tried to undermine the collective farm system, destroy the kolhozes and cause foodstuff difficulties in the Country. These degenerates planned to take away from us everything that we had acquired through collective work and convert the collective farm workers into slaves. The spy Beria and his gang be damned!"

The strength of the Soviet people rests on its unity and closeness with the Communist Party, in a limitless devotion to the idea of Communism. The unbreakable union of the peoples of the USSR constitutes the source for the strength of the Soviet State. The workers in our Country are constantly strengthening the brotherly friendship and cooperation of the peoples of the Soviet Union and guard it, like the apple of one's eye, against the infringements of all enemies. Comrade Zairov, a worker of the Tashkent Agricultural Machinery Plant, stated at the meeting of the collective:

---

* *Awakening.*

"The conspirators tried to make an encroachment on the friendship of nations of the USSR. But all their efforts are in vain. Nobody will be able to sow dissension in our one, single family. The nations of the Soviet Union became intimately connected with each other for all times in the fires of the Great October Revolution, in a victorious drive towards Communism. The strength of the Soviet Worker and Peasant State lies in our unity, in our friendship fostered by the Communist Party. The traitor Beria and his associates went against the people and the people will severely punish them."

At the meetings of workers or peasants or Soviet intelligentsia resolutions are being adopted unanimously that contain the demand to punish severely the traitors of the Fatherland. The sentiment of unanimity that reigns at the meetings of workers once more emphasizes the powerful force of the moral and political unity of our nation, its solidarity with the Party and Government.

The Party teaches the Soviet people to be at arms at all times against the intrigues of the imperialist reaction and its agents. Our duty is to increase in every possible way the vigilance and always repulse the hostile acts of the capitalist encirclement. Revolutionary vigilance constitutes a weapon against all enemies. This weapon therefore should be kept ready for action at all times.

The great power of our State lies in the unbreakable unity of the Party, the Government and the Nation. Rallied behind the Communist Party and the Soviet Government our Nation will rub off the face of the earth the pitiful pygmies who dared to raise their hand against our Socialist Fatherland. Under the leadership of the Communist Party the Soviet nation marches confidently along the path of building Communism.

(*Izvestia*, December 23, 1953)

In the next column of the same issue *Izvestia* announced the voices of angered Soviet citizens from all over the country, shaped in the article:

Soviet People Are Saying: There Is No Mercy and There Will Be None For the Enemies Of The People!
The Unity Of The Peoples of the USSR Is Indestructible

Tashkent, 22 December. (By telephone from our own correspondent.) In the plants, factories, scientific research establishments, collective and state farms of the Uzbekistan meetings of workers are taking place.

At the meeting of the collective of the Tashkent Plant *Elevator* Comrade Yusupov, a turner, made a speech. He said:

"The criminal gang of Beria established as their goal the destruction of our own Soviet Government for which the workers and peasants spilled their blood. The foul enemies of the people, acting on orders of capitalists, tried to sow dissension among the nations of the Soviet Union and undermine the strength of our Socialist State. The traitors miscalculated. The unity of the peoples of the USSR is indestructible. We are infinitely grateful to the Communist Party and to the Soviet Government for having unmasked Beria and his gang."

At the meeting of the collective of the Academy of Sciences of the Uzbek SSR the Secretary of the Academy, Comrade Yunusov, declared:

"The Soviet Government has shown to the nations of our Country the clear path leading toward a free and happy life. Uzbekistan changed in a short period of time from a backward Tsarist colony into one of the developing Republics, thanks to the Soviet Administration. We will not allow the bourgeois hirelings, spies and murderers to restore capitalism. The Soviet Court should severely punish Beria and his associates. No mercy should be given to the enemies of the people!"

Traitors Cannot Escape the Day of Reckoning

Kishinev, 22 December. (By telephone from our own correspondent.) In the cities and villages of Moldavia meetings of workers are taking place, gathering large crowds. The factory workers and the peasants on the collective farms and the intelligentsia are holding up to shame the hirelings of foreign capitalists—Beria and his associates. They are declaring that traitors cannot escape the day of reckoning.

"The contemptible degenerates overreached themselves," declared Comrade Shevchenko, a worker of the Kishinev Hosiery and Underwear Factory. "They wanted to disturb the friendship of nations in our Country and reestablish capitalism," she stated. "However, these perfidious plans of the enemies have been destroyed. Soviet people are rallying to the Central Committee of the Communist Party and to the Soviet Government. The people and the Party are united and invincible."

Unanimous Will of the People

Kuybyshev, 22 December. (By telephone from our own correspondent.) Everywhere in the Region workers' meetings are taking place in connection with the communication of the USSR Prosecutor's Office. At these meetings a unanimous will of the people is being expressed to severely punish the foul traitors of the Fatherland—Beria and his accomplices.

At the meeting in the Club of the Plant *Avtotraktorodetal** a blacksmith, Comrade Manukhin, made a speech. He said:

---

* Auto-tractor-parts.

"We will raise our revolutionary vigilance even higher and we will close our ranks around the Communist Party and the Soviet Government even closer."

Thousands of workers, engineers and technicians of the Kuybyshev repairing plant, in a unanimously adopted resolution declare that they demand a severe punishment for the enemies of the people.

To Do Everything in One's Power to Realize a Great Goal

With the feeling of great anger and indignation towards the traitors to the Fatherland, the Soviet people met the communication of the USSR Prosecutor's Office on the completion of the investigation in the case of Beria, the traitor to the Fatherland.

Beria and his associates used all means, as low as they could be, in order to accomplish their base goals: the liquidation of the Soviet system, the restoration of capitalism in our Country. The agent of international imperialism Beria used all means: the undermining of the economic and military strength of the Soviet Union, the fight against measures of the Party and the Government, taken with the view of developing agriculture and improving the material well-being of the Soviet people.

Beria tried to sow discord between the nations of our Country, to breathe life into the remnants of the bourgeois and nationalistic elements in the Union Republics.

Our Country constitutes a model of a multi-national state. The Communist Party insured a real equality of nations by strengthening by all means the bonds of friendship between the Nations of the Country of Socialism. Both the small as well as the large nations of our Country reached a high level of development of all their material and spiritual potentials. A striking example of this development is the Tatar SSR.

The Tatar Republic is recording an unprecedented growth of its economy and cultural life with the help of the great Russian people within the brotherly family of nations. The former Kazan province numbered a few small-capacity domestic and primitive enterprises and a primitive agriculture as well. The Kazan province ranked 44th among the 50 provinces of tsarist Russia in literacy. That is how it was. Look how the Tatar Republic is changed at the present time: Dozens of large plants and factories have been built there. The volume of industrial production increased 56 times as compared with 1913. Socialist agriculture has been supplied with powerful machinery.

At the present time there are 13 establishments of higher education, a branch of the USSR Academy of Sciences, 46 technical and pedagogical schools, 3,676 schools, out of which 1,659 have Tatarian as their language of instruction. Two million students are being instructed in the schools alone. There were 3,289 houses of culture, clubs, museums, theatres and other cultural and instructive establishments organized in the Republic.

The indestructible friendship of nations constitutes one of the most important achievements of the Socialist system. The despicable traitor Beria stretched his polluted hands to tear down this achievement. He tried to drive a wedge into the friendship of the peoples, using Jesuit methods, and by the same token to weaken our Country. In this he did not succeed. Nobody ever will succeed in dividing the nations of the USSR and bringing back conditions which were relegated to the past. The wheel of history cannot be turned back. Whoever will try to do it will be mercilessly swept aside. The great unity of the Party and the people is a guarantee of it.

We, the Soviet scientists, along with workers, peasants, and the intelligentsia, demand a severe punishment for the traitors of our Fatherland. Together with the entire Soviet nation we will ceaselessly build Communism in our Country and offer all our strength and knowledge to achieve this lofty goal.

Academician B. Arbuzov, City of Kazan.

Sacred Friendship of the Soviet People

Yerevan, 22 December. (By telephone from our own correspondent.) The workers of Armenia unanimously demand a severe punishment for the traitors of the Fatherland—Beria and his assistants.

At the meeting of workers and employees of the machine tool plant named after Dzerzhinsky a speech was made by the high-speed turner, T. Tumaykyan.

"The base hirelings of international capitalism who managed by deceit to occupy responsible Government positions were ready to take over power in order to deprive us of our happy way of life and push us into a capitalist slavery. The enemies of the people miscalculated. The friendship of the nations of the USSR is sacred and unbreakable. We, the workers, demand from the Supreme Court severe punishment for Beria and his stooges."

Comrade Tumaykyan urged the collective of the plant to increase the revolutionary vigilance and work without respite for the further strengthening of the might of our Fatherland.

At the meeting held in the Republican Academy of Sciences its President, Academician V. Ambarsumyan, took the floor and said:

"The communication of the USSR Prosecutor's Office shows that Beria and his accomplices were experienced professional provocateurs and murderers. Beria strived to sow hostility among the nations of the USSR. This will never happen! I shall express the general sentiment and conviction when I state that love and friendship and devotion towards the great Russian nation is the object of our pride and guarantee of the development of the Armenian as well as all other Soviet nations. The Soviet people will rally even closer around its Communist Party and the Soviet Government and will resolutely continue its march towards the victory of Communism."

Meetings, which gathered large crowds, were held at Yerevan plants and factories, at enterprises at Leninakan, Kirovakan, at collective and state farms of the Ararat Valley.

Participants of all meetings unanimously adopted resolutions in which they demand a severe punishment for the traitors of the Fatherland. The workers of Armenia are assuring the Central Committee of the Communist Party of the Soviet Union and the Soviet Government that they will apply all their efforts in order to fulfill the historic tasks set by the Nineteenth Party Congress and by the September Plenary Sessions of the Central Committee of the Communist Party of the Soviet Union.

The Traitors Be Damned!

Rustavi, 22 December. (By telephone from our own correspondent.) Steel melter Sh. Kukhaleyshvili took the floor at the meeting of the Transcaucasian metallurgical plant named after Stalin, and said:

"It is difficult to express in words the anger towards Beria and his gang. The hirelings of foreign capital planned to deprive the Soviet people of its free and happy life and in order to achieve their base goals they did not stop at any abomination. Judas Beria established secret connections with the agents of foreign Intelligence services, counterrevolutionary Menshevik-émigrés, the bloody enemies of the Georgian people. We demand merciless punishment for Beria and the band of his co-participants."

Let Us Rally Closer around the Party

Sverdlovsk, 22 December. (By telephone from our own correspondent.) Worker meetings are taking place at the enterprises of the Ural area in connection with the announcement of the USSR Prosecutor's Office regarding the case of Beria, the enemy of the people and the traitor of the Fatherland.

Rolling mill operator Comrade Zheleznyakov took the floor at the meeting of the workers and employees of the metallurgical plant named after Serov. He declared:

"A conspiratorial group knocked together by the most vile enemy of the people, Beria, has been made harmless and is being handed over to the court. There is no such power on earth that could turn history back. The robbers who tried to sell us into capitalist slavery should be severely punished. There should be no mercy for the traitors of the Fatherland! We, the metallurgical workers, like all toilers of our Country, will close our ranks even tighter around the Central Committee of the Communist Party and the Soviet Government. The collective of our shop fulfilled its annual production quota on schedule. We shall deliver by January 1 thousands of tons of rolled steel above the plan for our beloved Fatherland."

Team leader Comrade Kharlov addressed the meeting at the sheet rolling shop of the Alapayev metallurgical plant. He said:

"We will have no pity for all those who raise their hand against the achievements of the Great October Socialist Revolution."

In their resolution the sheet rolling mill operators demand that the severest punishment be applied to Beria and his co-participants.

State Criminals Should Be Severely Punished

Ryazan, 22 December. (By telephone from our own correspondent.) In plants and factories, in collective farms, machine tractor stations and in state farms crowds gather at meetings. The workers of the whole Region hold up to shame Beria and his associates, a gang of hirelings of the international capital and demand severe punishment for the criminals.

In the *Krasnyy Ugolok** of the Mervinskaya Machine Tractor Station a gathering of tractor and combine operators as well as agricultural specialists took place.

The chief engineer of the machine tractor station, Comrade Chikolodkov declared:

"The Beria group of conspirators established as their goal the seizure of power and the liquidation of the Soviet system in our Country in the interest of international capitalism. We are full of anger and indignation, we demand severe punishment of the criminals. We will even more resolutely strengthen the power of our Socialist Fatherland!"

Taking the floor at a meeting, the tractor operator Surov declared:

"There is no place on Soviet soil for the foul traitors of the Fatherland —Beria and his gang. They are not human, they are degenerates. They should be mercilessly punished. In the name of all tractor operators I declare: We will toil with all our might in order to strengthen our powerful Fatherland marching towards Communism. We shall rally even closer around the Communist Party and the Soviet Government."

The collective of the Mervinskaya Machine Tractor Station completed the quarterly tractor overhaul quota on time. Machine operators and agricultural specialists pledged at the meeting to overhaul all tractors and machines by February 1.

(*Izvestia*, December 23, 1953)

---

* *The Red Corner* (workers' recreation room).

Appendix 25

ALL NATIONS OF THE USSR ARE UNANIMOUS IN THEIR
DEMAND FOR SEVERE PUNISHMENT OF THE
SPIES AND TRAITORS TO THEIR COUNTRY—
BERIA AND HIS GANG

The Russian Federation

Employes' meetings are being held in the cities and villages of the Russian Federation. Workers, employes and farm laborers are unanimously demanding a severe punishment of Beria, the enemy of the Soviet Nation, and other participants of the group of conspirators which he organized.

Comrade Yemelyanova, a worker at the Cast Iron Shop No. 3 of the Moscow automobile plant, named after Stalin, has stated the following at the meeting of the collective:

"All actions of the Communist Party and the Soviet Government are directed towards the improvement of the nation's living conditions," she said. "Attempting to hamper the implementation of the necessary measures, undertaken by the Party and Government, intended to improve agriculture and to raise the material well-being of workers, Beria wanted to undermine the collective farm system, to drive a wedge between the working class and the peasantry, as well as to create difficulties in the Country's food supply system. Speaking for thousands of workers of our automobile plant I demand that Beria, the malicious enemy of the Soviet Nation, meets the deserved punishment for his crimes."

Comrade Dubrava, head of the Department of History of Technology, in an emotional speech at a meeting of professors, lecturers, students and employes of the Leningrad Mining Institute, stated:

"Beria, the rabid enemy of the Soviet Nation, and his conspirators, intended to put an end to the grandiose achievements not only of our people, but of workers of all countries: namely, he wanted to liquidate our Soviet workers' and peasants' system; intended to take away the free way of life from the Soviet Nation, its sublime laws; to revive the capitalist system and to restore domination by the bourgeoisie."

The orator, loudly applauded by the entire audience, also stated that: "The collective of the Institute, consisting of thousands of members, together with the entire Soviet Nation, demands that the Special Session of the Supreme Court of the USSR punish the foul conspirators, renegades and traitors without any mercy."

Mass meetings of workers and employes were held at establishments of Stalingrad, a heroic city. The toilers are unanimously demanding severe punishment of the odious enemies of the people.

Comrade Zabora, foreman, commented with indignation at the meeting of the blooming shop at the *Krasnyy Oktyabr** plant about the foul activities of Beria:

"Beria intended to use the organs of the Ministry of Internal Affairs in order to seize power and to put an end to the Soviet system. We, the metallurgists, demand severe punishment of the traitor and renegade, Beria, as well as of all the members of his vile gang of murderers and spies."

The miners of the Kuznetsk Coal Basin with indignation are holding up to shame the traitors to the Country. A coal loader, Comrade Cherepanov, at the meeting of workers of the mine named after Kirov, stated as follows:

"Beria, the worst enemy of the Soviet people, and his accomplices have effectively been exposed. Through all these years, Beria maintained and widened his treacherous connections with the foreign Secret Service. He could not have had and there was no popular backing for him in the Country; the only thing he could count on was assistance on the part of reactionary foreign powers. The Party has torn the mask from the foul conspirators. The vile creature will be destroyed without mercy!"

Pravda's correspondents are reporting about numerous meetings of workers from the following cities: Gorky, Rostov-on-the-Don, Petropavlovsk-in-Kamchatka, Ryazan, Vladivostok, Kuybyshev, Molotov, Kirov, Kazan, Makhachkala, and other cities.

Ukraine

At a spacious building of the thin sheet rolling shop of the *Zaporozhye Metallurgical Plant*, hundreds of smelters and rolling mill operators gathered here at the time of a shift change.

A rolling mill operator, Comrade Kapsheyev, declared: "It is difficult to express the anger and indignation that fill our hearts. Perfidious agents of international imperialism wanted to destroy our Soviet State, to restore the domination of the bourgeoisie, and to subject the Soviet Nation to the bondage of foreign capital. For this crime alone, the foul traitors should be destroyed like venomous snakes. In addition, these monsters committed also other serious crimes—they created lawlessness and arbitrariness, killed honest people by whom they feared to be exposed; they attempted to undermine the collective farm system, to create problems in the Country's food supply system to sow seeds of distrust and hostility among the nations of the USSR. They cannot expect any mercy: the Soviet Nation is unanimous in its demand for the most severe punishment for these foul and contemptible conspirators!"

---

* *The Red October.*

The thoughts and feelings of the *Zaporozhye's* metallurgists are being fully shared by the workers in the city of Lvov.

A locksmith, Comrade Grabovsky, at the meeting of the collective of the *Lvov Agricultural Machinery Plant*, stated as follows:

"Beria and his accomplices attempted to destroy the Soviet system. But this system, created by the people itself, is dear to and cherished by the people. They are the worst enemies of the people—that is, Beria and his gang. And the Soviet nation will severely punish the foul traitors."

Comrade Ivasyuta, a young scientist, came forward at the meeting of the staff of the Lvov branch of the Academy of Science of the Ukrainian Soviet Socialist Republic. He stated: "Traitor Beria has committed criminal acts in order to revive and to activate the bourgeois-nationalistic elements in the Union Republics, among others, also in our parts of the Country, in the Western regions of the Ukraine: to sow the seeds of misunderstanding among the nations of the USSR, and in the first place, to undermine the friendship of the nations of the USSR with the great Russian Nation. The criminal design of traitors had been shattered into smithereens by our indestructible solidarity, by our unity and friendship."

A meeting of the Soviet Writers of the Ukraine was held in Kiev. P. Tychin, a well-known Ukrainian poet, declared at the lectern:

"Beria wore a mask throughout his entire life, in order to seize power, to deceive the Party, to deceive the Nation.

"This villain wanted to undermine the basis of our multi-national State —that is, the friendship of the nations within the USSR; in particular, he wanted to wreck a centuries-old blood-cemented friendship of the Ukrainian Nation with the great Russian Nation. This provocative attempt has been exposed and liquidated. Let those reactionary imperialist circles abroad, which are basing their designs on such human scum as Beria and his gang, remember once and for all that all attempts aiming to destroy the Soviet system and to restore the domination by the bourgeoisie in our Country have been crushed and will be crushed in the future by the great and indestructible unity of the Party, Government and the entire Nation!"

Reports are coming in about the anger and indignation of the Ukrainian Nation from Kharkov, Kherson, Odessa, Voroshilovgrad, Poltava, Nikolayev, Uzhgorod, and other cities and areas of the Ukraine.

Byelorussia

The collective farm peasants, the workers of the Machine and Tractor Station and of the State farms, jointly with all working people of Soviet Byelorussia demand the highest penalty for Beria, the enemy of the

Nation, and for the members of the gang of traitors which he organized.

Over 300 collective farm workers gathered in the spacious club of the agricultural co-op named after Kirov in the Vetkovsk District of the Gomel Region.

Comrade Iokov, secretary of the collective farm Party Organization, read to the collective farm workers the communication of the USSR Public Prosecutor's Office.

Comrade Pysikov, manager of the collective farm asked to be heard. He declared: "Villain Beria and his gang attempted to encroach upon our collective farm system. They attempted to hinder the development of our agriculture under various pretexts. They impeded the vital decisions related to collective farm production problems; they wanted to create artificially problems in the food supply system of the cities and industrial centers. Let the Soviet Judiciary lower its penal sword on the heads of the despicable bandits, without mercy."

Comrade Golos, a worker of the machine shop of the Baranovichi railroad car barn, declared during the time of a discussion with regard to the communiqué of the Office of the Public Prosecutor of the USSR:

"We are working, sparing no sweat of our brow, in order for our Country to grow stronger, to become even more powerful, to move more swiftly towards Communism. But the contemptible conspirators attempted to interfere with our efforts; they were sabotaging and killing honest Party workers, who were standing in the way of the criminal designs of this gang. We demand that the traitors of the Nation receive the highest punishment."

Georgia

Well-attended workers' meetings were held in all shops of the Transcausian Metallurgical Plant named after Stalin in Rustavi. Comrade Kukhaleyshvili, smelter, spoke at the meeting of the open hearth furnace shop:

"It has been established," stated he, "that as far back as 1920, Beria made connections with the Menshevik Secret Political Police, which was a branch of British Intelligence. Throughout the subsequent years, he was tied in with the worst enemies of the Georgian Nation, i.e., with the counterrevolutionary Georgian émigrés—Mensheviks—who joined a foreign Intelligence Service long ago. This old spy and provocateur, who wangled his way into positions of leadership through slander and intrigues, conducted an infamous policy designed to undermine the friendship among the Soviet nations. The Georgian Nation demands severe punishment for the traitor and provocateur, Beria, and all participants of his gang."

In the unanimously adopted resolution, the metallurgists of Rustavi assure the Central Committee of the Communist Party of the USSR and the Soviet Government that they will spare no efforts and energy in order to successfully fulfill the decisions of the Nineteenth Congress of the Party, of the Fifth Session of the Supreme Council of the USSR, and of the September Plenary Session of the Central Committee of the Communist Party of the Soviet Union. The metallurgists demand that the Special Judicial Session of the Supreme Court of the USSR pass the severest sentence on Beria, enemy of the Nation, and his accomplices.

Similar demands were adopted at the meetings of workers and employes of plants and factories in Tbilisi, Kutaisi, Batumi, and other cities in the Georgian Soviet Socialist Republic.

Kazakhstan

Collective farm workers of the agricultural co-op named after Kalinin in the Alma-Ata District held a meeting in a spacious courtyard. Sarmulda Baymuldayev, a collective farm worker, having carefully listened to the communiqué of the Office of the Public Prosecutor of the USSR, asked to be heard. He said:

"The enemy and traitor Beria, together with his stooges wanted to divert our Country from the bright road along which our Party leads us. He nurtured a despicable design: to stir up discord among the nations of the USSR to undermine their friendship with the great Russian Nation. I, the old Sarmulda, say: this will never happen! We will not let our sacred friendship be broken. The Russian Nation, our own Communist Party and the Soviet Government helped us to make Kazakhstan a flourishing Country, to build many plants, to create collective farms, to open schools, clubs and hospitals. The stronger our friendship with all nations in the Soviet Union will become, the brighter will flourish our Kazakh Republic. This is why I, a collective farm shepherd, who does not want to be a hired man for a bey, demand with all the Soviet peoples: destroy the mad dog, Beria, and his accomplices!"

Zeynep Bekstayeva, a collective farm worker, warmly supported Baymuldayev. "Do you think it is possible," she exclaimed, "to spare those who wanted to make our life miserable and hopeless again as it was during the tsarist period!"

Raimbek Zhamankeyev, head of the dairy and cattle collective farm, spoke warmly and sincerely about the Communist Party, about the Soviet Government, which is vigilantly standing watch for the freedom and independence of all Soviet Nations and will never permit the Soviet people to fall into the bondage of the bourgeoisie.

Well-attended meetings of workers were held also at plants and factories in Alma-Ata, Semipalatinsk, Pavlodar, Karaganda, and other cities of the Republic.

Tadzhikistan

The Tadzhik Nation is filled with a deep indignation. It condemns traitors of the Country, Beria and his gang, and speaks with an anger and contempt about those criminals who lost all human qualities.

"Beria and his stooges," stated Kabul Sanginov, a foreman of a shift at the Stalinabad Cotton Gin-Mill, "wanted to turn us backwards into that dark past when we lived like slaves. What a vile treachery, what a heinous crime against the Nation! We demand severe punishment of the contemptible scoundrels, who traded our life and freedom!"

The voice of collective farm workers in Tadzhikistan has an angry tone. K. Razakov, a Hero of Socialist Labor, stated at the meeting of the collective farm named after Zhdanov, in Molotovabad District:

"The enemies of our Country attempted many times to undermine the friendship among nations of the Soviet Union. But the friendship among our nations is eternal and inviolable. This friendship makes our Country powerful and strong like granite. There is no place and there cannot be any place on our soil for traitors and provocatuers!"

Pravda's correspondents also report workers' meetings in Turkmenistan, Uzbekistan, Kirgizia, Azerbaijan, Armenia, Moldavia, Lithuania, Latvia, Estonia, the Karelian Autonomous Soviet Socialist Republic—from all the Soviet Republics. The nations of the USSR, time and again demonstrate a close solidarity in their support of the Party and Government and their unanimity in their demand of a severe sentence for the traitors of the Country—Beria and his accomplices.

(*Pravda*, December 23, 1953)

Appendix 26

NO MERCY FOR TRAITORS AND SPIES— SUCH IS THE UNANIMOUS DEMAND OF ALL SOVIET PEOPLES

Yesterday, meetings were taking place at establishments, in collective and State farms, on construction projects and in institutions. The Soviet Nation angrily censures Beria and his accomplices, demanding that these sworn enemies be banished from the face of the earth.

The Gang of Conspirators Should Be Destroyed

Poltava, 23 December. (By *Pravda's* correspondent.) A wave of the Nation's anger is rising in the villages of the Poltava Region; collective farm workers are holding up to shame the despicable degenerate of the human race, Beria, and his accomplices.

Ivan Cherednik, brigadier of the 5th field team, made a stirring speech at a meeting of the agricultural cooperative named after Stalin, in Reshetilov District:

"The Ukrainian Nation," he stated, "remembers well and will never forget the terror and the sufferings to which it was subjected during foreign enslavement under the yoke of invaders. Beria, a traitor of the Country, and spy, had a preposterous, conspiratorial design against the Soviet system and intended to thrust again our Nation into the bondage of the international capital. But this will never happen! We stand behind our own Soviet Authority, our own National Government, which has given us happy living conditions. Look, how flourishing are our Ukrainian villages in the brotherly family of happy nations! Cursing the robbers and traitors, we, the descendants of Bogdan Khmelnitsky say: nobody will ever succeed in wrecking the firm friendship of the Ukrainian Nation with the great Russian Nation."

Maria Yeremenko, team leader, expressing the unanimous feelings of all the collective farm workers present at the meeting declared:

"The Special Session of the Supreme Court of the USSR hears the angry voice of the entire Soviet Nation. The gang of killers and conspirators organized by the spy, Beria, should be wiped from the face of the earth!"

WE WILL CRUSH TRAITORS AS WE WOULD POISONOUS SNAKES

Frunze, 23 December. (By *Pravda's* correspondent.) Meetings of employes are being held at enterprises, collective and State farms, at establishments and educational institutions throughout the Republic. The intelligentsia of Kirgizia, jointly with the industrial and agricultural workers, censure the criminal, treacherous activities of Beria, the worst enemy of the Nation.

Comrade Fursunov, Candidate of Agricultural Sciences, speaking at a meeting of the Kirghiz Livestock Science and Research Institute, stated:

"Beria and his stooges, enemies of the Country, reached for the most precious thing—i.e., for our own Government of Workers and Peasants which was won with the blood of many sons of our Socialist Country. They wanted to reestablish capitalism, destroy the collective farm system and force the Soviet Nation under the domination of capitalism. Agents of international capitalism attempted to sow the seeds of discord among the nations of our multi-national Country. But the criminal designs of the enemies of the Country have been exposed and destroyed. The Soviet Nation holds up to shame the renegades of the Country and demands an imposition of the highest punishment for them by the Supreme Court of the USSR. We shall rally even closer around our native Communist Party and Soviet Government and we declare that everyone who attempts to take away the power from the Soviet Government, or the freedom and independence of our Country, shall be crushed like a poisonous snake."

EXPRESSIONS OF INDIGNATION BY THE BUILDERS OF THE KUYBYSHEV HYDROELECTRIC POWER PLANT

Stavropol (near Kuybyshev), 23 December. (Via telephone.) At the construction site of the Kuybyshev hydroelectric power project. The Soviet people work here strenuously day and night, building the largest hydroelectric plant in the world. Yesterday, well-attended meetings took place at the construction site. Builders expressed their anger and deeply felt indignation, while discussing the foul, treacherous acts of Beria and his stooges.

V. Khlyust, crew manager of the *Stalingrad 1001* suction dredge, whose members distinguished themselves by a remarkable work record, stated at the meeting of the workers and employes of the 3rd hydro-mechanization sector as follows:

"Beria, the foul renegade of the country, the sworn enemy of the people, became a spy of foreign Intelligence and a traitor to our Nation 'way back in 1919. Fulfilling instructions given by his bosses, the foreign reactionaries, he organized a conspiratorial group and jointly with his accomplices planned to seize power, to abolish the Soviet system and to restore the rule of capitalism. The Central Committee of the Party and the Soviet Government exposed and disarmed the conspirators. The mask has been torn from them. The criminals should be crushed like dangerous and poisonous snakes. Such is the unanimous and absolute demand of the Soviet people. We, the builders of the Kuybyshev Hydro-electric Power Plant join our voices with those of our people."

A. Lebedev, head of the youthful crew of a suction dredge, stated:

"We are building the largest hydroelectric power plant in the world. The energy of the Kuybyshev Hydroelectric Power Plant will strengthen even more the economy of the Country and permit the factories and plants to turn out even more products for national consumption. The enemies wanted to hamper this inspiring and important construction effort, which the Soviet Nation carries on under the leadership of the Communist Party. In order to achieve their criminal goal, they applied the lowest and most despicable means, attempting to use the organs of the Ministry of Internal Affairs with the intent of placing them above the Party and Government, to seize power in the Country, and to restore the capitalist system. These renegades and traitors will be given the highest penalty for their grave crimes. And we, the Soviet people, having cast aside the contemptible traitors shall close our ranks behind our Party and Government, and with even greater confidence move forward to new achievements in the building of Communism."

Pyotr Sukhov, a motor vehicle driver, one of the foremost men at the construction project, who drove over 125,000 miles in his vehicle without overhaul, declared at the meeting of the Motor Vehicle Section No. 7:

"Beria, the worst enemy of the Nation, an old spy and provocateur, has been exposed. His criminal accomplices have also been caught. Thanks to the fact that the Central Committee of the Party as well as the Government undertook decisive measures designed to put an end to the insidious, treacherous conspiracy, our State has become even stronger, even more powerful. The important constructive tasks, set by the Party and Government for the national economy shall be fulfilled at present, with even greater success.

"The small group of villains that was in our way has been exposed, and should be destroyed without mercy!"

Builders of the Kuybyshev Hydroelectric Power Plant hold up to shame the renegades and traitors of the Country, demanding for the latter the highest punishment, without mercy, in the resolutions passed at their meetings. The builders are proclaiming that they will even more closely rally behind the Central Committee of the Communist Party and the Soviet Government and that they will intensify the revolutionary vigilance and increase their efforts in the struggle of building a Communist society.

SPIES AND MURDERERS ARE DAMNED FOREVER!

Gorky, 23 December. (*Pravda*'s correspondent.) Well-attended meetings of workers, engineers, technicians and other personnel were held at all establishments in the city. The Soviet people, expressing their hate and contempt for the enemies of the Country, are declaring that they will fulfill the tasks assigned by the Central Committee and the Soviet Government with even greater energy and persistence.

"All of us know," stated Comrade Katayev, a well-known blacksmith of the automobile plant named after Molotov, "that our force consists in a firm unity of the Party, the Government and the Nation. Beria and his accomplices wanted to weaken this force, to wreck the unity of workers and peasants, to break the great friendship of the Nations of the USSR. They wanted to seize power in the Country, abolish everything that our

Nation has won by its efforts through the years under the Soviet system. I am standing here at our workers' meeting and I want the Soviet Court to hear my voice: There should be no mercy for Beria and his gang of enemies of our Country, for the traitors to the Nation!"

Comrade Kharlamov, smelter and the initiator of the competition for the fulfillment of the annual plan, came forward at the meeting in the malleable cast iron shop and said:

"There are no words to express the contempt and hate felt collectively by the many thousands of workers of our plant toward the foul renegades and traitors, Beria and his gang. While we, the Soviet people, are sparing no efforts nor labor to strengthen the power of our Country, to fulfill with honor tasks established by the Party and the Government in order to promote the welfare of the people, those mercenaries of capitalism attempted to stab us in the back, plotted various foul intrigues, intended to create problems in the Country's food supply system, to undermine the friendship among the Nations of the USSR and to use the organs of the Ministry of Internal Affairs against the Party, against our National Government and against the Nation. We have but one request, that is, that the foul agents of imperialism receive a stiff punishment, without mercy. Let them be damned forever!"

(*Pravda*, December 24, 1953)

Appendix 27

SENTENCE OF THE COURT—THE VERDICT OF THE NATION

The workers of our Country greeted with great satisfaction the sentence pronounced by the Special Session of the Supreme Court of the USSR in the matter of the traitor and spy Beria and the participants of the group of treacherous conspirators organized by him: Merkulov, Dekanozov, Kobulov, Goglidze, Meshik and Vlodzimirsky. The judgment of the Court condemning the conspirators to the highest degree of punishment for crime—sentence to be shot—and the decision of having this sentence carried out corresponds to the unanimous demand of the Soviet people.

"By his sentence," stated Comrade Yaremenko, a worker of the Kiev plant *Leninskaya Kooznitsa*,* "the Soviet Court expressed the will of the people. All workers commenting on the announcement of the USSR Prosecutor's Office unanimously asked for the liquidation, without any mercy, of the band of traitors and demanded that the Soviet soil be purged of these base conspirators, planning to undermine the Union of

---

* Lenin's Forge.

Workers and Peasants, to grasp power in their hands, liquidate the Workers and Peasants System and restore the rule of the bourgeoisie. The will of the people has been fulfilled!"

"All agricultural workers in the collective farms," said Comrade Gunin, the chairman of the collective farm *Krasnyy Kollektivist** of the Nekrasovsky District in the Yaroslavsky Region and a hero of Socialist Labor, "greeted this just sentence with unanimous approval. No rascal, no matter how he may try, will ever be able to undermine the power and greatness of our State, nor will he be able to undermine the collective farm system, the basis of our well-being. All attempts of our enemies will be blocked and the enemies themselves will be annihilated. The Communist peasantry will close its ranks even tighter around its own Communist Party and will redouble its efforts to bring about a big upswing in agriculture."

This is the voice of all industrial and agricultural workers and of the intelligentsia, of all toilers in our Country. They all express their unanimous satisfaction because the band of traitors and enemies of the Country has been apprehended, unmasked, and annihilated.

The affair of Beria and his associates again and again reminds the Soviet people about the fact that the reactionary imperialist forces abroad are stubbornly continuing their attempts to undermine our Country. They are activating the so-called "cold war," conduct in their press and over the radio interminable slandering campaigns against the USSR, attempt to infiltrate spies and saboteurs into our Country and set aside for these activities hundreds of millions of dollars.

The reactionary imperialist circles, by way of the Intelligence Agencies of their countries, feverishly try to find in the Soviet Union all kinds of corrupt people and renegades whom they could use in their subversive activities. They cannot count on anyone else in the USSR, the exploiting classes have been liquidated in our Country long ago and the entire Soviet society is pervaded by the great sense of political and moral unity. For this reason traitors on the order of Beria and his associates constitute for the foreign reactionary circles the only suitable acquisition.

As it has been established by the preliminary and judicial examination, the foreign reactionaries have every reason to believe that Beria is "their man" and that he is a reliable Intelligence agent and a scout.

As early as the year 1919, in Baku, Beria entered the service of the Mussavat Government as a Secret agent and was carrying out the most repugnant and bloody instructions of the English Intelligence Agencies. During his residence in Georgia in 1920, Beria again committed treason by establishing an underground connection with the Menshevik Secret

---

* The Red Collectivist.

Police, which also constituted a branch of the English Intelligence Service.

Through all the following years Beria was enlarging and strengthening contacts with foreign Intelligence agencies. Disguising his hostile activities in various ways he succeeded in gathering a treacherous group of conspirators which was joined by people who were bound together by a mutual guarantee by committing together a number of most severe crimes against the Soviet State. The conspirators established as their vile and criminal goal the elevation of the Agencies of the Ministry of Internal Affairs over and above the Communist Party and the Government of the USSR, the use of these Agencies against the Party and the Government as well as against the people in order to seize power, liquidate the Workers and Peasants System, restore capitalism and bring back the rule of the bourgeoisie in our Country.

In order to hide their criminal activity the conspirators staged terroristic reprisals against people on whose part they suspected the danger of being unmasked. They slandered honest Party and Soviet workers who stood in the way of their achieving power, intrigued in a base way against them and committed a number of crimes to the end of eliminating cadres devoted to the Communist Party and the Soviet Government.

After the demise of J. V. Stalin all international reactionary forces were stirred to a greater activity, counting on the weakening of the Soviet State. Betting on the general increased activity of the reactionary and imperialist forces the hireling and agent Beria increased also the scope of his activities. Preparing for the take-over of power he began with a feverish haste to place participants of his group of conspirators in leading positions in the Central Office of the Ministry of Internal Affairs as well as in its local Agencies. At the same time honest workers of the Ministry of Internal Affairs who refused to carry out the criminal instructions of the conspirators were summarily dealt with, subjected to reprisals, persecution and dismissal.

Among the perfidious treacherous schemes of Beria there was also the plan of sabotaging the measures undertaken by the Party and the Government with the view of increasing agricultural production. This was done for the purpose of undermining the union of workers and peasants, to weaken the collective farm system and to create production difficulties in the Country. Beria undertook also a number of criminal measures which included provocations leading to the revival and activation of the remnants of the bourgeois and nationalistic elements in the Union Republics, to sow discord and enmity among the nations of the USSR and, in the first place, to undermine the friendship of the peoples of the USSR with the great Russian nation.

While carrying out all these provocations and schemes Beria was hoping that the foreign lords—the imperialist circles—would "appreciate" the efforts of their old agent and would support his anti-Soviet conspiracy. And they indeed encouraged in many ways their toady, demanding that his anti-Soviet plans be carried out. The expectations, however, of the enemies to weaken the Soviet State proved to be in vain. Facing the increased activity of the imperialist forces our people closed its ranks around the Communist Party and the Soviet Government and did not spare its forces and efforts in order to realize the policy worked out by the Party. While he was increasing his subversive conspiratorial activities Beria was caught red-handed. The Central Committee of the Party and the USSR Government unmasked this perfidious traitor, found out and disarmed the group of conspirators that he organized. The counterrevolutionary plot of the cleverly disguised traitor and spy foundered on the highly attuned vigilance of our Party and our Government, being on watch for the interests of the people.

The affairs of Beria and his gang have been brought to an end. The participants of the most vile group of conspirators which at any time turned against the Soviet people have been condemned to be shot—the highest degree of penal punishment. The sentence has been carried out. The contemptible names of Beria and his associates have been three times cursed by the people. The affair of Beria reminds us again about the necessity to increase the political vigilance by every available means, in every field, and under any given set of circumstances. Measures taken by the Party and the Government concerning the establishment of a continuous and systematic control by Party organizations over the activities of all segments of the Soviet establishment, among them also over the activities of the Agencies of the Ministry of Internal Affairs, and in particular, measures providing strict control in the observance of the Soviet Law, are calculated to increase political vigilance. Putting these measures into operation the Party was guided by repeated instructions of V. I. Lenin dealing with the importance of the Soviet Law and reminding us that "the most insignificant act of lawlessness, the smallest breach in the Soviet system constitutes an opening which will be immediately utilized by the enemies of the workers."

An unslackening and systematic control by the Party Organizations over the activities of all—without any exceptions—segments of the State machinery, over a precise and unflinching observance of the Socialist Law will, without any doubt, help to increase the political vigilance of the Soviet nation and will make it even more effective and aggressive. And this would mean a continued strengthening of the Soviet State and a further increase of its power. This is how all Soviet people evaluate the fact of unmasking the gang of Beria's conspirators and that is how this fact is also being interpreted by all honest and objective people in the capitalist countries. The Indian newspaper, *Our Herald*, very objectively stated recently that the announcement about the unmasking of Beria and his associates "testifies to the stability of the Soviet Administration as well as to the confidence in its strength."

Having crushed and discarded the venomous snake from its path the Soviet nation confidently marches forward along the glorious road of Communist construction. The Communist Party and the Soviet Government are directing all work efforts and creative activities of industrial and agricultural workers as well as of the intelligentsia towards an all-around development of peace economy, towards a steep increase in the output of Socialist agriculture and consumer goods and towards a steady increase of the well-being of all city and agricultural workers. These noble, creative tasks are commensurate with the vital interests of our people and with the desire to maintain and strengthen peace in the whole world. Consequently, Soviet nation, led by the Communist Party, headed by its Central Committee, will spare neither effort nor forces in order to transform these tasks into reality.

(Pravda, December 25, 1953)

Selected Bibliography

WORKS IN ENGLISH

Agabekov, Georges. *OGPU: The Russian Secret Terror.* New York: Brentano's, 1931.

Alexandrov, Victor. *The Tukhachevsky Affair.* Englewood Cliffs, N. J.: Prentice-Hall, 1964.

Alliluyeva, Svetlana. *Only One Year.* New York: Harper & Row, 1969.

Alliluyeva, Svetlana. *Twenty Letters to a Friend.* New York: Harper & Row, 1967.

Amalrik, Andrei. *Will the Soviet Union Survive Until 1984?* New York: Harper & Row, 1970.

Anders, Wladislav. *An Army in Exile.* London: Macmillan and Co., Ltd., 1949.

Andrews, William G. *European Political Institutions.* Princeton: D. Van Nostrand Company, Inc., 1962.

Armstrong, Hamilton F. *Tito and Goliath.* New York: Macmillan Company, 1951.

Avtorkhanov, Abdukhman. *Stalin and the Communist Party.* New York: Frederick A. Praeger, Inc., 1959.

Basseches, Nikolaus. *Stalin.* New York: E. P. Dutton and Co., Inc., 1952.

Beck, F. and Godin, W. *Russian Purge and the Extraction of Confession.* New York: Viking Press, 1951.

Beria, Lavrenty P. *On the History of the Bolshevik Organizations in Transcaucasia.* Moscow: Foreign Languages Publishing House, 1939.

Berkman, Alexander. *The Bolshevik Myth.* London: Hutchinson, 1925.

Bethel, Nicholas. *Gomulka, His Poland and His Communism.* London: Longsmans, 1969.

Brzezinski, Zbigniew. *The Permanent Purge.* Cambridge: Harvard University Press, 1956.

Bulfinch, Thomas. *Bulfinch's Mythology.* New York: Crowell-Collier-Macmillan, 1967.

Burnham, James. *The Web of Subversion.* New York: The John Day Company, 1954.

Carlisle, Olga A. *Voices in the Snow.* London: Weidenfeld and Nicolson, 1962.

Carpozi, George, Jr. *Red Spies in Washington.* New York: Pocket Books, 1969.

Carr, Edward H. *The Bolshevik Revolution, 1917-1923.* Volume 1, Volume 2. Baltimore: Penguin Books, 1950.

Conquest, Robert. *The Great Terror.* New York: The Macmillan Company, 1968.

Conquest, Robert. *The Soviet Deportation of Nationalities.* New York: St. Martin's Press, 1960.

Crankshaw, Edward. *Khrushchev.* New York: Viking Press, 1966.

Crankshaw, Edward. *Khrushchev's Russia.* Baltimore: Penguin Books, 1959.

Crankshaw, Edward. *Russia Without Stalin.* New York: Viking Press, 1956.

Dallin, David J. *From Purge to Coexistence*. Chicago: Henry S. Regnery Company, 1964.

Dallin, David J. *Soviet Espionage*. New Haven: Yale University Press, 1955.

Dallin, David J. and Nicolaevsky, Boris I. *Forced Labor in Soviet Russia*. New Haven: Yale University Press, 1947.

Daniels, Robert V. *The Kronstadt Revolt of 1921*. Thesis, no date.

Daniels, Robert V. *Red October*. New York: Scribner's Sons, 1967.

Dedijer, Vladimir. *Tito*. New York: Simon and Schuster, 1953.

de Gramont, Sanche. *The Secret War*. New York: G. P. Putnam's Sons, 1962.

Deker, Nikolai K. and Lebed, Andrei (editors). *Genocide in the USSR*. New York: The Scarecrow Press, Inc., 1958.

Delarne, Jacques. *The Gestapo*. New York: Dell, Inc., 1965.

Deutscher, Isaac. *Stalin*. New York: Oxford University Press, 1950.

Deutscher, Isaac. *The Unfinished Revolution*. New York: Oxford University Press, 1969.

Djilas, Milovan. *Conversations with Stalin*. New York: Harcourt, Brace and World Inc., 1962.

Djilas, Milovan. *The New Class*. New York: Frederick A. Praeger, 1957.

Douglas, William O. *Russian Journey*. New York: Doubleday and Company, 1956.

Duranty, Walter. *Stalin and Co*. New York: William Sloane Associates, Inc., 1949.

Ebon, Martin. *Svetlana*. New York: The New American Library, 1967.

Ehrenburg, Ilya. *Post-War Years 1945-54*. New York: The World Publishing Company, 1967.

Fisher, John. "The Easy Chair—Some Guesses About the Next Kremlin Conspiracy." *Harper's Magazine*, March, 1969.

Fisher, John. *Why They Behave Like Russians*. New York: Harper & Brothers, 1947.

Fleming, Peter. *The Fate of Admiral Kolchak*. London: Rupert Hart-Davis, 1963.

Fotitch, Constantin. *The Political Situation in Yugoslavia Today*. Washington, D.C.: Central National Committee of Yugoslavia, 1945.

Futrell, Michael. *Northern Underground*. London: Faber and Faber, 1963.

Garthoff, Raymond. *Soviet Military Policy*. New York: Frederick A. Praeger, 1966.

Ginzburg, Eugenia S. *Journey into the Whirlwind*. New York: Harcourt, Brace and World, 1967.

Goldston, Robert. *The Soviets*. New York: Bantam Books, 1967.

Gorbatov, Aleksander. *Black Year*. London: Flagon Press, 1964.

Granovsky, Anatoli. *I Was a Soviet Spy*. New York: Paperback Library, 1963.

Grey, Ian. *The First Fifty Years, Soviet Russia, 1917-1967*. New York: Coward-McCann, Inc., 1967.

Gruber, Helmut. *International Communism in the Era of Lenin*. Greenwich, Conn.: Fawcett, 1967.

Gugushvili, Andrew. "The Struggle of the Caucasus Peoples for Independence." *The Eastern Quarterly*, Vol. IV, No. 4, October 1951.

Gunther, John. *Inside Russia Today.* New York: Harper & Brothers, 1958.

Gunther, John. *Meet Soviet Russia.* New York: Harper & Row, 1964.

Haywart, Max. *On Trial.* New York: Harper & Row, 1966.

Heibbrun, Otto. *The Soviet Secret Service.* New York: Frederick A. Praeger, 1966.

Hutton, J. Bernard. *School for Spies.* New York: Coward-McCann, Inc., 1962.

Hutton, J. Bernard. *Stalin—the Miraculous Georgian.* London: Neville Spearman, Ltd., 1961.

Jackson, J. Hampden. *Marx, Proudhon and European Socialism.* New York: Collier Books, 1966.

Karpinsky, V. *The Social and State Structure of the USSR.* Moscow: Foreign Languages Publishing House, 1951.

Karski, Jan. *Story of a Secret State.* Boston: Houghton Mifflin Company, 1944.

Katkov, George. *The Trial of Bukharin.* New York: Stein and Day, 1970.

Kazemzadeh, Firuz. *The Struggle for Transcaucasia 1917-1921.* New York: Philosophical Library, Inc., 1951.

Kennan, George F. *On Dealing with the Communist World.* New York: Harper & Row, 1964.

Kennan, George F. *Russia and the West Under Lenin and Stalin.* Boston: Little, Brown and Co., 1960.

Kerensky, Alexander. *Russia and History's Turning Point.* New York: Duell, Sloane and Pearce, 1965.

Khrushchev, Nikita S. *Khrushchev in America.* Full texts of the speeches made by N. S. Khrushchev. New York: Crosscurrents Press, 1960.

Khrushchev, Nikita S. *Khrushchev Remembers.* Boston: Little, Brown and Company, 1970.

Khrushchev, Nikita S. *On the Communist Programme.* Moscow: Foreign Languages Publishing House, 1961.

Kirchner, Walther. *A History of Russia.* New York: Barnes and Noble, Inc., 1966.

Koestler, Arthur. *Darkness at Noon.* London: Jonathan Cape, 1951.

Kolarz, Walter. *Russia and Her Colonies.* New York: Frederick A. Praeger, 1952.

Kramish, Arnold. *Atomic Energy in the Soviet Union.* Stanford: Stanford University Press, 1959.

Kramish, Arnold. *The Soviet Union and the Atom.* Santa Monica: The Rand Corporation, 1958.

Kravchenko, Victor. *I Chose Freedom.* New York: Charles Scribner's Sons, 1946.

Krivitsky, Walter G. *In Stalin's Secret Service.* New York: Harper & Brothers, 1939.

Kusnierz, Bronislav. *Stalin and the Poles.* London: Hollis and Carter, 1949.

Lamparski, Richard. *Whatever Became of . . . ?* New York: ACE Publishing Corp., 1970.

Lane, Arthur Bliss. *I Saw Poland Betrayed.* Boston: Western Island, 1965.

Lane, Theodore, H. Von. *Why Lenin? Why Stalin?* Philadelphia: J. B. Lippincott Company, 1964.

Lang, David. *A Modern History of Soviet Georgia*. New York: Grove Press, Inc., 1962.

Langsam, Walter C. *Historic Documents of World War II*. Princeton: D. Van Nostrand, 1958.

Laqueur, Walter. *The Fate of the Revolution*. New York: The Macmillan Company, 1967.

Lenin, Vladimir I. "On Cooperatives." A speech delivered at the Ninth Party Congress, April 3, 1920. Lenin, *Sochineniia* (Collected Works), 4th edition, vol. 30, pp. 447-448, Moscow: Politizdat, 1950.

Lermolo, Elizabeth. *Face of a Victim*. New York: Harper & Brothers, 1955.

Levine, Isaac Don. *The Mind of an Assassin*. New York: Farrar, Straus and Cudahy, 1959.

Levine, Isaac Don. *Stalin's Great Secret*. New York: Coward-McCann, 1956.

Loebl, Eugen. *Stalinism in Prague*. New York: Grove Press, Inc., 1969.

London, Artur. *The Confession*. New York: William Morrow and Co., 1970.

Lyons, Eugene. *Workers' Paradise Lost*. New York: Funk and Wagnalls, 1967.

McClosky, Herbert and Turner, John E. *The Soviet Dictatorship*. New York: McGraw-Hill Book Company, 1960.

Malaparte, Curzio. *Kaputt*. New York: E. P. Dutton and Co., Inc., 1946.

Malaparte, Curzio. *The Volga Rises in Europe*. London: Alvin Redman, Ltd., 1957.

Mandelstam, Nadezhda. *Hope Against Hope*. New York: Atheneum, 1970.

Massie, Robert K. *Nicholas and Alexandra*. New York: Atheneum, 1967.

Mayakovsky, Vladimir. *The Bedbug and Selected Poetry*. New York: Meridian Books, 1960.

Maynard, John. *Russia in Flux*. New York: Macmillan, Inc., 1951.

Menon, K. P. S. *Russian Panorama*. London: Oxford University Press, 1962.

Mikolajczyk, Stanislav. *The Rape of Poland*. New York: McGraw-Hill Book Company, Inc., 1948.

Monat, Pavel with Dille, John. *Spy in the U. S.* New York: Berkley, 1961.

Moorehead, Alan. *The Russian Revolution*. New York: Bantam Books, 1958.

Neugebauer, Norwid, M. *The Defense of Poland*. London: M. I. Kolin Ltd., 1942.

Nicolaevsky, Boris I. *The Crimes of the Stalin Era*. New York: The New Leader, 1962.

Nicolaevsky, Boris I. *Power and the Soviet Elite*. New York: Frederick A. Praeger, 1965.

O'Donnell, James. *Communism*. New York: Sadlier, Inc., 1964.

Orlov, Alexander. *The Secret History of Stalin's Crimes*. New York: Random House, 1953.

Page, Bruce, David Leitch and Phillip Knightley. *The Philby Conspiracy*. New York: Doubleday and Company, Inc., 1968.

Page, Martin and Burg, David. *Unpersoned. The Fall of Nikita S. Khrushchev*. London: Chapman and Hall, 1966.

Pares, Bernard. *Russia*. New York: Penguin Books, 1944.

Parvilahti, Unto. *Beria's Gardens*. New York: Dutton and Co., 1960.

Payne, Pierre S. R. *The Rise and Fall of Stalin.* New York: Simon and Schuster, 1965.
Payne, Robert. *Lenin.* New York: Simon and Schuster, 1964.
Payne, Robert. *Stalin.* New York: Simon and Schuster, 1965.
Petrov, Vladimir and Evdokia. *Empire of Fear.* London: Andre Deutsch, 1956.
Philby, Kim. *My Silent War.* New York: Grove Press, Inc., 1968.
Pipes, Richard. *The Formation of the Soviet Union.* Cambridge, Mass.: Harvard University Press, 1964.
Pistrak, Lazar. *The Grand Tactician.* London: Thames and Hudson, 1961.
Pollack, Emmanuel. *The Kronstadt Rebellion.* New York: Philosophical Library, 1959.
Pope, Arthur U. *Maxim Litvinoff.* New York: Fisher, 1943.
Randall, Francis B. *Stalin's Russia.* New York: Macmillan, Inc., 1965.
Rauch, Georg. *A History of Soviet Russia.* New York: Frederick A. Praeger, 1963.
Romanovsky-Krassinsky, H. S. H. *Dancing in Petersburg.* London: Victor Gollancz, 1960.
Rush, Myron. *Political Succession in the USSR.* New York: Columbia University Press, 1965.
Salisbury, Harrison E. *The 900 Days. The Siege of Leningrad.* New York: Harper & Row, 1969.
Schapiro, Leonard. *The Communist Party of the Soviet Union.* New York: Random House, 1960.
Schuman, Frederick L. *Soviet Politics.* New York: Alfred A. Knopf, 1946.
Schwarz, Fred. *You Can Trust the Communists.* Englewood Cliffs, N.J.: Prentice-Hall, 1960.
Seitz, Albert B. *Mihailovic Hoax or Hero?* Columbus, Ohio: Leigh House, 1953.
Seth, Ronald. *The Executioners.* New York: Hawthorn Books, 1968.
Seth, Ronald. *Spies at Work.* New York: Philosophical Library, 1954.
Seth, Ronald. *Unmasked.* New York:Hawthorn Books, 1965.
Shub, David. *Lenin.* New York: Doubleday and Company, 1948.
Smith, Edward Ellis. *The Young Stalin.* New York: Farrar, Straus and Giroux, 1967.
Smith, Walter Bedell. *My Three Years in Moscow.* New York: J. B. Lippincott Company, 1950.
Snow, Edgar. *The Pattern of Soviet Power.* New York: Random House, 1945.
Snow, Edgar. *Stalin Must Have Peace.* New York: Random House, 1947.
Solzhenitsyn, Alexander. *One Day in the Life of Ivan Denisovich.* New York: E. P. Dutton and Co., 1963.
Souvarine, Boris. *Stalin.* New York: Alliance Book Corporation, Longmans, Green and Co., 1939.
Spiro, Edward (E. A. Cookridge). *The Net That Covers the World.* New York: Henry Holt and Company, 1955.
Stalin, Joseph V. *Marxism and the National and Colonial Question.* London: Lawrence and Wishart, Ltd., 1947.
Stalin, Joseph V. *Mastering Bolshevism.* New York: New Century Publishers, 1945.

Sterling, Claire. *Masaryk Case.* New York: Harper & Row, 1969.

Svanidze, Budu. *My Uncle Joseph Stalin.* New York: G. P. Putnam's Sons, 1953.

Swianiewicz, Stanislav. *Forced Labour and Economic Development.* Toronto: Oxford University Press, 1965.

Szulc, Tad. *Czechoslovakia Since World War II.* New York: Viking Press, 1971.

Tarsis, Valeriy. *Ward 7.* New York: E. P. Dutton and Co., Inc., 1965.

Thayer, Charles W. *The Case of Richard Sorge.* New York: Harper & Row, 1966.

Thayer, Charles W. "M.V.D. Man's Declaration of Independence." *Life Magazine,* July 5, 1954.

Tietjen, Arthur. *Soviet Spy Ring.* New York: Coward-McCann, Inc., 1961.

Toland, John. *The Last 100 Days.* New York: Random House, 1965.

Trotsky, Leon. *Stalin.* New York: Stein and Day, 1967.

Trotsky, Leon. *Trotsky's Diary in Exile 1935.* Cambridge, Mass.: Harvard University Press, 1958.

Tucker, Robert C. *The Soviet Political Mind.* New York: Frederick A. Praeger, 1964.

Tucker, Robert C. and Cohen, Stephen F. *The Great Purge Trial.* New York: Grosset and Dunlap, 1965.

Weisberg, Alexander. *The Accused.* New York: Simon and Schuster, 1951.

Werth, Alexander. *Russia at War 1941-45.* New York: E. P. Dutton and Co., 1964.

Werth, Alexander. *Russia Under Khrushchev.* Greenwich, Conn.: Fawcett, 1966.

Westwood, J. N. *Russia 1917-1964.* New York: Harper & Row, 1968.

Wolfe, Bertram D. *Communist Totalitarianism.* Boston: Beacon Press, 1956.

Wolfe, Bertram D. *Khrushchev and Stalin's Ghost.* New York: Frederick A. Praeger, 1957.

Wolfe, Bertram D. *Strange Communists I Have Known.* New York: Stein and Day, 1965.

Wolfe, Bertram D. "The Struggle for the Soviet Succession." *Foreign Affairs, An American Quarterly Review,* July 1953, Vol. 31, No. 4.

Wolfe, Bertram D. *Three Who Made a Revolution.* New York: Dial Press, 1948.

Wolin, Simon and Slusser, Robert. *The Soviet Secret Police.* New York: Frederick A. Praeger, 1957.

Young, Gordon. *Stalin's Heirs.* London: Darek Vershayle, 1953.

Zhukov, Georgi K. *Marshal Zhukov's Greatest Battles.* New York: Harper & Row, 1969.

MISCELLANEOUS

Encyclopedia America, New York, 1957.

Encyclopaedia Britannica, Chicago, 1958.

Encyclopedia of Russia and the Soviet Union. New York: McGraw-Hill, 1961.

Facts and Documents Concerning Polish Prisoners of War Captured by the USSR During the 1939 Campaign (For private circulation only), February 1946.

Facts on Communism, Vol. II. The Soviet Union from Lenin to Khrushchev. Washington: U. S. Government Printing Office, 1961.

Foreign Affairs, An American Quarterly Review, July 1953, New York, 1953.

History of the Communist Party of the Soviet Union. New York: International Publishers, 1939.

Supplementary Report of Facts and Documents Concerning the Katyn Massacre (For private circulation only), October 1947.

The Crime of Katyn, Facts and Documents with a foreword by General Wladislav Anders. London: Polish Cultural Foundation, 1965.

The Katyn Forest Massacre: Hearings before the Select Committee to Conduct an Investigation of the Facts, Evidence, and Circumstances of the Katyn Forest Massacre, Eighty-Second Congress, First Session on Investigation of the Murder of Thousands of Polish Officers in the Katyn Forest near Smolensk, Russia, October 11, 1951. Washington: United States Government Printing Office, 1952.

The Katyn Forest Massacre: Hearings, Second Session, Part 2, February 4, 5, 6, and 7, 1952.

The Katyn Forest Massacre: Hearings, Part 3 (Chicago, Illinois), March 13 and 14, 1952.

The Katyn Forest Massacre: Hearings, Part 4 (London, England), April 16, 17, 18 and 19, 1952.

The Katyn Forest Massacre: Hearings, Part 5 (Frankfurt, Germany), April 21, 22, 23, 24, 25, and 26, 1952.

The Katyn Forest Massacre: Hearings, Part 6 (Exhibits 32 and 33 presented to the Committee in London by the Polish Government in Exile).

The Katyn Forest Massacre: Hearings, Part 7, June 3, 4, and November 11, 12, 13, 14, 1952.

The Katyn Forest Massacre: Interim Report. A Resolution to Authorize the Investigation of the Mass Murder of Polish Officers in the Katyn Forest near Smolensk, Russia, July 1952.

The Katyn Forest Massacre: Final Report, December 22, 1952.

The Katyn List of Prisoners of War at the Camps Kozelsk, Starobelsk, Otashkov, who disappeared in Soviet Russia (Polish), prepared by Adam Moszynski, London: Gryf Publications, 1949.

Keesing's Contemporary Archives, Weekly Diary of World Events, 1937-1940, London: Keesing's Ltd.

Polish-Soviet Relations 1918-1943. Official Documents. Confidential. Issued by the Polish Embassy in Washington by Authority of the Government of the Republic of Poland.

Red Russia after 50 Years, by the editors of *Look* magazine. New York: Cowles Books, 1970.

Soviet World Outlook, Washington: U. S. Department of State, 1959.

Speech of Nikita Khrushchev Before a Closed Session of the XXth Congress of the Communist Party of the Soviet Union on February 25, 1956.

World Communist Movement, Volumes I, II, III, IV. Washington: U. S. Government Printing Office, 1960, 1963, 1964, 1965.

PERIODICALS

New York Herald-Tribune; New York Times; Washington Post; Daily News; Washington Star; Time; Newsweek; National Geographic Magazine; Commentary, American Bar Association Journal; American Mercury; Daily Worker; Eastern Quarterly; Foreign Affairs; Harper's; The Christian Science Monitor; News Dispatches; New York World-Telegram and Sun.

WORKS IN FRENCH

Manport, Henri de. *La Massacre de Katyn.* Paris: La Table Ronde, 1966.
Rossi, A. *Autopsie de Stalinisme.* Paris: Pierre Haray, 1957.

PERIODICALS

Democratie Nouvelle; Defendre la Vérité; L'Histoire Pour Tous; L'Humanité.

WORKS IN ITALIAN

Il Giornale della Sera. Rome: April 18, 1946.

WORKS IN GERMAN

Der Spiegel. Hamburg: December 8, 1969.

WORKS IN RUSSIAN

Beria, Lavrenty P. *K Voprosu ob Istorii Bolshevitskikh Organizatsii v Zavkavkazye (On the History of the Bolshevik Organizations in Transcaucasia).* Moscow: 1st Edition, 1935, 9th Edition, 1952.
Dumbadze, Evgeny V. *Na Slushbe Cheka i Kominterna (In the Service of the Cheka and the Comintern).* Paris, 1930.
Khachapuridze, T. W. *Bolsheviki Gruzii v Boyakh za Pobedu Sovietskey Vlasti (The Georgian Bolsheviks in the Battles for the Victory of the Soviets).* Leningrad: Gosudarstviennoye Izdatelstvo Politicheskoy Literatury, 1947.

MISCELLANEOUS

Baku. Moscow: Izdatelstvo Progress.
Bolshaya Sovietskaya Encyclopedia (Great Soviet Encyclopedia). Moscow, 1950.
Politischesky Slovar (Political Dictionary). Moscow: Gosudarstviennoye Izdatelstvo Politicheskoy Literatury, 1958.

Sovietskaya Historicheskaya Encyclopedia (*Soviet Historical Encyclopedia*). Moscow, 1964.

PERIODICALS

Bolshevik; Izvestia; Na Rubezhe; Pravda; Izvestia Vremennogo Revolutsionnogo Komiteta Matrosov, Krasnoarmeytsev i Rabochik Goroda Kronstadta.

WORKS IN POLISH

Berling, Zygmunt. "Pamietniki" (Memoirs). Warsaw: *Kultura, a Weekly Magazine*, April 16, 23, 30, and May 7, 21, 1967.
Bregman, Aleksander. *Najlepszy Sojusznik Hitlera* (*The Best Ally of Hitler*). London: Orbis, 1958.
Daniszewski, Tadeusz. *Feliks Dzierzynski*. Warsaw: Ksiazka i Wiedza, 1951.
Dzierzynska, Zofia. *Lata Wielkich Bojow* (*The Years of Great Battles*). Warsaw: Ksiazka i Wiedza, 1969.
Mora, Sylvester and Zwierniak, Piotr. *Sprawiedliwosc Soviecka* (*Soviet Justice*). Italy, 1945.
Pomian, Andrzej. *Powstanie Warszawskie* (*The Warsaw Uprising*). Washington, Manuscript, 1970.

MISCELLANEOUS

Wielka Encyklopedia Powszechna (*Great Universal Encyclopedia*). Warsaw: Powszechne Panstwowe Wydawnictwo Naukowe, 1965.
Przewodnik po Wystawie F. Dzierzynskiego (Catalogue of the F. Dzerzchinsky's Exhibition). Warsaw, Ksiazka i Wiedza, 1951.

INDEX

Index